D1557109

THIRTY THOUSAND NAMES
OF
IMMIGRANTS

A COLLECTION

OF UPWARDS OF

THIRTY THOUSAND NAMES

OF

GERMAN, SWISS, DUTCH, FRENCH

AND OTHER

Immigrants in Pennsylvania

From 1727 to 1776,

WITH A

Statement of the names of Ships, whence they sailed, and the date
of their arrival at Philadelphia,

CHRONOLOGICALLY ARRANGED,

TOGETHER WITH THE

Necessary Historical and other Notes,

ALSO,

An Appendix containing Lists of more than one thousand German
and French Names in New York prior to 1712,

BY

Prof. I. DANIEL RUPP,

Reprint of the Second
Revised and Enlarged Edition
WITH AN ADDED INDEX

Reprint from the Second Edition (Philadelphia, 1876),
with the Index from the Third Edition (Leipzig, 1931),
and with added Publisher's Preface and Index to Ships
Genealogical Publishing Co., Inc.
3600 Clipper Mill Rd., Suite 260
Baltimore, Maryland 21211-1953
1965, 1971, 1975, 1980, 1985, 1994, 2000, 2006
Copyright © 1965
Genealogical Publishing Co., Inc.
Baltimore, Maryland
All Rights Reserved
Library of Congress Catalogue Card Number 65-26916
International Standard Book Number 0-8063-0302-6
Made in the United States of America

PUBLISHER'S PREFACE

To those engaged in the study of American genealogy, this work will require no introduction. Over the years it has achieved a remarkable reputation as one of the most useful tools for identifying persons who came to North American between 1727 and 1776, and the demand for copies of it has not ceased in spite of the fact that it has long been unavailable. Passenger lists have always been a desideratum to the genealogist, as they are often the means of forming the missing link which is the genealogist's boon. In recent years efforts have been made to sort out and print from old records lists of the early emigrants, but when Rupp's pioneer work appeared in the latter-half of the nineteenth century such compilations were rare. As the first attempt to bring together the thousands of persons who came to Pennsylvania, this work stands today as a cornerstone in the foundation of Pennsylvania genealogy.

In the belief that this work is of interest to the general public and invaluable to the genealogist and historian, we have reproduced the lists as published by Rupp. To add to the usefulness of the work, we have added an eighty-nine page name index which was originally published in Leipzig, Germany in 1931. To further add to its utility, we compiled an index to all ships' names. As it stands it is a facsimile edition of the work listed as Number 144 in the recently revised and enlarged edition of Lancour's *Bibliography of Ship Passenger Lists,* 1538-1825, and the best edition possible.

Genealogical Publishing Co.

Baltimore, Md.
1965

BIRDS EYE VIEW OF THE CENTENNIAL GROUNDS.

CARPENTERS' HALL, PHILADELPHIA.

INDEPENDENCE HALL, PHILADELPHIA.

INDEPENDENCE HALL, PHILADELPHIA, 1776.

MEMORIAL HALL, 1876.

INTERNATIONAL EXHIBITION

MAIN EXHIBITION BUILDING.

1776

1876

PHILADELPHIA, U. S. AMERICA

MAY 10 to NOVEMBER 10, 1876.

AGRICULTURAL HALL.

HORTICULTURAL HALL.

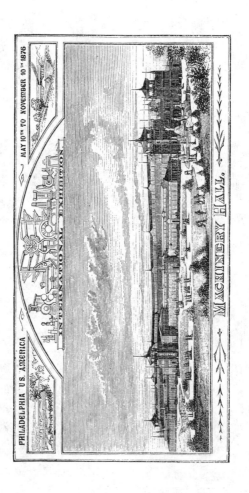

PHILADELPHIA U.S. AMERICA

INTERNATIONAL EXHIBITION

MAY 10TH TO NOVEMBER 10TH 1876

MACHINERY HALL.

PREFACE TO THE IMPROVED EDITION.

To meet the often-repeated requests of many who were anxious to ascertain, if possible, when such and such persons came to Pennsylvania, the Editor copied carefully the original Lists of the Names of German, Swiss and other immigrants on File in the Secretary's Office, at Harrisburg, and published an edition of *A Collection of Thirty Thousand Names, &c.*, in 1856.*

The first edition is now out of print, and cannot be had at any price. From $5 to $7 have been paid within the last five years for *second-hand* copies.

The second edition is a carefully revised one, and much improved. The names of males, not sixteen years of age, are inserted immediately under those above sixteen years old, instead of presenting them in the *Appendix*. There have also been added enlarged *Lists* of names of first settlers at Germantown, of early settlers in Lancaster county, in Tulpehocken, Berks county, &c.

This *Collection* contains upwards of *Thirty Thousand Names, &c.*, and some historical and biographical *notes*. The present descendants of the early German, Swiss and French immigrants, now numbering millions, living in Pennsylvania, New York, Maryland, Virginia, and in the Western States, will be enabled, if they procure this *Publication*, to ascertain the time of their ancestors' arrival, and other facts of value to most of them.

---

* The first edition was published in a *Monthly Serial* of 24 pages. Soon after issuing the first *number*, the Editor received orders for the *Collection* from persons in New York, New Jersey, Maryland, Virginia, North Carolina, Ohio, Kentucky and other Western States, and from persons in many counties in Pennsylvania.

(v)

It has been truthfully said: "That comparatively few of the living millions in the United States can tell when their forefathers came to this country." By the aid of this *Collection,* thousands of the descendants of early immigrants, can with certainty, determine the year of the arrival of their progenitors.*

Among other objects had in view in publishing this *Collection,* is the preservation of names, which indifference or accident might have forever placed beyond reach.

As many feel, naturally, curiously anxious to know the names of fellow-passengers, in crossing the ocean "in perils by sea," the Editor has sought to gratify this curiosity by the plan of arrangement adopted.

This *Collection* may also lead to the rightful recovery of inheritance of money, *held in abeyance,* in the old country. It is not, however, presumed, that this, in itself, is legal evidence, but it may aid materially in suggesting modes of proof to the right of such claims.

I. DANIEL RUPP,

43d AND HURON STS., WEST PHILADELPHIA.

1875.

---

* The late *Rev. Henry Harbaugh, D. D.,* in a letter to the Editor, 1856, said: "This *Collection* will place in the hands of *Subscribers* the means of tracing their ancestors, which must prove a great satisfaction to all who have not, under a false training, grown indifferent as to their earthly origin. We are among those who believe that any who care not about their earthly origin, care little as to anything higher. We are much mistaken if this work will not be much sought for."

Vorrede zur verbesserten Auflage.

Um der oft von Vielen wiederholten Nachfrage, welche gerne
zu erfahren wünschten, wann diese oder jene Personen sich in
Pennsylvanien niedergelassen, zu entsprechen, schrieb der Her=
ausgeber die in der Amtsstube des Staats=Sekretärs zu Har=
risburg aufbewahrten Original=Listen der Namen deutscher,
schweizerischer und anderer Einwanderer sorgfältig ab und
veröffentlichte dieselben in dem im Jahre 1856 unter dem
Titel „Eine Sammlung von über 30,000 Namen"
u. s. w. erschienenen Buche.*

Die erste Auflage ist jetzt vergriffen und um keinen Preis
zu bekommen. Alte Exemplare haben in den letzten fünf
Jahren von $5 bis $7 gebracht.

Die zweite Auflage erfuhr eine sorgfältige Prüfung und
bedeutende Verbesserung. Die Namen der männlichen Ein=
wanderer unter sechzehn Jahren folgen (anstatt im Anhang)
gleich nach der Liste der über sechzehn Jahre alten Personen.
Eine vermehrte Namenliste der ersten Ansiedler in
Germantown, in Lancaster County, in Tulpehocken, Berks
County u. s. w. ist dieser Auflage beigefügt.

Diese Sammlung enthält über 30,000 Namen 2c.,
nebst geschichtlichen und biographischen Anmerkungen.—Die=
selbe ermöglicht es, den jetzt zu Millionen zählenden Nach=
kommen der frühen deutschen, schweizerischen und französischen
Einwanderer, die in Pennsylvanien, New York, Maryland,
Virginien und den westlichen Staaten wohnen, wenn sie sich
dieses Werk anschaffen, die genaue Zeit der Ankunft ihrer

---

* Die erste Auflage erschien in monatlichen Nummern von 24 Seiten.
Bald nachdem die erste Nummer verbreitet war, kamen Bestellungen für
die Sammlung von Personen in New York, New Jersey, Maryland,
Virginien, Nord=Carolina, Ohio, Kentucky und anderen westlichen Staaten,
nebst vielen Counties in Pennsylvanien.

Vorfahren und andere wichtige Thatsachen, die den Meisten von großem Werthe sind, zu erfahren.

Wahr ist: „Daß verhältnißmäßig Wenige der von den in den Vereinigten Staaten lebenden Millionen wissen, wann ihre Voreltern in dieses Land kamen." Mit Hülfe dieser Sammlung können Tausende der Abkömmlinge früher Einwanderer mit Gewißheit das Jahr, in dem ihre Ahnen angekommen sind, bestimmen.*

Die Veröffentlichung dieser Sammlung hat einen weiteren Zweck darin, daß in ihr die Namen in ihrer eigentlichen ursprünglich richtigen Form enthalten sind, welche durch Gleichgültigkeit oder Zufall wohl für immer außerhalb jedes Bereichs gekommen sein würden.

Da Viele eine natürliche Neugierde haben, die Namen der Mitpassagiere zu wissen, die mit ihnen über das Meer kamen und mit ihnen die Gefahren des Wassers durchmachten, so bemühte sich der Herausgeber, in dem von ihm verfolgten Plane der Eintheilung solche Neugierde zu befriedigen.

Diese Sammlung kann ebenfalls zur rechtmäßigen Erlangung einer im alten Lande „in Anwartschaft gehaltenen" Erbschaft von Geld führen. Es wird jedoch nicht erwartet, daß das hier Gebotene an sich selbst gesetzliche Beweis-Urkunde sein soll, sondern es dürfte wesentlich dazu beitragen, Wege an die Hand zu geben, welche Beweise für die Rechtmäßigkeit solcher Ansprüche liefern.

J. Daniel Rupp,
43ste und Huron-Straße, West-Philadelphia.

1875.

---

* Der selige Pastor Dr. Heinrich Harbach schrieb in einem Briefe an den Herausgeber vom Jahre 1856: „Diese Sammlung ermöglicht die Unterschreiber, ihre Vorfahren zu erforschen, welches Denen, die durch eine falsche Erziehung nicht ganz gleichgültig gegen ihre irdische Abstammung geworden sind, großes Vergnügen gewähren muß. Wir gehören zu Denen, die glauben, daß Diejenigen, welche sich nicht um ihre irdische Abstammung bekümmern, sich ebensowenig um höhere Dinge kümmern. Wir würden uns sehr täuschen, wenn dieses Werk nicht einen reißenden Absatz fände."

CONTENTS.

Inhalt.

———

(X)

General Introduction.

BRIEF NOTICES OF THE PRINCIPAL GERMAN, SWISS AND FRENCH SETTLEMENTS IN NORTH AMERICA, DURING THE COLONIAL ERA.*

LOVE of fame, the desire to enlarge their dominion, eager to sway the sceptre over subjugated nations, influenced the ancient Germans to leave their hearths, and to achieve conquests, thus proving themselves, in days of yore, as in the middle ages, *Herren der Welt*, Lords of the World.

At different periods, various causes and diverse motives induced them to abandon their *Vaterland*. Since 1606, millions have left their homes, the dearest spots on earth, whither the heart always turns. Religious persecution, political oppression drove thousands to Pennsylvania—to the asylum for the harrassed and depressed sons and daughters of the relics of the Reformation, whither William Penn himself invited the persecuted of every creed and religious opinion.

From 1682 to 1776, Pennsylvania was the *central point* of emigration from Germany, France and Switzerland. Penn's liberal views, and the *illiberal* course of the government of New York toward the Germans, induced many to come to this Province.—*See Appendix* No. X.

In the first period of twenty years, from 1682–1702, comparatively few Germans arrived: not above two hundred families,—they located principally at Germantown. They were nearly all *Plattdeutsch*, Low Germans, from Cleves, a Duchy in Westphalia, and arrived in 1683–1685. Leaving their native country at *that* time, they providentially escaped the desolation of a French war, which in 1689 laid waste the city of Worms, near which town they resided; ravaged the countries

---

* In the *Fireside History of German and Swiss Immigrants,* a fuller account of these settlements is given.

for miles around, where the flames went up from every market place, every hamlet, every parish church, every country seat within the devoted provinces. When, in the same year were laid waste, Rohrbach, Laimen, Nussloch, Wissloch, Kirchheim, Bruckhausen, Eppelnheim, Wieblingen, Edingen, Neckerhausen; and *Handschuhsheim*, in the Duchy of Baden, in *which*, says *Kayser*, Johannes Schad and Ludwig Rupp were consumed in the flames.—*Kayser's Schauplatz von Heidelberg*, p. 505.

Francis Daniel Pastorius, born at Sommerhausen in Franconia, Germany, Sept. 26, 1651, arrived at Philadelphia in the ship America, captain, Joseph Wasey, Aug. 20, 1683, with his family. He was accompanied by a few German emigrants: Jacob Schumacher, George Wertmueller, Isaac Dilbeck, his wife and two children, Abraham and Jacob; Thomas Gasper, Conrad Bacher, *alias* Rutter, and an English maid, Frances Simpson. Others soon followed Pastorius. (For a List of their names, and of the first settlers at Germantown, *see Appendix* No. I.) Pastorius located where he laid out *Germantown* the same year in which he arrived in Pennsylvania. The land of the Germantown settlement was first taken up by him, the 12th of the 10th month (October) 1683. He commenced the town with thirteen families. In less than five years some fifty houses had been erected.

The period from 1702–1727 marks an era in the early German emigration. Between forty and fifty thousand left their native country—"their hearths where soft affections dwell." The unparalleled ravages and desolations by the troops of Louis XIV, under Turenne, were the stern prelude to bloody persecutions. To escape the dreadful sufferings awaiting them, German and other Protestants emigrated to the English colonies in America.

In 1705, a number of German Reformed, residing between Wolfenbüttel and Halberstadt, fled to Neuwied, a town of Rhenish Prussia, where they remained some time, and then went to Holland—there embarked, in 1707, for New York. Their frail ship was, by reason of adverse winds, carried into the Delaware bay. Determined, however, to reach the place for which they were destined—to have a home among the Dutch, they took the overland route from Philadelphia to New York. On entering the fertile, charming valley in *Nova Cæsaria*, New Jersey, which is drained by the meandering *Musconetcong*, the Passaic and their tributaries, and having reached a goodly land, they resolved to remain in what is now known as the *German* Valley of Morrison county. From this point, the Germans have spread into Somerset, Bergen and Essex counties.

At Elizabethtown, where the first English settlement was made in New Jersey, 1664, there were many Germans prior to 1730.* There was also a German settlement at a place known as *Hall mill*, which is some thirty miles from Philadelphia.†

A well supported tradition maintains, that a Polish colony, consisting of two hundred Protestants, settled in the early part of the eighteenth century, in the valleys of the Passaic and Raritan rivers, in New Jersey. They were led by Count Sobieski, a lineal descendant of the wide-world-known John Sobieski, king of Poland, who routed the Tartars and Turks in 1683. The name *Zabriskie*, still found in New Jersey and New York, seems to be corrupted from Sobieski.—*Bard's Rel. Am.*, p. 81.

In 1708 and 1709, thirty-three thousand, on an invitation of Queen Anne, left their homes in the Rhine country for London, where some twelve or thirteen thousand arrived in the summer of 1708.‡ These were, for some time, in a destitute condition—wholly depending upon the charity of the inhabitants of the English metropolis.

In the fall of 1709, one hundred and fifty families, consisting of six hundred and fifty Palatines, were transported, under the tutelar auspices of Christian De Graffenried and Ludwig Michell, natives of Switzerland, to North Carolina. As in all new countries, the Palatines were exposed to trials, privations and hardships incident to border life. One hundred of them were massacred by the *Tuskarora* Indians, Sept. 22, 1711.§

---

* „Den 16. Juni 1734, um 10 Uhr Morgens, kam ich nach Elisabeth-town, wo viele Deutsche wohnen. Dieser Ort ist etliche Meilen lang, allein es sind die Häuser bisweilen sehr weit von einander entfernt."—Von Reck: Ulsperger's Nachrichten p. 159.

† Rev. Michael Schlatter preached here in 1746.—*Magazine of the German Reformed Church*, II., p. 266.

‡ "There were books and papers dispersed in the Palatinate, with the Queen's picture on the books, and the title page in letters of gold, which, on that account, were called, 'The Golden Book,' to encourage the Palatines to come to England, in order to be sent to the Carolinas, or to other of Her Majesty's colonies, to be settled there."—*Journal of the House of Commons, England*, XVI., p. 467, 468.

§ The anniversary of this massacre was solemnized for many years as a day of fasting and prayer.—*Williamson's N. C.*, I., p. 193, 194.

The descendants of these Germans reside in different parts of the State.*

North Carolina received constant accessions of German immigrants. In the first third of the last century came Tobler, and the Rev. Zuberbühler, of St. Gaul, Switzerland, with a large number of his countrymen, located in Granville county. Tobler was soon appointed Justice of the Peace. Besides these, many Germans moved from Virginia and Pennsylvania, seated themselves in the mountainous regions. Lincolnton and Stokes, as well as Granville county, were settled by Germans. In 1785, the Germans from Pennsylvania alone in North Carolina, numbered upwards of fifteen hundred persons.—*Löher*, p. 69.

In 1707, a company of French Protestants arrived and seated themselves on the river Trent, a branch of the Neuse.—*Hale's U. S.*, p. 98.

At the time these Palatines left England for North Carolina, the Rev. Joshua Kocherthal, with a small band of his persecuted Lutheran brethren, embarked at London, 1708, for New York, where they arrived in December, and shortly thereafter he, with his little flock, settled on some lands up the Hudson river, which they had received from the crown of England. Two thousand one hundred acres, granted by a patent, Dec. 18, 1709.—*O' Calahan's Doc. His. N. Y.*, p. 591. The Queen also bestowed upon Kocherthal five hundred acres as a glebe for the Lutheran church. Newburg is the place of this settlement.†— Rev. *Kocherthal*, 1719.

In the meantime, while those were transported to North Carolina, and to New York, three thousand six hundred Germans were transferred to Ireland; seated upon unimproved lands in the county of Limerick, near Arbela and Adair; others, in the town of Rathkeale, where their descendents still reside, and are known to this day, as *German Palatines*, preserving their true German character for industry, thrift and honorable dealing. Persons who have lately visited them say, "They are the most wealthy and prosperous farmers in the county of Limerick."‡ They still speak the German language.§

---

* *See App.* No. VIII. and No. IX.

† *Brodhead's Documentary History of New York*, V., p. 67. The names of those who accompanied Kocherthal have been preserved, and are kept in the archives of the State of New York. — *See App.* No. IV. for a list of these names.

‡ *Journal H. C. Eng.*, XVI., p. 465; *Methodist Quarterly Review*, Oct. No. 1855, p. 489.

§ *Fliegende Blätter*, II., p. 672.

Of the large number that came to England, in 1708 and 1709, seven thousand, after having suffered great privations, returned, half naked and in despondency, to their native country. Ten thousand died for want of sustenance, medical attendance, and from other causes. Some perished on ships. The survivers were transported to English colonies in America. Several thousand had embarked for the Scilly Islands, a group south-west of England; but never reached their intended destination.

Ten sails of vessels were freighted with upwards of four thousand Germans for New York. They departed the 25th December, 1709; and after a six months' tedious voyage reached New York in June, 1710.* On the inward passage, and immediately on landing, seventeen hundred died. The survivors were encamped in tents, they had brought with them from England, on Nutting, now Governor's Island. Here they remained till late in autumn, when about fourteen hundred were removed, one hundred miles up the Hudson river, to Livingston Manor. The widowed women, sickly men and orphan-children remained in New York.† The orphans were apprenticed by Governor Hunter, to citizens of New York and of New Jersey.‡

Those settled on Hudson river were under indenture to serve Queen Anne as grateful subjects, to manufacture tar and raise hemp, in order to repay the expenses of their transportation, and cost of subsistance, to the amount of ten thousand pounds sterling, which had been advanced by parliamentary grant. A supply of naval stores from this arrangement, had been confidently anticipated. The experiment proved a complete failure.§ There was mismanagement.

The Germans, being unjustly oppressed, became dissatisfied both with their treatment, and with their situation. Governor Hunter resorted to violent measures to secure obedience to his demands. In this, too, he failed. One hundred and fifty fami-

---

* *John F. Watson* in his *Annals*, Vol. II., p. 258, says— this was a *six months' voyage*. They embarked Dec. 25, 1709, arrived at New York, June 14, 1710.—*See Brodhead's Doc. His. N. Y.*, V., p. 167.

† For a list of the names of families that remained in New York, *see App.* No. V.

‡ For a list of the names of apprenticed children, *see App.* No. VI.

§ For a list of names in Livingston Manor, *see App.* No. VII.

lies, to escape the certainty of famishing, left, late in the autumn of 1712, for Schoharie Valley, some sixty miles north-west of Livingston Manor. They had no open road, no horses to carry or haul their luggage—this they loaded on rudely con- structed sleds, and did tug these themselves, through a three- feet-deep snow, which greatly obstructed their progress—their way was through an unbroken forest, where and when the wind was howling its hibernal dirge through leaf-stripped trees, amid falling snow. It took them three full weeks. Having reached Schoharie, they made improvements upon the lands, Queen Anne had granted them. Here they remained about ten years, when, owing to some defect in their titles, they were deprived of both lands and improvements. In the Spring of 1723, thirty-three families removed and settled in Pennsylvania, in Tulpehocken, some fifteen miles west of Reading. A few years afterwards, others followed them.*

The other dissatisfied Germans at Schoharie, who did not choose to follow their friends to Pennsylvania, sought for and found a future home on the frontiers in Mohawk Valley.

New York was, at an early day, an asylum for the French Protest- ants, or Huguenots. As early as 1656, they were already numerous in that State; ranking in number and wealth next to the Dutch. New Rochelle, situated near the shore of Long Island sound, was settled solely by Huguenots from Rochelle in France. "The emigrants pur- chased of John Pell 6,000 acres of land. One venerable Huguenot, it is related, would go daily to the shore, when, directing his eyes to- wards (the direction) where he supposed France was situated, would sing one of Marot's hymns, and send to heaven his early morning de- votions. Others joined him in these praises of their God, and remem- brances of their beloved native clime, from which they had been ban- ished by the merciless fires of persecution."—*Weiss' His. of French Prot. Ref.*, II., p. 304.

In Ulster and Dutchess counties, many of their descendants still re- side. In Ulster are the descendants of Dubois, Dian or Deyo; Has- broucq, or Hasbrouck; Le Febre, Bevier, Crispell, Freir, &c.—*For names of males at New Rochelle in 1710, see App.* No. XIII.

Queen Anne, who well understood the policy of England, to retain her own subjects at home, encouraged the emigration of Germans, sent some of those whom she had invited in 1708 and 1709, to Virginia; settled them above the falls of the Rappahannock, in Spottsylvania county, where they commenced

* For a list of names of first settlers in Tulpehocken, *see App.* No. XIV.

a town, called *Germanna*. The locality was unpropitious. They moved some miles further up the river, "where they soon drove well."* From this settlement they spread into several counties in Virginia, and into North Carolina.

Shanandoah and Rockingham county in Virginia were settled by Germans from Pennsylvania, prior to 1746. Many of their descendants still speak the German language.

When George Washington and others were surveying lands in that part of Virginia, in April, 1748, "they were attended with a great company of people, men, women and children, who followed through the woods—they would never speak English; but when spoken to, they all spoke Dutch (German)."—*Spark's Washington*, II., p. 418.

In 1690, King William sent a large body of French Protestants to Virginia. In 1699, another body of six hundred Huguenots came to Virginia, under Philip Da Richebourg, and were assigned lands on the south side of James River about twenty miles from the present site of Richmond.—*Howison's Virginia*, II., p. 160, 161.

Some of the names of the Huguenots have been handed down, such as Chastain, David, Monford, Dykar, Neirn, Dupuy, Bilbo, Dutoi, Salle, Martain, Allaigre, Vilain, Soblet, Chambon, Levilain, Trabu, Loucadou, Gasper, Flournoy, Amis, Banton, Sasain, Solaigre, Givodan, Mallet, Dubruil, Guerrant, Sabattie, Dupre, Bernard, Amonet, Porter, Rapine, Lacy, Bondurant, Goin, Pero, Pean, Deen, Edmond, Benin, Stanford, Forqueran, Roberd, Brian, Faure, Don, Bingli, Reno, Lesueur, Pinnet, Trent, Sumter, Morriset, Jordin, Gavin.—*Weiss' H. Fr. Pro. Ref.* II., p. 322.

Because of relentless persecution and oppression in Switzerland, a large body of defenceless Mennonites fled from the Cantons of Zurich (the birth-place of Gessner, Zimmerman, Lavater and Pestalozzi); of Bern and Schaffhausen, about the year 1672, and took up their abode in Alsace, above Strassburg, on the Rhine, where they remained till they emigrated, 1708, to London, thence to Pennsylvania. They lived some time at Germantown, and in the vicinity of Philadelphia. In 1712, they purchased a large tract of land from Penn's agents, in Pequae, then Chester, now Lancaster county. Here this small colony erected some huts or log cabins, to serve temporarily as shelters. Here the time and again persecuted and oppressed Swiss, separated from friends and much that makes life agreeable, hoped to unmolestedly begin anew. Here, surrounded on all sides by several clans of Indians, they located in the gloomy, silent shades of a virgin forest, whose undisturbed solitude was yet

---

* *See App.* No. XII.

uncheered by the murmurs of the honey bee, or the twitterings of the swallow, those never-failing attendants upon the woodman's axe. For the hum and warblings of those, they had not only the shout and song of the tawny sons of the forest, but also the nocturnal howlings of the ever watchful dog, baying at the sheeny queen of night, as she moves stately on, reflecting her borrowed light. By way of variety, their ears were nightly greeted by the shrill, startling whoop of the owl, from some stridulous branches overhanging their cabins, and bending to the breeze of evening, or by the sinister croakings of some doleful night songsters in the contiguous thickets.

This Swiss settlement formed the nucleus, or centre of a rapidly increasing Swiss, French and German population, in the Eden of Pennsylvania.*

Hereafter, the influent accession from the European continent steadily increased, so much so, as to excite attention, and create no small degree of alarm among the "*fearful* of that day."†

It is stated, by a popular *Annalist*, upon the authority of another, that the first settlement in Lancaster county was made by some French families in 1704.— *Watson's Annals*, II., p. 112.

The families named were still at Bittingheim, in the latter part of May, 1708—and only arrived in New York late in December, 1708, as will appear from the sequel.

Mary Führe (Feree) of Bittingheim, High bailiwick of Germersheim, applied March 10, 1708, for a pass to come to the "Island of Pennsylvania"—these are the words in the pass—„auf die Insul Pennsylvanien per Holland und England sich zu begeben und allda zu wohnen vorhaben."

She and her family also applied for a certificate of church membership, May 10, 1708, which sets forth that they were of *La profession de la pure Religion Réformée, fréquente nos saintes assembles, et participe à la cene du Seigneur avec les autres fidèles.* The certificate is signed by *J. Roman*, Pasteur et Inspecteur, attested by the clerk.

Madam Feree, or Wemar, or Warembier, as she was called by all these names, her son Daniel Fiere, Isaac Feber, or La Fevre, and others, accompanied the Rev. Kocherthal to New York in 1708. Here, says current tradition, she remained till 1712. The records at Harrisburg show, that, Sept. 12, 1712, Maria Warenbür, Wemar, or Fiere, at the instance of Martin Kendig had 2,000 acres of land confirmed

---

* For names of first settlers in Pequa Valley, *see App.* No. III.

† Since the days of James Logan, an influential man of the Provincial Council, who, in 1724, said some unkind things of the Germans. In another work the *Editor* notices this charge more fully. Politicians have more than once, in their *threnodies*, complained to the Germans: "We piped, and ye did not dance."

to her at Pequae.—*His. Lan. Co.* p. 102; *O'Calahan's Doc. His. N. Y.*, III., p. 550.—*For the names of those who accompanied Kocherthal, see App.* No. IV.

Scarcely had the Mennonites commenced making their lands arable, when they sent a commissioner, Martin Kendig, to Germany and to Switzerland, to induce others to come to Pennsylvania. He was successful. There were large accessions to this new colony in 1711 and 1717 and a few years later. So great was the influx at this time of Swiss and German immigrants, as to call forth, as already stated, public attention, especially of those in office.

Governor Keith, says the Record, "observed to the Board—the Governor's council—that great numbers of foreigners from Germany, strangers to our language and constitution, having lately been imported into this Province, daily dispersed themselves immediately after landing, *without producing certificates from whence they came or what they are*, and, as they seemed to have first landed in Britain, and afterwards to have left without any license from government, or as far as they know, so, in the same manner, they behaved here, without making the least application to him or any of the magistrates. That, as this practice *might be* of very dangerous consequence, since, by the same method, any number of foreigners, from any nation whatever, enemies as well as friends, might throw themselves upon us." This was in 1717.

This observation by Gov. Keith led to the adoption of a measure, *which has prevented the loss* of the names of upwards of thirty thousand of the first German immigrants to Pennsylvania.* His jealously of

---

* The *Editor* wrote to the Secretary of the State of New York, and inquired of him whether similar Lists as those preserved at Harrisburg, are to be found in the Secretary's office at Albany. The following is the Secretary's reply:

STATE OF NEW YORK, SECRETARY'S OFFICE, } ALBANY, July 18, 1856. }

I. D. RUPP, Esq.

Dear Sir:—We have in our Office no Lists of the kind you refer to. We have indices of foreigners, who file what are called alien depositions, to enable them to hold real estate, and who have become citizens; but these would comprise a very small proportion of the entire number of immigrants, who are brought into the State.　　　　　　Yours, Truly,

M. L. SCHERMERHORN.

the Germans at this time, though he afterwards espoused their cause heartily, has been overruled to preserve the memory of the oppressed and persecuted.—*See Col. Rec.*, III., pp. 29, 228.

In 1719, Jonathan Dickinson remarked: "We are daily expecting ships from London, which bring over Palatines, in number about six or seven thousand. We had a parcel that came over about five years ago, who purchased land about sixty miles west of Philadelphia, and proved quiet and industrious."*

After 1716, Germans, a few French and Dutch, began to penetrate the forest or wilderness—some twenty, thirty, forty, others from sixty to seventy miles, west and north from the metropolis. Large German settlements had sprung up at different points within the present limits of Montgomery and Berks counties. At Goshenhoppen there was a German Reformed church, organized as early as 1717.† Some Mennonites coming from the Netherlands, settled along the *Pakihmomink*,‡ and *Schkipeck* (a) a few years later.

Germans and French located on the fertile lands of *Wahlink* (b) encompassed by hills. Here an opening was made for others— persecuted Huguenots. Amongst the prominent families in Oley were the Turcks or De Turcks, Bertolets, Berdos, De la Plaines, Delangs, Loras, Levans, Yoder, Keim, Herbein, Schaub, Engel, Weidner, Schneider, Alstadt.

Abraham De Turck, of Oley, in a note to the Editor, March 1844, says: "My ancestors, Isaac Turck and De Turck by name, lived in France. They were of the so called Huguenots, on account of which they were obliged to flee to the city of Frankenthal in the Palatinate. Thence they emigrated to America, and, at the time of Queen Anne, they settled in New York in the neighborhood of Esopus. They moved to Oley in 1712. The patent of my land is dated 1712."—*His. Berks Co.*, p. 88.

Isaac Turck, aged 23, husbandman, unmarried, was one of the number who accompanied Kocherthal. *See App.* No. IV.

In this connection, though apparently out of place, it may be stated that nineteen of the number who accompanied Rev. Kocherthal, turned *pietists* the first year; whereupon Kocherthal and Schüneman petitioned the Council, May 26, 1709, that these nineteen might be *deprived of*

---

* These were some of those who had come to Pennsylvania upon the invitation of Martin Kendig.—*His. Lan. Co.*, pp. 79–117.

† *German Reformed Messenger*, Aug. 3, 1842.

‡ Perkioming meaning *at the Cranberry place*. (a) Skippack, i. e. *stinking pool of water*. (b) Oley, by interpretation, *a cavern, cell, also a tract of land, encompassed by hills*.

their sustenance, "because they had withdrawn from the communion of the minister, and the rest of the Germans." June 18th a committee was appointed to inquire into the dispute between the Germans. June 21st this committee reported, "That none of the allegations brought against the *pietists* had been proved before them, and that they should be cared for in like manner with the others."—*O'Calahan's Doc. His. N. Y.*, III., p. 544.

Among the early settlers of Alsace, or Elsace township, Berks county, were many French Reformed or Huguenots; also Swedes who were Lutherans.

"Tradition has it, that the Huguenots, German Reformed and Lutherans held religious meetings within a mile or two of Reading, and in conformity with the good custom of their fathers in Europe, conducted their worship in the evening as well as during the day."—*Bucher.*

The Germans were principally farmers. They depended more upon themselves than upon others. They wielded the mattock, the axe and the maul, and by the power of brawny arms rooted up the grubs, removed saplings, felled the majestic oaks, laid low the towering hickory; prostrated, where they grew, the walnut, poplar, chestnut—cleaved such as suited the purpose, into rails for fences—persevered untiringly until the forest was changed into arable field. They were those of whom Governor Thomas said, 1738: "This Province has been for some years the asylum of the distressed Protestants of the Palatinate, and other parts of Germany; and, I believe, it may truthfully be said, that the *present* flourishing condition of it is in a great measure owing to the *industry of those people;* it is not altogether the fertility of the soil, but the number and industry of the people, that makes a country flourish."—*Col. Rec.* iv. 315.

England understood well the true policy to increase the number of the people in her American colonies,—she retained at home her own subjects, encouraged the emigration of Germans; by this England was the gainer, without any diminution of her inhabitants.

Unreasonable as it may seem, it was this class of Germans, that were so much feared, "whose numbers from Germany at this rate, would soon produce a German colony here, and perhaps such a one as Britain once received from Saxony in the fifth century."*

---

* *Watson's Annals,* II., p. 255.

In 1719, some twenty families of *Schwartzenau Täufer* arrived at Philadelphia. Some settled at Germantown, others located on the Skippack, in Oley, at Conestogo and Mülbach, Lancaster county.

About 1728 and 1729, the Germans crossed the Susquehanna, located within the present limits of York and Adams county, and made improvements under discouraging circumstances. Feuds, so common on the borders of States, existed between the people of Pennsylvania and Maryland—strife for ascendency among the rulers! Some were actually *"kansas'd!"*

In 1736, Thomas Cressap of Maryland, made himself captain—headed some fifty *"congenial spirits,"* for no other purpose, than to drive the Germans from their farms. To inspire his accomplices, he very generously proposed to divide the land owned and improved by the Germans, among his associates. To reward them for anticipated services, he promised each two hundred acres. The Germans were seized by force of arms—their houses demolished—and they themselves carried off and imprisoned, for no other reason than that they were subjects to the proprietory of Pennsylvania.—*Col. Rec.* iv. 69–122.

As early as 1710–1712, German emigrants came to Maryland, settled in the region between Monocacy and the mountain, on the spot where Fredericktown was subsequently laid out by Patrick Dulany, 1745. This first settlement soon extended to the Glades, Middletown and Hagerstown. Between 1748 and 1754, twenty-eight hundred Germans were brought to Maryland, many of whom settled in Baltimore.—*Rev. Zacharias' Centenary Sermon*, 1847. *Butler's History of Maryland*, pp. 51, 52, 61, 62.

The tide of emigration from the continent of Europe was strong. Various influences were brought to bear upon the increase of the influx. In Pennsylvania, the *Neuländer*, tools in the hands of shipowners, merchants and importers, contributed much to induce Germans to leave their homes. There was, besides these, another class, who were active in prevailing upon the inhabitants of Germany to abandon their country for the new world. These two classes, Neuländers and speculators, resorted to diverse arts in order to effect their purposes. They gave those, whom they desired to abandon their homes, assurances, endorsed by solemn promises, that the *Poet's Arcadia* had at last been found in America. To possess this, in Louisiana, on the banks of the Mississippi, several thousands left Germany in 1716 and 1717, under the leadership of the notorious John Law, who, instead of bringing them immediately on their arrival in America, to the promised Eden, on the banks of the Father of the Western Water, landed them on the pontines of Biloxi near the Mobile. Here they were exposed, without protection against their many foes, for five years. Not one of them entered the promised paradise. Two thousand were consigned to the grave. The pallid survivors—about three hundred, finally seated on the banks of the Mississippi, 1722, some thirty or forty miles above New Orleans. Law had, through his agents, engaged twelve thousand Germans and Swiss. The sad fate of those of Biloxi, was spread abroad, which deterred others from coming to participate in the promised blessings of the Elesyan fields, or to possess the *Eldorado!*

The three hundred on the Mississippi were very poor for some years. They had been reduced to the most extreme poverty. "From these poor, but honorable Germans, have sprung," says *Gayarre,* "some of the most respectable citizens of Louisiana, and some of the wealthiest sugar planters in the State." Their descendants forgot the German language, and have adopted the French; but the names of many clearly indicate the blood coursing in their veins; nevertheless more than one name has been so frenchified as to appear of Gallic parentage. The coast, so poor and beggarly at first, and once known as the German coast, has since become the producer and the receptacle of such wealth, as to be now known by the appropriate name of *Cote d'or,* i. e. *Coast of Gold.**

Father Du Poisson, Missionary to the Arkansas, in 1727, in passing along here, visited *Les Allemands,* the Germans, May 10th.—"We advanced six leagues, which is about as much as they can ever accomplish in ascending the river, and we slept, or rather encamped *aux Allemands* (at the Germans). These are the quarters assigned to the lingering remnant of that company of Germans most of whom had died of misery, some at the east,† and some on arriving in Louisiana. Great poverty is visible in their dwellings."—*Early Jesuit Miss.,* II., pp. 236, 262, 263, 267.

In the spring of 1734, some Lutherans, known in history as Saltzburgers, from Saltzburg, a city of Upper Austria, arrived in Georgia. In Europe, they too had been the victims of bloody persecution. "They had been driven from their country and their homes, on account of their unswerving attachment to the principles of the Gospel."‡

---

* *Gayarre's Louisiana,* pp. 360, 361. *Barbe Morbois' His. La.*

† Near Dauphin Islands, twenty-five miles south of Mobile.—*Brown's Illinois,* p. 163.

‡ *Rev. A. P. Strobel's His. of the Saltzburgers,* p. 21—a book that every German should have in his library.

This devotedly pious band of Christians was accompanied by their attached pastors, the Rev'ds. John Martin Boltzius and Israel Christian Gronau, and an excellent schoolmaster, Christian Ortman. The Saltzburgers located in Effingham county, and styled their first settlement Ebenezer, to express their unfeigned gratitude to the Lord, who had been to them, "A strong rock; a house of defence, to save them."*

The Schoolmaster was deemed no less important than the pastor. "The cause of education was not overlooked by the Germans. A fund was subsequently created for the schoolmaster's support; for our pious forefathers judged, and very correctly too, that no country can prosper in which provision is not made for the mental culture and improvement of the rising generation."—*Strobel.*

This German colony received accessions from time to time, until they reached, prior to 1745, several hundred families. There were also many Germans residing in Savannah; besides some forty or fifty Moravians in the same State, under the pastoral care of the Rev. David Nitschman.

"The Moravians made no permanent settlement in Georgia. When the Spanish war broke out, they removed, almost to a man, to the State of Pennsylvania, because it was contrary to their religious faith to take up arms in any cause."†

In 1738, some arrived in Pennsylvania and located at Bethlehem.‡ "In 1740, those who had remained, left Georgia and joined their brethren in Pennsylvania. Thus the mission among the Indians in Georgia, after a promising beginning, was at once suspended."§

Before the Moravians came to Pennsylvania, a respectable number of Schwenckfelders had arrived, settling in Bucks and Philadelphia county, now Montgomery, Berks and Lehigh. The Schwenckfelders had intended, before leaving their homes in Europe, to embark for Georgia. They, however, changed their minds and established themselves in the asylum for the oppressed, Pennsylvania.

In 1732, Monsieur Jean Pierre Pury, of Neuchatel, Switzerland, visited Carolina. Being encouraged by the Government

---

* For names of males of first settlers, *see App.* No. IX.

† *Strobel's Saltzburgers,* p. 80.

‡ For names of those who left Georgia and came to Pennsylvania, *see Addenda B.—Grantz' Brüder-Geschichte* p. 302.

§ *Loskiel,* Part II., p. 6.

both of England and Carolina, he undertook to settle a colony of Swiss there. In 1732, one hundred and seventy persons were transported. These were soon followed by others. In a short time the colony consisted of three hundred persons. They settled on the north bank of the Savannah, built a town called *Purysburgh*, about thirty-six miles above the mouth of the river. The colony still continued to increase. In 1734, Pury brought two hundred and seventy persons more from Switzerland. All these were brought from Switzerland at the expense of Pury and several of his friends, who advanced him money for that purpose, he having spent the greatest part of his fortune in the prosecution of that design, before he could bring it to execution. There were now nearly six hundred souls in this settlement.

"This was done in pursuance of a scheme, proposed by Mr. Pury to the Assembly of South Carolina; his scheme was to people the southern frontier of Carolina with brave and laborious people, such as the Swiss are known to be. The Assembly highly approved of this scheme; to assist him in the execution of it, they passed an act, August 20, 1731, which secured to him a reward of £400, upon his bringing over to Carolina a hundred effective men. In this act the Assembly promised also to find provisions, tools, &c., for three hundred persons for one year. Purysburgh in 1747, contained more than one hundred houses tolerably well built.

In Colleton county, on the north bank of North Ediston river, 12 miles from its mouth, stands *Wilton*, or New London, consisting of 80 houses built by Swiss under the direction of Zuberbühler, with leave from the Assembly. This town proved detrimental to Purysburgh, being in the heart of the country and near the capital; it drew people thither, who did not care to go to Purysburgh."—*Bowen's Geog.* ii. 645. *London edition*, 1750.

From 1740–1755, a great many Palatines were sent to South Carolina. They settled Orangeburg, Congaree and Wateree.[*] In 1765, upwards of six hundred from the Palatinate and Swabia were sent over from London, and had a township of land set apart for them.[†]

---

[*] *Ramsay's S. C.* i. 3, 4.

[†] *Holme's American Annals*, ii. 268.—*Proceedings of the House of Commons, England, Aug.* 1764.

Many of the Dutch colonists, dissatisfied with their situation in New York, after the submission of the colony to the crown of England, repaired to South Carolina, and contributed by their industry to the cultivation of the province. The success that attended them induced more of their countrymen to follow their example.—*Ramsay.*

In 1679, Charles II. sent at his own expense, in two ships, a company of Huguenots to South Carolina, in order that they might cultivate the vine, the olive, &c. In 1752, no fewer than sixteen hundred Protestants, chiefly French, settled in South Carolina.—*Holmes; Baird.*

In 1739, a number of Lutherans and German Reformed purchased a tract of land from General Waldo, and laid out the town Waldoborough, in Lincoln county, Maine. Bremen, a village in the same county, and Frankfort, in Waldo county, were undoubtedly laid out, or settled by Germans, as the names would indicate. During the Spanish and French war, in 1746, Waldoborough was laid in ashes by some Canadian Indians. Some of the inhabitants were massacred, others abducted. Not a few died from the ill-treatment received at the hands of the savages,—some made their escape, and were dispersed in Canada. Waldoborough remained in ruins until 1750. In 1751, invited by those in authority, thirty German families, and in 1752, fifteen hundred individuals from Europe, persons of means, settled in Maine. "The title of land from General Waldo proving unsound, many left the colony, and its numbers have never greatly increased."—*Hazelius,* pp. 34, 48, &c. *Löher,* 1772. "Some of them left Maine to join their countrymen at Londonderry, South Carolina, but most of these repented of having taken that step, and returned to Maine, where their descendants are to be found to this day."—*Baird.*

King George II. of Great Britain, held out strong inducements, through very liberal promises, to all who would emigrate into, and settle Nova Scotia, when a considerable body of Germans, principally Hanoverians, left their country, embarked for America, landed at Chebucto bay, near Halifax, the capital of Nova Scotia, where fourteen hundred and fifty-three re-embarked, and landed at Marliguish, on the 7th of June, 1753. "Here they laid out the flourishing town of Lunenburg. Here they were doomed to experience the same resistance from the natives which the colonists at Halifax had met with, in settling the Peninsula; and the early history of the place contains little else than a constant succession of struggles with the savages, in which, notwithstanding the powerful protection they received from the Government, they lost many lives. Their attempts at agriculture were therefore restricted within a very narrow compass, and the settlement of the adjoining country was retarded until the French power and influence in Nova Scotia were subdued."—*Haliburton's His. Nova Scotia*, I., p. 162; *Murray's Brit. Amer*, II., p. 55; *Löher*, pp. 68, 74; *M' Culloch's Uni.*, II., p. 498.

From 1735, settlements in Pennsylvania multiplied rapidly; extended over vast regions, west of the SAOSQUAHANAUNK,* whither the Scotch-Irish had led the way. The German settlements kept pace with the native. From the Susquehanna westwards, in Cumberland Valley, they had located prior to 1765 along the limpid CALLAPASSCINK (*a*), on either side of the sinuous SUNIPDUCKHANNET (*b*), and farther west, along the GUNNEUKISSCHIK (*c*); three principal streams, draining this fertile, highly improved district of country.

The KAU-TA-TIN-CHUNK (*d*), extending from the Delaware hundreds of miles westwards, was not an insurmountable barrier, —that they crossed, and laid out farms, "where shortly afterwards they, their wives and children, were exposed to the torch, hatchet and scalping knife of the savages, and their midnight assault and slaughter." Hundreds fell victims to the relentlessly cruel savage, along the Blue Mountains, south and north of them and along the Susquehanna, as far north as Penn's Creek, from 1754–1763, and even at a later period. Among the massacred were many Germans—more than three hundred in all.

Germans massacred, north of the Blue Mountain, within Monroe county, among others, were: Guldin, Höth, or Huth, Bömper, Vanaken, Vanflör, Schnell, Hartman, Hage, Brundich, Hellman, Gonderman, Schleich, Müller, Vandelap, Decker, Van Gondie, Brincker. South and north of the same mountain, within the present limits of Northampton, Carbon and Lehigh—more than one hundred were killed. Among them were: Sohn, Klein, Bittenbender, Roth, Schäffer, Anders, Nitschman, Senseman, Gattermyer, Fabricius, Schweigert, Leslie, Presser, Depu. Along the same mountain, within the limits of Berks, Lebanon and Dauphin county—Reichelsdörfer, Gerhart, Neidung, Klug, or Kluck, Linderman, Schott, Kraushar, Zeissloff, Wünch, Dieppel, Henly, Spitler, Nöcker, Maurer, Böshar, Fell, Kühlmer, Lang, Trump, Yäger, Sechler, Schetterly, Sauter, Geiger, Ditzler,

* Susquehanna, *i. e.* Long-crooked-river. (*a*) Yellow breeches, the signification of the Indian name is, Where-it-turns-back-again. (*b*) Canodoquinet, *i. e.* For-a-long-way-nothing-but-bents. (*c*) Canococheague, *i. e.* Indeed-a-long-journey. (*d*) The *Kittatiny* or Blue Mountain.

2*

Frantz, Schnebele, Mosser, Fincher, Hubler, Martloff, Wolf, Händsche, Weisser, Miess, Lebenguth, Motz, Noah, Winkelblech, Zeuchmacher, &c

Prior to 1770, the wilderness of Pennsylvania was penetrated beyond the Allegheny Mountains. Settlements were effected within the present bounds of Westmoreland and other western counties of this State. A number of German families had located on the Monongahela as far up as Redstone, Brownsville, Fayette county. Here settled the Weismans, Pressers, Vervalsons, Delongs, Jungs, Martins, Shutts, Peters, Schwartz, Hutters, Cackeys, Abrahams, and others,* whom that devoted minister of the cross, the *Rev. John Conrad Bucher*, visited in November, 1768.—*Col. Rec.*, IX., p. 508; *German Reformed Messenger*, May 24, 1854; *Rupp's History of Berks Co.*, p. 459. *For names of many other Germans in Westmoreland county, see the History of Western Pennsylvania, by the Editor.*

---

* The first Germans in Western Pennsylvania, located in Greene county. These were two brothers, the Eckerleins of Ephrata, who left there and settled in the depths of the wilderness, in 1745.—*Chronicon Ephratense*, pp. 158, 195, 197. *Col. Rec.*, V., p. 531. Prior to 1754, Wendel Braun, and his two sons, and Frederick Waltzer, located four miles west of Uniontown.—*Smith's Old Redstone*, p. 25.

Allgemeine Einleitung.

Kurze Bemerkungen über die bedeutendsten deutschen, schweizerischen und französischen Ansiedelungen in Nordamerika
während der Colonialzeit.*

Liebe nach Ruhm, das Streben nach Vergrößerung ihrer Herr-
schaft und die Begierde, ihr Scepter über unterjochten Völkern zu
schwingen, beeinflußten die alten Deutschen ihren Herd zu verlassen
und Eroberungen zu machen. Dadurch erwiesen sie sich vor Alters
wie im Mittelalter als die „Herren der Welt."

Mannigfaltig waren die Ursachen und Beweggründe, welche
sie zu verschiedenen Zeiten bewogen, ihr Vaterland zu verlassen.
Seit 1606 haben Millionen ihrer Heimath, dem Theuersten auf
Erden, nach dem sich die Seele immer wieder zurücksehnt, den
Rücken zugekehrt. Religiöse Verfolgungen und staatliche Unter-
jochung trieben Tausende nach Pennsylvanien, der Zufluchtsstätte
für die gequälten und unterdrückten Söhne und Töchter der
Reformation, und wohin auch William Penn selbst die Verfolgten
jeden Bekenntnisses und religiöser Anschauung einlud.

Von 1682–1776 war Pennsylvanien der Centralpunkt der
Einwanderung von Deutschland, Frankreich und der Schweiz.
Penn's liberale Ansichten und der höchst unliberale Weg, den die
Regierung von New York gegen die Deutschen eingeschlagen hatte,
brachten viele in diese Provinz. (Siehe Anhang Nr. X.)

In dem ersten Zeitabschnitt von 1682–1702 kamen verhältnißmäßig nur wenige Deutsche an: wohl nicht mehr als zwei hundert Familien, die sich meistens in Germantown niederließen. Dieselben waren beinahe sämmtlich Plattdeutsche aus Cleve, einem
Herzogthum in Westphalen, und langten hier in den Jahren
1683–1685 an. Da sie ihr Vaterland zu der Zeit verließen,
so entgingen sie, Dank der göttlichen Vorsehung, den Verheerun-

---

* In dem Werke "Fireside History of German and Swiss Immigrants"
findet der Leser umfassendere Auskunft über diese Ansiedelungen.

gen des französischen Krieges, welcher 1689 die Stadt Worms
zerstörte, in deren Nähe sie gewohnt hatten, und das Land meilen=
weit verwüstete. Von jedem Marktflecken, von jedem Dörfchen,
von jeder Pfarrkirche, von jedem Landsitze innerhalb der unglück=
lichen Provinzen loderten die Flammen empor. In demselben
Jahre wurden ebenfalls zerstört: Rohrbach, Laimen, Nußloch,
Wißloch, Kirchheim, Bruckhausen, Eppelnheim, Wieblingen,
Edingen, Neckerhausen und Handschuhsheim im Herzogthum
Baden, in welchem nach Kayser Johannes Schad und Lud=
wig Rupp verbrannt worden sind.—Kayser's Schauplatz
von Heidelberg, S. 505.

Franz Daniel Pastorius, geboren zu Sommerhausen in Fran=
ken am 26. Sept. 1651, landete in Philadelphia mit dem Schiffe
„Amerika", Capitän Joseph Wasey, am 20. August 1683 sammt
seiner Familie. Seine Begleiter waren einige deutsche Einwan=
derer: Jakob Schuhmacher, Georg Wertmüller, Isaak Dilbeck,
Frau und zwei Kinder, Abraham und Jakob, Thomas Gasper,
Conrad Bucher, alias Rutter, und ein englisches Mädchen, Namens
Franzes Simpson. Andere folgten Pastorius bald nach. (Für
eine Liste der Namen und der ersten Ansiedler von Germantown
siehe Anhang Nr. I.) Pastorius ließ sich in demselben Jahre,
in dem er nach Pennsylvanien gekommen, da nieder, wo er hernach
Germantown gründete. Der Grund zu dieser Niederlassung
wurde von ihm bereits am 12. Oktober 1683 aufgenommen. Den
Anfang der Stadt machten dreizehn Familien. In weniger als
fünf Jahren waren schon fünfzig Häuser errichtet.

Die Periode von 1702–1727 bezeichnet einen Zeitabschnitt in
der Geschichte der ersten deutschen Einwanderung. Zwischen vier=
zig und fünfzig tausend verließen ihre Heimath. Die beispiellosen
Verheerungen und Verwüstungen der Truppen Ludwig's XIV.
unter Turenne, waren das traurige Vorspiel blutiger Verfol=
gungen. Um diesen schrecklichen Leiden, die ihrer erwarteten, zu
entgehen, wanderten deutsche und andere Protestanten nach den
englischen Colonien in Amerika aus.

1705 flüchtete sich eine Anzahl Deutsch=Reformirter, die zwischen
Wolfenbüttel und Halberstadt wohnten, nach Neuwied und von
dort nach Holland, wo sie sich 1707 nach New York einschifften.
Widrige Winde trieben ihr Schifflein die Delaware Bay hinauf.
Da sie sich's jedoch vorgenommen hatten, an den Ort ihrer Be=
stimmung zu gelangen und ihre Heimath unter den Holländern
zu suchen, nahmen sie von Philadelphia den Ueberlandweg nach

New York. Als sie aber das entzückende Thal Nova Cäsaria in New Jersey zu Gesicht bekamen, welches durch den sich hinschlängelnden Musconetcong, Passaic und deren Zuflüsse getränkt wird, und gutes Land gefunden hatten, entschlossen sie sich daselbst zu bleiben. Diese Niederlassung ist jetzt unter dem Namen "German Valley von Morrison County" bekannt. Von diesem Punkt verbreiteten sich die Deutschen über die Counties Somerset, Bergen und Essex.

In Elisabethtown, der ersten englischen Niederlassung im Staate New Jersey vom Jahre 1664, gab es viele Deutsche schon vor 1730.* Zu Mill Hall, einem von Philadelphia etwa dreißig Meilen entfernten Orte, war ebenfalls eine deutsche Niederlassung.†

Eine wohlbegründete Ueberlieferung behauptet, daß am Anfang des achtzehnten Jahrhunderts sich eine aus zweihundert protestantischen Polen bestehende Colonie in den Thälern des Passaic und Raritan in New Jersey niedergelassen habe. Dieselbe hatte den Grafen Sobieski zum Führer, einen direkten Abkömmling des weltberühmten Polenkönigs Johann Sobieski, der im Jahre 1683 vor Wien die Türken auf's Haupt schlug. Der in New Jersey und New York sich noch findende Name Zabriskie scheint eine verdorbene Form von Sobieski zu sein.—Bard's Rel. Am., p. 81.

Auf eine Einladung der Königin Anna verließen in den Jahren 1708 und 1709 dreiunddreißig tausend ihre Heimath in den Rheinländern, von denen im Sommer 1708 etwa zwölf oder dreizehn tausend in London ankamen.‡ Diese Ankömmlinge waren eine Zeitlang in einer solch' hülflosen Lage, daß sie ganz und gar von der Mildthätigkeit der Bewohner der Hauptstadt England's abhängig sein mußten.

Im Spätjahr 1709 wurden ein hundert und fünfzig pfälzische Familien, bestehend aus sechs hundert und fünfzig Seelen, unter der Aufsicht und dem Schutze des Christian de Graffenried und Ludwig Michell, beide Schweizer von Geburt, nach Nord-Caro-

---

* "June 16th, 1734, at 10 o'clock A. M., I came to Elizabethtown, where many Germans reside. This place is several miles in length, but the houses are sometimes separated by a considerable distance."—*Reck, Ulsperger's Nachrichten*, p. 159.

† Pastor Michael Schlatter predigte hier 1746.

‡ "Bücher und Zeitungen wurden in der Pfalz verbreitet. Auf den Büchern war der Königin Bild und das Titelblatt mit goldenen Buchstaben verziert, weshalb sie auch das „goldene Buch" genannt wurden. Ihr Zweck war, die Pfälzer zu bewegen, nach England zu kommen, um nach den Carolinas oder andern Colonien Ihrer Majestät als Ansiedler geschickt zu werden."—Journal des englischen Unterhauses, XVI., S. 467, 468.

lina gesandt. Wie in allen neuen Ländern, so waren auch die
Pfälzer hier Prüfungen, Entbehrungen und Beschwerden, wie sie
sich im Grenzleben stets finden, ausgesetzt. Die Tuskarora India=
ner metzelten am 22. Sept. 1711 ein hundert derselben nieder.*
Die Abkömmlinge dieser Deutschen wohnen in verschiedenen Thei=
len des Staates zerstreut.†

Nord=Carolina erhielt einen beständigen Zufluß von deutschen Einwan=
derern. Im ersten Drittheil des letzten Jahrhunderts kam Toblar, und
zur selben Zeit ließ sich Pastor Zuberbühler von St. Gallen mit einer
großen Anzahl seiner Landsleute in Granville County nieder. Toblar wurde
bald darauf zum Friedensrichter ernannt. Außer diesen zogen viele Deutsche
aus Pennsylvanien und Virginien dahin und schlugen ihren Wohnsitz in
den gebirgigen Gegenden auf. Lincolnton, Stokes, sowie auch Granville
County haben Deutsche colonisirt. Die aus Pennsylvanien eingewanderten
Deutschen in Nord=Carolina zählten 1785 allein über fünfzehn hundert
Personen.—Löher, S. 69.

Im Jahre 1707 langte eine Gesellschaft französischer Protestanten an,
die sich am Flusse Trent, einem Arm der Neuse, den Ort ihrer Niederlas=
sung wählten.—Hale's Ver. St., S. 98.

Zur Zeit, als diese Pfälzer sich von England nach Nord=Caro=
lina einschifften, ging auch Pastor Josua Kocherthal mit einer
kleinen Herde seiner verfolgten lutherischen Glaubensbrüder in
London auf's Schiff (1708), um nach New York überzusegeln,
wo sie auch im December desselben Jahres ankamen und sich kurz
darauf an den oberen Ufern des Hudson auf einem Strichen
Landes, welches ihnen die Krone England's geschenkt hatte,‡ an=
siedelten. Die Königin genehmigte Pastor Kocherthal weitere
fünf hundert Acker als Kirchengut für die lutherische Kirche. Neu=
burg ist der Ort dieser Niederlassung.§—Pastor Kocherthal, 1719.

Während diese nach Nord=Carolina und New York geschickt
wurden, setzte man drei tausend sechs hundert Deutsche nach Ir=
land über, zum Bebauen uncultivirten Landes im County Lime=
rick in der Nähe von Arbela und Adair; Anderen wurde das
Städtchen Rathkeale zum Wohnort angewiesen, wo ihre Nach=

---

* „Der Jahrestag dieses Blutbads wurde viele Jahre lang mit Fasten
und Beten festlich begangen."—Williamson's N. C., I., S. 193, 194.

† Siehe Anhang Nr. VIII. u. IX.

‡ „Zwei tausend ein hundert Acker laut königlichen Befehls, 18. Decbr.
1709."—O'Calahan's Doc. His. N. Y., p. 591.

§ Brodhead's Doc. Gesch. von N. Y., V., S. 67. Die Namen von
Kocherthal's Begleitern wurden erhalten und sind im Staatsarchiv zu New
York zu finden.—Siehe Anhang Nr. IV.

kommen sich noch finden und heutiges Tages als „deutsche Pfäl=
zer" bekannt sind, und als solche auch ihrem ächten deutschen
Charakter, dem Fleiß, der Wirthschaftlichkeit und dem ehrlichen
Handeln, treu geblieben sind. Reisende, welche dieselben kürzlich
besucht, sagen von ihnen: „Sie sind die reichsten und wohlhabend=
sten Bauern in Limerick County."* Dieselben sprechen auch die
deutsche Sprache noch.†

Von der großen Anzahl, die in den Jahren 1708 und 1709
nach England gekommen waren, kehrten sieben tausend, nachdem
sie große Leiden ausgestanden, in halb nacktem und verzweifeltem
Zustand in ihr Vaterland zurück. Zehn tausend starben aus
Mangel an Nahrungsmitteln, ärztlichem Beistand und anderen
Ursachen. Andere kamen auf Schiffen um. Die noch Ueberleben=
den wurden nach den englischen Colonien in Amerika gebracht.
Etliche tausend wollten nach den südwestlich von England ge=
legenen Scilly=Inseln überschiffen, sind aber nie daselbst ange=
kommen.

Zehn Schiffe waren mit über vier tausend Deutschen beladen
und für New York bestimmt. Am 25. Decbr. 1709 segelten die=
selben und liefen im Juni 1710 nach einer sechsmonatlichen höchst
beschwerlichen Reise im Hafen von New York ein.‡ Auf ihrer
Reise in's Innere kurz nach dem Anlanden, starben siebzehn hun=
dert. Die Ueberlebenden schlugen ihr Lager in Zelten auf, welche
sie von England mitgebracht hatten, und zwar auf Nutting, dem
jetzigen Governor's Island. Hier verblieben sie bis spät im
Herbst, als etwa vierzehn hundert nach Livingston Manor, hun=
dert Meilen am Hudson hinauf, verlegt wurden. Die verwittweten
Frauen, kränklichen Männer und Waisen blieben in New York.§
Die Waisen gab Gouverneur Hunter Bürgern von New York
und New Jersey in die Lehre.‖

Die nach dem Hudson Geschickten waren unter Verpflichtung,
der Königin Anna als gehorsame Unterthanen dankbarst zu die=

* Journal des englischen Unterhauses, XVI., S. 465; Method. Quarterly Rev., Okt. 1855, S. 489.

† Fliegende Blätter, II., S. 672.

‡ Siehe Brodhead's Doc. Gesch. N. Y., V., S. 167.

§ Eine Namensliste der in New York zurückgebliebenen Familien findet
sich im Anhang Nr. V.

‖ Anhang Nr. VI. gibt eine Namensliste der in die Lehre gegebenen
Kinder.

nen, Theer zu kochen und Hanf zu bauen, um die vom Parlamente
gewährte Summe von zehn tausend Pfund Sterling, welche ihre
Ueberfahrt kostete, zurückzuerstatten. Man hatte erwartet, auf
solche Weise das Schiffsmagazin zu füllen. Grund übler Ver-
waltung erwies sich aber dieser Versuch als gänzlich mißlungen.*

Die so ungerecht unterdrückten Deutschen wurden mit ihrer
Behandlung und Lage unzufrieden. Gouverneur Hunter griff
zu gewaltthätigen Maßregeln, um seinen Befehlen Gehorsam zu
erzwingen. Auch dies mißlang ihm. Im Spätherbst 1712
brachen ein hundert und fünfzig Familien, um dem sichern Hun-
gertod zu entgehen, nach dem sechzig Meilen nordwestlich von
Livingston Manor gelegenen Schoharie=Thal auf. Da gab's
keine durchbrochene Straßen, keine Pferde, die ihr Gepäck getragen
oder gezogen hätten. Dies lud man auf grobgezimmerte Schlitten
und schleppte es mit eigener Hand durch den drei Fuß tiefen
Schnee, der ihr Vorwärtskommen sehr hinderte. Ihr Weg führte
durch das Dickicht des Urwaldes, durch dessen entlaubte Zweige
der schneidend kalte Wind pfiff und die fallenden Schneeflocken
zornig durcheinander jagte. Die Reise dauerte drei volle Wochen.
In Schoharie angelangt, bebauten sie die ihnen von der Königin
Anna verliehenen Ländereien. Hier verweilten sie zehn volle
Jahre, bis ihnen Grund eines Versehens in ihrer Urkunde ihr
sämmtliches Land mit allen Verbesserungen entrissen wurde. Im
Frühjahr 1723 brachen drei und dreißig Familien auf und
schlugen ihren Wohnort in Tulpehocken, etwa fünfzehn Meilen
westlich von Reading, auf. Einige Jahre darauf folgten Andere
nach.†

Die übrigen unzufriedenen Deutschen zu Schoharie, die ihren
Freunden nicht nach Pennsylvanien folgen wollten, suchten sich
im Mohawk Thale eine zukünftige Heimath.

New York war schon frühe ein Zufluchtsort für die französischen Protestanten, gewöhnlich Hugenotten genannt. Schon 1656 waren dieselben zahlreich im Staate vorhanden. An Zahl und Gütern kamen sie den Holländern am nächsten. New Rochelle, das nahe der Küste der Meerenge
von Long Island gelegen ist, wurde ausschließlich von Hugenotten aus
Rochelle in Frankreich gegründet. „Die Emigranten kauften von John
Poll 6000 Acker Land. Ein ehrwürdiger Hugenotte, so erzählt man, ging

---

* Im Anhang Nr. VII. findet sich eine Namensliste dieser Familien zu
Livingston Manor.

† Anhang Nr. XIV. gibt eine Namensliste der ersten Ansiedler in Tulpehocken.

täglich an die Küste und, indem er sein Auge Frankreich zu richtete, sang er eins von Marot's Liedern und schickte sein Morgengebet zum Himmel. Andere stimmten mit ein in das Lob ihres Gottes und in die Erinnerungen an ihr geliebtes Vaterland, aus dem sie die grausamen Feuer der Verfolgung vertrieben."—Weiß' Gesch. der franz. prot. Ref., II., S. 304.

In den Counties Ulster und Dutcheß wohnen noch viele ihrer Abkömmlinge. In Ulster finden sich die Sprossen von Dubois, Dian oder Deyo, Hasbroucq oder Hasbrouck, La Febre, Bevier, Crispell, Freir u. s. w.—Siehe die Namen der männlichen Einwohner von New Rochelle 1710, im Anhang Nr. XIII.

Die Königin Anna, welche die Staatsklugheit England's ausgezeichnet verstand, sorgte stets dafür, daß ihre eigenen Unterthanen zu Hause blieben, die Deutschen aber zur Auswanderung aufgemuntert würden. So schickte sie einige von denen, die sie in den Jahren 1708 und 1709 nach England gelockt hatte, nach Virginien, wo ihnen ein Stück Landes oberhalb der Wasserfälle des Rappahannock in Spottsylvania County angewiesen wurde. Daselbst gründeten sie die Stadt Germanna. Die Gegend war ungünstig. Sie zogen deshalb einige Meilen stromaufwärts, wo sie bald Glück hatten.* Von dieser Niederlassung verbreiteten sie sich über mehrere Counties von Virginien und Nord=Carolina.

Die Counties Shanandoah und Rockingham in Virginien wurden vor 1746 von Deutschen aus Pennsylvanien angesiedelt. Viele von ihren Nachkommen reden noch die deutsche Sprache.

Als George Washington und Andere im April 1748 in jenem Theil Virginien's ihre Ländereien vermaßen, „liefen ihnen Schaaren von Männern, Weibern und Kindern zu, die ihnen durch die Wälder nachfolgten und nie englisch sprachen, aber, wenn angeredet, in deutscher Sprache antworteten."—Spark's Washington, II., S. 418.

1690 schickte König William eine große Anzahl französischer Protestanten nach Virginien. Eine weitere Sendung von sechs hundert Hugenotten kam unter Philipp De Richebourg nach Virginien. Ihnen wurde eine Strecke Landes auf der Südseite des James=Flusses, etwa zwanzig Meilen von der jetzigen Lage Richmond's, angewiesen.—Howison's Virginien, II., S. 160, 161.

Einige der Namen dieser Hugenotten sind uns erhalten worden; z. B. Chastain, David, Monford, Dykar, Neirn, Dupuy, Bilbo, Dutoi, Salle, Martain, Allaigre, Vilain, Soblet, Chambon, Levilain, Trabu, Loucadou, Gasper, Flournoy, Arnis, Banton, Sasain, Solaigre, Givodan, Mallet, Ducy, Bondurant, Goin, Pero, Pean, Deen, Edmond, Benin, Stanford, Forqueran, Roberd, Brian, Faure, Don, Bingli, Reno, Lesueur, Pinnet, Trent, Sumter, Morriset, Jordin, Gavin.—Weiß' Gesch. der franz. prot. Ref., II., S. 322.

---

* Siehe Anhang Nr. XII.

3

In Folge der unaufhörlichen Verfolgung und Unterdrückung in der Schweiz floh eine große Menge schutzloser Mennoniten aus den Cantonen Zürich (dem Geburtsort von Geßner, Zimmermann, Lavater und Pestalozzi), Bern und Schaffhausen um's Jahr 1672 nach dem Elsaß und ließ sich oberhalb Straßburg am Rhein nieder. Von hier wanderten dieselben 1708 nach London und von dort nach Pennsylvanien aus. Eine Zeitlang wohnten sie in Germantown und in der Nähe Philadelphia's. 1712 kauften sie eine große Strecke Landes in Pequae, damals Chester, jetzt Lancaster County, von Penn's Agenten an, worauf dieselben dann Hütten und Blockhäuser errichteten, welche ihnen zeitweilig ein Obdach gewähren mußten. Hier hofften die immer und immer wieder verfolgten und unterdrückten Schweizer, getrennt von ihren Freunden und so manchen Annehmlichkeiten dieses Lebens, ungehindert von Neuem anfangen zu können. Auf allen Seiten von mehreren Indianerstämmen eingeschlossen, hatten sie sich da in den düstern, stillen Schatten eines jugendlichen Waldes zurückgezogen, dessen ungestörte Einsamkeit noch nicht von dem Summen der Biene oder den Flügelschlägen der Schwalbe begrüßt worden war, welche die nie fehlenden Begleiter der Axt des Holzhackers sind. Anstatt des Hummens und Geschwätzes dieser hörten sie nicht blos den Ruf und Gesang des rothbraunen Waldessohnes, sondern auch das nächtliche Geheul des stets wachsamen Hundes, der der lichten Königin der Nacht, wie sie so stattlich einherzieht und ihr geborgtes Licht wiederstrahlt, nachbellt. Um einer größeren Mannigfaltigkeit willen drang auch das schrille, erschreckende Gekrächze der Eule nächtlich in ihre Ohren, die auf einem verborgenen Aste über ihren Hütten die Abendluft einsaugt, oder das schauerliche, klägliche Geschrei eines Nachtvogels in seinem finsteren Dickicht.

Diese schweizerische Niederlassung bildete den Knoten- oder Mittelpunkt einer schnell zunehmenden Bevölkerung von Schweizern, Franzosen und Deutschen im Eden Pennsylvanien's.*

Der vom europäischen Continente hereinströmende Zuwachs mehrte sich beständig, so daß er die Aufmerksamkeit wach rief und bei den Furchtsamen jenes Tages nicht geringe Besorgniß verursachte.†

---

* Die Namen der ersten Ansiedler im Pequa Thale sind im Anhang Nr. III. angegeben.

† Seit den Tagen eines James Logan, eines einflußreichen Mannes im provincialen Concil, der 1724 den Deutschen höchst unschöne Dinge nach-

Ein volksthümlicher Geschichtschreiber berichtet auf die Behauptung eines andern, daß die erste Niederlassung in Lancaster County im Jahre 1704 die einiger französischen Familien war.—Watson's Annalen, II., S. 112.

Die genannten Familien waren Ende Mai 1708 noch in Bittingheim und kamen erst in der letzten Hälfte des Monats Dezbr. 1708, wie unten noch weiter gezeigt werden wird, in New York an.

Marie Führe (Feree) aus Bittingheim, Oberamt Germersheim, suchte am 10. März 1708 um einen Paß nach mit der Absicht „auf die Insul Pennsylvanien per Holland und England sich zu begeben und allda zu wohnen vorhaben."

Am 10. Mai 1708 erbat sie sich auch ein kirchliches Zeugniß für sich und ihre Familie; dasselbe bestätigt, daß „sie der lautern reformirten Glaubenslehre angehören, unsere öffentlichen Gottesdienste besucht und mit andern Gläubigen am Mahle des Herrn Antheil genommen haben." Unterzeichnet ist es von J. Roman, Pastor und Inspektor, und beglaubigt von einem Schreiber.

Frau Feree, oder Wemar, oder Warembier (wie sie genannt wurde) begleitete mit ihrem Sohne Daniel Fiere, Isaak Feber oder La Fevre und andern im Jahre 1708 den Pastor Kocerthal nach New York. Hier soll sie bis 1712 geblieben sein. Die Urkunden zu Harrisburg zeigen, daß am 12. Sept. 1712 durch die Vermittlung von Martin Kendig, Maria Warenbuer, Wemar oder Fiere 2000 Acker Land zu Pequae zugesprochen wurden.—Gesch. Lanc. Co., S. 102. O'Callahan's Doc. Gesch. N. J., III., S. 550. Die Namen der Begleiter Kocerthal's, s. Anhang Nr. IV.

Kaum hatten die Mennoniten ihre Ländereien baubar gemacht, so sandten sie schon Martin Kendig als Bevollmächtigten nach Deutschland und der Schweiz, um andere zu bewegen, nach Pennsylvanien zu kommen. Er hatte großen Erfolg. 1711 und 1717 und einige Jahre später erfuhr die Colonie einen bedeutenden Zuwachs. So zahlreich war die Einwanderung von Deutschen und Schweizern, daß, wie schon oben darauf hingewiesen, dieselbe besonders bei Beamten Bedenken erregte.

So erzählt die Staats=Chronik: „Gouverneur Keith wies sein Collegium, den Gouverneurs=Rath, auf die große Anzahl der Fremden aus Deutschland hin, die unsere Sprache und Verfassung nicht kennen und kürzlich in diese Provinz hereingebracht wurden. Dieselben zerstreuen sich gleich nach ihrer Ankunft, ohne zuvor schriftlich zu zeigen, woher sie kommen und wer sie sind, und wie sie sich in England betragen, welches sie ohne Erlaubniß der Re=

---

sagte, und seiner Nachbeter, die noch zu behaupten wagten, was er nur unter Furcht aussagte, hat die Vergangenheit festgestellt, daß solche Verdächtigungen ohne guten Grund waren. In einem andern Werk nimmt der Editor vollständigere Notiz von dieser Anklage. Politiker haben schon mehr als einmal das Klagelied über die Deutschen angestimmt: „Wir haben euch gepfiffen und ihr wolltet nicht tanzen."

gierung verlassen haben, so auch hier, da sie sich weder bei ihm
noch bei einer anderen obrigkeitlichen Person gemeldet. Solche
Handlungsweise könnte sich als sehr gefährlich erweisen, da auf
gleichem Wege irgend eine beliebige Anzahl Fremder, von welcher
Nation sie immer sein mögen, Freunde oder Feinde, uns zuströmen
möchte." So geschrieben 1717.

Diese Bemerkung des Gouverneurs Keith führte zur Annahme einer
Maßregel, die das Verlorengehen von über dreißig tausend Namen der ersten
deutschen Einwanderer in Pennsylvanien verhinderte.* Sein Mißtrauen,
das er damals gegen die Deutschen hegte, obwohl er nachher ihre Interesse
eifrig vertrat, mußte dazu ausschlagen, daß das Gedächtniß der Unterdrückten
und Verfolgten nicht ausgewischt wurde.—Siehe Col. Rec., III., S. 29, 228.

1719 bemerkte Jonathan Dickinson: „Täglich erwarten wir
Schiffe von London, die von sechs bis sieben tausend Pfälzer her=
überbringen sollen. Ein Theil derselben kam vor etwa fünf Jahren
herüber; dieselben kauften sich sechzig Meilen westlich von Phila=
delphia Land an und erweisen sich als friedliche und arbeitsame
Leute."†

Nach dem Jahre 1716 begannen die Deutschen, etliche Fran=
zosen und einige wenige Holländer, wohl zwanzig, dreißig, vierzig,
und Andere, sechzig und siebzig Meilen weit westlich und nördlich
von der Hauptstadt die Wälder zu durchbrechen. Große deutsche
Ansiedelungen entstanden in den jetzigen Berks und Montgomery
Counties. In Goschenhoppen organisirte sich schon 1717 eine

---

* Verfasser dieses schrieb an den Staatssekretär von New York, um von
ihm zu erfahren, ob sich solche Listen, wie die zu Harrisburg erhaltenen, auf
dem Amtszimmer des Sekretärs von New York befänden, und erhielt fol=
gende Antwort:

Staat New York, Amtsstube des Sekretärs, }
Albany, 18. Juli 1856.   }

Herrn J. D. Rupp.

Lieber Herr! In unsrer Office haben wir keine Listen
von der Art, welche sie angeben. Wir haben wohl Register von Fremden,
welche eine eidliche Aussage betreffs ihrer Person niederlegen, die es ihnen
dann ermöglicht, liegendes Eigenthum zu halten und Bürger zu werden;
dies ist aber immerhin nur eine kleine Anzahl im Vergleich zur ganzen Masse
von Emigranten, die in den Staat gebracht werden.

Ihr ergebenster
M. L. Schermerhorn.

† Diese sind von denen, welche auf die Einladung von Martin Kendig
nach Pennsylvanien gekommen waren.—Gesch. von Lanc. Co., S. 79–117.

deutsch=reformirte Gemeinde.* Einige niederdeutsche Mennoniten †
ließen sich am Pakihmomink entlang und einige Jahre später am
Schkipeck (a) nieder.

Deutsche und Franzosen wählten sich die fruchtbare Landschaft
Wahlink (b) zu ihrem Wohnort. Hier öffnete sich bald Anderen,
den verfolgten Hugenotten, eine Heimath. Unter den hervorragen=
den Familien in Oley waren: Turcks oder de Turcks, Bertolets,
Berdos, de la Plaines, Delangs, Loras, Levans, Yoder, Keim,
Herbein, Schaub, Engel, Weidner, Schneider, Alstadt.

Abraham de Turck von Oley schrieb an den Herausgeber in einem März
1844 datirten Briefe: „Meine Vorältern, Namens Isaak Turck, de Turck,
wohnten in Frankreich, waren von den sogenannten Hugenotten, flüchteten
wegen Religion nach der Pfalz, in die Stadt Frankenthal, von dorten
wanderten sie aus nach Amerika, ließen sich nieder im Staat New York,
in der Gegend Esopus, in der Zeit der Königin Anna; zogen nach Oley
um 1712. Das Patent von meinem Land ist 1712."—*His. Berks Co.*, p. 88.

Isaak Turck, ein Landmann, 23 Jahre alt, war einer der Begleiter des
Pastors Kocherthal.—Anhang Nr. IV.

Es mag hier bemerkt werden, obwohl es etwas außer Ordnung erscheint,
daß neunzehn von denen, die mit Pastor Kocherthal waren, im ersten Jahre
Pietisten wurden. Hierauf ersuchten Kocherthal und Schünemann am 26.
Mai 1709 den Rath, diesen Neunzehn den Unterhalt zu entziehen „weil sie
sich der Seelsorge des Predigers und den übrigen Deutschen entzogen
hätten." Am 18. Juni ernannte man einen Ausschuß, um die Schwierig=
keiten unter den Deutschen zu untersuchen. Derselbe berichtete am 21.
Juni: „daß keine der den Pietisten zur Last gelegten Dinge vor andern
erwiesen werden konnten."—O'Calahan's Doc. Gesch. N. Y., III., S. 544.

Unter den ersten Ansiedlern von Elsaß Township, Berks County,
waren viele französische Reformirte oder Hugenotten, ebenfalls
schwedische Lutheraner. „Man erzählt, daß die Hugenotten,
Deutsch=Reformirte und Lutheraner innerhalb einer oder zweier
Meilen von Reading ihre Gottesdienste gehalten und sich nach
guter Weise ihrer Väter in Europa Abends sowohl als den Tag
über versammelt haben."—Bucher.

Die Deutschen waren hauptsächlich Landleute. Sie verließen
sich mehr auf sich selbst als auf Andere. Sie schwangen den Karst,
die Axt und den Schlägel, und mit ihren sonnenverbrannten
Armen rotteten sie die Wucherpflanzen aus, fällten die majestäti=
schen Eichen und die schlanken Wallnußbäume, die Kastanien und

---

* German Ref. Messenger; Aug. 3, 1842.

† Perkioming heißt der Preiselbeere=Platz. (a) Skippack, d. h. eine
stinkende Wasserlache. (b) Oley heißt eine Höhle, Zelle, auch eine von
Bergen eingeschlossene Landschaft.

Pappeln. Was brauchbar war, spalteten sie zu Schwellen für Zäune. Ihr unermüdlicher Eifer wußte keine Schranken, bis er die ganze waldige Wildniß in urbares Land umgeschaffen hatte. Von ihnen sagte Gouverneur Thomas im Jahre 1738: „Diese Provinz hat seit Jahren als Zufluchtstätte für verfolgte Protestanten der Pfalz und anderer Theile Deutschland's gedient, und ich glaube mit Wahrheit sagen zu können, daß sie ihren gegenwärtigen blühenden Zustand größtentheils dem Fleiße dieses Volkes zu verdanken hat. Es ist nicht die Güte des Bodens allein, sondern die Anzahl und Arbeitsamkeit eines Volkes, die ein Land wohlhabend machen."—Col. Rec., IV., S. 315.

England verstand seine Politik in der schnellen Bevölkerung der amerikanischen Colonien: seine Unterthanen behielt es zu Hause, betrieb hingegen die Auswanderung der Deutschen. England zog seinen Gewinn daraus, ohne von seinen Einwohnern zu verlieren.

Es mag unvernünftig scheinen, daß man ängstlich auf die Schaaren deutscher Einwanderer sah, „die, wenn sie in solchen Massen herüberströmen, eine deutsche Colonie hier gründen möchten, und vielleicht eine solche, wie die der Angelsachsen im fünften Jahrhundert in Britannien."*

Im Jahre 1719 kamen etliche zwanzig Familien der Schwarzenau-Täufer in Philadelphia an. Einige zogen nach Germantown, andere nach dem Schippack in Oley, nach Conestogo und Mülbach in Lancaster County.

Um 1728 und 1729 überschritten die Deutschen den Susquehanna und ließen sich innerhalb der jetzigen Grenzen der Counties Adams und York nieder. Dort richteten sie sich, obwohl unter vielen Hindernissen, ein. Es entspannen sich, wie es leider oft zwischen Bewohnern der Grenze der Fall ist, Fehden zwischen den Maryländern und Pennsylvaniern, und Streit um die Oberhand unter den Führern.

Thomas Cressap von Maryland machte sich 1736 zum Hauptmann von fünfzig gleichartigen Geistern, lediglich dazu, um die Deutschen von ihren Bauereien zu jagen. Um seinen Gesellen Muth einzuflößen, schlug er vor, das Land, welches die Deutschen angebaut hatten, unter sie zu vertheilen. Für die zu leistenden Dienste sollte ein jeder zweihundert Acker erhalten. Die Deutschen wurden mit Waffengewalt angegriffen, ihre Wohnungen zerstört und sie vertrieben und gefangen genommen, und das blos aus dem Grunde, weil sie der Regierung Pennsylvanien's treu geblieben waren.— Col. Rec. iv., S. 69-122.

---

* Watson's Annalen, II., S. 255.

Schon in den Jahren 1710–1712 kamen Deutsche nach Maryland und ließen sich in der Gegend zwischen dem Monocacy und den Bergen, da, wo nachher Patrick Dulany (1745) Fredricktown auslegte, nieder. Dieselben dehnten sich aber bald bis nach den Glades, Middletown und Hagerstown aus. Zwischen 1748 u. 1754 wurden achtundzwanzig hundert Deutsche nach Maryland gebracht, von denen Viele sich nach Baltimore wandten.— Pastor Zacharias, Predigt beim hundertsten Jahresfest, 1847. Butler's Gesch. v. Md., S. 51, 52, 61, 62.

Die Fluth der Auswanderung vom europäischen Continent war mächtig. Einflüsse verschiedener Natur trugen dazu bei, dieselbe nur noch zu verstärken. In Pennsylvanien waren es die Neuländer, Werkzeuge in der Hand der Schiffsbesitzer, Kaufleute und Importeure, welche viele Deutsche bewogen, ihren Herd zu verlassen. Außer diesen gab es noch eine weitere Classe, die sich große Mühe anthat, den Einwohnern Deutschland's Auswanderungs=Gelüste einzuflößen. Diese zwei Sorten, die Neuländer und Speculanten, nahmen Zuflucht zu verschiedenen Kunstgriffen, um ihren Zweck auszuführen. Sie machten allerlei Versprechungen und stellten den Leuten vor, in dem neuen Land flögen ihnen die gebratenen Tauben in's Maul. Um dieses Paradies zu besitzen, folgten Tausende dem berüchtigten John Law in den Jahren 1716 und 1717, um es in Louisiana an den Ufern des Mississippi zu finden. Anstatt daß er sie aber in's verheißene Eden brachte, landete er dieselben an den Wassern des Biloxi, nahe Mobile. Fünf Jahre lang waren sie hier obdachlos Wind und Wetter ausgesetzt. Nicht einer betrat das verheißene Land. Zwei tausend verschlang das Grab. Die blassen Ueberlebenden, drei hundert an der Zahl, bauten sich schließlich am Mississippi, etliche dreißig oder vierzig Meilen oberhalb New Orleans, an. Law's Agenten hatten auf zwölf tausend Deutsche und Schweizer gerechnet; aber das traurige Schicksal derer am Biloxi hatte sich verbreitet wie ein Lauffeuer, und die übrigen von dem Wagniß für die vorgebildeten Güter und Besitzthümer abgeschreckt.

Jahre lang befanden sich die Dreihundert am Mississippi in dürftigen Umständen. Sie waren in den äußersten Nothstand versunken. „Aber," sagt Gayarre, „von diesen armen, jedoch ehrbaren Deutschen stammen viele der angesehensten Bürger Louisiana's und viele der reichsten Zuckerpflanzer im Staate." Ihre Nachkommen vergaßen die deutsche Sprache und nahmen die französische an; aber die Namen Vieler deuten klar auf ihr Herkommen, obwohl manche so gallisirt oder französirt sind, daß es scheint, als wären sie von französischer Herkunft. Die Küste, welche ehe=

dem so arm und dürftig war, und die „deutsche Küste" genannt
wurde, hat seitdem solche Reichthümer hervorgebracht und in sich
aufgenommen, daß sie jetzt unter dem geeigneten Namen Cote d'or,
„Goldküste", bekannt ist.*

Am 10. Mai 1727 besuchte Vater Du Poisson, ein zu den Arkansas ge=
sandter Missionar, in seiner Durchreise die Deutschen. Er sagt: „Wir
drangen achtzehn Meilen weit den Fluß hinauf vor, etwa so viel, als sie je
zu Stande bringen können, und schlugen unser Lager bei den Deutschen
auf. Dies sind die Aufenthaltsplätze, welche den Ueberresten der Deutschen,
die vom Elend im Osten† und in Louisiana verschont geblieben, angewiesen
worden sind. Große Armuth herrscht in ihren Wohnungen."—Early
Jes. Miss., II., S. 236, 262, 263, 267.

Im Frühjahr 1734 kamen die Salzburger Lutheraner (aus
Salzburg, einem Herzogthum in Oestreich) in Georgia an. Auch
sie hatten in Europa schwere Verfolgungen zu erleiden. „Sie
wurden aus ihrer Heimath vertrieben und aus dem Lande gejagt,
weil sie den Lehren des Evangeliums mit unverrückter Treue an=
hingen."‡

Diese ernste und fromme Gesellschaft von Christen wurde von
ihren theuren Seelsorgern, den Pastoren Johann Martin Boltzius
und Israel Christian Gronau, sammt ihrem ausgezeichneten
Schulmeister, Christian Ortmann, begleitet. Die Salzburger
ließen sich in Effingham County nieder und benannten ihre An=
siedelung „Ebenezer", um dadurch ihrem Herrn ihren aufrichtigen
Dank zu sagen, der ihnen seither „ein starker Fels" gewesen war
und ihnen „bis hierher geholfen" hatte. §

Den Schulmeister dachte man nicht weniger wichtig, als den Pfarrer.
„Die Erziehungssache wurde von den Deutschen nicht übersehen. Für den
Unterhalt des Schulmeisters schuf man nachher einen Fond; denn unsere
frommen Vorfahren urtheilten sehr richtig, daß kein Land gedeihen könne,
welches für die geistliche Pflege und Ausbildung des aufwachsenden Ge=
schlechts keine Vorsorge treffe."—Strobel.

Diese deutsche Colonie erfuhr einen Zuwachs von Zeit zu Zeit,
bis sie noch vor 1745 mehrere hundert Familien zählte. In Sa=
vannah wohnten ebenfalls viele Deutsche; außer diesen befanden
sich unter der geistlichen Pflege des Pastors David Nitschmann
noch viele Mährische Brüder im Staate.

* Gayarre's Louisiana, S. 360, 361. Barbe Morbois' Gesch. v. Louis.
† Nahe den Dauphin Inseln, fünf und zwanzig Meilen südlich von
Mobile.—Brown's Illinois, S. 163.
‡ Pastor A. P. Strobel's Gesch. der Salzburger, S. 21.—Dieses Buch
sollte sich in den Händen jedes Deutschen befinden.
§ Anhang Nr. IX. gibt die Namen der ersten Ansiedler.

„Die Mährischen Brüder gründeten keine bleibende Nieder=
laſſung in Georgia. Als der Krieg mit Spanien ausbrach, zogen
ſich faſt alle nach Pennſylvanien zurück, weil es gegen ihren Glau=
ben verſtieß, in irgend einer Sache zu den Waffen zu greifen."*
Im Jahre 1738 kamen Einige in Pennſylvanien an und ließen
ſich zu Bethlehem nieder.† „Diejenigen, welche noch in Georgia
zurück geblieben waren, verließen daſſelbe 1740 und zogen zu ihren
Brüdern nach Pennſylvanien. So wurde die Miſſion unter den
Indianern in Georgia nach einem vielverſprechenden Anfange
wieder aufgegeben."‡

Ehe die Mährischen Brüder nach Pennſylvanien kamen, hatte
ſich ſchon eine beträchtliche Anzahl Schwenckfelder eingefunden,
und die Counties Bucks und Philadelphia, jetzt Montgomery,
Berks und Lehigh, ausgewählt. Es war ihre Abſicht, bei ihrem
Abzug aus Europa Georgia zuzuſteuern. Sie änderten ihr Vor=
haben und wandten ſich dieſer Zufluchtsſtätte aller Unterdrückten zu.

1732 beſuchte Herr Jean Pierre Pury von Neuchatel aus der
Schweiz Carolina, und, beeinflußt von den Regierungen England's
und Carolina's, unternahm er es, eine ſchweizeriſche Anſiedelung
daſelbſt zu gründen. Ein hundert und ſiebzig Perſonen kamen
1732 herüber. Ihnen folgten bald andere. Kurz darauf zählte
die Colonie drei hundert Bewohner. An den nördlichen Ufern
des Savannah ließen ſie ſich nieder und bauten etwa ſechs und
dreißig Meilen oberhalb der Mündung des Fluſſes eine Stadt,
welche ſie Purysburgh hießen. Die Colonie vermehrte ſich
zuſehends. Pury brachte 1734 weitere zwei hundert und ſiebzig
Perſonen aus der Schweiz. Dieſe kamen ſämmtlich auf Koſten
Pury's und einige ſeiner Freunde, die ihm zur Ausführung ſeines
Planes Mittel an die Hand gaben, da er ſein ganzes Vermögen
bereits daran gewandt hatte, noch ehe er denſelben völlig verwirk=
licht ſah. Jetzt befanden ſich beinahe ſechs hundert Seelen in
dieſer Niederlaſſung.

„Herr Pury that dies infolge eines von ihm der Geſetzgebung
von Süd=Carolina gemachten Entwurfs, deſſen nämlich: das
ſüdliche Grenzland Carolina's mit tapferen und arbeitſamen

---

* Strobel's Salzburger, S. 80.
† Die Namen derer, die Georgia verließen und nach Pennſylvanien wan=
derten, ſind in Zuſatz B enthalten.—Grantz' Brüder=Geſchichte, S. 302.
‡ Loskiel, Th. II., S. 6.

Leuten, was bekanntlich die Schweizer sind, zu bevölkern. Die Assembly zeigte sich ganz mit diesem Vorschlag einverstanden, und bewilligte ihm am 20. August 1731 400 Pfund Sterling, wenn er hundert tüchtige Männer nach Carolina bringe. In diesem Beschluß verpflichtete sich die Regierung ebenfalls, drei hundert Personen ein Jahr lang mit Unterhalt, Werkzeugen u. s. w. zu versehen. 1747 hatte Purysburgh über hundert ordentlich ge=baute Häuser.

In Colleton County, am nördlichen Ufer des North Ediston Flusses, 12 Meilen von dessen Mündung, liegt Wilton, oder Neu London, mit achtzig Häusern, welche die Schweizer mit Er=laubniß der Assembly unter Zuberbühler gebaut hatten. Dieser Ort erwies sich nachtheilig für Purysburgh wegen seiner Lage im Mittelpunkt des Landes und nahe der Hauptstadt. Viele, die nicht nach Purysburgh wollten, zogen da hin."—Bowen's Geogr., ii., S. 645. Londoner Ausgabe von 1750.

In den Jahren 1740–1755 brachte man viele Pfälzer nach Süd=Carolina. In Orangeburg, Congaree und Wateree setzten sie sich fest.* Ueber sechs hundert aus Schwaben und der Pfalz wurden 1765 von London herübergeschickt auf ein eigens für sie bestimmtes Township. †

Viele der holländischen Colonisten, die nach der Uebergabe der Colonie an die Krone England's mit ihrer Lage in New York nicht mehr zufrieden waren, brachen nach Süd=Carolina auf und steuerten durch ihre Arbeitsam=keit nicht wenig zum Wohlstand der Provinz bei. Ihr Erfolg bewog auch andere ihrer Landsleute, ihrem Beispiele zu folgen.—Ramsay.

1679 sandte Karl II. in zwei Schiffen eine Anzahl Hugenotten nach Süd=Carolina, um daselbst den Weinstock, die Olive u. s. w. zu pflanzen. Nicht weniger als sechzehn hundert Protestanten, meistens Franzosen, ließen sich 1752 in Süd=Carolina nieder.—Holmes; Baird.

Im Jahre 1739 kauften mehrere Lutheraner und Deutsch=Re=formirte ein Stück Grund von General Waldo, und legten darauf die Stadt Waldoborough in Lincoln County, Maine, an. Bre=men, ein Dorf in demselben County, und Frankfort in Waldo County sind, wie aus den Namen ergeht, zweifelsohne von Deut=schen entweder angelegt oder angesiedelt worden. Im Laufe des spanisch=französischen Krieges wurde Waldoborough durch die

---

* Ramsay's Süd=Carol., i., S. 3, 4.

† Holme's Am. Annalen, ii., S. 268.—Verhandlungen im engl. Unter=haus, Aug. 1764.

Hände canadischer Indianer 1746 zum Aschenhaufen. Viele der
Einwohner wurden niedergemacht, andere abgeführt. Nicht wenige
starben infolge der grausamen Behandlung seitens der Wilden;
einige entkamen durch die Flucht und zerstreuten sich in Canada.
Bis 1750 blieb Waldoborough ein Schutthaufen. Im Jahre
1751 kamen auf Einladung der Regierung dreißig deutsche Fa=
milien, und 1752 fünfzehn hundert bemittelte Leute von Europa
nach Maine. „Da jedoch der Rechtstitel des General Waldo sich
als fehlerhaft erwies, so verließen Viele die Colonie. Ihre Be=
völkerung nahm nie bedeutend zu."—Hazelius, S. 34, 48 2c.
Löher, 1772. „Einige zogen aus Maine, um mit ihren Lands=
leuten in Londonderry, Süd=Carolina, zu wohnen, von denen
aber die Meisten diesen Schritt hernach bereuten und nach Maine
zurückkehrten, wo sich ihre Nachkommen jetzt noch finden."—Baird.

Auf große Versprechungen des Königs Georg II. von Groß=
Britannien hin, welche er denen aussetzte, die nach Nova Scotia
auswandern würden, machte sich eine bedeutende Anzahl Deutscher,
meist Hannoveraner, auf den Weg nach Amerika, wo sie in der
Chebucto Bay, nahe Halifax, der Hauptstadt von Nova Scotia,
ankamen. Vierzehn hundert und dreiundfünfzig schifften sich wie=
der ein und landeten am 7. Juni 1753 in Marliguish. „Hier
legten sie die blühende Stadt Lünenburg an, hatten aber dieselben
Schwierigkeiten auszustehen, mit denen die Colonisten zu Halifax
in Ansiedlung der Halbinsel zu kämpfen hatten. Die Urgeschichte
jenes Ortes erzählt von wenig Anderem, als einer fortwährenden
Wiederholung von Kämpfen mit den Wilden, in denen, ungeachtet
der kräftigen Hilfe, die ihnen die Regierung stellte, doch Viele ihr
Leben verloren. Feldbau hatten sie deshalb nur innerhalb eng ge=
gezogener Grenzen zu betreiben, und die Urbarmachung des an=
stoßenden Landes mußte überliegen bleiben, bis die französische
Macht in Nova Scotia gebrochen war."—Haliburton's Gesch.
von Nova Scotia, I., S. 162; Murray's Brit.=Amer., II., S. 55;
Löher, S. 68, 74; M'Culloch's Uni., II., S. 498.

Von 1735 vermehrten sich die Ansiedelungen in Pennsylvanien
zusehends und dehnten sich über unabsehbare Gegenden, westlich
von Saosquahanaunk,* aus, wohin ihnen die schottischen

---

* Susquehanna, d. h. „lang=gebogener=Strom." (a) Gelbe Hosen.
Die Bedeutung des indianischen Namens ist „Wo es sich wieder zurück=
dreht." (b) Canodoquinet, d. h. „Eine große Strecke lang nichts als Krüm=
mungen." (c) Canococheague, d. h. „Sicher eine lange Reise." (d) Der
Kittatiny oder „Blaue Berg".

Irländer den Weg gezeigt hatten. Die deutschen Niederlassungen konnten sich, verstärkt durch die immerwährend zufließende Einwanderung, mit den Eingeborenen messen. Vor 1765 hatten sie sich westlich vom Susquehanna im Cumberlandthal und den Ufern des klaren Callapaßcink (a) entlang, und auf beiden Seiten des geschlängelten Sunipduckhannet (b), und weiter nach Westen am Gunneukißchik (c), drei diese fruchtbare Gegend bewässernde Ströme, niedergelassen

Der Kau-ta-tin-Chunk (d), der sich vom Delaware hunderte von Meilen westwärts zieht, war ihnen kein unüberwindliches Hinderniß. Sie schritten darüber hinweg und legten da ihre Bauereien an, „wo sie kurz nachher sammt Weib und Kind der Fackel, dem Beil und Scalpirmesser der Wilden und ihrem mitternächtlichen Angriff und Blutthaten ausgesetzt waren." In den Jahren 1754—1763, und noch später, fielen Hunderte den unerbittlich grausamen Wilden zum Opfer, und dies den Blauen Bergen entlang in südlicher und nördlicher Richtung, und am Susquehanna hinauf bis zu Penn's Creek. Unter den Dahingeschlachteten waren viele Deutsche—mehr als drei hundert im Ganzen.

Unter den erschlagenen Deutschen nördlich von den Blauen Bergen und innerhalb Monroe County waren: Guldin, Höth, oder Huth, Bömper, Vanaken, Vanslör, Schnell, Hartmann, Hage, Brundich, Hellmann, Gondermann, Schleich, Müller, Vandelap, Decker, Van Gondie, Brincker. Innerhalb der Counties Lehigh, Northampton und Carbon, südlich und nördlich der Berge, fielen über Einhundert. Unter diesen waren: Sohn, Klein, Bittenbender, Roth, Schäffer, Anders, Nitschmann, Sensemann, Gattermyer, Fabricius, Schweigert, Leslie, Presser, Depu. Innerhalb der Counties Berks, Lebanon und Dauphin, denselben Bergen entlang: Reichelsdörfer, Gerhart, Neidung, Klug oder Kluck, Lindermann, Schott, Kraushar, Zeißloff, Wünch, Dieppel, Henly, Spitler, Nöcker, Maurer, Böshar, Fell, Kühlmer, Lang, Trump, Yäger, Sechler, Schetterly, Sauter, Geiger, Ditzler, Frantz, Schnebele, Mosser, Fincher, Hubler, Martloff, Wolf, Händsche, Weisser, Mieß, Lebenguth, Motz, Noah, Winkelblech, Zeuchmacher u. s. w.

Vor 1770 war man in der Wildniß Pennsylvanien's bis über das Allegheny Gebirge vorgedrungen. Innerhalb der jetzigen Grenzen von Westmoreland und anderen westlichen Counties dieses Staates bestanden bereits Ansiedelungen. Eine Anzahl deutscher Familien hatte sich am Monongahela bis hinauf nach Redstone, Brownsville, Fayette County, niedergelassen. Unter ihnen waren: Weismann, Presser, Vervalson, Delong, Jung, Martin, Schutt, Peter, Schwartz, Hutter, Cackey, Abraham und andere,* welche jener treue Diener Christi, Pastor Johann Conrad Bucher, im Nov. 1768 besuchte.—Col. Rec., IX., S. 508; German Reformed Messenger, 24. Mai 1854; Rupp's Geschichte von Berks Co., S. 459. Die Namen vieler anderer Deutschen in Westmoreland County sind in der vom Verfasser dieses zusammengestellten Geschichte vom westlichen Pennsylvanien zu finden.

---

* Die ersten Deutschen im westlichen Pennsylvanien ließen sich in Greene County nieder. Es waren die beiden Brüder Eckerlein, welche 1745 Ephrata verließen, um sich in der Tiefe der Wilderniß einen neuen Wohnort zu suchen.—Chronicon Ephratense, pp. 158, 195, 195. Col. Rec., V., S. 531. Vor 1754 bauten sich Wendel Braun mit seinen beiden Söhnen und Friedrich Walzer vier Meilen westlich von Uniontown an.—Smith's Old Redstone, p. 25.

PROLEGOMENA,

TO WHICH THE SPECIAL ATTENTION OF THE READER IS RESPECTFULLY INVITED.

GERMANS, Swiss, Dutch and French formed a large portion of the first settlers of Pennsylvania. Between forty and fifty thousand names of these Immigrants are to be found in the Records of the State—in Land warrants, Acts of naturalization, and in Lists of imported foreigners. Much time has been spent in laborious researches, to copy from these Records the names of Immigrants, and arrange them in chronological order; especially, the names of those who came to Pennsylvania prior to 1727. As that *Collection*, embracing the period from 1682–1727, is not as complete as it might be, it is withheld from the public for the present. The *Collection* now published, embraces a period of fifty years, and contains upwards of thirty thousand names of the ancestors "*of toiling millions.*"

The great influx of these Immigrants began about the year 1707. Since then, thousands of Germans, Swiss and others bade their friends adieu, left their *Vaterland*, their homes—"the hearth where soft affections dwell,"—for this foreign country. So vast became their numbers in Pennsylvania, as to excite public attention as early as 1717, and, finally, to lead the provincial Council to adopt, Sept. 14, 1727, and enforce the following Resolution:

"*That* the masters of vessels, importing *Germans and others from the continent of Europe*, shall be examined whether they have leave granted them by the Court of Great Britain for the importation of these foreigners, and that a LIST be taken of all these people, their several occupations, and place from whence they came, and shall be further examined touching their intentions in coming hither; and that a writing be drawn up for them to sign, declaring their allegiance and subjection to the King of Great Britain, and fidelity to the Proprietary of this Province, and that they will demean themselves peaceably towards all His Majesty's subjects, and observe and conform to the Laws of England and of the Government of Pennsylvania."—*Col. Rec.,* III., pp. 29, 283.

(39)

LISTS were taken by the masters of vessels, and attested as being "*exact* and *true*." These are still preserved in the Secretary's Office at Harrisburg. Many of them are *triplicates*. All have been carefully examined by the Editor. For convenience of reference, the Lists are designated in this *Collection*, A, B, C.

A. The master's or captain's Lists contain the names of all male passengers above the age of sixteen, and some of them, the names of all the passengers. If any had *died*, or were *sick*, on the arrival of the ship, they are marked accordingly.

B. This List contains all the names of males above the age of sixteen, who were made to repeat and subscribe the *Declaration* of allegiance, with their own hands, if they could write, if they could not. the name was written by a clerk, and the qualified person *made his mark*. Lists A and B are preserved in detached papers.

C. This List is an *autograph* duplicate of B, signed in the same way, and is preserved in Book form.

LIST A was at the time of presentation, Sept. 21, 1727, to Oct. 19, 1736, copied *literatim* into the *Provincial Records*—containing 2,536 names. These were lately published by authority of the Legislature, "*as a faithful and literal copy of the original*," in the III. and IV. Colonial Records. The printed List does not present the true orthography of one-half of the *autographs*, or the names written by the qualified persons themselves. This remark is not intended as invidious. It is a mere statement of the fact, that English scholars may not always be able to spell German names correctly.*

B and C are made the basis of this edition. The orthography of *cognomens*, or family names, is given as in the *autographs*, or as written by clerks, though the latter do rarely present the correct spelling of German names. To distinguish names written by clerks, from *autographs*, this mark (*) has been appended to the former. Some of the

---

* Hundreds of instances might be cited from the printed Colonial Records to sustain the assertion. Two must suffice. In September, 1727, a person subscribed the Declaration thus: G. M. Weis, V. D. M.—In the Col. Rec. III. 284, the name is printed G. M. Wey, V. D. M. Rev. Weis was born at Stebbeck, in Neckarthal, Germany—graduated at Heidelberg—was for some years pastor of the German Reformed Congregation in Philadelphia—died at Goshenhoppen 1763.—*Rupp's His. Lan Co.255. Rupp's His. Lebanon Co. 442.* In September, 1728, another person subscribed the Declaration, Johann Caspar Stœver, S. S., Theol. Stud. In the Col. Rec. III. 331—Johan Casper Steffer jr. Rev Stœver was born in Strassburg, Germany—was for many years a minister of the Lutheran Church at Lebanon—he died near that place, May 13, 1779, aged 71 years, 3 months and 2 days. His descendants still reside in Pennsylvania.—*Rupp's His. of Rel. Denom. U. S. Rupp's His. of York Co. 692.*

German *autographs* are difficult to decipher. When a doubt remains as to the orthography, a note of interrogation (?) has been added.

In List A there are names of males above sixteen years old, marked *sick*, which are not found in B and C, and some are marked *dead*. To complete this *Collection*, these names have been added, and designated accordingly. Where this (♂) is added to a name, it indicates the person was *sick*.

Determined to make this publication as satisfactory as possible, the names of males under sixteen years of age have been copied with the utmost care, and will be presented in an Appendix, in which the correct spelling of names, as far as can be ascertained by collating all the Lists, is represented. By adopting the plan pursued, several thousand names will be added, which would otherwise not have appeared. Foot notes have occasionally been added, for reasons fully explained in the Introduction.

Some of the *notes* are of a historical, others of a biographical character. The most important are those containing the names of early settlers, who had landed at some port, other than that of Philadelphia, but who afterwards came into Pennsylvania, and whose descendants still reside here. An attempt has been made to place the different spellings of names in juxtaposition, showing the orthography of the ancestor's autograph and that of his descendants, as in the case of the well-known Hiester family. An ancestor signed his name to the Declaration, Sept. 26, 1737, the time of his arrival, *Jost Hüsterr—Hiester* is the orthography adopted by his descendants.

It is not the only design of this publication to preserve names, which indifference or accidents might forever place beyond reach, or to lead to the recovery of rights to inheritances abroad, that might otherwise remain unestablished; but to enable thousands to determine with certainty the time of their ancestors' arrival in Pennsylvania.— Prominent and intelligent individuals may be met with, who, when asked: *When did your ancestors arrive?* can give only a conjectural answer. The descendants of MATHIAS SMYSER, who, numbering in 1845, 1,162 say: "*Mathias*, with his brother *George* and his sister *Margaretta*, emigrated to America *about* the year 1738, or probably at an earlier period." * By the aid of this *Collection*, the year, month of arrival and day of his signing the Declaration can be determined. The *conjectured* time is *seven years—"far* from the *mark!"*

* Minutes of the Centennial Celebration, held by the descendants of the Elder Mathias Smyser, May 3d, 1845, on the farm of Samuel Smyser, West Manchester Township. York County, Pa.

4*

Vorbemerkungen,

welche dem Leser zur aufmerksamen Durchsicht besonders empfohlen sind.

Deutsche, Schweizer, Holländer und Franzosen bildeten einen großen Theil der ersten Ansiedler Pennsylvanien's. Zwischen vierzig und fünfzig tausend Namen dieser Einwanderer sind im Staatsarchiv aufbewahrt, und zwar in Landvollmachten, Naturalisirungs=Acten und in Listen angelangter Fremder. Ausgedehnte Nachforschungen, das Abschreiben der Namen der Auswanderer von diesen Urschriften, und die geschichtliche Zusammenstellung derselben nahmen viel Zeit in Anspruch, und besonders ist dies der Fall bei den Namen derer, die vor 1727 nach Pennsylvanien kamen. Da die Sammlung, welche die Namen der in dem Zeitraum von 1682–1727 Eingewanderten in sich schließt, nicht so vollständig ist, als sie gemacht werden könnte, so wird dieselbe wenigstens für die Gegenwart dem Publikum vorenthalten. Die jetzt veröffentlichte Sammlung schließt eine Periode von fünfzig Jahren in sich, und enthält über dreißig tausend Namen der Ahnen emsiger Millionen.

Der große Strom dieser Einwanderung wurde flüssig im Jahre 1707. Seitdem haben Tausende von Deutschen, Schweizern und anderen Nationen ihren Freunden die Hand zum Abschied gereicht, ihr Vaterland verlassen und ihre Heimath, „des Herdes traute Feuerstätte", um in einem fremden Lande ihr Glück zu versuchen. So zahlreich wurden sie in Pennsylvanien, daß sie schon im Jahre 1717 das öffentliche Augenmerk auf sich richteten und endlich den Provinzialrath am 14. September 1727 zwangen, folgenden Beschluß zu fassen und durchzusetzen:

„Daß die Capitaine von Schiffen, auf denen Deutsche und Andere von dem Festlande Europa's herübergebracht werden, untersucht werden sollen, ob sie für die Einfuhr solcher Fremden von der Regierung England's Erlaubniß eingeholt haben, und daß eine Liste von allen diesen Leuten genommen werde, nebst ihren Berufsarten und den Orten ihrer Herkunft, und dieselben weiter über die Absicht ihres Hierherkommens befragt werden, und daß eine Schrift zur Unterzeichnung ihrerseits entworfen werde, in der sie ihren Gehorsam und Unterthänigkeit gegen den König von Groß=Britannien und gegen den Besitzer dieser Provinz ihre Treue erklären, und

(43)

daß sie sich ferner gegen alle Unterthanen Seiner Majestät friedlich benehmen und die Gesetze England's und der Regierung Pennsylvanien's befolgen und gemäß denselben handeln."—Col. Rec. III., S. 29, 283.

Listen wurden demgemäß von den Schiffs-Capitainen angefertigt, welche sie als genau und wahr zu beschwören hatten. Diese sind noch auf der Amtsstube des Staatssecretairs zu Harrisburg erhalten. Viele davon sind dreifach vorhanden. Alle wurden vom Herausgeber sorgfältig untersucht. Aus Rücksicht für Bequemlichkeit im Nachschlagen sind die Listen mit A, B, C bezeichnet.

A. Die Capitainslisten. Dieselben enthalten die Namen aller männlichen Passagiere über sechzehn Jahre, und einige die Namen sämmtlicher Reisenden. Diejenigen, welche auf dem Schiffe starben oder krank gewesen waren, wurden nach der Ankunft demgemäß bezeichnet.

B. Diese Liste enthält alle Mannsnamen über sechzehn Jahre, die ihre Anhänglichkeit an ihre frühere Regierung zu widerrufen und ihren Gehorsam gegen den König von England eigenhändig zu bezeugen hatten; konnten sie nicht schreiben, so unterzeichnete der Beamte den Namen, und die betreffende Person setzte ihr Zeichen bei. Die Listen A und B sind auf besonderen Schriftstücken aufbewahrt.

C. Diese Liste ist ein eigenhändiges Duplicat von B, und ist in Buchformat aufbewahrt.

Die Liste A war zur Zeit ihrer Vorzeigung vom 21. September 1727 bis 19. October 1736 buchstäblich für die Provinzial-Berichte abgeschrieben. Sie enthält 2,536 Namen. Diese wurden kürzlich im Namen der Gesetzgebung im Band III. und IV. des Colonial-Berichts als eine getreue und buchstäbliche Abschrift des Originals veröffentlicht. Die gedruckten Listen geben für die Hälfte der eigenhändig oder von den beauftragten Personen geschriebenen Namen die unrichtige Schreibweise. Diese Bemerkung ist aber aller Gehässigkeit bar. Es wird dadurch nur die Thatsache festgestellt, daß englische Gelehrte deutsche Namen nicht immer richtig buchstabiren können.*

---

* Hunderte von Beispielen könnten von den Colonial-Berichten angeführt werden, um dies zu bestätigen. Zwei müssen genügen. Im September 1727 unterzeichnete eine Person die Declaration so: G. M. Weis, V. D. M.; im Colonial-Bericht III., 284, ist der Name gedruckt G. M. Wey, V. D. M. Pastor Weis wurde zu Stebbed im Neckarthal, Deutschland, geboren, graduirte zu Heidelberg, war einige Jahre lang Pastor an der deutsch-reformirten Kirche in Philadelphia, und starb 1763 zu Goschenhoppen.—Rupp's Gesch. v. Lanc. Co. 255. Rupp's Gesch. v. Lebanon Co. 442.—Im September 1728 unterzeichnete eine andere Person diese Declaration so: Johann Caspar Stöver, S. S., Stud. theol. In den Colonial-Berichten III., 331, Johan Casper Steffer jr. Pastor Stöver wurde in Straßburg, Deutschland, geboren, war viele Jahre lang Prediger an der lutherischen Kirche zu Lebanon, und starb am 13. Mai 1779 in der Nähe, im Alter von 71 Jahren, 3 Monaten und 2 Tagen.

B und C sind diesem Werke zu Grunde gelegt. Die Schreibweise der Eigen= oder Familiennamen ist die der Unterschrift der Personen selbst, oder der Angestellten; letztere jedoch geben selten die richtige Schreibweise deutscher Namen. Um die von Angestellten geschriebenen Namen von der eigenhändigen Namensunterschrift zu unterscheiden, ist ersteren ein Stern (*) beigesetzt. Viele der deutschen Unterschriften sind höchst schwierig zu entziffern. Wo ein Zweifel bezüglich der richtigen Schreibweise obwaltet, ist ein Fragezeichen (?) hinzugesetzt.

In Liste A sind die Namen der kranken und verstorbenen männlichen Personen über sechzehn Jahre beigefügt, welche sich in B und C nicht finden. Um diese Sammlung zu vervollständigen, wurden deshalb diese Namen aufgenommen und demgemäß bezeichnet. Wo das Paragraphzeichen (§) steht, bedeutet es, daß benannte Person krank war.

Entschlossen, diese Sammlung möglichst vollständig zu machen, findet sich im Anhang eine höchst genaue Abschrift der Namen der unter sechzehn Jahren stehenden Mannspersonen; daselbst ist auch die richtige Schreibweise, wie sie bei Vergleichung aller Listen ersichtlich ist, angegeben. Durch Verfolgung dieses Plans werden einige tausend Namen mehr hinzugefügt, die sich sonst nicht hätten einreihen lassen. Randglossen wurden hin und wieder beigesetzt aus Ursachen, die in der Einleitung weiter auseinandergesetzt sind.

Einige der Glossen oder Bemerkungen sind geschichtlichen, andere biographischen Charakters. Die wichtigsten sind die, welche die Namen von frühzeitigen Ansiedlern enthalten, die in einem anderen Hafen, als dem zu Philadelphia, angekommen und nachher nach Pennsylvanien eingewandert sind, und deren Nachkommen noch jetzt hier wohnen. Auch machte man einen Versuch, die verschiedenen Schreibweisen desselben Namens neben einander zu stellen, um dadurch zu zeigen, wie der Ahne seinen Namen buchstabirte, und wie ihn die Nachkommen jetzt schreiben. Ein bekannter Fall ist der in der Hiester=Familie. Ihr Stammvater unterzeichnete am 26. September 1737 seinen Namen Jost Hüsterr zur Declaration; seine Abkömmlinge haben die Schreibweise Hiester angenommen.

Der Zweck dieser Schrift ist nicht blos, Namen zu erhalten, welche durch Gleichgültigkeit oder Zufall für immer unzugänglich gemacht werden könnten, oder zur Entdeckung von auswärtigen Erbrechten zu führen, welche sonst unbegründet geblieben sein könnten, sondern um Tausenden es zu ermöglichen, die Ankunft ihrer Voreltern in Pennsylvanien mit Genauigkeit zu erfahren. Man kann oft hervorragenden und verständigen Personen begegnen, die auf die Frage: Wann kamen Ihre Ahnen an? nur eine

---

Seine Nachkommen wohnen noch in Pennsylvanien.—Rupp's Gesch. der rel. Benennungen in den Ver. St. Rupp's Gesch. v. York Co. 692.

unbestimmte Antwort zu geben vermögen. Die Nachkommen von M a t h i a s S m y s e r, die 1845 1,162 zählten, sagen: „M a t h i a s wanderte um's Jahr 1738, oder w a h r s c h e i n l i c h früher, mit seinem Bruder G e o r g und seiner Schwester M a r g a r e t t a nach Amerika aus."* Mit Hilfe dieser S a m m l u n g kann das Jahr und der Monat der Ankunft, und der Tag der Unterzeichnung der Declaration bestimmt werden. Die m u t h - m a ß l i c h e Z e i t i s t s i e b e n J a h r e—w e i t a b v o m Z i e l!

---

* Protokoll der hundertjährigen Feier, die von den Nachkommen des Aeltesten Mathias Smyser am 3. Mai 1845 auf dem Gut des Samuel Smyser in West-Manchester Township, York County, N. Y., gehalten wurde.

NAMES

OF

German, Swiss and other Immigrants.

At a meeting of the Board of the Provincial Council, held at the Court House * in Philadelphia, Sept. 21, 1727, one hundred and nine Palatines appeared, who, with their families, numbered about four hundred persons. These were imported into the Province in the ship William and Sarah, William Hill, Master, from Rotterdam, last from Dover, England, as by clearance from the officers of His Majesty's customs there. The said Master being asked if he had any license from the Court of Great Britain for transporting those people, and what their intentions were in coming hither, said that he had no license or allowance for their transportation other than the above clearance, and that he believed they designed to settle in this Province.— *Col. Rec.* III. 283.

All male persons above the age of sixteen did repeat and subscribe their names, or made their *mark*, to the following *Declaration :*

"We subscribers, natives and late inhabitants of the Palatinate upon the Rhine and places adjacent, having transported ourselves and families into this Province of Pennsylvania, a colony subject to the crown of Great Britain, in hopes and expectation of finding a retreat and peaceable settlement therein, Do solemnly promise and engage, that we will be faithful and bear true allegiance to His present MAJESTY, KING GEORGE THE SECOND, and His successors, kings of Great Britain, and will be faithful

---

* Immigrants were usually qualified at the Court House, occasionally elsewhere. October 15, 1766, at the dwelling house of John Lawrence, Mayor of Philadelphia. January 13, 1767, and October 6, 1767, at the Office of Thomas Willing, Esq. December 8, 1773, at the house of Peter Miller, Esq., in Philadelphia.—(*Editor.*)

(47)

to the proprietor of this Province; and that we will demean ourselves peaceably to all His said Majesty's subjects, and strictly
observe and conform to the Laws of England and of this Province,
to the utmost of our power and the best of our understanding."

Namen
der
deutschen, schweizerischen u. andern Einwanderer.

Bei einer im Gerichtshaus* zu Philadelphia am 21. Sept.
1727 gehaltenen Versammlung des Collegiums des Provinzial=
Rathes erschienen ein hundert und neun Pfälzer, welche mit ihren
Familien etwa vier hundert Personen ausmachten, und mit dem
Schiffe William und Sarah, Capitain William Hill, von Rotter=
dam über Dover in England mit Erlaubniß zur Abfahrt von
den Beamten in Seiner Majestät Zollhause nach der Provinz
abgeführt wurden. Auf die Frage an den Capitain, ob er vom
englischen Hofe Vollmacht zur Ueberschiffung dieser Leute erhalten
habe und aus welcher Ursache dieselben herüberkämen, antwortete
derselbe, daß er keine Bewilligung oder Erlaubniß für deren
Ueberfahrt habe als die obgenannte Genehmigung der Zollbeamten,
und daß er glaube, daß ihr Vorhaben sei, sich in dieser Provinz
niederzulassen.—Col. Rec. III. 283.

Alle männlichen Personen über 16 Jahre wiederholten die nach=
stehende Declaration, und dieselben unterzeichneten eigenhändig
mit ihrem Namen oder ihrem Zeichen:

„Wir, die Unterzeichneten, geboren und weiland wohnhaft in
der Pfalz am Rhein und in den angrenzenden Plätzen, und nun
selbst sammt unseren Familien in diese Provinz von Pennsyl=
vanien, eine der Krone England's angehörende Colonie, in der

---

* Einwanderer wurden gewöhnlich im Gerichtshause qualificirt, gelegent-
lich anderswo. Am 15. Oktober 1766 im Wohnhause des John Lawrence,
Mayor von Philadelphia. 13. Januar 1767 und 6. Oktober 1767 in der
Amtsstube des Thomas Willing, Esq. 8. December 1773 im Hause des
Herrn Peter Miller zu Philadelphia.—(Herausgeber.)

Hoffnung und dem Glauben, dahier eine Zufluchtsstätte und eine friedliche Niederlassung zu finden, ausgewandert, versprechen und verpflichten uns, Seiner gegenwärtig regierenden Majestät, König Georg dem Zweiten, und Dessen Nachfolgern, Königen von Großbritannien, Treue und Anhänglichkeit beweisen, uns dem Besitzer dieser Provinz treu erweisen, und uns gegen alle Unterthanen besagter Majestät friedlich benehmen zu wollen, und zu unserem besten Wissen und Willen die Gesetze England's und dieser Provinz zu befolgen."

G. M. Weis, V. D. M., a
Rudolph Beyl,
Sebastian Gräff,
Tobias Frey,
Johan Peter Fritz,
Jacob Jost,
Rudolph Wellecker,
William Herry,*
Jacob Bausel,
Philip Rutschly,
Elias Meyer,
Johannes Leib,
Hans Georg Ziegler,
Henrich Meyer,
Christoph Walter,*
Johannes Huth,
Philip Zigler,*
Joseph Albrecht,
Michael Böttle,
Georg Petter,
Johannes Barth,
Hans Ernst Rudy,
Hans Georg Hertzer,
Jacob Meyer,
Henrich Meyer,*
Hans Philipp Schweickhardt,

Philip Jacob Rheinlender,
Johann Friderich Hilligass,
Hans Michael Zimmerman,
Johann Georg Schwab,
Hans Bernhart Wolff,
Johannes Eckman,
Hans Martin Wellmer,*
Hans Caspar Spangler,
Hans Martin Will,
Johann Jacob Cuntz,
Hans Georg Welcker,
Alexander Dübendöffer,
Johan Friderick Rudi,
Hans Michael Pfautz,
Hans Michael Diel,
Hans Jerg Anspacher,
Georg Schumacher,
Hans Georg Nögelle,
Hans Georg Kremer,
Andreas Holsbacher,
Hans Adam Wilder,*
Hans Georg Wolff,
Hans Martin Liebenstein,
Johan Henrich Hartman,
Johannes Haberacker.

---

a G. M. Weis was for many years a minister of the Gospel in the German Reformed Church in Pennsylvania.

a G. M. Weis war viele Jahre lang ein Prediger des Evangeliums in der reformirten Kirche.

In vol. iii. 284. Colonial Records, it is stated, "sundry of these foreigners lying sick on board, never came to be qualified." I have compared Lists A, B and C and find in List A, besides those given above, the following names:

S. 284 Col. Rec. III. heißt es: „Einige dieser Fremden, welche krank an Bord lagen, wurden nie qualificirt." Ich habe die Listen A, B und C zusammengestellt, und finde außer den oben angegebenen in Liste A noch folgende:

Benedict Strome,*
Henericus Bell,*
Daniel Levan,*
Willm Jurgeins,*
Adam Henrich,*
Sebastian Vink,*
Hans Georg,*
Hans Georg Bowman,*
Hans Martin Shoomaker,*
Hieronimus Milderd,*
Jon Barnd Lerinstey,*
Steven Frederick,*
Hans Jacob Eckinan,*
Hendrick Wittser,*
Jacob Plause,*
Johannis Strome,*
Philip Swyger,*
Jacob Swartz,*
Christian Snyder,*
Jacob Mast,*
Johanes Balt,*
Albert Swoap,*
Abraham Beni,*
Johan Willm Mey,*
Johannes Hier,*
Ulrich Sieere,*
Jacob Swicker,*
Philip Feruser,*
Johan Wester, §
Martin Prill,*
Peter Seytz,*

Bastian Smith,*
Nicholas Adams,*
Ulrich Hetzell,*
Henrich Gonger, §
Clement Eise,*
Philip Rödesell,*
Uldrich Staffon,*
John Tobias Serveas,
Johan Hend Gyer, §
Johanes Barteleme,*
Christopher Walter,*
Hans Adam Stoll,*
Hans Jerig Viegle,*
Hans Jerig Roadebas,*
Christopher Wittmer,*
Hans Mich Pagman,*
Hans Mich Triell,*
Hans Mich Weider,*
Hans Jerrick Wigler,*
Hans Fillkeysinger,*
Hans Georg Kley, §
Andro Saltzgerber,*
Christopher Labengyger,*
Hans Georg Schaub,*
Johannes Tiebindorf,*
Conrad Milder,*
Hans Adam Beinder,*
Abraham Farne,*
Hans Georg Milder,*
Rudolph Wilhelm,*
Johanes Michel Peepell.*

The following are reported as having died:

Die Folgenden werden als gestorben berichtet:

Leonard Seltenrich, Jac. Milder, Christopher Milder and Hans Georg Ahrnold.

---

2) Sept. 27, 1727. Fifty-three Palatines with their families, about two hundred persons, imported in the ship James Good-will, David Crocket, Master, from Rotterdam, last from Falmouth, appeared, repeated and signed the Declaration.—*Col. Rec.* III. 284.

Sept. 27, 1727. Drei und fünfzig Pfälzer, die mit ihren Familien, etwa zwei hundert Personen, auf dem Schiffe James Good-will, Capitain David Crocket, von Rotterdam über Falmouth ge= bracht wurden, erschienen, wiederholten und unterzeichneten die Declaration.—Col. Rec. III. 284.

Michael Danner,	Hans Häge,
Joseph Schurgh,*	Hans Lieman,
Georg Müller,	Jacob Weygerdt,
Ulric Staufer,	Ulric Zug,
Peter Zug,	Jacob Fritz,*
Adam Kiener,	Ulrich Kiener,
Hans Kiener,	Christian Weber,
Joseph Clap,*	Georg Steinerger,
Christian Miller,*	Jacob Walder,
Georg Klapp,	Paul Hein,
Hans Debalt Leteman,	Henry Zeug,
Georg Michael Kuntz,	Jacob Siegel,
Hans Michael Kuntz,	Hans Furster,
Michael Syegrist,	Henrich Wolff,
Hans Langnecker,*	Georg Valentin Klop,
Reinhardt Jung,	Johan Jacob Walder,
Wilhelm Weygerdt,	Christoph Kirchhoff,
Abraham Ebersohl,	Michael Leiberth,
Hans Michael Friedler,*	Heinrich Eberli,
Jacob Gass,	Bartholomeus Siegrist,
Friederich Gass,	Johan Adam Volpel,
Jacob Gass, §	Johan Ludwig Klop,
Hans Müller,	Hans Georg Koch,
Jacob Arndt,	Johannes Müller,
Hans Hein,*	Joseph Müller,

Bastian Müri,   Heinerich Schultz,
Jacob Gangwyer,*   Georg Zeug.
Hans Altorffler,

---

3) Sept. 30, 1727. Seventy Palatines with their families,
about three hundred persons, imported in the ship Molley, John
Hodgeson, Master, from Rotterdam, last from Deal, appeared,
repeated and signed the Declaration.—*Col. Rec.* III. 287.

Sept. 30, 1727. Siebzig Pfälzer mit ihren Familien, etwa
drei hundert Personen, die auf dem Schiffe Molley, Capitain John
Hodgeson, von Rotterdam über Deal gekommen sind, erschienen, wie=
derholten und unterzeichneten die Declaration.—Col.Rec.III.287.

Hans Stuber,*   Michel Sebastian, 0
Andries Börns,*   Hans Georg Dieter,
Johannes Krauss,   Georg Ludwig Gesell,
Martin Hausser,   Hans Jergle Schellenberg,0
Marx Fuchs,   Henrich Kauffmann,
Hans Ring,   Michel Schenck,0
Hans Mosser,   Hendrich Kryebiel, 0
Michael Krebil,   Frantz Stupp,
Hans Kobel,   Hans Jacob Bender,
Michael Frantz,   Hans Jerig Keel,
Peter Gut,   David Mardtin,
Ludwig Bortz,   Jacob Marttin,
Andreas Ihllig,   Christian Velte,
Felix Guth,   Jacob Scherer,
Wygan Diell,*   Jacob Bähr,
Hannes Steyer,   Hans Funk,§
Hans Guth sen.,   Samuel Gut,
Henrich Fultz, §   Martin Kindigh,
Samuel Behr,   Ulrich Leib,
Hans Ludwig Dederer,   Tobias Horch,
Hans Heinrich Bernhardt,   Hans Mich. Aso,*
Hans Georg Huber,   Christian Miller,
Hans Leonard Hofman,*   Johannes Büller,
Hans Michel Guth,   Augustin Weder,
Michael Spowner,*   Stephanus Reppert,
Hans Georg Harger,   Ulrich Schellenberger,
Michel Schmidt,   Henrich Mayer, 0
Burckhard Hoffmann,   Samuel Oberholtz,

Hans Jacob Riedt,
Christian Solderman, §
Rudolph Lanckes,*
Hans Hooghstadt,*
Christian Wenger,
Hans Erick Feilter,*
Joh. Matheis Egener.

In List A are reported dead:

Liſte A berichtet als todt:

Hans Ulrich Shumacher and Jacob Horrester.

---

4) Oct. 2, 1727. Fifty-three Palatines with their families, about one hundred and forty persons, imported in the ship Adventurer, John Davies, Master, from Rotterdam, last from Plymouth.—*Col. Rec.* III. 288.

In the printed *Col. Rec.* only twenty-seven names appear. In A fifty-five, in B thirty-two.—(*Editor.*)

Oct. 2, 1727. Drei und fünfzig Pfälzer mit ihren Familien, etwa hundert vierzig Perſonen, kamen auf dem Schiffe Adventurer, Capitain John Davies, von Rotterdam über Plymouth an.—Col. Rec. III. 288.

In den gedruckten Colonial-Berichten finden ſich nur ſieben und zwanzig Namen, in A fünf und fünfzig und in B zwei und dreißig.—(Herausgeber.)

Johannes Lehman,
Michael Müller,
Peter Shilling,*
Jacob Bauman,
John Seyham,
Johannes Kurtz,
Nicklas Chron,
Jacob Wilhelmus,
Caspar Ney,
Jacob Leidy,
Michael Eickert,
Peter Rule,*
Baltas Leim,
Ulrich Riesser,
Nocolas Keyser,
Christopher Ulrick,*
Johann Peter Weissner,
John Cari Harlacher,*
Christophel Miller,*
Jacques Simonet,
Johannis Ullerich,
Johannes Beydeler,
Hans Adam Osser,*
Mathias Risling,*
Frans Baltzar Frans,*
Johann Peter Hess,
Christopher Ulrick,*
Christian Bickler,*
Daniel Bowman,*
Johan Dieter Borleman,
Johann Jacob Stutzman,
Georg Christoph Æchstein.

Besides these, who signed the Declaration, List A has the following:

5*

Außer den obigen, welche die Declaration unterzeichneten, ent=
hält Liste A noch Folgende:

Ulrich Pitcha,*

Michael Thar,*

Jacob Bowman,*

Nicholas Kern,

Hans Marteler,*

Joost Coope,*

Jacob Fisher,*

Henry Smith,*

Jacob Meyer,*

Jacob Smith,*

Jno. Sower,*

Jacob Riser,*

Jacob Filler,

Hans Hisly,*

Benedict Null,*

Leonard Rodennill,*

Derrick Rowshower,*

Hendrich Horlogh,*

Jaspar Mingale,*

Alexander Fritley,*

Christian Frier,*

Christoph Hoffman,

Hans Haldeman,

Christian Piger,

Christo Exell,*

Adam Pisher,*

Jacob Hoofman,*

Peter Boorlinger,*

Hans York Heriger.*

5) Oct. 16, 1727. Forty-six Palatines with their families,
about two hundred persons, imported in the ship Friendship,
of Bristol, John Davies, Master, from Rotterdam, last from Cowes,
whence the ship sailed June 20th.—*Col. Rec.* III. 290.

In B are thirty names; in A fifty-two, including sick and dead.

Oct. 16, 1727. Sechs und vierzig Pfälzer mit ihren Familien,
etwa zwei hundert Personen, kamen mit dem Schiff Friendship,
von Bristol, Capitain John Davies, von Rotterdam, und am
20. Juni über Cowes an.—Col.=Ber. III. 290.

In B sind dreißig und in A zwei und fünfzig Namen, mit
Einschluß der Todten und Kranken.

Peter Hagman,

Jacob Hiestandt,

Johannes Bense,

Martin Scheleren,*

Adam Liphart,

Valentin Kratz,

Hans Riess,

Michel Eberhart,

Nicolas Piere,*

Christian Mayer,

Peter Pixseler,*

Peter Leeman,*

Henrich Lohr,

Illess Kassel,

Niclaus Bucher,

Nicklas Crösman,

Peter Welde,

Peter Eberhardt,

Philip Reemer,*

Johannes Schönholtzer,

Johann Georg Hoffmann,

Andreas Schwartz,

Hans Jerig Lauman,
Jeramia Miller,
Johann Georg Müller,
Matheis Schweitzer,
Jacob Sneppley,*
Johan Vincens Mayer,
Johannes Kassel,
Johannes Forrer,

Henrich Strickeller,
Johannes Hiestandt,
Christian Creyebiel,*
Albrecht Bauman,*
Heinrich Schnebli,
Michel Miller,*
Abraham Schwartz,
Johann Philip Ried.

Besides these, who signed the Declaration, List A has yet:

Außer biesen, welche bie Declaration unterzeichneten, enthält Liste A noch Folgende:

Jacob Hiestandt,*
Ulrich Scheren, §
Peter Folock, §
Peter Fennima, §
Jno. Crybile, §
Christian Fide, §
Nicholas Bogert, §

Michael Eberam, §
Peter Hansberger, §
Ulrich Leemer, §
Lodowick Bentze,*
Joseph Eberam, §
Peter Clucksclear, §
Nicholas Chasrood. §

In List A these are reported dead:

Als tobt berichtet Liste A:

Andrew Urmi, Jacob Trycler, Jacob Snyder, Henry Croo, Jno. Overholser and Falkert Adest.

---

6) Aug. 24, 1728. Eighty Palatines with their families, about two hundred persons, imported in the ship Mortonhouse, John Coultas, Master, last from Deal, whence the ship sailed June 15th.—*Col. Rec.* III. 327.

According to List A two hundred and five persons were imported. Eighty males above sixteen, sixty-nine women and fifty-six children.—(*Editor.*)

Aug. 24, 1728. Achtzig Pfälzer mit ihren Familien, etwa zwei hundert Personen, wurden mit dem Schiff Mortonhouse, Capitain John Coultas, über Deal, von wo das Schiff am 15. Juni abfuhr, herübergebracht.—Col.-Ber. III. 327.

Nach Liste A waren es zwei hundert fünfzig Personen: achtzig männliche über sechzehn Jahre, neun und sechzig weibliche und sechs und fünfzig Kinder.—(Herausgeber.)

Georg Bechtell,
Philip Noldt,

Abraham Wolff,
Hans Erdt,

Johannes Bär,
Baltas Gerringer,*
Andres Ewy,*
Steph. Haltsbieller,
Johannes Roth,
Jacob Storm,
Frederick Leeder,
Johannes Edesma,
Uli Schürch,
Johan Scharch,
Jacob Jost,
Peter Denckelberg,*
Vincent Stoufer,*
Johannis Christ,*
Frans Latshow,*
Henrich Wilh. Dielinger,
Johann Dietrich Hengst,
Peter Mittelkauff,
Christ. Newswanger,*
Hans Weldgrau,*
Johannes Bölla,
Jacob Heidschuh,
Bernerd Henssel,*
Hans Michel Dettmer,
Michael Saipell,*
Johannes Weygandt,
Johan Georg Doderer,
Johan Georg Roth,
John Jacob Hack,*
Johann Michael Ranck,
Johan Christoph Meng,
Christoffel Bencker,
Johannes Huber,
Michael Köhler,
Johan Stock,
Johann Rör,
Johan Herer,*
Philip Engert,

Derick Oordt,*
Jacob Brulasher,*
Felde Kille,*
Hans Frih,
Johannes Bär,
Jacob Wissel,*
Hans Hauff,
Rudolph Heller,
Hans Philip,
Jacob Coger,*
Conrad Keer,*
Jonas Köhler,
Martin Schaub,
Jacob Brunner,
Johan Er,
Ury Schürch,
Georg Schmidt,
Hans Wolf Dielinger,
John Henry Raan,
Henrich Eschelmann,
Johannes Morgenstern,
Johannes Kitsmiller,*
Johannes Lägerhän,*
Kasper Heydrukee,*
Johan Jost Schmidt,
Martin Vogelhütter,
Johannes Franckhauser,
Johannes Naycommet,*
Hans Martin Miller,
Hans Leonard Miller,
Denius Dunckelberg,
Frederick Denckelberg,
Johan Peter Mölich,
Gottfried Henke,
Johan Albrecht Köhler,
Christopher Sullenger,
Hans Jacob Miller.*

---

7) Sept. 4, 1728. Thirty Palatines with their families, about one hundred persons, imported in the ship Albany, Lazarus

Oxman, Master, from Rotterdam, last from Cowes, whence the ship sailed June 22d.—*Col. Rec.* III. 329.

Sept. 4, 1728. Dreißig Pfälzer mit ihren Familien, etwa ein hundert Personen, kamen mit dem Schiffe Albany, Capitain Lazarus Ormann, von Rotterdam über Cowes, welches sie am 22. Juni verließen, herüber.—Col.=Ber. III. 329.

Simon Scholler,	Georg Frid V. Berbisdorff,
Casper Riedt,	Frid Christf. von Steysplatz,
Jacob Weis,*	Johann Philip Glasser,
Matheis Koplin,	Heinrich Stellfeldt,
Lorentz Belitz,	Friederich Eichelberger,
Casper Hoot,*	Hans Jacob Donbach,
Conrad Duboy,	Georg Wendel Biehel,
Michel Keim,	Johannes Shönfeldt,
Hans Georg Metz,	Johan Daniel Bengel,
Georg Gerttner,	Philip Shoman,*
Hans Miller,*	Hans Jacob Biehel,
Johan Carl Keil,	Alexander Zarthmann,
Andrew Ablin,*	Hans Georg Buch,
Jän Blömen,	Hans Jerick Riger,*
Martin Calb,*	Jerig Fred. Bergenstott.*

8) Sept. 11, 1728. A number of Palatines with their families, about ninety, imported in the ship James Goodwill, David Crocket, Master, from Rotterdam, last from Deal, whence she sailed June 15th.—*Col. Rec.* III. 331.

Sept. 11, 1728. Eine Anzahl Pfälzer mit ihren Familien, wohl neunzig, kamen auf dem Schiffe James Goodwill, Capitain David Crocket, von Rotterdam über Deal, welches das Schiff am 15. Juni verließ.—Col.=Ber. III. 331.

Ulrich Englert,	Leonard Hicker,
Georg Graff,	Jacob Lentz,
Michael Neff,	Johan Ruspag,
Hans Gurtz,*	Adam Sommer,
Isaac Werthon,	Andreas Graff,
Hans Martin Valck,	Jacob Fuchs,*
Hans Mich. Rider,*	Jacob Herman,*
Friederich Scholl,	Martin Moser,
Sebastian Dörr,	Jacob Bayer,
Bastian Ederle,?	Adam Engeler,§

Jacob Kuhn,
Martin Valk,*
Johann Caspar Stöver,
   Missionaire.
Johann Caspar Stöver,
   S. S. Theol. Stud.
Johan Leonhart Holsteiner,
Johan Egidius Grimm,
Matheus Fernsler,
Thomas Kopenhaver,*
Georg Schuhmacher,
Theobald Mechling,

Andreas Strickli,
Johan Leonhart Keller,
Johan Christof Groff,
Philip Henrich Söller,
Johan Adam Mosser,
Hans Jerick Seyler,*
Hans Urich Bontz,*
Hans Jacob Schlauch,
Hans Georg Medtler,
Jacob Meckling,
Michael Korr.

9) Aug. 19, 1729. Seventy-five Palatines with their families, about one hundred and eighty persons, imported in the ship Mortonhouse, James Coultas, Master, from Rotterdam, last from Cowes, whence the ship sailed June 21st.— *Col. Rec.* III. 367.

Aug. 19, 1729. Fünf und siebenzig Pfälzer mit ihren Familien, wohl hundert und achtzig Personen, brachte das Schiff Morton=house, Capitain James Coultas, von Rotterdam über Cowes, welches es am 21. Juni verließ.—Col.=Ber. III. 367.

Dielman Kolb,
Michael Borst, *a*

Rudolph Moor,*
Uldric Root,*

a Michael Borst, the Editor's maternal great-grandfather, who lived and, in 1741, died near Lebanon.—*See Rupp's History of Lebanon Co., pp.* 303, 304.

a Michael Borst, der Urgroßvater des Herausgebers mütterlicherseits, wohnte bei Lebanon und starb 1741.—Siehe Rupp's Gesch. von Leb. Co., S. 303, 304.

Note —In the year 1729, Conrad Weiser left Schoharie with his wife and five children; Philip, Frederick, Anna, Madlina and Maria, settled near the present site of Womelsdorf, Berks County. He was usefully employed in various capacities by the Government until within a few weeks of his demise. He died July 13, 1760, aged 63 years, 8 months and 13 days. His remains rest near Womelsdorf.—*Rupp's His. Berks Co., pp.* 195, 222.

Anmerkung.—Im Jahre 1729 verließ Conrad Weiser Schoharie und zog mit seiner Frau und fünf Kindern in die Nähe des jetzigen Womels=dorf, Berks Co. Die Regierung verwandte ihn bis kurz vor seinem Tode zu mancherlei Diensten. Er starb am 13. Juli 1760 im Alter von 63 Jah=ren, 8 Monaten und 13 Tagen. Sein Leichnam ruht in der Nähe von Womelsdorf.—Rupp's Gesch. von Berks Co., S. 195, 222.

Carl Ernst Musselbach,
Johan Philip Ranck,
Konradt Wörntz,
Henrich Schlengeluff,
Heinrich Dubs,
Heinrich Blimm,
Christ. Brown,*
Andreas Meys,
Jacob Obere,*
Ulrich Croll,*
Conrad Kilner,
Rudolph Walder,*
Simon Rohl,
Baltzar Rör,*
Georg Threhr,
Hans Müller,
Casper Dorest,
Johannes Hoock,
Nicolas Peffel,
Ultimer Schnebler,*
Christ. Kroll,*
Jacob Crebil,
Peter Wecher,
Adam Orth,
Johannes Reis,
Michel Weber,*
Nicolas Carver,*
Valtin Keiser,
Johannes Orde,*
Wendel Wyant,*
Richd. Fetter, §
Jacob Reyer, §
Peter Weeger, §
Jacob Sellser,
Friderich Marsh, §
Andrew Bastian, §

Jacob Fetter, §
Moret Creeter, §
Hans Ulrich Vry,*
Johan Niclas Printschler,
John Daniel Worley,*
Valentine Ficus,*
Hans Michel Heides,
Johan Stephan Riemer,
Jacob Eschelmann,
Abraham Kensinger,*
Hans Michel Fröhlich,
Hans Jacob Roodlys,*
Hans Ulrich Hüber,
Gerhardt Müller,
Heinrich Zurtere,
Jacob Bowman,*
Johannes Müller,
David Montandon,
Georg Adam Weidel, a
Christoph Schambach,
Henrich Killhaver,*
Reynard Halder,*
Christ. Bumgarner,*
Friederich Marsteller,
Johann Peter Moll,
Johann Middle,*
Adam Bastian, §
Henry Daniel Back, §
Johann Georg Crössman,
Georg Crössman,
Christian Longenacre,*
Martin Alstadt, §
Philip Jacob Back, §
Hendrick Sneevele,*
Jacob Reif, *formerly of Pa.*
Jacob Seller, *of Germantown.*

---

a Georg Adam Weidel, the paternal grand-father of *Jacob Weidel,*
Esq., of Lebanon, Pa.

a Georg Adam Weidel, der Großvater vaterseits des Herrn Jakob Weibel in Lebanon, Pa.

Jacob Reif and Jacob Seller were probably both *Neuländer,* a class of persons fully noticed in *Rupp's Fireside History of the Germans in Pennsylvania.* Jacob Reif was once a conspicuous person in the early history of the German Reformed Church.

In A are the names of fifty-five females; among others, the wife of Jacob Reif, Veronica Reif; Eliza Seller, Anna Christiana Schlengeluff, Apalis Schlengeluff, Anna Barbara Ranck, Mary Ann Crössman.

Jacob Reif und Jacob Seller waren wahrscheinlich beide Neuländer, eine Art Leute, welche in „Rupp's Gesch. der Deutschen in Pennsylvanien für den häuslichen Kreis" gründlich behandelt sind. Jacob Reif war seiner Zeit eine bedeutende Persönlichkeit in der Geschichte der deutsch=reformirten Kirche.

In A sind die Namen von fünf und fünfzig Frauen; unter anderen: die Frau von Jacob Reif, Veronica Reif; Elisa Seller, Anna Christiana Schlengeluff, Apalis Schlengeluff, Anna Barbara Ranck, Marie Anna Crößmann.

---

10) Sept. 15, 1729. Fifty-nine Palatines with their families, one hundred and twenty-six persons, imported in the ship Allen, James Craigie, Master, from Rotterdam, last from Cowes, whence the ship sailed July 7th.—*Col. Rec.* III. 368.

Sept. 15, 1729. Neun und fünfzig Pfälzer mit ihren Familien, ein hundert und sechs und zwanzig Personen, brachte das Schiff Allen, Capitain James Craigie, von Rotterdam über Cowes, welches das Schiff am 7. Juli verließ.—Col.=Ber. III. 368.

Johannes Mack,	Jacob Wiss,
Velten Mack,	Jacob Snider,*
Hans Gunde,	Jacob Lesle,*
Andreas Bony,	Paul Lipkip,*
Hisbert Benter,*	Johannes Kipping,
Pieter Lesle,	Conrad Eill,?
Jacob Bosserdt,	Alexander Mack, *a*

---

a Alexander Mack sen., was born at Schriesheim, in the Palatinate, 1679. He married Anna Maria Kling of his native town. They had sons and daughters: John Valentin, Johannes, Alexander, Christina and Anna Maria. Both daughters died young. His wife died in Germany 1720. He settled near Germantown—died 1735—buried in the Brethren burying ground. The *epitaph* on his tombstone is brief: Hier

Alexander Mack, *der junge,*
Jacob Kalcklöser,
Wilhelmus Knepper,
Johan Henrich Kalckgleser,
Christophel Kalckglässer,
Johan Christ. Crobf,
Hans Slaughters,*
Hans Jacob Kiebel,
Rinehart Hammer,*
Johann Martin Kress,
Johannes Meinterfeer,*
Johannes Perger,*
Andreas Kropp,
Matheis Schneider,
Mathias Ulland,*
Georg Dieter,
Alexander Dihll,
Daniel Cropp, §
John Hissle, §
Velten Becker,
Christian Matler,
Ulrich Œllen,

Saml. Galler,*
Joseph Brunner,
Jerrich Hoffart,
Feltin Rafer,*
Jacob Cropp, §
Joh. Jacob Knecht,
Georg Vetter,
Philip Mich. Fiersler,*
Hans Georg Klauser,*
Christian Schneider,
Johannes Flückiger,
Christian Kropf,
Johannes Petenkoffer,
Hans Georg Koch,
Hans Caspar Kolb,
Jno. Jacob Hopbach,
Leonhart Amweg,
Johannes Wightman,*
Valentine Gerhart Hisle,
Henrich Peter Middeldorff,
Christian Ketzendander,*
Heinrich Holtzstein.

A contains six names of males under sixteen, also the names of thirty-nine females above sixteen; among these are Agnus Kalklöser, Joanna Margaret Bony, Veronica Knepper, Anna Margaretta Mack, Philippina Mack, Anna Kipping, Sivilla Kipping, Johanna Kipping, Eva Bossert, Maria Kalklöser, members, with their husbands, of the *Schwartzenau - Täufer,* of whom Alexander Mack sen. was *Urheber,* or founder, about the year 1708. He seceded from *Hochman,* with whom he had co-operated for some time, accompanying him in his religious visits in

---

ruhen die Gebeine A. M., geboren 1679, gestorben 1735, seines Alters 56 Jahr.

a Alexander Mack sen. wurde 1679 zu Schriesheim in der Pfalz geboren. Er verheiratete sich mit Anna Maria Kling aus seinem Geburtsort. Söhne und Töchter wurden ihnen geboren: Johann Valentin, Johannes, Alexander, Christina und Anna Maria. Beide Töchter starben jung. Seine Frau starb 1720 in Deutschland. Er ließ sich nahe Germantown nieder, starb 1735 und liegt auf dem Brüder-Begräbnißplatze begraben. Die Inschrift auf seinem Grabstein ist: Hier ruhen die Gebeine A. M., geboren 1679, gestorben 1735, seines Alters 56 Jahr.

Germany and Switzerland. Some of the *Täufer* had come to America ten years before Mack.—*Rupp's His. Relig. Den. U. S.*

A enthält sechs Namen der Mannspersonen über sechzehn Jahre, ebenfalls die Namen von neun und dreißig Weibspersonen über sechzehn; unter diesen sind: Agnus Kalklöser, Joanna Margaret Bony, Veronica Knepper, Anna Margaretta Mack, Philippina Mack, Anna Kipping, Sivilla Kipping, Johanna Kipping, Eva Bossert, Maria Kalklöser, mit ihren Männern zu den Schwartze=nau=Täufern gehörend, deren Gründer der ältere Alexander Mack um's Jahr 1708 war. Er trennte sich von Hochmann, dessen Mitarbeiter er eine Zeit lang gewesen und den er auf seinen Re=ligionsreisen nach Deutschland und der Schweiz begleitet hatte. Einige der Täufer waren zehn Jahre vor Mack nach Amerika ge=kommen.—Rupp's Gesch. der rel. Ben. in den Ver. St.

---

11) Aug. 29, 1730. Palatines with their families, two hundred and sixty persons, imported in the ship Thistle, of Glasgow, Colin Dunlap, Master, from Rotterdam, last from Cowes. —*Col. Rec.* III. 283.

Aug. 29, 1730. Das Schiff Thistle von Glasgow, Capitain Colin Dunlap, brachte Pfälzer mit ihren Familien, zwei hundert und sechzig Personen, von Rotterdam über Cowes.—Col.=Ber. III. 283.

Valentin Grisemer,	Hans Menigh,
Johannes Dunckel,	Nichol Fiser,
Christof Batter,	Johan Zwinger,
Christian Leman,*	Jacob Nagel,
Jeremias Hes,*	Ulrich Scherer,
Joh. Georg Ludwig Hass,	Philip Groscost,*
Bernhart Siegmund,	Casper Bittner,*
Hans Jacob Dohl,	Nickel Cünter,
Johan Peter Ohller,	Johannes Scherer,
Johan Henrich Schmidt,	Johannes Haus,*
Caspar Fiehman,	Philip Hautz,*
Steven Remer,*	Lorentz Hoff,
Rudolph Draugh,*	Thomas Hamma,
Johannes Kun,*	Jacob Stiffel,
William Keim,*	Wolfer Sperger,*
Ludwick Delman,*	Ulrich Steyner,*
Gerhart Zinn,	Thomas Hes,

Henrich Hes,
Hendrich Gutt,*
Caspar Krieger,
Christoph Anckenbrant,
Jean Henri Fortineaux,*
Frederich Reimer,
Peter Beswanger,*
Johan Caspar Schmidt,
Johan Paulus Düttenhöffer,
Johan Augustus Scherrer,
Hans Georg Hofman,
Abraham Transu,
Casper Hartman,*
Christian Shram,
Leonhart Köpplinger,
Rudolp Andreas,

Frederick Peifer,
Johannes Kepplinger,
Felte Meidelman,
Dietrich Beidelman,
Elias Meidelman,
Jacob Ammon,
Johan Nickel Lukenbell,*
Hans Simon Mey,
Henrich Lukebill,
Ludwig Mohler,
Lönhart Hochgenug,
Peter Federolff,
Peter Müller, a
Friederich Lienberger,
Peter Frawiener,
Bernhard Renn,

a Peter Müller was a native of Oberamt Lautern, Germany. He graduated at Heidelberg. He was a man of profound erudition—of more than ordinary powers of mind—a finished scholar, as is evident from testimony born him by the Rev. Jedediah Andrews. In a letter dated Philadelphia, 10 mo., (Oct.) 14th, 1730, "There is," says Andrews, "lately come over a Palatine candidate of the ministry, who, having applied to us at the synod for ordination, 'tis left to Tenant, Andrews and Boyd to do it. He is an extraordinary person for sense and learning. We gave him a question to discuss about *Justification*, and he answered it, in a whole sheet of paper, in a very notable manner. His name is John Peter Müller, and speaks Latin as readily as we do our natural tongue." In 1735, he connected himself with the *Siebentägers*, of Ephrata. He died Sept. 25, 1796. His remains rest at Ephrata, Lancaster County, Pa.—*Rupp's His. Lan. Co., p.* 229.

a Peter Müller ist im Oberamt Lautern in Deutschland geboren. Er grabuirte auf der Heidelberger Universität. Er war ein Mann von tiefer Gelehrsamkeit und besaß außergewöhnliche Geisteskräfte, wie aus dem Zeugniß des Pastors Jedediah Andrews ersichtlich ist. In einem, Philadelphia, den 14. Oct. 1730 datirten Briefe sagt er: „Es ist kürzlich ein theologischer Candidat herübergekommen aus der Pfalz, der auf seine Anmeldung bei der Synode zur Ordination an Tenant, Andrews und Boyd verwiesen wurde. Er ist eine außerordentliche Persönlichkeit, was Verstand und Gelehrsamkeit anbetrifft. Wir legten ihm eine Frage bezüglich der Rechtfertigung vor, welche er auf einem ganzen Bogen Papier ausgezeichnet beantwortete. Sein Name ist John Peter Müller und er spricht Latein so fließend, wie wir unsere Muttersprache." 1735 verband er sich mit den Siebentägern zu Ephrata. Er starb am 25. Sept. 1796. Seine Ueberreste ruhen zu Ephrata, Lancaster Co., Pa.—Rupp's Gesch. Lanc. Co., S. 229.

Dietrich Kober,
Georg Hützel,
Ludwig Hützel,
Georg Undetenard,*
Carl Valentin Michaels,

Christopher Henerich,
Johann Matheis Theis,
Michael Thomas,
Christian Thomas.

---

12) Sept. 5, 1730. Forty-five Palatines with their families, one hundred and thirty persons, imported in the ship Alexander and Ann, William Clymer, Master, from Rotterdam, last from Cowes.—*Col. Rec.* III. 386.

Sept. 5, 1730, brachte das Schiff Alexander und Ann, Capitain William Clymer, von Rotterdam über Cowes fünf und vierzig Pfälzer mit ihren Familien, etwa ein hundert und dreißig Personen.—Col.=Ber. III. 386.

Anthony Miller,
Daniel Christman,*
Adam Phillipot,*
Martin Müller,
John Peter Waller,*
Frantz Blum,
Jacob Müller,
Fredrick Meyer,*
Carl Keller,
Eberhart Meyer,
Adam Schuler,
David Süsholtz,
Martin Creiner,
Marger Jerger,
Michael Belscher,
Conrad Stamm,
Leopold Helligas,
Mattheis Seltzer,
Hans Gerham,?
Michael Beyerle,
Christof Steinlein,
Hans Mich. Wiedes,
Johan Carl Hornberger,

John Adam Stadtler,*
Hans Veltin Breneissen,
Hans Lanciscus,
Henrich Lanciscus,
Johannes Herbert,
Baltes Lanckhär,
Michael Bürger,
Hans Jacob Oberholtz,
Martin Bucher,
Johan Friederich Weber,
Henrich Marte,
Geo. Michel Breneissen,
Johan Philip Emmert,
Peter Edelman,*
Johannes Widner,
Michel Ackermann,
Rudolph Messerschmidt,
Henrich Clemmer,*
Johannes Klemmer,
Johann Volckmann,
Joh. Sebastian Graff,
Hans Bartel Hornberger,
Joh. Fried. Lanciscus.

---

13) Nov. 30, 1730. Palatines with their families imported in the ship Joyce, William Ford, Master, from Boston.—*Col.*

Rec. III. 389. In this ship there were twenty-eight males above sixteen years, six males under sixteen; twenty-four females, of whom eight were under sixteen years.—(*Editor.*)

Nov. 30, 1730. Pfälzer mit ihren Familien kamen auf dem Schiff Joyce, Capitain William Ford, von Boston.—Col.=Ver. III. 389. Auf diesem Schiffe befanden sich acht und zwanzig Mannspersonen über sechzehn, und sechs unter sechzehn Jahren, außerdem vier und zwanzig Frauen, von denen acht unter sechzehn Jahren waren.—(Herausgeber.)

Christian Miller,
Nicolas Swort,*
Daniel Swort,*
Hans Wichel,*
Joseph Dommi,
John Bear,*
Leonhart Kolb,
Henry Shever,*
Egram Hall,
Johannes Cuntz,
Marck Nitzen,
A. G. Schultze,

Johan Ludwig Heintz,
Hans Jacob Bear,*
Friederich Elberscheidt,
Johann Adam Hoff,
Andreas Hoffmann,
Hans Ulrich Mayer,
Leonhardt Pfudere,
Johan Michael Fischer,
Henrich Kilian,
Johannes Oberbäck,
Zacharias Barth.

Passengers under sixteen years of age:

Reisende unter sechzehn Jahren:

Hans Lenhart Schäffer, Lorentz Mayer, Christian Schwartz, Jacob Schwartz, Hans Schwartz, Ludwich Weichel, Hen. Bär.

---

14) Aug. 17, 1731. Palatines imported in the ship Samuel, Hugh Peircy, Master, from Rotterdam, last from Cowes.— *Col. Rec.* III. 410. Males, thirty-nine above sixteen, sixteen boys under sixteen; thirty-three women above sixteen, and twenty-one girls under sixteen.—(*Editor*)

Aug. 17, 1731. Pfälzer, die auf dem Schiffe Samuel, Capi-tain Hugh Peircy, von Rotterdam über Cowes gebracht wurden.— Col.=Ver. III. 410. Männliche neun und dreißig über sechzehn, und sechzehn unter sechzehn Jahren; drei und dreißig weibliche Personen über sechzehn und ein und zwanzig unter sechzehn.— (Herausgeber.)

Joh. Georg Kirschner,
John Fisher,*

Philipp Knopp,
Casper Holtzhausen,

Conrad Eckert,
Ludwig Han,
Johannes Metzger,
Jacob Wenst,*
Conrad Möller,
Christo Ritter,*
Johannes Diterichs,
Andreas Erlewyne,*
Johan Millbürger,
Hans Ritter,
Joh. Georg Koch,
Barent Tisen,*
Johannes Spengler,
Georg Balser Wentz,
Hans Georg Plüger,
Johann Michael Gleim,
Engelberd. Schraidt,

Johan Henrich Knopp,
Johann Jacob Krauss,
Johann Jacob Scheibe,
Johann Henrich Hammel,
Frederick Babenmeyer,*
Lodwick Goodbrood,*
Hans Georg Bender,
Georg Sebald Madriger,*
Hans Georg Lohrman,
Philip Friederich Vogel,
Johann Christoph Bauer,
Ludwig Sauermilch,
Johannes Stuntz,
Hans Adam Warthman,
George Henderich,
Hans Georg Lohrman.

Passengers under sixteen years:

Reifende unter ſechzehn Jahren:

Martin Griesemer, Johannes Schraidt, Georg Kropp, Peter
Knopp, Georg Hahn, Georg Han, Joh. Han, Carl Müller, Joh.
Dietrichs, Abraham Warthman, Jac. Hofminich, Balzer Vogel,
Henrich Mülberger, Georg Gutbrod, Anthony Schniding.

In this ship came, according to List A, Ludwig Heck, his
wife Mary and daughter Elizabeth.

Mit dieſem Schiffe kamen nach Liſte A Ludwig Heck mit ſeiner
Frau Mary und ſeiner Tochter Eliſabeth.

---

15) Sept. 11, 1731. Palatines imported in the ship Pennsylvania Merchant, Jno. Stedman, Master, from Rotterdam, last
from Dover.—*Col. Rec.* III. 413. Males, fifty-seven above sixteen, twenty-five under sixteen; females, fifty-seven above sixteen, thirty-three under sixteen.

Sept. 11, 1731. Pennſylvania Merchant, Capitain John
Stedman, von Rotterdam über Dover, brachte Pfälzer.—Col.=
Rec. III. 413. Männer ſieben und fünfzig über und fünf und
zwanzig unter ſechzehn; ſieben und fünfzig Weiber über und
drei und dreißig unter ſechzehn Jahren.

Michael Geberth,
Michael Feder,

Ludwig Wulheit,
Jacob Lanius,

Peter Smit,*
Abraham Sahler,
Johan Niclas Weiss,
Martin Boger,
Georg Heinrich,
Jacob Steiner,
Christian Weiser,
Johannes Diehl,
Abram Freeman,*
Friedrich Geberth,
Friedrich Strubel,
Valentin Schults,*
Frantz Krück,
Heinrich Krämer,
Baltzer Seyler,*
Christoph Beier,
Johannes Schenkel,
Conrad Sybert,
Nicklaus Fuss,
Laurence Roodt,*
Conrad Hoogh,*
Jacob Mumma,
Adam Sauer,
Michael Geyger,*
Johannes Rymert,*
Johann Bartel Gucker,
Hans Adam Kremer,

Johann Michael Moll,
Martin Hunsecker,*
Christian Schmidt,
Hans Georg Kelchner,
Christian Schmidt,
Johann Georg Mayer,
Joh. Georg Bergströsser,
Johan Henrich Schmidt,
Johan Bernhardt Arndt,
Christophel Moll,
Johan Jacob Krück,
Joh. Nicklaus Steinmetz,
Hans Adam Echelen,
Joh. Jacob Woltzhoffer,
Valentein Schneider,
Johann Philip Beyer,
Hans Martin Schultz,
Rudolph Casman,*
Johannes Rynert,
Joh. Engelbert Lack,
Johan Georg Schmidt,
Burckhart Küllmer,
Johannes Bischoff,
Johannes Shaak,*
Andreas Beyer,
Hans Michael Horlacher,
Melchior Wistholtz.

Passengers under sixteen:

Reifenbe unter fechzehn Jahren.:

Bernhardt Geberth, Matthias Geberth, Gottl. Geberth, Christian Krämer, Henrich Gehr, Adam Krämer, Christian Gehr, Georg Henrich Gehr, Jacob Mumma, Johannes Sahler, Jacob Arndt, David Arndt.

---

16) Sept. 21, 1731.* Palatines imported in the ship Britania, of London, Michael Franklyn, Master, from Rotterdam,

---

* While the Synod of South Holland was in session in Dort, 1731, eight hundred exiled Palatines passed through the place to take ship at Rotterdam for America. They were visited by the whole Synod

last from Cowes.—*Col. Rec.* III. 414. One hundred and four
males above sixteen, thirty-seven under sixteen; eighty-one
females above sixteen, forty-five under sixteen—in all two hundred and sixty-nine.—(*Editor.*)

Sept. 21, 1731. Das Schiff Britania von London, Capitain
Michael Franklyn, von Rotterdam über Cowes, brachte Pfälzer.*
—Col.-Ber. III. 414. Ein hundert und vier männliche Personen
über und sieben und dreißig unter sechzehn, ein und achtzig weib=
liche über und fünf und vierzig unter sechzehn. Im Ganzen zwei
hundert neun und sechzig.—(Herausgeber.)

Hisbertus Barsch,	Michel Horsh,*
Johannes Barsch,	Daniel Hubert,*
Henrich Geber,	Christian Hubert,*
Han Henrich Geber,	Jacob Carl,
Johannes Geber,	Ulrich Keyser,
Jacob Räsch,	Henrich Kram,
Lucas Vetler,	Jacob Kobel,
Henry Blicher,*	Nicholas Känele,
Leonard Bock,*	Abraham Kern,
Hans Boschung,	Gotfried Kraft,
Johannes Ægender,	Valentin Kleim,
Johannes Frey,	Wilhelm Kerkes,*
Joseph Beyer,*	Michel Meyer,*
Jacob Gunt,*	Jacob Meyer,
Hans Garner,	Jacob Mier,
Rudolph Holsinger,	Michel Mothes,*
Hen. Herbertz,	Johannes Batholommay Rieger,
Jacob Hachman,*	*Hochteutscher Prediger, a*
Johan Heistand,*	Louis Timothee,

in a body and were furnished by them with provisions and medicines.
After Christian exhortation, prayer and singing, they were dismissed
with the assurance that they might rely upon the Church of Holland
for support in their new abode.—*Ger. Ref. Almanac, p.* 22 *for* 1865.

* Während die Synode von Süd-Holland 1731 in Dortrecht ihre Sitzung
hatte, zogen acht hundert vertriebene Pfälzer durch die Stadt, um in Rotterdam auf's Schiff zu gehen. Der ganze geistliche Körper besuchte sie, gab ihnen
Nahrungsmittel und Arzeneien mit auf den Weg. Nach einer christl. Auf-
munterung, Gesang und Gebet, wurden sie mit der Versicherung entlassen,
daß sie sich auf die Kirche Holland's um Unterstützung in ihrem neuen
Wohnorte verlassen können.—Deutsch-ref. Kalender für 1865, S. 22.

a Rev. Rieger was a native of Oberingelheim, Palatinate, Germany.
He studied at Basel and Heidelberg and had charge of several German

Gelert Gelehren,
Jacob Sevenköl,*
Johannes Albert,
Abraham Halshaus,
John Henrich Bahn,
Hans Michael Blattner,
Veith Bruningher,*
Johan Jacob Beyer,*
Johan Adam Beyer,*
Hans Georg Ebert,
Hans Michel Ebert,
Johannes Eschelman,
Hans Michel Debilbissen,*
Hans Georg Debilbissen,*
Hans Michel Wilhelm,
Hans Georg Friedle,*
Hans Georg Gunt,
Hans Michel Henning,
Hans Lenhard Holtzapfel,
Erasmus Holtzapfel,*

Johannes Kirschner,
Georg Dietrich Köhl,
Wilhelm Lautermilch,
Christian Lehman,
Johann Philip Lutz,
Hans Peter Lederman,
Hans Jacob Mautz,
Johan Thomas Meyer,
Hans Henrich Martin,
Johan Caspar Müntz,
Christian Miller,*
Herman Miller,*
John Nehs,
Mathias Nehs jr.,
Hans Georg Nöss,
George Passage,*
Gab. Bösher,*
Johannes Roth,
Jacob Rohr,
Matheis Smeisser,* b

Reformed Congregations in Pennsylvania. He died at Lancaster, Pa.,
March 14, 1769, aged 62 years, 2 months and 4 days. His remains
rest in the grave yard of the German Reformed Church, Lancaster
City.—*Rupp's History of Lancaster County, pp.* 226, 460.

a Paſtor Rieger war in Oberingelheim in der Pfalz geboren. Er ſtudirte
in Baſel und Heidelberg, bediente mehrere deutſch-reformirte Gemeinden in
Pennſylvanien und ſtarb am 14. März 1769 in Lancaſter, Pa., im Alter
von 62 Jahren, 2 Monaten und 4 Tagen. Sein Leichnam ruht auf dem
Kirchhofe der deutſch-reformirten Kirche in der Stadt Lancaſter.—Rupp's
Geſch. von Lancaſter Co., S. 226, 460.

b Matheis Smeisser was born in Rugelbach, Germany, February 17,
1715; on his arrival in Pennsylvania, he settled in York County, where
he died 1778. He was one of the ancestors of the numerous *Smysers,*
whose descendants now number upwards of twelve hundred.

In List A appear the names of *Barbara Smeisser,* aged 50 years, and
Margareth Smeisser, aged 20 years, the former undoubtedly the mother
of, and the latter sister to MATHEIS, aged 16, and *George Smeisser,*
aged 9 years, at the time of their arrival.

b Matheis Smeiſſer, am 17. Februar 1715 in Rugelbach, Deutſchland,
geboren, ließ ſich nach ſeiner Ankunft in Pennſylvanien in York County
nieder, wo er 1778 ſtarb. Er war einer der Vorväter der zahlreichen
Smyſer, deren Abkömmlinge jetzt über zwölfhundert zählen.

In Liſte A erſcheint der Name Barbara Smeiſſer, 50 Jahre alt, und

Mich. Stocker,*
Christophel Drübe,
Hans Vogler,
Lenhart Fieohr,
Oswald Wald,
Caspar Weis,
Jacob Wirtz,
Jacob Nehs,*
Johann Adam Ruppert,
Leonhart Steininger,
Hans Georg Möller,
Joh. Leonhart Bihlmeier,

Joh. Christian Sackreider,
Joh. Michl Schrotner,
Georg Willem Schwartz,
Henrich Ludwig Schwartz,
Johann Adam Schröter,
Valentine Siegmund,*
Jacob Schumacher,
Johannes Schmidt,
Hans Martin Wetzell,
Georg Wannmacher,
Michael Ness,
Joh. Jacob Weynandt.

Under sixteen: (Unter ſechzehn):—Peter Timothee, Ludwig Timothee, Carl Timothee, Daniel Geber, Peter Räsch, Nicholas Frey, Georg Michael Blattner, Hans Brunninger, Hans Adam Brunninger, Leohard Bock, Hans Michael Bock, Hans Boschung, David Brecht, Casper Debelbissen, Henrich Ægender, Ludwig Ægender, Lorentz Friedle, Hans Georg Friedle, Hans Georg Gundt, Joseph Hirsch, Peter Hirsch, Johannes Kern, Hans Georg Köhl, Johannes Lehman, Rudolph Martin, Hans Jacob Nöss, Hans Jacob Roth, Georg Bindeissen, Justus Rupertus Schwartz, Johannes Schwartz, Johann Michael Schröter, Hans Georg Schröter, Johann Henrich Welde, Martin Wetzell, Johannes Moll, Conrad Henning.—Hans Boschung 39 years old, Barbara Boschung 37, Hans Philip Boschung 9, Anna Barbara Boschung 6, Christianna Boschung 3 years.

---

17) Oct. 14, 1731. Palatines imported in the Snow Louther, Joseph Fisher, Master, from Rotterdam, last from Dover.—*Col. Rec.* III. 417. Thirty-three males above sixteen, fifteen under sixteen, and thirty females of different ages, and *two infants* unbaptized—in all 81.—(*Editor.*)

Oft. 14, 1731. Im Snow Louther, Capitain Joſeph Fiſher, von Rotterdam über Dover, kamen Pfälzer an.—Col.=Ber. III. 417. Männliche drei und dreißig über und fünfzehn unter ſechzehn, und dreißig weibliche Perſonen verſchiedenen Alters nebſt zwei kleinen ungetauften Kindern: 81 im Ganzen.—(Herausg.)

Margaretha Smeiſſer, 20 Jahre. Erſtere iſt wohl die Mutter und Letztere die Schweſter des ſechzehnjährigen Matheis und des neunjährigen Georg Smeiſſer.

Gottfried Lehman,
Jacob Michael,
Jacob Keesey,*
Henrich Baum,
Philip Eckford,
Ulrich Michel,
Jacob Holtzinger,
Johann Christian Lehmann,
Johan Wendel Gisse,?
John Jacob Brunner,
Johann Mathias Cramer,
Hans Georg Hamerich,
Philip Peter Visanant,
Johan Peter Fissnand,
Melchior Häyden,*
Philip Kinss,
Dorst Hoste,*

Hans Rösch,
Johannes Ullerich,
Jacob Snevely,*
Christo Newbert,*
Caspar Betschen,
Georg Schöltz,
Daniel Weisiger,
Henrich Havervass,
Christoffel Amborn,
Anton Banckauff,
Johan Nickel Schmid,
Johann Conrad Franck,
Frantz Philip Ulerich,
John Christoph Knauer,
Christ. Ernst Stägenmüller,
Caspar Baumann.

Under sixteen: (Unter ſechzehn):—Johannes Gottfried Lehman, David Giesse, Conrad Giesse, Ulrich Giesse, Jeremias Brunner, Johannes Albrecht, Michael Brunner, Henrich Brunner, Paul Hamerich, Johann Georg Merchand, Johann Ludwig Merchand, Johann Adam Fessingen, Johannes Straub, Philip Lorentz Michael, Jacob Holtzinger.

---

18) May 15, 1732. Palatines imported in the ship Norris, Thomas Lloyd, Master, from Boston.—*Col. Rec.* III. 429.

Mai 15, 1732. Das Schiff Norris, Capitain Thomas Lloyd, brachte Pfälzer von Boston. Col.-Ber. III. 429.

Casper Schirch,
Martin Gasner,
Mathias Weber,
John Phil. Weber,
Johan Mäncher,
Johannes Behn,
Michael Andreas,

Johan Michael Siegmund,
Joh. Dietrich Jungmann,
Christian Rennenger,*
Johannes Herman,
Valentine Westheber,
Joh. Georg Liebenstein.

---

19) Aug. 11, 1732. Palatines imported in the ship Samuel, of London, Hugh Piercy, Master, from Rotterdam, last from Cowes.—*Col. Rec.* III. 431. One hundred and six males above sixteen, thirty-four under sixteen; eighty-nine females above

sixteen, and fifty under—in all two hundred and seventy-nine.—
(*Editor.*)

Aug. 11, 1732. Pfälzer wurden auf dem Schiffe Samuel
von London, Capitain Hugh Piercy, von Rotterdam über Cowes
gebracht.—Col.-Ber. III. 431. Einhundert und sechs männliche
Personen über und vier und dreißig unter sechzehn, nebst neun
und achtzig weiblichen über und fünfzig unter sechzehn. Im
Ganzen zwei hundert neun und siebenzig. (Herausgeber.)

Martin Gerhard,
John Bendler,
Nicklas Körper,
Laurentz Knockel,
Matheus Böckle,
Ulrich Böchle,
Samuel Brandt,
John Heneberger,
Michel Dirstein,
Henrich Ebby,
Gotfried Stahl,
Michel Georg,
Johann George Nungesser,
Georg Philip Windemuth,
Hans Jacob Beclie,
Christoph Böckle,
Johan Jacob Behlerdt,
Hans Georg Klingmann,
Jacob Oberholtzer,
Johan Adam Andress,
Christ. Frantz sen.,*
Samuel Scherer,
Leonhart Döbler,
Oswald Hostetter,
Hans Muselman,
Christ. Frantz jr.,
Friedrich Kieffer,
Jacob Crist,*
Jacob Fleiser,
Georg Döbler,
Georg Bender,
Jacob Stauffer,
Martin Weigell,

Johannes Miller,
Christian Beudler,
Hans Adam Neidig,
Julius Dehr,
Christian Biry,
Andreas Müller,
Christian German,
Benedict German,
Peter Balsbach,
Jacob Knechell,*
Martin Giller,
Jacob Kieffer,
Ulrich Burkhalter,
Jacob Gut,
Hans Paulus Boger,
Johannes Ziger,
Georg Heyl,
Peter Stey,*
John Bumgardner,*
Jacob Albrecht,
J. H. Hartmann,
Wendel Gerlach,
John Helford,*
Jacob Weyes,*
Henrich Berret,*
Jacob Gochnauer,
Peter Frit,
Andreas Shetler,
Carl Seyl,
Philip Wendel,
Eliseus Mayer,
Johannes Lentz,
Johannes Brechbil,

Johan Nickel Strass,
Hans Georg Gödeke,
Joh. Leonhardt Kieffer,
Frederich Mulchslager,*
Michael Kreiderr,
Henrich Ramsauer,
Johan Georg Glassbrenner,
Johan Sebalt Kremer,
Wendel Brechbühll,
Johan Georg Kleinhauss,
Hans Wendel Höll,
Wilhelm Bergheimer,
Andreas Slantzeberger,
Johannes Uhrich,
Johan Peter Heylmann,
Joh. Leonhart Ziegler,
Joh. Friederich Schütz,
Joh. Phillip Schütz,
Johan Jacob Erdman,

Georg Ludwig Horning,
Caspar Wartman,
Georg Klingman,
Johan Philip Bager,?
Hans Michel Balmer,
Christian Balmer,
Friderich Aldorffer,
Anastasius Uhler,
Hans Jerg Steger,
Wendel Bernheisel,
John Bernheisel,
Hans Mich. Baumgertner,
Hein Ulrich Fischer,
Peter Schellenberger,
Hans Georg Queichel,
Wendel Wörbel,
Augustus Wendell,
Peter Schneider,*
Adam Hillegas.

Under sixteen: (Unter fechzehn):—Henrich Böchle, Georg Ebby, Georg Stahl, Heinrich Eberle, Samuel Oberholtzer, Johannes Frantz, Michael Frantz, Johannes Hosteller, Valentin Nungesser, Johannes Lentz, Abraham Wollschläg, Christian Wollschläg, Johannes Ramsauer, Philip Neidig, Gottlieb Heyl, Conrad Bergh, Jacob Kieffer, Michael Boger, Matthias Boger, Jacob Zerger, Georg Berger, Michael Albrecht, Georg Hartman, Jacob Bereth, Henrich Bereth, Caspar Bereth, Georg Schellenberger, Georg Kremer, Friedrich Kremer, Gottfried Kremer, Johannes Wörbel, Michael Mayer, Adam Mayer, Christian Böhler.—Johann Sebald Kremer aged 32, Margaretta Kremer 27, Georg 12, Friedrich 9, Gottfried 7 years old.

20) Sept. 11, 1732. Palatines imported in the ship Pennsylvania, Jno. Stedman, Master, from Rotterdam, last from Plymouth.—*Col. Rec.* III. 452. Seventy-three males above sixteen; women and children, of both sexes and different ages, ninety-eight—in all, one hundred and seventy-one.—(*Editor.*)

Sept. 11, 1732. Mit dem Schiffe Pennsylvanien, Capitain John Stedman, von Rotterdam über Plymouth kamen Pfälzer. Col.=Ber. III. 452. Drei und siebenzig männliche Personen über

fed)zehn; Weiber und Kinder verschiedenen Alters neun und acht=
zig; im Ganzen hundert und ein und siebenzig.—(Herausgeber.)

Adam Klingen,
Joseph Caspering,?
Jacob Giss,
Conrad Frick,
Michael Rein,
John Jacob Buss,
Michael Wüll,
Johan Seleberger,*
Philip Frank,
Jacob Rod,
Simon Carle,
Adam Louer,*
Hartman Lauer,*
Jacob Haus,
Wendel Fiser,
Philip Kebelbe,
Cornelius Kram,
Hans Rootelee,*
Johannes Weber,
Conrad Schönig,
Daniel Müller,
Johannes Hoorle,*
Paulus Ryter,*
Henrich Ryter,*
Georg Mertz,
Michael Schnager,*
Ditrich Gauff,
Johannes Faas,
Jacob Schaad,*
Michael Capp,
Gabriel Konigh,
Carl Ohliger,
Adam Zeyler,*
Friederich Emy,
Mathias Shaub,*

Hendrick Christian,
Leonard Immel,
Michael Immel,
Geo. Michael Hohlstein,
Hans Georg Graff,?
Hans Georg Smit,*
Hans Georg Cuntz,
Christofel Stedler,*
Johan Georg Kauger,
Matheias Hauser,
Simon Peter Holsteiner,
Hans Michel Much,
Han Niclaus Müller,
Johann Peter Strack,
Benedict Eiselman,
Michael Witmer,*
Geo. Michel Schweinhart,
Han Michael Krumrein,
Wolf Copenhäer,*
Michael Copenhäer,*
Mattheis Menchen,
Johann Georg Amend,
Christian Steinbach,
Albrecht Wolffgang,
Paulus Linsenbigler,
Hans Jacob Meyer,
Johann Georg Bätz,
Bernhart Wolffinger,
Bastian Wagner,
Georg Friedrich Capp,
Georg Palsgraff,
William Chriesmerg,*
Hans Leond Conrad,
Wendel Weinheimer,
Hans Georg Minhard.

Matthias Zollicoffer, V. D. M.,

Under sixteen: (Unter fed)zehn):—Philip Ulrich, Jacob Ulrich, Benedict Bartholomäus, Henrich Christian, Hans Kuntz,

Andreas Schweinhart, Christian Müller, Michael Müller, Georg
Hottel, Henrich Hottel, Johannes Hottel, Johan Mayer, Rein-
hart Mayer, Paul Reuter, Caspar Reuter, Michael Schweighart,
Peter Gunst, Bastian Wolfinger, Peter Wolfinger, Jacob Isaac,
Friederich Isaac, Friederich Ermich.

---

21) Sept. 19, 1732. Palatines imported in the ship Johnson,
of London, David Crocket, Master, from Rotterdam, last from
Deal.—*Col. Rec.* III. 453. One hundred and twelve males
above sixteen, ninety-eight under sixteen; ninety-eight females
above sixteen, and eighty-five under sixteen—in all three hundred
and thirty.—(*Editor.*)

Sept. 19, 1732. Pfälzer auf dem Schiffe Johnson, Capitain
David Crocket, aus London, von Rotterdam über Deal.—Col.-
Ber. III. 453. Hundert und zwölf männliche über und acht und
neunzig unter sechzehn; acht und neunzig weibliche Personen
über und fünf und achtzig unter sechzehn: drei hundert dreißig
im Ganzen.—(Herausgeber.)

Hans Steinmann,	Andreas Hemler,
Laurens Hartman,	Nicolas Ewick,*
John Harwich,	Johan Ewick,§
Paulus Wegerlein,	Joh. Henrich Baum,
Valtin Beyer,	Ludwig Friedle,
Henrich Sien,	Anthorn Gilbert,
Conrad Behn,*	Valentin Wield,*
Jacob Müller,	Nicolas Wield,*
Thomas Matern,*	Adam Hummel,
Andreas Overback,*	Fredrich Miller,*
Jacob Cruir,*	Johannes Dieter,
Jacob Rouse,*	Thomas Sauder,
Daniel Schew,*	Johanes Söffrens,
Isac Cuschuah,*	Joh. Georg Steinmann,
Bernhart Peffer,	Hans Jacob Meller,
Conrath Bollon,	Johan Georg Meller,*
Andreas Lohr,	John Michel Lochtner,
Lorentz Weber,	Hans Henrich Jegner,
Tobias Hegelle,	Valentine Renner,
Christoph Riss,	Joh. Martin Schilling,
Friederich Riss,	Johannes Mössinger,
Adam Himler,	Mathias Brownwart,*

Johan Jacob Rower,*
Christof Ehrenhart,
Johan Jacob Kuntz,
Joh. Wilhelm Köllin,
Joh. Conradt Scheimer,
Joh. Martin Bullinger,
Hans Martin Bullinger,
Han Phil. Zimmerman,
Johan Michel Deeter,
Paulus Weinheimer,
Johannes Bastian,
Lorentz Bastian,
Joh. Balthasar Bott,
Joh. Philipp Görich,
Joh. Adam Werner,
Joh. Valtin Umstadt,
Joh. Georg Baltz,
Nicolas Evelandt,*
Joh. Martin Bauer,
Johannes Ebermann,
Johannes Albrecht,
Johan Henrich Jung,
Johan Adam Leberger,
Bartholomeus Morth,?
Johan Christoph Beyer,
Lenhart Mumma,
Lorentz Kuntz,
Ludwig Leeman,
Christoff Englert,
Henry Oswald,*
Leonard Weyer,*
Laurentz Bawder,*
Rudolph Bonner,*

Henrich Appel,
Pieter Derber,*
Peter Gabele,
Peter Seyler,
Philip Smit,*
Conrath Sieber,
Jacob Tray,*
John Shullmeyer,*
Johannes Frey,
Thomas Cryle,*
Friederich Mayer,*
Joh. Georg Sehm,
Johannes Kreuel,
Johannes Schmitt,
Joh. Frid. Baumgärdtner,
Joh. Henrich Miller,
Joh. Peter Schmidt,
Joh. Jacob Neihältzer,
Han Georg Tray,*
Michael Schullmeyer,*
Johannes Hannar,*
Joh. Hen. Messerschmidt,
Martin Caplinger,*
Hans Wilhelm Brant,
Christian Shneyder,*
Conrad Schneider,
Joh. Leonhardt Herman,
Joh. Peter Genther,
Johan Frantz Russ,
Joh. Paulus Lederer,
Joh. Georg Gumpp,
Joh. Adam Kreil,
Joh. Georg Oberkagler.

Under sixteen: (Unter ſechzehn):—Paulus Harwich, Jacob Harwich, Nickolaus Harwich, Jacob Wegerlein, Johan Jacob Müller, Johannes Oberbeck, Philip Oberbeck, Ludwig Schuey, Michael Mössinger, Paul Mössinger, Johann Bauer, Johannes Lauer, Herman Lauer, Henrich Weber, Martin Ebeland, Adam Vogel, Johann Kuntz, Friederich Riss, Jacob Umstadt, Conrad Stock, Jacob Ebeland, Johannes Eberman, Jacob Albrecht, Ludwig Albrecht, Conrad Sattler, Johannes Sattler, Anthoni

Mumma, Michael Seyler, Valentin Seyler, Lorentz Sieber, Johann Conrad Frey.

———

22) Sept. 21, 1732. Palatines imported in the ship Pink Plaisance, John Paret, Master, from Rotterdam, last from Cowes.—*Col. Rec.* III. 459. Seventy-seven males above sixteen, twenty-eight under sixteen; sixty-eight females above sixteen, and fifteen under sixteen—in all one hundred and eightyeight.—(*Editor.*)

Sept. 21, 1732. Auf dem Schiffe Pink Plaisance, Capitain John Paret, von Rotterdam über Cowes kamen Pfälzer.—Col.= Ber. III. 459. Sieben und siebenzig männliche Personen über und acht und zwanzig unter sechzehn; acht und sechzig weibliche über und fünfzehn unter sechzehn Jahren: hundert und acht und achtzig im Ganzen.—(Herausgeber.)

Georg Bast,	Balthasar Schönberger,
Joh. Clinc,*	Tobias Pechtluf,*
Melcher Feler,	Johan Fulker,*
Bastian Rudi,	Carl Wagner,
Christian Huber,	Jacob Kutz,
Samuel Mayer,	Stephen Long,*
Martin Mayer,	Christian Strom,*
Jacob Schere,	Rudolff Christen,
Paulus Hertzel,	Peter Bicker,*
Hans Huber,	Hans Stömply,
Felix Fissler,	Ulrich Stalley,
Rudolph Reichert,	Paulus Keyser,*
Mathes Müller,	Hans Danler,*
Johan Philip Müller,	Jacob Bloom,*
Johannes Müller,	Jacob Swisser,*
Conrath Scharff,	Frantz Städel,*
Daniel Stauffer,	Nicklaus Peni,?
Hans Zimmerman,	Andreas Wolff,
Hans Georg Wagner,	Jacob Stauffer,
Georg Peter Knecht,	Johan Landis,
Christian Besicker,	Hans Gesell,*
Christian Martin,	Elias Wagner,
Johann Jacob Koch,	Philip Ott,
Johannes Huisiner,	Ulrich Resser,*
Johan Frantz Fuchs,	Hans Lechteni,?

7*

Hans Jacob Keyser,
Matthias Kramer,
Nicol Zimmerman,
Ulrich Zimmerman,
Samuel Harnisch,
Andreas Pflückinger,
Christoff Albrecht Lang,
Joh. Wilhelm Straub,
Georg Bernhart Mahr,
Joh. Philip Kistner,
Joh. Adam Zimmerman,

Hans Albrecht Bucher,
Henrich Hertzell,
Hans Melchior Werffel,
Nicolaus Carn,*
Hans Ulrich Wagner,
Henrich Harstlich,*
Hans Leonhart Hertzell,
Andreas Cramer,*
Michael Schärer,
Johan Wolff Berlett.?

A. Sick: (Krank):—Johannes Gross, Nicolas Ish, John Jac. Felker, Ulrich Hottell.

Under sixteen: (Unter sechzehn):—Hans Zimmerman, Christian Zimmerman, Bastian Zimmerman, Jacob Mann, Hans Martin Huber, Jacob Huber, Jacob Born, Jacob Mayer, Christoph Mayer, Hans Dickleder, Hans Peter Stalley, Martin Marte, Johan Emanuel Brallion, Conrad Böchtold, Bastian Rudy, And. Stättel, Reinhart Reichart, Ulrich Wilhelm Kern, Jacob Treiler, Christoph Müller, Hans Georg Müller, Philip Müller, Jacob Baseaur, Joh. Bernhart Straub, Matthias Klein, Henrick Klein.

---

23) Sept. 23, 1732.   Palatines imported in the ship Adventurer, Robert Carson, Master, from Rotterdam, last from Cowes.— *Col. Rec.* III. 455.   Fifty-eight males above sixteen, nineteen under sixteen; forty-three females above sixteen, and twenty-seven under sixteen—in all one hundred and forty-seven.—(*Ed.*)

Sept. 23, 1732.   Mit dem Schiffe Adventurer, Capitain Rob. Carson, von Rotterdam über Cowes kamen Pfälzer.—Col.=Ber. III. 455.   Acht und fünfzig männliche Personen waren über und neunzehn unter sechzehn; drei und vierzig weibliche über und sieben und zwanzig unter sechzehn: hundert sieben und vierzig im Ganzen.—(Herausgeber.)

Michael Brandt,
Michael Gross,
Johannes Artz,*
Georg Mosser,
Balthas Stüber,
Andreas Kilian,
Andreas Horn,*

Mathias Walder,
Han Michael Müller,
Johan Georg Präuner,
Friedrich Tendelspach,*
Hans Georg Able,*
Hans Martin Ranger,
Han Paulus Zantsinger,

David Holtzeder,
Hieronymus Glantz,
David Fischer,
Michael Moser,
Simon Meyer,
Georg Unruh,
Conrath Lang,
Michel Potts,
Johannes Schott,
John Wingleplech,*
Henrich Steger,
Malteis Riegel,
Henrich Lips,
Michael Koogh,*
Simon Gillinger,*
Andreas Wise,*
Georg Riegel,
Conrad Clewer,
Nicolaus Bartle,*
Tobias Moser,
Andreas Schaup,*
Leonhard Moser,

Hans Leonart Gam,
Lorentz Zwirner,
Baltzar Bortner,
Han Leonhard Nydy,*
Johannes Heberling,
Hans Jacob Gander,
Daniel Kolmer,
Mattheas Wagner,
Hans Ulrich Hey,
Bernhart Shertle,*
Johannes Becker,*
Paul Le Cene,
Jean Le Cene,
Vallentin Scheib,
Nicholas Bogerdt,
Johannes Grawius,
Hans Georg Lehner,
Han Melcher Stecher,
Hans Michael Hagg,
Georg Michael Mäck,
Hans Peter Steyger,*
Leonard Aam, *sick.*

Under sixteen: (Unter ſechzehn):—Hans Adam Trump, Hans Michael Glantz, Hans Holtzeder, Bastian Mosser, Simon Mosser, Hans Georg Mosser, Georg Meyer, Hans Meyer, Georg Adam Steger, Hans Michael Potts, Hans Peter Heberling, Bastian Schönle, Hans Peter Winckelbleck, Lorentz Lessing, Johan Jacob Gander, Johann Georg Gander, Jacob Bortner, Simon Benedict, Johannes Artz.

---

24) Sept. 25, 1732. Palatines imported in the ship Loyal Judith, of London, Robert Turpin, Master, from Rotterdam, last from Cowes.—*Col. Rec.* III. 456.

Sept. 25, 1732. Mit dem Schiffe Loyal Judith von London, Capitain Robert Turpin, von Rotterdam über Cowes kamen Pfälzer.—Col.=Ber. III. 456.

Andreas Gaar,?
Jacob Steli,
Matthes Baarsteyn,*
Rudolph Brown,*

Matthes Schmidt,*
Henrich Papst,*
Jacob Spansailer,
Christian Reep,*

Peter Kreiter,
Johannes Kreiter,
Jacob Miller,*
Henrich Göbell,
John Auterbach,*
Peter Rauch,
Michael Pentz,*
Jacob Küntzel,
Joh. Christian Shultz,
    Minister, (aged 30),
Johann Adam Gaar,
Johan Michael Ebert,
Johann Adam Abel,
Johann Jacob Abel,
Johan Georg Schmidt,
Hans Philip Spansailer,
Hans Peter Schäfer,
Hans Burghart,
Hans Georg Noll,
Friederich Kühller,
Hans Georg Wagner,
Hans Georg Pelman,*
John Michael Royer,
Johann Carl Reyer,
Fridrich Ehley,
Jacob Lishire,
Ludwig Happel,
Conrad Fey,
Philip Raup,
Leonhart Hegell,
Bernard Walter,
Henrich Acker,
Wilhelm Berne,*
Hans Kuntz,
Paulus Müller,
Cronomus Miller,*
Hans Weldtli,
Peter Saudter,
Samuel Griffe,*
Martin Heilman,
Andreas Schenk,*

Michael Emmert,
Phil. Ernst Krüber,
Geo. Mich. Rey,*
Hans Georg Able,
Johannes Vogel,
Johannes Bentz,
Jonas Wolf,*
Lenhart Lotz,
Marcus Jung,
Henrich Leibacher,
Johan Becker,
Baltzer Conkell,
John Geo. Furkill,*
Johannes Bintnagel,*
Hans Georg Raub,
Johan Shuman,?
Georg Müller,
Christian Gum,
Friedrich Schäffer,
Johannes Reep,*
Casper Krämer,
Conrad Walther,
Jacob Pretz,
Joh. Geo. F. Emmert,
Joh. Martin Reier,
Hans David Ely,
Matthäus Schultz,
Philip Ludwig Güfi,?
Hans Georg Riser,
Georg Adam Riser,
Philip Jacob Acker,
Johann Georg Rück,
Hans Michl Criger,*
Hans Georg Kuntz,
Hans David Lentz,*
Joh. Philip Sauter,
Joh. Georg Hoffmann,
Johannes Heilman,
Martin Weybrecht,
Joh. Geo. Obermüller,
Georg Christoph Lay,

Johan Geo. Friederich,
Johan Georg Honnig,
Johann Veit Jorger,
Geo. Michael Schmidt,
Jacob Bühlmayer,
Joh. Michael Hoffacker,
Georg Peter Schultes,
Johann Peter Kucher,
Joh. George Nadderman,
Hans Jacob Stambach,
Joh. Friedrich Hesser,
Joh. Fried. Burghart,

Andreas Cochenderff,
Hans Antoni Gasser,
Hans Henrich Eckler,
Johan Nicklas Rämer,
Johannes Züsser,?
Hans Martin Bau,
Hans Georg Tran,
Johannes Schmeltzer,
Johannes Rebmann,
Han Martin Weybrecht,
Hans Georg Birstler.

A. *Sick*—George Ritter. *Dead* (tobt)—Jacob Lishire.

25) Sept. 26, 1732. Palatines imported in the ship Mary, of London, John Gray, Master, from Rotterdam, last from Cowes.—Sixty-nine males above sixteen, one hundred and twenty-two women and children—in all 183.

Sept. 26, 1732. Das Schiff Mary von London, Capitain John Gray, von Rotterdam über Cowes, brachte Pfälzer.—Neun und sechzig männliche Personen über sechzehn, und ein hundert und zwei und zwanzig Weiber und Kinder—im Ganzen 183.

Nicolas Staller,*
Jacob Reitlershan,
Conrath Miller,
Dewald Kase,*
Christian Kling,
Jacob Stempel,
Nicolas Stemple,*
Jacob Haub,*
Christoph Kiser,*
Reinholt Ezle,*
Cornelius Teele,*
Daniel Billiger,
Albrecht Strauss,
Andreas Moser,*
Casper Miere,*
Jacob Würth,
Georg Schüssler,
Henrich Chesler,*

Jacob Walter,
Jacob Walder,
Herman Sin,
Simon Müller,
Winnale Cattler,
Albrecht Hass,
Carl Lisa,*
Georg Kling,
Johannes Werth,
Michael Dörr,
Pierre Fleury,
Martin Ernst,
Nicolaus Kint,*
Han Georg Froschauer,
Michael Eberman,
Hans Jacob Eberman,
Johann Laudermilch,*
Hans Adam Miller,

Georg Phillip Pier,
Joh. Jacob Dreibelbiss,
Conrad Aberman,*
Hans Georg Ebenno,*
Hans Michel Walck,
Hans Jacob Würth,
Stephen Kennamer,*
Johannes Mäyer,
Henry Cheesler,*
Hans Jacob Cheesler,*
Joh. F. Rauschenberger,
Jacob Marcus Imler,
Christian Minier,*

Hans Georg Minier,*
Hans Henrich Teny,*
Hans Adam Robetes,
Jean Louis d'Avier,
Johann Georg Kohl,
Hans Georg Embright,*
Hans Peter Verley,*
Georg Felte Pickel,*
Hans Michel Mentz,
Johannes Schaffner,?
Johannes Huber,
Christopher Bickel.

A. *Dead*—Hans Georg Dörr, aged 16, Leonard Sable, 40, Hans Georg Smith, 44, and Baltas Click, 33.

---

26) Sept. 30, 1732. Palatines imported in the ship Dragon, Chas. Hargrave, Master, from Rotterdam, last from Plymouth.— In all 185.

Sept 30, 1732. Mit dem Schiff Dragon, Capitain Charles Hargrave, von Rotterdam über Plymouth, kamen Pfälzer.—Im Ganzen 185.

Peter Matern,*
Michel Dirr,*
Christ. Hoffmann,*
Jacob Leipersburger,*
Hans Laabour,*
George Road,*
Leonhard Slosser,
Leonhard Miller,*
Peter Raudenbusch,
Henrich Gruber,
Johannes Witman,
Jacob Klein,
Peter Schlosser,
Christian Huber,
Hans Georg Hegi,
Simon Belsner,
Andreas Schlauch,
Henrich Basler,

Lenhart Bentz,
Michael Graff,
Tobias Ball,
Georg Fantz,
Georg Hayle,*
Georg Seib,
Ludwig Sype,*
Frantz Seib,
Henrich Klein,
Joh. Friedrich Romich,
Hans Georg Dirr,*
Martin Weidknecht,
Hans Adam Bender,
Johan Adam Romich,
Joh. Wilhelm Franck,
Hans Jacob Schörck,
Hans Peter Wolff,
Johan Heerbürger,

Johannes Geiger,
Johan Georg Greiner,
Joh. Dietrich Greiner,
Han Wilhelm Ziegler,
Johannes Schreyiackh,
Joh. Nicklaus Müller,
Johan Phil. Hopmann,
Johan Philip Schlauch,
Hans Michel Reisner,

Hans Rudolph Illig,
Hans Martin Kappler,
Georg Ludwig Schütz,
Christophel Beser,
Johann Jacob Beyerle,
Hans Ulrich Ber,
Hans Georg Heill,
Felix Brunner,
Hans Georg Soldnier.

A. *Sick*—Andreas Beetel, Wilhelm Keyser, Daniel Steinmetz, Johan Hagea, Jacob Hagea, Georg Tsober, George Bär, Henry Zowck, Laurence Bechtle, Nichlas Musloch, Dietrich Bucher, Jacob Dubbs, Wolfgang Birle, Friederich Engelhart Uhlmann.—Simon Baserer, *dumb* (ſtumm).

27) Oct. 11, 1732. Palatines imported in the ship Pleasant, J. Morris, Master, from Rotterdam, last from Deal.—In all 150.

Oct. 11, 1732. Das Schiff Pleasant, Capitain James Morris, von Rotterdam über Deal, brachte Pfälzer.—Im Ganzen 150.

Henrich Spengler,
George Bär,*
Friedrich Bassler,*
Ulrich Badner,
Johann Georg Senck,
Baltzer Spengler,
Jacob Friederich Klem,
Johan Jacob Timanus,
Ulrich Peters,
Georg Hans Ped,?
Georg Spengler,
Georg Keller,
Henrich Roth,
Jacob Padum,?
Henrich Eckert,
Conrath Kolb,
Felix Miller,?
Johannes Gamber,
Friederich Notz,
Johannes Moak,*
Ulrich Basler,*

Georg Mess,*
Valentin Müller,
Conrad Rowp,*
Georg Michel Favian,*
Isaac Raudenbusch,
Matthias Jurian,*
Hans Georg Falck,
Phillip Schilling,*
Conrad Glasbrenner,
Jacob Hornberger,*
Hans Peter Siegmund,*
Hans Bern Kuntzer,*
Hans Philip Kresler,
Matheis Ambrossi,
Hans Adam Schilling,*
Joh. Casper Wenterott,
Geo. Philip Schnatterly,
Han Michel Schatterly,
Hans Michel Hoffman,
Johannes Taffelmeyer.?

A. *Sick*—Leonard Lutes, George Pisell, Conrad Ralsure, Peter Ralsure, Conrad Hellebrun, David Menner, Mich. Favon, Andrew Schweitzer, Jacob Froch, George Karne, Johannes Kleffer, Christoph Sprecher, David Menein, J. Georg Passage.

---

28) Oct. 17, 1732. Palatines imported in the ship Pink John and William, of Sunderland, Constable Tymperton, Master, from Rotterdam, last from Dover.—Sixty-one men above sixteen, one hundred and nine women and children of both sexes of different ages—in all 170.—(*Editor.*)

Oct. 17, 1732. Auf dem Schiffe Pink John und William, von Sunderland, Capitain Constabler Tymperton, von Rotterdam über Dover, kamen Pfälzer.—Ein und sechzig Männer über sechzehn, nebst ein hundert und neun Weibern und Kindern verschiedenen Alters—im Ganzen 170.—(Herausgeber.)

Moretz Lorentz,	Hans Peter Brechbill,*
C. Vielgar,?	Benedict Brechbill,*
Georg Albright,*	Hans Brechbill,*
Laurens Kieffer,*	Michael Blömhauer,
Jacob Brakebill,*	Casper Willauer,
Stephen Mattes,*	Conrad Low,*
Bartel Maul,	Ludwig Hugel,*
Hans Emich,*	Jacob Weber,*
Johannes Jägi,	Johannes Schook,*
Johannes Nagel,*	Abraham Dubo,*
Peter Smidt,*	Adam Wilt,*
Baltzer Gurlach,	Antoni Albrecht,
Christian Lau,	Conrad Getts,
Stephan Matz,	Nicklaus Koger,?
Nicholas Paschon,	Matheus Mauser,
Hans Georg Martin,	Gideon Hoffer,*
Bernhard Weymer,*	Hans Riehl,
Hans Ehr. Vosselmann,	Henrich Geck,
Felten Schydecker,*	Johannes Vögle,
Johannes Deymen,*	Jacob Henrich,
Pieter Hayvigh,*	George Veibert,*
Michael Weissel,	Han Georg Sprecher,
Fridrich Wyssel,*	Joh. Michael Hoffman,*
Ludwig Johan Herr,	Joh. Nicklaus Boschung,
Joh. Philip Reinhardt,	Hans Jacob Reyel,

Georg Adam Stis,*
Hans Georg Rohbach,*
Joh. Nicklaus Schmid,
Hans Philip Gleis,*
Sebastian Truckmüller,*
Johan Martin Schöffer,
Johan Paul Derst,
Mathias Rubichon,
Philip Melchior Meyer,
Joh. Georg Wahnsidel,
Johan Peter Apfel,
Johan Jacob Scherr.

A. Sick—Frederick Kuhler, Philip Melchner, Bartel Noll, Jac. Brechbill, Johan Vinterhelver, Philip Jac. Probst, Mich. Müller, Philip Dubo, Hans Woolf Doopel, Joseph Hously, Michael Probst.

Under sixteen:—Nicholas Emich, Joh. Emich, Jacob Emich, Johann David Helfer, Christopher Helfer, Andreas Boschung, Henrich Boschung, Johannes Weymer, Christ. Lau, Christian Bieber, Jacob Bieber, Joh. Schrögen, Jacob Lorentz, Jacob Reyel, Jacob Frey, Caspar Müller, Hans Müller, Mich. Müller, Peter Albrecht, Joh. Albrecht, Bernhardt Hublich, Michael Hublich, Michael Rihl, Michael Martin, Carl De Meyerer, Johann Rubichon.

---

29) Aug. 17, 1733. Palatines imported in the ship Samuel, of London, Hugh Percy, Master, from Rotterdam, last from Deal.—Males eighty-nine above sixteen, females eighty-six; males under sixteen, fifty-four, females sixty-two—in all 291.—(Ed.)

Aug. 17, 1733. Auf dem Schiffe Samuel von London, Capitain Hugh Percy, von Rotterdam über Deal, kamen Pfälzer.— Neun und achtzig männliche und sechs und achtzig weibliche Personen über sechzehn, und vier und fünfzig männliche unter, und zwei und sechzig weibliche unter sechzehn—im Ganzen 291.— (Herausgeber.)

Hans Peter Frey,*
Elias Theiler,*
Abraham Kuhn,*
Friedrich Kuhn,
Jacob Rausher,*
Christian Kröbs,
Henrich Bischof,*
Peter Kuntz,*
Andreas Frey,
Friederich Leiby,
Michael Schmidt,
Mattheis Ley,
Hans Peter Beissel,
Michael Sturtzebach,*
Han Georg Strohauer,
Johan Lechtenwallner,
Johan Jacob Zimmer,
Hans Georg Ruch,*
Johan Georg Ruch,
Hans Jacob Ruch,*
Johannes Jacob Ritt,
Hans Leonhart Leher,

8

Hans Georg Peck,*
Friederich Alldörffer,
Hans Georg Wervel,
Hans Leonard Wolff,
Hans Casper Jost,*
Hans Wolf Eiseman,*
Hans Fries,
Hans Werfel,*
Martin Scheib,
Solomon Miller,*
Hans Jacob Hoff,*
Kilian Schmid,
Christian Löffel,
Milchor Wagner,
Michael Probst,
Andreas Wigner,
Johann Kauffmann,
Caspar Millhouse,*
Andreas Weltz,
Jacob Fegely,
Jacob Wenger,
Johan Lorig,*
Johannes Schnep,*
Lorentz Schnepp,
Martin Wanner,
Henrich Beter,
Henrich Roth,
Peter Cornelius,
Nicolaus Kan,*
Marx Gleim,
Elias Hasele,*
Heinrich Haller,
Jacob Krater,

Peter Drachsel,
Henry Meder,
Lorentz Seyboot,
Hans Jacob Mathis,
Johan Lenhart Weiss,
Joh. Jacob Griesinger,
Johan Philip Hötzer,
Hans Kaspar Eysseman,
Justus Simon Wagner,
Han Jacob Kämmerlin,
Hans Adam Lang,
Han Michael Probst,
Han Georg Zoller,
Joh. Caspar Körber,
Joh. Henrich Fischer,
Joh. Henrich Adam,
Joh. Wilhelm Fischer,
Hans Casper Brenner,
Joh. Conrad Kämpff,
Peter Ensminger,
Christian Kämpff,
Gilbert Kämpff,
Jacob Gerckenhauser,
Han Lehnard Eimiger,?
Joh. Peter Knöbell,
Joh. Caspar Schaffner,
Ulrich Flickiner,*
Han Adam Stuckroth,?
Valentin Sneider,*
Hans Peter Mack,*
Christian Danner,
Henrich Fessler,*
Han Bernhardt Trostell.

Sick—Han Jac. Gamooroon.

Under sixteen:—Valentin Frey, Hans Peter Frey, Christian
Frey, Hans Peter Strohauer, Philip Adam Thäler, Hans Martin
Thäler, Hans Georg Kuhn, Michael Ruch Kuntz, Hans Georg
Kuntz, Georg Ritt, Hans Jac. Ritt, Hans Georg Leitner, Hans
Mich. Kämmerlin, Christopher Frey, Jacob Leiby, Hans Peter
Beissel, Hans Jacob Beissel, Lenhart Wirbel, Martin Scheib,
Hans Georg Scheib, Christian Lang, Jacob Fischer, Jac. Fegely,

Hans Georg Lörch, Joh. Schnepp, Lorentz Schnepp, Christian
Wanner, Henrich Peter, Henrich Ensminger, Hans Philip Ensminger, Friederich Kämpff, Wilhelm Ritt, Lorentz Cornelius,
Michael Kahn, Hans Adam Dieminger, Marx Gleim, Henrich
Haller, Philip Drachsel, Georg Drachsel, Jacob Drachsel, Gottfried Drachsel, Peter Drachsel, Daniel Drachsel, Benedict Seyboot, Georg Rossel, Georg Meder.

---

30) Aug. 27, 1733. Palatines imported,—ship Eliza, of London, Edward Lee, Master, from Rotterdam, last from Dover.—
Males fifty-eight above sixteen, females fifty; males forty-one
under sixteen, females forty-one—in all 190.—(*Editor.*)

Aug. 27, 1733. Das Schiff Eliza von London, Capitain
Edward Lee, von Rotterdam über Dover, brachte Pfälzer.—
Männliche Personen acht und fünfzig, und weibliche fünfzig über
sechzehn; ein und vierzig männliche und ein und vierzig weibliche
unter sechzehn—im Ganzen 190.—(Herausgeber.)

Johannes Kirschner,
Johannes Mohn,
Conrad Schott,*
Johan Philip Saner,
Joh. Michael Grauel,
Johan Georg Petry,
Michael Ruth,
Carl Hetrich,*
Henrich Slentz,
Johannes Jung,*
Ulrich Schuh,*
Jaro Schuh,
Johannes Loatz,
Henrich Still,
Simeon Linder,
Simon Linder jr.,
Michael Faber,
Aron Doganer,*
Stephan Lauman,
Jaques Bonet,
Jacob Müller,
Johannes Knoll,*
Jacob Kobbler,*

Frantz Weiss,
Georg Ohr,*
Johannes Ohr,
Jacob Serber,*
Jacob Serber jr.,
Jacob Hänrich,
Jacob Zettle,
Jacob Dellinger,
Henry Stricker,*
Balser Metz,*
Joh. Henrich Schötte,
Johann Philip Faust,
Johan Philip Faust,
Joh. Henrich Dänig,
Han Peter Hoffman,
Johan Peter Paust,
Johan Philip Paust,
Jacob Michael Eyb,
Matthias Weidman,
Geo. Friederich Anselt,
Hans Georg Perger,
Wolfgang Müller,
Simon Schermann,

Georg Scherman,
Johan Debalt Traudt,
Hans Martin Traudt,
Johannes Herrgeröder,
Joh. Henrich Dewess,
Joh. Philip Schmidt,
Hans Jacob Metz,*

Hans Georg Nordt,
Andreas Klebsattel,
Georg Henrich Mertz,
Johann Ulrich Gaul,?
Johannes Vögelin,?
Michael Reinhard.*

Sick—Johann Joseph Faller, *schoolmaster*, Matthew Weidman, Hans Georg Ley, Nicholas Sly.

Under sixteen:—Conrad Kirschner, Joh. Georg Kirschner, Martin Mohn, Ludwig Mohn, Conrad Kobel, Johannes Schötts, Johan Jacob Paust, Johan Adam Paust, Joh. Henrich Paust, Michael Ruth, Johannes Hetterich, Johann Heinr. Hetterich, Wilhelm Hetterich, Hans Jacob Slentz, Michael Jost, Johannes Jost, Johann Peter Jost, Andreas Eyb, Hans Michael Lutz, Johannes Weidman, Christoph Weidman, Matthias Weidman, Simon Linder, Lorentz Linder, Michael Faber, Johann Tobias Bogner, Stephan Lauman, Jean Simeon Bonet, Jacob Müller, Philip Scherman, Johannes Traudt, Johann Henrich Traudt, Casper Horsveldt, Philip Schmidt, Tobias Nordt, Joh. Friederich Dellinger, Mattheis Gaul.

---

31) Aug. 28, 1733. Palatines,—ship Hope, of London, Dan. Reid, Master, from Rotterdam, last from Cowes.—Males eighty-three above sixteen, females eighty-one; males and females two hundred and twenty-five under sixteen—in all 389.—(*Editor.*)

Aug. 28, 1733. Pfälzer mit dem Schiffe Hope von London, Capitain Daniel Reid, von Rotterdam über Cowes.—Drei und achtzig männlichen Geschlechts und ein und achtzig weiblichen über sechzehn; unter sechzehn beiderlei Geschlechts zwei hundert fünf und zwanzig—im Ganzen 389.—(Herausgeber.)

Ulrich Wissler,
Hans Steinman,*
Peter Steinman,
Hans Steinman,
Hans Rat,
Ulrich Reinhardt,
Hans Grumbacher,
Christian Stouder,*
Nicholas Timberman,*

Hans Timberman,*
Joseph Flure,
Johannes Flure,
Christian Kerr,*
Michael Whitmer,*
Ulrich Whitmer,*
Peter Whitmer,*
Jacob Bürki,
Hans Snabley,

Friderick Becker,
Rudolph Brock,
Christian Reblet,*
Barnard Keller,*
Conrad Rauf,*
Georg Richter,*
Peter Aarond,*
Daniel Roth,*
Frantz Klebsattel,
Andreas Lauch,
Herman Arand,*
Peter Schmück,
Henrich Umberger,
Peter Sayler,
Christian Johnle,*
Georg Kreisseman,
Andreas Besinger,
Abraham Miller,*
Jacob Bart,
Henrich Tace,*
Benedict Wise,*
Michael Ably,*
Jacob Rubman,
Henrich Fegly,
Barnard Fegely,
Steven Slonacker,*
Rudolph Schnebele,
Peter Eschelman,
Christian Eschelman,
Ulrich Loninacre jr.,*
Hans Georg Weittner,

Hans Georg Brimmer,
Christian Blank,
Jacob Lachbaum,
Heinrich Schmidt,
Hans Georg Schreyack,
Joh. Henrich Vonreth,
Johan Adam Reistel,
Han Geo. Eichelberger,
Joh. Leonahart Stein,
Hans Georg Kohler,
Hans Georg Höffner,
Johan David Deschler,
Johan Jacob Mückli,
Johan Carl Gramp,
Bastian Tryster,*
Han Leonhart Umberger,
Georg Michael Treitter,
Hans Georg Gobel,
Hans Jacob Gerber,
Joh. Christopf Cumm,
Joh. Ad. Simon Cumm,
Martin Spitelmayer,?
Han Adam Spittlemire,*
Wilhelm Krauss,
Han Michael Steinbren,
Abraham Kreutter,
Hans Jacob Schreiber,
Daniel Hüselman,
Jacob Schreyack,
Han Michael Schreyack.

A. *Sick*—Michael Umberger and Jacobus Linck.

Under sixteen:—Hans Peter Ebly, Hans Adam Ebly, Hans Michael Ebly, Hans Rollman, Hans Adam Linck, Jac. Eschleman, Caspar Schnebele, Michael Becker, Friederich Brock, Hans Reiff, Henrich Schmidt, Ludwig Busse, Geo. Huselman, Georg Adam Gobel, Jacob Gensman, Michael Klebsattel, Hans Georg Klebsattel.

---

32) Sept. 18, 1733. Palatines,—brigantine Pennsylvania Merchant, of London, John Stedman, Master, from Rotterdam,

last from Plymouth.—Seventy-one males above sixteen, fifty-six females; and sixty-four males and females under sixteen—in all 191.—(*Editor.*)

Sept. 18, 1733. Das Rennschiff Pennsylvania Merchant von London, Capitain John Stedman, von Rotterdam über Plymouth, hatte Pfälzer an Bord.—Ein und siebenzig männliche und sechs und fünfzig weibliche Personen über und vier und sech=zig männlichen und weiblichen Geschlechts unter sechzehn—im Ganzen 191.—(Herausgeber.)

Johann Klemm,
Gotlob Klemm,
Georg Scholtz,
David Scholtz,
Johannes Naas,
Pierre Marot,
Andreas Kleim,*
Georg Kleim,
Georg Schait,?
Johannes Riegel,
Johannes Riegel jr.,
Michael Walter,
Georg Knop,
Jacob Ott,
Ludwig Ewalt,
Michael Ludwig,*
Daniel Ludwig,*
Philip Schmyer,
Peter Ruth,*
Hans Lauer,
Mattheis Gisch,
Adam Vollmer,
Ludowick Evaldt,*
Frederick Gotz,*
Johannes Mihm,
Peter Schmidt,*
Paulus Schäffer,
Andreas Frey,*
Bernhart Mauss,
Andreas Bauer,
Peter Straub,

Friederich Glass,
Johannes Gordner,
Mattheus Büchler,
Andreas Mosemann,
Christian Mosemann,
Hans Burchard,
David Burchard,
Johann Schönfeldt,
Johan Aullenbacher,
Joh. Valentin Pressel,
Carolus Burckhard,
Joh. Philip Weynandt,
Johan Michael Ott,
Alexander Gasser,*
Joh. Michael Staudt,
Joh. Jost Ohlwein,
Philip Angelberger,
Michael Seydenbender,
Johan Daniel Endt,
Johan Valentin Endt,
Johan Peter Saling,
Hans Georg Winter,
Hans Martin Santer,*
Johann Adam Beyer,
Joh. Christoph Igelsbach,
Michael Kelchner,
Georg Barthol. Schäffer,
John Ludwig Sees,
Hans Georg Hauk,
Johann Jacob Karst,
Christian Hook,*

Hans Georg Grondt,	Johann Georg Grimm,
Georg Adam Koch,*	Henrich Schmidt.
Justus Osterrath,	

A. *Sick*—Melchior Gronsaum, Henrich Reet, Jacob Unger.

Under sixteen:—Henrich Souchonet, Guilliam Marot, Philip Marot, Benjamin Marot, Daniel Marot, Hans Georg Ritt, Caspar Klemm, Abraham Riegel, Johannes Ewalt, Johann Schmyer, Johannes Gasser, Matheis Gasser, Joh. Ruth, Jacob Ruth, Peter Ruth, Georg Winter, Hans Winter, Andreas Stehlin, Johannes Stehlin, Matheis Stehlin, Jacob Schultz, Joh. Götz, Johannes Reuter, Peter Ingold, Jacob Frick, Paulus Schäffer, Georg Schäffer, Georg Stoubig, Christian Striebig, Joh. Schäffer, Christopher Frey, Christian Fischer, Jacob Straub, Peter Straub, Georg Hauck, Paulus Gardner, Andreas Büchler.

---

33) Sept. 28, 1733. Palatines,—brigantine Richmond and Elizabeth, Christopher Clymer, Master, from Rotterdam, last from Plymouth. — Forty-four males above sixteen, thirty-four females; twenty-four males under sixteen and thirty-five females—in all 137.—(*Editor.*)

Sept. 28, 1733. Auf dem Rennschiffe Richmond und Elisa= beth, Capitain Christopher Clymer, von Rotterdam über Plymouth, kamen Pfälzer.—Vier und vierzig Männer und vier und dreißig Frauen über, und vier und zwanzig männlichen und fünf und dreißig weiblichen Geschlechts unter sechzehn—im Ganzen 137.— (Herausgeber.)

Frantz Schuller,	Ulrich Burghalter,*
Jacob Greib,	Mattheis Beck,
David Mertz,	Hans Schürer,
Georg Lipp,*	Jacob Christ,*
Mattheus Bausser,	Marcus Christ,*
Matheis Bausser jr.,	Marx Bigler,
Christian Bausser,	Johannes Weber,
Philip Mire,*	Mattheis Resch,
David Edelman,*	Hans Michael Mertz,
Adam Spohn,	Hans Conrad Lipp,*
Jacob Hennel,	Philip Jacob Edelman,
Michael Wise,*	Johan Georg Schuster,
Jacob Lebegood,*	Johan Jost Heck,
Jacob Herman,*	Jacob Huntzecker,

Hans Jacob Utz,
Hans Georg Utz,
Hans Peter Somey,*
Hans Jacob Somey,*
Hans Peter Somey jr.,
Otto Fredrick Somey,*
Joseph Schumacher,
Johann Nicolas Seeger,

Georg Schönmansgruber,
Johannes Wollett,
Henry Winterberger,
Georg Angstet,
Philip Dedigman,
Johannes Rosenstiel,*
Abraham Wotring.?

A. *Sick*—Ludwig Rigerd.

Under sixteen:—Johan Peter Mertz, Balthaser Edelman, Daniel Bausser, Johan Henrich Spohn, Johannes Schuffart, Johann Dan. Heck, Johan Jacob Lebenguth, Dewald Herman, Jacob Herman, Hans Herman, Hans Peter Herman, Hans Michael Somey, Johannes Somey, Hans Peter Burchhalter, Hans Henrich Seeger, Johann Christian Seeger, Anthony Beck, Joh. Henrich Beck, Georg Angstet, Johannes Angstet, Philip Fahrismann, Hans Peter Wotring.

---

34) Sept. 29, 1733. Palatines,—ship Pink Mary, of Dublin, James Benn, Master, from Rotterdam, last from Rotterdam.— Fifty-five males above sixteen, thirty-seven females; thirty males under sixteen, forty-nine females—in all 171.—(*Editor.*)

Sept. 29, 1733. Pfälzer,—Schiff Pink Mary von Dublin, Capitain James Benn, von Rotterdam.—Fünf und fünfzig männlichen und sieben und dreißig weiblichen Geschlechts über sechzehn, und dreißig Knaben und neun und vierzig Mädchen unter sechzehn—im Ganzen 171.—(Herausgeber.)

David Karcher,
Gottfried Reich,
Hannes Yorde,
Andreas Dries,*
Cornelius Dries,*
Peter Dries,*
Jacob Spengler,*
Peter Hite,*
Elias Stickler,
Hans Georg Harlacher,
Johann Adam Dries,
Johann Michael Noll,
Philip Thomas Trump,

Johannes Wingertmann,
Johannes Teutscher,
Johann Peter Theusler,
Johann Georg Riebell,
Johann Arnold Billig,
Johannes Stickler.
Henrich Sauer,
Christian Blaser,
Jacob Franck,
Friederich Funck,
Michael Friedly,
Nicolaus Soder,
Andreas Ney,

Christian Sooter,*
Georg Pfaffenberger,
Georg Pfaffenberger jr.,*
Georg Düry,
Jacob Hoffman,*
Asemus Rambach,
Jacob Berkel,*
Nicolaus Moretz,
Peter Apple,
Johannes Lap,*
Johannes Reichenbach,
Johan Martin Braun,
Philip Jacob Rothrock,
Johannes Rothrock,

Hans Michael Hammer,
Johan Michael Dill,
Christian Retelsberger,*
Friederich Dörfflinger,
Hans Michael Keller,
Hans Jacob Berkel,
Baltzer Breuninger,
Johan Adam Wärner,
Geo. Friederich Köhler,
Johan Peter Göttel,
Johan Jacob Göttel,
Johannes Slabach,*
Jacob Löscher,
Joh. Henry Slabach.*

A. *Sick*—Johannes Holtz.

Under sixteen:—David Karcher, Hans Georg Yorde, Johannes Yorde, Balthasar Reich, Christopher Spengler, Johan Stickler, Adam Stickler, Henrich Stickler, Johann Philip Wingertmann, Joh. Adam Blaser, Hans Martz Blaser, Nicolaus Blaser, Christopher Teutscher, Jac. Teutscher. ☞ *One boy of Funck, not baptized, seven weeks old.* Hans Henrich Sauer, Johan Jacob Braun, Hans Michael Ney, Adam Pfaffenberger, David Hoffman, David Rambach, Hans Jacob Rambach, Hans Mich. Köhler, Hans Jacob Berkle, Hans Jacob Breninger, Peter Göttel, Rudolph Lapp, Dewald Schlabach, Hans Geo. Löscher.

---

35) Oct. 12, 1733. Palatines,—ship Charming Betsy, John Ball, Master, from London.—Sixteen males above sixteen, twelve females; fifteen males under sixteen, twenty females—in all 63.—(*Editor.*)

Oct. 12, 1733. Pfälzer,—Schiff Charming Betsy, Capitain John Ball, von London.—Sechzehn Männer und zwölf Frauen über sechzehn; fünfzehn Knaben und zwanzig Mädchen unter sechzehn—im Ganzen 63.—(Herausgeber.)

Johann Kettner,
Henrich Möcklei,
Samuel Ludi,
Ulrich Leibegood,*
Adam Spag,*

Peter Stocker,*
Johannes Lang,
John Lang jr.,
Geo. Michael Kettner,
Hans Peter Gruber,*

Christian Anderich,   Hans Paul Vogt,
Johan Leibegood,*   Nicholas Hetzel.*
Nicholas Burger,*
A. *Sick*—Wilhelm Imler.

Under sixteen:—Johann Henrich Kettner, Henrich Adam
Kettner, Martin Gruber, Adam Lebenguth, Jacob Lebenguth,
Adam Spag, Philip Bürger, Georg Breidengross, Ludwig Imm-
ler, Johannes Immler, Andreas Vogt, Caspar Vogt, Johann
Georg Lang, Christopher Hetzel, Hans Jacob Hetzel.

---

36) Sept. 12, 1734.* Palatines,—ship Saint Andrew, John
Stedman, Master, from Rotterdam, last from Plymouth.—Eighty-

---

* There is a slight discrepancy between the statement, in a German
book, printed 1771, giving account of the voyage and arrival of those
imported in the ship Saint Andrew, and the original papers. From
the book alluded to it appears the ship Saint Andrew, John Stedman,
Master, was freighted with *Schwenckfelders*, followers of Casp. Schwenckfeld, born in Lower Silesia, 1490. These left their homes in April
1734, embarked at Altoona, Denmark, May 14, arrived at Philadelphia
September 22, and on the 23d they declared their fealty: "On September 23d all male persons above the age of sixteen had to appear
in the Court House, in order to swear allegiance to the rules of the
country, to wit: The King of Great Britain and His successors to the
Crown of England.—*Description of the Journey, &c.*, pp. 450–461. These
settled in Berks, Lehigh and Montgomery.—*Rupp's His. Rel. Denom.
U. S.*, pp. 663–667.—*Rupp's His. Berks Co.*, pp. 222, 427.—For a full
account see Chapter *Schwenckfelders*, in *Rupp's History of the Germans
in Pennsylvania*.

Here it may be noted, that these were not the first Schwenckfelders
in Pennsylvania. September 18, 1733, a number of them arrived at
Philadelphia, in the brigantine Pennsylvania Merchant; among these
were Johann Klemm, Gottlob Klemm, Georg Scholtz, David Scholtz.
It would appear they remained for some time in Philadelphia. Mr.
von Beck in his *Reise-Diarium* von Ebenezer in Georgia nach den Nord-
ländern, under date, Philadelphia, June 6, 1734, says: "Here are of
all denominations and sects: Lutherans, Reformed, Episcopals, Pres-
byterians, Catholics, Quakers, Tunkers, Mennonites, Sabbatherians,
Seventh-day Baptists, Seperatists, Böhmists, Schwenckfeldians, Tuch-
feldtians, Eucthelists, Jews and Pagans, &c."—*Ulsperger News*, I, p.156.

* Betreffs der Fahrt und Ankunft der mit dem Schiffe Saint Andrew
gebrachten Personen findet sich in einem 1771 gedruckten deutschen Buche
von den Urkunden. Von dem angeführten Buche scheint es, das Schiff
Saint Andrew, Capitain John Stedman, sei mit Schwenckfeldern, Nachfolger des 1490 in Niederschlesien geborenen Caspar Schwenckfeld, beladen

nine males above sixteen, forty-one males under sixteen; women and female children one hundred and thirty-three—in all 263.— (*Editor.*)

Sept. 12, 1734.* Das Schiff Saint Andrew, Capitain John Stedman, von Rotterdam über Plymouth, brachte Pfälzer, und zwar neun und achtzig männliche über und ein und vierzig männliche Personen unter sechzehn, nebst hundert und drei und dreißig Weibern und Kindern weiblichen Geschlechts—im Ganzen 263.— (Herausgeber.)

Christopher Wiegner,	Caspar Jäckel,
Georg Hübner,	Melchior Hübner,
Georg Kribel,	Christoph Schubert,
Baltzer Jäckel,	Melchior Kribel sen.,
Georg Jäckel,	Balthaser Hoffman,*
Caspar Kribel,	Melchior Kribel jr.,
Georg Ander,	Georg Hoffman sen.,*
Abraham Jäckel,	Baltzer Hoffman jr.,*
Georg Reinwald jr.,	Jeremias Jäckel,
Hans Wiegner,	Christoph Jakele,*
Georg Wiegner,	Gregorius Meisther,*
Baltzer Jäckel jr.,	Christoph Reinwald,

gewesen. Dieselben verließen ihre Heimath im April 1734, gingen zu Altona in Dänemark am 14. Mai auf das Schiff, kamen am 22. Sept. in Philadelphia an und am 23. gelobten sie Treue: „Den 23. September mußten alle Manns-Personen, so über 16 Jahr, auf's Rathhaus, um dem Herrn des Landes, nämlich dem König von Groß-Brittanien und Successores der Krone England's, den Eid der Treue ablegen."—Reise-Beschreibung 2c., S. 450-461. Diese ließen sich in Berks, Lehigh und Montgomery nieder.—Rupp's Gesch. rel. Ben. der Ver. St., S. 663-667.—Rupp's Gesch. von Berks Co., S. 224, 427. Eine eingehende Abhandlung findet sich in Rupp's Gesch. der Deutschen Pennsylvanien's, im Kapitel „Schwenckfelder."

Es wäre auch bemerkenswerth, daß diese nicht die ersten Schwenckfelder in Pennsylvanien sind. Am 18. Sept. 1733 kamen einige mit dem Schnellfahrer Pennsylvania Merchant in Philadelphia an, darunter waren Johann und Gottlob Klemm und Georg und David Scholtz. Es scheint, als blieben sie eine Zeit lang in Philadelphia. Herr von Beck schreibt unter dem 6. Juni 1734 über Philadelphia in seinem Reise-Diarium von Ebenezer in Georgia: „Hier sind von allen Religionen und Secten: Lutheraner, Reformirte, Bischöfliche, Presbyterianer, Catholiken, Quäcker, Dumpler, Mennonisten, Sabbatherians, Siebentäger, Separatisten, Böhmisten, Schwenckfeldianer, Tuchfeldter, Wohlwünscher, Juden und Heiden, u. s. f.— Ulsperger's Nachrichten, I, S. 156.

Hans Henrich Jäckel,
Melchior Mentzel,
Georg Mentzel,
Georg Weiss,*
Caspar Heydrich,
Georg Scholtze,
Christoph Wiegner,
Georg Anders,
David Seibb,
Christoph Seibb,
Georg Heydrich,
Georg Drescher,
Melchior Meishter,*
Baltzer Anders,
Georg Scholtze,
Caspar John,
Friederich Schöps,
Christoph Pauss,
David Schubert,
Wilhelmus Pott,
Degenhart Pott,
Peter Schämker,*
Nicolas Dek,*
Nicolas Winder,
Ulrich Spies,*
Peter Jäger,*
Peter Treidel,
Conrad Frey,
Valentin Dihl,*

Abraham Dihl,
Melchior Neuman,
Tobias Hertteranfft,
Balthaser Heydrich,
Christoph Neuman,
Matthias Jäckel,
Christopher Jäckel,
Gregorius Scholtze,
David Meschler,
Christoph Drescher jr.,
Melchior Scholtze,
Christopher Scholtze,
Hein. Ludwig Urickhaus,?
Bernhard Steinbach,
Georg Bansche,
Hans Hübener,*
Wilhelm Witzen,
Johannes Van Duliken,?
Jacob Friederick Rieger,
Johann Georg Rutz,?
Valentin Veruch,
Jacob Rumpfellt,
Johannes Wildfang,*
Jacob Wilhelmi,
Johan Caspar Störller,*
Johannes Senger,
Matthias Marcker,
Heinrich Rumpfeld.

Sick—Christopher Kriebel, David Hübner, Georg Reynold, David Jackle, Andreas Warner, Hans Martin Tryster.

Under sixteen:—David Neuman, Abraham Wiegner, Georg Wiegner, Caspar Seibb, Andreas Heydrich, Georg Anders, Melchior Hübner, David Schubert, Peter Labach, Johann Wilhelm Pott, Johannes Pott, Georg Heinrich Ruth, Jacob Frey, Johann Henrich Deck, Johannes Deck, Johann Michael Wolfgang, Johannes Wolfgang, Jacob Wilhelmi, Valentin Wilhelmi, Wilhelm Hertteranfft, Friederich Drescher, Johann Jacob Spies, Johann Nicolaus Steiner, Johann Jacob Steiner, Philip Freidel, Hans Georg Völcker, Johann Jacob Hildebrand, Clement Dubach, Christopher Kribel, Christopher Hübner, David Schubert.

Georg Kribel, Christopher Hoffman, Christopher Reinhold, Melchior Wiegner, Christopher Meister, Balthasar Jäckel, Georg Hertteranft, Melchior Hertteranft, Christopher Heydrich.

---

37) Sept. 23, 1734. Palatines imported in the ship Hope, Daniel Reid, Master, from Rotterdam, last from Cowes.—Forty-nine males above sixteen, forty-five females; fourteen boys and seventeen girls—in all 125.—(*Editor.*)

Sept. 23, 1734. Das Schiff Hope, Capitain Daniel Reid, von Rotterdam über Cowes, brachte Pfälzer.—Neun und vierzig männliche und fünf und vierzig weibliche Personen über sechzehn, und vierzehn Knaben und siebenzehn Mädchen—im Ganzen 125. (Herausgeber.)

Jacob Bauman,	Simon Beil,
Jacob Hoffer,	Joh. Henrich Otter,
Michael Gerber,	Antony Nobel,
Christian Huser,	Antony Nobel jr.,
Michael Fickel,	Johannes Richter,
Ulrich Buhler,*	Christian Farnie,
Bernhart Richer,*	Johannes Keinsman,*
Han Henrich Hoffman,*	Johan Adam Schroff,
Han Jacob Fischbach,	Johan Peter Gross,
Johann Wilhelm Graff,	Joh. Henrich Klöckner,
Johan Albert Langerfeld,	Aug. Henrich Kunstman,
Gottfried Schierwager,	Joh. Henrich Heissman,
Philip Esping,	Joh. Philip Doldt,*
Johannes Keiser,	Zacharias Flamerfeld,*
Peter Stam,	Joh. Wilhelm Ahlbach,
Christoph Rabe,	Joh. Peter Schmidt,
Henrich Stettz,	Han Henrich Otterpach,
Zacharias Ahlbach,	Joh. Herbert Weberd,
Johannes Jung,	Joh. Arnold Reisch,
Jost Shmith,*	Joh. Hen. Weschenbach,
Johannes Nöh,	Joh. Geo. Antony Müller,
Georg Lübcken,	Joh. Andreas Müller,
Johannes Artger,	Christian Otto Schultz,
Simon Kirbach,*	Cornelius Parät.

Under sixteen:—Johann Caspar Kratz, Johann Philip Kratz, Nicholas Husar, Hans Michael Keiser, Anthony Heinsman, Johan Henrich Gross, Johan Gerhard Klöckner, Johann Wilhelm Ahlbach, Johan Gerhard Ahlbach, Johann Peter Ahlbach, Herman Jung, Johann Jacob Noch, Johannes Lescher, Joseph Heinsman, Henrich Wilhelm Reisch.

---

38) May 29, 1735. Palatines and Switzers imported in the ship Mercury, William Wilson, Master, from Rotterdam, last from Cowes.—Sixty-four men, fifty-one women, thirty-seven boys and thirty-four girls—in all 186.—(*Editor.*)

Mai 29, 1735. Pfälzer und Schweizer mit dem Schiffe Mer= cury, Capitain William Wilson, von Rotterdam über Cowes.— Vier und sechzig Männer, ein und fünfzig Frauen, sieben und dreißig Knaben und vier und dreißig Mädchen—im Ganzen 186. (Herausgeber.)

Conrad Würtz,	Jacob Weidman,
Jacob Beshar,	Hans Conrad Käller,
Jacob Schenckel,*	Jacob Madler,
Heinrich Huber,	Henrich Schreiber,
Jacob Neff,	Martin Shellberg,*
Jacob Täntzler,*	Jacob Maurer.*
Johann Weiss,	Henrich Scheuchzer,
Henrich Merk,	Jacob Shellenberg,*
Hans Meier,?	Henry Mosock,*
Caspar Netzli,	Jacob Wiest,*
Jacob Frey,	Rudolph Egg,
Jacob Meyer,	Rudolph Walter,*
Hans Huber,	Jacob Schmit,*
Conrad Naffe,*	Conrad Meyer,*
Hans Müller,	Jacob Näff,
Hans Ott,	Caspar Gut,
Johannes Heit,	Jacob Matz,
Henry Surber,*	Philip Klein,
Abraham Weidman,	Hans Ulrich Amon,*
Rudolph Weidman,	Rudolph Aberly,*
Hans Jacob Radtgäb,	Jacob Conrad Naffe,*
Johan Ulrich Aner,*	Caspar Plauler,
Baltzer Bossert,	Abraham Weckerly,
Caspar Schweitzer,	Conrad Rütschi,
Henrich Oswald,	Christoph Neumeister,
Jacob Perdschinger,*	Johannes Mölich,
Henry Brunner,*	Henrich Forst.

Sick—Kilian Mertz, Jacob Homberger, Jacob Bücher, Henrich Müller, Conrad Zuppinger.

The following are marked *absent:*

Die Folgenden werden als abwesend bezeichnet:

Henry Götschy, Johan Henrich Maurer, Henrich Zurber, Jacob Schmid, Melchior Meyer.

Under sixteen:—Rudolph Götschy, Moritz Götschy, Rudolph Beschar, Rudolph Huber, Jacob Dentzler, Rudolph Dentzler, Abraham Dentzler, Abraham Dübendörffer, Hans Ulrich Brunner, Felix Ahner, Caspar Beschar, Henrich Beschar, Rudolph Beschar, Hans Matz, Hans Conrad Matz, Lenhart Meyer, Jac. Meyer, Heinrich Frey, Hans Jacob Meyer, Jacob Hubler, Rudolph Dübendörffer, Jacob Weidman, Matthias Käller, Jacob Bucher, Hans Ulrich Zupinger, Jacob Walther, Hans Jacob Neff, Felix Schmidt, Hans Henrich Plauler, Hans Jacob Plauler, Felix Metzger, Jacob Rütschi, Henrich Rütschi, Heinrich Mölich, Andreas Mölich, Gottfried Mölich.

39) June 28, 1735. Palatines imported in the brig Mary, of Philadelphia, James Marshall, Master, from London.—Thirteen men, ten boys, eighteen women and girls—in all 41.—(*Editor.*)

Juni 28, 1735. Auf der Brigg Mary von Philadelphia, Capitain James Marshall, von London, kamen Pfälzer.—Dreizehn Männer, zehn Knaben, achtzehn Frauen und Mädchen—im Ganzen 41.—(Herausgeber.)

Melchior Scholtze,	Zacharias Friedrich,
Henrich Boshart,	Henrich Würchman,
Peter Schwaab,	Johannes Würchman,
Andreas Brinker,*	Jacob Weidmer,
Wilhelm Gesel,*	Solomon Rückstul sen.,
Andreas Widmer,	Solomon Rückstul jr.

Under sixteen:—Caspar Boshart, Henrich Boshart, Conrad Brünckner, Henrich Würchman, Jac. Wiedmer, Hans Brückner, Henrich Rückstuhl.

40) Aug. 26, 1735. Switzers, late inhabitants of the Canton of Bern, in Switzerland, imported in the ship Billander Oliver, Samuel Merchant, Master, from South Carolina.—Eighteen men, eighteen women, six boys and three girls—in all 45.—(*Editor.*)

Aug. 26, 1735. Schweizer aus dem Canton Bern auf dem Schiffe Billander Oliver, Capitain Samuel Merchant, von Süd=Carolina.—Achtzehn Männer, achtzehn Weiber, sechs Knaben und drei Mädchen—im Ganzen 45.—(Herausgeber.)

Hans Bucher,
Lazarus Wenger,
Hans Koller,*
Christian Zwaller,
Johannes Marti,
Jacob Stelly,*
Ulrich Yilia,*
Johannes Etter,
Peter Henckels,

Christian Brenholtz,*
Hans Michael Pingley,
Hans Lüdenbörg,
Abraham Mäusslin,
Ulrich Mischler,
Christian Weber,*
Jacob Wilhelm Naath,
Hans Leyenberger,*
Hans Bucher jr.

Under sixteen:—Benjamin Bucher, Christian Bucher, Jacob Koller, Peter Leinberger, Hans Weber, Christian Weber.

41) Sept. 1, 1736. Palatines imported in the ship Harle, of London, Ralph Harle, Master, from Rotterdam, last from Cowes. One hundred and fifty-six men, sixty-five women, one hundred and sixty-seven boys and girls—in all 388.—(*Editor.*)

Sept. 1, 1736. Pfälzer, die mit dem Schiffe Harle von London, Capitain Ralph Harle, von Rotterdam über Cowes kamen.—Ein hundert sechs und fünfzig Männer, fünf und sechzig Frauen und ein hundert sieben und sechzig Knaben und Mädchen—im Ganzen 388.—(Herausgeber.)

Frantz Heckert,
Johannes Krück,
Johannes Lorentz,
Abraham Tiegarden sen.,
Johannes Hannewald,
Abraham Tiegarden,
Jacob Gemling,
Georg Zeisloff,
Wilhelm Hetterling,
Daniel Nargarg,*
Nicklaus Trewer,
Michael Jochim,*
Karl Kern,
Nicklas Rebell,*
Jacob Amandus,

Andreas Jochim,*
Vincent Schackie,
Jacob Hostedler,*
Jacob Eysen,
Hans Ruppele,
Frederick Beegel,*
Jacob Jayser,
Andreas Kurtz,
Frederick Memart,
Jacob Sontag,
Adam Seider,
Nilaus Lang,
Adam Boher,
Ludwig Lay,
Christian Erb,

Peter Rentsch,
Matthias Speck,
Dietrich Martin,
Andreas Grimm,
Nicolas Post,
Heinrich Dubs,
Joh. Van Laschet,
Joh. Peter Van Laschet,
Christian Van Laschet,
Joh. Philip Wageman,
Johan Philip Wick,
Johan Valentin Voigt,
Johan Mathias Voigt,
Johan Daniel Braun,
Johan Michael Graul,
Geo. Nicolas Sysloop,*
Johan Baltzer Zeisloop,*
Johan Peter Nargary,
Joh. Christophel Treber,
Johann Georg Jäky,
Leonhardt Cronbach,
Rudolph Hackmann,
Jacob Fellmann,
Cornelius Weygandt,
Hans Melchior Beyer,
Andrias Nargang,
Johannes Bütler,
Clemens Slottenbecker,
Johan Jacob Weyl,
Joh. Wilhelm Speck,
Peter Slottenbecker,
Johannes Willems,
Heinrich Slottenbecker,
Heinrich Gerhart,
Joh. Jacob Daubenspeck,
Andreas Haillman,
Johan Mathias Bruch,
Johan Peter Feglin,*
Johan Georg Mein,
Johannes Rothrock,
Johan Jacob Barth,

John Jacob Zyderman,
Andreas Cratz,
Jacob Libbert,
Valentin Neu,
Nicolaus Melcher,
Eberhart Ebeler,
Christian Schryack,
Conrad Frankenberger,
Johannes Rossinger,
Daniel Meyer,
Johannes Hess,
Paulus Brunner,
Christian Landes,
Andreas Gross,
Leonhart Jäger,
Peter Rupp,
Michael Noll,
Johannes Meyer,
Nicolas Ængne,
Caspar Meyer,*
Ludwig Mauerer,
Caspar Stelling,
Dewalt Beyer,
Johan Brand,
Mathias Deck,
Christian Suder,
Johannes Gerber,
Jonathan Heger,
Mattheus Röser,
Jacob Cuntz,
Jacob Hollinger,
Jacob Kochenauer,*
Andreas Franck,
Adam Wambolt,
Johannes Fuchs,
Gottfried Grüll,
Michael Linder,
Christoph Rudolpf,
Peter Hironimus,
Thomas Hummel,
Johannes Schneider,

9*

Johannes Zacharias,
Balthaser Stephanus,
Joh. Ludwig Weicker,
Joh. Henrich Bruner,
Johan Georg Basel,
Joh. Ludwig Kammerer,
Joh. Michael Weygell,
Laborius Merschrath,
Johannes Rissmann,
Joh. Christoph Windemuth,
Johann Georg Wambolt,
Johann Georg Scheidler,
Johann Conrad Grimm,
Johann Adam Schauss,
Zacharias Setzler,
Johan Valentin Scherer,
Isaac Adolphus Delb,
Johan Jacob Christler,
Christian Stöckly,

Johann Jacob Nuss,
Johan Conrad Bab,
Heinrich Wohlgemuth,
Abraham Wohlgemuth,
Joseph Wohlgemuth,
Georg Adam Werner,
Jacob Lädtermann,
Johan Philip Müntz,
Henrich Weydebach,
Caspar Kupferschmidt,
Johannes Franckeberger,
Han Georg Handtwerch,
Joh. Adam Hohenschilt,
Johan Peter Wambold,
Georg Michael Friedrich,
Johan Peter Marsteller,
Johan Georg Lehnert,
Joh. Georg Windemuth.

Sick—Jacob Eysen, Abraham Saaler, Michael Hochstädter, Ludwig Meyer.

---

42) Sept. 16, 1736. Palatines with their families, in all 330, imported in the ship Princess Augustus, Samuel Merchant, Master, from Rotterdam, last from Cowes.

Sept. 16, 1736. Pfälzer sammt ihren Familien, 330 an der Zahl, kamen auf dem Schiffe Princeß Augustus, Capitain Samuel Merchant, von Rotterdam über Cowes.

Georg Mayer,?
Stephen Schust,
Jacob Meyer,
Georg Meyer,*
Rudolph Essig,
Wilhelm Huber,
Jacob Müller,
Simon Carl,
Jacob Früh,
Lorentz Früh,
Leonhart Stein,?
Lorentz Simon,

Christian Simon,
Friederich Gärdner,*
Henrich Meyer,
Sebastian Graff,
Daniel Hekendorn,*
Bastian Stoler,
Friederich Greier,*
Martin Greider,
Durst Thomme,
Martin Domey,*
Hans Jacob,
Durst Thomme,

Joseph Kratzer,
Jacob Kese,*
Rudolph Rauch,
Hans Spiteler sen.,
Hans Spiteler,
Nicolaus Tenne,?
Jacob Baire,*
Hans Jacob,*
Stephen Jacob,*
Henry Books,*
Christian Buchty,
Abraham Jacke,
Jean Comer,
Hans Fiseler,*
Nicolas Jewdie,*
Joh. Gabriel Lämmle,
Joh. Georg Baumgärtner,*
Han Philip Fleckser,?
Johan Georg Ritter,
Johan Jost Dubs,
Hans David Bilman,
Hans Thomas Keer,
Hans Michael Carl,
Gottfried Lautermilch,
Philipp Gullmann,
Hans Michael Essig,
Georg Abraham Essig,
Johan Jacob Busch,*
Han Nicolas Schmidt,
Han Georg Trautman,*
Hans Georg Graff,
John Adolph Wenssel,
Han Jacob Beitert,
Christian Schenblein sen.,
Christian Schenblein jr.,
Han Hegendorn sen.,*
Han Hegendorn jr.,
Han Jacob Greider,*
Thielman Hirnschall,
Hans Jacob Dups,

Hans Georg Gerster,
David Löwenstein,
Sebastian Caquelin,
Dieterich Caquelin,
Jean Caquelin,
Daniel Kommer,
Dieterich Werlie,
Hans Imberman,
Hans Jacob Keller,
Benedict Yühli,
Christian Däppen,?
Waltes Baumann,
Hans Rudolph Erb,
Melchior Detweiler,
Jonas Joner,
Jacob Joner,
Hans Siber,
Hans Zwalle,
Hans Stockie,
Peter Binckly,*
Hans Binckly,*
François Oriths,
Nicholas Orich,
Eneas Noel,*
Joseph Noel,
Jacob Altlandt,
Peter Weyer,
Christian Schlächten,
Rudolph Baumgärdner,
Jean François Chrestien,
Collas Drasbart,*
Johannes Keller sen.,
Jacob Christman,
Michael Haalling,
Marcus Merky,*
Hans David Merky,*
Nicklaus Mesling,*
Johan Conrad Ganger,
Georg Nicolas Ganger.

Sick—Georg Maurer, Jacob Domme, Dietrich Marschall,

Hans Georg Knaab, Jacob Brüderle. *Dead*—Sebastian Caquelin, Hans Joner.

---

43) Oct. 19, 1736. Palatines with their families, 110 persons, imported in the brigantine Perthamboy, George Frazer, Master, from Rotterdam, last from Dover.

Oct. 19, 1736. Pfälzer mit ihren Familien, 110 Personen, kamen auf dem Schnellsegler Perthamboy, Capitain Geo. Frazer, von Rotterdam über Dover an.

Abraham Beer,	Peter Apfelbaum,
Johan Frantz,	Joh. Georg Micklein,
Johannes Siegel,*	Johan Ludwig Seib,
Jacob Keller,	Ludwig Stred. Vollsteller,
Caspar Struwel,	Johan Philip Quickel,*
Caspar Lambert,	Johan Peter Pritz,
Georg Keg,*	Joh. Michael Quickel,
Paulus Andoni,	Francis Joseph Hornig,
Johannes Geier,	Joh. Caspar Schmidt,
Johannes Schler,	Friederich Bleibtreu,
Peter Kohl,	Johan Adam Rausch,
Daniel Speth,	Johan Jost Mohr,?
Jacob Bleicher,*	Johan Georg Quickel,*
Peter Haas,	Joh. Christian Heininger,
Johannes Herr,	Joh. Heinrich Schmidt,
Deobald Veit,	Abraham Dumbaldt,
Dirk Schutten,*	Ernst Fried. Dumbaldt,
Nicolas Stop,*	Gottfried Eberhard.
Pierre D'Veau,	

---

44) Aug. 30, 1737. Palatines imported in the ship Samuel, Hugh Percy, Master, from Rotterdam, last from Cowes.—In all 318.

☞ After this date none of the names of Palatines are published in the *Colonial Records.*—(*Editor.*)

Aug. 30, 1737. 318 Pfälzer mit dem Schiffe Samuel, Capitain Hugh Percy, von Rotterdam über Cowes.

☞ Nach diesem Datum werden keine Namen der Pfälzer mehr in den Colonial-Berichten veröffentlicht.

Abraham Farni,
Henrich Werlle,
Christian Müller,
Henrich Müller,
Jacob Schober,*
Peter Tost,*
Nicolas Marret,*
Jacob Kuntz,
Benedict Tomas,
Hans Ebler,
Friederich From,
Darius Ruff,
Philip Becker,*
Ludwig Bothner,
Weyrich Rutisieli,
Jacob Volck,*
Johannes Ries,
Jacob Offenbacher,
Wilhelmus Beyer,
Johannes Kohr,
Henrich Guthard,
Daniel Filbert,
William Strub,
Johannes Lang,
Lorentz Becker,
Lorentz Schreiber,
Simon Mineehr,*
Peter Minich,*
Paul Frantz,
Friederich Eberhart,
Joseph Bischoff,
Peter Budniger,
Ulrich Bickell,
Lenhart Glaser,
Conrad Schütz,
Nicolas Meyer,*
Francis Fordene,*
Michael Fortineh,
Johan Georg Wichel,
Johannes Schöffler,
Johannes Drachsell,

Johan Peter Drachsell,
Christan Brengel,
Andreas Aulenbacher,
Hans Adam Staut,*
Hans Georg Hüttner,
Hans Michael Hetzer,
Johann Georg Ziegler,
Johan Jacob Kolb,
Johan Friederich Krafft,
Johan Jacob Nuss,
Heinrich Steinmetz,
Johan Thomas Kern,
Simon Hönninger,
Michael Pfingstag,
Hans Georg Lale,*
Johann Georg Roth,
Johan Christoph Meckel,
Ludwig Kornmann,
Johan Paul Geiger,
Johan Valentin Lang,
Johan Peter Stembell,
Johan Jacob Eichholtz,
Johannes Cashnetz,*
Hans Jacob Castnitz,
Hans Adam Biedniger,
Johan Adam Schneider,
Johan Georg Sauerbier,
Johan Jacob Maag,
Johan Lenhart Volck,
Johan Heinrich Klein,
Johan Nicolas Finck,
Johan Adam Drumm,
Johan Conrad Müller,
Bernhart Womer,*
Johan Christian Doll,
Melchior Fordene,*
Jacob Baum,
Andreas Müller,
Johannes Baum,
Jacob Lower,*
Michael Lower,*

Georg Weyrich,
Peter Hugett,
Jacob Lang,
Jacob Wolff,
Peter Wolff,
Peter Bier,
Johannes Haust,
Ludwig Klein,*
Johannes Staudt,
Christian Ruth,*
Johan Christian Dascher,
Philip Fenstenmacher,*
Michael Spengler,*

Johannes Peter Doll,
Johan Wilhelm Welsch,
Johan Jacob Welsch,
Michael Schumacher,
Johann Peter Licht,
Wilhelm Rabenwalt,
Johann Henrich Moll,
Johann Jacob Kintzer,
Johann Georg Geiss,
Ludwig Becker,
Johann Adam Löffler,
Johan Jacob Staudt.

---

45) Sept. 10, 1737. Palatines imported in the ship Snow Molly, John Howell, Master, from Amsterdam, last from Dover.— In all 95.

Sept. 10, 1737. Pfälzer auf dem Schiffe Snow Molly, Capitain John Howell, von Amsterdam über Dover.—Im Ganzen 95.

Valentin Stober,
Valentin Stober jr.,
Jacob Stober,
Friederich Reitzel,
Nicolaus Kachelriess,
Michael Hertlein,
John Winter,
Jacob Meier,
Joh. Jacob Geyer,*
Valentin Rohleber,
Christophel Gomer,
Phil. Jacob Schaaff,
Frederick Horn,*
Joh. Peter Han,
John Mart. Fröhlich,
Joh. Jac. Schaaff,

Hans Jonas Reitzel,
Johan Christoph Grohmann,
Johan Albrecht Schaller,
Johan Georg Albert,
Georg Albrecht Schaller,
Johan Lenhart Wulfart,?
Georg Simeon• Christ,
Hans Mich. Herdlein,
Georg Fried. Wollenweber,
Philip Gottleib Meintz,
Johan Philip Kratzer,
Johan Adam Gomer,
Philip Adam Endler,
Johannes Reitzmann,
Johan Christoph Schäcke.

---

46) Sept. 24, 1737. Palatines imported in the ship Virginus Grace, John Bull, Master, from Rotterdam, last from Cowes.— In all 225.

Sept. 24, 1737. Pfälzer mit dem Schiffe Virtuous Grace, Capitain John Bull, von Rotterdam über Cowes.—Im Ganzen 225.

Antoni Rüger sen.,
Antoni Rüger jr.,
Jacob Schaub,*
Isaac Hoffman,
Hans Hoffman,
Christoph Stauffer,
Leonhart Heier,
Rudolph Lützler,
Bernard Haup,*
Jacob Schwartz,
Jacob Remel,*
Jacob Graff,
Jacob Rimy,
Ludwig Born,
Jacob Stokee,*
Simon Stokee,*
Jeremiah Smitt,*
Peter Konder,
Peter Staut,*
Adam Weiss,
Abraham Wize,*
Michael Ulrich,
Jacob Wolff,
Adam Dill,
Baltzer Hartsoc,*
Christian Toll,*
Jacob Croyter,
David Bruch,
Georg Heck,
Hans Weis,
Jacob Springer,
Johannes Tasker,
Jacob Hubler,
Christian Piner,*
Henrich Grimm,
Michael Carle,?
Albert Lebolt,

Burckhart Rüger,
Isaac Hoffman jr.,
Martin Hegendorn,
Johannes Stauffer,
Hans Jacob Groller,
Hans Jacob Kobler,*
Hans Georg Schwartz,
Hans Georg Reimmel,
Albrecht Graff,
Simon Schunck,
Frederick Cromer,*
Hans Georg Dillmann,
Henrich Jacob Dillmann,
Hans Michael Ulrich,
Christian Bullinger,*
Hans Georg Konder,*
Rudolph Duckwell,*
Jacob Hollinger,
Andrew Sunwald,*
Hans Georg Friederick,
Friederich Kiester,
Henrich Schwerdt,
Jacob Bollinger,
Wilhelm Fischer,
Henrich Shamberger,*
Henrich Crössman,
Hans Georg Meyer,*
Johan Jacob Conradt,
Henrich Wideabach,*
Johannes Weiss,*
Henrich Engel,
Johannes Hunsecker,
Michael Rausch,
Christian Bauer,
Hans Jacob Inhof,*
Simon Hunsecker.

47) Sept. 26, 1737. Palatines imported in the ship Saint
Andrew Galley, John Stedman, Master, from Rotterdam, last
from Cowes.—In all 450.

Sept. 26, 1737. Auf dem Schiffe Saint Andrew Galley kamen
unter Capitain John Stedman von Rotterdam über Cowes. 450
Pfälzer.

Jacob Kintzer,
Jacob Niss,
Philip Hefft,
Jacob Fries,*
Philipp Fritsch,
Peter Rapp,
Caspar Hüter,
Valentin Steinmetz,
Georg Kern,
Georg Schissler sen.,*
Johannes Stöhr,
Georg Schissler jr.,*
Philip Stöhr,
Georg Des,
Georg Hefft,*
Jacob Lentz,
Jacob Kuster,*
Nicolas Koch,*
Andreas Smith,*
Christian Meyer,*
Johann Meyer,*
Conrad Reich,
Michael Brown,*
Georg Wambold,
Elias Ratgen,*
John Spycker,
Georg Rahn,
Conrad Rahn,
Philip Schmidt,
Baltzer Beil,
Georg Neihart,
Lorentz Kayser,
Conrad Wall,
Jacob Werry,*
Henrich Kreyter,*

Peter Lin,
Nicolas Scherer,*
Henrich Smith,*
Nicolaus Holler,
Wilhelm Ohler,
Paulus Lingel,
Henrich Wisler,
Georg Kocher,
Johan Georg Kälsch,
Michael Neihart,
Johan Lenhart Jerling,
Philip Lebengut,*
Joh. Christian Bürger,
Wilhelm Scheffer,
Georg Hen. Wamboldt,
Johan Conrad Jost,
Johan Asinus Gerling,*
Joh. Jac. Schindeldecker,
Johannes Schnauber,
Johan Georg Kläppinger,
Tobias Böckell,
Johannes Meyer,
Jacob Neiswanger,*
Hans Jost Meier,
Hans Martin Amwäg,
Nicolaus Scheyer,
Nicolaus Biettel,
Michael Andreas,*
Johan Georg Schneider,
Gerhardt Hübschman,
Johan Jacob Lingel,
Johan David Bühler,
Johan Peter Spycker,
Johannes Mevius,
Johan Philip Wisman,

Johan Friederich Heim,
Johan Ludwig Kolb,
Johan Philip Seger,
Bernhart Dickhoff,
Johan Jacob Rosenmann,
Georg Fried. Neihart,
Johannes Schlotter,
Johan Georg Kuntz,
Johan Christian Thron,
Matthias Lederman,*
Valentine Baumgärdner,*
Johannes Altenberger,
Johan Justus Erdmann,
Johan Peter Drass,
Johan Rudolph Henrich,
Christopher Schaub,*
Albrech Fig,?
Ulrich Horn,
Peter Weiland,*
Martin Cron,
Georg Conrad,
Jacob Conrad,
Daniel Zopff,
Ulrich Sollberger,
Christian Estu,*
Mattheis Weber,
Casper Heyser,
Valentin Diebel,
Casper Rabe,*
Conrad Delp,*
Johan Funck,*
Peter Knepper,*
Nicolas Rattge,*

Joseph Zolenberger,*
Henrich Frantz,
Andreas Heid,*
Adam Strauch,*
Daniel Ries,
Nicolas Ries,
Jost Hüsterr,
Christoph Krause,
Johannes Dreichler,
Johan Philip Streiter,
Georg Caspar Zeigner,
Johan Ludwig Wildanger,
Johan Georg Gist,
Johan Jacob Weller,
Daniel Zacharias,
Christoph Schwenck,
Georg Dietrich Helt,
Johan Philip Steffen,
Johan Herman Weber,
Johan Henrich Märtz,
Henrich Schieffler,
Georg Ludwid Denner,
Johannes Geltbach,
Johan Philip Edinger,
Georg Gernandt,
Johannes Köhler,
Friederich Schönfelder,
Ernst Seydel,
Abraham Wagner,
Christoph Hübner,
Joh. Herm. von Basten,
Candidatus S. Th.

Sick—Dan. Hüster, Jac. Keim, John Erdman, John Appel.
Absent—Georg Test, Caspar Heyser.

48) Oct. 5, 1737. Palatines, in all 231, imported in the bilander Townshead, Thomas Thompson, Master, from Amsterdam, last from Cowes.

Oct. 5, 1737. 231 Pfälzer mit dem kleinen Lastschiffe Townshead, Capitain Thomas Thompson, von Amsterdam über Cowes.

Christian Ewig,
Georg Egnel,?
Conrad Holbe,
Peter Schad,
Jacob Wogel,
John Peter Wilt,*
Conrad Lauterbach,
Peter Lauderbach,
Johan Georg Joh,
Johan Casper Neuer,
Jean Corbo,
Christian Fredrick,
Simon Ersame,*
Anthony Hidler,*
Jacob Acker,*
Balthasar Süsz,
Peter Rausch,
Valentin Kiffer,
Georg Spengel,
Johan Küstler,*
Vincent Küster,*
Casper Wendel,
Andreas Epple,
Georg Schutz,
Conrad Preiss,
Leonard Kugel,
Georg Arnoldt,
Christian Aspech,
Elias Obelhart,*
Peter Graff,
Ludwig Frantz,
Michael Balmer,
Peter Wagner,
Johan Schlieger,*
Johannes Geseller,
Conrad Rippert,*
Peter Hotner,

Johannes Lowra,*
Jacob Schantz,
Sebastian Bisch,*
Silvester Holber,
Christian Friederich,*
Johan Georg Heyer,?
Johan Georg Euler,
Johan Casper Premauer,
Eberhard Geschwind,
Valentin Henneberger,*
Hans Georg Friederich,
Hans Georg Krause,
Andreas Camerer,
Peter Mahrsteller,
Hans Georg Ehemann,
Anthony Hempele,
Hans Georg Mentzer,
Wendel Zwecker,
Hans Matthias Pfeil,
Johan Jacob Sauer,
Georg Friederich Arnoldt,
Johannes Schlegel,
Martin Pfatteicher,
Conrad Reinhart,
Johan Ægidius Hoffman,
Johan Stephan Bernhardt,
Hans Georg Bray,
Hans Mich. Henneberger,
Johan Michael Kärber,
Johan Frantz Wilhelm,
Joh. Philip De Bertholt,
Johan Peter Bonnet,
Valentin Himmelberger,
John Peter Ysterloh,
Joh. Martin Dieffenbacher,
Johan Georg Seger,
Georg Casper Fernsler.

Sick—Balthasar Sies, Casper Wendel.

---

49) Oct. 8, 1737. Palatines imported in the ship Charming
Polly, of London, Charles Stedman, Master, from Rotterdam,

last from Plymouth.—One hundred and five men, twenty-five boys, and one hundred and seven women and girls.—237 passengers.—(*Editor.*)

Oct. 8, 1737. Pfälzer auf dem Schiffe Charming Polly von London, Capitain Charles Stedman, von Rotterdam über Plymouth.—Ein hundert und fünf Männer, fünf und zwanzig Knaben, und ein hundert und sieben Weiber und Mädchen.—237 Reisende.—(Herausgeber.)

Johannes Beitzel,	Jacob Mast,
Hans Georg Götz,	Ulrich Spiker,*
Michael Somer,	Elias Schreiber,
Andreas Ziegler,	Peter Brucker,
Jacob Hubele,	Claus Erb,
Gottlieb Reisinger,	Claus Erb jr.,
Heinrich Voltz,	Johannes Erb,
Jacob Sontag,	Adam Pfeller,
Jacob Sontag jr.,	Jacob Dester,*
Johannes Krauth,	Matthias Riechart,*
Jacob Schumacher,	Jacob Raisch,
Christian Geiger,	Georg Gross,
Jacob Baumann,	Johan Martin Becher,
Marin Funck,	Hans Peter Schipp,
Christian Hapeger,	Hans Peter Bernhart,
Joseph Habeger,	Johan Ludwig Heger,
Henrich Karli,?	Hans Georg Heiss,
Georg Mauntz,	Johan Heinrich Heiss,
Jacob Schantz,	Johan Stephan Conrad,
Hans Schantz,	Hans Georg Heiss,
Hans Gerber,	Hans Peter Küder,
Hans Gerber sen.,*	Hans Martin Reisinger,
Hans Holl,	Hieronimus Eberle,
Hans Koffel,*	Hans Jacob Fachler,
Isaac Holl,	Johan Philip Bötzer,
Wendel Holl,	Hans Jacob Kauffmann,
Hans Wenger,	Hans Jacob Hobbecher,*
Christian Kurtz,*	Hermanus Orendorff,*
Jacob Miller,*	Thielmanus Weschenbach,
Christian Müller,	Mattheis Hoffmann,
Valentin Jung,	Christian Lichte,*
Benedict Lehman,	Peter Eschbacher,*
Jacob Beiler,	Hans Michael Punch,*

Abraham Müller,
Johann Jost Kunz,
Hans Zimmermann,*
Daniel Zacharias,
Jacob Underkoffer,
Michael Zurger,*
Christian Hertzberger,*
Nicolaus Schreiber,
Christian Bürcki,
Jacob Wilhelm Weiss,
Johan Jeremias Jünghen,
Johan Jacob Wetzel,
Johan Valentin Haan,
Frederick Hoffman,*
Johan Georg Ilgenfritz,
Johan Jacob Dester,
Abraham Hann,
Andreas Hagenbuch,
Hans Georg Kübler,
Johan Dietrich Branner,
Peter Lohrmann,
Christian Gross,

Lorentz Nolff,
Wendel Heinrich,
Dietrich Uhler,
Andreas Weber,
Christoph Krauth,
Peter Freydinger,
Ulrich Strickler,
Jacob Schopff,
Christopher Ecker,
Thomas Schiri,
Johannes Bowman,*
Georg Ludwig Wagner,
Valentin Uhler,
Balthasar Huber,
Georg Henrich Ernsperger,
Johan Matthias Albrecht,
Georg Titus Cap,
Johannes Köhler,
Hans Jacob Strickler,
Georg Philip Fuhrmann,
Georg Michael Düntz.

Sick—Abraham Dannahauer, Hans Georg Dannahauer, Hans Stephan Conradt, Georg Michael Hollinger, Johan Henrich Grimm, Hans Georg Bäcker.

Under sixteen:—Abraham Dannenhauer, Paul Schumacher, Georg Schumacher, Adam Fachler, Johann Ludwig Sontag, Wilhelm Geiger, Abraham Kauffman, Joseph Karle, Christian Schantz, Hans Lehman, Abraham Holl, Jos. Wenger, Christian Eschbacher, Benedict Lehman, Christopher Beiler, Peter Herschberger, Johann Georg Schreiber, Philip Schreiber, Christian Erb, Friederich Hoffman, Hans Georg Ilgenfritz, Wilhelm Rieger, Georg Martin Cap, Christian Baumann, Johann Jacob Baumann.

———

50) Oct. 31, 1737. Palatines imported in the ship William, John Carter, Master, from Rotterdam, last from Dover.—180 passengers.

Oct. 31, 1737. 180 Pfälzer kamen auf dem Schiffe William, Capitain John Carter, von Rotterdam über Dover.

Michael Reuter,
Jacob Vechtel,*
Wendel Bohn,
Johannes Schantz,
Caspar Sürber,
Peter Schäffer,
Johannes Gett,*
Heinrich Rode sen.,
Henrich Rode jr.,
Daniel Rode,
Dietrich Uhle,
Matthias Switzer,*
Jacob Hauer,
Christian Miller,
Jost Ficcus,*
Niclaus Mufli,
Christian Jagi,
Andreas Kessinger,
George Fitheim,*
Jacob Krom,*
Simon Schedel,*
Thomas Bauer,*
Michael Bauer,
Philip Jacob Reuter,
Hans Adam Kletle,
Johannes Madlung,
Johan Dietrich Uhle,
Johannes Maurer,
Hans Georg Meister,
Johan Fried. Muthhardt,
Hans Michael Hauer sen.,
Hans Michael Hauer jr.,
Johan Michael Gesel,

Johannes Küchle,
Hans Peter Hauth,
Joh. Theobold Schalck,
Johan Nicholas Fischer,
Hans Georg Becholtt,
Johan Georg Kessinger,
Johan Michael Boltz,
Johan Carl Haffelee,*
Johan Balthas Rathgeber,
Johan Michael Spiegel,
Johan Fried. Heinnoldt,
Johan Peter Baumgertner,
Geo. Hein Valen. Hencke,
Conrad Braun,
Joseph Keller,*
Jacques Creuccas,
Mattheis Schmidt,
Theobald Lange,*
Johannes Schwing,
Johannes Miller,*
Joh. Peter Wilms,
Christian Winderbauer,
Joh. Gerh. Brenner,
John Casper Zunfft,*
Hans Jacob Faber,*
Hans Adam Faber,
Georg Jacob Bentz,
Johan Michael Nees,
Johan Conrad Ernst,
Heinrich Weidtmann,
Johannes Weidtmann,
Johan Georg Beyer,
Johan Wendel Ernst.

Sick—Friederich Will, Peter Fickus. *Drowned* (ertrunken)
Matthew Switzer.

---

51) July 27, 1738. Palatines imported in the brigantine
Catharine, Jacob Philips, Master, from London.—15 passengers.

Juli 27, 1738. 15 Pfälzer auf dem Schnellfahrer Catharine,
Capitain Jacob Philips, von London.

10*

Hans Boach,*
Jacob Zuch,
Hans Seiler,*
Ulrich Seiler jr.,*

Christian Zug,
Hans Schneider sen.,*
Hans Ludwig Falbeystan.

---

52) Sept. 5, 1738. Palatines, in all 252, imported in the ship Winter Galley, Edward Paynter, Master, from Rotterdam, last from Deal.

Sept. 5, 1738. Im Ganzen 252 Pfälzer auf dem Schiffe Winter Galley, Capitain Edward Paynter, von Rotterdam über Deal.

Nicholas Elie,*
Christoph Heller,
Simon Heller,
Johannes Roth,
Henry Weishart,*
Andreas Beier,
Martin Beier,
Johannes Light,*
John Sauvage,*
Lorentz Heim,
Albrecht Eberhart,
Gottlieb Eberhart,
Wendel Drauth,
Johannes Berntz,
Ludwig Meyer,*
Peter Wagner,
Adam Mayer,
Johan Jacob Stahl,
Johan Peter Müller,
Frantz Ludwig Barth,
Abraham Körper,
Johan Philip Bayer,
Hans Adam Schreiner,
Joh. Henrich Eschbach,
Joh. Michael Schreiner,
Johan Wendel Laschett,
Johan Michael Römer,
Johan Friederich Hase,
Johan Martin Mayer,

Johan Wilhelm Mayer,
Johan Philip Wagner,
Johannes Wagner,
Sebastian Zettlemeier,*
Johan Philip Sebolt,
Johan Nehs,
Rudolph Schler,
Johan Miller,*
Conrad Shmit,*
Philip Beyer,*
Philip Weber,
Wilhelm Janss,
Henry Teich,*
Jacob Bin,
Andreas Bin,
Markes Miller,*
Friederich Haas,
Frantz Seel,
Henrich Becker,
Samuel Moch,
Friederich Krafft,
Melchior Stall,*
Henry Feelt,*
Adam Stoop,*
Henry Klengler,*
Georg Joughein,*
Simon Deck,*
Philip Beyer jr.,*
Jacob Hee.

Peter Bucher,*
Augustus Pönsy,*
Jacob Thebelt,*
Philip Harlas,*
Andreas Hoock,
Wilhelm Best,*
Casper Berger,*
Conrad Dust,*
Andreas Seim,*
Georg Seiberth,
Adam Wall,
Julius Rübell,
Jacob Venig,
Jacob Runck,
Christian Jani,?
Laz. Palin,
Jacob Saddler,*
Jacob Bach,
Stephan Lang,
Hans Mich. Hochländer,
Johan Peter Hoffman,
Georg Hoffman,
Jacob Barthelm,
Nicholas Walter,*
Hans Geo. Gerth, *dumb*,
Johan Michael Knab,
Mattheus Ulrich,
Henrich Landgraff,*
Johannes Jäger,*
Johan Michael Rusler,*
Johan Martin Schreiner,
Paulus Kirchner,?
Joh. Daniel Trölich,
Johan Michael Preis,
Johan Christoph Wagner,
Daniel Butterfass,
Johan Jacob Krafft,
Johan Adam Schäffer,
Georg Ernst Lintell,*
Johan Jacob Hust,*
Wilh. Zacharias Andich,

Conrad Zimmerman,
Hans Jacob Tatweiler,
Johan Melchior Weiss,
Han Nicolas Preis,
Christophel Ambrüster,
Hans Adam Heinder,*
Andreas Frederick,*
Geo. Martin Lohmüller,*
Georg Andreas Stupp,
Johan Jacob Müller,
Johan Philip Weicker,
Hans Philip Köhler,
Johan Georg Faass,
Johan Philip Faass,
Johan Valentine Stocker,
Joh. Balthas Sartorius,
Joh. Valentin Lemerd,?
Daniel Drumberg,*
Johan Jacob Beyer,
Friederich Fahrion,
Adam Hoffmann,
Charle Gillion,*
Claude Charle,
Isaac Vial,
Matthias Gensle,
Conrad Ettinger,*
Henry Sturf,*
Ludwig Fillinger,
Johannes Ewert,
Paul Prack,
Henrich Bullinger,
Johan Georg Hayd,
Johannes Bechtolt,
Georg Philip Dollinger,
Frid. Ambrose Tranberg,
Johan Michael Mattes,
Georg Michael Hyltel,
Johannes Cranester,
Hans Georg Schmidt,
Wilhelm Gelsendorf,
Johannes Lingenfeldter.

53) Sept. 9, 1738. Palatines, in all 349, imported in the ship Glasgow, Walter Sterling, Master, from Rotterdam, last from Cowes.

Sept. 9, 1738. 349 Pfälzer an der Zahl mit dem Schiffe Glasgow, Capitain Walter Sterling, von Rotterdam über Cowes.

Valentin Krantz,
Melchior Clos,
Ehrhard Kless,
Johannes Zinn,*
Philip Jacobs,*
Nicolas Mock,
Johannes Hüppel,
Adam Albert,
Nicolas Kleh,
Debalt Guth,
Philip Drumm,
Daniel Staudt,*
Peter Staudt,*
Theobald Klee,*
Conrad Wolff,
Jacob Bernhard,
Daniel Corell,*
Gottfried Zerfass,
Johannes Miller,*
Daniel Schneider,*
Johannes Dreher,
Carl Neumann,
Henry Lowrence,*
Philip Gebhart,
Peter Koch,*
Jacob Mann,*
Wilhelm Daub,*
Jacob Grub,
Thomas Schneider sen.,
Thomas Schneider jr.,
Johan Adam Schneider,
Johan Philip Rihl,
Matheis Fenstermacher,
Wilhelm Fenstermacher,
Johan David Diel,
Johan Nicklas Fischer,*

Johan Nicolas Wolff,
Johannes Pontius,
Johan Nicolas Rausch,
Johan Philip Heintz,
Johan Marx Heintz,
Johannes Battelm,
Johan Henrich Walter,
Johan Bernhard Rauch,
Johan Jacob Seibert,
William Mombaur,*
Christopher Kauffeld,
Johan Nicklas Bower,*
John Peter Bower,*
Conrad Rebman,*
Jacob Finstermacher,
Johan Georg Mill,*
Henrich Jacob Anspach,
Henrich Radebaugh,*
Sebastian Haupt,
Heinrich Bömmer,
Peter Jost,
Johannes Jost,
Johannes Kuntz,
Wilhelm Diel,
Jost Mitzler,
Georg Klein,
Jacob Tiel,*
Philip Cunius,
Killian Noll,*
Jacob Triess,
Stephan Braun,
Peter Engell,
Leonhart Georg,*
Anthony Erford,*
Johannes Boos,
Johannes Berger.

Michael Luteinger,*
Michael Müller,*
Peter Daub,
Abraham Heintz,
Albertius Koch,
Michael Maurer,
Martin Wall,*
Deobalt Weber,
Georg Stohler sen.,*
Georg Stohler jr.,*
Bernhart Stohler,
Johan Adam Bömmer,
Philip Bartholomy,
Johan Adam Steyn,
Johan Henrich Koller,
Johan Peter Oberkehr,
Johan Wilhelm Gerhart,
Johan Nickel Peck,
Johannes Bobenheiser,*

Andreas Bobenheiser,
Johan Adam Hubert,
Johannes Guckes,
Johan Nickel Emrich,
Johan Nickel Michael,
Johan Frid. Michael,
Hans Adam Miller,*
Johan Dieter Frey,
Hans Adam Shade,*
Frantz Carl Huyet,
Johan Christ. Neuman,
Christopher Bernhart,*
Frantz Gildner,
Thomas Gärniger,*
Johan Adam Hartman,
Heinrich Bernhard,?
Mathias Stohler,*
Bernhart Dahlheimer.

54) Sept. 9, 1738.† Palatines imported in the snow Two Sisters, James Marshall, Commander, from Rotterdam, last from Cowes.—Forty-one men, thirty women, twenty-three boys and sixteen girls—in all 110.

Sept. 9, 1738.† Mit dem Seeschiffe Two Sisters, Commandant James Marshall, von Rotterdam über Cowes.—Ein und vierzig Männer, dreißig Weiber, drei und zwanzig Knaben und sechzehn Mädchen—im Ganzen 110.

Johannes Dadinger,
Johan Wildermuth,
Melchior Schedle,
Dietrich Benedict,

Hans Wendel Hoff,?
Christophel Schneider,
Hans Georg Wagner,
Hans Adam Heylman,

† This year, 1738, Rev. A. G. Spangenberger, a Moravian, arrived from Georgia in Pennsylvania. Through him the Moravians were made attentive to the conversion of the Indians, having received some accounts of them through Conrad Weiser.

† In diesem Jahre, 1738, kam Pastor A. G. Spangenberger, ein Herrnhuter, von Georgia nach Pennsylvanien. Durch ihn wurden die Herrnhuter bewogen, der Bekehrung der Indianer mehr Aufmerksamkeit zu schenken, da ihm Conrad Weiser von ihnen erzählt hatte.

Wolfgang Braun,
Johannes Solder,
Jacob Hauser,
Philip Friederich,
Andreas Frey,*
Leonhart Notz,
Henrich Funck,
Johannes Johe,
Christian Everhart,*
Philip Smit,*
Simon Creysmeyer,*
Matthias Keyger,*
Balthas Bahret,
Johannes Merckel,
Hans Mich. Reiss,

Hans Georg Greiser,*
Hans Martin Halter,
Johan Gotlieb Breuninger,
Hans Martin Breuninger,
Hans Michael Easterly,*
Michael Friederich Zeyler,
Hans Georg Brendel,
Hans Georg Brücker,
Johan Philip Brendel,
Johan Henry Rydenstock,*
Johan Wilhelm Wentzel,
Hans Georg Coon,*
Johan Wolfgang Unger,
Johan Bernhart Reber,
Johan Henrich Meyer.

Under sixteen:—Johann Wilhelm Simon, Melchior Ruch,
Friederich Schupp, Ludwig Holtzhefer, Hans Peterly, Christian
Schenck, Jacob Dür, Hans Peter Ziegler, Johan Henrich
Brendel, Hans Lenhart, Hans Geiger, Hans Michael Kuhn,
Andreas Huber, Christian Schwartz, Hans Jacob Hoffer, Frantz
Joseph Eileshauer, Hans Horst, Georg Friederich, Jacob Frey,
Hans Grube, Peter Grube.

---

55) Sept. 11, 1738.   Palatines imported in the ship Robert
and Oliver, of Dublin, Walter Goodman, Commander, from Rotterdam, last from Dover.—320 passengers.

Sept. 11, 1738. Das Schiff Robert und Oliver von Dublin,
Commandant Walter Goodman, von Rotterdam über Dover,
brachte 320 Pfälzer.

Caspar Scheck,
Lorentz Biesang,?
Paulus Baliett,
Peter Heydrich,
Peter Kister,
Alex. Scheffer,*
Reinhart Alspach,
Jacob Frantz,
Matheis Alsbach,
Paulus Bufle,*
Philip Herzog,

Melchior Kolp,
Peter Kolp,*
Johannes Förch,
Peter Seubert,
Johannes Röhrer,
Melchior Yand,*
Ludwig Boos,*
Jacob Bricker,*
David Nagle,*
Gerhart Henry,*
Nicolas Miller,

Gottfried Betzele,
Daniel Klingenschmidt,
Christopher Heydrich,
Michael Clementz,
Johan Peter Phiel,*
Johan Paulus Kutz,
Johannes Trautmann,*
Georg Michael Buch,
Johan Adam Schnell,*
Johan Gottfried Röhrer,
Georg Michael Kolb,
Johannes Huntzinger,
Hans Mich. Torenberger,
Valentin Schultz,
Frantz Klingenschmidt,
Johan Georg Friederich,
Casper Weisgerber, §
Johan Jacob Klunt,*
Hans Caspar Dortst,
Hans Adam Gesler,*
Hans Jacob Reyman,*
Hans Michael Reyman,*
Adam Daniel,*
Peter Heyel,
Johannes Brown,*
Tobias Steuer,
Theobalt Schäffer,
Theobalt Schäffer jr.,
Andreas Meyer,*
Paulus Mosser,*
Johannes Bricker,*
Michael Müller,*
Jacob Dommer,*
Johan Shneyder,*
Andreas Bader,
Hans Martin,
Joseph Kensel,*
Philip Tofort sen.,
Philip Tofort jr.,
Henrich Shengle,*

Conrad Hayt,*
Peter Hayt,*
Christian Grub,
Theobald Fick,
Anthony Biehler,
Ulrich Bullher,*
Peter Ruby,*
Jacob Beck,
Peter Reitenauer,
Georg Gottfried,
Adam Dick,
Joh. Christoph Welterich,
Johan Nicolaus Schneyder,
Johan Frid. Schneyder,
Joseph Kentzel jr.,
Johan Philip Weiss,
Johan Jacob Gugerle,
Jacob Koppenheffer,*
Leonhart Nachbar,*
Johan Nicolas Wolff,
Henrich Thomme,
Joh. Jacob Schumacher,
Johannes Schumacher,
Johan Nicklas Holl,*
Abraham Holl,
Balthaser Reydenauer,
Hans Georg Roth,
Johan Philip Fehl,
Johannes Eskusen,*
Peter Eskusen,* (Escoque,)
Michael Shumaker,*
Stephan Durabercher,*
Johannes Schleyfard,*
Johan Peter Karch,
Johan Adam Graner,?
Hans Martin Startzman,
Hans Hen. Reitenauer,
Christian Stetler,
Johan Nicolas Nagle,*
Christian Cassell.*

56) Sept. 16, 1738. Palatines imported in the ship Queen
Elizabeth, Alexander Hope, Master, from Rotterdam, last from
Deal, England.—In all 300.

Sept. 16, 1738. 300 Pfälzer mit dem Schiffe Queen Elisa=
beth, Capitain Alexander Hope, von Rotterdam über Deal in
England.

Wilhelm Brant,
Andreas Felsinger,*
Andreas Lerch,*
Peter Lerch,
Johann Lerch,
Christian Laubach,
Reinhart Laubach,
Johan Ludwig Seipel,
Johan Otto Yserloch,
Johan Georg Bergman,
Johan Bernhard Roth,
Hans Otto Schlächer,
Georg Casper Schlächer,
Johan Jost Schlächer,
Johannes Schimmel,
Johannes Kunckel,*
Caspar Lörch,
Christoph Streter,
Nicolas Fege,?
Johannes Hetrich,
Henrich Koch,
Johannes Schmidt,
Georg Loroy,
Nicolas Winholdt,*
Johan Schneider,
Paul Geissel,
Ernst Scharp,
Georg Scharp,*
Ludwig Thomas,*
Johannes Strohl,
Johannes Bager,
Johannes Starr,*
Georg Dörr,
Martin Weitzel,*
Christoph Ried,*

Johannes Stein,
Henrich Zeller,
Johannes Lörch,
Johannes Schäffer,
Johannes Möser,
Nicholas Hyches,*
Bernhart Lintze,*
Georg Scharp,*
Isaac Scharp,
Theobald Schmidt,
Conrad Hergle,
Casper Leap sen.,
Casper Leap jr.,
Johannes Alt,
Carl Nagel,
Henrich Wilhelm,
Johannes Homan,
Conrad Miller,
Philippus Medh,
Casper Scheffer,*
Conrad Göbe,
Jacob Ewald,*
Johan Georg Schlächer,
Johan Henrich Seitz,
Johan Henrich Silvius,
Johan Siegmund Henle,
Johan Adam Shisler,
Johan Peter Specht,
Johan Henrich Weber,
Johan Henrich Koch,
Johan Gabriel Vogell,
Johan Henrich Schmidt,
Johan Peter Schmidt,
Johan Carl Reichart,*
Johannes Reiffschneider,

Joh. Con. Reiffschneider,
John Michael Leroy,*
Johan Marx Seypell,
Johan Ulerich Sibel,*
Johan Georg Ellinger,
Johan Henrich Weiss,
Johan Werner Wetzel,
Daniel Eiglebonner,*
Johan Conrad Stichel,
Heinrich Schleucher,
Christian Morietz,
Johan Henry Hyches,
Johan Henrich Nichter,
Johan Martin Schwedener,
Johan Georg Kunkel,*

Heinrich Weitzel,
Ernestus Schlegel,
Johan Henrich Grist,
Johan Henry Gabel,*
Johan Casper Schreiber,*
John Jost Sulsbach,
Christian Nudhart,*
Conrad Lieppert,
Johannes Gunckel,
Wilhelm Lieppert,
Casp. David Dumernicht,
Johan Gottwals,
Johannes Rister,
Nicolaus Schrack,
Nicolaus Ziegler.*

57) Sept. 19, 1738. Palatines imported in the ship The
Thistle, John Wilson, Commander, from Rotterdam, last from
Plymouth, England.—300 passengers.

Sept. 19, 1738. 300 Pfälzer auf dem Schiffe The Thistle,
John Wilson, Befehlshaber, von Rotterdam über Plymouth, Engl.

Daniel Draichler,
Wilhelm Bischoff,
Isaac Ommell,
Valentin Heiss,*
Jacob Kener,*
Abraham Stetler,
Jacob Sligh,*
Thomas Reigh,*
Johannes Gers,*
Daniel Schneider,
Lorentz Gutt,
Andreas Neumann,
Henrich Becholdt,*
Johann Keller,
Jacob Carle,
Christian Lutz,*
Caspar Lutz,
Jacob Cloder,
Johannes Hedrigh,*

Johannes Cron,
Jacob Meyer,
Elias Zöller,
Michael Thiel,*
Michael Friess,
Johannes Friess,*
Martin Grimm,
Johannes Krimm,
Jost Freueller,
Johannes Cön,*
Bernhart Smith,*
Melchior Smith,*
Conrad Rühmle,
Christian Lotter,
Paul Shiffer sen.,
Bernhart Shiffer,
Paulus Shiffer jr.,
Philip Kuhn,*
Valentin Wildt,

11

Jacob Bender,
Christian Brechbüll,
Johannes Schligter,
Christian Stettler,
Peter Habacker,*
Henrich Brightbill,*
Georg Elias Amendt,?
Peter Fonderburgh,*
Valentin Fonderburgh,*
Johan Adam Schneider,
Joseph Keller,*
Johan Georg Lotz,
Johannes Weinmüller,
Jost Birckenstock,
Georg Michael Grötz,*
Johan Leonhart Müller,
Hans Georg Mayer,
Joh. Jacob Schuhmann,
Conrad Weymiller,
Andreas Mendung,?
Johan Simon Friess,
Caspar Kühner,
Hans Martin Biller,*
Hans Jacob Pfarr,*
Hans Adam Leidy,*
Michael Underkoffer,
Martin Mansperger,
Johan Herman Schäffer,

Joh. Hen. Riemenschneider,
Henry Bartholom. Shäffer,
John Rudolph Auchenbach,*
Michael Hubach,
Andreas Hannewalt,
Johan Ludwig Müller,
Johan Conrad Ziegler,
Johan Peter Schneider,
Nicolaus Freitag,
Elias Nicolas Bender,
Jacob Nicolas Bender,*
Johan Philip Schmeltzer,
Dietrich Six,*
Johan Frank,
Georg Günther,
Peter Günther,
Wendel Lentz,
Johannes Wiest,
Hans Meyer,
Ulrich Segen,?
Johann Rudolph,
Jacob Kalladay,*
Georg Mattheis Weller,
Jacob Hubach,
Michael Ströbel,
Hans Schmauss,?
Joh. Mich. Geisselmann.

----

58) Sept. 20, 1738. Palatines imported in the ship Nancy and Friendship, William Wallace, Commander, from Rotterdam, last from Dover.—Eighty-seven males above sixteen, and one hundred women and children—in all 187.

Sept. 20, 1738. Pfälzer auf dem Schiffe Nancy und Friend=schip, Befehlshaber Wm. Wallace, von Rotterdam über Dover.—Sieben und achtzig Männer über sechzehn Jahre, und ein hundert Weiber und Kinder—im Ganzen 187.

Johan Bübinger,
Jacob Rost,*
Stephan Glaser,

Michael Karcher,
Johannes Kulm,
Lorentz Debong,*

Johannes Negele,
Adam Krebs,*
Philip Stover,
Heinrich Seibel,
Adam Pence,*
Jacob Wallrecht,
Jacob Vollmer,
Jacob Fulmer,*
Tobias Dittis,
Jacob Zorn,
Michael Hubrich,
Jean Granget,
Casper Messner,*
Leopold Jost,
Georg Müller,
Paulus Hime,*
Jacob Hime,*
Jacob Stamler,
Jean Jurdan,
Jacob Durie,*
Nicolas Strauss,
Jean Gausfres,
Johan Wendel Braun,
Valentin Schaller,
Hans Georg Becher,
Theobald Klinger,
Johannes Hannecker,
Abraham Ecker,
Johannes Schreiber,
Hans Peter Rausenberger,*
Christian Meyer,*
Theobald Sterner,*
Hans Georg Buch,
Johannes Schwartzwelder,
Johannes Schaller,
Hans Jacob Huber,
Michael Messner,*
Bartholomäus Bach,
Hans Adam Bach,
Hans Georg Hartman,*
Johannes Schwanner,
Hans Georg Mahler,*

Johannes Stinglie,*
Friederich Pfünder,
Bernhart Matz,
Hans Michael Brauch,
Valentin Pence,*
Christopher Weiss,
Valentin Reintzel,
Abraham Wendel,
Adam Ritter,
Peter Laucks,*
Philip Sowber,*
Jacob Schup,*
Georg Kern,*
Bernard Ege,*
Jacob Ege,
Friederich Karle,
Sebastian Neas,*
Henrich Hermes,
Vite Bechtoldt,
Jacob Wagner,
Lorentz Hautz,*
Marx Schmidt,
Friederich Heyly,*
Martin Speck,
Christian Jung,
Johannes Freyling,*
Georg Michael Boret,*
Joh. Georg Kauffman,
Eberhard Drollinger,
Joh. Ad. Schwartzwälder,
Christoph Wendel Jacoby,
Johan Michel Ege,
Adam Drollinger,
Georg Daniel Henner,*
Johannes Längle,
Johannes Gensemer,
Johannes Friederich,*
Joh. Martin Karcher,
Dan. Friederich Reinetz,?
Hans Georg Bauch,*
Hans Georg König.

59) Sept. 20, 1738. Palatines imported in the ship Nancy, Henry Beach, Commander, from Rotterdam, last from Dover.— 150 passengers.

Sept. 20, 1738. 150 Pfälzer auf dem Schiffe Nancy, Befehligender Henry Beach, von Rotterdam über Dover.

Johannes Brientz,
Johannes Baltzer,
Jacob Lassall,*
Michael Jacob,
Henry Meyer,*
Michael Scholl sen.,
Michael Scholl jr.,*
Christoph Meyer,
Henrich Kemper,
Jacob Meyer,
Johann Meyer,*
Nicolas Onas,*
Joseph Meyer,*
Matheus Leazer,*
Johannes Rollen,*
Jacob Reese,*
Philip Haimes,
Philip Trap,*
Peter Meesmer,*
Jacob Klatz,
Casper Mantz,
Johan Peter Lautermann,
Caspar Hoffmann,
Christian Bergman,

Johannes Betschler,
Antonius Engelbret,
Johannes Ehrholt,
Ernst Hausknecht,
Nicholas Robertus,*
Ulrich Sheydecker,*
Georg Michael Roth,
Johannes Memminger,*
Frantz Ackermann,
Hans Michael Meyer,*
Martin Peter Meyer,*
Martin Springenklee,
Wilhelm Karst,
Joh. Philip Bensch,
Joh. Dieterich Hesselbeck,*
Jacob Pavelieats,*
Johannes Kastinitz,*
Jacob Œsterlin,
Jacob Barth,
Johannes Bosch,
Johannes Hass,
Melchior Bellman,*
Michael Kemperle.

60) Oct. 12, 1738. Palatines imported in the snow Fox, Chas. Ware, Commander, from Rotterdam, last from Plymouth.—95 passengers.

Oct. 12, 1738. 95 Pfälzer auf dem Seeschiffe For, Befehligender Charles Ware, von Rotterdam über Plymouth.

Michael Grün,
Jacob Balmer,
Adam Heisser,
Adam Ullrich,
Philip Hess,

Martin Rein,*
Peter Hesterman,*
Bastian Felte,
Michael Krieger,*
Jacob Stieger,

Adam Ulmer,*
Thomas Reusch,?
Johannes Asper,*
Michael Potz,*
Martin Cludy,*
Hans Diebalt Drog,
Georg Michael Balmer,
Joachim Stöber,
Hans Martin Rein,
Hans Georg Wüst,
Hans Georg Pauth,

Hans Georg Zimerly,
Johannes Goldenberger,*
Hans Georg Frey,*
Jacob Hoffman,*
Christian Hohlmann,
Philip Jacob Bub,
Christopher Bub,
Christian Kauff,
Ulrich Hübster,*
Hans Georg Fetter.

61) Oct. 25, 1738. Palatines imported in the ship Davy,
Wm. Patton, Commander, from Amsterdam, last from Cowes.—
180 passengers.
Oct. 25, 1738. 180 Pfälzer auf dem Schiffe Davy, Comman=
dant William Patton, von Amsterdam über Cowes.

Nicolas Hoffener,
Andreas Born,*
Valentin Alt,
Valentin Nicklaus,*
Christian Schmidt,
Conrad Waldman,*
Simon Lampert,
Ulrich Reichart,*
Georg Stoltz,
Han Adam Jök,*
Baltzer Lampert,
Hans Timmer,*
Michael Lange,*
Jacob Hoffman,*
Gottfried Braun,
Johan Stephen Rausch,*
Johan Jacob Kintzer,
Johan Nicolas Theiss,
Joh. Wendel Seibert,
Johan Friederick Bartz,

Johan Adam Schreyack,*
Johannes Halftzmer,?
Johan Mattheis Scherer,
Johan Casper Stein,*
Johan Philip Wickert,
Johan Henry Fleck,*
Johan Henrich Scherer,
Johan Friederich Stembel,
Johan Valentin Fliegel,*
Johan Georg Bickes,
Georg Lutz,*
Jacob Schram,*
Joh. Geo. Krebs,
Joh. Bert. Sender,?
Georg Schram,*
Hans Michael Tillshöffer,*
Hans Jacob Schmuck,*
Johan Andreas Kauffman,
Johan Nicolas Kienser,*
Johan Jacob Herbert.

62) Oct. 27, 1738. Palatines imported in the ship Saint
Andrew, John Stedman, Master, from Rotterdam, last from
Cowes.—300 passengers.

11*

Oct. 27, 1738. Auf dem Schiffe St. Andrew, Capitain John Stedman, von Rotterdam über Cowes, 300 Pfälzer.

Peter Light,*
Jost Shumacher,
Hannes Hoffer,
Stephan Ackerman,
Conrad Nagel,
Andreas Sin,
Reinhart Bene,*
Martin Dellinger,
Christoph Berger,
Martin Schwartz,
Wilhelm Risser,
Christian Heinrich,
Hans Wisler,
Peter Böhm,
Michael Messer,
Johannes Hertt,
Henrich Sauer,
Christopher Leiss,
Jacob Öttiner,
Andreas Wacker,*
Michael Syder,*
Johannes Ambrecht,*
Vite Ambrecht,*
Johannes Utzman,
Johannes Greber,
Jacob Beyer,
Jacob Stern,
Henrich Hoffman,
Christian Meyer,*
Mattheus Hirt,
Lorentz Kriger,
Johannes Althauss,
Johan Georg Kiehl,
Johann Henrich Ertz,
Frantz Herman Diel,
Manus Sassemanhaus,
Johan Jacob Kehler,
Johan Georg Grauell,
Johan Conrad Bittenbender,
Johan Peter Spiess,
Joh. Christopher Kintzel,
Hans Jacob Künerein,?
Georg Conrad Schreier,
Friederich Buckenmeyer,
Joh. Thomas Eberhart,
Hans Georg Behringer,
Johan Henrich Wald,
Johan Nicolas Stähler,
Hans Jacob Shertzer,
Joh. Arnold Shröder,
Michael Hiltenbrandt,
Philip Martin Füsel,
Georg Bernhart Lauman,
Hans Jacob Kattermann,
Hans Michael Schyver,
Adam Hambrecht,
Michael Scheissle,
Hans Casper Hindertruther,
Hans Jacob Esler,
Hans Jacob Brauss,
John Peter Voyzin,
Georg Nicolas Mayer,
Johannes Althauss,
Johan Christ. Altoch,
Bastian Bremer,
Berdolf Meyer,
Johannes Bosfeld,*
Johannes Hoffman,
Johannes Mercher,
Johan K. Röser,
Daniel Bibighaus,
Johan Georg Althaus,
Conrad Hambrecht,
Hans Martin Waltz,
Johan Georg Weber,
Jost William Blücher.*

Sick †—Johannes Krieve, Casper Hukabach, Vict. Walter,
Christ Wagner, Lewis Vansant, Simon Derrick, Jacob Walter,
Johan Schenkel, Anthon Kinter, Samuel Beem, Peter Yosey,
Christian Sauder, Georg Grevener, Christian Trewett, Henrich
Behn, Elias Bald, Hans Ulrich Katerman, Hans Michael Shef-
fer, Christian Stein Claither, Thomas Everhard, Hans Philip
Smith, Martin Adam Brows, Ulrich Tow, Hans Georg Webber,
Johan Neveling, Georg Bibighaus, Andreas Genberger, Jacob
Welsh, Johan Heinrich Hoffman, Johan Jacob Wagner.

63) Oct. 28, 1738. Palatines imported in the bilander Thistle,
George Houston, Commander, from Rotterdam, last from Cowes.
Forty-two men, thirty-six boys, sixty-four women and girls—
in all 142.

Oct. 28, 1738. Pfälzer auf dem Lastschiffe Thistle, Comman=
dant Georg Houston, von Rotterdam über Cowes.—Zwei und
vierzig Männer, sechs und dreißig Knaben, und vier und sechzig
Weiber und Mädchen—im Ganzen 142.

Jacob Lantz,	Abraham Huntzicker,
Michael Lantz,	Peter Huntzicker,
Johannes Gyser,*	Johannes Kleingenny,*
Peter Gyser,*	Hans Martin Hertz,
Conrad Mehriam,?	Hans Nicolas Ensminger,
Peter Coger,*	Samuel Eberhart Kopp,
Marcus Reminger,*	Gottfried Harlacher,*
Casper Maspeck,*	Hans Peter Lantz,*
Friedrich Müller,	Hans Georg Dietz,*

† Lloyd Zachary and Th. Bond, physicians, stated in a certificate,
under date of October 27, 1738: "We have carefully examined the
state of health of the marines and passengers on board of the ship
St. Andrew, Captain Stedman, from Rotterdam, and found a great
number laboring under a malignant, eruptive fever, and are of the
opinion, they cannot, for some time, be landed in town without the
danger of infecting the inhabitants."—(*Editor.*)

† Die Aerzte Lloyd Zachary und Th. Bond erklären in einem Certificat
vom 27. Octbr. 1738: „Wir haben den Gesundheitszustand der Reisenden
und Seeleute des Schiffes St. Andrew, Capitain Stedman, von Rotter=
dam, genau untersucht, und gefunden, daß eine große Anzahl an einem bös=
artigen, mit Ausschlag verbundenen Fieber leidet, und sind der Ansicht, daß
sie vorderhand nicht an's Land können, ohne die Bewohner anzustecken."—
(Herausgeber.)

Johann Jacob Dietz,
Has Bern Stiganer,*
Hans Adam Fehler,
Joh. Wilhelm Bossler,
Nicolas Liser,
Christian Frelich,*
Ludwig Meier,
Henrich Jung,?
Christian Gysler,
Daniel Müller,
Michael Burn,*
Friederich Brotsman,

Friderich Sculpes,*
Georg Miller,*
Johann Georg Grob,
Hans Jacob Sefüs,*
John Georg Lilie,*
Johann Georg Delpp,
Ludwig Joseph Biehel,
Johan Peter Stegel,
Hans Georg Lintz,
Johan Georg Hess,
Uhlerich Dietz,
Michael Dietz.

Under sixteen:—Peter Dietz, Michael Stockhalter, Daniel Mischler, Wilhelm Stockhalter, Ludwig Ensminger, Philip Christian Kopp, Hans Nicolaus Lantz, Johann Lantz, Michael Kocher, Ulrich Karle Klein, Johann Christian Keyser, Andreas Heinrich Klein, Andreas Seifuss, Hans Christopher Seifuss, Henrich Seifus, Friederich Jacob Jung, Ulrich Jacob Jung, Christopher Henrich Jung, Johannes Jung, Daniel Rehsauer, Hans Adam Braun, Jacob Henrich Brotzmann, Ludwig Kopp, Caspar Stückle, Daniel Skulpius, Hans Peter Lentz, Paul Herbold, Hans Adam Herbold, Jacob Herbold.

☞ After this date, no names of persons under sixteen years old appear in the *Captains' List.*

☞ Nach diesem Datum geben die Capitainslisten die Namen keiner unter sechzehn Jahren alter Personen an.

---

64) Oct. 30, 1738. Palatines imported in the ship Elizabeth, George Hodgson, Commander, from Rotterdam, last from Cowes.—95 passengers.

Oct. 30, 1738. 95 Pfälzer auf dem Schiffe Elisabeth, Commandant Georg Hodgson, von Rotterdam über Cowes.

Ludwig Nicola,
Johannes Mühr,
Daniel Heenig,
Christoph Egen,
Johannes Meisters,
Conrad Neidigh,*
Nicolas Hodely,*
Johannes Carl,

Conrad Renner,*
Lorentz Raus,*
Philip Besa,*
Friederich Kehler,
Mathias Poriger,*
Jacob Frantz,*
Jacob Gern,
John Yeites,*

Matheis Christ,*
Christian Lesch,*
Mattheus Döbler,
Elias Beringer,*
Ludwig Pfantzler,
Jacob Schiltknecht,
Johan Georg Arnold,
Philip Jacob Lendenberger,
Conrad Wannemacher,
John Jacob Kesler,
Matthias Bartholome,*
Hans Ulerich Fritz,*
Hans Georg Petery,*

Georg Ernst Meyer,
John Ludwig Potts,
Hans Conrad Vogelman,*
Hans Jacob Bener,*
Andreas Rothenheffer,
John Adam Kintzel,
Hann Georg Windlinger,
Hans Michael Deinie,
Martin Degenbeck,*
Ulrich Raudenbusch,
Christoph. Theophil. Creutz,
Georg Adam Yegold.*

65) Nov. 9, 1738. Palatines imported in the ship Charming
Nancy, Charles Stedman, Commander, from Rotterdam, last from
Cowes.—200 passengers.

Nov. 9, 1738. 200 Pfälzer auf dem Schiffe Charming Nancy,
Befehlshaber Charles Stedman, von Rotterdam über Cowes.

Jacob Dieterich,*
Markus Tholhaver,*
Jeremias Zämer,*
Abraham Berlin,*
Hans Etimers,*
Samuel Schust,*
Peter Kreitzer,*
Andreas Kreitzer,*
Christoph Abel,*
Andreas Beyerle,
Michael Klein,*
Georg Hatz,*
Christoph Trenkel,*
Stephen Trenkel,*
Jacob Corrt,*
Conrad Fleck,
Christian Miller,*
Hans Bollman,*
Hans Fletiger,*
Nicklas Klagh,*
Ludwig Klotz,

Henrich Meiss,
Hans Siegman,*
John Siegman,*
Ferdinand Dörtzbach,
Christian Miller,*
Henrich Kistner,
Martin Utz,*
Peter Butz,
Jac. Wannemacher,
Hans Geo. Strobel,
Hans Christian Gerber,
Hans Michael Rein,*
Han Georg Reisser,*
Hans Adam Didel,*
Hans Philip Mauerer,*
Hans Jacob Kuntz,*
Hans Jacob Kuntz jr.,*
Georg Michael Kerber,*
Hans Jacob Berlin,*
Georg Frederich Berlin,*
Johan Jacob Müller,

Joseph David Trissler,
Peter Baldesberger,*
Johan Adam Zehman,*
Abraham Hauswirth,
Jacob Hochstetter,*
Abraham Kunzig,*
Christoph Siegman,*
Georg David Boos,*
Hans Georg Holtz,*
Johan Michael Maurer,

Hans Georg Siegman,
Bernhart Siegman,*
John Peter Waltz,*
Johan Baltas Kneerster,
Johan Henry Kepele,*
Hans Georg Schenck,
Joh. Stephan Guthman,
Hans Jacob Shank,*
Hans Henry Pohl,*
Hans Jacob Müller.

66) Dec. 6, 1738. Palatines imported in the snow Enterprize Lynell Wood, Master, from London.—120 passengers.

Dec. 6, 1738. 120 Pfälzer mit dem Seeschiffe Enterprize, Capitain Lynell Wood, von London.

Vincent Pieler,*
Jacob Hertzel,*
Conrad Hertzel,*
Jacob Hertzel jr.,
Jacob Saxer,*
Thomas Lang,
Georg Nodhardt,
Hans Jac. Vander Weyt,
Johannes Richter,
John Georg Weber,*
Jacob Rothweiler,
Jacob Mansinger,*
David Mansinger,*
Melchior Mantzinge,
Fritz Böcker,

Johannes Becker,*
Hans Ruth,*
Henry Berger,*
Martin Greider,*
Casper Horner,*
Jacob Horner,*
Caspar Keller,*
Felix Hausecker,*
Jacob Kestenholtz,
Hans Rudi Bürgi,
Martin Tschudi,
Rudolph Meyerhoffen,*
Hans Jacob Fröli,
Hans Michael Müller,
Matheis Baumgärtner.

Sick—Friederich Erter and Jacob Hertzell.

67) Jan. 10, 1739. Palatines imported in the bilander London, Joshua Pipon, Commander, from London.—60 passengers.

Jan. 10, 1739. 60 Pfälzer mit dem Lastschiffe London, Befehlshaber Joshua Pipon, von London.

Felix Lang,
John Long,*
Henry Long,*

Henry Ortley,*
Jacob Bantz,*
Caspar Widter,

Marcus Koch,*
Jacob Koch,*
Martin Koch,*
Peter Thomas,
Michael Meyer,*
Georg Hans Pfiester,
Georg Henrich Pfiester,
Johannes Gassmann,

John Georg Albert,*
Christopher Koch,*
Michael Sautter,
Johannes Thomas,
Burghart Weaver,*
Christopher Bader,*
Jacob Dispionit.

---

68) Feb. 7, 1739. Palatines imported in the ship Jamaica Galley, Robert Harrison, Commander, from Rotterdam, last from Cowes.—320 passengers.

Feb. 7, 1739. 320 Pfälzer auf dem Schiffe Jamaica Galley, Befehlshaber Robert Harrison, von Rotterdam über Cowes.

Jacob Müller,
Hans Eppli,
Henrich Hauser,
Casper Mayer,*
Peter Huber,
Henrich Müller,
Lenhart Fürer,
Henry Galler,*
Conrad Ackert,*
Heinrich Ackert,
Henry Better,
Ulrich Schmidt,*
Jacob Fehr,
Hans Conrad Rösli,
Johannes Wittersinn,
Henrich Hostman,
Hans Henry Angst,*
Joachim Hanslay,
Rudolph Baumer,*
Hans Henrich Sommer,
Hans Michael Schwinck,
Christopher Müller,
Adam Schwinck,
Rudolph Decker,
Conrad Bauchler,*
Andreas Nabniger,*

Jacob Schwärber,*
Hans Moog,*
Casper Freneir,*
Jacob Kuntz,
Hans Meier,
Jacob Meyer,
Hans Nüsli,
Jacob Hina,*
Henrich Otto,
Henry Glattly sen.,*
Henry Glattly jr.,
Felix Bossert,*
Jacob Bossert,*
Henry Meyer,*
Felix Schutz,*
Rudolph Schutz,
Lawrence Rieger,*
Henry Stally,*
Henry Rokoop,*
Bernard Riga,*
Johannes Trenner,*
Rudolph Kamp,*
Johannes Scheibley,*
Felix Leinbaker,*
Henry Leinbaker,*
Hans Zolinger,*

Jacob Dunkel,*
Jacob Meyer,*
Felix Clatley,*
Henrich Gantz,
Hans Anard,*
Henry Scheibly,*
Henry Brunder,*
Rudolph Shutz,
Henrich Schellenberg,
Jacob Hopman,*
Hans Jacob Hopman,*
Felix Bachman,*
Georg Brunder,*
Christoph Weidman,
Jacob Bucher,*
Heinrich Bachman,
Ulrich Swartzenberg,*
Johannes Boshart,
Hans Ulrich Hoffman,

Jacob Baumann,
Hans Jac. Baumann,
Melchior Dünck,?
Ulrich Bäninger,
Hans Bachman,*
Henry Overholtz,*
Hans Jacob Bäninger,
Hans Ulrich Näff,
Hans Ulrich Meyer,*
Hans Jacob Schaub,
Heinrich Dünck,
Hans Jacob Kern,
Heinrich Kremer,
Ulrich Nüssli,
Jacob Nargang,*
Henry Wert,*
Casper Wideman,*
Felix Frankfelder.*

69) Aug. 27, 1739. Palatines imported in the ship Samuel, Hugh Percy, Commander, from Rotterdam, last from Deal.—340 passengers.

Aug. 27, 1739. 340 Pfälzer im Schiffe Samuel, Befehlshaber Hugh Percy, von Rotterdam über Deal.

Johannes Fischer,*
Caspar Meth,
Johannes Meth,
Henrich Thorwarte,
Michael Adam,
Peter Rule,*
Jean Daniel Bouton,
Johannes Braunmiller,*
Michael Schmöhl,
Johan Leonhart Hortung,
Johannes Schneyder,
Johan Georg Bartmann,
Peter Welschans,
Georg Freeman,*
Matheis Claus,*

Peter Steinman,*
Conrad Hausman,*
Frederick Gerhard,*
William Gerhard,*
Peter Grub,*
Georg Sneyder.*
Johan Lamenick,?
Daniel Kockart,*
Peter Moor,*
Ludwig Geib,*
Jacob Fuchs,
Sebastian Doll,*
Christian Seyfert,
Philip Lentz,
Johannes Beyer,

Paul Michael,*
Michael Hahn,*
Johannes Hahn,
Michael Simon,
Simon Geres,
Peter Schöffer,
Adam Becker,
Michael Miller,
Michael Baur,*
Lorentz Minich,
Abraham Faust,
Jacob Reiss,
Philip Hirsch,
Jacob Wolff,
Michael Miller,*
Christian Schug,
Peter Scholl,
Otto Riedy,
Simon Drom,
Peter Nickom,*
Frederick Nickom,*
Daniel Bürger,
Paul Samsel,
Nicolas Kniesel,*
Peter Mombauer,*
John Michael Bartmann,
Johan Matheis Bartman,
Johan Georg Heyer,
Johan Lorentz Hänsell,
Johannes Ermentraudt,
Johan Philip Ermentraudt,
Joh. Fried. Ermentraudt,
Johan Peter Dressler,
Joh. Daniel Crub,
Johannes Bischoff,
Hans Adam Diehl,
Johan Daniel Diehl,
Carl Adam Diehl,

Joh. Adam Schneider,
Peter Schwenck,
Abraham Hendrick,*
John Nicolas Hendrick,*
Johan Georg Nickel,
Joh. Christ. Zimmerman,
Joh. Henrich Ehrhard,*
David Lautenbach,*
Sebastian Guckert,
Joh. Adam Klein,*
Christian Schöpffer sen.,
Christian Schöpffer jr.,
Philip Jacob Schell,
Johan Henrich Freys,
Johan Peter Priem,
Johan Philip Serfass,
Johan Peter Stüber,
Johan Georg Schauss,
Abraham Schreiner,
Johan Christopher Ruth,
Johan Georg Faust,*
Johan Adam Müller,
Johan Friederich Gabel,
Johan Philip Gabel,
Johan Jacob Kockert,
Michael Mombauer,*
Joh. Nicolas Mombauer,*
Johan Jacob Riedy,
John Peter Riedy,*
Michael Helffenstein,
Casper Doll,*
Christopher Doll,*
Joseph Bederie,*
Joh. Bern. Bederie,
Johan Philip Klein,*
Joh. Adam Gottwals,
Abraham Solomon,*
John Nicolas Bach.*

70) Aug. 27, 1739. Palatines imported in the snow Betsy, Richard Buden, Commander, from Rotterdam, last from Deal.—190 passengers.   12

Aug. 27, 1739. 190 Pfälzer mit dem Seeschiffe Betſy, Com=
mandant Richard Buden, von Rotterdam über Deal.

Nicklaus Leinberger,
Daniel Dalwig,
Johannes Küner,?
Martin Adam,
Caspar Herde,
Martin Barth,
Peter Blaser,*
Friederich Seitz,*
Johannes Martin,*
Georg Becker,*
Jacob Berkel,*
Conrad Becker,
Valentin Becker,
Valentin Ertel,
Andreas Weldi,*
Martin Haag,
Conrad Graff,
Jonas Klein,
Matheis Hertsel,*
Johannes Koch,
Frantz Welchel,*
Jacob Guth,*
Jacob Lantz,
Johannes Back,
Jacob Ernst,
Henrich Strickert,
Michael Becker,
Conrad Unbehand,*
Martin Hoch,*
Jacob Allen,

Hans Jacob Geiger,
Sebastian Unberhent,*
Joh. Melchior Kiener,
Johan Georg Scherer,
Johann Peter Hoffman,
Christian Rodenbach,
Hans Michael Ernst,
Hans Jacob Maron,
Gerh. Henrich Schütz,*
Geo. Wilhelm Höcker,
Johan Daniel Œsterlen,
Johan Daniel Müller,
Johan Hasselwanger,*
Johan Peter Meyer,*
Georg Daniel Schall,*
Johannes Reinhardt,
Johan Michael Roth,
John Henrich Miller,*
Andreas Engelhard,
Friederich Ehrenfeichter,?
Joh. Gottfried Straube,
Pierre Aubertien,
Conrad Hackensmitt,
Georg Friederich Schaffer,*
Jacob Unbehand,*
Valentin Unbehand,*
Hans Martin Bär,*
Johannes Weibell,
Nicklas Leyberger.*

71) Sept. 3, 1739. Palatines imported in the ship Robert
and Alice, Walter Goodman, Commander, from Rotterdam, last
from Deal.—Seventy-eight men, fifty-seven women and eightyeight children—in all 213.

Sept. 3, 1739. Pfälzer kamen auf dem Schiffe Robert und
Alice, Befehligender Walter Goodman, von Rotterdam über

Deal.—Acht und siebenzig Männer, sieben und fünfzig Frauen und acht und achtzig Kinder—im Ganzen 213.

Hans Schantz,	Christian Hirschi,
Peter Riesser,	Hans Jacob Schneider,*
Jost Ebersohl,	Nicolaus Ellenberger,
Michael Hahn,	Frantz Leyenberger,
Jost Diehl,	Hans Jacob Reiff,*
Carl Schallin,	Joh. Martin Hoffmann,
Henrich Steiner,	Johannes Hoffmann,
Johannes Steiner,	Johan Peter Hoffmann,
Jacob Steiner,	Christopher Bollinger,
Caspar Shever,*	Johannes Baumann,
Hans Müller,	Hans Michael Reitenauer,
Samuel Brant,*	Johan Martin Böhler,
Jost Brant,*	Johannes Havecker,*
Peter Bieber,	Joseph Kubhold,*
David Schäffer,	Abraham Böchtel,
Jacob Stambach,*	Christopher Hovell,*
Jacob Smith,*	Johannes Votrin,
David Miller,*	Johannes Beihn,?
Jacob Zerchert,*	Peter Hoffmann,
Matthis Obolt,*	Daniel Hoffmann,
Hans Schants,*	Johan Peter Volck,
Georg Honi,	Abraham Welshans,*
Nicklas Honi,*	Samuel Helburgher,*
Jacob Burgher,*	Henry Bambergher sen.,*
Philip Burgher,*	Henry Bambergher jr.,*
Bernhart Yauser,*	Christian Erhart,*
Benedict Lesseir,*	Christian Ellenberger,
Christian Treit,*	Hans Peter Treit,*
Theobald Cleiver,*	Albrecht Vonderlind,
Nicklas Fisher,*	Philip Martzloff,
Christian Klein,*	Adam Wilhelm,*
Lorentz Brua,	Simon Mendinger,*
Lorentz Biever,*	Hans Adam Geri,
Bastian Klein,*	Joseph Welschhans,
Jacob Gerry,*	Hans Mich. Diebolt,
Theobald Correl,*	Hans Peter Gemberlin,
Johannes Müller,	Hans Mich. Diebolt,*
Benedict Bisser,	Hans Michael Leiser,
Nicklas Lieser,*	Johannes Ebersohl.

72) Sept. 3, 1739. Palatines imported in the ship Friend-ship, William Vittery, Commander, from Rotterdam, last from Deal.—150 passengers.

Sept. 3, 1739. Auf dem Schiffe Friendship, Commandant William Vittery, von Rotterdam über Deal, kamen 150 Pfälzer

Johannes Mayer,
Egidi Mayer,
Michael Kraus,*
Michael Blatner,
Nicklas Schwartz,*
Andreas Hack,
Jacob Franck,
Jacob Kübortz,
Justinus Hoffman,
Stephan Lasch,
Johannes Wolfart,
Conrad Florans,*
Martin Beniger,*
Jacob Loch,
Johannes Loch,
Johannes Nicol,
Martin Leid,*
Jacob Farne,
Henrich Ullerich,
Frantz Brossman,
Michael Trolers,
Veit Miller,
Henrich Heyl,
Conrad Schwartz,
Leonhart Florer,*
Lorentz Fridtel,
Ludwig Hevener,*
Johannes Werner,
Wilhelm Werner,
Martin Jack,*

Johan Philip Illig,
Balthassar Hissong,*
Georg Jacob Burchert,
Georg Ernst Bühler,
Daniel Reinhart,*
Joh. Michael Laub,
Johan Jacob Franck,
Georg Michel Bender,*
Hans Peter Adich,
Johan Conrad Engel,
Anthony Fischbach,?
Philip Stambach,
Georg Michael Wolf,*
Johan Conrad Wolf,*
Gottfried Christian,
Hans Peter Müller,
Peter Zimmerman,
Christian Ehrgott,
Georg Henry Hensell,*
Philip Christoph Werner,
Georg Thomas Heyl,
Hans Thomas Heyl,*
Bernhart Herbolt,
Johan Henrich Rump,
Johan Veit Bachler,*
Henry Bleistein,*
Johan Conrad Philipin,*
Hans Ad. Haushalder,*
Joh. Nicolas Mauerer,
Henry Bleistein.§

73) Sept. 3, 1739. Palatines imported in the ship Loyal Judith, Edward Painter, Commander, from Rotterdam, last from Deal.—315 passengers.

Sept. 3, 1739. 315 Pfälzer mit der Loyal Judith, Comman=
dant Edward Painter, von Rotterdam über Deal.

Henrich Keffer,
Gottfried Mang,
John Georg Shup,
Bartholomæ Ieserding,
Johannes Bollmar,
Carl Heiser,*
Erasmus Frantz,*
Johannes Frantz,*
Bastian Albert,
William Albert,*
Peter Martger,*
Nicklas Weighel,
Nicklas Schild,*
Johannes Bebertz,*
David Fortney,*
Jost Liesser,
Jacob Hough,*
Valentin Shey,*
Peter Kern,
Martin Sebelie,
Nicklas Small,*
Christian Rohrbach,
Jacob Rohrbach,
Bernhart Warth,
Matheas Reemer,*
Nicholas Reemer,
Peter Becker,
Jacob König,
Ludwig Danney,*
Philip Denigh,*
Christian Hütter,
Henry Bough,*
Johannes Rupperter,
Sebastian Jacoby,
Henrich Wolffrum,
Peter Bucher,
Bartel Bucher,
Carl Scholl,*
Georg Laub,

Tobias Weber,
Ludwig Mans,*
David Weisser,
Philip Riss,
Abraham Staudt,
Mathias Felden,*
Martin Schaffner,
Georg Michael Iserding,
Johan Georg Ramseyer,
Johan Nickel Bollmar,
John Peter Lauch,*
Joh. Philip Schneider,
Hans Nickel Klein,
Johan Frantz Albert,
Hans Adam Teetze,*
Hans Adam Haledii,
Johan Christoph Frantz,
Johan Nicklas Shild,*
Johan Georg Threer,*
Johan Peter Wolff,
Johan Nickel Doll,
Johan Peter Hauch,
Caspar Leydäcker,*
Johan Georg Burghart,*
John Adam Small,*
Henry Adam Klein,*
Joh. Nicolas Schatteau,
Johan Henrich Kohde,
Johan Carl Hey,
Johan Adam Reemer, *
Johan Adam Tanny,
Philip Hasselberger,
Johan Jacob Tanny,
Johan Nickel Kleh,
Hans Adam Wolffrum,
Hans Peter Bouger,*
Philip Burghart,*
John Jacob Stuhl,
Adam Schiedenhelm,

12*

Johann Carl Geres,
Johan Nickel Glesser,
Christopher Schmidt,
Nicklas Rodenburger,
Johan Georg Staudt,

Henry Handwerck,*
Nicklaus Hantwerck,
Johann Dehlbauer,
Georg William Thur,*
Hans Jacob Madöri.

NOTE.—On the 26th of December, 1738, a ship of 300 tons was cast
away on Block Island. † This ship sailed from Rotterdam in August,
1738, last from Cowes, England. John Wanton, the Governor of Rhode
Island, sent Mr. Peter Bouse and others from Newport to Block Island,
to see how matters were. On the 19th of January, 1739, these returned to Newport, R. I., reporting that the ship was commanded by
Captain Geo. Long, that he died on the inward passage, and that the
mate then took charge of the ship which had sailed from Rotterdam
with 400 Palatines, destined for Philadelphia, that an exceedingly
malignant fever and flux had prevailed among them, only 105 landing
at Block Island, and that by death the number had been reduced to
90. The chief reason alleged for this great mortality was the bad condition of the water taken in at Rotterdam. It was filled in casks that
before had contained white and red wine. The greater part of the
goods of the Palatines was lost.—*Penn. Gazette, Feb. 8, 1739.*

Anmerkung.—Am 26. December 1738 scheiterte ein Schiff von 300
Tonnen Gehalt an Block Island. † Dieses Schiff segelte im August von
Rotterdam über Cowes in England. John Wanton, Gouverneur von
Rhode Island, sandte Herrn Peter Bouse und andere von Newport nach
Block Island, um den Zustand der Dinge zu erfahren. Am 19. Januar
1739 kehrten diese nach Newport, R. J., zurück und berichteten, daß Capitain Georg Long, der das Schiff befehligte, auf der Herfahrt gestorben
,ei und dann der Steuermann die Leitung des Schiffes übernommen habe,
welches von Rotterdam mit 400 Pfälzern abgefahren und nach Philadelphia
bestimmt gewesen sei; daß ein sehr schlimmes Fieber und Ruhr unter ihnen
geherrscht habe; daß nur 105 auf Block Island landeten und daß der Tod
auch diese auf 90 vermindert habe. Die Hauptursache des Fiebers will
man in dem schlechten Wasser finden, das in Rotterdam gefaßt und in
Fässern, die zuvor rothen und weißen Wein enthielten, aufbewahrt worden
war. Die meisten Güter der Pfälzer gingen verloren.—Pennf. Gazette,
3. Feb. 1739.

74) Dec. 11, 1739. Palatines imported in the ship Lydia,
James Allen, Commander, from London.—75 passengers.

---

† Block Island lies in the Atlantic, south of the State of Rhode Island. It is eight
miles in length and from two to four miles in breadth. It constitutes the township of
New Shoreham, Newport Co., R. I. There are no forests, the only fuel is peat.—I.D.R.

† Block Island liegt im Atlantischen Ocean, südlich vom Staate Rhode Island. Dasselbe ist acht Meilen lang und von zwei bis vier Meilen breit, und bildet das Township New
Shoreham, Newport Co., R. J. Es ist waldlos, die Einwohner brennen Torf.—(J. D. R.)

Dec. 11, 1739. 75 Pfälzer kamen mit dem Schiffe Lydia, Com=
mandant James Allen, von London an.

Ludwig Frick,*
Johannes Frick,*
Andreas Krug,*
Ulrich Steiner,
Henry Seetz,*
Henry Seetz jr.,*
Rudolph Bär,
Henry Grob,*
Caspar Frick,*
Hans Bär,
Heinrich Bär,

Hans Jacob Hauser,
Hans Jacob Free,*
Hans Jacob Grop,*
Johannes Schleiffer,
Johannes Weber,*
Henrich Hobert,*
Johannes Kagie,*
Hans Ulerich Weber,*
Johannes Reittenaur sen.,*
Johannes Reittenaur jr.,*
Joh. Conrad Fromm.

---

75) Sept. 23, 1740. Palatines and Switzers imported in the
ship Friendship, William Vittery, Commander, from Rotterdam,
last from Cowes.—120 passengers.

Sept. 23, 1740. 120 Pfälzer und Schweizer auf dem Schiffe
Friendship, Commandant William Vittery, von Rotterdam über
Cowes.

Johan Christy,
Johann Mann,
Johannes Kapp,
Moritz Milhaus,*
Bast. Schaub,
Wittus Hartweg,
Jacob Lübrick,
Martin Schaup,*
Heinrich Woher,
Henrich Brobeck,*
Gottlieb Briegner,
Hans Frey,*
Martin Rauff,*
Johannes Süss,
Lenhart Witz,
Heinrich Feger,
Jacob Dägen,
Derst Tschopp,
Jacob Hensi,*
Friederich Grieger,

Friederich Gerahn,
Andreas Eschenbach,
Johan Thomas Reinhard,
Rudolph Kürntglein,
Hermanus Heffeling,
Ludwig Wessinger,*
Nicolaus Braubeck,
Nicklaus Steinhauer,
Jacob Steinhauer,
Johannes Seiler,*
Heinrich Spohnhauer,
Hans Georg Schneider,*
Henrich Unkenbacher,
Hans Jacob Fetterley,?
Hans Slebacher,*
Jacob Slebacher,*
Georg Anastasius Bern,
Hans Lebemith,
Marx Hüfrefege.?

76) Sept. 27, 1740. Palatines imported in the ship Lydia, James Allen, Commander, from Rotterdam, last from Dover.—In all 180.

Sept. 27, 1740. 180 Pfälzer mit dem Schiffe Lydia, Commandant James Allen, von Rotterdam über Dover.

Simon Hirsch,*
Christian Weber,*
Christian Holenberger,*
Arnold Schneider,*
Nicklas Couwald,
Johannes Wil. Beck,
Johannes Arnold,*
Christian Coos,
Peter Altonius,*
Philip Fritz,*
Jacob Keyser,*
Henry Keyser,*
Michael Eichhart,
Jost Lang,
Matheis Käffer,*
Philip Petry,*
Philip Tülman,
Daniel Schneider,*
Daniel Lucas,*
Christoph Geist,
Matthias Fuchs,
Wilhelm Lang,*
Johann Ditrich,*
Johan Teis,
Johannes Kichler,
Arnold Schuman,*
Caspar Wirth,*
Nicklas Beyer,*
Peter Lorentz,*
Peter Lamm,*
Henrich Reussen,

Johan Georg Crässmann,
Johan Georg Lohss,
John Georg Torenberger,*
Johan Herman Lehr,*
Johan Jacob Hollenberger,
Johan Jost Presen,
Johan Wilhelm Folberg,*
Johan Henry Beck,*
Johan Jacob Beck,*
Johan Henrich Tiewes,
Christian Shwaigermeyer,*
Peter Henry Shook,*
Johan Michael Jacks,*
Johan Nickel Beckeles,
Johan Fried. Althoniuss,
Johan Adam Fritz,*
Ludwig Hartenstein,
Johan Peter Loie,
Johan Georg Brosius,
Christopher Fuchs,
Valentin Pracht,*
Elias Gottlieb Stein,
Johannes Berckhyser,*
Johann Gerhart Schneider,
Johann Adam Schneider,*
Johan Peter Schuman,*
Wilhelm Heldebrand,*
Johannes Kagelberger,*
Johann Simon Denner,
Abraham Kirchhoff,
Johann Jost Plöhger.

---

77) Sept. 30, 1740. Palatines imported in the ship Samuel and Elizabeth, William Chilton, Commander, from Rotterdam, last from Deal, England.—In all 206.

Sept. 30, 1740. 206 Pfälzer auf dem Schiffe Samuel und
Elisabeth, Commandant William Chilton, von Rotterdam über
Deal, England.

Frantz Epgardt,
Johannes Schnog,
Peter Berger,
Johannes Hoffman,
Joh. Peter Anders,
Paul Dünschman,
Johan Christ Kräffeller,
Johannes Theis Fiser,*
Johan Christ. Schmidt,
Johan Christ. Frantz,
Johan Jacob Fischer,
Christ. Peter Fischer,*
Martin Schmidt,
Philip Bosser,*
Christian Kirbach,
Georg Wilhelm,
Friederich Löhner,
J. Adam Luckenbach,
Joh. Georg Rörich,
Joh. Ernst Rörich,
Joh. Moritz Kohn,*
Herman Betzer,*
Johannes Hadorn,
Henricius Schneider,
Jost Kremer,
Theis Schneider,
Conrad Hirsch,*
Thomas Schneider,

Joh. Peter Schneider,
Joh. Henry Arth,?
Johannes Wergraf,
Christian Schumacher,
Johan Wilhelm Klein,
Carl Jacob Weymer,
Johan Adam Meyer,*
Johan Adam Schneider,
Johan Adam Müller,
George Wilhelm Kirbach,*
Johan Friedrich Schneider,
Johannes Brandenbürg,
Johan Hubrecht Dimott,*
Joh. Henrich Luckenbach,
Johan Simon Erlegner,
Johan Georg Eller,
Joh. Gerhart Luckenbach,
Joh. Adam Hammacher,
Joh. Hubrecht Hammacher,
Johan Peter Schreiner,
Johann Theis Müller,
Johan Adam Bender,*
Joh. Peter Shoemaker,*
Joh. Peter Harhaussen,*
Johan Adam Rörich,
Johan Bertram Klein,
Johan Simon Hüller,*
Hans Henry Müller.*

78) Nov. 25, 1740. Palatines imported in the ship Loyal
Judith, Lovell Paynter, Commander, from Rotterdam, last from
Deal.—265 passengers.

Nov. 25, 1740. 265 Pfälzer kamen mit dem Schiffe Loyal
Judith, Commandant Lovell Paynter, von Rotterdam über Deal.

Anthony Keller,*
Christian Brentzer,

Wilhelm Saur,*
Henry Thielbon,*

Andreas Beck,
Conrad Schneider,
Georg Viantt,
Jacob Kichler,
Simon Wehr,
Lenhart Gerhart,
Wilhelm Ohl,
Johann Wolff,
Henry Wagner,*
Friederich Becker,*
Peter Sheetz,
John Henry Legire,*
Johan Wilhelm Oster,
Johan Abraham Haas,
Johan Jacob Theobalth,
Andreas Refschneider,
Wilhelm Jost Becker,
Johan Baltzer Hoffmann,
Johan Nicolas Zöll,
Justus Lindeman,
Henrich Lindeman,
Johannes Keilman,
Wilhelm Schmidt sen.,
Wilhelm Schmidt jr.,
Johannes Schmidt,
Valentin Schneider,
Jacob Lindeman,
Heinrich Brem,
Jacob Breem,*
Valentin Krimm,*
Jacob Krimm,*
Ulrich Hartman,
George Conrad,*
Adam Maurer,*
Conrad Wishong,*
Peter Becker,
Carle Gro,
Johannes Werbel,
Mathias Schmidt,
Peter Grauel,*
Conrad Schmidt,

Johannes Adam,
Johannes Wagner,
Frantz Jost,
Caspar Boner,
Andreas Schmidt,
Johannes Diehl,
Philip Kauff,
Johannes Ley,
Jacob Wolff,
Johannes Becht,
Johannes Frantz,
Conrad Schney,
Philip Wishong,
Jean Ganty,
Peter Sell,*
Johan Jacob Koch,*
Johan Georg Schneider,
Johan Nicolas Bröder,
Johan Friedrich Engel,
Johan Wilhelm Betz,
Johan Dieterich Becker,
Johan Bernhard See,
Johan Abraham Bollenbacher,
Johan Nicolas Fey,*
Johan Ulrich Scheier,
Johan Jacob Schertel,
Johannes Müller,
Johann Michael Busch,
Johan Peter Diehl,
Johan Peter Mohr,
Herman Heyman,
Johan Friederich Loritz,
Friederich Wilhelm Nagel,
Joh. Georg Gottschalck,*
Isaac Dieterich,
Johan Peter Wolff,
Johann Georg Epple,
Johan Georg Meier,
Johan Wilhelm Esich,
Johan Nicklas Haubt,
Johan Peter Hans,

Johan George Esling,*
Johan Peter Müller,

Joh. Georg Seyter,
Jacob Sell.*

79) Dec. 3, 1740. Palatines imported in the ship Robert and Alice, Walter Goodman, Master, from Rotterdam, last from Cowes.—185 passengers.

Dec. 3, 1740. 185 Pfälzer kamen mit dem Schiffe Robert und Alice, Capitain Walter Goodman, von Rotterdam über Cowes.

Johannes Seydel,*
Johann Eader,*
George Zohnleyter,*
Andreas Höller,
Andreas Sheyb,*
Henry Steiner,
Frederick Hanet,*
Philip Balthaser Crössman,
Johan Henrich Crössman,
Johan Wilhelm Stadellmaner,
Johan Georg Kramer,
Christian Anderbach,
Hans Michel Holschuh,
Johan Jacob Radge,
Johannes Brein,
Peter Reppert,*
Christoph Magel,*
Daniel North,*
Blastius Bear,*
Antoni Feltman,
Joseph Walther,
Johannes Vogel,*
Andreas Bentz,
Johannes Bückell,
Johannes Göttlich,
Henrich Göttlich,*
Rubert Reinbracht,*
A. Kurtz,
Henry Hanroth,*
Philip Shamele,*

Jacob Becker,*
Jacob Cress,*
Jacob Barthel,
Johannes Bruch,
Peter Grantzer,*
Joh. Caspar Œther,
Hans Theobald Grim,*
Johan Jacob Diemer,
Johan Henrich Neuman,
Johann George Schmit,*
Johan Adam Gass,
Johan Jost Hensel,
Joh. Wilhelm Volprecht,
Joh. Friederich Fichthelm,
Hans Jacob Green,*
Johan George Smitt,*
Johann Jacob Zimmerman,
Johan Philip Heileger,
Geo. Michael Lingeveldt,*
Wilhelm Moritz Vitel,
Johann Georg Rauch,
Johan Melchior Hangerer,
Christoffel Hillebrandt,
George Philip Cress,*
Conrad Schweighauser,
Hans Martin Conrad,*
Johan Christoph Beserer,
Johan Nicklaus Hippel,
Johan Peter Sebolt.

80) Dec. 3, 1740. Palatines imported in the ship Samuel, Hugh Percy, Captain, from Rotterdam, last from Deal.—175 passengers.

Dec. 3, 1740. 175 Pfälzer kamen mit dem Schiffe Samuel, Capitain Hugh Percy, von Rotterdam über Deal.

Nicklas Kuntz,
Heinrich Wolff,
Johannes Schreiber,
Conrath Schneiss,
Johann König,
Georg Born,
Nicklas Zöller,*
Peter Spengler,*
Peter May,
Jacob Maurer,
Paulus Huey,
Henry Giessler,*
Georg Keyser,
Samuel Taner,*
Wilhelm Marx,
Philippus Küpperter,
John Adam Stump,
Jacob Schuster,*
Caspar Klöckner,*
Johan Henrich Fröhlich,
Adam Schneider,
Georg Bombach,
Johan Nicolas Schwingel,
Johan Nickel Schmidt,
Johannes Stool,*
Gottfried Walter,*
Georg Schwingel,
Johan Nicolas Zerfass,
Parthal Osterman,*
Thomas Dörner,
Nicklas Gruber,*
Philip Leaber,*
Jacob Fuchs,*
Georg Maus,
Andreas Miller,
Philip Kreber,
Henrich Kreber,
Bastian Vey,*
Joh. Peter Werner,*
Peter Bischoff,
Urban Aschenbrenner,
Abraham Schellberg,*
Johannes Zimmermann.
Johan Nicolas Wuff,
Joh. Nicolas Zimmermann.

Sick—Ludwig Vivel, Peter König, Jacob Ruperter, William Bishof, Thomas Fuse, Isaac Hencker, Joseph Neigh, Adam Bushart, Jacob Bley, Georg Kreger, Valentin Singrove.

Dead—Mathias Klein.

NOTE.—During 1739 and 1740 a number of *Moravians* came from Georgia into Pennsylvania, and settled at Bethlehem and Nazareth. For a list of these see ADDENDA, B.

Anmerkung.—Während 1739 und 1740 kam eine Anzahl Herrnhuter von Georgia nach Pennsylvanien und ließ sich zu Bethlehem und Nazareth nieder. Abbenda B enthält eine Namenliste.

81) May 30, 1741. Palatines imported in the snow Francis and Ann, Thomas Coatam, Master, from Rotterdam, last from St. Christophers.†

Mai 30, 1741. Pfälzer kamen auf dem Seeschiffe Francis und Ann, Capitain Thomas Coatam, von Rotterdam über St. Christophers.†

Peter Holl,
Geo. Philip Clem,*
Johannes Immel,
Jacob Kipper,
Martin Bittner,*
Michael Bigler,
Johan Peter Herbel,

George Adam Koch,*
Hans George Koch,*
Samuel Georg Tössler,
Johan Conrad Schmidt,
Georg Adam Ernst,
Johan Wendel Hornung.

82) Sept. 23, 1741. Palatines imported in the ship Marlborough, Thomas Bell, Master, from Rotterdam, last from Cowes.

Sept. 23, 1741. Pfälzer kamen mit dem Schiffe Marlborough, Capitain Thomas Bell, von Rotterdam über Cowes.

Peter Kuhn,*
Joh. Jacob Ick,
Ulrich Naffzir,
Johannes Ladsher,*
Friedrich Meyer,*
Jacob Hill,
Johan Ludwig German,
Johan Friederich Freyss,
Johann Wilhelm Welsch,
Johan Jacob Kuhn,
Johan Georg Wagner,
Johan Nicklas Beyer,*
Simon Vogelgesang,
Friedrich Zöllner,
Michel Kreischer,
Michael Seipert,*
Peter Staudt,
Lenhart Kleim,*

Bernhard Kapp,
Daniel Simon,
Johannes Doll,
Johannes Meyer,*
Jost Gasserd,
Philip Kuntz,
Jacob Bernhartt,
Peter Deiss,*
Abraham Hess,
Johannes Kühl,
Georg Ruth,
Nicklas Martin,
Philip Lein,
Nicolas Süss,
Peter Brent,
Michael Swyng,*
Johannes Kleim,
John Nicholas,*

† One of the British West India Islands.—*Editor.*
† Eine der britisch-westindischen Inseln.—Herausgeber.

13

Johannes Horn,
Caspar Modus,*
Jacob Gerdheir,*
Peter Kieffer,*
Daniel Kieffer,*
Michael Neumer,
Johan Jacob Hegel,
Johan Michael Welsch,*
Johan Nickel Œhl,
Johan Daniel Gröninger,
Georg Jacob Glug,
Johan Jacob Nicolaus,
Joh. Wilhelm Engelman,
Johan Adam Kascht,
Johannes Worscheber,
Johannes Deiss,
Joh. Jacob Kemper,
Johan Peter Engel,

Johannes Dielbohn,
Friederich Bals Ratsmith,*
Johannes Kuhn,
Joh. Ludwig Hen. Kohl,
Peter Bartoleme,*
Johan Tobias Rühm,
Melchior Stahlman,
Hans Nicholas Smith,*
Henry Bernhart,*
Joh. Nicolaus Schmucker,
Philippus Schneider,
Anthonius Œhler,
Johan Adam Kamp,
Joh. Ludwig Hanckstein,
John Jacob Personz,*
Johan Jacob Dietz,
Johan Karl Fishahason,*
Johan Carl Metz.*

---

83) Sept. 26, 1741. Palatines imported in the ship St Mark,
—— Wilson, Master, from Rotterdam, last from Cowes.

Sept. 26, 1741. Pfälzer kamen mit dem Schiffe St· Mark,
Capitain —— Wilson, von Rotterdam über Cowes.

Nicklas Gebhard,*
Peter Criling,*
Conrad Stellweg,?
Mathias Fols,*
Jacob Matteis,
Wilhelm Müller,
Mattheus Borich,
Johann Arnold Steeg,
Johann Nicklaus Steeg,
Hans Philip Auert,
Johannes Von Erdre,?
Johan Henrich Müller,
Johan Peter Bernhart,
Johan Henrich Müncker,
Conrad Funck,
Philip Mees,*
Georg Davahrt,

Ernst Braun,
Nicklas Seyler,*
Johannes Wieder,
Wilbertus Lutz,
Ulrich Weis,*
Johannes Scherrer,
Christoffel Stumb,
John Harst,*
Peter Jacob,
Michael Folber,*
Hans Amweg,
Philip Swiger,*
Nickel Mensch,*
Friederich Hertzog,
Martin Becker,
Philip Hass,
Michael Riess,

Johannes Corell,
Martin Edenborn,*
Adam Rener,*
Peter Hoffman,
Hans Moore,*
George Yearst,*
Conrad Funck,
Martin Leey,*
Cenes Mook,*
Abraham Dencey,*
Philip Yeist,*
Henrich Stahl,
Johannes Scheider,
John Shider,*
Jacob Gerhardt,*
Peter Gaberd,*
Johan Johnloft,*
Philip Kalbach,
Conrad Dolch,*
William Prickes,*
Henrich Kroh,
Michael Geest,*
Johannes Engel,
Lorentz Eranmach,
Johan Herman Gell,
Johan Martin Spegt,
Joh. Adam Von Erden,*
Johan Friederich Heinrich,
Johan Adam Schmahl,
Johann Conrad Michell,
Johann Starffinger,*
Johan Friederich Römer,

Johan Wilhelm Hoffmann,
Just Lorentz List,
Joh. Adam Gundacker,
Joh. Walther Fischbach,
Johan Georg Schmaltz,
Johan Caspar Ahls,
Johan Nickel Steinert,
Johan Philip Beick,
Hendrick Korst,*
Johan Georg Metz,
Johan Jacob Corell,
Johan Samuel Mühl,*
Hans Jacob Meltzer,*
Johann Philip Mann,
Johann Henrich Mauerer,
Leonhard Korn,
Johann Niclas Hauer,*
Johannes Bockius,
Friederich Kleppert,
Johann Jost Schneider,
Johannes Kerstrich,
Johann Vallstapp,
Jacob Stoffelbein,
Johannes Wehler,
Johannes Schaum,
Johannes Rehwalt,
Christian Arhndarff,
Adam Schreiber,
Michael Dreydel,
Philip Hoffman,
Johann Christian Orendorff,
Johann Georg Warth.

84) Oct. 2, 1741. Palatines imported in the ship St. Andrew, Charles Stedman, Master, from Rotterdam.

Oct. 2, 1741. Pfälzer kamen mit dem Schiffe St. Andrew, Capitain Charles Stedman, von Rotterdam.

Johan Conrath,
Peter Buhl,
Peter Voigt,

Nicklaus Jungblud,
Johannes Butterweh,
Jacob Albrecht,

Ulrich Schömig,
Philip Ulmer,
Jacob Gerges,?
Michael Will,
Jacob Worst,
Paulus Michael,
David Delatter,*
Nicolaus Bauer,
Hans Uhlerich,
Johannes Pfeil,
Conrad Giesy,*
Jacob Meyer,
Johan Peter,
Johan Philip,
Frans Grau,
Jacob Pfeiffer,
Jacob Klein,
Wilhelm Gauff,
Johannes Roll,*
Nicklas Neezer,*
Peter Müller,
Jacob Aseby,*
Jacob Meyer,
Wilhelm Ludwig Becker,
Daniel Henrich Elch,?
Friederich Christian Becker,

Carl Jung Eurvett,?
John Michael Behler,*
Joh. Georg Daniel Kübortz,
Carl Philip Wirtz,
Johan Philip Ebärtz,
Augustus Kauffmann,
Hans George Lägner,*
Johannes Anthoni,
Joh. Michel Prenger,
Ulrich Stambach,
Hans Philip Hoffman,*
Reinhart Böckney,
Rudolff Steinman,*
George Caspar Hälle,*
Lorentz Schwenk,*
Johan Moritz Dupel,*
Gotfried Orbig,*
Joh. Nic. Schappert Bernhart,
Bernhart Lachart,
Valentin Sees,*
Hans Rutschmann,
Jacob Saltzberger,*
Heinrich Weissmüller,
Simon Henrich Höcker,
Johan Henrich Walter,
Hans Surber.*

---

85) Oct. 12, 1741. Palatines imported in the ship Friend-ship, Alex. Thomas, Master, from Rotterdam, last from Cowes.

Oct. 12, 1741. Pfälzer kamen mit dem Schiffe Friendship, Capitain Alex. Thomas, von Rotterdam über Cowes.

Paulus Müller,
David Dreher,
Jacob Diehl,
George Hirt,*
Jacob Herth,
Joh. Geo. Wilhelm Berger,
Andreas Hubert,*
Johan Peter Braun,
Wilhelm Erhart,*

Johannes Erhart,
Adam Enler,
Valtein Scheck,
Matheis Schreth,
Jacob Lies,
Peter Haldriter,*
Daniel Hubert,*
George Hubert,*
Nicklas Bundry,*

Nicklas Klan,*
Carl Schneyder,*
Wilhelm Antes,*
Valentin Embs,
Cassimir Wessel,*
Friederich Helwig,
Peter Jung,
Jacob Simon,*
Adam Weber,
Jacob Dinges,
Peter Baal,*
Peter Durny,*
Johan Handeise,
Johannes Melchior,
Andreas Kranmer,
Joh. Jacob Schäck,
Hans George Haldriter,*
Philip Haldriter,*

Caspar Rauland,*
Nicklas Holtzleeder,
Johan Georg Embs,
Johan Caspar Schneider,
Johann Georg Koch,
Valentin Hohwerder,
Johan Nickel Schuster,
Johan Wilhelm Hoster,
Johannes Fiehman,
Wilhelm Zimmer,*
Simon Jacob Boor,
Johan Georg Riegel,
Joh. Conrad Lechleiter,
Daniel Korstmann,
John Philip Oliger,
Johan Jacob Schleiff,
Joh. Christoff Schmuckheyde.

---

86) Oct. 17, 1741. Palatines imported in the ship Molly, Thos. Oliver, Commander, from Rotterdam, last from Deal.

Oct. 17, 1741. Pfälzer kamen mit dem Schiffe Molly, Commandant Thos. Oliver, von Rotterdam über Deal.

Joseph Hobian,
Michael Miller,*
Martin Giese,*
Michael Boracker,*
Jacob Rimli,
Wilhelm Schwarm,*
Veldin Weissig,*
Daniel Gillmann,
Peter Godfried,*
Johannes Müller,
Peter Mantz,*
Daniel Ecron,
Michael Spindel,
Christoffel Heine,*
Michael Simon,*
Johann Georg Druck,
Johann Adam Scheib,

John Nicklas Klein,*
Johan Lenhart Beyer,
Phil. Conrad Weydner,
Johan Jacob Moltz,
Johannes Stockschleger,
Christian Commens,*
Bartolomæ Conselman,*
John Frederick Schipp,*
Johan Simon Hein,
Johannes Mattheis,
Johannes Zellman,
Johan Michel Keyser,
Michael Höpster,
Matheus Kilian,
Philip Daum,
Herman Sauer,*
Jacob Engelman,

13*

Johan Ruddiss,
Daniel Zinck,*
Michel Seuberlich,
Martin Regelman,
Lenhart Lämmer,*
Peter Krammer,
Alex. Stockschleder,
Henrich Becker,
Samuel Spiegel,
Joh. Michel Herb,
Diterich Shweyzey,
Conrad Riegelman,
John Peter Siesler,*
Matheus Meyer,*
Bernhart Switzig,
Joh. Peter Bender,
John Geo. Hubeny,*
Hans Georg Sterrles,
Andreas Unger,*

Johan Georg Küntzel,
Sebastian Herlieman,
Johan Jacob Gerst,
Jacob Engellmann,
Johan Jacob Kron,
Johan Peter Eitergall,
Hans Michel Schwartz,
Joh. Henrich Schmitt,
Johan Michel Krämer,
Johan Henrich Weydner,
Johan Michael Weicker,
Georg Philip Rühl,
Hans George Riegelman,*
Johan Friederich Klein,
Johan Christophel Stimbi,
Johan Wilhelm Saner,
John Lenhart Siesler,*
Johann Caspar Gress,
Johan Jacob Decker.

87) Oct. 26, 1741. Palatines imported in the snow Molly,
John Cranch, Master, from Rotterdam, last from Deal.

Oct. 26, 1741. Pfälzer kamen mit dem Seeschiffe Molly,
Capitain John Cranch, von Rotterdam über Deal.

Peter Schmitt,
Jacob Schmid,
Jacob Theis,
Henrich Pfeil,
Johannes Hess,
Georg Funk,*
Stephan Rüb,
Friederich Ott,
Georg Keck,
Joachim Berger,
Peter Meyer,*
Michael Jung,
Peter Simon,
Baltzer Hamman,?
Anthony Adam,*
Peter Metz,*

Johan Heinrich Gräff,
Johan Wilhelm Huey,
John George Meylander,*
Johan Peter Herbach,
Johann Peter Haass,
Joh. Geo. Wilhelm Küsterman,
Joh. Theobald Brauchler,
Valentin Benedict Hardt,
Johan Michael Süs,
Johannes Metzler,
Hans Adam Sontag,
Johan Philip Desch,
Hans Peter Hess,
Hans Dewald Siber,*
John Gothart Armbriest,*
Joh. Henrich Daniel,

Peter Weber,*   Theobald Weber,
Johannes Ermel,*   Hans Adam Cresman.*

---

88) Nov. 7, 1741. Palatines imported in the snow Thane of
Fife, William Weems, Master, from Rotterdam, last from Aberdeen, Scotland.

Nov. 7, 1741. Pfälzer kamen mit dem Seeschiffe Thane of
Fife, Capitain William Weems, von Rotterdam über Aberdeen,
Schottland.

Gabriel Jung,   Johann Bolander,*
Jacob Fortine,   Johan Adam Kircher,*
George Creim,*   Vallentin Esman,*
Carl Grim,   Valentin Winterstein,
Adam Grim,*   John Henry Bob,*
Johannes Boss,*   Anthony Schneyder,*
Matteas Kolb,*   Lenhart Zarburger,*
Ludwig Essig,   John Nicklas Kelch,*
Peter Semier,*   John George Weyman.*
John Sebastian,*

---

89) Nov. 20, 1741. Palatines imported in the ship Europa.

Nov. 20, 1741. Pfälzer, die mit dem Schiffe Europa anlangten.

Joh. Mich. Marx,   Jacob Lomger,*
Paulus Furmann,   Conrad Cornman,
Paul Furman sen.,*   Philip Wirbel,*
Dewald Shanck,*   Henrich Ensminger,
Caspar Rubert,*   Joh. Christian Hausknecht,
Johan Jost,   John Daniel Begly,*
Peter Walmer,*   Johan Paul Bauer,
Henry Kuhntz,*   Hans Arnold Meyer,
Henrich Udry,   Henrich Christman,
Johannes Henrich,   Johan Jacob Löser,
Konradt Rahm,   Johan Christian Löser,
Simon Gross,   Hans Niclas Eisenhauer,
Theobald Gross,   Johan Peter Eisenhauer,
Ludwig Breit,   Johann Isenhauer,*
Andreas Lann,*   Hans George Shneyder,*
Jacob Shneyder,*   Michael Haberstück,
Philip Crentz,*   Henry Nicklas Hostein,*

Johann Nicolaus Ander,
Johannes Corell,
Joh. Christoph Wagner,
Johan Peter Schreiber,
Nicolaus Wagner,

Johan Andreas Krieger,
Philip Nair,*
Peter Main,
Johan Peter Krieger,
Johann Henrich Krieger.

NOTE.—*Count Nicolaus Ludwig Zinzendorf* arrived at New York in the latter part of November, 1741. For a full account of *Zinzendorf,* see *Rupp's History of Northumberland County,* p. 391, and *History of Northampton County,* pp. 79, 86.

Anmerkung.—Graf Nicolaus Ludwig von Zinzendorf kam in New York gegen Ende November 1741 an. Eine vollständige Behandlung über Zinzendorf findet der Leser in Rupp's Geschichte von Northumberland Co., S. 391, und Northampton Co., S. 79, 86.

---

90) May 28, 1742. Foreigners imported in the snow Catharine, —— Gladman, Commander.

Mai 28, 1742. Fremde, die mit dem Seeschiffe Katharine, Commandant Gladman, angekommen sind.

Johannes Brücker,
David Bischoff,
Michel Miesch,?
Henry Almers,
Nathanael Seidel,
Jacob Lischy, *a*
George Wiessener,*

Matheus Wittgie,
Georg Kast,
Georg Emder,
Georg Schneider,
Joseph Möller,
Friederich Post, *b*
Gottlieb Petzold,

---

a This was the *Rev. Jacob Lischy,* a Moravian minister, who officiated for several years as a German Reformed minister in York, Pa.— See *Rupp's History of York County,* p. 694.

a Dies war Pastor Jacob Lischy, ein Herrnhuter Geistlicher, welcher einige Jahre als deutsch-reformirter Pfarrer in York, Pa., amtete.—Siehe Rupp's Geschichte von York Co., S. 694.

b Post was an unassuming, honest German, a Moravian. In 1743 he accompanied the missionaries Pyrläus and Senseman to Shekomeko, an Indian village bordering on Connecticut, where he married a baptized Indian woman. Having preached the Gospel among the Indians for several years, he was maltreated by being arrested at Albany and imprisoned in New York. After his liberation, he returned to Europe, 1749. He afterwards returned to Pennsylvania, and while at Bethlehem was prevailed upon, 1758, to carry a message from the Government to the Delaware, Shawanese and Mingo Indians in the West.— See *Post's Journal of* 1758 in *Rupp's History of Western Pennsylvania. Edition of* 1846.—(*Editor.*)

John Adolph Meyer,
Johan Brandmüller,
Paul Daniel Bryzelius,
Heinrich Joachim Sensemann,
Michael Tannenberger,
Johan Georg Hardtner,
Johann Philip Mauerer,

Johann Leonhart Schnell,
Christian Werner,
Joh. Christoph Heyne,
Johan Georg Heydecker,
Johann Reinhard Rona,
Johann Michael Huber.

91) Aug. 25, 1742. Foreigners imported in the brigantine Mary, John Mason, Master, from Rotterdam, last from Cowes.

Aug. 25, 1742. Frembe kamen mit bem Schnellfahrer Mary, Capitain John Mason, von Rotterbam über Cowes.

Valentin Kraft,
Daniel Etter,
Johannes Seivert,*
Andreas Straub,*
Martin Arnold,*
Jacob Reeder,*
Martin Schmidt,
Georg Kiester,
Peter Burgener,
Rupertus Bender,
Peter Welch,
Hans Trachsell,
Abraham Liettel,*
Jacob Nägli,

Johann Philip Bertz,
Johan Michael Zeister,
John Henry Kookes,*
Constantinus Stilling,
Hans George Sneyder,*
Johan Friedrich Ricker,
Christoffer Danner,*
Jacob Baumann,
Georg Friederich Heranus,
Johannes Bergerhoff,
Gerret van Kouten,
Jan De Mars,
Peter Burckner,*
Christian Bugner.

92) Sept. 3, 1742. Foreigners imported in the ship Loyal Judith, James Cowie, Master, from Rotterdam, last from Cowes.

b Post war ein bescheidener, ehrlicher Deutscher und Herrnhuter. 1743 begleitete er die Missionare Pyrläus und Sensemann nach Shekomeko, einem Indianerdorf, das an Connecticut grenzt, wo er auch eine getaufte Indianerin heirathete. Nachdem er den Indianern mehrere Jahre lang das Evangelium verkündigt hatte, wurde er durch Gefangennehmung zu Albany und Einsperrung in New York mißhandelt. Nach seiner Befreiung kehrte er 1749 nach Europa zurück. Einige Zeit nachher besuchte er Pennsylvanien wieder und während seines Aufenthalts in Bethlehem bewog ihn 1758 die Regierung, eine Botschaft den Delaware, Shawanese und Mingo Indianern im Westen zu überbringen.—Siehe Post's Journal von 1758 in Rupp's Geschichte vom Westlichen Pennsylvanien. Ausgabe von 1846.— (Herausgeber.)

Sept. 3, 1742. Frembe kamen mit bem Schiffe Loyal Jubith, Capitain James Cowie, von Rotterdam über Cowes.

Bernhart Janson,
Kilian Fischel,
Johan Fishel,*
Georg Metzger,
Gottfried Schnelie,
Friederich Keher,*
Wendel Vetter,
Jacob Berentpeller,*
Daniel Lang,
Johannes Schultz,
Johannes Mertens,
Dieterich Hobbach,
Reymund Laufflenter,*
Johannes Dernheimer,
Simon Wischhan,
Friederich August,
Johannes Lehn,
Felbert Sochus,
Simon Jonas,
Jacob Taubetishel,*
Johan Jacob Winterehle,
Johan Peter Jung,
Johan Jacob Schühler,
Johan Georg Weninger,?
Wilhelm Anspach,
Friederich Schollenberger,
Johan Jacob Sheer,*
Johan Paul Weytzel,
Johann Henrich Dörr,
Johann Michel Sternn,
John Adam Turinger,*
Johann Jacob Rath,
Henricus De Hooff,
Friederich Germerjung,
Joh. Andreas Strassbürger,
Henrich Wolffskehl,
Philip Henrich Erben,

Johann Henrich Wagner,
Theobald Nabinger,
Johannes Lorentz,
Philip Cronenberger,
Peter Frey,
Johannes Rab,
Peter Klein,
Ludwig Schott,
Johannes Rühl,
Zacharias Heller,*
Friederich Pfeil,
Johannes Fissel,
Christofiel Heucher,
Valentin Grün,
Johannes Domie,
Lorentz Place,
Johannes Rühl,
Peter Barth,
David Schäll,*
Johan Jacob Grub,
Johann Georg Jäger,
Johann Lehnhart Führ,
Johannes Peter Frey,
Paulus Westenberger,?
Johann Michel Paulis,
Johann Baltzer Schäffer,
Johann Valentin Gloninger,
Hans Georg Shaffer,
Samuel Fortinnix,
Christoph Plantz,
Christoph Bergman,
Ludwig Metzger,
Conrath Hartman,*
Johannes Schumacher,
Christoffel Geller,
Jonas Furtuly,*
Johann Simon Gräff.

93) Sept. 21, 1742. Foreigners imported in the ship Francis and Elizabeth, George North, Master, from Rotterdam, last from Deal.

Sept. 21, 1742. Frembe famen mit bem Schiffe Franzis unb Elifabeth, Capitain George North, von Rotterbam über Deal.

Michel Kolb,	Johann Wilhelm Werth,
Michael Thesser,	Johan Nicklaus Cuntz,
Johannes Withman,	Wilhelm Ruff,
Ulrich Halber *	Martin Meyer,
Jacob Geiger,	Peter Laaber,*
Johannes Eckel,	Jacob Binder,
Peter Rubel,*	Melchior Hirtzel,
Jacob Klein,*	Jonas Metzger,
Frederich Haussman,	Adam Säbert,
Nicklaus Walder,*	Johannes Grob,
Christian Newcomer,*	Philip Shleyhouff,*
Andreas Waltaich,	Andreas Heintz,
Christian Henrich,	Hans Ewert,
Conrad Bassel,*	Johannes Schäfer,
Henry Cerber,*	Conrad Gerhart,
Christoph Schmidt,*	Heinerich Hirt,
Jacob Schenck,	Anton Faust,
Paulus Daterer,	Nicklaus Röhrig,
Michel Coppelger,	Martin Kirschner,
Johann Friederich Iollgo,	Peter Stam,
John Henrich Stoll,	Adam Odt,
Christian Adam Höbel,	Adam Ott sen.,
Johan Michael Waidele,	Conrad Ott,
Johann Jacob Holbein,	Johannes Odt,
Joh. Michael Käschstler,	Johannes Reusswig,
Johann Henrich Stes,	Christian Rügner,
Hans Adam Klein,	Johannes Weber,
Ullrich Neuschwanger,	Johannes Bohm,*
Christian Newcomer jr.,	Jacob Yoder,*
Johann Peter Waller,	Friederich Meyer,
Christian Hürd,	Jacob Kurtz,
Hans Michel Fohl,	Jacob Guth,
Thomas Heunemeyer,	Peter Faust,*
John Gottfried Rieger,*	Conrad Bloss,
Johann Georg Weith,	Jacob Hanck,
Johan Peter Kochlein,	Johann Peter,

Moritz Zug, *a*
Christian Zug,
Johannes Zug,
Christof Geiser,
Hans Georg Binder,
Hans George Shenk,*
Matthäus Wendnagel,
Samuel Wohlegemuth,*
Hans Georg Knödler,
Hans Michael Bauer,*
Johan Matthias Plantz,
Rudolph Wollenweiller,
Hans George Ruthy,*
Ludwig Jacob Friedburg,
Johann Adam Stam,
Johann Henrich Rengel,
Johan Henrich Wolff,
Johan Georg Schüssler,
Nicolaus Gottschalck,
Johann Peter Odt,
Johann Henrich Odt,
Johan Henrich Dessler,
Leonhardt Michael Rüger,
Johann Henrich Ahl,
Johann Christian Hörner,
Johan Jacob Bohn,
Christian Jotter,
Christian Jotter jr.,
Christian Miller,*
Johannes Knäg,*
Johannes Gerber,
Uhllerich Ställy,*
Johan Adam Heydrig,*
Johan Georg Faust,*
Johan Henry Creesman,

Johannes Walther,
Hans Jacob Huber,
Philip Deter Huber,*
Johan Peter Köhler,
Stephan Bopenmeier,
Abraham Kolman,
Johan Michel Truckenmüller,
Jost Fuchs,*
Henry Miller,*
Ludwig Huber,
Gabriel Köhler,
Jacob Sarbach,
Georg Schultz,
Moses Binder,*
Christian Ecket,*
Andreas Bachman,
Bernhart Kober,*
Melchior Schäner,
Abraham Gross,
Johannes Koohn,*
Martin Stouver,*
Ludwig Schmaltzhaff,
Georg Adam Müller,
Hans Michael Krafft,*
Christian Dannewald,*
Johann Henrich Schertz,
Carl Philip Schultz,
Hans Michael Doll,
Johann Michael Bucher,
Johann Michael Seitz,
Abraham Schnutz,
Matheus Massiman,
David Rotheheffer,
Christian Müller.

---

a Moritz Zug was the grandfather of *Shem Zook*, of Mifflin County, Pa., favorably known by his agricultural essays in the Patent Office Reports within the last few years.

a Moriß Zug war der Großvater von Shem Zook von Mifflin County, Pa., der durch seine Aufsäße über Landwirthschaft in den Patent-Office-Berichten während der lezten paar Jahre rühmlichst bekannt ist.

94) Sept. 24, 1742. Foreigners imported in the ship Robert and Alice, Martley Cussack, Master, from Rotterdam, last from Cowes.

Sept. 24, 1742. Frembe famen mit bem Schiffe Robert unb Alice, Capitain Martley Cuffad, von Rotterbam über Cowes.

Philippus Bärger,
Cornelius Miller,
Friederich Müller,
Ludwig Miller,*
Conrad Pooff,*
Veltin Paul,
Philip Farenthal,
Jacob Stübigh,*
Hans Rub,
Friederick Becker,
Michel Axer,
Michel Wolff,
Johannes Heydt,
Peter Geris,
Philip Geris,*
Nicklaus Hartt,*
Paulus Bang,
Johannes Binackel,
Adam Gucker,*
Christian Gucker,*
Michel Weiss,
Henry Stave,*
Durst Ziegler,
Johannes Ziegler,
Johann Georg Christ,
Georg Christian Ulrich,
Johann Jacob Metzger,
Johan Nicklas Hyl,*
Johann Jacob Benedick,
Hans Adam Christ,*
Simon Jacob Theil,*
Johann Georg Schissler,
Hildebrand Heckman,
Johann Philip Kercher,
Johann Christoffel Peter,

Johan Jacob Bome,*
Simon Peter Diehl,
Johan Friederich Heimer,
Johann Henrich Werner,
Johann Simon Drum,
Johann Jacob Schmitt,
Johann Casper Schell,
Johann Michel Koch,
Johannes Brosius,
Joh. Abraham Brosius,
Johann Georg Riess,
Johann Jacob Riess,
Johann Jacob Wagner,
Jacob Weber,
Jacob Stein,
Lorentz Riess,
Peter Herber,
Johannes Herber,
Andreas Harter,
Johannes Kerch,
Matheas Meyer,*
David Weil,
David Mackly,*
Johannes Krape,*
Peter Maus,*
Andreas Kessler,
Hans Adam Holdt,*
Hans Adam Furtig,*
Friederich Schmidt,
John Jacob Zervin,*
Philip Jacob Ehrenfelter,
Adam Furchtig,*
Joh. Paulus Reuther,?
Hans Peter Woolf,*
Hans Geo. Katzenstein,*

14

Matheis Heinrich,?   Michael Danner,
Dietrich Danner,   Hans Michael Spaar.*

NOTE.—Rev. *Henry Melchior Muhlenberg,* D. D., Patriarch of the
Evangelical Lutheran Church in America, arrived from Charleston,
S. C., at Philadelphia, Nov. 28, 1742.—See *Rupp's History of Berks
and Lebanon Co.,* p. 433.

Anmerkung.—Paſtor Henry Melchior Mühlenberg, Dr. Theol. und
Patriarch der evangeliſch=lutheriſchen Kirche in Amerika, kam am 28. Novbr.
1742 von Charleſton, S. C., in Philadelphia an.—Siehe Rupp's Geſch.
von Berks und Lebanon Co., S. 433.

95) Aug. 30, 1743. Foreigners imported in the ship Francis
and Elizabeth, George North, Master, from Rotterdam, last from
Cowes.

Aug. 30, 1743. Fremde kamen mit dem Schiffe Franzis und
Eliſabeth, Capitain George North, von Rotterdam über Cowes.

Hans Bucher,
Henry Coughly,*
Hans Zoblei,
Rudolph Mertz,
Hans Meier jr.,
Henry Rudolph,*
Henrich Müller,
Uhllerich Näff,*
Henry Leer,*
Casper Spery,*
Henry Shwitzer,*
Casper Crop,*
Johannes Hug,
Henry Naff,*
Kilian Gild,*
Hans Meyer,*
Henry Rudsh,*
Hans Heinrich Hübner,
Hans Heinrich Näff,
Christopher Bosser,*
Henry Weidman,*
Henry Hebrecht,*
Hans Gütinger,
Hans Henry Naff,*
Henry Baumgardner,
Hans Jacob Naff,*
Hans Heinrich Scheuerer,
Hans Ulrich Bladman,
Henry Leinbach,*
Henry Poldesberger,*
Hans Jacob Usser,*
Heinrich Bauerdt,
Rudolph Kleinpeter,*
Jacob Wegmann,
Peter Scheurer,
Johannes Meier,
Ely Walder,*
Henry Good,*
Felix Leea,*
Henrich Eck,
Johannes Büch,
Jacob Boumer,*
Hans Kuhn,*
Hans Dups,
Johannes Bär,
Jacob Bär,
Henrich Grob,
Henrich Hitz,
Jacob Franck,
Henrich Suter,

Henry Zutter,*
Henry Shmit,*
Daniel Harner,
Hans Jacob Würst,
Felix Hierlyman,*
Johannes Boser,
Melchior Steheli,
Lenhart Alterfer Schmied,
Henry Dubydorffer,*
Felix Christ. Wagner,
Hans Rurckons,*

Hans Jacob Meyer,
Hans Jacob Rüttlinger,
Lenhart Schnebeli,
Henrich Schleypfer,
Johannes Schildemrad,
Jacob Bachman,
Caspar Snabily,*
Hans Jacob Pfister,
Hans Ulrich Dinges,
Hans Ulrich Hegnetsweiller.?

96) Sept. 2, 1743. Foreigners imported in the ship Loyal Judith, James Cowie, Master, from Rotterdam, last from Cowes.

Sept. 2, 1743. Frembe kamen mit bem Schiffe Loyal Jubith, Capitain James Cowie, von Rotterbam über Cowes.

Bartel Zöller,
Johannes Becker,
Philip Christian,*
Martin Dincky,?
Johannes Lärer,
Michel Seitz,
Henrich Moag,*
Jacob Maag,
Johan Jacob,
Johannes Kirst,
Friedrich Feltberger,
Lorents Laffersweiler,
Nickel Runckel,
Johan Runckel,
Adam Brech,
Johannes Jäger,
Johannes Krämer,
Daniel Märtz,
Bernhard Lauffersweiler,
Nicklaus Scherstenberger,
Johan Conrad Schütz,
Johann Georg Eppelman,
Johan Jacob Gittelman,
Johan Wendel Dannefelser,

John Valentin Hammer,*
Johann Wilhelm Becker,
Johan Adam Moses,
John George Miller,*
Johannes Hönig,
Johan Peter Braun,
Johann Philip Odewelder,
Philip Carl Angel,
Johan Adam Mohr,
Johann Philip Beier,
Johan Philip Gambach,
Johan Adam Uehrbass,
Johannes Gambach,
Ulrich Freyhofer,
Rudolff Buchy,*
Wendel Horst,
Valentin Wentz,
Gerhart Fichker,*
Bastian Bongart,
Christian Weiss,
Johannes Bott,
Andreas Walter,
Nicklas Keller,
Adam Kappel,

Lorentz Schmahl, a
Adam Shmaal,*
Jacob Haussman,
Johannes Schreyer,
Johannes Habersod,*
Mattheas Hoffer,
Simon Küstener,
Peter Roth,*
George Fitterer,*
Peter Miller,*
Jacob Möhner,
Lorentz Hardt,
Adam Schmahl,
Wentz Schmahl,
Valentin Grosch,
Friederich Fichgus,
Bernhart Becker,
Johannes Becker,
Johannes Bermes,
Jacob Bentli,
Jacob Keyser,*
Philipp Hoffman,
Johann Philipp Wentz,
Christoph Weisskopff,
Christopel Grossert,
Johannis Schwindt,

Johann Jacob Wilhelm,
Johann Jacob Huth,
Jacob Grosskopff,*
Johan Henrich Scheurer,
Hans Georg Sheyer,*
Johan Adam Reyd,*
Johann Jacob Petry,
Johan Adam Fuchs,
Johannes Brückbauer,
Johannes Mondshauer,*
Johann Phillipp Böhm jr.,
Johann Phillipp Böhm,
Hans Wolf Waltz,*
Andreas Weybrich,
Hermanus Höffer,
Johann Philip Hardt,
Johann Emrich Bott,
Johan Georg Wolffskehl,
Mattheus Butterfass,
Nicolas Maneubach,
Johan Philip Schrieger,
Joh. Philip Schrieger jr.,
Johann Henrich May,
Johann Georg Störy,
Hans Heinrich Maag,
Johan Balthasar Groh,

---

a *Lorentz Schmahl*, a native of the Middle Palatinate, settled as a farmer six miles from York, Pa., where he pursued assiduously and successfully his calling to the close of his life, leaving four sons: *Jacob*, who, when young, moved to Baltimore, whose son, Col. Jacob Small, was Mayor of the city; *John Schmahl* moved to and settled in Beaver County; *Kilian* and *Lawrence* remained in York. From the former, the greater part of the numerous *Smalls* in York County descend.— *Rupp's History of York County*, p. 743.

a Lorenz Schmahl, in der mittleren Pfalz geboren, ließ sich als Bauer sechs Meilen von York, Pa., nieder, wo er seinem Beruf bis zum Ende seines Lebens treu und eifrig oblag. Er hatte vier Söhne: Jakob, der in seiner Jugend nach Baltimore zog und dessen Sohn, Col. Jakob Small, Mayor der Stadt war; John Schmahl ließ sich in Beaver County nieder; Kilian und Lorenz blieben in York. Von ersterem stammt der größere Theil der in York County so zahlreichen Smalls.—Rupp's Geschichte von York County, S. 743.

Georg Frederich Gribel,*
Peter Schweikharth,
Johannes Hoffman,

Lorentz Miller,*
Johan Daniel Hoff,
Joh. Jacob Fossbendler.

97) Sept. 5, 1743. Foreigners imported in the snow Charlotte, John Mason, Master, from Rotterdam, last from Cowes.

Sept. 5, 1743. Frembe famen mit bem Seeschiffe Charlotte, Capitain John Mason, von Rotterbam über Cowes.

Adolph Eiler,
Henrich Hant,
Mattheis Basting,
Henry Shoemaker,*
Wilhelm Bretz,
Jacob Bretz,
Johannes Lees,*
Johannes Lisch,
Johannes Schiffer,
Phillippus Maurer,
Jacob Enck,
Johannes Gross,
Anthon Schnieder,
David Dautderer,?
Nicklas Wolfart,
Henrich Eckenroth,
Johannes Koch,
Valentin Lörch,
Johannes Riesset,
Henrich Meyer,*
Anton Zehmer,
Gottlieb Werth,
Johannes Bopp,
Johannes Söhn,

Johan Nickel Schnell,
Johan Peter Schwager,
Johann Philip Schnell,
Johannes Ickrath,
Johan Friederich Thor,
Johan Jacob Enck,
Joh. Andoni Hellenthal,
Johann Georg Miller,
Johan Georg Herman,
Johan David Schmidt,
Johan Conrath Guthmann,
Johan Balthaser Gir,?
Johann Jacob Stamm,
Johannes Niemand,
Johann Henrich Mertz,
Friederich Krämer,
Johannes Hermann,
Hans Georg Albrecht,*
Mattheis Heimbach,
Jacob Granable,*
Johannes Albenächt,
Johannis Clossheim,
Johannes Ulmstadt,
Johannes Mumrich.

98) Sept. 20, 1743. Foreigners imported in the ship Lydia, James Abercrombie, Master, from Rotterdam, last from Cowes.

Sept. 20, 1743. Frembe famen mit bem Schiffe Lybia, Capitain James Abercrombie, von Rotterbam über Cowes.

Jost Folmer,*
Johannes Bender,*

Johannes Benner,
Frantz Bricker,

14*

Dietrich Fohl,
Johannes Zepter,*
Johan Christian Walther,
Joh. Christian Rischstein,
Joh. Henrich Hoffman,
Johan Jacob Gücker,
Johan Henrich Gücker,
Simon Dreissbach,
Johannes Weller,*
Johannes Hünche,
Dielman Schütz,*
Johannes Ax,
Hieronimus Weber,
Konradt Wirdt,
Johannes Jung,
Hermanus Bruch,
Johannes Gring,
Johannes Ffister,
Peter Althen,
Wilhelm Hehbel,
Henry Schwartz,*
Matheus Lentz,*
George Frieh,
Conrath Kohl,
Andreas Schmitt,
Johannes Roth,
Johannes Peltz,*
Valentin Roth,*
Jeremias Weidy,*
Frantz Greulich,
Casper Gastner,
Henry Frey,*

Johannes Bauer,
Johannes Dörr,
Philip Heger,*
George Ament,*
Johan Jost Dreissbach,
Johan Ludwig Rudolph,
Johan Peter Rühl,
Johannes Blattenberger,*
Johan Gerhart Weick,
George Wilhelm Eckart,*
Johan Wilhelm Eckroth,
Joh. Wilhelm Krautter,
Johan Adam Gaul,
Johann Andreas Gutman,
Joh. Nickel Seidenbach,
Henrich Lepkücher,
Johan Philip Amendt,
Johan Christian Neff,
Joh. Bernhart Gesell,
Johan Jacob Hacker,*
Johan Georg Schwartz,
Christian Härshy,*
Joh. Friederich Sänger,
Valentin Schmidt,
Johan Nickel Sauer,*
Johan Christoffel Looss,*
Valentin Kletter,*
Joh. Friederich Heyer,
Valentin Heyer,
Conrad Sallam,*
John Goodman.*

---

99) Sept. 26, 1743. Foreigners imported in the ship Rosannah, James Reason, Master, from Rotterdam, last from Cowes.

Sept. 26, 1743. Frembe kamen mit bem Schiffe Rosannah, Capitain James Reason, von Rotterbam über Cowes.

Jacob Hoffman,
Andreas Spring,*
Jacob Schäueffele,

Casper Kessler,
Hans Ferdinandt,
Casper Meier,

Jacob Fincky,*
Rudy Keyser,*
Johannes Jooghly,*
Henrich Christoph Heroldt,
Hans Georg Bentzinger,
Johan Wilhelm Satler,
Hans Georg Stärner,
Georg Christoph Schoch,
Hans Georg Fuchs,
Hans George Markwart,*
Hans Martin Müller,
Hans Conrad Bruner,*
Jacob Schuster,*
Hans Müller,*
George Müller,*
Gregorius Müller,*
Hans Brunner,
Henry Müller,*
Martin Wirth,
Johannes Fischer,*
Jacob Prela,
David Schatz,
Friederich Stall,
Jacob Legler,

Samuel Wolff,
Leonhart Ströbel,
Andreas Strele,
Christian Haller,
Jacob Haller,
Michael Wyland,*
Henrich Burckart,
Hans Jacob Gassner,
Hans Ulerich Huber,*
Hans Melchior Fischer,*
Johannes Fischer jr.,
Bernhart Pflaugner,
Hans Jacob Remmler,
Hans Jacob Hummel,
Johannes Ketterman,*
Georg Christoff Herals,
Georg Philip Hummel,
Hans Georg Kater,
Hieronimus Henning,
Hans Georg Etzweiller,
Hans Leonhart Wyland,*
Casper Bindschädler,
Johannes Roodsman.*

---

100) Sept. 30, 1743. Foreigners imported in the ship Phœnix, William Wilson, Commander, from Rotterdam, last from Cowes.

Sept. 30, 1743. Frembe kamen mit bem Schiffe Phönir, Commanbant William Wilson, von Rotterbam über Cowes.

Wilhelm Hölty,
Otto Hai,
Lenhart Wintergress,
Johannes Dandoner,
Matheis Treuckel,
Johannes Ungear,*
Christoff Holwer,*
Jacob Rubly,*
Michael Bauer,*
Michael Leavy,
Johannes Schnee,

Philip Reesher,*
Philip Spegel,
Jacob Gänsle,
David Säusert,?
Frederich Köhler,
Jacob Siherrer,*
Michael Eller,
Isaac Will,
Henry Meyer,*
Dewald Hochstädt,*
Johann Henrich Hauss,

Lorentz Protzmann,
Henry Reydmeyer,*
Paulus Behringer,
Phillippus Bayer,
Hans Michael Stumpf,
Joh. Nicklas Lohman,
J. Ernst Reiffschneider,*
Johannes Gänsle,
Johan Frederich Esch,
Johann Jost Köhler,
Georg Klingmann,
Johan Georg Sternbirger,
Johan Valtin Reul,
Johann Georg Schäffer,
Friederich Miller,*
Johan Henrich Wagner,
Peter Handwercker,
Benedict Nussbaum,*
Jacob Geiger sen.,
Jacob Geiger jr.,
Matheis Kent,
Johannes Bär,*
Johannes Stamm,*
Peter Gör,
Jacob Böm,
Melchior Bär,
Christophel Bär,
Melchior Bär jr.,
Melchior Seydler,
Daniel Schwartz,

Henry Dornig,*
Michael Masserly,*
Daniel Mauss,
Peter Bartolomes,
Philipus Bartheus,
Nicklaus Fey,
Lorentz Cuntz,
Georg Huber,
Conrad Wirth,
Adam Richman,
Nicklas Hoffman,*
Bernhart Mackler,*
Henry Georg Nees,*
Johann Niclas Gauer,
Johann Jost Vetter,
Michael Steckbek,
Anthon Bensinger,
Hans Adam Felbaum,*
Conrad Felbaum,*
Caspar Reithnauer,*
Johannes Reudenauer,*
Joh. Michael Füchthorn,
Christian Rorbagh,*
Johannes Nusbaum,*
Johan Adam Herbes,
Bernhart Müller,
Hans Michael Miller,*
Johannes Schmidt,
Cal. August Erlwein.*

---

101) Sept. 30, 1743. Foreigners imported in the ship Robert and Alice, Hartly Cussack, Commander, from Rotterdam, last from Cowes.

Sept. 30, 1743. Frembe famen mit bem Schiffe Robert und Alice, Commanbant Hartly Caffucf, von Rotterbam über Cowes.

Johannes Zäner,
Simon Zenger,
Nicklas Baker,*
Jacob Baker,*

Johannes Good,*
Joseph Ziebly,*
Deobold Bauer,*
Jacob Shock,

Andreas Liess,
Kasper Strom,
Michael Deato,
Johannes Shalley,*
Christian Shalley,*
Matheas Baum,*
Johannes Schütz,
Karl Schwartz,
Johann Philip Emig,
Johannes Martin,
Johann Philip Emig sen.,
Baltzer Schwerdt,
Phillip Fredrick May,
Joh. Ludwig Schalle,
Hans Adam Shally*,
Johannes Obenheyser,
Nicklas Schreiber,
John Henry Butz,
Johan Kolmangreuer,?
Jacob Schmidt,
Hans Georg Stucki,
Christoff Sheaneman,*
Hans Jacob Köller,
Peter Guthman,
Samuel Landes,
Conrad Œsterlen,
Johannes Bender,
Henry Gilbert,
Hans Hardt,
David Sarbach,
Samuel Bechtel,

Jacob Bucki,
Abraham Derst,
Mattheis Meier,
Oswald Neff,
Johannes Young,*
Bardel Miller,
Henry Fanner,*
Felix Fanner,*
Baltzer Gilbert,*
Conrad Toll,*
Ulrich Cress,?
Joseph Sheffer,*
Hans Georg Œsterle,
Christoff Œsterlin,*
Joh. Ludwig Truckenmüller,
Johann Georg Frey,
Andreas Hemberger,
Hans Georg Endes,
Hans Michael Ott,
Christian Müller,
Hans Georg Müller,
Henrich Stertzenacker,
Philip Heinetsch,
Hans Georg Begtel,
Johan Georg Schwartz,
Felix Zollinger,
Heinrich Zwick,
Wilhelm Spats,*
Jacob Gillinger,
Bernhart Gilbert.

102) Oct. 7, 1743. Foreigners imported in the ship St. Andrew, Robert Brown, Captain, from Rotterdam, last from Cowes.

Oct. 7, 1743. Fremde kamen mit dem Schiffe St. Andrew, Capitain Robert Brown, von Rotterdam über Cowes.

Jacob Walter,*
Friderich Stoll,
Johannes Moak,*
Andreas Wollinger,*

Ulrich Wechlid,
Adam Heyler,
Jacob Striey,
Joseph Hartman,

Johannes Hauser,
Herman Busch,
Georg Gärtner,
Lenhart Stein,
Leonhart Dewalt,*
Gottlieb Zigel,*
Johan Mergel,*
Gottlieb Schleer,
Jacob Clausser,*
John Nicklas Zeisinger,*
Joh. Adam Gerber,
Geo. Mich. Weiss Müller,
Hans Georg Maurer,
Johan Simon Kern,
Hans Peter Grumbach,
Hans Michel Striey,
Friederich Jayter,
Georg Philip Kürr,
Hans George Eatter,*
Hans Martin Fischer,
Philip Jacob Buttman,
Johan Michel Wagner,
Hans Adam Sommer,
Georg Friederich Zügel,
Johann Jacob Ringer,*
Daniel Meidinger,
Jacob Eichhorn,
Lenard Fuchs,*
Andreas Güllam,
Martin Ruth,
Jacob Hesse,*
Heinrich Brunner,
Hans Burger,
Ernest Amon,*
Christle Casper,
Johannes Ulerich,*
Frederick Hubely,

Johannes Mayer,
Peter Werner,
Johannes Widmann,
Leonhardt Kern,
Heinrich Wagner,
Friederich Ziegler,
Johannes Rieger,
Anthon Knauss,
Ludwigh Dewys,
Abraham Hüller,
Valentin Shutter,*
Henry Shutter,*
Jacob West,*
Johannes Eberhart,
Hyronimus Trauttmann,
Bernhart Dübinger,*
Joh. Ludwig Kraft,
Hans Ulrich Hegli,
Hans Jerg Backastos,*
Hans Ulrich Jakly,
Hans Ulrich Odt,
Hans Henry Bossart,*
Jac. Fried. Dochterman,
Hans Jacob Goldner,*
Hans Jerg Amon,
Melchior Bührly,
Johan Georg Wittmann,
Hans Georg Œhler,
Michael Wolfgang,*
H. Peter Fronkhousen,*
Johan Henrich Knauss,
Daniel Debüs,
Joh. Henrich Gackenbach,
Han Adam Zimmerman,
Niclaus Kobelentz,
Johan Philip Schneider.

---

103) Nov. 10, 1743. Foreigners imported in the snow Endeavor, Thomas Anderson, Captain, from London.

Nov. 10, 1743. Fremde kamen mit dem Seeschiffe Endeavor, Capitain Thomas Anderson, von London.

Matheis Braunefelder,	Matheis Braunefelder jr.,
Adam Schaub,*	Hans Ulrich Schaub.
Jacob Frounwalder,*	

NOTE.—Sometime in the summer of 1743, the ancestor of the KEL-KERS (Swiss) left his native country for America. His great-grandson, *Rudolph F. Kelker*, son of *Frederick*, has in his possession interesting family papers, from which the Editor has made some extracts. Among others is a certificate of church-membership, viz: L. B. S.

It is shown by these presents, that Heinrich Köllicker, born in 1705 at Herrliberg, on Lake Zurich, is the son of estimable parents, and has, by holy Baptism, been united with the Reformed Christian Church. Likewise, it is also the intention of Barbara Brätscheri, his wedded wife, together with their three sons and two daughters, all of good repute, as far as is known, to leave their fatherland of their own accord and emigrate to Pennsylvania or Carolina, in order there permanently to settle and herewith take with them their churchright for themselves and for their descendants.

To this journey we wish them success, the divine blessing, health and the attainment of their object. For the sake of greater security I have written the above with my own hand and certified it with my seal.

HANS CONRAD ZIEGLER,

HERRLIBERG, } Minister at Herrliberg
the 8th day of June, 1743. } and Wezwyl. [L. S.]

Family tradition says, they were 28 weeks in crossing the ocean. The date of their actual departure from Switzerland, and of their arrival in this country, and place of landing, are all (up to the present) unknown. As the name does not appear on the lists of immigrants to Pennsylvania, it has been surmised that they landed in Carolina. Henry Köllicker settled about four miles from Lebanon, now Lebanon, then Lancaster County, Pennsylvania, and we learn from the Records of the Church that he was an Elder in the "Berg Kirch," near Lebanon, in 1745. His son Anthony, and daughter Susanna are his only children supposed to have reached America with him. The others, it is believed, died before his arrival.

Anmerkung.—Im Sommer 1743 verließ der Ahne der Kelker (aus der Schweiz) sein Vaterland, um nach Amerika auszuwandern. Sein Ur-enkel, Rudolph F. Kelker, Sohn des Friedrich, besitzt interessante Familien-schriften, aus denen der Herausgeber Auszüge machte. Unter denselben ist folgendes ihm von seinem Prediger ausgestellte Zeugniß:

Mit gegenwärtigen attestiren das Heinrich Köllicker von Herrliberg am Zurich See gebürtig, gebohren werden von ehrlichen Eltern, im jahr unseres Heilands gezelt 1705 und durch den Heiligen Tauff der Reformirten Christ-lichen Kirchen einverleibet. Item, Barbara Brätscheri sein Eheweib samt 3 Söhnen und 2 Töchtern, alles unverläumbte leut, so vil im wüssen, frey

unb ungezwungen ſich entſchloſſen ihr Vaterland zu verlaſſen unb nach
Pennſylvanien ober Carolina zu reiſen; daſelbſt ſeßhaft nieber zu laſſen,
hiemit ihr Mannen unb Gemeindrecht für ſich unb ihre Nachkommen
mitnehmen.

In welcher Reis ihnen glück, ſegen, geſundheit unb erreichung ihres
Zwecks angewunſcht wirb. Zu mehreren ſicherheit hab ich obiges mit hanb
unb bitſchafft unberſeßt.

Hans Conrad Ziegler,
Herrliberg,   }   Pfarrer zu Herrliberg unb
ben 8 tag Heumonat 1743. }   Wezwyl.   [L. S.]

Eine Familien-Ueberlieferung ſagt, daß bie Ueberfahrt über ben Ocean
28 Wochen in Anſpruch genommen habe. Das genaue Datum ihrer Ab=
reiſe von ber Schweiz unb ihrer Ankunft in dieſem Lanbe ſinb, wie auch
ber Lanbungsplaß, bis auf ben heutigen Tag unbekannt. Da ber Name
auf ben Liſten ber Einwanderer nach Pennſylvanien nicht ſteht, ſo glaubte
man, dieſelben ſeien in Carolina gelandet worden; Henry Köllicker ließ ſich
etwa vier Meilen von Lebanon, damals Lancaſter, jeßt Lebanon County,
Pennſylvanien, nieber, unb aus ben Berichten lernen wir, baß er 1745 ein
Aelteſter ber „Berg=Kirche", nahe Lebanon, war. Man iſt ber Meinung,
baß ſein Sohn Anthony unb ſeine Tochter Suſanna bie einzigen mit ihm
in Amerika angekommenen Kinber unb baß bie übrigen vor ſeiner Ankunft
geſtorben ſinb.

---

104) Oct. 8, 1744. Foreigners imported in the ship Aurora,
Robert Pickeman, Captain, from Rotterdam, last from Cowes.

Oct. 8, 1744. Fremde kamen mit bem Schiffe Aurora, Capi=
tain Robert Pickeman, von Rotterbam über Cowes.

Jost Vrevel,	Pontius Wiern,?
Johan Dornbach,*	Johann Christian Kell,
Conrad Rörig,*	Johan Adam Hirter,
Joh. Thieffelbach,?	Johan Adam Hierte,*
Joh. Phil. Fost,*	Johan Henrich Bock,
Daniel Foost,*	Johan Adam Shog,*
Peter Schäffer,	Johan Christ Wirth,*
Pierre Aune,	Johann Adam Wagner,
Johannes Baker,*	Hans Valtein Streder,
Johan Besenger,	Johan Georg Müller,
Matteas Meyer,*	Johan Adam Meyer,*
Matteas Meyer jr.,*	Joh. Hermanus Frevel,
Nicklas Meyer,*	Johan Peter Sheeff,*
Jean P. Pavon,	Joh. Wilh. Ganderman,
Johannes Michael,*	Joh. Henrich Rörich,
Phillipus Fackert,	Georg Wilhelm Berger,

Joh. Christian Berger,
Joh. Wilhelm Sage,
Mattheis Hem,
Georg Nölen,?
Godhart Löre,*
Andreas Pichnöster,
Jacob Scheyer,
Johan Noll,
Matthis Noll,
Bernhart Neyzart,*
Marcus Andres,
Joh. Paul Krebs,
Joh. Jacob Henn,
Joh. Peter Henn,
Joh. Hen. Dornbach,*
Joh. Härfstenbach,
Joh. Adam Geyer,
Joh. Geo. Shuster,*
Joh. Geo. Kell,
Joh. Jac. Reyman,*
Joh. Wil. Weiss,
Joh. Pet. Jung,
Joh. Donis Shmit,*
Joh. Wilh. Weyer,

Joh. Adam Schumacher,
Frantz Wilh. Kaulbach,
Johan Konrad Weyre,
Johan Wilhelm Lands,*
Johan Christ Kohl,*
Joh. Wilhelm Koch,*
Johan Peter Weingerer,?
Johan David Dornbach,
Joh. Peter Neytzert,
Joh. Peter Feyzer,
Johan Peter Meyer,
Joh. Christof Stiegeler,
Johan Georg Stiegeler,
Johan Bastian Miller,
Johan Henrich Häffer,
Joh. Henrich Schlemer,
Joh. Georg Schuster,
Johan Peter Cheert,?
Johan Wilhelm Kell,
Johan Ludwig Ehrman,
Johan Martin Köhler,
Johan Peter Strunck,
Johan Matteas Dexter.*

105) Oct. 20, 1744. Foreigners imported in the ship Phœnix, William Wilson, Captain, from Rotterdam, last from Cowes.

Dct. 20, 1744. Frembe kamen mit bem Schiffe Phönir, Capitain William Wilfon, von Rotterbam über Cowes.

Henrich Hartmann,
Johannes Herberth,
Georg Schön,*
Lorentz Erbach,
Adam Fischborn,
Antonius Fischborn,
Nicklas Peteo,
Theobald Klein,
Conrad Fuchs,
Andonius Weyrich,
Mattheis Kolb,

Philip Bretz,
Martin Kolb,
Lewalt Laub,*
Jacob Rau,
Johan Wendel Metzler,
Johann Adam Wegel,
Johan Adam Morgen,
Casper Schneider,
Joh. Philip Mauck,
Johan Peter Götz,
Christoph Westerberger,

15

Joh. Georg Wahnsiller,
Friederich Partemer,
Johannes Schneider,
Philip Wendel Klein,
Johan Jost Tizler,*
Joh. Henry Mattinger,
Johan Herman Mohr,
Joh. Nicolaus Wagner,
Jacob Buchman,
Georg Odt,
Johannes Klein,
Johannes Kuhn,
Philip Krebe,
Johannes Flück,
Paulus Eberhardt,
Paul Schneider,
Martin Etter,?
Joh. Fiehlt,
Conrad Hefling,
Henrich Platt,
Friederich Gresser,
Wendel Benödes,
Martin Kiester,
Andreas Eshbacher,*
Johannes Wayemer,*
Johannes Dieckert,
Friederich Stelwag,
Peter Faust,
Gerhardt Fircus,
Jacob Stephen,*
Jacob Wagner,
Andreas Sörger,
Conrath Jung,
Friederich Huby,*
Anthonius Höblich,
Andreas Grübel,
Henry Pad,*
Bastian Morian,
Heinrich Liess,
Herman Decreiff,*
Philip Flugh,*

Rudolph Fiehl,
Valentin Huss,?
Johann Kuntz,
Weymar Strunck,
Valentin Winesheim,
Jerg Wilhelm Staudt,
Joh. Nic. Messerschmidt,
Joh. Balthas Fischborn,
Peter Tauschhäus,
Gerhardt Schlesser,
Friederich Michael,
Johann Philip Andreæ,
Christian Eberhart,
John Georg Westberger,*
Johan Nickel Hen,
Friederich Huber,
Johan Philip Wagner,
Johan Reinhart Waltz,
Christoffel Dinckenschiet,
Johann Georg Schäffer,
Fried. Christian Müller,
Johann Valentin Hue,
Joh. Peter Breyvogel,
Joh. Georg Meisenheim,*
John Adam Klein,*
Johan Philip Höflich,
Johan Philip Kerchner,
Johan Henrich Kuntz,
Johan Adam Braun,
Peter Philipp Hahn,
Joh. Friederich Sauer,
Johann Dierlhoffner,
Philip Peter Grassert,
Johan Peter Fuchs,
Johan Peter Kolb,
Christoffel Fiehl,
Diellman Diekenschiedt,
Anton Schneider,
Philip Jacob Bäder,
Johan Philip Roth,*
Han Dewalt Seltenreich.

106) Nov. 2, 1744. Foreigners imported in the ship Friendship, John Mason, Captain, from Rotterdam, last from Cowes.

Nov. 2, 1744. Frembe kamen mit bem Schiffe Frienbship, Capitain John Mason, von Rotterbam über Cowes.

Herman Weber,
Wilhelm Weber,
Caspar Weber,
Gerhart Will,
Jacob Fughs,*
Jacob Engel,
Peter Bogert,
Valentin Voyt,
Georg Bernhart,
Conrath Förster,
Nicklaus Kusig,
Jachim Joan,
Christoph Koble,*
Albrecht Müller,
Johannes Gräber,
Johannes Moll,
Peter Williar,
Abraham Mischat,
Peter Hann,
Johann Wohlleben,*
Dewald Sperk,*
Georg Bieber,
Johannes Bieber,
Dewald Beaber,*
Wolfgang Siess,
Johannes Weber,
Johann Schlögel,*
Bernhart Roobe,*
Johan Lobach,?
Johannes Tieze,
Philip Waghmer,*
Dietrich Schattler,*
Debalt Werner,
Philip Shaffer,*
Peter Gesell,

Joh. Adam Radebusch,*
Johan Jacob Ferber,
Anthonius Dillan,
Joh. Philip Ehrenhardt,
Joh. Henrich Vätter,
John Peter Cusick,*
John Jacob Summer,*
John Wilhelm More,*
Theodorus Krahl,*
Adam Schölkopf,
Johan Wilhelm Reuel,
Geo. Emig Haartz,*
John Adam Haartz,*
Johann George Weber,
Johan Adam Weber,
Andreas Reiffschneider,
Johannes Schmidt,
Johan Georg Schmidt,
John Peter Noss,
Michael Baumann,
John Jacob Bildhous,*
Johann Jacob Stoltz,
Johan Georg Schädel,
Johann Nickel Grob,
Georg Konrad Grob,
Heinrich Jacob Krebs,
Johan Baltzer Köhler,
Johann Michael Klein,
Johann Ernst Solomo,
Johannes Wildt,
Heinrich Scheffer,
Heinrich Scheffer jr.,
Henrich Fayerbach,*
Henrich Koppelberger.

107) Dec. 11, 1744. Foreigners imported in the ship Carteret, —— Stevinson, Captain, from Rotterdam, last from Cowes.

Dec. 11, 1744. Frembe kamen mit bem Schiffe Carteret, Capitain —— Stevinson, von Rotterbam über Cowes.

Philip Stein,
Jacob Graff,
Johannes Zörlin,
Han Peter Schühlein,
Hans Henry Dobler,
Hans Georg Klein,*
Michael Häut,
Johannes Dewalt,
Rudolph Meeke,*
Hans Forster,*
Philip Bickler,
Jacob Bickler,
Walter Miller,*
Valentin Young,*
Michael Anthon,*
Henry Shwenk,*

Nicolas Herman,*
Nicklas Steinmetz,
Friederick Kop,
Joh. Georg Schaaff,
Albrecht Fried. Binder,
Johan Philip Binder,
Balthazar Armgast,*
Christophel Weber,
Jacob Lambrecht,
Christoph Bittenbender,
Johannes Mayer,
Joh. Christian Rehkopp,
Friederich Deobeld,
Friederich Deobeld jr.,
Johannes Kautz,
Wilhelm Jungck.

108) Dec. 22, 1744. Foreigners imported in the ship Mascliffe Galley, Georg Durell, Commander, from Rotterdam, last from a port in Dorsetshire, England.

Dec. 22, 1744. Frembe kamen mit bem Schiffe Mascliffe Galley, Commanbant Georg Durell, von Rotterbam über einen Hafen in Dorsetshire, Englanb.

Christian Stauffer,
Johannes Staube,*
Jacob König,*
Henry Dochman,*
Christian Coots,*
Hans Lynter,*
Stephan Kurtz,*
Hans Eyer,*
Jacob Engel,*
Jacob Sharff,*
Christian König,*
Samuel König,*

Christian Lang,
Hans Lichti,
Frantz Gernandt,
Valentin Heger,*
Elias Dietrich,
Christian Florig,*
Jacob Höffling,*
Conrad Notz,
Conrad Meckes,
Philip Haible,
Johannes Meister,*
Ulrich Gotter,*

Johann Jacob Meyer,
Valentine Tallebach,*
Christian Herford,?
Lenhart Klopert,*
Christian Krebill,
Abraham Steiner,
Adam Jacob Maurer,
Johan Adam Gess,
Leonhard Müller,
Andreas Henr. Pattheuer,
Michael Trahman,
Joh. Melchior Bruder,
Johan Adam Werntz,
Philip Ludwig Werntz,
Johan Jacob Werntz,
Hans Georg Graff,
Hans Georg Schneider,
Hans Adam Young,*
Hans Peter Burye,
Hans Georg Dewalt,
Caspar Schertzer,
Christian Mosser,*
John Showalter,*
Johannes Mosieman,
Henry Thomas,*

Bernhart Bear,*
Philip Vetter,*
Jacob Ebi,
Jost Yotter,*
Peter Jutzy,*
Jacob Müller,
Peter Weiss,
Peter Looh,*
Peter Mayer,*
Jacob Juncker,
Elias Rieth,*
Jacob Pregly,*
Andreas Mosselman,*
Hans David Ern,
Jacob Dauerschauer,
Johannes Albrecht,*
Johannes Sauder,*
Christian Frätz,*
Rudolph Hand,?
Peter Wittmer,
Henrich Schlichter,
Rudolph Herdte,
Josua Caspar Herdte jr.,
Rudolph Herdte jr.,
Geo. Wilh. Heydelbach.

NOTE.—For 1745 no Lists found in the Archives. This year the Rev'ds *Peter Brunnholtz, Herman Heinrich Lempke, J. N. Kurtz* and *J. H. Schaum*, Lutheran ministers, arrived in Pennsylvania.—*Rupp's Original History of Religious Denominations, &c.*, p. 384; *Stœver's Memoir of the Life and Times of Mühlenberg*, p. 59.

Anmerkung.—Von 1745 sind keine Listen im Archiv aufbewahrt. In diesem Jahre kamen die lutherischen Pastoren Peter Brunnholtz, Hermann Heinrich Lempke, J. N. Kurtz und J. H. Schaum in Pennsylvanien an.—Rupp's Original-Geschichte religiös. Benennungen 2c., S. 384; Stöver's Memoir des Lebens Mühlenberg's, S. 59.

109) Sept. 27, 1746.† Foreigners imported in the ship Ann Galley, William Wilson, Captain, from Rotterdam, last from the Orkneys, Scotland.

† This year the Rev. *Michael Schlatter*, of St. Gall, Switzerland, embarked for America, June 1st, arrived at Boston July 21st, came to

15*

Sept. 27, 1746. † Fremde kamen mit dem Schiffe Ann Galley, Capitain William Wilson, von Rotterdam über die Orkneys, Schottland.

Philip Bohn,
Johannes Bohn,
Johannes Dammer,
Christopher Thamer,*
Thomas Hahn,
Johannes Hahn,
Conrad Räber,
Carl Heyderich,*
Caspar Heyderich,*
Daniel Zwier,
Johan Peter German,
Johan Georg Godschalk,*
Johan Baltzer Bohn,
Johan Balthasar Damer,
Christoph Hoffman,*
Johan Ludwig Lauman,
Johan George Knabe,*
Rubert Harttoffel,
Joseph Egenbrohen,*
Johannes Kauffman,
Michael Egolf,
Michael Egolf jr.,
Simon Dohster,
Martin Lauman,
Heinrich Müller,
Martin Blisky,*

Johannes Ott,
Johannes Sheck,
Michael Batz,
Jacob Wetzel,
Jacob Ziegler,
Andreas Endt,
Johannes Kraus,
Balthasar Stauf,
Mattheus Hohl,
Christian Lentz,
John Lentz,
Philip Ziegler,
Christoph Lentz,
Matheas Bleakly,*
Conrad Dress,
Michael Dieter,
Johannes Sigle,
Jacob Ziegly,*
Christian Stram,
Peter Reshe,
Georg Stram,
Georg Ruth,
Georg Betz,
Joseph Alber,
Georg Hetrich,
Jacob Dauttel,

Philadelphia Sept. 6. He was one of the first missionaries and founders of the German Reformed Church in America.—*Rupp's History of Berks County*, p. 443; *Rupp's History of the Germans in Penna., Chapt. History of the German Reformed Church; Rev. H. Harbaugh's Memoirs of Rev. M. Schlatter.*

† In diesem Jahre schiffte sich Pastor Michael Schlatter von St. Gallen in der Schweiz am 1. Juni nach Amerika ein, wo er dann auch in Boston am 21. Juli und in Philadelphia am 6. Sept. ankam. Er war einer der ersten Missionare und Begründer der deutsch=reformirten Kirche in Amerika.—Rupp's Gesch. von Berks Co., S. 443; Rupp's Gesch. der Deutschen in Pennsylvanien, Capitel über die Reform. Kirche; Pastor H. Harbach's Erinnerungen an Pastor M. Schlatter.

Valentin Staffel,*
Hans Peter Dornhauer,
Johannes Sheck jr.,
Joh. Gottlieb Wehner,
Johannes Hummel,
Johan Adam Heindel,
Hans Georg Bresthle,
Joh. David Schaihing,
Bernhart Bochner,
Ludwig Falkenstein,
George Shneering,*
Johan Andreas Jetter,
Hans George Trasher,*
Hans Mich. Neuhauser,
Johan Baltes Bücher,
Christian Kauffmann,
Abraham Rösch,

Friederich Eichholtz,
Joh. Wilhelm Horst,
Johann Schröter,
Jacob Freymann,
Caspar Schneider,
Johannes Stöffel,
David Küntzel,
Geo. Albrecht Hillegass,
Hans Grünewaldt,
Michel Zimmerman,
John Michael Sekel,
Christian Wagner,
Melchior Mill,
Michael Sekel,
Michael Klawer,*
Mathias Streihl.

110) Oct. 25, 1746. Foreigners imported in the Neptune,
Thomas Wilkinson, Master, from Rotterdam, last from England.

Oct. 25, 1746. Frembe kamen mit bem Schiffe Neptune, Capi=
tain Thomas Wilkinson, von Rotterbam über England.

Johannes Kauffeld,
Arenne Consul,
Henry Eller,
Henry Miller,*
Jacob Shnyder,*
Johannes Heindt,
Joh. Friedrich Windst,
Joh. Fried. Windst jr.,
Johan Peter Funck,
Johan Jacob Pfeiffer,
Peter Sutter,
Jacob Rauch,
Jacob Bauman,
George Kauffeld,
Adam Kogh,*
Daniel Jacob,
Frantz Reynhart,
Nicklas Felle,*

Jacob Baab,
Peter Willem,
Johannes Gobel,*
Jacob Steiner,
Georg Weber,
Michel Werntz,
Jacob Huntz,
Dewalt Angny,*
Caspar Dewalt,
Jacob Leisser,
Carl Risch,
Georg Ernst,
Pierre Gerro,*
Jean Duesto,*
Saule Ruibec,
Francoi Conrieu,
Joseph Gerra,*
Pierre Vaintvas,

Valentin Leonhardt,
Jacob Bauman jr.,
Nicklas Kauffeld,
Joh. Christoff Hausmann,
Andreas Reinhart,
Isaac Steiner,
Joh. Peter Langenberger,
Wilhelm Baussman,
Philip Ginder,
Johannes Steiner,
Joh. Philip Reinhart,
Lorentz Baussman,
Henrich Steiner,

Christoffel Pausch,
Conrad Conrath,*
Philip Wissner,
Henry Shneyder,*
Joh. Bernhart Fer,
Christian Steiner,
Peter Grosnickel,
Michel Fischer,
Johannes Breitenbach,
George Zimmerman,
Joh. Christian Leibrock,
Friederich Reinhart,*
Alexander Gibbo.*

111) Aug. 1, 1747. Foreigners imported in the bilander Vernon, Thomas Ricks, Master, from Rotterdam, last from Leith, Scotland.

Aug. 1, 1747. Frembe kamen mit bem Laftschiffe Vernon, Capitain Thomas Ricks, von Rotterbam über Leith, Schottland.

Andreas Bürge,*
Christoffel Bär,
Jacob Steinbring,
Christoff Cressel,*
Dewald Sheyder,*
Jacob Leesher,*
Marx Ehli,
Henry Goub,*
Abraham Funck,*
Jacob Shappy,*
Felix Weiss,
Henrich Startzman,
Johannes Grünwald,
Hans Michael Kuntz,*
Heinrich Büttner,
Hans Mich. Büttner,
Samuel Witmer,*
Tobias Wagheman,*
Joh. Georg Meingästner,
Hans Caspar Feerer,
Johannes Rooghel,*

Hans Jacob Shappy,*
Hans Bickell,
Jacob Schnebeli,
Rudolph Hornecker,*
Ulrich Hornecker,*
Henry Herker,*
Peter Bawman,*
Johannes Walder,
Ludwig Weiter,
Rudolph Huber,
Georg Wampfler,
Henrich Huber,
Henrich Huber jr.,
Hans Friedt,
Kilian Indorff,
Heinrich Fiett,
Wilhelm Otz,
Hans Nickel Schmitt,
Hans Wilhelm Weidner,
Hans Henrich Weiss,
Hans Bleigestaufer,

Rudolph Hornecker jr.,
Hans Jacob Walder,
Hans Henrich Walder,
Hans Casper Walder,
Han Michel Eysenmann,
Joh. Christian Wampfler,

Joh. Ludwig Wampfler,
Hans Niclaus Bär,
Jacob Steinbrachel,
Hans Georg Schar,
Friederich Wirtz.

112) Sept. 24, 1747. Foreigners imported in the ship Lydia, William Tiffin, Captain, from London—inhabitants of Switzerland.

Sept. 24, 1747. Frembe famen mit bem Schiffe Lybia, Capitain William Tiffin, von London—Bewohner ber Schweiz.

Johannes Vogel,*
Jacob Verner,*
Hans Peiffer,
Hans German,
Peter Verner,*
Michael Meyer,*
Henrich Danner,*

John Jacob Meishter,*
Hans Martin Wehrner,
Mich. Vogelfanger Tölly,
Hans Jacob Grüllmann,
Daniel Heinrichs,
Georg Jacob Nudell,
Thom. Hen. Breymayer.

113) Oct. 9, 1747. Foreigners imported in the ship Restauration, James Hall, Captain, from Rotterdam, last from Leith—inhabitants of the Palatinate and places adjacent.

Oct. 9, 1747. Frembe famen mit bem Schiffe Restauration, Capitain James Hall, von Rotterbam über Leith—aus ber Pfalz unb angrenzenben Länbern.

David Scherch,
Martin Lesch,
Johannes Schanz,
Nicolaus Miller,
Tobias Pflieger,
Leonhart Horein,*
Johannes Knecht,
Andreas Seitle,
Hieronimus Greber,
Johannes Löffler,
Joh. Georg Sürmer,
Joh. Georg Kühner,
Martin Pfiengstag,

Johan Peter Beyl,
Joh. Adam Kauffman,
Hans Georg Jung,
Jacob Müller,
Jacob Röder,
Philip Hinsch,
David Dietterich,
Martin Streicker,
Andreas Riess,
Thomas Zigler,*
Jacob Houpt,*
Georg Lertschle,
Lucas Flak,*

Caspar Ber,*
Jacob Endi,
Georg Klees,
Georg Rohrer,
Johannes Yetter,
Baltas Mauerer,
Jacob Hacke,
Michael Wagner,
Peter Mosser,
Peter Mosser jr.,
Hans Guth,
Andreas Beyer,
Jacob Wetzler,
Simon Isbod,*
Christian Eller,
Johannes Fuchs,
Jost Kobel,
David Kobel,
Peter Wittmer,
Samuel Rosser,
Jacob Beysely,*
Michael Funck,
Jacob Gross,
Adam Tamas,
Christian Rupp,
Henry Righter,*
Hans Lay,
Michael Föss,
Bernhart Beck,
Georg Beyer,
Martin Moll,
Michel Meyer,
Johannes Leonner,
Joh. Lorentz Sträueker,
Christoph Wagner,
Georg Fried. Klingel,
Hans Georg Klingel,
Heinrich Rösch,
Joh. Philip Busch,
Joh. Daniel Busch,
Joh. Paulus Misser,

Hans Adam Sebaldt,
Hans Georg Törr,
Joseph Bentzinger,
Joseph Lobwasser,
Johan Georg Wendel,
Hans Georg Hoffman,
Johan Peter Lutz,
Johannes Schemmlein,
George Wallmiller,*
Heinrich Hauptman,
Michael Hoffman,*
Joh. Frantz Lemmlein,
Joh. Philip Stock,
Joh. Michael Weckesser,
Philip Hebeisen,
Johan Jacob Ebener,
Christoph Homan,
Friederich Rohrer,
Conrad Bisecker,
Joh. David Klemm,
Joh. Gottfried Bohner,
Michael Reinardt,
Hans Georg Eberhartt,
Hans Georg Shmitzer,*
Joh. Philip Hopff,
Gottfried Rattenauer,
Joh. Christoph Silberberg,
Johannes Hermann,
Johannes Feldmayer,
Georg Muckenberger,
Hans Leonard Butz,
Hans Michel Schlauch,
Christoph Mühleissen,
Gottfried Lauerer,
Andreas Bosshardt,
Michel Schill,
Balthes Zericher,
Jacob Rösch,
Mattheus Mauck,
Jacob Hettler,
Jacob Scherich,

Samuel Wendel,
Christian Mühleissen,
Geo. Friederich Kasper,
Philip Jacob Mayer,
Georg Daniel Eppler,

Johannes Weissman,
Hermanus Mumau,
Johan Jacob Schof,
Christian Tragher,*
Christian Schneider.

114) Oct. 13, 1747. Foreigners, inhabitants of the Palatinate and places adjacent, imported in the ship Two Brothers, Thomas Arnott, Master, from Rotterdam, last from Leith.

Oct. 13, 1747. Frembe aus ber Pfalz unb ben angrenzenben Länbern kamen mit bem Schiffe Two Brothers, Capitain Thomas Arnott, von Rotterbam über Leith.

Johannes Fuchs,
Johannes Bosse,
Johannes Adam,
Johannes Buch,
Peter Steinmetz,
Johannes Opp,
Jacob Arnold sen.,
Jacob Arnold jr.,
Mattheis Kern,
Johannes Hermann,
Johan Peterey,
Georg Schantz,?
Carl Baumberger,
Johannes Eberhart,
Nickolas Woolfe,*
Henrich Kirch,
Georg Kärch,
Johannes Bischoff,
Jost Fullmer,*
Johannes Udner,
Christian Eydam,*
Henrich Julius,
Daniel Sauerwalt,
Johannes Scheffer,
Johannes Enck,
Jacob Hüppel,
Johan Henrich Kuntz,
Joh. Christof Müller,

Johan Jacob Schmidt,
Joh. Bernhart Schneider,
Joh. Jacob Hilgert,
Johan Peter Bausmann,
Johan Philip Thomas,
Johan Ernst Kurtz,
Johan Frantz Hammer,
Frantz Henrich Gress,
Johan Georg Roth,
Johan Peter Conradt,
Johan Adam Kröber,
Joh. Philip Klonninger,
Joh. Leonhart Negele,
Johan Conrad Momma,
Johan Philip German,
Frantz Peter Lorentz,
Joh. Peter Meisteuch,
Joh. Wendel Eberhart,
Joh. Jacob Bischoff,
Joh. Diet. Schmidt,
Joh. Balthas Hieronymus,
Joh. Frantz Hieronymus,
Adam Ingebrand,*
Georg Philip Groh,
Philip Fidler,
Henry Beyl,*
Costiniös Ortmann,
Michel Reidenauer,

Sebastian Bauer,
George Wendling,
Anthon Armrester,*
Heinrich Scharff,
Herman Woöst,*
Nicklas Gebhart,
Dewald Knapff,
Georgius Boronii,
Johannes Schnepp,?
Henrich Kern,
Matheis Bischop,
Johannes Böhm,
Johan Seitzius,
Johann Georg,
Frantz Gerligh,*
Paulus Dilgard,
Philip Kolp,
Ernestus De Switzerdediefryer,
Johan Niclaus Sträitz,
Joh. Christoph Strohman,

Johan Philip Nachtgall,
Johan Georg Huth,
Joh. Valentin Harth,
George Greenemeyer,*
Johan Nickel Wüst,
Frantz Michel Bischop,
Johan Christoph Lehr,
Johan Conrad Geib,
Johannes Sassemanshause,
Johan Jost Reese,*
Joh. Jost Bebighausen,
Georg Herrmann,
Frantz Willhan,
Leonhart Müller,
Baltzer Mohn,
Uhllerich Moan,*
Valentin Buchaker,*
Adolff May,
Conrad Waagenær.

---

115) Oct. 20, 1747. Foreigners imported from Rotterdam, last from Leith.

Oct. 20, 1747. Frembe kamen von Rotterbam über Leith.

Johannes Gress,
Peter Koch,*
Henry Bawngwar,*
Jacob Spring,*
Jacob Frey,
Niclaus Lantz,
Wilhelm Dauber,
Adam Birger,
Hans Sheyer,*
Adam Schmitt,
Johannes Meyer,*
Charles Shmit,*
Christian Wenger,
Georg Schuster,
Johannes Stumpf,
Ludwig Tecker,*

Hans Conrad Beck,
Joh. Christian Petersohn,
Philip Henrich Seng,
Jacob Allimang,
Jacob Allimang jr.,
John Henry Schneyder,
Jacob Schwanger,
Johannes Wenger,
Christoff Gottschall,*
Hans Adam Furny,*
Abraham Frantz,
Hans Georg Lantz,
Christian Gärtner,?
Hans Philip Baron,
Sim. Con. Steinuth,
Joh. Wilhelm Yef,*

Georg Wirth,
Henry Frantz,
Peter Kennel,*
Peter Frantz,
Johan Küstner,

Hans Michel Kleim,*
Hans Dewalt Leyty,*
Nicklaus Wenger,
Henry Likwilder.*

---

116) Sept. 5, 1748.† Foreigners imported in the ship Edin‑ burgh, James Russel, Master, from Rotterdam, last from Ports‑ mouth.

Sept. 5, 1748.† Frembe famen mit bem Schiffe Ebinburgh, Capitain James Ruffel, von Rotterdam über Portsmouth.

Andreas Staut,
Jacob Schumacher,
Christoph Kumm,
Lorentz Reyder,
Dietrich Strubel,
Adam Rauch,*
Johan Lorentz,
Thomas Kirch,
Conrath Claus,
Sebastian Barthol,
Peter Wingert,
Philip Haller,
Peter Pfeiffer,*
Peter Ott,?
Friederich Gerhardt,
Peter Döst,
Lorentz Werthes,
Simon Pilanus,
Michel Gugesk *

Valentin Huth,
Valentin Huth jr.,
Valentin Sherer,*
Valentin Müller,
Felix Sautter,
Jacob Veirling,
Lenhard Œhler,
Joh. Valentin Opp,
Joh. Philip Schmitt,
Joh. Adam Schuster,
Joh. Stephan Franck,
Johan Peter Heger,
Joh. Valentin Klages,
Jacob Hilssheimer,
Joh. Philip Lorentz,
Joh. Valentin Lorentz,
Adam Kirchner,?
Joh. Leonard May,
Frantz Peter May,

---

† In 1748 several German Reformed ministers arrived in Pennsyl‑ vania. Aug. 13, 1748, Rev. *Dominicus Bartholomæus,* and Rev. *John Jacob Hochreutener;* Sept. 15, Rev. *Johann Jacob Leydig.*—*Dr. Bütt‑ ner's Reform. Kirche in America,* p. 11; *Rev. H. Harbaugh's Memoirs of Germ. Reform. Ministers in the U. S.*

† Im Jahre 1748 famen mehrere beutsch=reformirte Geistliche in Penn= sylvanien an. Am 13. August bie Pastoren Dominicus Bartholomäus unb Johann Jafob Hochreutener; am 15. Sept. Pastor Joh. Jafob Leybig.— Dr. Büttner's Ref. Kirche in Amerika, S. 11; Pastor H. Harbach's Erin= nerungen an bie beutsch=reform. Geistlichen in ben Ver. St.

Joh. Wilhelm Gärtner,
Joh. Peter Van Kännen,
Joh. Jacob Brommer,
Joh. Jacob Eyler,
Johan Nickel Buch,
Joh. Nickel Mayer,
Joh. Nickel Leu,?
Joh. Jacob Schlosser,
Joh. Herman Clauss,
Peter Wil. Caffroth,
Joh. Wilhelm Fuchs,
Joh. Nicolas Döst,
Caspar Franckfurther,*
John Georg Kirshner,*
Adam Anders,
Melchior Brown,*
Jacob Hoffman,
Heinrich Merckel,
Michel Theiss,
Georg Jantz,*
Matheas Krammer,*
Bernhart Diehl,
Reinhart Gaul,
Johannes Diehl,
Johannes Diehl jr.,
Conrath Graff,
Balthes Erbach,
Peter Schäffer,
Jacob Julius,
Peter Meetzler,
Matheas Betz,*
Philip Mook,*
Baltazar Essig,*
Peter Krebs,*
Ludwig Bronholtz,*
Henrich Klatz,
Adam Reem,*
Martin Klein,*
Abraham Stein jr.,
Peter Stein,
Abraham Stein,*

Henry Stein,*
Valentin Reiner,
Conrad Fritz,*
Matheas Ebert,*
Jacob Ebert,
Esaias Carl,*
Wilhelm Nick,*
Johannes Upp,
Conrath Buber,
Johan Lorentz Herschfänger,
Phil. Reinhart Gossler,
Geo. Lenhart Krumrein,
Johannes Weydenhauer,
Baldazar Spitznagel,*
Joh. Anton Bucholtz,
Johan Peter Bronnen,
Johan Michel Hoffner,
Joh. Nickel Eberhart,
Joh. Ulrich Hainman,
Joh. Friederich Antes,
Vallentin Kübatz,
Justinus Scherer,
Heinrich Scherer,
Hans Georg Betz,
Wilhelm Hans Mann,
Nicolaus Müller,
Johan Peter Weber,
Christopher Weber,§
Ludwig Lindenschmidt,
Nicolaus Lenhardt,
Georg Jacob Hartman,
Michael Hartman,
Philip Jacob Koch,
Friederich Herget,
Joh. Dan. Lindenschmidt,
Dominicus Rädel,
Michael Wagner,
Johan Peter Michel,
Jacob Schammo,
Johan Julius Reem,*
George Leuthenfer,

George Erdmayer,*
Paul Ulrich,
Johannes Riehm,

Johannes Foltz,*
Adam Uffner.?

---

117) Sept. 7, 1748.† Foreigners imported in the ship Hampshire, Thomas Cheesman, Captain, from Rotterdam, last from Falmouth.

Sept. 7, 1748.† Frembe kamen mit bem Schiffe Hampshire, Capitain Thomas Cheesman, von Rotterbam über Falmouth.

Johannes Faust,
Philip Hap,*
Adum Mayer,*
Johannes Bischoff,
Michael Widman,
Peter Ferdig,*
Jacob Rühl,
Johannes Mayer,
Hartman Adam,
Johannes Adam,
Georg Steyerwald,*
Conrath Maul,
Johannes Deffithal,*
Nicholaus Christ,*
Jacob Runckel,
Friederich Hammer,
Tobias Schall,
Jacob Holtz,
Andreas Hollinger,*
Caspar Höberling,
Philip Merckel,
Carl Engel,
Philip Koch,
Michael Basserman,

Jacob Sherr,
David Hag,
Anthony Ermolt,*
Frantz Grove,*
Henrich Cron,
Johannes Engel,
Jacob Schmidt,
Georg Lembcher,
Christopher Rubi,
Lorentz Wentzel,
Wolfgang Wolff,*
Jacob Hammer,
Anselmus Schreiner,
Andreas Miller,*
Rev. Joh. Albert Weygand,
Joh. Adam Wilhelm,
Joh. Georg Stimmel,
Johan Peter Schäfer,
Adam Immerhausser,
Johan Adam Schmid,
Johan Jacob Bentz,
John Georg Wäbeber,
Hans Peter Kucheller,
Hans Georg Hag,

---

† In the same year the Rev'ds. *Handschuh, Weygand, Kurtz, Schaum,* and *Klug,* Lutheran ministers, arrived in Pennsylvania.—See *Rupp's* ῾Η πᾶσα ἐκκλησία, (the entire Church), p. 385.

† In bemfelben Jahre kamen bie lutherifchen Geiftlichen Handfchuh, Weygand, Kurtz, Schaum unb Klug in Pennfylvanien an.—Siehe Rupp's ῾Η πᾶσα ἐκκλησία, (bie ganze Kirche), S. 385.

Joh. Andreas Riegler,
Joh. Adam Müller,
Johan Henrich Bott,
Phil. Ludwig Hütig,
Joh. Ludwig Wagner,
Joh. Dietrich Matthey,
Johan Frantz Noll,
Joh. Henrich Noll,
Joh. Friederich Ritz,
Joh. Anthon Maul,
Philip Wendel Helsel,*
Johan Tobias Höltzel,
Johan Michel Didah,?
Johan Philip Baum,

Johan Michel Ohrig,
Johan Georg Wieil,
Joh. Erhart Baumgertel,*
Johan Henrich Krom,
Joh. Caspar Lederholt,
Joh. Wilh. Leymeister,
Johan Daniel Hamm,
Johan Georg Weittman,
Philip Carl Piller,
Hans Jacob Osterman,
Philip Henrich Mohr,
Johan Adam Weiss,
Joh. Friderich Plotz.

118) Sept. 7, 1748. Foreigners imported in the Mary Galley, George Lawson, Captain, from London.

Sept. 7, 1748. Frembe famen mit ber Mary Galley, Capitain George Lawfon, von London.

Niclas Deederich,
Michael Konig,*
Nicklas Thinges,
Peter Edeborn,
Nicolaus Wolff,
Friederich Heff,
Caspar Klehr,
Peter Levan,
Conrad Cunner,
William Kohl,*
Jacob Back,
Georg Weber,

Peter Hans Schneeder,
Heinrich Schuhen,
Johan Georg Roth,
Joh. Gottfried Sommerlad,
Johan Peter Rauch,
Phil. Jacob Sommerlad,
Johannes Hieppel,
Abraham Geebs,*
David Sudder,*
Johan Adam Weber,*
Johannes Willerich.

119) Sept. 15, 1748.† Foreigners imported in the Two Brothers, Thomas Arnott, Master, from Rotterdam, last from Portsmouth.

---

† In Sept. 1748, *Peter Kalm*, the Swedish Nat. Phil. came to Philadelphia; he was born 1715, died 1779.—See *Davenport's Biogr. Dict.*

Sept. 15, 1748. † Frembe kamen mit bem Schiffe Two Bro=
thers, Capitain Thomas Arnott, von Rotterbam über Portsmouth.

Johannes Herrmann,
Peter Bier,
Peter Bier jr.,
Johannes Knecht,
Casper Kieffer,*
Abraham Kieffer jr.,
Jacob Scherer,
Jonas Eberst,
Christoffel Heck,
Nicolaus Clementz,
Johannes Wörner,
Johannes Laubach,
Jonas Somerlad,
Johannes Stein,
Jacob Hendel,*
Jacob Höck,
Michael Günter,*
Johannes Heckert,
Phillippius Stein,
Johannes Koller,
Conrad Köhler,
Johannes Schlegel,
Johan Burckhart Braun,
Johan Casper Apffel,
Johan Daniel Wirth,
Johan Peter Denig,
Siegmund Bassermann,
Joh. Friederich Hötz,
Georg Carl Hötz,
Johan Casper Engel,
Johan Philip Steffan,
Joh. Conrad Viehman,
Johan Conrad Rauch,
Johan Just Eberth,
Johan Baltes Schäffer,

Johan Peter Enogel,
Johan Matheus Etter,
Johan Caspar Räumer,
Johannes Huntzecker,*
Johan Friederich Reber,
Johan Paul Junger,*
Michael Reiffsnyder,*
Joh. Georg Messerschmidt,
Johannes Achtung,
Ulrich Wirth,
Ewalt Gantler,
Johannes Waltz,
Matteis Dilhart,
Johannes Deyh,
Candias Messert,
Johannes Nees,
Jacob Jirarden,
Johannes Schlegel,
Michael Hesler,
Henrich Frantz,
Georg Engel,
Johannes Braun,
Peter Dauber,*
Jacob Niess,
Augustus Peffer,
Johannes Müller,
Daniel Kober,
Nicolaus Kuntz,
Peter Felte,*
Michael Berges,
Carl Mahrt,
Philip Heim,
Jacob Bretzius,*
Jeremias Runckel,
Daniel Angst,

† Im Sept. 1748 kam Peter Kalm, ber schwebische Naturforscher, nach
Philabelphia; er war geboren 1715 unb starb 1779.—Siehe Davenport's
Biogr. Dict.

16*

Johannes Bitterwein,
Johan Nicklaus Kindt,
Johannes Gestner,
Johann Jost Dörr,
Johan Peter Messert,
Conrad Alex. Haug,
Johann Georg Fass,
Joh. Daniel Schneider,
Joh. Wilhelm Engel,
Joh. Henrich Engel,
Ludwig Daubnüstel,?
Johannes Neuhauss,
Joh. Wilhelm Müller,

Philip Jacob Schäffer,
Johan Philip Schwab,
Joh. Henrich Specker,
Joh. Michael Brücker,
Johan Jost Runckel,
Johan Peter Lenhart,
Matheus Hütwohl,
Han Adam Ströher,
Joh. Mattheis Ströher,
Michel Christman,*
Johannes Stöhr,
Johann Rouller,*
Joh. Mattheis Ströhr.

120) Sept. 15, 1748. Foreigners imported in the ship Judith, James Tait, Captain, from Rotterdam, last from Cowes.

Sept. 15, 1748. Frembe famen mit bem Schiffe Jubith, Capitain James Tait, von Rotterbam über Cowes.

Conrad Hinkel,*
Philip Knöbel,
Augustus Eygenbrod,
Henry Althaus,*
Valentin Welcker,
William Cuntz,*
Christian Schmid,
Johannes Stehr,
Casper Amhyser,
Friederich Gass,
Erhart Miller,*
Johannes Mayer,
Hans Peter Shaller,
Hans Michael Göhr,
Johan Adam Leidig,
Joh. Nicolaus Copia,
Johan Adam Meyer,
Christ Peter Sauerman,
Joh. Lorentz Weygandt,
Nicklas Ackermann,
Joh. Michael Serfriedt,
Christian Dapper,*

Joh. Esaias Weisskob,
Johannes Hassinger,
Ulrich Rathmacher,
Conrad Weigand,
Valentin Ardt,
Johannes Schall,
Michael Ungar,*
Johannes Schuey,
Jacob Becker,
Mattheis Lescher,
Jacob Seyvert,*
Peter Glick,
Conrath Rhein,
Thebus Spees,*
Jacob Motz,
Johan Jacob Hassinger,
Joh. Michel Baussmann,
Phil. Anthon Sauermann,
Joh. Peter Heckmann,
Johan Georg Haster,
Johan Henrich Beitzel,
Paulus Bender.

Geo. Michel Wamkessel,
Han Georg Arend,
Heinrich Bub,

Georg Melchior Stuber,
Christophel Sauer,
Joh. Henrich Brosius.

---

121) Sept. 16, 1748. Foreigners imported in the ship Paliena, John Brown, Master, from Rotterdam, last from Cowes. Sept. 16, 1748. Frembe famen mit bem Schiffe Paliena, Capitain John Brown, von Rotterbam über Cowes.

Adam Kastner,*
Jacob Beege,
Jacob Heissel,
Christoph Dang,
Henrich Deissinger,
Nicolaus Meisner,
Peter Petermann,
Valentin Katler,
Conrad Weiss,
Dietrich Sahl,
Andreas Rudolff,
Valentin Casser,
Johannes Kunckel,
Johann Kunckel jr.,
Georg Kuss,
George Nutz,*
Friederich Hofner,*
Joseph Pfeind,?
Erdman Koppe,
Friederich Bösch,
Martin Fannes,
Sebastian Leininger,
Ludwig Drackes,
Carolus Peier,
Johan Georg Entes,
Hans Georg Romel,*
Philip Peter Gniser,
Valentin Rummel,
Joh. Henrich Erlenbach,
Johan Georg Wack,
Johan Peter Laux,
Philip Carl Haas,

Geo. Mich. Rothermel,
Joh. Caspar Höpper,
Bertholomäus Scheib,
Johan Conrad Bohner,
Johan Peter Voltz,
Philip Höffelbauer,
Geo. Balthas Höffelbauer,
Georg Adam Neidig,
John Adam Dieterich,
Johan Ernst Kiesecker,
Joh. Gottfried Kunstman,
Johan Jacob Marthin,
Johan Jost Mertz,
Joh. Conrad Leininger,
Johan Biedenbender,
Joh. Philip Hertzel,
Johannes Macht,
Peter Mumma,*
Peter Heissler,
Johannes Miller,*
Philip Wolfe,*
Henrich Schwab,
Johannes Göter,*
Johannes Gether,
Friederich Hagner,
Bernhart Kuber,*
Hans Kunckel,
Matheis Berger,
Jacob Haller,
Conradt Bübelt,
Johannes Habinger,
Henderich Kuyl,*

Hans Zöbeli,
Jacob Ærig,
Pierre Cellier,
Jacob Margel,*
Jacob Fans,
Jost Kleiss,
Hans Sillmann,
Christoph Berth,
Nicklas Womser,*
Jacob Weber,
Casper Gerster,
Hans Wenger,
Stephan Wenger,*
Peter Bergtoll,
Christian Wenger,*
Samuel Fries,
Ludwig Eberling,
Henrich Nätter,
Andreas Keller,
Carl Blaser,
Johannes Holl,
Joh. Nicolaus Weicker,
Johan Jacob Müller,
Georg Balthas Kleber,
Geo. Philip Wuhlhauer,
Joh. Friederich Forster,
Han Adam Kunckel sen.,
Han Adam Kunckel jr.,
Johannes Summerauer,

Antoni Winkotz,
Adam Böhringer,
Andreas Böhringer,
Johannes Schmidt,
Heinrich Summerauer,
Georg Seidenspinner,
Henrich Bücher Deiss,
Casper Phil. Widerwenig,
Henrich Zöbeli,
Jacob Laudenberger,
Jacob Bleckenstorfer,
Hans Ulrich Bucher,
Heinrich Müdtschi,
Adam Hartmann,
Joh. G. Bernhart Stögli,
Joh. Rudolph Grendel,
Hans Yerick Miller,*
Henrich Adam Müller,
Michael Christmann,
Johan Jacob Carle,
Johann Kasper Carle,
Johann Jacob Schäfer,
Johan Nickel Kind,
Michael Kessler,
Joh. Christoph Speicher,
Georg Adam Karnagel,
Georg Adam Bauman,
Jacobus Müller.

122) Oct. 25, 1748. Foreigners imported in the ship Paliena and Margaret, John Govan, Captain, from Rotterdam, last from Leith.

Oct. 25, 1748. Frembe kamen mit dem Schiffe Paliena und Margaret, Capitain John Govan, von Rotterdam über Leith.

Ludwig Pflüger,
Henry Knobloch,*
Dietrich Reinharth,
Philip Zimmer,*
Andreas Spieller,*

Henry Seeman,*
Michael Bihl,
Johannes Fantler,?
Christian Hahn,
Johannes Kneith,

Johannes Lantz,
Jonas Dietz,
Richard Langer,*
Jacob Löffner,*
Peter Groll,
Hannes Klam,
Gottfried Fremauer,
Wilhelm Wagner,*
Balzer Fleischer,
Henrich Kropff,
Peter Schmid,
Carle Janckbach,
Jacob Landes,*
Antonius Brost,
Balzar Schwab,
Jacob Overkirsh,*
Michael Overkirsch,
Henrich Contter,
Friederich Mauss,
Henrich Busch,
Johannes Busch,
Wendel Keeffer,*
Joh. Nicolas Korndörfer,
Carl Balthasar Kern,
Johan Peter Nieth,
Johan Henrich Phul,
Johan Ludwig Seeman,

Friederich Panheimer,
Johan Peter Nay,*
Johan Jacob Mattheis,
Johan Adam Göbe,
Johan Michael Dietz,
Johan Diel Wentz,
Georg Henry Fuchs,
Johannes Meininger,
Johan Peter Han,
Johan Friederich Geiger,
Jan. Gottfried Stöy,
Johan Adam Schneider,
Joh. Michael Dreyerling,
Joh. Henrich Bentheis,?
Joh. Philip Schmäck,
Johan Georg Schad,
Joh. Melchior Kräuter,
Johan Peter Galler,*
Johan Nicol. Polch,
Joh. Michael Reinhart,
Joh. Matteis Gell,*
Johan Casper Prach,
Johan Jacob Hardt,
Johannes Unverzagt,
Johan Nickel Jung,
Anton Hamscher,
Johannes Boltz.

123) Oct. 25, 1748. Foreigners imported in the ship Elliot, James Adams, Captain, from Rotterdam, last from Cowes.— 240 persons, males and females.

Oct. 25, 1748. Frembe kamen mit bem Schiffe Elliot, Capitain James Abams, von Rotterbam über Comes.—240 Perfonen.

Heinrich Christian,
Gottlieb Schwarth,
Peter Räsch,*
Jacob Hoffman,*
Anthon Wolff,
Joh. Friederich Boserman,
Johann Georg Wien,

Johan Jost Kreuscher,
Johan Philip Jantz,
Johan Georg Bernhart,
Carle Helwig,
Gottlieb Bösler,
Philip Vorbach,
Jacob Drenth,

Matthäus Vorbach,
Peter Buth,*
Peter Hop,*
Conrad Wysner,*
Johannes Gross,
Engel Jonas,
Philip Kreischer,
Johann Paulus,
Jacob Kirch,*
Nicolas Necum,*
Nickel Nükom sen.,
Peter Nickum,*
Johannes Jacoby,
Johannes Staudter,
Michael Jost,
Conrad Gebhart,
Conrad Benner,
Johannes Degen,
Jacob Teitz,*
Jonas Hecht,
Peter Klein,*
Jacob Baum,
Philip Welmslehr,
Herman Beltz,
Johannes Bintzel,
Peter Marckert,
Philip Windermeyer,*
Anton Windermeyer,*
Simon Frankenfelt,*
Joh. Georg Toster,*
Andreas Wolff,
Conrad Henrich Eckhard,
Georg Peter Besel,

Johan Martin Hoffman,
Johan Martin Tüsch,
Johan Henrich Beriss,
Johann Strohschneider,
Johan Georg Ritz,
Johan Nicklas Kreischer,*
Johann Philip Biehl,
Johan Anthon Simon,
Johan Philip Breidenbach,
Johan Georg Blumer,
Joh. Nicolas Preire,*
Nicklaus Hasselbach,
Johan Jacob Gasser,
Christo. Sam. Bildmann,
Joh. Georg Rymisus,*
Hans George Haas,*
Johan Jacob Mertz,
Johann Nickel Lang,
Joh. Georg Schmucker,
Henrich Anthon König,
Joh. Peter Tressler,
Joh. Reinhart Schwein,
Joh. Daniel Miller,
Jacob Christian Gleim,
Johan Philip Peisser,
Georg Adam Gossler,
Joh. Conrad Gontler,?
Johannes Heydenreyd,*
Johann Adam Geyer,
Georg Paul Geyer,*
Georg Friederich Küper,
Joh. Casper Grosmuck,
Joh. Martin Bernheusel.

124) Aug. 30, 1749. Foreigners imported in the ship Crown, Michael James, Master, from Rotterdam, last from Cowes.— In all 500 persons.

Aug. 30, 1749. Frembe kamen mit dem Schiffe Crown, Capitain Michael James, von Rotterdam über Cowes.—Im Ganzen 500 Personen.

Hans Markly,*
Claus Berschman,
Hans Jacob Markly,*
Hans Georg Markly,*
Hans Erb,
Martin Weaber,*
Hans Heiney,
Jacob Groff,
Heinrich Seile,
Jacob Sally,*
Jacob Ruber,
Henrich Buser,
Frederick Bruker,*
Michael Beler,
Michael Danner,
Henrich Buser,
Hans Weber sen.,
Hans Weber jr.,*
Henrich Spahr,
Philip Schmid,
Matheis Läpli,
Hans Hawly,*
Durst Hawly,*
Martin Grumm,
Jacob Giesie,
Durst Duren,
Hans Eumler,
Henry Garster,*
Jacob Seiler,
Jacob Shootin,*
Hans Stohler,
Martin Seyler,*
Jacob Rohrer,
Ernst Endress,
Georg Vundi,
Hans Madery,*
Adam Weybel,*
Jacob Weibel,
Philip Omme,*
Durst Amme,
Matheas Seyler,*

Hans Scholtes,*
Hans Busser,*
Jacob Domme,*
Heinrich Thome,
Adam Thome,
Hans Mesemer,*
Hans Georg Groff,
Hans Henrich Pahr,
Johannes Ischadt,
Samuel Neuschwander,
Jacob Werenfels,
Hans Jacob Ställy,*
Joh. Emanuel Pfiffer,*
Martin Meierhofer,
Martin Tschudi,
Jacob Schweitzer,
Reinhart Gunstenhauser,
Hans Jacob Blonk,*
Johannes Tschuti,
Friederich Swonder,*
Adam Browbak sen.,*
Adam Browbak jr.,*
Heinrich Brabek,
Martin Walleset,*
Jacob Wiesener,*
Baltzer Strowman,*
Hans Flubacher,
Johannes Shitzer,*
William Derdamer,
Henry Handshy,*
Hans Ulrich Ehrenstieger,
Lenhart Booser,*
Christophel Seiler,
Martin Schneider,
Hans Jacob Hasler,*
Hans Jacob Gass,
Jacob Wallsener,*
Daniel Messerly,*
Hans Jacob Massener,*
Lorentz Morty,*
Johannes Marti,

Jaus Jacob Honegger,
Martin Dätwyler,
Hans Jacob Zaller,*
Heinrich Schneider,
Hans Ulrich Möstmer,
Friederich Litzler,
Hans Georg Reiniger,
Hans Ruben Brubeck,
Hans Dege,
Henry Leety,*
Daniel Lüdie,
Jacob Tschopp,
Henry Bruner,*
Martin Tschop,*
Johannes Seiler,
Hans Lüte,
Henry Shaffner,*
Jacob Greider,
Leonard Hey,
Nicklaus Dill,

Johannes Meyer,*
Conrad Ziegler,
Martin Herbster,
Heinrich Buda,
Bernhart Romstein,
Sebastian Hassler,*
Hans Jacob Greenblat,*
Martin Greenblat,*
Christoph Weeslin,*
Mattheas Spitler sen.,*
Mattheas Spitler jr.,*
Hans Jacob Spitler,*
Hans Greber,
Joh. Ludwig Buda,
Andreas Donner,*
Uhllerich Feeler,*
Hans Jacob Trawinger,*
Abraham Houser,*
Nicklas Makhold,*
Joh. Nicolas Macholt.

Sick—Jacob Furman, Hans Greber, Jacob Wurtz, Stephen Spenhover, George Sholtes, Hans Messner, Martin Gash.

---

125) Sept. 2, 1749.   Wirtembergers imported in the ship Chesterfield, Thomas Coatam, Master, from Rotterdam, last from Cowes.—In all 255.

Sept. 2, 1749. Württemberger kamen mit dem Schiffe Chester=field, Capitain Thomas Coatam, von Rotterdam über Cowes.—Im Ganzen 255.

Gallus Gulde,
Johannes Maurer,
Joseph Weidel,
Johannes Keller,*
Jaques Moris,
Martin Waghter,*
Friederich Gosner,
Frantz Schweitzer,
Nicolaus Reyer,
Solomon Gansle,
Jacob Reyer

Jacob Gast,
Jacob Aller,
Jacob Deible,
Martin Schooler,*
George Limbert,*
Martin Getz,
Georg Jäckel,
Hans Jacob Allerth,
Balthasar Maurer,
Jacob Schlotterer,
Martin Schauwecker,

Hans Conrad Schauwecker,
Martin Schlotterer,
Jacob Schlotterer,
Phil. Georg Müller,
Hans Mich. Lötterhe,
Hans Conrad Katz,
Maximilian Speidell,
Hans Georg Speidell,
Johan Jacob Ries,
Christian Käpple,
Johan Martin Beck,
Balthas Zimmerman,
Jacob Scheiffeler,
Hans Bernhart Klotz,
Bastian Meyer,
Jacob Klotz,
Gottfried Fuchs,
Elias Steeb,
Michael Steeb,
Hans Stecher,
Werner Sauder,*
Joseph Seitz,
Adam Wanner,
Johannes Kleim,
Joseph Hiller,
Michael Fanz,
Michael Kiele,
Jacob Metzger,
Christoph Gross,
Simon Schmidt,

Baltas Mayer,
Elias Ebirhardt,
Ludwig Hoch,
Joseph Eckert,
Jacob Hauch,
Conrad Wolf,
Johannes Michael Christman,
Christoph Wunder,
Johannes Henche,
Simeon Heritho,
Ludwig König,
Heinrich Seytter,
Mattheis Schlatterer,
Joh. Conrad Schlatterer,
Hans Christ Beuthler,
Hans Georg Kloss,
Hans Georg Haisch,
Hans Ebert Hordt,
Johan Martin Hoyst,
Mattheis Laudenschläger,
Michael Tompprät,
Jacob Reinthaler,
Christoph Schäffer,
Georg Fried. Fisher,
Hans Jacob Haar,
Hans Georg Hauselmann,
Johan Georg Weiss,
Philip Gübler,
Michael Stierlo.

Sick—Johannes Mayer, Sebastian Mayer, Hans Ulrich Suller, Jacob Klotz.

---

126) Sept. 2, 1749.   Wirtembergers from Erbach,—ship
Albany, Robert Brown, Master, from Rotterdam, last from
Cowes.—285 passengers.

Sept. 2, 1749. 285 Württemberger von Erbach kamen mit
dem Schiffe Albany, Capitain Robert Brown, von Rotterdam
über Cowes.

Johannes Schinf,
Johannes Gerber,
Friederich Gätzinger,
George Shwartz,*
Joh. A. Winckler,
Nickel Heist,
Matheas Schöuk,*
Vallentin Edelman,*
Hans Redman,*
George Truke,*
Wendel Scherr,
Joh. Nicolaus Porrath,
Joh. Philip Beyer,*
Joh. Henrich Möths,
Joh. Balthas Hetzler,
Joh. Georg Kroft,
Joh. Michel Kabel,
Joh. Michael Kabel sen.,
Hans Peter Gembler,*
Hans Mich. Gembler,*
Joh. Hen. Blumenschein,
Johan Peter Heist,
Michel Beed,
Joseph Scholl,
Johannes Grauer,
Christoph Nutts,*
Johannes Buchter,
Johannes Nibling,
Adam Edelman,
Gotlieb Volck,*
Andreas Welker,*
Johan Adam Joh,
Johan Jacob Joh,
Johannes Jotter,
Augustinus Ginter,
Peter Schäffer,*
Casper Walser,
Frederick Lewy,*
Johannes Müller,
Adam Luick,
Philip Lautenschleger,

Phil. Jacob Kreysh,*
Johannes Graber,*
Christoffel Nagel,*
Peter Brunner,*
Joh. Adam Getz,
Adam German,*
Adam Geisinger,
Joh. Philip Gerg,
Johannes Klinger,*
Martin Rausch,
J. Balthas Jegel,*
J. George Folk,*
Valentin Schuck,
Martin Schäffer,
Peter Kill,*
Alexander Klinger,
Nickolaus Beissel,
Conrad Menges,
Peter Brunner,
J. Adam Beiffweg,*
Joh. Philip Heist,
Geo. Adam Ewald,*
Joh. Philip Iaxthemer,
Hans Jacob Wagner,
Joh. Christof Kintzinger,
Hans Georg Fischer,
Joh. Martin Schuck,
George Michael Herold,*
Hans Martin Strein,*
Hans Georg Dreher,
Hans Georg Edelman,
Joh. Wilhelm Volck,
Johan Peter Hörg,
Johan Michel Ioh,
Hans Peter Jotter,
Hans Conrad Rärich,
Johan Georg Menges,
Mattheus Nunnenmacher,
Joh. Adam Heckman,
Hans George Nagel,*
Johannes Häckman,

Joh. Wilhelm Süfer,
Joh. Nicolas Delp,*
Joh. Zacharias Erdroth,
Joh. Georg Schäffer,
J. Leonhart Meyer,
Joh. Georg Dersler,
Hans Adam Peetsh,*
Joh. Antoni Walther,
Hans Philip Krichbaum,

Johann Adam Gorm,
Johan Lenhart German,
Adam Laudenschlager,*
Georg Michael Frantz,
Philip Jacob Walther,
Joh. Adam Krichbaum,
Johan Adam Rausch,
Johan Georg Rettig,
Johan Wilhelm Krichbaum.

Sick—Hans Kabel, Hans Balthaser Schäffer, Peter Belman, Hans Georg Hochzig.

---

127) Sept. 9, 1749. Palatines,—ship St. Andrew, James Abercrombie, Master, from Rotterdam, last from Plymouth.— 400 passengers.

Sept. 9, 1749. 400 Pfälzer kamen mit dem Schiffe St. Andrew, Capt. James Abercrombie, von Rotterdam über Plymouth.

Andreas Emmert,
Joseph Bergtohlt,
Arnold Kramer,*
Johannes Mebel,
Johannes Runkel,*
Henry Hamer,*
Adam Humberger,
Jost Streilhoff,
Jacob Linke,*
Christian Halte,
Peter Bauman,*
Jacob Rohr,
Peter Finger,
Christian Graff,
Christian Stauffer,
Johan Schnebeli,
Johannes Rohr,
Johannes Woosing,*
Michael Wagner,
Christian Hasseler,
Jacob Hertzler sen.,
Jacob Hertzler jr.,
Hans Dierstein,

Johannes Böhner,
Marcus Grull,*
Jacob Kern,
Johannes Haan,*
Jacob Leydig,
Samuel Meyer,*
Peter Ihrich,
Jacob Brandt,
Johannes Berr,
Ulrich Saufert,
Daniel Saufert,
Daniel Berr,
Peter Wilhelm,
Franz Jans,
Johannes Heisser,
Conrad Stichter,
Joh. Friederich Emrich,
Albrecht Ellenberger,
Samuel Kauffman,
Christian Eschbacher,
Casper Herschberger,
Benedict Mellinger,
Hans Rudy Frey,

Jacob Herschberger,
Joh. Georg Vallendin,
Hans Michael Vallendin,
Johannes Blickesterfer,*
Ulrich Blickestörfer,
Jacob Mashberger sen.,
Johan Henricus Wenig,
Joh. Jacob Küblinger,
Joh. Daniel Küblinger,
Peter Sterneman,*
Bartholomäus Voss,
Johann Peter Lach,
Christoph Weber,
Bernhart Kessler,
Johan Peter Druck,
Friederich Neuhoff,
Joh. Friederich Bohr,
Andreas Keller jr.,
Andreas Keller sen.,
Henrich Casper Racke,
Johannes Corell,
Joh. Engelbert Morgenstern,
Conrad Hoffmann,
Baltzer Weinberger,
Christian Kirschberger,
Joh. Wilhelm Franck,
Ulrich Hackmann,
Abraham Brübacher,
Johan Adam Stahler,
Joh. Conrad Seybell,
Hans George Garner,*
Joh. Henrich Gerndt,
Henry Slawffer,*
Valentin Stichler,

Johannes Walder,
Jacob Herbig,
Valentin Haag,
Jacob Eshelman,*
Johannes Jung,
Johannes Funck,
Christian Wenger,*
Hannes Wenger,
Jacob Eimann,
Christian Fuchs,*
Martin Spreng,
Adam Helweg,
Johannes Huth,
Peter Ahles,
Matheas Weise,*
Ulrich Jordte,
Christian Eschbacher,
Johannes Mellinger,
Johannes Brubacher,
Peter Eschelmann,
Johannes Eppelman,
Hans Jacob Weyse,*
Johan Adam Dörr,
Hermanius Heger,
Simeon Zeherman,
Johan Peter Krämer,
Christoffel Henry,
Jacob Weiss sen.,
George Shambach,*
Johannes Hackman,
Henrich Stauffer,
Uhellerich Staver,*
Hans George Hobler,
Jac. Fried. Debert Yäussler.

---

128) Sept. 11, 1749. Foreigners imported in the ship Priscilla, William Meier, Captain, from Rotterdam, last from Cowes.
299 passengers.

Sept. 11, 1749. 299 Fremde kamen mit dem Schiffe Priscilla,
Capitain William Meier, von Rotterdam über Cowes.

Johannes Kraun,
Johannes Miller,*
Friederich Lier,
Rudolph Bär,
Henry Barr,*
Henry Huber,
Johannes Bür,
Melchior Leeder,*
Henrich Kunst,
Jacob Stehli,
Hans Merky,
Hans Surber,*
Hans Schneebly,
Georg Funck,
Ulrich Hohsteter,
Johannes Weiss,
Rudolph Huber,
Jacob Huber,
Jacob Bär,
Jacob Baumann,
Henrich Wollenweider,
Hans George Isseller,*
Müller Heinrich,
Jacob Gützinger,
Joh. Reinhardt Uhl,
Mattheis Gallman,
Hans Rudolph Gallman,
Hans Jacob Meyer,
Hans Jacob Gübler,
Jacob Bodenreider,
Reinhart Scherer,
Johannes Hoffecker,
Joh. Philip Mühlhoff,
Joh. Peter Mühlhoff,
Johan Michael Boor,
Joh. Nickel Lorentz,
Johan Peter Franck,
Friederich Stroh,

Urich Hauber,
Casper Pfester,
Rudolp Näff,
Jacob Näff,
Casper Huber,
Rudy Kuntz,
Jacob Kuntz, §
Hans Kern,
Jacob Mawer,*
Rudy Mawer,*
Jacob Hauser,
Jacob Shnabely,*
Jacob Bart,*
Friederich Shurp,*
Johannes Shurp,*
Paulus Schorb,
Michael Franck,
Hans Zubler,*
Henry Meyer,*
Joh. Ludwig Küstner,
Joh. Philip Küstner,
Georg Peter Dürr,*
Joh. Jacob Walther,
Joh. Henrich Beiger,
Joh. Friedrich Frütschie,
Johan Nickel Göbel,
Joh. Michael Malfier,
Joh. Matheis Bohr,
Johan Adam Bohr,
Joh. Matheis Ströher,
Joh. Nicolaus Wedartz,
Joh. Matheis Becker,
Johan Nickel Neu,
Joh. Adam Neu,
Joh. Peter Müller,
Henrich Rütschi,
Joh. Burkhart Hoffmann.

129) Sept. 13, 1749. Foreigners from Wirtemberg, Alsace and Zweibrücken,—ship Christian, Thomas Brady, Captain, from Rotterdam, last from Cowes.

Sept. 13, 1749. Württemberger, Elsässer und Zweibrückner kamen mit dem Schiffe Christian, Capitain Thomas Brady, von Rotterdam über Cowes.

Paulus Brod,
Andreas Vogel,
Friederich Erb,*
Valentin Kern,*
Christoph Ludwig,
Ernst Münckel,
Heinrich Albrecht,
Frantz Ziegler sen.,
Frantz Ziegler jr.,
Benjamin Cuny,
Adam Schneck,
Johannes Schäffer,
Daniel Altik,*
Wilhelm Hältz,*
Joseph Ressener,*
Andreas Braun,
Karl Volden,
Philip Kaupt,*
Friederich Gelbach sen.,
Frantz Gelbach,
Friederich Gelbach jr.,
Joh. Andreas Auler,?
Hans Jacob Stotz,
Hans Adam Hackman,
George Ludwig Burg,*
Johannes Mischeb,
Martin Bernharth,
Julius Christo Bachman,
Hans Georg Michele,
Johan Georg Erig,
Joh. Caspar Geisinger,
Joh. Ludwig Bäuerle,
Michael Shoemaker,*
Ludwig Maintzger,
Joh. Phil. Hen. Hauer,
Georg Michel Derr,
Georg Hummel,*
Jacob Hieman,

David Pfautz,
Michael Hauff,
Weybegt Rupp,
Christian Romich,*
Michael Haupt,
Johannes Tilly,*
Matheis Ostertag sen.,
Matheis Ostertag jr.,*
Abraham Selman,*
Michael Rummel,*
John Ehrait,*
Baltasar Glisser,*
Wilhelm Heyshe,*
Martin Danner,
Conrad Bosch,
Matheis Weiss,
Joseph Schmidt,
Christian Limbacher,
Johannes Reuter,
Jacob Wälckly,
Isaac Jung,
Christian Ostertag,
Balthasar Dock,
Peter Gascha,
Samuel Mosser,
Jacob Ribelet,
Henrich Dock,
Hans Meck,
Peter Hamman,*
Philip Kugler,
Antony Ecki,
Jacob Rumel,
Georg Bernhart Braun,
Georg Michael Braun,
Joh. Andreas Weckeffer,
Joh. Jacob Datismann,
Martin Schlachenhauff,
Michael Hechelman,

Joh. Michael Mayer,
Hans Georg Haffer,
Hans Georg Haupt,
Hans Georg Schumacher,
Joh. Michael Sommer,
Joh. Abrecht Eshelman,*
Hans Georg Ungast,*
Hans Jacob Uber,*
Hans Georg Merckly,*
Jacob Risternholtz,
Johan Georg Limbacher,
Johan Adam Ebert,
Johan Jacob Sim,
Johannes Schmerber,

Hans Peter Jung,
Hans Peter Ribelet,
Joh. Nicolaus Koch,
Abraham Ribellet,
Phil. Thomas Hull,*
Christian Eichart,
Johan Jacob Barnitz,
Christian Glässer,
Michael Hauswird,*
Joh. Erhart Knappenberger,
Christian Gutknecht,
Martin Hisch,*
Berhart Schweighart,*
Hans Adam Krieger.

130) Sept. 14, 1749. Foreigners from the electorate Palatinate,—ship Two Brothers, Thomas Arnot, Master, from Rotterdam, last from Cowes.—312 passengers.

Sept. 14, 1749. 312 Pfälzer kamen mit dem Schiffe Two Brothers, Capitain Thomas Arnot, von Rotterdam über Cowes.

Weygand Schneider,
Christian Humbold,*
Jacob Gruber,
Joh. Gerhart Schneider,
Johan Peter Schneider jr.,
Johan Peter Shneyder sen.,*
Teys Refy,*
Michael Reyffener,*
Peter Reiffener,
Henry Wagner,*
Peter Ammo,
Philippus Löhr,
Johannes Osseler,
Johan Hermannis,
Christian Birkingbey,*
Jacob Cambeck,
Wilhelm Pfeiffer,
Johannes Damfuchs,
Johan Beisbeker,*
Peter Heinrich,

Simon Höller,
Johan Phillipus,
John Vemisbaker,*
Henry Weller,*
Johannes Hilbisch,
Matheus Trawn,*
Wilhelm Kusche,
Johannes Böhmer,
Ernst Schäffer,
Wilhelm Ditz,
Matheis Baker,*
Joh. Balthas Shmit,*
Joh. Christ Klein,
Joh. Ludwig Schiess,
Joh. Ernst Greiss,
Joh. Adam Becker,
Joh. Peter Hess,
Christian Steltz,
Joh. Jacob Carl,
Johannes Dirwess,

Joh. Peter Dihl,
Bastian Braun,
Johan Säger,
Wilhelm Helt,*
Joh. Deys Rüb,
Joh. Christ Rüb,
Ernst Becker,
Michael Durschman,
Joh. Wilh. Jäger,
Wilhelmus Jacobus Gruber,
Johan Conrad Refi,
Adam Henrich Prentz,
Johannes Hermanes,
Johan Henry Wagner,*
Hans Peter Lehr,*
Johan Jost Blecher,
Johan Peter Miller,*
Johan Jost Fischer,
Johan Peter Hilfisch,
Joh. Haubrich Löhr,
Johan Peter Lay,
Joh. Christ Löhmer,
Joh. Albert Strecker,
Johan Jost Shäffer,*
Joh. Daniel Hoffman,
Joh. Henrich Fuchs,
Joh. Henrich Schmit,
Georg Jacob Wird,*
Christian Matheis Göbeler,
Johan Henrich Gruber,
Johan Philip Sauer,
Johan Peter Lupp,
Johan Ernst Krämer,

Joh. Balthasar Schmidt,
Friederich Gottfried Schmidt,
Johan Peter Schuman,
Joh. Martin Schmitgen,
Joh. Adam Schmitgen,
Joh. Wilhelm Mallert,
Joh. Martin Greiss,
Joh. Jacobus Hoffman,
Johan Peter Jung,
Johan Adam Jung,*
Joh. Philip Becker,
Joh. Christ Badenheinner,
Johan Peter Aller,
Johan Peter Braun,
Johan Georg Schultz,
Johan Theis Durschman,
Johan Jacob Haner,
Johan Michael Gessel,
Johan Julius Schmidt,
Christoph Lentart,*
Johannes Fonn,
Johannes Küm,
Henrich Schmieg,
Joh. Deis Bäcker,
Christian Baker,*
Joh. Peter Stath,
Johan Wilhelm Schmidt,
Johan Christ Schneyder,
Johan Adam Gemmer,*
Johann Peter Seyn,
Johan Wilhelm Jung,
Johan Peter Schaaff,
John Peter Miller.*

131) Sept. 15, 1749. Palatines imported in the ship Edinburgh, James Russel, Master, from Rotterdam, last from Portsmouth.—380 passengers.

Sept. 15, 1749. 380 Pfälzer kamen mit dem Schiffe Edinburgh, Capitain James Ruffel, von Rotterdam über Portsmouth.

Heinrich Conrad,
Abraham Jung,
Peter Lang,
Georg Conrad,*
Johannes Schmidt,
Philip Mertz,*
Herman Mauer,
Jeremias Bär,
Wilhelm Tuchembel,
Valentin Scherer,
Henrich Miedel,
Adam Lambe,*
Christoph Lambert,
Philip Diehl,
Hannes Spicker,
Julius Spicker,
Johannes Bauer,
Friederich Klärr,
Peter Laub,*
Jacob Hamman,
Georg Fengel,
Peter Gübrit,
Waller Schmidt,
Valentin Heil,
Jacob Wirth,
Adam Bauer,
Georg Wachter,
Adam Goos,*
Andreas Stein,
Peter Tamerus,
Johan Friederich Ditz,
John Philip Hame,*
Johan Jacob Becker,
Philip Peter Becker,
Nicklas Biedeman,*
Daniel Sheimer,*
Friederich Scheimer,
Michael Scheimer,
Johan Daniel Koller,
Johann Henrich Lang,
Johan Philip Dick,

Joh. Friederich Martin,
Johan Conrad Lutz,
Johan Georg Meundel,
Johann Jacob Schäffer,
Johannes Rüdinger,
Johannes Senffelder,
Johan Henrich Schmidt,
Valentin Petry,
Adam Scheimer,
Johannes Schwerdt,
Johannes Laudenschläger,
Johannes Schneider,
Johan Georg Steiner,
Christoph Ridlein,
Georg Henry Risser,*
Wilhelm Schwerber,*
John Georg Hendershit,
Phillipp Metzger,
Heinrich Schmidt,
Bernhart Scherer,
Friederich Schwob,*
Dewalt Schmidt,
Samuel Kerch,
Jacob Kerch,
Nickel Renner,
Michael Penss,
Stofel Schuman,
Michael Mauerer,*
Christian Shmit,*
Conrad Knepper,
Johann Adam,
Andreas Bieber,*
Jacob Bieber,*
Rudolph Rauch,
Christian Axer,
Stephan Leyer,
Philip Dinges,
Jacob Klein,
Philip Bucke,*
Peter Brauch,
Philip Rickart,*

Henry Shmit,*
Jacob Zerel,*
Jacob Zinn,
Simon Hörch,
Johannes Althaus,*
Carl Sirer,
Jacob Becker,
Christian Egyr,
Johannes Bender,*
Henry Bender,*
Wendel Essig,
Friederich Dick,
Conrad Miller,*
Nicklas Grusius,*
Jacob Kulman,?
Fritz Schäffer,*
Jacob Mohr,
Gerlach Strich,
Georg Land,
Henry Zoll,*
Henry Marsh,*
Lothareus Pfannenbecker,
Nickolas Seltzer,*
Johan Peter Geis,
Hans Jacob Tamet,
Frantz Nicolaus Faber,
Henrich Faber,
Johann Buchharner,
Erasmus Bockius,
Johan Nicklas Fellenberger,
Mattheis Bolland,
Christoph Gideon Myrteties,
Nicklaus Eisenmänger,
Johan Georg Klein,
Simeon Charmely,
Frantz Hartman,
Johan Jacob Dästerr,

Georg Michael Mauer,
Georg Friederich Seil,
Antony Hargesheimer,
Joh. Wilhelm Schreiner,
Johannes Dietz,
Jacob Pfannkuchen,
Conrad Schweitzer,
Erasmus Althaus,
Adam Diehhart,
Benedictus Thom,
Christoffel Klärr,
Johannes von der Lindt,
Johann Michel Lawall,
Jacob Brubacher,
Johan Adam Sachs,
Johan Michel König,
Johan Nickel Scheffer,
Joh. Walther Schwob,
Joh. Wilhelm Pfeil,
Joh. Gerlach Huhn,
Joh. Daniel Huhn,
Samuel Neitlinger,
Friederich Zerfass,
Jacob Goodman,*
Phillip Goodman,*
Christian Bernhart,
Joh. Martin Neubecker,
Johannes Adler,
Bastian Wenig,*
Johannes Fritz,
Henry Steinmetz,
Friederich Conradt,
Jacob Hattebach,
Joh. Michel Hoffman,
Johan Jacob Kapp,
Johan Peter Weiler,
Henry Shermillin.*

132) Sept. 15, 1749. Foreigners from Zweibrücken, Nassau, Wirtemberg, and Palatinate,—ship Phœnix, John Mason, Master, from Rotterdam, last from Cowes.—550 passengers.

Sept. 15, 1749. 550 Ausländer von Zweibrücken, Nassau, Württemberg und der Pfalz kamen mit dem Schiffe Phönix, Capitain John Mason, von Rotterdam über Cowes.

Samuel Notoing,*
Caspar Bruner,*
Andreas Creiner,
Henrich Lüta,
Georg Härther,
Jacob Anthoni,
Nicklas Roath,*
Nicklas Ricksaker,
Andreas Tevental,*
Simon Walter,*
Johannes Gross,
Conrath Jost,
Jacob Schneider,
Jacob Meserli,
Joseph Han,
Henrich Ginder,
Michael Traxel,*
George Traxel,*
Henry Mishit,*
Dewald Stecker,*
Peter Gerret,*
Ulrich Stoller,
Georg Altman,
Anthon Altman,
Solomon Barher,*
Theobald Kuntz,
Niclas Eisseman,*
Michael Köppel,
Georg Caspar Heuss,
Hans Ulrich Ott,
Georg Wanenmacher,
Joh. Ludwig Strauss,
Samuel Wanenmacher,

Joseph Kauffman,
Georg Frantz Philippi,
Hans Georg Windenauer,
Hans Nickel Ott,
Hans Adam Bauss,
Hans Peter Rösser,
Georg Adolph Kräber,
Hans Lenart Hinckel,*
John George Shneyder,*
J. Rudolph Ginder,*
Joh. Jacob Mestenbach,
Abraham Nonnemacker,*
Hans Georg Cleiss,
Bernhart Traxel,*
John Jacob Mitshit,
Johan Michel Schmidte, a
Hans Peter Eichede,
Hans Philip Bison,
Hans Georg Eisseman,*
Peter Eisenmann sen.,
Peter Eisenmann jr.,
Johan Nickel Köppel,
Nicolaus Schneider,
Jacob Keppel,*
Paulus Keppel,*
Peter Keppel,*
Peter Isch,
Christof Brunner,
Daniel Duval,*
Johan Drugrare,*
Daniel Daam,*
Jacob Dormeyer,*
J. Lutwig,

a *Schmidte* has "*Arzt*," *physician*, appended to his name, indicative of his profession.—(*Editor.*)

a Schmidte fügte, um seinen Beruf anzuzeigen, „Arzt" seinem Namen bei.—(Herausgeber.)

Henry Schauff,*
Martin Klein,
Jacob Klein,*
Johannes Hort,
Andreas Gratt,
Johannes Creat,*
Georg Müller,
Philip Miller,*
Nicola Delon,
Peter Grieger,
Jacob Schneider,
Michael Nike,*
Jacob Nike,*
Mattheus Krasch,
Herman Batur,
Jacob Batur,
Marx Springel,*
Christian Creesle,*
Weirich Seltzer,
Johannes Gross,*
Felix Kley,
Hans Reese,*
Michael Shaffer,*
Heinrich Luteer,
Philip Laure,*
Christian Weiss,
Nicklas Bob,
Jacob Walter,*
Martin Walter,*
John Bender,*
Jacob Bieber,
Jacob Jonger,*
Samuel Spiger,*
Jacob Altman,
Wilhelm Altman,
Han Joh. Barhitz,
Hans Georg Jundt,
Johann Michael Mallo,
John Frederich Hister,*
Henrich Wilh. Mählich,
Samuel Dormeyer,*

Hans Jacob Witmer,*
Frantz Jacob Zühl,
John Nicklas Miller,*
Jeremias Schönbach,
Jacob Zollicker,
Adam Grantadam,*
Josephe Chavlier,
Johan George Ker,*
Josephe Courteuer,
Abraham Scherdrong,
Johan Georg Mölig,
Johan Reinhart Keller,
Conrad Wohlfahrt,
Andreas Rütsieler,
Daniel Greberger,
Christopher Reger,
Frantz Soal,*
François Grandadam,
Johan Adam Walter,*
John Matheas Shöman,*
Wilhelm Longhauer,*
Anthony Nieve,*
Christian Tathouer,*
Christian Brost,
Simon Roorig,*
Johannes Roorig,*
Johannes Geeber,*
Daniel Roorig,*
Anthoni Bieber,
Hans Nickel Bieber,
Hans Adam Herman,*
Hannes Müller,
Ulrich Kindlishberger,*
Johannes Weller,
Johannes Lamot,
Stephan Alman,*
Samuel Perquy,*
Jacob Schmidt,
Jacob Widmer,
Hans Sölli,
Hans Meier,*

Johannes Boushy,*
Jacob Miller,*
Christian Miller,*
Peter Miller,*
Johannes Keefer,
Peter Rett,
Jacob Misseler,*
Joseph Mischler,
Jacob Seiler,
Christian Staufer,
Jacob Klein,
Martin Ritter,*
Hans Lantz,
Jacob Hörnlie,
Antoni Kratzer,
Jacob Has,
Simon Degler,
Jacob Gratze,
Jacob Hünler,
Peter Kaufman,
Johannes Riehm,
Felix Sailor,*
George Bentz,
Jacob Bence,*
Johannes Sumer,
Christian Summer,*
Matheis Nafzger,
Johannes Farne,
Peter Crapy,*
Jacob Stauch,
Johannes Rupp,
Jacob Rupp,
Peter Nofsker,*
Erhart Bom,*
Philip Henkel,*
Johannes Reber,*
Daniel Rynolle,
Christian Fischer,
Nicolaus Dartwiller,*
Daniel Dörtweiler,
Martin Dartwiller,*

Michael Wüsel,
Hans Strubhar,
Christoph Spanler,*
Hans Georg Springer,*
Michael Dormeyer,*
Abraham Drachsel,
Durst Deretinger,*
Benedict Leman,*
Joh. Georg Steinroth,
Anton Beavenaw,*
François Hognon,
Joh. Michael Steng,
Joh. Michael Heller,
Friederich Wohlfahrt,
Hans Georg Keim,
Han Philip Grünewalt,
Sebastian Bissahr,
Joh. Ludwig Bentz,
Christian Hartman,*
Frantz Marshall,*
Christian Schowalder,
Rudolph Nafzger,
Christian Kauffman,*
Jacob Kauffman,
Johannes Lans,
Hans Georg Stauch,
Abraham Kurtz,
Anton von Gumden,
Georg Christian Sim,
Christian Kurtz,
Jan Hendrick Reckman,
Theobald Hoschar,
Hans Peter Hoschar,
Heinerich Hoschar,
Andre de Grange,
Georg Hertzog Dering,
Kilian Zimmerman,
Michael Ridelsberg,*
Christian Hochstätter,
Georg Hertzog,
Peter Obersteg,

18

Ulrich Hostetter'*
Simon Steckel,
Hans Schrantz,
Conrad Wagner,
Matheus Seygor,
Peter Herb,*
Jost Mayer,
Jacob Mann,
Frantz Griebel,
Nicklaus Hochstätter,

Johannes Schöndeman,
Ulrich Reinhart,
Ulrich Mischler,
Ludwig Eerlman,
Hans Nickel Mayer,
Martin Obersteg,
Casper Fretter,
Conrad Altvater,
Hans Michael Walther,
Joh. Ludwig Gribeler.

133) Sept. 19, 1749. Palatines and persons from the duchy of Wirtemberg,—ship Patience, Hugh Steel, Captain, from Rotterdam, last from Cowes.—270 passengers.

Sept. 19, 1749. 270 Pfälzer und Württemberger kamen mit dem Schiffe Patience, Capitain Hugh Steel, von Rotterdam über Cowes.

Engelbert Jung,
Herman Schneider,
Henrich Hartman,
Jacob Ernst,
Henry Righart,*
Jacob Richart,*
Johan Bauman sen.,
Johan Bauman jr.,
Andreas Hecker,*
Christian Eslinger,*
Michael Müller,
Bernhart Müller,
Andreas Müller,
Friederich Rübman,
Joh. Georg Bauman,
Conrath Röger,
Casper Kilian,
Adam Keltinger,
Georg Lutz,
Georg Lindenmuth,
Valentin Gramly,*
Carl Kayser,
Heinrich Magasch,

Christoph Kylbach,
Michael Schlör,
Andreas Unangst,
Johannes Steinseiffer,
Hermanus Battenberg,
Johan Jacob Grisse,
Johan Michel Stoltz,
Joh. Jost Zimmerman,
Dielman Grydelbach,
Johan Henrich Güthing,
Johan Wilhelm Hart,
Hans Henrich Wehler,
Joh. Friederich Schello,
Johan Georg Haffner,
Georg Ludwig Sommer,
Johan Jacob Bähr,
Hans Adam Gramlich,
Philip Jacob Ernst,
Hans Adam Gramlich jr.,
Johan Martin Hasee,
Hans Georg Meeder,
Joh. Wilhelm Rittelbach,?
Joh. Adam Zangmeister,

Georg Fried. Zangmeister,
Franz Georg Bacher,
Hans Peter Liewel,
Georg Henrich Urangst,
Georg Peter Glick,
Joh. Christoph Œllinger,
Daniel Camp,*
David Kamp,
Christ Zimmerman,
Peter Spohn,
Christoph Stroh,
Mattheis Milling,
Ludwig Lindenmuth,
Martin Leeser,*
Michel Billing,
Wilhelm Besch,
Andreas Beuschlein,
Andreas Fendig,
Johannes Endress,
Johannes Eulon,
Martin Bawer,*
Martin Riess,
Ferdinand Reed,*
Joseph Buyghart,
Georg Koster,
Johannes Eberts,*
Jacob Glasser,
Joseph Dummey,
Samuel Ehring,
Philip Herr,*
Johannes Wagner,*
David Keller,
George Smith,*
George Hoffner,*
Mattheis Heinlen,
David Heinlen,
Michael Okser,*
Andreas Föhl,
Joseph Hausser,
Daniel Finck,
Peter Finck,

Peter Stetzler,
Johannes Kast,
Adam Ernst,
Georg Peter Vogt,
Joh. Casper Senghaass,
Joh. Bernhard Fehr,
Hans Georg Kantz,
Hans Georg Martin,
Hans Peter Uhrig,
Hans Philip Brenner,
Philip Adam Brenner,
Hans Adam Ludwig,
Hans Peter Ludwig,
Georg Michel Röger,
Hans Martin Yler,
Hans Georg Hertel,
Hans George Linemuth,*
Joh. Christoph Wollet,
Johan Adam Gessner,
Johan Ludwig Barth,
Friederich Dörflinger,
Johannes Heillmann,
Johan Peter Zimmerman,
Joh. Friederich Gall,
Johan Adam Diem,
Johan Adam Hoffman,
Georg Michel Gibler,
Hans Georg Schuhmann,
Georg Himmelberger,
Joseph Kauffman,
Johannes Sauerzapff,
Abraham Baumann,
Gottlieb Baumann,
Lorentz Seyfriedt,
Bernhart Pangert,*
Daniel Kurtz,
Joh. Friederich Strauss,
Johannes Feyler,
Heinrich Häffner,
Bernhart Schmidt,
Andreas Müller.

Sick—Johan Ebert Stein, Jacob Ludwig, Johannes Ender.

NOTE.—At the same time the ship Patience arrived, two other vessels were about landing. In the *Archives* is found this *Memorandum:*— "The foreigners, in number 49, imported in the ship Francis and Elizabeth, Captain Beach, being sickly, were not permitted to be landed. Likewise the foreigners, in number 53, imported in the ship Rachel, Captain Armstrong, were so sickly that it was thought dangerous to suffer them to land altogether; whereupon the sick were ordered to be separated from the well, and such as recovered, with the well, were to be qualified *occasionally*."

Anmerkung.—Zur Zeit als dieses Schiff ankam, waren auch zwei andere am Landen. In den Archiven ist dieses Memorandum aufbewahrt: „Den auf dem Schiffe Franzis und Elisabeth, Capitain Beach, befindlichen 49 Ausländern, welche kränklich waren, wurde das Anlanden nicht erlaubt. Ebenfalls nicht den 53 Fremden auf dem Schiffe Rachel, Capitain Armstrong; diese litten so sehr, daß man es für gefährlich glaubte, sie überhaupt an's Land kommen zu lassen. Die Kranken wurden von den Gesunden ausgeschieden und zeitweise, wenn sie genesen waren, qualificirt."

134) Sept. 25, 1749. Foreigners from Wirtemberg, Alsace, and Hanau,—ship Speedwell, James Creagh, Captain, from Rotterdam, last from Cowes.—240 passengers.

Sept. 25, 1749. 240 Fremde von Württemberg, Elsaß und Hanau kamen mit dem Schiffe Speedwell, Capitain James Creagh, von Rotterdam über Cowes.

Peter Sadler,	Jacob Ham,*
Hans Müller,	Andreas Ham,*
Joseph Hengher,	Jacob Miller,*
Christian Hemler,	Adam Layar,
Dewald Metz,*	Burghart Ertinger,
Jacob Gryffing,	Johannes Yowch,*
Heinrich Zeiner,	Michael Kientz,
Johannes Berth,	Mattheus Sprutt,
Johannes Weiss,	Friederich Wentz,
Michael Shak,*	Johannes Hell,*
Christoph Meyer,*	Johannes Geradewohl,*
Michel Meyer,	Hans Jost Hausser,
David Hamm,*	Johannes Hausser,
Adam Buchman,*	Hans Georg Pfauty,*
Jacob Wächter,*	Joseph Freymiller sen.,*
Hans Diebolt,	Joseph Freymiller jr.,*
Michael Kleim,	Hans Jacob Held,

Ludwig Held,*
Johannes Amstedt,
Hans Morgedaller,*
Andreas Gossweiller,*
Joh. Erhardt Müller,
Johannes Tuckermann,
Hans Jacob Schiedt,
Joh. Friederich Lein,
Johan Peter Källner,
Joh. Michael Müller,
Matheas Onzinger,*
Ludwig Moser,*
Gisbetus Ignatius Knipp,
Johan G. Weydner,*
Joh. Egydius Deschner,
Hans Georg Achenbacher,
Georg Schütterlin,?
Hans Jacob Stöss,
Leonhart Ziffe,*
Johannes Scherban,
Philip Seifert,*
Jacob Fanheel,?

Christoph Stormer,*
Martin Wurffel,*
Jacob Hecht,
Andreas Töhms,
Hans Plach,
Hannes Plach,
Georg Stöss,
Isaac Vetter,*
Isaias Grieb,
George Silber,*
Hans Armgast,*
Andreas Herster,*
Andreas Sauer,
Andreas Flach,
Samuel Stheryders,
Han Jacob Hummerle sen.,
Han Jacob Hummerle jr.,
Hans Georg Wall,
Mattheis Lorentz,
Christian Strahling,
Hendrick Wookman.*

135) Sept. 26, 1749. Foreigners from Hanau, Wirtemberg, Darmstadt, and Eisenberg,—ship Ranier, Henry Browning, Master, from Rotterdam, last from ——, England.—277 passengers.

Sept. 26, 1749. 277 Frembe von Hanau, Württemberg, Darmstadt und Eisenberg kamen mit dem Schiffe Ranier, Capitain Henry Browning, von Rotterdam über ——, England.

Johannes Raber,*
Martin Katz,
Jacob Katz,
Martin Gloss,
Philipp Dähn,
Johann Schaller,?
Jacob Clem,
Jacob Katz,
Johannes Shnyder,*
Jacob Boller,

Sebastian Weitzel,
Friederich Weitzel,
Thomas Appel,*
Jacob Grauel,*
Christian Knipe,*
Abraham Hess,
Caspar Streader,*
Dewald Schust,?
Ekard Keyser,*
Leonhart Keyser,*

18*

Thomas Erich,
Johannes Albrecht,
Nicklaus Hess,
Joh. Christoph Brüst,
Christoph Heyndel,*
P. Hans Haytzmer,?
Johannes Landmann,
Johan Wilhelm Geyer,
Johan Conrad Riedel,
Hans Jacob Slener,
Johan Heinrich Weitzel,
Johan Adam Appel,
Joh. Philip Wygant,*
Philip Lauterbach,*
Conrad Lauterbach,*
Johan Nicolaus Hess,
Johan Ludwig Hess,
Johann Henrich Ströder,
Johannes Ströder jr.,
John Henry Streader,*
Georg Christian Eberhardt,
Johan Henrich Lehr,
Joh. Friederich Höck,
Johan Conrad Heck,
Joh. Conrad Lutz,
Hans Jacob Lutz,
Mattheis Graff,
Martin Lutz,
Christian Lutz,
Christian Mösser,
Johannes Messert,
Jacob Förster,
Johannes Weber,
Adam Hopff,
Johannes Conrad,
Johannes Shertel,*
Michael Henckel,*
Benedict Weiss,
Carl Schermann,
Peter Harting,
Peter Becker,

Joachim Vogel,
Andreas Heerreder,
Johannes Heerreder,
Jacob Engel,
Johannes Falick,
Philip Sultzbach,
Johannes Appel,
Heinrich Eckel,
Wilhelm Leberle,
Johannes Hohn,
Henrich Hartwich,
J. Henry Shreffer,*
Johannes Graber,
Johan Steygerwaldt,
Johann Landgraff,
Melchior Gebhart,*
Conrad Gebhart,*
Erasmus Rosenberger,
Johannes Krebs,
Conrad Wagner,
Johan Jacob Hettrich,
Hans Melchior Hammer,
Joh. Jacob Keich,
Joh. Georg Trippner,
Andreas Messert,
Ambrosius Habermehl,
Johan Heinrich Printz,
Johann Henrich Peter,
Fried. Wilhelm Geist,*
Joh. Adam Fasnacht,
Joh. Conrath Fassenacht,
Joh. Henrich Leppich,
Joh. Philipp Lehnig,
Johan Peter Feppel,
Johan Casper Schmidt,
Johan Conrad Geyer,
Johan Henrich Geyer,
Johan Georg Schultz,
Joh. Michael Schmaltz,
Joh. Peter Scharmann,
Georg Ernst Schmidt,

Wolff Casper Geyer,
Joh. Reinhart Rohrbach,
Joh. Thomas Schmidt,
Joh. Henrich Lorey,
Joh. Michael Oberheuser,
Johan Georg Hörtzel,
Joh. Henry Heppel,*
Joh. Jacob Dänderich,

Georg Ernst Maurer,
Michael Reiffschneider,
J. Michael Gunkel,
Johan Peter Steygerwaldt,
Johan Jacob Eckhardt,
Johan Conrad Gräll,
Joh. Daniel Baueshar,
Johan Philippus Jung.

Sick—Johan Sans, Melchior Heppel, Johannes Michler.

136) Sept. 26, 1749. Foreigners from the Palatinate and Zweibrücken,—ship Dragon, Georg Spencer, Master, from Rotterdam, last from Deal.—563 passengers.

Sept. 26, 1749. 563 Frembe von ber Pfalz unb Zweibrücken kamen mit bem Schiffe Dragon, Capitain Georg Spencer, von Rotterbam über Deal.

Christoph Eich,*
Johannes Gödtel,
Christian Fuchs,
Jacob Leber,
Johannes Eckel,
Georg Hostman,
Johannes Hust,
Bastian Leinthrick,?
Simon Richter,
Hans Gauffs,*
Valentin Weber,
Johannes Weber,
Jacob Weber,
Anthony Ohber,
Jonas Bohrer,
Martin Sier,*
Anthony Moor,*
Jacob Wey,?
Peter Heimbach,
Henrich Brill,
Jacob Brown,*
Jacob Miller,*
Adam Gerber,
Matheas Miller,*

Bernhart Wacker,
Friederich Minler,*
Peter Sühn,
Johannes Wagner,*
Matheis Wagner,
Johannes Zwalle,*
Casper Zirn,
Tobias Fey,
Johann Diwall,
Kilian Hagert,
Antony Müller,
Leonard Waller,*
Adam Egart,*
Jacob Bruner,*
Adam Brommer
Valentin Weber,
Dewald Shnyder,*
Johannes Ross,
Johan Nickel Eich,
Johan Georg Fedel,
Johan Peter Weyand,
Johan Jacob Peterman,
Joh. Christ. Heinrich Beck,
Andreas Gustus Seytz,

Hans Katzenbacher,
Ludwig Haspelhorn,*
Johan Philip Bauer,
John Nicklaus Hayn,
Joh. Nicklaus Reisinger,
Joh. Peter Reisinger,
Johan Peter Eckert,
Philip Jacob Schmit,
Joh. Heinrich Pengler,
Philip Jacob Eger,
Joh. Heinrich Sies,
Johan Nickel Wentz,
Jacob Byshall,
Johan Georg Dellen,
Wilhelm Hoffmann,
Melchior Benedict,
Michael Zyndelbach,*
Kilian Duvinger,
Joh. Nicolaus Schneider,
Johan Henrich Weber,
Joh. Peter Schlarbst,
Jacob Wendling,
Friederich Schütz,
Philip Jacob Schmidt,
Georg Philip Hartung,
Johann Martin Kolter,
Friederich Schweickhart,
Christian Hoffstättle,*
Hans Georg Hartlieb,
Michael Lenard,*
Henry Weber,*
Johan Valtin Weber,
Jacob Kraus,
Paulus Hartman,

Joh. Heinrich Hartman,
Michael Kilian,*
Ludwig Heitz,
Jacob Heitz,
Jacob Ness,
Martin Loroh,*
Stephan Bauer,
Jacob Frey,*
Peter Dagon,*
Georg Cump,*
Wilhelm Müller,
Weyrich Beck,
Jacob Roth,
Jacob Fihr,
Tobias Lawer,*
Martin Föll,
Johannes Partts,*
Jacob Beck,*
Johan Georg Ludwig,
Philip Müller,
Ambrosius Bender,*
Frantz Wittman,
Johan Georg Krauss,
Johannes Dürr,*
Johan Nicklas Shaffer,*
Michael Schneider,
George Jacob Shaffer,*
Johannes Enders,
Johan Friederich Widman,
Balthaser von Können,
Martin von Können,
Jacob Weidler,
Johann Henrich Eyrt,
Anthoni Œhler.

---

137) Sept. 27, 1749. Palatines in the ship Isaac, Robert Mitchell, Captain, from Rotterdam, last from Cowes.—206 passengers.

Sept. 27, 1749. 206 Pfälzer kamen mit dem Schiffe Isaac, Capitain Robert Mitchell, von Rotterdam über Cowes.

Rudolph Haberly,*
Heinrich Greb,
Hans Hug,
Henry Greb,*
Felix Mägli,
Peter Becker,
Andreas Linck,
Velty Kurtz,
Hans Kunrad,
Albert Shutz,*
Uhllerick Coppy,*
Baltas Shreiber,
Michael Fischer,
Johan Jahller,
Matheas Kehler,*
Leonhart Lasher,*
Conrad Weiss,
Johannes Klippel,
George Fisher,*
Andreas Bussart,
Jacob Klippel,
Hans Rudolph Fisher,*
Jacob Plehman,
Johan Heinrich Grün,
Michael Reedelmos,*
Johannes Storm,*
Hans Jacob Mägli,
Rudolph Fries,
Henrich Boshart,
Johan Jacob Stucki,
Johan Henrich Cramer,
Joh. Christian Schella,
Joh. Adam Shreiber,*
Christian Mechel,
Joh. Valentin Steinbring,
Hans Adam Maurer,
Johannes Henlein,

Johan Nickel Gerst,
Johan Peter Rit,
Johan Nickel Schäffer,
Georg Adam Fischer,
Joh. Casper Langenberger,
Wendel Becker,
Jacob Wissman,*
Henrich Landes,
Johannes Miller,
Johannes Landert,
Peter Mackhart,
Frantz Hemmle,
Christian Hemmle,
Henrich Huber,
Jacob Vesseler,
Johannes Bauer,
Philip Haber,
Ludwig Krebs jr.,
Ludwig Krebs sen.,
Georg Schlosser,
Johannes Wolff,
Johannes Jungblud,
Johan Adam Wolf,
Matthias Echternach,
Johan Friederich,
Joh. Nicolas Senderling,
Joh. Henry Weyermann,
Joh. Georg Schnabel,
John Michael Stumpff,
Joh. Daniel Weber,
Heinrich Burckhart,
Joh. Henrich Beck,
Johan Henrich Kleine,
Johan Georg Batz,
Nicolaus Bricker,
Joh. Simonus Schreiner.

Sick—Hans Conrath, Nicolaus Franger, Lorentz Haffner, Herman Haust.

138) Sept. 28, 1749. Foreigners from Basel, Wirtemberg, Zweibrücken, and Darmstadt,—ship Ann, John Spurier, Master, from Rotterdam, last from Cowes.—242 passengers.

Sept. 28, 1749. Frembe famen aus Bafel, Württemberg, Zweibrücken und Darmstadt mit dem Schiffe Ann, Capitain John Spurier, von Rotterdam über Cowes.—242 im Ganzen.

Philip Laidyg,
Wilhelm Rübel,
Johannes Danesus,?
Heinrich Braun,
Johann Spitler,*
Jacob Swoob,*
Johan Switzer,*
Jacob Weeser,*
Rudolph Viunt,
Adam Schaulling,
Daniel Schnebly,
Heinrich Mock,
Peter Elser,
Johannes Weber,
Thomas Lubek, §
Wendel Keller,*
Johannes Mertz,
Andreas Scholl,
Friederich Meyer,
Hans Adam Hacker,
Melchior Lippert,
John Jacob Sutz,*
Michael Hengst,
Jean Thoulouzan,
Johannes Straudman,
Jacob Landgraff,
Joh. Friederich Zimmermann,
Joh. Michael Zimmermann,
Johannes Zimmermann,
Johan Philip Weber,
Jacob le Jeunes,
Johan Paul Traub,
Johan Adam Schwartzbach,
Johan Peter Beissel,
Johan Georg Schreiner,

Hans Georg Schönperlen,
Engelhardt Kutern,
Johan Philip Falch,
Lorentz Henger,
Martin Eyer,
Graff Hünner,
Jacob Salathe,
Jacob Tschudy,
Blasius Hauck,*
Melchior Anter,
Conrad Renninger,
Jacob Sheybethal,*
Simon Kraus,*
Adam Heinrich,
Christian Shott,*
Johannes Sucher,*
Jacob Weichert,
Jacob Fecks,
Martin Brabnith,
Michael Breisah,
Michael Gassler,
Hans Nees,
Henrich Vogt,
Johannes Vogt,*
Jacob Schnell,
Adam Scharer,*
Hans Kuhn,*
Hans Shutty,*
Jacob Koller,*
Gotlieb Walter,
Conrad Mayer,
Jacob Shupp,*
Hans Ulrich Bussy,
Joseph Gallmann,
Bernhardt Hauck,

Georg Michel Schurtz,
Hans Rudolph Kittwiler,
Johan Jacob Kreiss,
Casper Derstenbecher,
Hans Jacob Vogt,
Johan Ewald Breyer,
Hans Georg Huber,
Georg Henrich Shott,*
Joseph Schnülbein,
Hans Michael Schuster,
Jacob Schnülbein,
Hans Michael Hauck,
Jacob Amman,*

Hans Jacob Nees,
Hans Michael Schwab,
Johannes Hummel,
Niclaus Motheri,
Jan Paul Imno,
Han Friedrich Schaffner,
Jacob Schaffner,
Jora Dangoranslo,
Johan Philip Henneman,
Sebastian Schneider,*
Joh. Paulus Eystelohr,
Johannes Dummer,*
Sick—Thomas Lubek.*

---

139) Oct. 2, 1749. Foreigners from Swabia, Wirtemberg, and Darmstadt,—ship Jacob, Adolph de Grove, Captain, from Amsterdam, last from Shields, England.—290 passengers.

Oct. 2, 1749. Ausländer aus Schwaben, Württemberg und Darmstadt kamen mit dem Schiffe Jacob, Capitain Adolph de Grove, von Amsterdam über Shields, England.—290 in Allem.

Friederich Bückel,
Christoph Fürstner,
Friederich Walles,*
Conrad Bauster,
Philip Storm,*
Martin Wust,
Michael Miller,*
Georg Hoffman,
Johan Jacob Sinn,
Johan Georg Sinn,
Hans George Keplinger,*
Hans Georg Hoffman,
Georg Christian Spängler,
Johan Henrich Herget,
Johan Christoph Kees,?
John Georg Steigleder,
George Bachert,*
Joseph Ritter,
Paul Lebing,
Jacob Uhllerich,*

Johannes Becker,
Daniel Freysinger,*
Conrad Reese,*
Johannes Roth,
Jacob Sinder,
Peter Seyds,*
Martin Treibel,
Martin Erch,
Georg Schweigers,
Jacob Traudt,
Jacob Rupp,
Jacob Gilbert,
Lorentz Hoch,
Johann Jabbes,?
Johannes Neier,
Marcus Gönner,
Henry Rubert,
William Hofman,*
Matheis Hartman,
Johannes Rohm,

Henry Krahmer,
Jacob Kautzman,
Johann Bauman,
Adam Eichholtz,
Valentin Villib,
Friederich Becholt,
Adam Shnyder,*
Henry Wirdt,
Christoph Heiply,*
Philip Stumpff,
Peter Seyler,*
Jacob Heibly,*
Melchior Wolfart,*
Joseph Volck,
Johannes Folck,*
Martin Dötter,
Johan Conrad Lebing,
Georg Michael Laubinger,
Hans Georg Krafft,
Friederich Pfœrsching,
Jacob Fleischmann,
Johan Henrich Knöss,
Martin Bleymeyer,
Georg Eberharth,
Heinrich Hoffman,
Joh. Conrad Leitheiser,
Eberhart Windmeyer,
Christian Fried. Häberlin,

Hans Georg Bauer,
Johan Georg Stein,
Bernhart Gilbert,
Simon Grossman,
Hans Adam Fakler,*
Hans Philip Schöster,
Georg Carl Rubert,*
Johan Henrich Rohm,
Hans Georg Münig,*
Joh. Georg Hunkinger,
Gotfried Samuel Welper,
Johan Georg Heinrich,
Joh. Adam Hiltenbeittel,*
Joh. Martin Eichholtz,
Joh. Wendel Kühner,
Johannes Zimmermann,
Joh. Michael Schneyder,
Hans Michael Gandner,
Johan Jacob Heil,
Johann Adam Roth,
Johan Georg Gröther,
Melchior Vogelmann,
Johan Georg Störner,
Hans Michael Gintner,
Nicolas Dötter,
Matheis Dötter,
Claudt Reinaldt.

Sick—Fried. Seydler, Baltaser Bauer, Johannes Hartman.

---

140) Oct. 7, 1749. Palatines from Mannheim and Zweibrücken,—ship Lesbie, J. Balledium, Captain, from Rotterdam, last from Cowes.—450 passengers.

Oct. 7, 1749. Pfälzer kamen aus Mannheim und Zweibrücken mit dem Schiffe Lesbie, Capitain J. Balledium, von Rotterdam über Cowes.—450 im Ganzen.

Conrad Valentine,*
Hannes Henrich,*
Wendel Wahl,
Jacob Hamels,*

Martin Andreas,*
Ulrich Ichle,
Johannes Hess,*
Friederich Schott,

Johannes Eckman,*
Henry Mohler,*
Peter Klein,*
Casper Klein,
Friederich Fuchs,
Anthon Koch,*
Michael Shmeyer,*
Peter Kraut,
Philip Mäuer,
Peter Kuntz,
Conrad Wolfe,*
Martin Kind,
Wendel Jung,
Christophel Jung,
Johannes Ritcher,*
Friederich Mey,
Balser Schmit,
Michael Klee,
Philip Klein,
Wendel Schmertzen,*
Johannes Becker,
Valentin Petry,
Michel Huyet,
Jacob Womer,
Christian Melchert,
Philip Kärcher,
Johannes Pfeil,
Michel Cuntz,
Jacob Strauss,*
Michel Dinger,
Peter Weber,
Christoph Geigenberger,
Peter Grünenwalt,
Christoph Lesch,
Johann Adam Mäuer,
Martin Vösener,
Johannes Wessener,*
Rudolph Hoffman,*
Johan Philip Griessemann,
Johan Herman Metz,
Johann Jacob Metz,

Johan Bernhart Neiman,
Joh. Paul Rothgerber,
Johan Peter Wickert,
Johan Paul Wickert,
Martin Schwenck,
Johan Peter Stimmel,
Johan Georg Kind,
Johann Michael Messemer,
Simon Baumgärttner,
Gottfried Grünzweig,
Hans Georg Scheistlen,
Johann Diehl Klein,
Johan Jacob Engler,
Joh. Wilhelm Irrendt,
Jacob Hoffman,
Peter Imbsweiller,
Anthoni Petersheimer,
Jacob Harberger,
Michael Wommer,*
Christ. Adam Müller,
Johan Jacob Ninies,*
Johan Adam Correll,
Johan Michael Deobalt,
Johan Philip Matheis,
Johan Nicolas Müller,
Johan Jacob Walter,
Gottfried Finderer,
Gottfried Kommell,
Hans Georg Fischer,
Jacob Cratz,
Stephan Hepp,
Georg Hepp,
Johannes Müller,
Valentin Behler,*
Conrad Behler,
Georg Müller,
Johannes Lang,*
Andreas Supper,
Jacob Mauerer,*
Peter Grem,*
Adam Stein,

19

Philip Haubt,
Jost Fischer,
Peter Miller,
Jacob Jäger,
Georg Imich,
Jost Engler,
Jacob Meyer,
Henry Boce,*
Georg Martin Hausser,
Bernhardt Hepp,
Jacob Leonhart,*
Johannes Harmonie,
Hans Georg Brodbeck sen.,
Hans Georg Brodbeck jr.,

John Rudolph Espidt,
Johan Philip Supper,
Johan Adam Dörffling,*
Joh. Reinhardt Böhm,
Johannes Klossmayer,
Johan Adam Bath,
Friederich Bender,
Christian Schneider,
Nicklas Diemus,*
Philipp Otto Wagner,
Joh. Ludwig Dengeiss,
Nicolas Deterich,*
Joh. Christoph Fackler.

Sick—Matheis Knauss, Bartholomæ Mertz, George Shmit, Philip Adam.

---

141) Oct. 10, 1749. Palatines, persons from Wirtemberg, Durlach, and Zweibrücken.

Oct. 10, 1749. Frembe famen aus ber Pfalz, Württemberg, Durlach unb Zweibrüden.

Jacob Bock,
Steffe Mausch,
Johannes Beck,
Henrich Bachman,
Michael Kipp,
Leonhardt Meyer,
Georg Wagner,
Henry Heyser,*
Joseph Balick,
Konrat Linss,
David Bast,
Georg Berger,
Adam Wollmer, §
Reinhart Heiss,
Heinrich Haffer,
Jacob Adams,*
Georg Conrad Bloss,
Matheas Oberfeld,*
Henrich Hübener,

Bernhart Miller,*
Andreas Gembler,
Georg Friedrich Schmidt,
Johannes Hanfwerck,
Johann Michael Bast,
Michael Steinborn,
Johannes Ohlinger,
Johann Peter Clemmentz,
Wilhelm Arnold,
Peter Arnold,
Johannes Arnold,
Georg Simon Bresler,
Ludwig Herrmann,
Jacob Kneiss,
Nicklas Bresler,*
George Bresler,*
Michael Bahrt,
Henrich Koch,
Friederich Jung,

Nickolas Simon,
Christian Lentz,
Michael Barth,
Michel Schock,
Jacob Shaak,*
Peter Rap,*
Ambrose Remly,
Michael Messer,
Matheas Keller,
Johannes Schmidt,
Philip Häny,*
Conrad Geidlinger,*
Ludwig Hach,
Johannes Vogt,
Daniel Bock,
Andreas Vogler,*
Baltzer Heyl,
Johannes Barth,
Hans Grätsch,
Jacob Schantz,
Carl Shantz,*
Henry Miller,*
Casper Dorn,
Joseph Gebhart,*
Adam Lotz,
Johannes Koch,
Georg Rögler,
Johannes Kau,
Jacob Stadtler,
Jacob Tonner,
Jacob Ulmer,
David Kehm,
Friederich Doll,
Georg Breining,
Jacob Brücker,
Georg Crassan,
J. William Shaak,
Georg Jacob Wagner,
Johannes Oberle,
Johann Peter Oberle,
Conrad Glück,

Johan Georg Schreiber,
Georg Henrich Wüst,
Cornelius von Starweg,
Johann Georg Hammer,
John Jacob Messer,*
Anthonius Gedelo,
Hans Georg Huff,
Johan Henrich Hettich,
Johannes Scherrer,
Jacob Schweinfurth,
Hans Michael Seitz,
Johan Jacob Rahn,
Michael Bastian,
Nicolaus Schäffer,
Johannes Uhllerich,*
Georg Küher,
Georg Adam Löble,
Wilhelm Löble,
Johannes Himmelreich,*
Johan Jacob Weyden,
Johan Philip Œhlweiler,
Peter Kratringer,*
Georg Jacob Shierman,*
Johan Georg Lutz,*
Valentein Schallus,
Bastian Shalles,*
Hans Georg Kau,
Henry Reinhart, §
Nicklaus Moclotz,
Joh. Philip Hausman,
Philip Martin Hammel,
Jacob Schriffele,
Bernhart Breininger,
Stephan Tieffelmeyer,
Christianus Hentz,
Johannes Gelisen,
Nicklaus Gelisen,
Michel Brücker,
Christian Seyder,*
Georg Kremer,
Edmundus Tholl,

Georg Reilenbach,
Valentin Keller,
Johannes Storm,*
Jacob Kantz,*
Michael Kantz,*
Jacob Bertsch,
Philip Bodomer,
Andreas Ecker,
Ruprecht Haug,
Mathias Müller,
Wilhelmus Savelkorl,
Georg Christoph Müller,

Nicolaus Forschberge,
Georg Ludwig Hoffmann,
Joh. Peter Hickenauer,
Joh. Stephan Dietewig,
Valentin Schweitzer,
Johan Nickel Klein,
Johan Michael Mintz,
Christian Carl Brandt, *a*
Johann Menle Brandt,
Johan Christian Brandt,
Joh. David Wöpperck.

142) Oct. 17, 1749.   Palatines, Wirtembergers and Alsatians, (from Alsace,)—ship Dragon, Daniel Nicholas, Master, from Rotterdam, last from Portsmouth.—244 passengers.

Oct. 17, 1749.   Pfälzer, Württemberger und Elsäſſer kamen mit dem Schiffe Dragon, Capitain Daniel Nicolas, von Rotterdam über Portsmouth.—244 im Ganzen.

Andreas Mohr,
Martin Shrätter,*
Nicklaus Brickner,*
Conrad Roth,
Felix Gartom,*
Jacob Wolff,
Andreas Hertz,
Hans Danzel,*
Henry Jacob,*
Conrad Engel,*
Philip Fischer,
Valentin Bender,
David Shantz,*
Andreas Bircker,
Stephan Purman,
Peter Fischer,*

Jacob Fisher,
Andreas Kerschner,
Johannes Müller,
Johannes Sauter,
Johannes Rumffel,
Hans Georg Danbach,
Wilibald Gambert,
Wilhelm Menges,
Hans Peter Voltz,
Michael Schmidt,
Christian Duchmann,
Peter Tuchman,*
Hans Michael Kuntz,
Hans Georg Stambach,
Joh. Eberhart Balthas,
David Kleidens,

a This name is written in beautiful *Roman Script*, with the professional appendix—*Christian Carl Brandt, Chirurg.*

a Dieser Name iſt in ſchöner lateiniſcher Schrift geſchrieben mit dem profeſſionellen Titel „Chirurg".

Heinrich Kübarts,
Johannes Stiebler,
Johan Adam Stiebler,
Hans Georg Burkhard,
Johan Nicklas Wyner,*
Johannes Waall,*
Andreas Euerling,
Wilhelm Hoffmann,
Johan Jacob Alles,
Johan Simon Groh,
Heinrich Fischer,
Jacob Griess,
Peter Diehl,
Abraham Keiler,
Johannes Bigler,*
Adam Sprengel,
Jacob Kiefer,
Simon Metziger,
Peter Grow,*
Conrad Shyd,*
Georg Shyd,*
Conrad Grumbach,
Simon Eshbagh,*
Jacob Grumbach,
Casper Iba,

Johannes Schmidt,
Johannes Eberle,
Johannes Gehr,
Bastian Gernaut,
Wilhelm Zimerle,
Tobias Horein,
Anthony Zürch,
Balthas Schneider,
Conrad Vieman,
Johan Georg Krumlauf,
Georg Henry Shyd,*
Hans Michael Haudesch,
Heim Heydersh,*
Hans Mich. Haudenscheidt,
Johan Adam Meier,
Johan Martin Ferster,
Joh. Andreas Wagner,
Johan Henrich Theiss,
Hans Michael Rosser,
Geo. Hen. Witler Gründell,
Johan Jacob Wirth,
Johannes Hoffmann,
Johan Georg Schneider,
Phil. Lorentz Zimmerle,
Arnold Klehass.

143) Oct. 17, 1749. Foreigners from the Palatinate, Wirtemberg and Rittenheim,—ship Fane, William Hyndman, Captain, from Rotterdam, last from Cowes.—596 passengers.

Oct. 17, 1749. Ausländer aus der Pfalz, Württemberg und Rittenheim kamen mit dem Schiffe Fane, Capitain William Hyndman, von Rotterdam über Cowes.—596 im Ganzen.

Gottlieb Söhner,
Tobias Manich,
Jacob Schneider sen.,
Jacob Schneider jr.,
Leonhart Lang,
Christian Reiner,
Georg Reiner,
Adam Seifert,

Michael Biner,
Casper Wagner,
Paul Geiger,
Jacob Stier,
Christian Stein,
Georg Geiger,
Adam Hugly,*
Ludwig Triber,*

Mattheis Stier,
Christoffel Graf,*
Christoph Graf jr.,
Christoph Willet,
Johan Martin Offner,
Sam. Henry Abentschon,*
Reinhold Abendschön,
Christian Abendschön,
Gottlieb Baumgärttner,
Christoph Altneth,
Joh. Henrich Gerlach,
Hans Georg Huber,
Johan Georg Huber,
Georg Michael Haas,
Johannes Schilling,
Johan Adam Keilinger,*
Joh. Christoph Wethwein,
Joh. Conrad Häussler,
Jacob Plantz,
Jacob Weyand,
Heinrich Benner,
Henry Mise,
Arnold Althaus,
Ludwig Benner,
Johannes Benner,
Herman Weber,*
Jost Weber,
Conrad Stenger,
Conrad Crum,
Konrath Kremer,
Johannes Keim,
Johannes Gross,
Adam Spies,
Wilhelm Shätz,*
Jacob Klein,
Johannes Pfeil,*
Johann Graffhos,
Jacob Hahn,
Jacob Zeller,
Conrad Zeller,
Johannes Zeller,

Michael Meyer,
Martin Willer,
Martin Faigile,
Martin Pefferle,
Johannes Herter,
Jacob Kelling,
Casper Zesseler,*
Johannes Algeyer,*
Andreas Scherle,
Henrich Priest,
Melchior Ram,*
Christian Reiner,
Paul Müller,
Gottfried Tietz,
Leonhart Jung,*
Lorian Eisely,*
Johannes Krämer,*
Conrad Hirsh,
Johan Leonhard Jung,
Leonhardt Plantz,
Johan Jacob Schneider,
Georg Jacob Plantz,
Jost Sasmanhaus,
Daniel Marburger,
Johan Henrich Rentzel,
Jost Wilhelm Rentzel,
Johan Henrich Schmidt,
J. Engel Stokman,*
Johan Philip Stockmann,
Johan Casper Klein,
Johannes Klein,
Daniel Benner,
Johan Georg Zachrias,
Martin Schneider,
Christoph Schneider,
Joh. Martin Hausser,
Johannes Wahl,
Johan Martin Hertz,
Johan Martin Reisser,
Christian Damselt,
Christoffel Wimer,*

Hans Georg Mayer,
Georg Friederich Höhn,
Hans Georg Plocher,
Samuel Beck,*
Johannes Fischer,
Melchior Heckman,
Johannes Schweitzer,
Hans Jacob Bötz,
Hans George Kern,*
Hans Norffkoh,?

Georg Philip Reiber,
Hans Jacob Keller,*
Melchior Rinehold,
Joh. Dietrich Reiner,
Wilhelm Claussenius,
Ulrich Heininger,
Jacob Adam Kraut,
Joh. Conrad Biehn,
Joh. Friederich Stieg.

144) Nov. 9, 1749. † Foreigners imported in the snow Good Intent, Benjamin Boswell, Master, from Rotterdam, last from Cowes.—76 passengers.

Nov. 9, 1749. † Ausländer kamen mit dem Seeschiffe Good Intent, Capitain Benj. Boswell, von Rotterdam über Cowes.— 76 im Ganzen.

Johannes Hausman,
Joseph Hausman,
Paulus Hausman,
Dietrich Mertz,
Johannes Kreiner,
Peter Hetzer,
Mattheas Plenninger,*
Ludwig Stumb,*
Jacob Mäsner,
Michael Jung,
Georg Meyer,
Peter Matter,
Friederich Bassler,

Hans Georg Bössmer,
Joh. Christoph Besmer,
Johan Adam Kurtz,
Johannes Heinninger,
Jacob Heinninger,
Hans Georg Hentzelmann,
Christian Pfingstag,
Georg Henrich Reinöhl,
Jacob Reinholtz,
Johannes Kessler,*
Ludwig Werentz,
Henry Seyder.

145) Aug. 11, 1750. Foreigners imported in the ship Patience, Hugh Steel, Captain, from Rotterdam, last from Cowes.

† This year Rev. *J. Conrad Steiner,* a Swiss from the Canton Zurich, a German Reformed Minister, came to Pennsylvania.—*Büttner's Ref. Church,* p. 11.—(*Editor.*)

† In diesem Jahre kam Pastor J. Conrad Steiner, ein Schweizer aus dem Canton Zürich und reform. Geistlicher, nach Pennsylvania.—Büttner's Ref. Kirche, S. 11.—(Herausgeber.)

Aug. 11, 1750. Ausländer kamen mit dem Schiffe Patience, Capitain Hugh Steel, von Rotterdam über Cowes.

Stephan Beck,
Henrich Lentz,
Peter Groff,*
Christoff Bener,*
Andreas Müller,
Georg Schnedh,
Jacob Jacoby,*
Adam Jacobi,
Matheis Jacobi,
Peter Jacobi,
Jacob Burkard,
Jacob Bär,
Jacob Conrath sen.,*
Jacob Conrath jr.,
Daniel Miller,
Jacob Reichert,
Samuel Werner,
Johannes Halm,*
Peter Wieland,
Hans Peter Treger,
Jacob Heckendorn,
Hans Peter Graff,
Hans Jacob Groff,*
Johannes Peter Klein,
Johan Nickel Müller,
Johan Nickel Cuntz,
Joh. Wilhelm Fuchs,
Joh. Christoph Orpertag,
Johan Peter Fitz,
Johan David Junge,*
Joh. Henrich Leineweber,
Joh. Conrad Wölffle,
Christian Ulrich Lentz,
Christoph Ketteman,
Johan Georg Ketteman,
Joh. Jacob Rappoldt,
Georg Friederich Groh,
Johan Georg Bader,
Friedcrich Waltzer,

Jacob Schwob,*
Georg Loadig,*
Geo. Adam Eckerdt,
Joh. Peter Wohner,
Balthasar Vetterman,
Georg Hamen,
Conrad Velten,
Jacob Mühleysen,
Nicklas Mühleysen,
Wilhelm Diedrich,
Henrich Reinhardt,
Johannes Roller,*
Christoph Fritz,*
Jacob Lentel,
Henrich Georg,
Christian Mener,
Matheas Oberkirsch,*
Nicklas Conrad,*
Jacob Deremot,
Abraham Ritner,
Andreas Rost,*
Paulus Reylandt,
Johannes Eischby,
Dewald Gerst,*
Friederich Gerst,*
David Smith,*
Peter Poland,*
Stephen Poland,*
Peter Foltz,
Jacob Dobeler,*
Hans Kawffman,*
Christian Shmitt,*
Philip Heiber,
Jacob Keellenthal,*
Michael Juncker,
Johannes Palm,*
Johannes Reichle,
Casper Greiter,
Anthon Derffus,

Carl Vollunte,*
Jacob Dannether,
Hans Michael Melber,
J. Michael Leidich,
Johan Georg Bauer,
Georg Adam Eckart,*
Johan Christoph Kuntz,
Johan Wilhelm Wann,
Johan Arnold Reinhart,
Johannes Nickel Henrich,
Johann Peter Schütz,
Johannes Adam Lauch,
Johan Jacob Weirich,
Johann Nickel Brod,
Johan Michel Conrad,*
Johan Nickel Hasber,
Johan Jacob Lüsbes,
Johan Peter Diedrich,
Johan Nickel Jung,
Philip Jacob Maurer,
Johan Friederich Pfeil,
Hans Georg Eslinger,

Hans Georg Sing,
Johan Conrad Bross,
Johannes Baumgärtner,
Hans Georg Nagel,
Georg Friederich Haug,
Johan David Görges,
Joh. Andreas Mühlschlägel,
Joh. Adam Satson,*
Johan Philip Ost,
Johan Matheis Georg,
Friederich Henrich,
Johan Michael Leib,
David Stadelmayer,
Bartholomä Lentzinger,
Johan Adam Fetzer,
Johan Adam Stiehl,
Joh. Albrecht Velter,
Johannes Esbenstein,
Johan Adam Dentzell,
Johan David Limbech,
Johan Jacob Müller.

146) Aug. 13, 1750. Foreigners imported in the ship Bennet Galley, John Wadham, Master, from Rotterdam, last from Portsmouth.—260 passengers.

Aug. 13, 1750. Fremde kamen mit dem Schiffe Bennet Galley, Capitain John Wadham, von Rotterdam über Portsmouth.— 260 im Ganzen.

Jacob Lange,*
Adolph Riehl,
Isaac Gunst,*
Jacob Dencker,*
Georg Acker,
Michael Gallater,*
Carl Gustav,
Johanes Koch,*
Peter Bucks,
Jacob Lazarus,
Jacob Valentine,*

Joseph Eck,*
Christoff Grindler,*
Adam Steffan,
Wendel Insel,
Martin Bender,
Johannes Jacob,
Peter Merckel,
Gylyan Geused,
Uhlerich Steiner,*
Casper Stattler,
Hans Bergher,*

Peter Gutman,
Bentz Horny,*
Balzer Leibrock,*
Bastian Ledig,
Jacob Schäffer,
Hans Rughty,*
Nicklaus Mercklin,
Peter Funck,
Andreas Müller,
Michael Kuntz,
Hans Düringer,
Johannes Bley,*
Benjamin Kelhover,*
Dewald Wantlin,*
Friederich Reys,*
Jacob Reiss,
Johanes Hoon,*
Hans Michael Beyer,*
Hans Jacob Silander,
Johan Georg Ott,
Joh. Jacob Shützlin,
John Friederich Ott,*
Johan Jacob Wüppel,
Johan Adam Bayer,
Johan David Neumann,
Michael Neumann,
Hans Georg Baldes Pargel,
Johannes Philip Schmit,
Hans Peter Shrantz,*
Heinerich Leininger,
Johan Frantz Friess,
Johann Michel Kloss,
D. Carl Gottlieb Diesbergen,
H. Jacob Sander,*

Hans Georg Wetzel,
Hans Georg Hallifas,*
Hans Georg Schenckel,
Johann Georg Süss,
Hans Peter Peters,*
Hans George Hoon,*
Georg Friederich Hoon,*
George Friederich Hetzel,*
Hans Michael Hetzel,*
Hans Michel Reber,
Henrich Jacob Vandeburg,
Christoff Ackerman,
Hans Michael Roth,
Julius Friederich Vollandt,
Johan Georg Ronister,
Hans Georg Shlaybouer,*
Hans Georg Reichart,
Hartman Leibengut,*
Christian Fried. Knauss,
Hans Michael Hell,
Hans Adam Miller,*
Georg Jacob Brünsholtz,
Benedict Peter,
Adam Fixe,*
Peter Lazarus,*
George Lees,
Diebolt Schwenck,
Hans Mich. Leby,*
J. Adam Printzholtz,*
Hans Thomas Leininger,
Hans Michael Bonet,*
Johan Nickel Post,
Joh. Phil. Jacob Schott,
Johann Georg Hafer.

Sick—Johannes Miller, Friederich Lauderbrunn, H. Nicklas Blader, Henry Peter.

147) Aug. 13, P. M., 1750. Ship Edinburgh, James Russel, Master, from Rotterdam, last from Portsmouth.—314 passengers.

Aug. 13, Nachmittags, 1750. Das Schiff Edinburgh, Capitain James Russel, von Rotterdam über Portsmouth, brachte 314 Passagiere.

Johann Corngibel,*
Johannes Beyer,*
Johannes Beyer jr.,
Michel Hamburgeis,*
J. George Kirshner,*
Valentin Sösttel,
Stoffel Bruning,*
Ludwig Gassler,
Jost Schneider,
Thomas Kegel,*
Thomas Klosse,*
Henrich Kloss,
Andreas Huck,
Jacob Möler,
Georg Schäffer,
Johannes Wien,
Michael Lemer,
Daniel Klein,
Jacob Schäfer,
Johan Fasnacht,*
Johannes Telcher,*
Johannes Delcher,
Jacob Werntz,
David Herbster,*
Jacob Lanish,
Georg Heyle,*
Jacob Loch,
Casper Strohl,
Andreas Ditz,
Philip Conrad Aumüller,
Johann Seybert Gertz,
Johann Henrich Lotz,
Johann Philip Heck,
Casper Bröning,
Joh. Peter Seyfert,
Johan Georg Rabe,
Johan George Flour,*
Johann Georg Müller,

Johan Adam Stein,*
Johan Casper Rötter,
Johann Georg Klein,
Johan Philip Hölsel,
Lorentz Baum,
Christophel Spahr,
Philippus Bücksell,
Johannes Gertz,
Johan Peter Leib,
Johannes Feuerstein,
Hans Georg Renninger,*
Johan Herman Dippel,
Johannes Eulert,
Wendel Renninger,*
Ludwig Pretzman,
Frederick Brinkman,*
Daniel Meerbagh,*
Andreas Spielman,*
Peter Sickenberger,
Valentin Kreischer,
Henrich Pilgram,
Peter Nees,*
Peter Bohre,
Andreas Keanig,*
Carel Keanig,*
Philip Shmith,*
Nicklas Hirt,*
Johannes Kniss,
Christian Haffner,*
Jacob Flug,*
Nicklas Spring,*
Johannes Philips,*
Andreas Bensell,
Jacob Daunneberger,?
Jacob Merckle,
Simon Merckle,
Carl Stedt,
Johannes Mohl,

Peter Marcus,*
Conradt Böhm,
Gottlieb Wyda,*
Casper Mug,*
Michael Heinle,
Peter Collep,*
Conrad Haffer,
Theobald Cuntz,
Frantz Cuntz,
Peter Spengler,*
Johannes Shmit,*
Severimus Sheffer,*
Christian Kempt,
Jacob Michael,
Jacob Schaffner,
Anthony Heanz,*
Jacob Walter,*
Ludwig Bauer,
Nicklas Spiri,
Nicklaus Bard,
Henry Coller,*
Philip Balbierer,
Jacob Metziger,*
Thomas Bough,*
Philip Begtholt,
Casper Conradi,
Friederich Hoffmann,
Johann Rüdelbach,?
Valentin Chitzrieth,?
Casper Dieffebacher,
Michael Matinger,
Johannes Wölschläger,
Johann Jacob Brang,
Simon Peter Ternantz,*
Johan Ulrich Daumer,

Johann Gottlieb Rabi,
Johann Martin Schäffer,
Johan Georg Höltzer,
Johan Christoffel Scharff,
Samuel Falckenhahn,
Johannes Schmidt,
Johan Philip Stang,
Johan Georg Dum,
Johannes Haffner,
Johannes Möller,
Christoffel Möller,
Johann Bernhard Christ,
Johan Adam Huber,*
Jacob von de Balt,
Georg Fried. Heilbrunn,
Johan Fried. Heilbrunn,
Johan Daniel Bübel,
Ludwig Schreiner,
Wilhelm Schreiner,
Christ. Sam. Bachmann,
Joh. Ludwig Widtmann,
Joh. Ludwig Seysser,
Johan Georg Esch,
Hans Adam Wagner,
Georg Adam Hobel,
Ludwig Spannagel,
Johan Adam Regel,
Johan Henry Shöman,*
Andreas Brandner,
Georg Sebastian Krausser,
Johan Ludwig Ehrhart,
Johannes Fisser,
Matthias Heiss,
Johannes Wagner,
Nicolaus Gerlach.

---

148) Aug. 15, 1750. Ship Royal Union, Clement Nicholson, Commander, from Rotterdam, last from Cowes.

Aug. 15, 1750. Das Schiff Royal Union, Commandant Clement Nicholson, von Rotterdam über Cowes, brachte Fremde.

Jacob Grob,*
John Brenhauer,*
Jacob Karner,*
J. J. O. Driesch,
Adam Staub,
Casper Schmidt,
Philip Prike,*
Hans Prike,*
Conradt Arnoldt,
Jacob Stehr,
Hans Weertz,*
Matheas Rost,*
Anthoni Emrich,
Daniel Braun,
Martin Schrenck,*
Andreas Haas,*
Andreas Hotz,
Adam Long,*
Gottlieb Utz,
Michael Eyrich,
Matheas Eyrich,*
Felix Jung,
Johann Georg,
Philip Eberhart,
Jacob Steebly,*
Martin Schmitt,
Nickel Faust,
Abraham Gerhart,*
Jacob Shmith,*
Peter Hambro,
Nickel Fass,
Matheas Fesbely,
Johannes Hartman,
Peter Mann,*
Daniel Düdi,
Johann Wilhelm Lochmann,
Herman Schwamm,
Frederick Schnitzer,
Johan Conrad Scheffer,
Stephan Mürlich,
Christoffel German,

Henrich Hauenstein,
Hans Michael Bauersachs,
Andreas Hertzog,
Hieronymus Schleider,
Gustav Friederich Schleider,
Heinrich Holtzman,
Michael Luttman,
Hans Georg Young,*
Johan Martin Schwartz,
Peter Ulrich Bauer,
Johann Georg Utz,
Hans Adam Kautzmann,
Bernhard Œsterle,
Joh. Friederich Glassbrenner,
Johan Jacob Ebenth,
Ludwig von der Schmidt,
Matheis Bernhardt,
Johann Michael Schül,
Johann Adam Berger,
G. Adam Renecker,*
Hans Martin Wurtz,
Philip Peter Theyl,*
Johan Georg Spiettler,
Fried. Christ. Kappeberger,
Joachim Wilhelm Storck,
Johan Philip Kirschbaum,
Johan Michael Hollich,
Johann Peter Perster,
Johan Friederich Brecht,
Johannes Trümper,
Simon Leyteker,*
Jacob Beensly,*
Henrich Müller,
Wilhelm Discher,
Jonas Vogt,
Henrich Bauer,
Andreas Röth,
Friederich Süber,
Johann Gelberee,
Hans Shoub,*
Martin Shoub,*

Philip Dick,
Wendel Bretz,
Philip Fuchs,
Philip Lenius,
Johannes Bauer,
Valentin Fidler,
Martin Rubbert,
Christian Rust,
Jacob Handshy,*
Friederich Paff,
Friederich Miesch,
Johannes Miesch,
Joseph Zug,
Martin Imhoff,
Johannes Willar,
Jacob Urering,*
Valentin Schmeltzer,*
Anthon Kräber,
Johannes Paffler,
Peter Wolff,
Philip Welde,
Johannes Grimb,
Philip Wilhertzbach,
Frantz Brunnholtz,
Philip Jacob Stümpel,
Valentin G. Bast,
Friederich Jacob Cummer,
Georg Hoffmann,
Hans William Statily,*
Henry Ully Statily,*
Johan Andreas Jüngst,
Johan Peter Dick,
Dielman Fuchs,
Nicol Merckhäusser,
Johan Dietrich Duey,

Johann Christian Duey,
Wilhelm Müller,
Johann Millerschurl,?
Johan Adam Kern,
Johann Jacob Helwig,
Johan Philip Ludwig,
G. Michael Kraus,*
J. Nickolaus Sanger,
Johann Peter Schneider,
Joh. Nicolaus Wertingisch,
Johannes Schnebli,
Johann Adam Schmeltzer,
Johannes Christ. Brammeret, a
Philip Wendel Opp,
Friederich Wolff,
Johannes Gamber,
Matthäus Bastenmeye,
Kilian Ganther,
Johann Peter Benner,
Isaac Widmer,
Johannes Rohr,
Henrich Wolff,
Jacob Crebler,*
Achior Crebler,*
Jacob Rorrer,*
Jacob Rincker,*
Melchior Keeper,*
Friederich Keeper,*
Johannes Zünd,
Henry Smith,*
Henrich Felty,
Puthy Weyss,*
Rudolff Sherrer,*
Henry Trölly,*
Jacob Bercher,

---

a Johannes Christian Brammeret is an unusually well written chi-
rograph, having appended to it, "*going through the land.*" No doubt,
a mere sojourner.—(*Editor.*)

a Diese Handschrift ist ungewöhnlich gut und hat den Zusatz: „durch's
Land gehend." Wahrscheinlich nur ein Reisender.—(Herausgeber.)

Henry Weys,*
Rudolff Widmer,*
Hans Scheurer,
Weirich Wagner,
Henry Brinker,*
Jacob Thumy,*
Caspar Waldy,*
Philip Bruner,*
Jost Funck,*
Johannes Knob,
Rudi Mauerer,
Anthony Suder,*
Henry Redlinger,*
Joseph Shomony,*
Gallus Fricker,*
Henry Sifry,*
Jacob Schüredt,
Georg Prall,
Jacob Waasser,
Tobias Pfister,*
Jacob Lostatter,*
Jacob Lostetter jr.,
Conrad Tshakky,
Johannes Turny,*
Peter Balsam,*
Abraham Arb sen.,
Christian Mosser,*
Johannes Housser,*
Isaac Greber,
Hans Jacob Meyer,
Leonhardt Vonruff,
Lenhart Fröly,
Rudolph Hemming,
Hans Georg Meyer,*
Conrad Kuntzly,*
Henrich Koch,
Hans Michel Neracker,
Hans Conrad Steinman,
Hans Jacob Zöble,
Joseph Lenggenhar,

Melchior Winkelman,
Jacob Haassler,*
Abraham Hasseler,*
Hans Georg Shan,*
Uhlerich Bitsferker,*
Johannes Weidman,
Johannes Bimmesdörffer,
Abraham Imoberstüch,
Heinrich Harneist,
Hans Jacob Bär,
Heinrich Aleiss,
Ludwig Engel,*
Solomon Cauffman,
Uhllerich Waldmer,*
Heinrich Bauinger,
Andreas Shneyder,*
Johannes Zöpner,
Hans von Huber,
Rudolph Guttinger,*
Conrad Weydman,*
Christian Pfäher,
Conrad Bucher,*
Caspar Bucher,
Heinrich Haller,
Friederich Alenbach,
H. Nicholas Helling,*
Michael Singer,*
Conrad Kramer,*
Heinrich Boshart,
Hans Georg Hennold,
Felix Housser,*
Rudy Hausser,
Jacob Fischer,*
Adam Cheseches,?
Jacob Wäspy,*
Johannes Waspy,*
Joachim Diehrig,
Johannes Schneider,
Johann Casper Schaff,
Johann Adam Meng,

Johan Nickel Jung,   Hans Adam Seydler,*
Friederich Specht,   Johan Paul Glehas.

Marked "on board."—Probably confined by sickness:

Bezeichnet „an Board".—Wahrscheinlich wegen Krankheit zu=
rückgehalten:

Hans Smith, Henry Wurtz, Philip Bauer, Henrich Hambach, Henry Bretz, Ludwig Bretz, Sander Sanger, Jacob Urering, Lorentz Ampel, Henry Bousman, Anthony Samber, Christoph Eyerman.

------

149) Aug. 21, 1750. Ship Anderson, Hugh Campbell, Captain, from Rotterdam, last from Cowes.

Aug. 21, 1750. Schiff Anderson, Capitain Hugh Campbell,
von Rotterdam über Cowes.

Christian Botz,	Johannes Marquardt,
Ludwig Horst,*	Johannes Bretz,
Johannes Gunderman,*	Johann Beck,*
Martin Weber,	Matheas Weymer,*
Peter Hentzel,	Jacob Lyme,*
Gottfried Büttner,	Henry Reinfeld,*
Samuel Lüthy,*	Johan Engel Gonderman,
Christoph Metz,	Johann Henrich Fick,
Johannes Shmit,*	Johannes Peter Jung,
Jacob Rüter,	Johann Henrich Cuntz,
Christian Widman,	Johan Georg Schneider,
Oswald Dups,*	Johannes Henrich Ham,
Conrad Hauser,	Johan Jacob Sturm,
Gerhart Führ,	Johan Christian Sturm,
Conrad Derr,	Johan Heinrich Schuster,
Lorentz Hauck,	Joh. Heinrich Mauden,
Jacob Dengler,	Johannes Ludwig Beel,
Valentin Maitlin,*	Johan Wilhelm Beel,
Jonas Mütschler,	Johan Daniel Rheiner,
Johannes Hebel,	Johan Henrich Schneider,
Johan Miller,*	Johann Michel Huber,
Johannes Schauerer,	Johan Jacob Huber,
Christoph Miller,	Johan Martinus Reinhardt
Michael Wagenmann,	Johann Georg Reichman,
Gerhart Birkenbeyly,*	Johann Christian Rick,

Johan Baltzer Schmith,
Christian Kauffman,*
Hans Georg Singer,
Johan Georg Miller,
Johannes Jacob Blässer,
Johann Philip Benner,
Georg Deobalt Aner,?
Johan Philip Rambach,
Hans Georg Rath,
Johan Peter Weiss,
Johan Christophel Bretz,
Johan Wilhelm Britzing,
Melchior Bruner,*
Jacob Beaver,*
Georg Melcher,?
Andreas Shaad,*
Jacob Ackermann,
Lenhart Zebolt,*

Philip Pop,*
Jacob Heillman,
Johannes Naumann,
Christoph Steiner,
Conrad Plesher,?
Urban Friebele,
Johann Ludwig Etter,
Johann Peter Batz,
Johann Peter Becker,
Johann Philip Noll,
Johann Jacob Bop,
Reinhart Hasenbürger,
Johann Theis Schmidt,
Johannes Schwartzhaud,
Johann Gottlieb Naumann,
Johan Conrad Ruff,
Henrich Leuchthold.

---

150) Aug. 24, 1750.   Ship Brothers, Muir, Captain, from Rotterdam, last from Cowes.—271 passengers.

Aug. 24, 1750. Schiff Brothers, Capitain Muir, von Rotterdam über Cowes.—271 Passagiere.

Adam Shnyder,*
Adam Weaber,*
Erasmus Hess,
Jacob Gerdner,*
Johannes Koch,
Johannes Œhrle,
Philip Kawtzman,*
Christian Shott,*
Jacob Keller,
Johannes Walder,*
Joseph Nagel,*
Abraham Schneider,
Adam Mensch,*
Abraham Glass,*
Christian Fried,
Johannes Friessner,
Friederich Miller,*

Peter Meyer,*
Benedict Krieger,
Andreas Frey,
Casper Caarel,*
Daniel Cabel,*
Nickolas Rome,*
J. Nickolas Holl,*
F. Philip Holl,*
J. Adam Lucas,*
Johann Jacob Kimmel,
John Lenard Miller,*
Johann Leonhard Groh,
Johann Peter Seger,
Johann Henrich Keller,
Johan Georg Keller,
Johann Adam Körner,
Johann Georg Weiss,

20*

Johann Philip Weiss,
Johannes Blumenschein,
Johan Georg Höring,
Johann Georg Gans,*
Johan Nickel Ganss,
Johan Nicklaus Helm,
Joh. Georg Scheunberger,
Johann Matheis Schäffer,
Jacob Friederich Sahn,
Johan Peter Schmunck,
Johan Georg Drear,*
Hans Martin Sürfes,
Hans Peter Müller,
Johann Daniel Hoffmann,
Johan Heinrich Hauck,
Johann Georg Zerr,
Johann Philip Hüller,
Hans Georg Frey,
Engelhart Wagner,*
Jost Jacoby,
Mattheis Miller,
J. Jacob Freysh,*
Martin Dreisbach,
Martin Reich,?
Martin Weaber,*
Otto Dan. Neuer,
J. Leon. Reish,*
Hans Geo. Stauch,

J. Jacob Reybolt,*
Martin Ulmer,*
Hans Geo. Ganshorn,
Johannes Stroll,
G. Adam Bartholt,*
Adam Eberle,
Con. Israel Oberle,
Joh. Hen. Leeseman,
George Adam Barttel,*
G. Michael Rommigh,*
Hans Georg Rommigh,*
Johann Jacob Schuster,
Joh. Jacob Wagner,
Johann Henrich Gamber,
Georg Michael Gamber,
Johann Peter Krämer,
Johann Jacob Bernauer,
Hans Philip Bender,
Johan Georg Koop,
Johann Adam Franck,
Johan Conrad Schultz, *chir.*,
Johann Georg Müller,
Johann Adam Edelmann,
Johan Peter Laudenschleger,
Johan Ludwig Rauhzahn,
Johan Peter Fölker,
Georg Adam Young.*

---

151) Aug. 28, 1750. Ship Two Brothers, Thomas Arnt,
Captain, from Rotterdam, last from Cowes.

Aug. 28, 1750. Schiff Two Brothers, Capitain Thomas
Arnt, von Rotterdam über Cowes.

Philip Peter,*
Frederich Prophet,*
Christopher Gerner,
Johannes Kreutzwisser,
David Metzger,
Jacob Stein,
Christoph Albrecht,*

Peter Hergedt,
Baltazar Löffler,*
Stephan Kneisel,*
Johannes Kerlinger,
Daniel Sommer,*
Johannes Battenfeld,
Philip Battenfeld,

Sebastian Werner,*
Leonhart Heichel,*
Johannes Stoll,
Johannes Böhmer,
Lucas Schäffer,
Johan Georg Huber,
Johan Matheis Gerner,
Hans Georg Gerner,
Johann Adam Holtz,*
Georg Michael Schupp,
Hans George Seacoist,*
Hans Martin Eche,
Hans Adam Pfisterer,
Hans Adam Pfesterer,*
Philip Peter Huff,
Hans Adam Battenfeld,
Johann Heinrich Leibling,
Johann Friedrich Thomas,
Johann Jacob Schäffer,
Johann Wilhelm Stoll,
Johann Peter Böhmer,
Johann Wilhelm Gölb,
Johann Paulus Müller,
Johann Wilhelm Schneider,
Michael Mell,
Jacob Roller,
Martin Dups,
Christian Matheis,
Jacob Rosch,
Andreas Wentz,
Michael Waltz,*
Jacob Keble,
Jacob Bloss,
Johannes Becker,*
Jacob Weis,*
Martin Weis,*
Jacob Daniel,
Bernhart Berch,*
Tobias Muller,*
Tobias Müller jr.,
Matheus Brundle,

Mattheis Seufried,
Eberhart Bichel,
Matheis Rössler,
Jacob Volltzer,?
Michael Tybly,*
Peter Martin,
Mattheis Martin,
Johannes Warner,*
Lorentz Spatz,
Henry Hillinger,*
Mathias Berger,*
Johannes Jung,
Hans Martin Kollmer,
D. Bernhart Rothbaus,*
Hans Christoph Englerth,
Jacob Adam Nonnenmacher,
Hans Balthas Buck,
Johann Jacob Klein,
Hans Georg Sauerbreu,
Johannes Billheimer,*
Hans Adam Shmit,*
Hans Georg Geltz,*
Hans Georg Weiss,
Johan David Bichel,
Hans Georg Rudel,
Johann Jacob Braun,
Christoph Friedrich Reutter,
Hans Georg Müller,
Hans Wendel Seufried,*
Joseph Seufried,
Joh. Christoph Breitzinger,
Hans Georg Marich,
Christoph Buckbeck,
Hans Georg Dischler,
Johan Friederich Risch,
Christoph Meyer,*
Hans Georg Saal,
Philipp Dellinger,
Joseph Stumbff,
J. Daniel Printz.

236   NAMES OF GERMAN, SWISS

Sick—J. Gottlieb Weniger, Baltazar Munster, Andreas Dürr, Hans Jacob Metzger.

---

152) Aug. 28, 1750. Ship Phœnix, John Mason, Captain, from Rotterdam, last from Cowes.—339 passengers.

Aug. 28, 1750. Schiff Phönix, Capitain John Mason, von Rotterdam über Cowes mit 339 Passagieren.

Erdman Schultz,
Johannes Seltzer,
Simon Peter,
Christian Bernhardi,
Jacob Saber,*
Jacob Patz,
Johann Georg Leyss,
Johan Ludwig Schleber,
Johan Nickel Vogelgesang,
Johan Conrad Protzman,
John Henry Weydigh,*
Johan Georg Kalteisen,
Jean Drapet,
Caspar Bruner,*
Michel Peter,
Henrich Gerlart,
Hans Wirheiner,
Jacob Moog,*
Ernst Böhm,
Conrad Zellner,*
Georg Betzler,
Peter Seigendaller,*
Ulrich Seigendaller,*
Johannes Peter,
George Hultzler,*
Jacob Sheel,*
Jacob Frison,*
Henry Yeal,*
George Yure,*
George Saling,*
George Kop,*
Jacob Werly,*
Conrad Hay,*

Dewald Theil,*
Jacob Reb,
David Frarry,*
Jacob Muni jr.,*
Jacob Muni sen.,*
Debolt Beck,
Peter Dinck,
Henry Herman,*
Michael Cuntz,*
Andreas Hotz,
Georg Hauss,
Peter Schmitt,
Jacob Riffel,
Peter Erhart,*
Dietrich Erhart,*
Debalt Frantz,
Frantz Anton,
Georg Gees,*
Joseph Waltz,
Philip Hind,*
Jacob Anthoni,
Solomon Phillips,
Johan David Schmitt,
Johan Wilhelm Hertzog,
Johan Jacob Peter,
Michael Forbringer,*
Heinrich Eberhard,
Johann Wilhelm Weiss,
Johan Gottfried Rüger,
Carl Ernst Rüger,
Georg Siegenthahller,
Johan Jacob Reich,
Philip Jacob Volandt,

Hans Michel Nothstein,
John George Debald,*
Henry Haberman,*
Michael Lehman,
Christian Muni,*
Conrad Muni,*
Hans Ulrich Schleppi,
Andreas Muni,*
Christopf Durrenberger,*
Michael Berger,*
Hans Jacob Seuter,
Nicklaus Yeisly,*
Johann Georg Herman,
Andreas Diemer,
Johan Friederich Röhn,
Dewald Kuntz,
Johan David Ziffel,
Johannes Zurbrück,
Martin Buchman,*
Jacob Buchman,*
Georg Hans Anthoni,
Nicklaus Jacob,
Georg Friederich Lintz,
Johannes Meyer,*
Carl Seusterditz,
Christoph Fischer,
Adam Hiltenbrandt,
Abraham Shopffer,*
Martin Burchhardt,
Michael Straub,
George Lindeman,*
George Hatzinger,*
Henry Meyer,*
Michael Kapp,
Ulrich Fooks,*
Dewalt Fooks,*
George Lohr,*
Jacob Werner,
Peter Bem,
Nicklaus Hegi,
Jacob Haber,

Peter Schirmer,
Hans Braun,
Valentin Mochel,
Heinrich Müller,
Jacob Paule,
Johannes Lips,*
Abraham Enderly,*
Christian Gross,
Carl Heiser,
Jacob Heck,
Johan Solomon,*
Jacob Meyer,*
Jacob Fisher,*
Adam Weiss,
Paul Weber,
Johan Grimm,
Hans Miller,*
Godlieb Bobe,*
George Matler,*
Henrich Presler,
Debalt Farringer,*
Killian Jaac,*
Conrad Hefer,?
Georg Voltz,
Martin Jost,*
Philip Finck,*
Michael Fischer,
Gottlieb Thurm,
Nicklaus Kiffer,*
Jacob Schoch,
Philipp Ferber,
Andreas Engel,
Peter Will,
Hans George Eter,*
Anthoni Grieser,
Georg Henrich Etter,
Jacob Friederich West,
Johannes Wedel,
Johan Friederich von Rohr,
Joh. Andonus von Rohr,
Gottfried Thiele,

Christophel Pfuller,
Johan Otmansdorff,*
Jacob Laubenhauer,
Michael Shalleberger,*
Ernst Jacob Dippberger,
Michael Lederman,
David Dieterich,
Christian Andræ,
Johann Jacob Heiser,
Gottfried Peuckert,
Johan Tobias Zimmerman,
Friederich Zimmerman,*
Joh. Michael Heuschkell,
Joh. Christof Heuschkell,
Benjamin Heuschkell,
David Ensminger,
George Reinhart,*
Hans Heinrich Nächt,
Abraham Rithmüller,
Paneratius Reichhelt,
Hans Weckerling,
Adam Haberling,*
Philip Friederich Winther,
Johan Georg Malle,
Andreas Wittenmeyer,
Joseph Gerber,
Johannes Phillipi,
Johannes Phillipi jr.,
Andreas Phillipi,
Christian Philipy,
Hans Jacob Liebenguth,
Hans Jacob Liebenguth jr.,
Peter Liebenguth,
Johann Jacob Leininger,
Nicklaus Jost,

Hannes Gerber,*
George Shep,*
Dewalt Nagel,*
Caspar Shmit,*
Georg Clauss,
Christian Gurdner,*
Johannes Philipi,
Marx Dahleth,
Christian His,?
Hans Blasser,*
Hans Deterig,*
George Viet,*
Jacob Klöti,
Philip Stock,
Ulrich Eggler,
Sirach Schultz,
Hans Wagner,*
Adam Reistebacher,
Ludwig Wohlfahrt,
Joseph Peter Bauer,
Georg Engelhart,?
Ludwig Wittenmeyer,
Heinrich Sterchi,
Philipp Waletein,
Joh. Gottfried Zichelhart,
Wilhelm Ehrman,
Thomas Shlighter,*
Nickolaus Shlighter,*
Han Geo. Dierenberger,
Paulus Christian,
Hans Georg Ludwick,
Peter Haberstick,*
Johannes Steckel,*
Hans Georg Schultz,
Jacob Guntzerhausser.

---

153) Aug. 31, 1750. Ship Nancy, Thomas Cautom, Master, from Rotterdam, last from Cowes.—270 passengers.

Aug. 31, 1750. Schiff Nancy, Capitain Thomas Cautom, von Rotterdam über Cowes mit 270 Reisenden.

Johannes Vollmer,
Daniel Bohset,
Martin Müller,
Lorentz Schenck,
Joseph Stähle,
Friederich Gans,
Johann Gans,
Thomas Gans,*
Georg Heuling,
Johannes Zweigle,
Michael Rieder,
Andreas Brauer,
Michel Hensel,
Johannes Heide,
Christoph Kendtel,
Johannes Glasser,
Jonas Raub,
Friederich Weiss,
Wilhelm Gettling,
Geo. Hen. Lutz,
Joh. Bernhardt Riede,
Balthas Federhoff,
Bernhart Rockenstihl,
Daniel Haubersack,
Joh. Conrad Raisch,
Joh. Tobias Rudolph,
Hans Georg Hetle,
Martin Jommel,
Johan Georg Bauer,
Joh. Bernhart Wünsch,
Johann Georg Sieger,
Johann Georg Musse,
Geo. David Schneider,
Hans Georg Kuhm,
Johan Jacob Cantz,
Han Georg Beiterman,
Han Jacob Beiterman,
Joh. Fried. Unrath jr.,
Geo. Henrich Lutz jr.,
Geo. Wilhelm Marx,
Joh. Geo. Marx,

Christian Fautz,
Joh. Jacob Weiss,
Michael Ferster,
Jeremias Horngacher,
Christian Hornberger,
Andreas Rahnfelder,
Bernhart Gilbert,*
Christoph Wetzel,
Frantz Kühlwein,
Jacob Würth,
Andreas Singel,
Johann Herbolt,
Christian Blosser,*
Johannes Löw,
Christian Giebeler,
Tilman Creutz,
Johann Gitting,
Johannes Rehbach,
Johannes Jung,
David Nuss,
Philip Grabeman,
Immanuel Bager,
Henrich Wil. Stiegel,
Joh. Ludwig Traber,
Han Georg Benner,
Joh. Nicklaus Gilbert,
Joh. Jacob Gobel,
Joh. Georg Gilbert,
Johan Jacob Baum,
Hans Georg Gilbert,
Han Adam Herbalt,
Joh. Philip Hautz,
Han Jacob Gilbert,
Joh. Jacob Barth,
Jost Henrich Wehler,
Joh. Peter Gutelius,
Joh. Jacob Brumbach,
J. Daniel Sheyder,*
Dilmanus Weissgerber,
Johan Peter Kleim,*
Joh. Henrich Comrath,

Johan Henrich Klein,
J. Henry Seidensticker,*

Johan Henrich Jung,
Joh. Georg Braunsberg.

---

154) Sept. 12, 1750. Ship Priscilla, William Wilson, Captain, from Rotterdam, last from Cowes.—210 passengers.

Sept. 12, 1750. Schiff Priscilla, Capitain William Wilson, von Rotterdam über Cowes.—210 Reisende.

Christian Reutzel,
Johannes Grack,
Conrad Grack,
Peter Hartman,*
Nicklaus Weininger,
George Cunkel,*
Andreas Schuster,
Valentin Born,
Nicklaus Schäffer,
Johannes Guckel,
Johannes Rauck,
Johannes Mayer,
Conrad Hertzog,
Kaspar Oberdorff,
Daniel Resseler,*
John Henry Ritzel,*
Joh. Wilhelm Reutzel,
Friederich Steinberger,
Han Mich. Wissner sen.,
Han Mich. Wissner jr.,
Joh. Henrich Rössler,
Geo. Henrich Räsch,
George Ernst Rish,*
Joh. Georg Keyser,
Joh. Georg Rössler,
Joachim Gottschalck,
Eberhart Steygerwaldt,
Johan Adam Börner,
Georg Ernst Becker,
Han Andreas Kachel,
Johannes Stang,
Johannes Huth,
Wilhelm Adelman,

Johannes Mauss,
Andreas Oberdorff,
Friederich Shnyder,*
Johannes Ommerth,
Valentin Corngiber,*
Henrich Lotz,
Michael Roth,*
Thomas Bertholt,*
Peter Günder,
Johannes Plott,
Johannes Heyl,*
Georg Waihdel,
Ludwig Shmith,
Balzer Jäger,
Johannes Föller,
Balthazar Filler,*
Johannes Lamb,*
Carl Russ,*
Andreas Œtzel,
Joh. Jacob Newman,*
Wendel Lawmeister,
Johan Straushaar,
Balthazer Simmons,*
Christian Hartting,
Johan Melchior Orth,
Johan Adam Roth,
Joh. Baltzer Stockel,
Ernst Phil. Kirscher,
Johannes Schuman,
Johann Peter Muth,
Nicklas Berninger,*
Melchior Kleinfelter,*
Johannes Möller,

Joh. Simon Oberdorff,*
Carl Miller,*
Johannes Diemer,
Joh. Michael Stoffel,*

Joh. Henry Rulley,*
Simon Schierher,
Conrad Rössler,
Joh. Henrich Liff.

155) Sept. 29, 1750. Ship Osgood, William Wilkie, Captain, from Rotterdam, last from Cowes.—480 passengers.

Sept. 29, 1750. Schiff Osgood, Capitain William Wilkie, von Rotterdam über Cowes.—480 Reifende.

Hendrich Bronk,*
Yerrick Wisht,*
Jacob Wist,*
Laurantius Wüst,
Jacob Wüst,
Christoph Shmit,*
Michael Shmit,*
Johannes Greiner,
Conrad Toll,*
Georg Becker,
Johannes Seyl,
Jacob Clauser,*
Henry Clauser,*
Nicklaus Burg,*
Nicholaus Hörner,
Friederich Hörner,
Han Geo. Hautzenbieler,
Andre Baudemont,
Hans Adam Kney,
Valentin Petermann,
Wilhelm Humbert,
Heinrich Hörner,
Johannes Schwab,
Gabrial Leydy,*
Friederich Reist,
Gottlieb Kauffman,*
Mattheis Schnepp,
Bartolomæus Eppler,
Hans Baltas Otz,
Han George Zigler,*
Joh. Martin Neher,

Joh. Georg Speidel,
Michael Peterman,*
Georg Dick,*
Christian Faas,*
Jacob Krebs,*
Eder Deghe,*
Jacob Schoch,
Peter Stotz,
Ludwig Sotz,
F. Schweitzer,
Rudolph Christi,
Jacob Keamigh,*
Jacob Glohser,
Lorentz Dobbler,*
Ludwig Readwile,*
Georg Ulrich,
Philip Jacob,
Durst Cantick,*
Frederich Kuntz,
Michel Bele,
Ludwig Bitzer,
Ludwig Eiszele,
Hans Netischeh,
Ludwig Moritz,
Friederich Gauss,
Johannes Wolffer,
Christian Schmoller,
Anthony Shnyder,*
Jacob Frasch,
Matheas Meyer,*
Michael Eusinger,

21

Heinrich Dietmar,
Christian Eyserloh,
Emanuel Brittschedt,
Christian Heussler,
Michael Heinrich,*
Andreas Knödler,*
Christian Knotz,
Sebastian Rayster,
Johan Michael jr.,
Christoph Albrecht,
Conrad Bender,
Johannes Schnell,
Joh. Fried. Sautter,
Jacob Schneider,
Georg Scheufflen,
Christian Schuhler,
Jacob Scheufflen,
Hans Georg Crietz,
Han Martin Wolffer,
Andreas Herther,
Johannes Moritz,
Joh. Michael Rietweill,
Johan Arnold Kuntz,
Johannes Dinges,
Conrad Wittman,
Gottlieb Mittelberger,
Nicolaus Haugendobler,
Joh. Wendel Ackerman,
Joh. Georg Ackerman,
Han Bastian Eberhard,
Loren Marque Daudt,
Hans Georg Marti,
Joh. Georg Ludwig,*
Hans Martin Waltz,
Hans Jacob Binder,
Johann Georg Gauss,
Hans Georg Meyer,*
Han Martin Kienstein,

Han Mart. Kienstein jr.,
Joh. Henrich Binder,
Joh. Christian Seindel,
Joh. Gottfried Richter,
Joh. Gottolb Hoppe,
Han Geo. Koberstein,
Johann Martin Kast,
Jacob Fried. Kümmerley,
Han George Fackler,*
Han Georg Knödler,
Han Geo. Schweigarth,
Han Georg Murr,
Han Georg Kreutz,
Hans Geo. Schnawffer,*
Han Mich. Dentzer,
Joh. Daniel Bosch,
Valentin Heygis,
Georg Heigis,
Mattheis Miller,
Christian Stotz,
Bernhardt Rüst,
Jacob Ehele,
Jacob Eilheim,
Jacob Uhllerich,*
Andreas Hertcher,*
Hans Jac. Shanker,*
Louis Gerizeh,
Johan Jacob Bosch,
Hans Georg Hutekunst,
Johan Peter Bender,
Johan Peter Bender jr.,
Johan Philip Mofhel,?
Hans Ludwig Zimmerman,
Hans Georg Mofhel,?
Hans Ludwig Stein,
Hans Martin Müller,
Philipp Joseph Schilling,
Hans Georg Basch.

156) Sept. 17, 1750. Brigantine Sally, William Hassleton, Captain, from London.

Sept. 17, 1750. Schnellfahrer Sally, Capitain William Haßleton, von London.

Christoff Reushaw,*
Joseph Reiff,*
Peter Millend,*
Ludwig Falck,
Jacob Winkler,*
Hans Stuber,*
Nicklas Dick,*
Hans Stohl,*
Hans Ammich,*
Hans Stuber,*
Jacob Furrer,*
Jacob Dick,*

Hans Uhlerich Winsh,*
Johan Gottfried Kiele,
Hans Christian Scheffeler,
Friederich Schärschler,
Johannes Kuhn,
Hans Georg Keller,
Christoff Coblet,*
Christian Stober,
Hans George Frey,*
Hans Knerr,*
Jacob Miller,*
Abraham Yarsing.*

157) Nov. 3, 1750. Ship Brotherhood, John Thomson, Captain, from Rotterdam, last from Cowes.—300 passengers.

Nov. 3, 1750. Schiff Brotherhood, Capitain John Thomson, von Rotterdam über Cowes.—300 Reisende.

Conrad Laubsher,*
Johannes Schäffer,
Simon Minch,
Teobalt Williahr,
Matheis Hoffner,
Jacob Stark,*
Jacob Sicher,*
Peter Sicher,
Mattheis Brückert,
Johan Jacob Laubscher,
Johann Nicolaus Schäffer,
Johann Elias Williahr,

Johan Adam Heys,*
Georg Friederich Bayer,
Johann Peter Brickli,
Johann Jacob Maag,
Hans Georg Schaufler,
Johann Nicolaus Meck, a
Pierre Paris,
Isaac Paris,
Henrie Jeune,
Michael Swing,*
Johannes Schock,
Peter Hahn,

a Died at Harrisburg, April 16, 1803, aged 71 years, 4 months and 4 days. He was the *Editor's* wife's *Proavus.*

a Starb zu Harrisburg am 16. April 1803 in einem Alter von 71 Jahren, 4 Monaten und 4 Tagen. Er war der Urgroßvater der Frau des Herausgebers.

Jacob Frey,
Michael Seitz,
Johannes Albrecht,*
Johannes Kreuss,
Nicolaus Bonn,
Johannes Bonn,*
Nicklas Weisman,*
Michael Weisman,*
Paul Iemel,
Wilhelm Trün,
Philip Leister,
Hans Ziesser,
Nicklas Leyster,*
Peter Bassler,
Joseph Bassler,
Jacob Bassler,
Jacob Schowalter,
Henry Stigel,*
Peter Fahren,
Joseph Fahren,
Johannes Rub,*
Jacob Lichty,*
Johannes Mast,
Peter Stuky,*
Hans Konig,*
Hans Zorr,*
Joseph Meyer,*
Michael Hölley,
Peter Fisher,*
Philip Feillem,
Michael Wurm,*
Ludwig Fetzer,*
Peter Knabe,*
Hans Blauch,
Hans Knebel,
Michael Stuky,*
Hans Siegrist,
John Jost Shwalb,*
Johan Jacob Wolkemer,
Peter Ratenbürger,
Joh. Henrich Küblinger,

Joh. Christoffel Hembel,
Sebastian Käppler,
Christian Däublin,
Johannes Lehman,
Johannes Showalter,
Christian Showalter,
Peter Lugenbiehl,
Christian Eidenes,
Christian Bleich,
Heinrich Schwartz,
Christian Kauffman,
Johann Philipp Eckell,
Johan Jacob Lösch,
Johannes Rohrer,
Johan Adam Stöhr,
Johannes Schneider,
Johannes Bassler,
Jacob Schowalter sen.,
Peter Schowalter,
Simon Wisham,*
Christian Rub,*
Jacob Bürth,
Johannes Holly,
Nicolaus Mihller,
Christian Furrer,*
Andreas Hölley,
Peter Delebach,
Christian Neycomer,*
Johan Georg Beck,
Wilhelm Werner,*
Hans Gundelfinger,*
Jacob Naftziger,
Christian Knebel,*
Hans Hertzler,
Johannes Hertzler,
Johann Jost Weigandt,
Georg Daniel Orth,
Melchior Geissert,
Jacob Mössinger,
Jacob Berg,
Jacob Reif,*

Georg Weiss,
Jacob Graf,
Jacob Behr,
Hans Funck,
Paul Roth,*
Christian Neuman,

Martin Funck,
Georg Rebschleger,
Jacob Hausser,
Nicolaus Schmidt,
Johannes Hausser,
Johan Georg Bauer.

158) Nov. 30, 1750. Ship Sandwich, Hazelwood, Captain, from Rotterdam, last from Cowes.—200 passengers.

Nov. 30, 1750. Schiff Sandwich, Capitain Hazelwood, von Rotterdam über Cowes.—200 Reisende.

Jacob Simre,
Johan Ludwig,
Peter Sallatin,*
Christian Fiess,
Jacob Rumel,*
Daniel Fahrne,
Joseph Klöpster,
Jacob Traub,
Heinrich Schmidt,
Johannes Koch,*
Adam Weygel,
Daniel Debuss,
Henry Hartzel,*
Johannes Moll,
Hans Bollinger,
Andreas Mentz,
John Eshbach,*
Paulus Groundler,*
George Brech,*
Johannes Leitz,
Philip Gassman,
Michael Möggy,*
Henrich Stumpf,
George Casper,*
John Martin,*
Henry Haan,*
Peter Mantz,
Casper Peter,
Johannes Reel,*

Jacob Breys,
Jacob Shmit,*
Michael Frankhauser,
Johann Georg Gass,
Georg Philip Rumel,
Johan Philip Körgert,
Leonhart Rupperter,
Johannes Willdanger,
Mattheis Wilfanger,
Martin Deinberger,
Johannes Knauss,
Johannes Weygel,
Johann Peter Gläffer,
Nicolaus Lorentz,*
Peter Huffshmit,*
Jacob Bollinger,*
Johannes Fuchs,
Johan Peter Lamberty,
Hans Adam Biebel,
Joh. Christoph Laubach,*
Joh. Bernhardt Kessler,
George Christ. Deull,*
Georg Philip Teul,
Joh. Henrich Wäydemann,
Johan Adam Gross,
Georg Adam Wagner,
John Georg Wagner,
Kasper Ristnach,
Wendel Hermann,*

Friederich Schenckel,
Johan Jacob Koch,
Johannes Fleisher,*
Michael Fünfrock,
Peter Shmit,*
Martin Nazurus,*
Philip Leher,
Ulerich Tuxly,*
Rolandt May,
Georg Œss,
Daniel Bricker,
Moritz Wöber,
Jacob Spitler,
Martin Piere,
Jost Habgehes, ?
Friederich Schor sen.,
Friederich Yor jr.,

Hans Weber,
Michael Schor,
Nicklaus Schande,
Joh. Friederich Bager,
Joh. Anthon Schwartz,
Joh. Philip Schwartz,
Joh. Anthonius Körner,
Christian Hagen,
Konrath Imhoff,
Lorentz Shmitly,*
Michael Hans Peter,
Jacob Behrt,*
Wolfgang Joh. Henhey,
Engelhart Yeiser,
Gottlieb Beckley,*
Caspar Mayer.

159) Aug. 26, 1751. Ship Anderson, Hugh Campbell, Master, from Rotterdam, last from Cowes,—fifty Roman Catholics.—236 passengers.

Aug. 26, 1751. Schiff Anderson, Capitain Hugh Campbell, von Rotterdam über Cowes,—fünfzig Römisch-Katholische.—236 Reisende.

Lorentz Durst,*
Mathias Rost,*
Jacob Maud,*
Joseph Strosle,*
Hans Martz,*
George Hoozer,*
Sebastian Greim,
Adam Greim,
Hans Riter,
Peter Klein,
Martin Clain,*
Joseph Voltz,
Hans Adam,
Hans Shaver,*
Philip Kinder,*
Andreas Hyder,

Peter Wehrner,
Hans Scheffer,
Michael Morith,*
Lorentz Leble,
Jost Stroh,
Hans Georg Hummerle,
Johannes Frick,
Hans Georg Hook,
Michael Chrisback,*
Johannes Bower,*
Ludwig Werner,*
Joh. Friederich Geyer,
Peter Breelinger,
Anthony Yauble,*
Abraham Rinehart,*
Ulrich Bernhart,*

Hans Jacob Bernath,
Hans Georg Schneider,
Michael Dannerinborgen sen.,
Michael Dannerinborgen,
Johannes Zimmer,*
Hans Casper Stündter,
Joseph Riebell,
Georg Arbengast,
Hans Michael Koonts,*
Michael Sommer,
Matheis Flach,
Lorentz Shiney,*
Michael Barle,
Michael Weidt,
George Reyser,*
Adam Storch,*
Otto Haase,
Johannes Fürster,
Henrich Fürster,
Valentin Clamdy,
George Miller,*
Joseph Wittemer,*
Hans Petersheim,
Christoph Fleur,
Hans Straub,*
Hans Metz,*
Christian Ritz,
Adam Gehrich,
Peter Weber,
Jacob Meier,
Jacob Minjan,*
Bastian Nögle,

Johannes Geiger,
Daniel Miller,*
Henrich Erferdt,
Joseph Joram,
Henry Demanche,*
Johan Jost Franck,
Carl Wiederholt,
Bartholomäus Weid,
Valentine Loomyer,
Joh. Abraham Arbeiter,
Joh. Christian Schauer,
Wilhelm Hammer,
Joh. Kilian Feltmann,
Johannes Seyffarth,
Joh. Michael Deininger,
Hans Georg Spang,
Dominique Fleur,
Jacob Tschieringer,
Joh. Dietrich Hostender,
H. Michael Metz,
H. Martin Vaudalin,
Joh. Caspar Jungmann,
Jeremias Taubenheim,*
Matthias Schwartzwelder,
Hans Georg Felber,
Johannes Hildebrand,
Johan Georg Reichwein,
Joh. Christoph Ohle,
Joh. Michael Gistelbarth,
Johan Christian Alter,
Augustus Milchsack.

160) Sept. 5, 1751. Ship Shirley, James Allen, Captain, from Rotterdam, last from Orkney, Scotland,—three Roman Catholics.—288 passengers.

Sept. 5, 1751. Schiff Shirley, Capitain James Allen, von Rotterdam über Orkney, Schottland,—drei Römisch-Katholische. 288 Reisende.

Leonard Maas,
Johannes Fähr,
Mattheus Keuffer,
Henry Uhrer,*
Heinrich Wagner,
Jacob Huth,
Michael Schneider,
Gottlieb Roth,*
Johannes Heiss,
Michael Weiss,
Hans Georg Betz,
Christoff Ludewig,*
Georg Jacob Fisar,?
Johan Michael Sholty,
Joh. Georg Schumacher,
Johan Caspar Spring,
Johan Martin Kroll,
Johan Philip Wagner,
Hans Georg Klobly,*
Johann Georg Curr,
Johan Lorentz,
Georg Giebler,
Heinrich Crafft,
Thomas Geiner,*
Friederich Zinn,
Georg Schörth,
Jacob Schauckert,
Jacob Shack,*
Henrich Curr,
Martin Leyer,
Nickolas Mildeberger,*
Lorentz Ludwig,*
Ludwig Schüttler,
Fredrick Shetz,*
George Frantz,*
Georg Kleeh,
Johann Grosskopff,*
Daniel Pracht,*
Georg Balsbach,
Georg Kreuller,
Andreas Kuhn,*

Christoph Gnässle,
Burkhart Heinrich,
Wendel Miech,
Isaac Paris,
Johannes Ney,*
Stephan Schertzer,
Samuel Shweyart,*
Balzar Henning,*
Veit Meister,
Conrad Sampel,
Johannes Gilbert,
Frederick Krafft,
Christian Mook,
Christian Sholl,*
Lenhart Sumer,*
Michael Arnold,*
Dietrich Röhm,
Peter Mugler,
Christian Riger,*
Frederich Gross,
David Frank,
Hans Martin Seyfeird,
Georg Adam Stör,
Hans Adam Gramlich,
Joh. Bernhard Shrauk,*
Hans Georg Schrauck,
Johann Michael Wagner,
Johannes Jacob Braun,
Hans Andreas Zilling,
Geo. Conrad Schweighart,
Hans Adam Franck,
Johan Friedrich Teibz,*
Hans Henrich Kautzmann
Georg Michel Walcker,
F. Johannes Schweitzer,
Hans Stephan Martin,
Georg Simon Baum,
Johann Georg Gassinger,
Johann David Herbst,
H. George Ney,*
Hans Jacob Schoch,

Johan Henrich Schirm,
Johann Martin Seltzer,
Hans Georg Wurteberger,*
Christoph Horlacher,
Georg Michel Gretter,
H. Michael Wurtenberger,*
Johann Georg Kühlein,
Johan Conrad Beyrer,
Hans Jacob Fogelmann,*
Michael Fägelman,*
Johann Michael Sommer,
Friederich Wielandt,
Frederich Shwartz,*
Johann Georg Blintzinger,
Georg Martin Carle,
Hans Michel Ott,
Jacob Bernard Danecker,*
Johannes Reys,*

Melchior Lauall,*
Hans Georg Hand,*
Gabriel Rössler,*
Johan George Epson,*
David Edlinger,
Francis Edelberger,
Ludwig Ernst,
Michael Fölix,*
Jacob Sheyder,*
Hans Shauman,*
Jacob Gerringer,*
Johan Michael Leytecker,*
Melchior Reysal,*
Andreas Schmeltzer,*
Christopher Ederly,*
Johan Elias Horrst,
Nickolas Mittelburger.*

161) Sept. 9, 1751. Ship Patience, Hugh Steel, Captain, from Rotterdam, last from Cowes,—eight Roman Catholics.— 255 passengers.

Sept. 9, 1751. Schiff Patience, Capitain Hugh Steel, von Rotterdam über Cowes,—acht Röm.-Katholische.—255 Reisende.

John Hendrick,*
Pierre Balmas,
Diewald Hig,
Andreas Bleshor,*
Daniel Tien,
Jacob Wenigard,*
Stephen Deer,*
Abraham Wild,
Isaac Reno,
Matthieu Moret,
Daniel Ehart,
Christian Gran,*
Michel Farckart,
Johannes Bock,*
Christian Gally,*
Jacob Wolf,

Jacob Wolf,
Philip Hering,
Jacob Enckisch,
Philip Gob,*
Blasius Isele,
Michael Wieder,
Martin Erdman,
Jacob Stöhr,
Ludwig Rimmel,
J. Peter Andrea,
Peter Haubert,*
Peter Thomas,*
Frantz Host,*
Peter Haut,*
Georg Ludwig Math,
Eberhart Chappelle,

Jean Henri Tien,
Johann Andreas Bersch,
Johannes Strohschneider,
Johan Fried. Strohschneider,
Michael Strohschneider,
Hans Michael Mauer,*
Hans Georg Worthlin,*
Hans Worthlin,*
Jacob Danninger,
Michael Mauch,
Samuel Pauser,
Hans Peter Enck,
Christian Gabriel Conver,
H. George Gerhart,
Johan Henrich Hering,
Philip Wendel Höring,
John George Reely,
Johann Georg Babb,
Johann Andreas Hütig,
Philip Carl Jüdii,
Johann Andreas Becher,
Carl Anton Bergman,
Johann Christoph Wieder,
Johann Georg Ruoff,
Johan Diterich Weitzen,*
Johann Henrich Weitzel,
Johann Frantz Huber,
Hans Peter Huber,*
Peter Martin,
Joh. Deitschmall,
J. Henry Dietzel,
Jacob Martin,*
Michel Drabach,
J. Adam Trarbach,*
Jacob Trarbach,*

J. Peter Thomas,*
Conrad Miller,*
Henry Miller,*
Nicola Matter,
Johannes Rust,
Daniel Hess,*
Jost Karger,*
Melchior Spery,*
Johannes Block,*
George Block,
Nicklas Wolff,*
Peter Wolcher,*
Friederich Möbs,
Bernhard Bauer,
Philip Conrad Zeiler,
Johann Henrich Stöhr,
Johan Martin Freitag,
Georg Henrich Joseph,
Johann Peter Müller,
Johann Henrich Dull,
Johann Philip Haubert,
Johann Philip Litz,
Hans Peter Shutz,*
Johan Nicol. Bass,
Joh. Adam Oberkirch,*
Johannes Schwarbach,*
Johann Jacob Weyll,
Johann Peter Holderbaum,
Johan Adam Barthnies,
Johan Peter Ströher,
Johann Georg Scherbeann,
Hans Adam Didrich,
Jacob Leibrock,
Christian Lindner,*
Petrus Trauenstack.

162) Sept. 14, 1751. Ship St. Andrew, James Abercrombie, Captain, from Rotterdam, last from Cowes,—eight Roman Catholics, ten Mennonites, the remainder Calvinists.—230 passengers.

Sept. 14, 1751. Schiff St. Andrew, Capitain James Abercrombie, von Rotterdam über Cowes,—acht Römisch-Katholische, zehn Mennoniten, die Uebrigen Calvinisten.—230 Reisende.

Johannes Lenn,
Peter Eckman,*
Wendel Hanst,
Peter Berringer,*
Jacob Brandt,
Martin Shwab,*
Jacob Kimmel,
Adam Kimmel,
Christoph Foth,
Jacob Stahl,
Johannes Ehrman,
Michael Spengler,
Thomas Vreytach,*
Valentin Daubenberger,
Ludwig Dewalt,*
Georg Ludwig Stutzenberger,
Peter Jacob Weiss,
Rudolph Schöppi,
Henrich Seydenbender,*
Johann Philip Kimmel,
Johann Henrich Lohmann,
Georg Henrich Rösch,
Hans Peter Henrich,
Philipp Ihringer,
Johann Conrad Bäuerle,
Hans Georg Spengler,*
Johann Peter Schmeher,
Johann Michael Friedle,
Johan Jacob Daubenberger,
Hans Georg Hitman,*
J. Philip Liss,*
Johannes Frick,*
J. Jacob Shumber,*
Augustus Hub,
Valentin Kimmel,
Melchior Seib,
Caspar Wilghart,*
Albrecht Reinhardt,

Andreas Lemel,
Peter Arnold,*
Albrecht Dederer,
Friederich Biebler,
Tacitus Geiger,*
Alexander Holder,
Martin Bender,*
Martin Dietz,
Peter Bininger,*
H. Matheus Miller,*
Kilian Destermüller,
J. William Volck,
Conrad Erich,*
J. Adam Diersen,*
Gottlieb Ihrich,
Abraham Gusman,
Hans Mauerer,*
J. Wendel Shwob,*
Johannes Frick,*
Stephan Rigler,
Andreas Kramer,*
Hans Georg Scheu,
Joseph Bender,
Joseph Ehrman,
Weybrecht Nushagen,*
J. Adam Kirschbaum,
Georg Wilhelm Friedrich,
Hans Georg Uhrich,
Johann Jacob Selig,
Johann Georg Hub,
Johann Ludwig Ziegler,
Georg Adam Allbrecht,
Johan Georg Threer,
Johann Georg Kochendörffer,
Johann Philip Teutsch,
Hans Peter Strein,
Johann Frantz Biebler,
Johann Georg Schäffer,

Johann Georg Feick,
Hans Adam Hetter,*
Georg Peter Hüter,
Joh. Christoph Steirschildt,
Johan Henrich Eisenmenger,
Johan Friederich Mindisch,
Georg Simon Schramm,
Georg Thomas Henneberger,
Peter Henrich Eysenmenger,
Johann Jacob Haffner,
Johan Conrad Friedle,

Johann Adam Stückle,
Johann Gottfried Stückle,
Johann Dietrich Sauer,
Johann Daniel Betz,
Johann Georg Weiss,
J. Balth. Eysenmenger,
Michael Casper Fuchs,
Johannes Georg Bäcker,
Johann Georg Lasch,
Georg Michael Weeber.

163) Sept. 14, 1751. Ship Duke of Bedford, Richard Jefferys, Master, from Rotterdam, last from Portsmouth,—nine Roman Catholics, one hundred and twenty Calvinists.—260 passengers.

Sept. 14, 1751. Schiff Duke of Bedford, Capitain Richard Jefferys, von Rotterdam über Portsmouth,—neun Römisch=Katholische, ein hundert und zwanzig Calvinisten.—260 Reisende.

Friederich Zabooy,*
Friederich Zabooy jr.,*
Johann Henrich Weickel,?
Hans Michel Scherster,
Abraham Beck,
Isaac Wengert,
Andreas Beck,*
Nicklas Münder,*
Samuel Weiss,*
Adam Koch sen.,
Adam Koch jr.,
Michel Koch,
Andreas Knauer,
Johannes Knauer,
Christian Reich,
Caspar Scherffig,
Andreas Schäffer,
Michael Pisserth,
Georg Fetzer,
Peter Gerbrich,
Valentin Huth,

Michael Huth,*
Joseph Fuchs,
Frantz Bruner,*
Erhart Grimm,
Jacob Hobler,*
Abraham Holl,
Christian Gally,*
Christoph Heller,
Henrich Heller,
Caspar Müller,
Philip Liebener,*
Jacob Thürig,*
Henry Shloder,*
Caspar Metz,*
Henry Derker,*
Johannes Bender,
Valentin Shaffer,*
Peter Weber,
Johannes Weber,
Peter Blügner,
Henrich Lummel,

Michael Heyler,
Simon Burchhart,
Johannes Dewetten,
Jacob Vaser,
Jacob Lallemand,
Johann Georg Beck,
H. Michael Meyer,*
Johan Jacob Zigler,*
Joh. Michael Koch,*
Johan Melchior Rudi,
Hans Peter Knauer,
Caspar Weinmer,*
Georg Balthes Wecker,
Christoph Albert,
Matthäus Fetzer,
Johan Henrich Krebs,
Michael Gerbrich,
Johann Adam Koller,
Hendrick Courpenning,
Jeremias Geiger,
Joh. Rennigius Spiegel,
Christian Künther,
Johann Gottlieb Zinck,
Johan Peter Kammer,*
Friederich Mutschler,
Valentin Mutschler,
Johan Christian Lentz,
Johannes Schmuck,*
Hans Georg Bender,
Johan Georg Bender jr.,
Johann Marcus Beck,
Johannes Kleinpeter,
Hans Peter Schiffarth,
Martin Mattheis Schielie,
Georg Adam Krauss,
Georg David Reinhard,
Hans Michael Knab,*
Johann Lorentz Stindtler,
Johann Philip Schmidt,
Johan Georg Stotz,
Johan Jacob Gehemann,

Johan Georg Burckhardt,
Johann Andreas Heldt,
Johann Adam Schick,
Johann Wendel Weichstnir,
Johann Philip Diehl,
Lorentz Hünckel,
Hans Peter Kelinsteller,
Jacob Rewold,*
Christoph Zieger,*
Andreas Jund,
Peter Herr,
Georg Kleinpeter,
Nicklaus Schultz,
Rudolph Hoffer,*
Johannes Schäffer,
Peter Grauel,*
Martin Müller,
Andreas Kolb,
Christian Krebs,
Jacob Klein,
Paulus Sherly,*
Jacob Gally,*
Johannes Stumpp,
Jacob Geiger,
Carl Shaffer,*
Nicklas Shmith,*
Jacob Hildebrandt,
Solomon Heisch,
Hans Georg Resh,*
Martin Henrich,
Hans George Miller,*
Matthias Röckhele,
Hieronimus Kömmele,
Hans Jacob Kurtz,
Hans Georg Hauser,
Johann Jacob Fischer,
Mattheus Schöllhorn,
Johann Ludwig Einsel,
Johan Peter Heygiss,
Peter Ludwig Häyer,
Hans Georg Klein,*

Friederich Würth,
Johan Martin Heugeld,
Johann Martin Fleischman,
Henrich Bernhardt Diener,
Johann Adam Brentzinger,

Johan Adam Pole,*
Hans Georg Mercker,
Johann Adam Stock,
Johan Henrich Haber,
Nicolas von Münchler.

---

164) Sept. 16, 1751. Ship Edinburgh, James Russel, Master,—ten Roman Catholics.—345 passengers.

Sept. 16, 1751. Schiff Edinburgh, Capitain James Russel, zehn Römisch-Katholische.—345 Reisende.

Jacob Bauer,
Peter Maurer,
Lorentz Kuntzman,*
Conrad Zanck,*
Johannes Göttges,
Gottlieb Wagner,
Wilhelm Œrdter,
Conrad Bachman,
Henrich Katz,
Casper Wisser,
Henry Stumpff,
Johannes Doren,
Peter Fleck,*
Joseph Hombro,
William Saltzman,
Henrich Pfeffer,
Johann Adam Allan,
Philipus Jacob Wagner,
Johann Jacob Huser,
Hans Adam Miller,
Hans Michel Gerber,
Johann Henrich Ginterman,
Johann Henrich Völckner,
Johann Jacob Völckner,
Adam P. Kness,
Frantz Wilhelm Jerholtz,
Johann Peter Mengen,
Johann Henrich Stein,
Wilhelm Kupferschmied,
Hans Adam Matter,

Hans Henrich Noll,
Johann Adam Walther,
Georg Matter,
Jacob Keisser,
Andreas Keyser,*
Jacob Matter,
Michel Hardman,
Balthasar Jung,
Lorentz Schweissguth,
Peter Prim,*
Andreas Wier,*
Nicolaus Schoppert,
Hieronimus Textur,*
Abraham Schnell,*
Nicholas Lindeman,*
Peter Pfliester,
Henrich Pfliester,
Christian Luther,
Christian Scheib,
Michel Weber,
Nickel Weber,
Johannes Henrich,*
Michael Burger,*
Johannes Ort,*
Peter Schlosser,
Wilhelm Weigerich,
Frantz Highart,
Martin Schuh,
Frederick Greenewald,*
Carl Smith,*

Peter Lang,
Carl Schell,
Peter Rhein,
David Rhein,
Adam Kober,
Christian Kober,
Michel Bauerman,
Johannes Schlater,
Christian Hahn,
Peter Dötzter,
Nicholas Mathias,*
Martin Maties,
Johannes Mathias,*
Friederich Mehl,
Johann Wilhelm Heintz,
Philip Friederich Meyer,
Hans Adam Ferber,
Georg Justanus Noll,
Wilhelm Adam Wolff,
Georg Christophel Brem,
Johann Gottfried Kroh,
Johann Wilhelm Ferber,
Henrich Wilhelm Kochler,
Johann Michel Eberth,
Johann Philip Ebert,
Johann Nicolas Ebert,
Johann Georg Schnell,
Johann Michel Stemler,
Johann Nickel Weber,
Johann Nickel Weber jr.,
Johann Peter Stilling,
Johann Abraham Dauber,
Johann Friederich Conrad,
Johann Nickel Henrich,
Johann Georg Reinheimer,
Johann Friedrick Gräff,
Joh. Nicklaus Weyerbacher,
Isaac Weyerbacher,
Johannes Weyerbacher,
Johann Andreas Wagner,
Joh. Wilhelm Gräff,

Johann Friederich Fahss,
Heinrich Adam Scherer,
Jacob Zilchart,*
Johann Henrich Rhein,
Hans Adam Kober,
Johann Jacob Muller,
Johann Nicklaus Ker,
Johan Valentine Brenighoff,
Johan Philip Brenighoff,
Johan Friederich Brenighoff,
Johann Nicklaus Mehl,
Johann Wilhelm Nagel,
Johann Conrad Jost,
Abraham Wenbacher,
Hans Georg Kast,
Jacob Inder,*
Simon Burchart,*
Johannes Arbengast,
Jacob Fridrich,
Jacob Hoover,*
Frans Hoover,*
Johannes Schmid,
Johannes Klein,
Johannes Schmidt,
Jacob Funck,
Anthony Blum,
Nicklas Zegler,*
Johan Reys,*
Zachary Reys,
Blasius Weg,?
Georg Walcker,
Johann Philip Küster,
Johann Michael Heuler,
Philip Hasselbacher,
Johannes Schneider,
Johan Jacob Bitter,
Jacob Shnaudy,*
Johan Nicklaus Marheffen,
Georg Segman,*
Christian Steyerwaldt,
Daniel Lehmbacher,

Christoph Metz,
Henrich Daniel Deitt,
Johannes Schleich,

Philipp Henrich Weis,
Israel Burchart,
Johann Nickel Schmidt.

---

165) Sept. 16, 1751. Ship Nancy, Thomas Coatam, Captain, from Rotterdam,—one Roman Catholic.—200 passengers.

Sept. 16, 1751. Schiff Nancy, Capitain Thomas Coatam, von Rotterdam,—ein Römisch-Katholischer.—200 Reisende.

Jacob Guth,
A. Conrad Koder,
Conrad Koder,
David Mäuerle,
Michael Friess,
Johannes Hackeler,
Johannes Hopff,
Michael Capp,
Andreas Berensteher,
Jacob Kauffmann,
Elias Bär,
Jacob Kennely,*
Conrad Mäurly,
Jacob Scheible,
Sebastian Schnell,
Andreas Messerschmidt,
Hans Wuchter,
Andreas Bitinger,
Christian Nagel,
Jacob Kapp,
Daniel Kapp,
Hans Jacob Klett,
Johann George Rösch,
Hans Georg German,
Hans Georg Mäuerle,
Johann Friedrich Rooss,
Johann Friederich Würster,
Johann Martin Lang,
Johan Georg Goonner,
Hans Jacob Pfester,
Hans Michel Schnauster,
Johann Jacob Supper,

Hans Fredrick Brendley,*
Jacob Fredrick Sooper,
Hans Georg Reinthaler,
Johann Henrich Fischer,
Johann Ludwig Nonnemacher,
Hans Georg Reynthaller,*
Johan Jacob Scherick,
Johann Michel Rühl,
Hans Georg Schnell,
Johan David Weissmann,
Michel Mauser,
Johann Mauser,
Johannes Heydel,*
William Swindel,*
Jacob Haug,
Elias Mayer,
Hans Mayer,
Jacob Haag,*
Johannes Kimmerlein,
Conrad Steiger,
Wilhelm Hammer,
Daniel Keuler,
Johannes Keuler,
Johannes Kohler,
Jacob Raub,
Hans Hay,
Baltzer White,
Hans Bernhardt Messerschmidt,
Hans Jacob Wizer,
Hans Georg Koder,
Hans Martin Kimmerlein,
Hans Martin Mohr,

Hans Conrad Steiger,
Hans Georg Schnell,
Hans Georg Reichenächer,
Hans Martin Entiemann,
Johannes Kircher,*
Johann Lorentz Wilhelm,
Johann Philip Gerig,
Johann Friederich Billinger,
Michael Schmidt,
Johann Hay,
Johann Balthasar Geyer.

---

166) Sept. 16, 1751. Ship Brothers, William Muir, Captain, from Rotterdam.—200 passengers.

Sept. 16, 1751. Schiff Brothers, Capitain William Muir, von Rotterdam.—200 Reisende.

Johannes Leinberger,
Henry Shneyder,*
Johannes Bieber,
Joseph Kennel,*
Paul Mercker,
Henrich Seistel,
Friederich Millefelt,*
Erhart Millefelt,*
Michel Bieber,
Henrich Bieber,
Christoph Weber,*
Georg Hackir,
Peter Abert,
George Mader,
Valentin Walter,
Michael Oberly,
Andreas Klein,
Peter Moore,*
Peter Dingis,*
Peter Heyser,*
Johannes Seyfarth,
Johann Jacob Zigenfuss,
Johann Philip Schneck,
Joh. Melchior Swerer,*
Hans Jacob Farnie,
Hans Adam Wagner,
Friederich Entzminger,*
Johan Jacob Schmidt,
Johannes Schmidt,
Johannes Schnitt,
Johann Nicolaus Merckel,
Georg Conrad Meffet,
Philip Brentz,
Johann Jacob Ahlem,
Johan Adam Stein,
Johannes Zössler,
Ludwig Friedland,*
Johann Michel Mohr,
Johann Jacob Blum,
Johan Jacob Maul,*
Joh. Peter Sheesler,*
Johann Georg Hötzele,
Jacob Ludwig,
Martin Wolff,*
Henry Wolff,*
Adam Adams,*
Friederich Kirchner,*
Christoff Heuer,
Christoph Hauck,
Jacob Hauer,*
Sebastian Nagel,
Jacob Lehme,
Jacob Heit,
Joachim Nagel,
Georg Obermeyer,
Michael Weber,
Andreas Mohr,*
Georg Meintzer,

Conrad Menser,*
Anthony Graff,*
David Bietch,*
Michael Bietch,*
Jacob Roth,*
Ludwig Weltnes,
Jacob Ritter,
Daniel Zoller,
Jacob Frantz,
Christian Peter,
Joh. Jacob Gerling,*
Valentin Blumenstein,*
Johan Wendel Beylstein,
Joh. Georg Kirchner,*
Bernhard Hauer,*
Martin Mäintzer,
Johann Michael Hause,
David Musgnug,

Michael Raub,
Johann Georg Stählein,
Anthony Hauer,
Anthony Nagel jr.,
Anthony Nagel sen.,
Hans Georg Kappes,
Hans Georg Dillman,
Johannes Munster,
Hans Georg Uhlerich,
Johan Adam Heiser,
Georg Bastian Eigelberger,
Ludwig Schlincker,
Johannes Monitzer,*
Friederich Daniel Müller,
Georg Hoffheintz,*
Ludwig Bender,
Johan Henry Past,
Henrich Mag.

167) Sept. 21, 1751. Ship Two Brothers, Thomas Arnet, Master, from Rotterdam, last from Cowes.—239 passengers.

Sept. 21, 1751. Schiff Two Brothers, Capitain Thomas Arnet, von Rotterdam über Cowes.—239 Reisende.

Johannes Bausum,
Philippus Bausum,
Johannes Decker,
Johannes Rahn,
Jacob Jung,
Abraham Jung,
Johan Steinmetz,*
Georg Romel,
Jacob Pander,
Melchior Jung,
Joh. Christ. Fried. Wolff,
Christofel Gerhart,
Johann Henrich Decker,
Melchior Jung,
Caspar Steinmetz,*
Johan Jacob Steinmetz,
Johan Christian Lupp,

Johan Wilhelm Staudter,
Joh. Michael Lung,
Johan Georg Etzler,
Christian Rohr,*
Johannes Stauffer,
Simon Weier,
Andreas Brendle,
Georg Lupp,
Johannes Lupp,
Adam Lung,
Caspar Augenstein,
Ludwig Beickle,
Gregorius Richter,*
Henrich Arndt,
Carl Löhe,
Johannes König,
Daniel Becker,

Johannes Hein,
Johannes Henrich,
Johannes Orth,
Valentin Fey,
Johannes Lappe,
Andreas Grätz,
Anthonius Seemisch,
Conrad Christian,?
Jacob Eberhart,
Philipp Thomas,
Philipp Hetz,
Ludwig Gleissinger,
Johannes Werbung,
Georg Straub,
Jacob Fegert,
Mattheis Hunolt,
Wilhelm Hunolt,
Jacob Schauer,*
Simon Lung,
Johannes Shrout,*
Baltzer Kentzler,*
Henry Matheas,
Nicolaus Stoltz,
Johannes Bentz,
Han Martin Schers,
Jacob Heinberger,
Wolfgang Rüttichell,
Johann Georg Schneck,
Johan Philip Eyster,
Caspar Kalckglösser,*
Henrich Kalckglösser,
Georg Henrich Solinus,
Johann Wilhelm Weyman,
Hans Michael Herzog,
Hans Georg Schmitt,*

William Maltzberger,*
Johan Conrad Kreger,*
Johannes Becker,
Johann Georg Henrich,
Johannes Heintz,
Johan Henrich Heym,
Johan Jost Giersbach,
Johann Daniel Hoffman,
Johan Henrich Gring,*
Johann Henrich Hartman,
Johann Georg Decker,
Johan Jacob Hoffheintz,
Johan Henrich Ebes,?
Joh. Henry Mauerbach,*
Joh. Henrich Nicodemus,
Johan Jost Gring,
Philip Henrich Nöll,
Johan Martin Bender,
Johan Michael Wieg,
Johan Daniel Will,
Johan Adam Schmidt,
Johan Friederich Perlet,
Martin Christoph Röder,
Johannes Kristmann,
Johannes Molssberger,
Friederich Klarwein,
Joh. Christoph Georgey,
Fried. Wilhelm Herman,
Joh. Wilhelm Weinandt,
Johan Jacob Göbler,
J. Gerhart Zimmerman,
Johan Henrich Adam,
Joh. Gerhart Schuhmacher,
Joh. Wilhelm Cromberg,
Joh. Wilhelm Bodenheimer.

---

168) Sept. 23, 1751. Ship Neptune, James Wier, Captain, from Rotterdam, last from Cowes.—154 passengers.

Sept. 23, 1751. Schiff Neptun, Capitain James Wier, von Rotterdam über Cowes.—154 Reisende.

Anthoni Weinnert,
Jacob Hetzel,
Johannes Gies,
Michael Wennert,*
Adam Weiser,
Mattheus Lippoth,
J. Conrad Koch,
Johannes Manderbach,
Johannes Müller,
Jacob Pool, (Puhl),*
Johannes Greis,
Henrich Gerhart,
Johannes Schütz,
Nicolas Reybolt,*
Johannes Busch,
Johannes Meyer,
Michael Lauffer,
J. Michael Lauffer,
Johannes Vetter,
Johannes Œxle,
Johannes Beer,
Paulus Graninger,
Johannes Hombert,
Johannes Baker,*
Balthas Gressmann,
Matheis Lutz,
Joh. Engl. Cünrad,
Johannes Geistweit,
Joh. Georg Christ,
Johann Thomas,*
Andreas Steyger,*
Everhart Thomas,*
Henry Zimmerman,*
Jost Henry,*
Joh. Phil. Sesberger,
Joh. Ebert Steyner,*
Joh. Engel Bucher,
Christian Schmidt,
Christian Haffer,
Johannes Wilhelm Seyn,
Johan Phillippus Böhmer,
Johan Wilhelm Böhmer,

Johan Heinrich Vetter,
Johan Friederich Gettner,
Johan Bernhart Beatt,
Johann Georg Seckel,
Johan Alexander Schütz,
Johan Ludwig Klein,
Johan Conrad Wulleweber,
Johan Christ. Zimmerman,
Johan Henrich Kochling,
Johan Henrich Greiss,
Johan Philip Anhorn,
J. Henry Tillman,
Johann Peter Schaaff,
Johan Nickel Weber,
Johannes Peter Reusel,
Johannes Engelberth Jung,
J. Jost Walter,*
J. Friederich Shreiber,*
J. Henry Shmitt,*
Johan Philip Krum,
Philip Henry Sholtz,*
Johan Jacob Gonderman,
Hans Jacob Müller,
Johan Michel Nisch,?
Johan Christian Baum,
Johan Christian Benner,
Johan Christian Leidtorff,
Joh. Phil. Daniel Pfeiffer,
Georg Andreas Carle,*
Herm. Adolph Schoppenmeyer,
Johan Henrich Bucher,
Johann Egidus Hecker,
Johann Christian Schmidt,
Johann Henrich Schmidt,
Johan Henry Reinhart,*
Johannes Henrich Peiffer,
Joh. Peter Flick,
Joh. Philip Flick,
Johan Martin Flick,
Joh. Christian Zimmerman,
Gerlach Paul Flick.

169) Sept. 24, 1751. Ship Neptune, John Mason, Captain, from Rotterdam, last from Cowes.—284 passengers.

Sept. 24, 1751. Schiff Neptun, Capitain John Mason, von Rotterdam über Cowes.—284 Reisende.

Christian Armbrüster,
John Pieters,
Conrad Newmeyer,*
Henderich Boous,*
Jacob Sheyco,*
Philip Klinger,
Abraham Pons,
Johannes Höring,
Johannes Hering,*
Johannes Saum,
Johannes Redig,
J. Adam Ewig,*
Melchior Trautmann,*
Bernhart Jagel,*
Adam Pfeiffer,*
Christoph Cotz,*
Georg Kleinbach,*
Michael Link,*
George Crope,*
Johannes Henrich,
Frantz Horn,
David Maisheller,*
Johannes Gessner,
Elias Emminger,*
Conradt Schmidt,
Jacob Frith,
Jacob Gruber,*
Conrad Rawher,*
Balthaser Hess,*
George Kimmel,
Johannes Hock,*
Johannes Geiss,
Daniel Erhart,*
Peter Binger,
Andreas Miller,
Johannes Laurentius Schmidt,
Med. et Chirg Doctor.

Jean Pierre Arnoul,
Leonhart Mentzinger,
Hans Georg Anstein,
Johann Ludwig Höring,
Henrich Lautenschleger,*
Johann Bernhart Göth,
Johann Adam Trinckhauss,
Johann Adam Wirdeberger,
Johann Georg Erhardt,
Johann Philip Meyer,
Joh. Michael Knotz,*
Jacob Walter Wagner,*
Conrad Scheffnit,
Johan Wilhelm Grell,
Johan Georg Schäfer,
Johann Peter Schindel,
Johann Adam Geiss,
Martin Heckendorn,*
Andreas Drüchsel,
Johann Georg Eisenbeiss,
Wilhelm Göttman,
Hans Georg Heisy,
Hans Georg Spohn,
Johann Adam Heiss,
Johan Georg Heiss,
Tobias Daumiller,
Johann Peter Trautmann,
Christoph Hollobach,
Joh. Adam Issener,*
Andreas Reybold,
Friederick Zimmerman,
Jacob Zettelmeyer,*
Georg Zettelmeyer,*
Caspar Spann,
Jacob Bogus,
Henry Deutch,*
Clementz Frey,

Jacob Summer,*
Ludwig Knoll,
Nicklaus Schey,
Adam Weys,*
Caspar Kessler,*
Johannes Welt,
Jacob Nagel,
Christoph Schropp,
Johannes Vetter,
Stephan Herth,
Henrich Hall,
Casper Hoffmann,
Casper Hoffman jr.,
Jacob Buch,
Jacob Buch jr.,
Johannes Lemer,*
Georg Schill,
Andreas Berlib,*
Conrad Bower,*
Jacob Frey,*
Baltes Laub,
Jean Coulties,
Georg Creesh,*
Conrad Schäffer,
Siegmund Cosia,
Benedict Ervig,*
Henry Shröder,*
Michael Sattler,
Frederick Sullinger,*
David Kullem,
Jacob Peterman,*
Peter Klases,
Georg Eppenzeller,
Georg Adam Weys,*
Johannes Schniringer,

Lorentz Schniringer,
Johann Georg Vollert,
Heinrich Eyssenmenger,
Johann Michel Hag,
Johann Georg Heist,
Johan Ludwig Bilger,
Johann Jacob Gottwalt,
Antonius Lambrecht,
Johan Jacob Artzt,
Joh. Daniel Scharmann,
Johan Jacob Schneider,
Christian Hoffman,*
Conrad Selhoff,
Christoph Vanterberg,*
Johan Conrad Essy,*
Martin Schaickel,
Joseph Lehmann,
Ewald Trummaner,*
Jacob Höllerman,
Albrecht Schleppy,*
Johan Georg Must,
Joseph Zugmayer,
Phillip Mallycoat,*
Johan Bernhard Schäffer,
Johan Leon. Trautman,
Joh. Wilhelm Müller,
Johan Peter Klump,
Joh. Michael Dür,
Joh. Georg Hummer,
Uhllerich Schwenckel,*
Ludwig Klemmer,
Martin Kagel,
Michael Hahn,
Hans Georg Stehle.

170) Sept., Wednesday, the 25th, 1751. Ship Phœnix, John Spurrier, Captain, from Rotterdam, last from Portsmouth, England.—412 passengers.

Mittwoch, den 25. Sept. 1751. Schiff Phönir, Capitain John Spurrier, von Rotterdam über Portsmouth, England.—412 Paſſagiere.

Martin Maurer,
Jacob Bauer,
Christian Laufaner,
Michael Meyer,
Georg Volpp,
Antoni Stehrn,*
Georg Stirn,
Conrad Höffler,*
Jacob Jordan,
Andreas Roth,
Jacob Heegy,
Albert Schneck,
Michel Hoffman,
Christian Pfeiffer,
Martin Wagner,
Martin Engelberth,
Balthas Widenmeyer,
Martin Ziegler,
Peter Denler,
Martin Ludi,
Martin Herter,
Jacob Rosli,*
Hans Rosli,*
Georg Rosli,*
Jacob Riger,*
Georg Bänssle,
Simon Widmayer,
David Herrmann,
Carle Hey,*
Albrecht Heu,
Mathias Laufer,
Jacob Pfeiffer,*
Georg Hollinger,
Jacob Wörner,
Peter Hoffman,
Michael Hudere,*
Jacob Veigenbaser,
Conrad Host,

Bernhard Brand,
Baltzer Bümbel,
Matheis Bastian,
Anthoni Blesinger,*
Johannes Conrad Lauer,
Georg Matias Weig,
Johann Adam Bauer,
Hans Georg Weber,
John Georg Kappis,
Hans Michael Baunich,
Joh. Michael Lerchenzieler,
Hans Jacob Schletzer,
Philip Ernst Wagner,
Johan Melchior Mils,
Johan Friederich Fürber,
Joh. Valentin Hoffman,
Johann Conrad Frech,
Joh. Balthas Schölhorn,
Joh. Michel Schumacher,
Johann Georg Kiderer,
Michael Lautenschlager,
Johann Conrad Krügele,
Johan Tobias Hang,
Andreas Hildenbrandt,
Hans Jacob Stambach,
Hans Georg Betsch,
Ludwig Teussel,
Hans Georg Hägele,
Johan Gottfried Schmelzer,
Hans Jacob Geis,
Johann Gottfried Fuchs,
Hans Georg Schotebecker,
Georg Friederich Baisch,
Christian Küchler,
Johannes Gramm,
Michael Bossert,
Michael Kaucher,
Mattheis Hipscher,

Johann Georg Gehringer,
Albrecht Hübscher,
Baltus Schlichter,
Gottlieb Lunenmacher,
Johannes Dietrich,
Friederich Veit Schanss,
Friederich Dannwolff,
Joseph Böhringer,
Samuel Dirstein,
Elias Stocki,
Graff Hannold,
Christoph Lück,
Jacob Geigle,
Martin Off,
Jacob Hauber,
Matheus Kern,
Jacob Huber,
Jacob Hauher,
Jacob Alt,
Samuel Hitzer,*
Georg Hetzer,
Frederick Heins,
Jacob Seller,*
Jacob Waltz,
Georg Teuffell,
Philip Müller,
Mathias Diesch,
Jacob Harz,
Christian Neuffes,?
Thomas Fisher,*
Jacob Fischer,
Michael Laver,*
Dieterich Löffler,
Mattheus Walter,
Heinrich Fritz,
Baltes Beyer,
Abraham Hausser,
Georg Ziegler,
Jacob Walder,*
Michael Müller,
Friderich Wogt,*

Jacob Hermann,
Michel Ernst,
Michael Wörnner,
Matheis Schimpff,
Michael Mayer,
Simon Brener,
Friederich Hirsch,
Philip Poutmant,
Georg Carle,
Joh. Siegmund Kühler,
Christ. Friederich Weyler,
Franciscus Stür,
Mattheis Plocherr,
Jacob Bückel,
Johannes Albrecht,
Hans Jacob Kiechner,
Johannes Waltschmidt,
Johannes Hauer,
Christian Blaser,
Johannes Rathgeb,
Martin Eilting,
Bernhardt Schneider,
Hans Conrad Küchli,
Hans Georg Christein,
Christian Christein,
Peter Christein,
Johannes Demuth,
Friederich Kerchel,
Philipp Jacob Geis,
Johan Adam Stoltz,
Jean Diedier Moret,
Jacob von Können,
Lorentz Schmiedt,
Georg Michel Weimann,
Matheis Haufstein,
Jacob Hermann jr.,
Andreas Eissenhardt,
Johan Michel Wörnner,
Christian Schmidt,
Johannes Schmidt,
Jacob Bürkhardt,

Joh. Georg Fried. Bayer,
Gabriel Wachter,
Adam Hettinger,
Theophilus Hübbertz,
Samson Mittelberger,
Georg Baumann,
Michael Altrich,
Konrad Leuser,
Michael Leuttel,
Hans Georg Ehrman,

Jonas Rupp, *a*
Christoph Hofman,
Phillipp Müller,
Balthas Schwinkes,
Hans Jacob Meyer,
Johan Jacob Wörnner,
Hans Georg Blesser,*
John George Blazer,*
Hans Georg Bläser jr.

171) Oct. 4, 1751. Ship Queen of Denmark, Georg Parish, Commander, from Rotterdam, last from Cowes.—252 passengers.

Dct. 4, 1751. Schiff Queen of Denmark, Commandant Georg Parish, von Rotterdam über Cowes.—252 Reisende.

Christoph Berg,
Georg Wolff,
Hartmann Fritz,
Daniel Meyer,
Baltzer Martin,
Valentin Brock,*
Jacob Wolff,
George Bicker,
Balzar Konig,*
Johann Friederich Hering,
Georg Jacob Ullrich,
Michael Kremer,
Hans Georg Erbolt,

Melchior Zigler,*
Martin Shewerman,*
Hardlie Sallade,
Jacob Georjan,
Hans Georg Martin,
Jacob Kügel,*
Hans Suter,
Jacob Regennas,
Johannes Wagner,*
Peter Rehrer,
Heinrich Stohler,
Johannes Oxeman,*
Johannes Martin,

a Jonas Rupp, the Editor's paternal grandfather, was born Octbr. 23d, 1729, at *Reihen*, near Sinsheim, Grand Duchy of Baden. From 1751 to 1772 he lived in Lancaster Co., now Lebanon Co., in 1772 he moved to Cumberland Co., six miles west of Harrisburg. He died May 21st, 1801. His remains rest in the graveyard at *Friedens-Kirch*, three miles east of Mechanicsburg.

a Jonas Rupp, der Großvater des Herausgebers vaterseits, wurde am 23. Octbr. 1729 in Reihen, nahe Sinsheim, im Großherzogthum Baden, geboren. Vom Jahre 1751 bis 1772 wohnte er in Lancaster Co., jetzt Lebanon Co., 1772 zog er nach Cumberland Co., sechs Meilen westlich von Harrisburg. Er starb am 21. Mai 1801. Seine Gebeine ruhen auf dem Kirchhof der Friedenskirche, drei Meilen östlich von Mechanicsburg.

23

Jacob Geesseler,*
Andreas Fridli,
Stephan Bieg,
Andreas Roth,
Nicklas Rippel,
George Happes,*
Durst Grüner,
Jacob Joder,*
Hans Blanck,
Hans Reizer,*
Henry Süss,*
Michael Meyer,*
Christian Blanck,
Wilhelm Bosch,
Friederich Ruthy,
Johannes Shulty,*
Bastian Mengell,
Caspar Fisher,*
Conrad Fisher,*
Martin Fries,
Andreas Lantz,
Conrad Weiss,
Hans Geisser,*
Henrich Seitz,
Jacob Stehli,
Heinrich Stehli,
Jacob Shob,*
Nicklas Weiss,*
Heinrich Grell,
Georg Wolff,
Friederich Dirkerhoff,*
Johann Michel Hartmann,
Heinrich Bachman,
Johann Philip Bieg,

Johannes Carmane,*
Georg Grauss,
Conradt Schneider,
Johann Henrich Graff,
Christian Bernhart,
Hans Schneeberger,
Hans Jacob Weiss,
Marx Oberhäussle,
Hans Ulerich Hess,
Casper Schneider,
Johannes Schaad,
Hans Schallenberg,
Johannes Eymeyer,
Martin Dreysbach,
Johan Friederich Mertz,
Johan Henrich Hoffman,
Hans Henrich Wiest,
Hans Henry Shneyder,
Johannes Pampus,
Antonius Stütte,
Johan Wilhelm Friess,
Jacob Ruthlinger,
Heinrich Stehli,
Weinbert Tschucki,
Johannes Strub,
Joh. Friederich Steiner,
Friederich Lander,*
Johannes Possert,
Johann Friederich Mentzer,
Georg Schweyler,
Hans Melchior Anderegg,
Valentin Meyer,
Daniel Wolff,
Anthony Carmone.*

---

172) Oct. 7, 1751. Ship Janet, William Cunningham, Captain, from Rotterdam, last from Cowes.—220 passengers.

Oct. 7, 1751. Schiff Janet, Capitain William Cunningham, von Rotterdam über Cowes.— 220 Reisende.

Johannes Waller,*
Michael Hollstein,
Peter Ganns,*
Peter Rossburger,*
Philip Pfeiffer,*
Mathias Pfeiffer,*
Adam Jacobi,
Marx Breinig,
Adam Beckebach,*
Caspar Beckebach,*
Peter Ulmer,
Georg Welter,
Kilian Hausser,*
Nickolas Steyn,*
Henry Carle,*
Martin Bigler,*
Georg Bigler,*
Johannes Lap,*
Christ. Peifer,
Stephen Zweyer,*
Eberhart Kreiling,
Michael Alt,*
Adam Jordan,
Jacob Holtz,*
Carl Wagner,
Abraham Konig,*
Philip Enes,
Jacob Neiman,
Leonhart Bückel,
Johannes Hahn,
Wilhelm Ewig,*
Michael Leonhart,*
Matheas Nass,*
Henry Haushalter,*
Heinrich Friedle,
Melchior Krautter,
Jacob König,
Enoch Weber,
Jacob Sprecher,
Jacob Weimmer,*
Dewald Storch,*

Jacob Diether,
Ehrhardt Thürwächter,
Leonhart Simon,*
Georg Adam Beckenbach,
Johan Georg Beckenbach,
Georg Bernhart Beckenbach,
Johan Valentin Sommer,
Nickolas Eshwyn,*
Jacob Hauswirth,*
Jacob Kämmerer,
Heinrich Hetzel,
Johann Nickel Stumm,*
Johannes Kauffmann,
Johan Adam Best,
Johannes Schmidt,
Johan Peter Schang,
Andreas Altendorff,
Johan Lenardt Gösel,
Johann Jacob Lapp,
Joh. Christoph Weysbach,*
Han George Zweyer,*
Hans Adam Diem,*
Han George Odewalt,*
Joh. Andreas Engelman,
Georg Jacob Schirmer,
Michael Währlich,
Hans Conrad Bauman,
Johann Georg Geisler,
Johann Nicklas Wolff,*
Johan Valentin Ross,
Johan Jost Shweiger,*
Johann Jacob Weltz,
Johann Simon Schober,
Eberhart Gochnat,
Abraham Bitilion,
Johann Georg Busch,
Johann Michael Hoffmann,
Philip Jacob Hagenbuch,
Matheus König,
Hans Jacob Hübbert,
Christoph Ketteman,

Hans Georg Sprecher,
Philip Jacob Künbe,
Jacob Hahn,
Friederich Humbert
Diewald Matter,
Jacob Gallman,*
George Shend,*

Jacob Shaffer,*
Hans Georg Wallhuter,*
Johann Georg Steiner,?
Philip Jacob Humbert,
Johann Michael Drion,
Philip Jacob Meder,
Andreas Kisselberg.*

---

173) Oct. 16, 1751. Ship Duke of Wirtemberg, Montpelier, Captain, from Rotterdam, last from Cowes.—406 passengers.

Oct. 16, 1751. Schiff Duke of Wirtemberg, Capitain Montpelier, von Rotterdam über Cowes.—406 Reisende.

Ludwig Heinrich,
A. Mattheis,
Theodor Larber,
Johannes Wissner,
Andreas Schlenckfer,
Ulrich Bräitinger,
Conrad Ram,*
Jacob Umensetter,
Jacob Umensetter,?
Christoph Sündel,
Mattheus Reich,
Michael Weyhenger,
Johannes Schott,
Christian App,
Friederich Zoller,
Johannes Gräuttler,
Friederich Hering,
David Duett,*
Andreas Leaderer,*
Johannes Doll,*
Martin Dohl,
Johannes Notz,
Peter Strückel,
Martin Ecker,
Johannes Meiger,
Eberhardt Martin,
Leonhart Behl,
Balthas Götz,

Jacob Schäffer,
Bernhart Frick,*
Graff Pillab,*
Jacob Greiner,
Georg Christoph Reichle,
Johann Andreas Mayer,
Johann Georg Mayer,
Johan Andreas Mayer jr.,
Johann Adam Meckle,
Johann Georg Weisser,
Johann Georg Maisch,
Christian Gertzinger,
Jacob Ludwig Cäppele,
Johan Conrad Held,
Johannes Brodbeck,
Johannes Weyhenger,
Georg Wilhelm Bantlion,
Christ. Friederich Bantlion,
Hans Georg Schäffer,
Hans Georg Dute,*
Conrad Eisenhardt,
Georg Adam Schlegel,
Christophel Schlegel,*
Sebastian Wunder,
Johannes Wunderlich,
Johann Georg Hoch,
Mattheus Sabererick,
Joseph Brendlinger,

Georg Adam Franckenberger,
Georg Michael Kern,
Conrad Klingemeyer,
Joh. Conrad Leibbrand,
Georg Adam Gaab,
Hans Jacob Baum,
Daniel Baumann,
Conradt Grietzinger jr.
Conrad Merckle,
Friederick Keppert,
Jacob Zerch,
Johannes Winter,
Martin Ebbly,*
David Ansel,
Jacob Beyerly,*
Friederich Wibel,
Jacob Stahlman,
Joseph Ahner,
Adam Herman,
Jacob Jüngling,
Jacob Scherrer,*
Johann Nadem,?
Ulrich Hirschmann,
Matheus Hirschman,*
Johannes Stucky,*
Jacob Schwartz,
Johannes Augenstein,
Simon Nagel,
Philip Nagel,
Michael Deiss,
Johannes Mayer,
Johannes Mayer jr.,
Johannes Bischoff,
Bernhardt Merkle,
Michael Fritz,
Ludwig Fritz,
Casper Meyer,*
Peter Printly,*
Christian Fuchs,
Joseph Karg,
Jacob Karg,

Michael Rosch,
Michael Rosch jr.,
Jacob Esch,
Baltas Folck,*
Christoph Folck,*
Conrad Stöhr,
Philip Müller,
Stephan Katz,
Michel Waltz,
Martin Brodbeck,
Conrad Grietzinger,*
Johannes Brodbeck,
Dieterich Kämmerer,
Peter Kämmerer,
Christian Kämmerer,
Johann F. Brodbeck,*
Johan Georg Sendel,
Hans Georg Winter,
Hans Georg Heim,
Hans Georg Wehr,
Christ. Gottlieb Scheiberle,
Hans Peter Path,?
Joh. Friederich Dorff,
Joh. Michael Zehntbauer,
Johannes Schultheiss,
Andreas Hirschman,
Johan Adam Hirschman,
Hans Michael Moser,
Mattheus Dullnick,
Johann Georg Häman,
Johan Friederich Stiess,
Hans Georg Augenstein,
Philip Jacob Werner,
Hans Ludwig Roth,
Hans Philip Roth,
Hans Martin Bischon,?
Lorentz Wessener,
Hans Adam Meyer,
Hans Martin Fisser,
Michael Hirnneise,
Hans Georg Hirnneise,

23*

270 NAMES OF GERMAN, SWISS

Michael Hehnle,?
Johann Georg Dürr,
Jacob Widdenmann,
Michael Katz,
Hans Georg Schneider,
Johan Bardel Gottwalt,
Hans Bernhart Frantz,
Johann Jacob Waltz,
Andreas Weidhorn,*
Hans Georg Eckert,*
Michael Werner,
Wilhelm Koch,*

Benedict Funck,
Abraham Eckert,
Andreas Huttich,
Conrad Gensly,
Friederich Heyl,
Johannes Eberhart,*
Johannes Eberhart jr.,
Hans Georg Schinck,
Michael Wolff,
Andreas Kappler,*
Hans Georg Ege.

NOTE.—In a communication from Rev. *S. S. Schmucker*, D. D., to the Editor, March 18th, 1856, it is stated, the Rev. *John Dietrich Matthias Heinzelman* and Rev. *Emanuel Schultz*, Lutheran Ministers, arrived in Pennsylvania in the year 1751.—(*Editor.*)

Anmerkung.—In einer Mittheilung vom 18. März 1856 von Paſtor Dr. S. S. Schmucker an den Herausgeber ſagt derſelbe, daß die lutheriſchen Geiſtlichen Joh. Dietrich Matthias Heinzelmann und Emanuel Schulz im Jahre 1751 in Pennſylvania angekommen ſind.—(Herausgeber.)

174) Sept. 15, 1752. † Ship Two Brothers, commanded by Thomas Arnot, from Rotterdam, last from Cowes.

† Rev. *Michael Schlatter*, having revisited Germany, returned to America—arrived at New York, July 28th, 1752, accompanied, says *Lewis Mayer*, D. D., in his History of the German Reformed Church, in America, by six young ministers of the Gospel—Revds. *Wilhelm Stoy, Johannes Waldschmidt, Theodore Franckenfeld*, —— *Rubel*, —— *Wissler*, and *Philip Wilhelm Otterbein*. The latter was for many years a minister of the German Reformed Church. He is regarded, generally, as the founder of that now numerous denomination, "THE UNITED BRETHREN IN CHRIST."

"Rev. *Otterbein* was, says Lewis Mayer, more attentive to internal piety than to external forms........ In his person, Mr. Otterbein was portly and dignified; in his manner, urbane and affectionate, and of child-like simplicity. He had been well educated; and to the close of his life read Latin authors with as much ease as those in his vernacular tongue. His piety was unfeigned and glowing; his preaching solemn and impressive."—*Rupp's Hist. of Berks Co.*, pp. 445, 446.

P. W. Otterbein was born in Dillinberg, Nassau, Germany, Nov. 6, 1726. He died in Baltimore, Md., Nov. 17, 1813. He had, it is said, a peculiar attachment to *Jacob Wagner's* family of *Eibelshausen*, who, it is thought, emigrated to America at the time Otterbein came.

Sept. 15, 1752. † Schiff Two Brothers, befehligt von Tho=
mas Arnot, von Rotterdam über Cowes.

Georg Eisenmenger,	Paulus Bohm,
Friederich Mäyer,	Johan Deiswers,*
Joh. Christo Friederich Kohler,	Conrad Hahns,*
Kilian Eisenmenger,	Casper Krämer,
Jacob Müller,	Johannes Wilhelmus,
Christoph Arnoldt,	Adam Beck,
Nölgen Kremmer,	Johannes Jacob,
Peter Schock,*	Anthon Sheyed,*
Peter Hommer,*	John Antoni Statt,*
Paulus Gross,*	Wendel Frey,
Philip Bornn,*	Thomas Gramlich,
Wilhelm Huner,*	Jacob Lips,?
Jacob Müller,	Gottfried Kappes,
Conrad Winegarden,*	Casper Lichtenberger,
Bertram Behm,*	Michael Dietrich,
Paulus Huders,*	Joseph König,*
Moritz Hene,	Johannes Metzem,*
Jacob Anders,*	Borkhardt Unangst,
Johannes Gerhardt,	Jonas Pool,* (Puhl),
Peter Dilss,	Jacob Helbach,
Jost Ferschbach,	Joachim Sodt,?

† Nachdem Pastor Michael Schlatter Deutschland einen Besuch abge=
stattet, kehrte er am 28. Juli 1752 wieder nach New York zurück. Mit ihm
kamen, nach Dr. Mayer's Geschichte der reformirten Kirche in Amerika,
sechs junge Prediger, nämlich Wilhelm Stoy, Johannes Waldschmidt,
Theodor Franckenfeld, —— Rubel, —— Wißler und Philipp Wilhelm
Otterbein. Letzterer war viele Jahre lang ein Geistlicher in der deutsch=
reformirten Kirche. Er wird gewöhnlich für den Gründer der jetzt zahlrei=
chen Benennung der „Vereinigten Brüder in Christo" angesehen.

„Pastor Otterbein, sagt Louis Mayer, legte mehr Gewicht auf innere
Frömmigkeit, als auf äußere Form..... In seinem Aeußeren war er stattlich
und würdig, im Umgang höflich und liebreich, und von kindlicher Einfalt.
Er war gut geschult, und las gegen Ende seines Lebens lateinische Schrift=
steller mit derselben Fertigkeit, wie die in seiner Muttersprache. Seine
Frömmigkeit war ungeheuchelt und ernsthaft; seine Predigt würdevoll und
gewaltig."—Rupp's Gesch. von Berks Co., S. 445, 446.

P. W. Otterbein wurde in Dillinberg im Nassauischen geboren und zwar
am 6. Novbr. 1726. Er starb in Baltimore, Md., am 17. Novbr. 1813.
Man sagt, daß er eine besondere Vorliebe für Jakob Wagner's Familie zu
Eibelshausen hatte, welche, wie man glaubt, zur Zeit, als Otterbein kam,
nach Amerika auswanderte.

Johannes Lutz,
Conrad Welder,
Joh. Silas Bonn,*
Joh. Peter Bon,
Johann Martin Gans,
Johann Peter Lentz,*
Johan Peter Schock,*
Leopoldt Valentin Gross,
Johannes Henrich Metz,
Johann Friederich Beck,
Georg Michael Eberly,
F. Conrad Leberling,*
George Michael Miller,*
John Peter Rodebagh,*
John Peter Blom,*
Diedrich Wilhelm Dischong,
Johan Wilhelm Ahlbach,
John Peter Blom sen.,
John Christian Ottinger,*
Herbert Schumacher,
Johann Christian Hoffman,
Wilhelm Peterwelles,
Johan Wilhelm Meyer,
Conrath Schneider,
Joh. Herbert Lör,*
Joh. Antonius Krämer,
Johan Adam Imboten,*
Johan Gottfried Kring,
Johann Christian Seyler,
Johann Jacob Beyer,

Johan Christ. Eulenber,
Joh. Christ. Lichtenthäller,
Johann Christ. Meyer,
Johan Paulus Seehl,
Johan Steffy Drybler,*
Johan Peter Hauer,?
Johan Christian Albirger,
John Jacob Œlgarden,*
Johann Henrich Wirth,
Hans Henrich Münch,
Johann Wilhelm Böttger,
Johann Georg Metzger,
Georg Andreas Raab,
Georg Michael Gebhart,
Johan Gerlach Meyer,
Johan Georg Spiess,
Conrad Leinenberg,*
Nicolas Leinenberg,*
Jacob Dilss,
Moritz Wilh. Dills,
Joh. Peter Aller,
Joh. Wilh. Weller,
Johan Sebastian Onangst,
Johan Peter Schmidt,
Simon Ludwig Himroth,
Johan Herbert Wingert,
Wil. Henrich Brandenbürger,
Johan Thomas Schumacher,
Johan Peter Putterbach.

175) Sept. 19, 1752. Ship Edinburgh, James Russel, Captain, from Amsterdam, last from Cowes.

Sept. 19, 1752. Schiff Edinburgh, Capitain James Ruffel, von Amsterdam über Cowes.

Peter Renau,
Johan Valentin,
Henry Hollinger,*
Paulus Harting,
Frantz Renau,

Franciscus Dilier,
Michel Kümell,
Leonhart Claus,
Siegfried Billlng,
Martin Harsch,

Jacob Heerd,*
Jacob Beck,
Paulus Schmidt,
Nicolaus Mayer,
Jacob Fried,
Paulus Mauerer,*
Wilhelm Keller,*
Christoph Hummel,*
Paulus Walter,*
Peter Müh,
Jacob Küber,*
Johannes Roth,
Friederich Roth,
Johannes Bauer,*
Georg Shneyder,*
Georg Zerman,
Michael Fetzer,*
Christian Shneid,*
Christian Wenger,
Leonhard Lauter,
Sebastian Waas,
Johann Georg Denler,
Jacob Bildman,
Joh. Samuel Huth,
Georg Casper Bohrmann,
Johann Martin Schnepf,
Georg Leonhardt Pfüster,
Johannes Bernhardt,*
Michael Hibscher,*
Johan Georg Bauman,
Johannes Krieharst,?
Andreas Gabriel Dietrich,
Johan Wilhelm Trautwein,
Bartholomäus Lederer,
Georg Antony Schebble,
Johan Carl Häyer,
Johan Jacob Helm,
Johan Friederich Kiess,
Hans Martin Kirschman,
Martin Kuntzman,*
Hans Michael Weismeyer,*
Christoph Hardtmann,

Adam Christoph Behning,
Johannes Schwartz,*
Hans Jacob Roth,
Johann Christoph Bentz,
Stephan Nerlinger,*
Johan Christian Benish,*
Sebastian Dreher,
Jacob Friederich Blaser,
Jos. Bernhard Speth,?
Johan Jacob Häydt,
Johannes Zürn,
Georg Schild,*
Jacob Hauser,
Jacob Rincker,
Isaac Buck,*
Jacob Meysel,*
Johannes Gemser,
Carl Horn,
Friederich Rosslein,*
Leonhardt Rosslein,*
Adam Stock,
Andreas Fetzer,*
Friederich Fens,
Michael Dür,
Joseph Shennal,*
Frantz Fischer,
Johannes Hendel,
Johan Adam Schwartz,
Joh. Friederich Huss,*
Johann Jacob Kerffer,
Johannes Hüthler,
Heinrich Ottinger,
Jacob Wietdemann,
John Adam Rey,*
Michael Friederich,
Johann Rischerd,
Valentin Brüttschiett,
Johannes Schweller,
Hans Jacob Seltzer,
Joseph Shünal,*
Christoph Bauer.*

Sick on Board (krank an Bord):—Johannes Kerlin, Erhart
Kuhrbocker, Baltzer Fahringer, Jacob Müller, Johannes Jung,
Caspar Deilinger, Jacob Weller, Michael Karch, Jacob Roth,
Georg Braun, Michael Schäffer, Conrad Guth.

176) Sept. 22, 1752. Ship Brothers, William M'Nair, Captain, from Rotterdam, last from Cowes.

Sept. 22, 1752. Schiff Brothers, Capitain William M'Nair,
von Rotterdam über Cowes.

Johannes Stauch,	Georg Jacob Ehresmann,
Carl Fuchs,	Georg Henrich Gramlich,*
Martin Karch,	John George Edelman,*
Andreas Leisser,	Lenhart Hertell,
Peter Hellman,	Antonius Müller,
Jacob Seltzer,	Jacob Lorentz,
Johannes Unruh,	Hans Schüberli,
Daniel Utz,	Matheis Geyler,
Stephan Goss,	Andreas Geyler,*
Johannes Eckert,	Hans Gergerich,
Peter Bechtel,*	Michael Lupp,
Peter Seig,	Jacob Ybach sen.,
Johannes Bab,*	Jacob Ybach,
Jacob Miller,*	Diebolt Dietrich,
Bastian Hellman,	Hans Moltz,
Andreas Ott,*	Peter Bensel,
Georg Lentz,*	Mattheis Haas,
Samuel Herrmann,	Jacob Braun,
Johan Michael Lindemuth,	Johannes Sommer,
Johann Peter Schwartz,	Peter Hickman,
Johannes Edelman,	Philip Seydelman,
Hans Adam Heckman,	Conrad Heylman,*
Wilhelm Heckman,	Killian Pührer,
Joh. Conrad Kriechbaum,	Joseph Scheffer,?
Joh. Jacob Rudisielie,	Johann Georg Schmeltz,*
Johann Jacob Winter,*	Johann Georg Ester,
H. Nicolaus Berringer,*	Han Georg Edeler,*
Johan Jacob Wilhelm,	Johann Erhard Lobstein,
Johan Peter Gabel,*	Hans Georg Dammer,*
Hans Adam Gerig,*	Hans Georg Mauss,
Hans Peter Edelman,*	Philip Jacob Gottschalck,

Anthony Zimmermann,
Hans Ulrich Beutler,
Abraham Billing,
Heinrich Rahausser,
Hans Georg Sommer,
Hans Georg Holtzschuh,*
Johannes Cölus,*

Hans Adam Leh,
Hans Georg Marquard,*
Andreas Rotenbürger,
Hans Jacob Merckel,
Hans Jacob Hage,
Hans Adam Schnäbele,
Hans Jacob Burghen.*

Sick—Jacob Lasch, Johann Nicklas Schneider.

177) Sept. 22, 1752. Ship Halifax, Thomas Coatam, Captain, from Rotterdam, last from Cowes.

Sept. 22, 1752. Schiff Halifax, Capitain Thomas Coatam, von Rotterdam über Cowes.

Christophel Witmer,
Philip Engel,
Nicolas Kohler,*
Friederich Eberhart,*
Martin Decker,
Johannes Griese,
Hans Feltz,
Anthony Zinck,*
Johannes Paulus,*
Christian Herman,*
Jacob Olenthin,
Philip Hoffman,*
Bartholomæ Evar,*
Jonas Imschmiedt,
Peter Reeb,
Johan Melchior Brombach,
Johan Conrad Blecher,
Johann Georg Kuntze,
Michael Springer,
Johann Georg Kreybach,?
Johannes Josephus Roth,
David Sasmanhaussen,
Hans Georg Doctor,*
Johan Jacob Bersey,
Johan Ludwig Bersey,
Johan Jacob Brucker,*
Hans Michael Geyer,*

Hans Michael Hammer,
Hans Philip Elter,
Han Jac. Serber Zimmerman,
Friederich Fleckstein,*
Henry Meyer,*
Peter Duweiler,
Heinrich Maag,
Lorentz Dürr,*
Philip Hirdt,
Jacob Müller,
Jacob Sürber,
Heinrich Zolli,
Henry Kuntz,*
Ulrich Kreyser,
Caspar Wincker,*
Henrich Mercki,
Friederich Hörsch,
Johannes Meyer,*
Johannes Jordan,*
Johann Rudolph,*
Friederich Kämmer,
Jacob Klein,
Jacob Schaaff,
Johannes Gehr,*
Matheas Roth,*
Otto Pegy,*
Martin Varninger,*

Michael Wentz,
Anthony Rush,*
Jacob Hanick,*
Friederich Schaaff,*
Matheis Kientz,
Jacob Dietrich,
Jacob Juncker,
Peter Wendling,
Andreas Stöber,*
Michael Conradt,
Jacob Hisner,?
Johannes Riegeler,
Augustus Urban,
Joseph Held,*
Joseph Rübel,*
Georg Rübel,*
Johannes Patt,
Martin Hutter,*
Leonhart Weidman,
Hans Jacob Müller,
Conrad Müller,
Johannes Sürber,
Hans Jacob Rümmen,
Hans Heinrich Weiss,?
Hans Conrad Wirth,*
Hans Casper Schladter,
Wilhelm Haussaman,
Hans Michael Eigel,
Georg Hans Dietrich,
Johann Philip Göress,
Johann Georg Weber,
Hans George Gleysler,*
Jacob Weissenberger,*
Johannes Müller,
Paulus Schäffer,*

Johan Ludwig Ache,
Hermannius Ache,
Joseph Weigandt,*
Lorentz Reinhart,*
Martin Brungart,
Joh. David Wildenmuth,
Georg Wilhelm Müller,
Johann Jacob Hess,
Georg Ludwig Marburger,
Johann Kraffthorn,*
Johannes Jacob Ache,
Johan Henrich Gütting,
Hieronimus Spies,
Johannes Michael,
Johannes Schreiber,
Joh. Daniel Steinseiffer,
Hans Henrich Kauffer,
Hermanus Limper,*
Joh. Michael Kantzer,*
Johan Jacob Brentz,
Johan Georg Büssung,
Johann Dieterich,
Joh. Jacob Müller,
Johan Wennertblecher,
Johan Michael Bäcker,
Ulerich Glökil,*
Johannes Meyer,
Conrad Ziegler,*
Joseph Altheer,
Jacob Gross,
Hans Nickel Quinrin,?
Johan Nicklaus Hoffman,*
Johan Nicklaus Farringer,*
Joseph Onzemiller.*

Sick—Jacob Roth, Henrich Frey, Christian Bruchhart, Johannes Bruchhart, Matheis Müller, Daniel Fischer, Hans Dewald Wandlin, Hans Georg Mauser, T. Nicklas Mauser, Ludwig Gross, Johannes Köttring, Peter Bring, Johannes Ludwig, Johannes Ewers, Hieronimus Schneider, Georg Adam Schütz, Hans Jacob, Michael Gross.

178) Sept. 23, 1752. Ship St. Andrew, James Abercrombie, Captain, from Rotterdam, last from Plymouth, England.

Sept. 23, 1752. Schiff St. Andrew, Capitain James Abercrombie, von Rotterdam über Plymouth, England.

Jacob Baltzer,
Henrich Horn,
Hans Dommi,
Andreas Bartruff,
Ulrich Scherch,*
Abraham Zety,*
Jacob Orth,
Philip Becker,*
Christian Bühler,
Valentin Becker,*
Andreas Lintz,*
Ulerich Zercher,*
Daniel Blim,
Ulrich Scherr,
Leonhart Bremer,*
Jacob Blanck,*
Nickolus Blanck,*
Mathias Ecks,?
Johannes Ruts,*
Nicolas Buch,*
Hans Blanck,*
Joseph Gropff,
Ulrich Hauser,*
Leonard Hedly,*
Ulrich Fischer,
Johan Friederich Zeller,
Hans Martin Zeller,
Johan Christoph Rissel,
Hans Martin Hang,*
Dewalt Billman,*
John Philip Krimb,?
Philip Killinger,*
Jacob Hiestandt,
Johannes Webrecht,
Johan Georg Knoch,
Ludwig Spannagel,
Gabriel Spannagel,

Hans Georg Naffzer,*
Wilhelm Reiter,
Johan Jacob Bauer,
Jacob Kauffman,*
Johan Henrich Kräss,*
Johan Valentin Kräss,
Daniel Reinhold,
Christian Schmücker,
Johan Jacob Boltz,
Dorstius Alleman,*
Joh. Michael Mauerer,
Joh. Bernhart Eytel,
Ulrich Lautenbach,
Joseph Gall,
Jacob Fried,
Philip Wissler,
Johannes Moll,
Peter Moll,
Dietrich Schmitzer,
Eberhart Luttman,
Michael App,
Christian Stäbler,
Christian Meyer,
Henrich Schenck,
Heinrich Gebhart,
Jacob Lutz,
Andreas Zorn,
Jacob Schäffer,
Christoph Carl,
Christian Lutz,
Simon Kricht,
Peter Adam,
Friederich Planck,
Jeremias Eberle,
David Aller,
Philip Schauer,
Friederich Müller.

24

Ulrich Stauffer,
Simon Brand,*
Frantz Kamman,*
Daniel Gerhart,*
Michael Eindesweiler,?
Johan Georg Gramlich,
John Georg Küffer,*
Frantz Jacob Häussler,
Bastian Bohrman,
Jacob Bernhart Friederich,
Johann Peter Lang,
Georg Adam Eberth,
Hans Georg Bader,
Johan Georg Kupper,
David Katterman,
Johannes Schmidt,
    Sick—Jacob Forney.

Hans Jacob Berner,
Martin Steinbrenner,
Jacob Steinbrenner,
Matheus Baritschwerd,
Joh. Leonhart Keuchert,
Hans Michel Hattenbach,
Johan Georg Hattenbach,
Hans Jacob Eberle,
Johan Michael Schlencker,
Johan Heinrich Riedel,
Christoph David Schauer,
Johan Georg Eberle,
Hans Georg Heiss,
Hans Georg Piesch,*
Johan Peter Bangman,
John Caspar Ginter.

---

179) Sept. 23, 1752. Ship Ann Galley, Charles Kenneway, Captain, from Rotterdam, last from Portsmouth, England.

Sept. 23, 1752. Schiff Ann Galley, Capitain Charles Kenneway, von Rotterdam über Portsmouth, England.

Bartholomæ Eibach,
Andreas Braun,
Philip Heyd,
Sebastian Eschbalt,?
Wilhelm Conrad,
Jacob Mattler,
Andreas Kissel,*
Michael Obrist,
Johan Friederich Pendtner,
Albrecht Hofmeister,
Johan Ludwig Büschler,
Johannes Jacob Rau,
Eberhart Christoph Schret,
Joh. Henrich Kuntz,*
Johan Georg Steiner,
Johan Georg Rihm,?
Henry Angculy,
Martin Schall,

Martin Wolff,
Ulrich Spohn,*
Balthaser Mante,
Joseph Mayer,
Rudolph Schaub,*
Simon Zeiner,*
Nicklas Leydecker,*
Peter Spengler,*
Henry Valentin,*
Peter Campo,
Jean Pigonie,*
Clementz Ober,
Georg Ludwig,
Michael Meck,*
Michael Muth,
Thomas Jeidler,
Christian Muor,
Peter Inäbmit,

Michael Schwar,
Jacob Butz,*
Martin Müller,
Johan Elias,
Phillip Bleck,
Christian Tomm,*
Jacob Müller,
Jost Martin Waltz,
Johan Valentin Seidel,
Johan Friederich Springer,
Johan Gabriel Springer,
Johan Casper Spohn,*
Martin Georg Wahl,
Friederich Reichenerder,
Hans Georg Hipp,
Daniel Nonnenmacher,
Ludwig Conrad Schneider,

Joh. Michael Miller,*
Hans Georg Schaal,
Joh. Georg Spengler,*
Benedict Spetzfendem,
Hans Georg Meck,*
Hans Martin Mäck,
Han Georg Schley,*
Johan Conrad Schenck,
Hans Georg Baltzer,*
Joh. Jacob Wintzberger,*
Joh. Georg Schwinederer,
Johan Friederich Braun,
Johan Georg Braun,
Georg Jacob Schneider,
Hans Georg Schwartz,
Wilhelm Conrad,
Rudolph Schoff. §

180) Sept. 26, 1752. Ship Richard and Mary, John Moore, Master, from Rotterdam, last from Portsmouth.

Sept. 26, 1752. Schiff Richard und Mary, Capitain John Moore, von Rotterdam über Portsmouth.

Peter Wönner,
Peter Emmert,
Casper Baltzer,*
Johannes Weyant,*
Johann Diehlbeck,
Michael Behm,*
Nicklas Bernhart,*
Peter Hollebach,*
Andreas Ham,*
Gabriel Armbriester,
Johannes Conrath,
Jacob Daniel Scherrer,
Henrich Jacob Knerr,
Johan Daniel Allsbach,
Johan Nicklas Karcher,*
Johan Georg Gensheimer,
Johan Georg Emmerich,
Johan Philip Taules,

Johan Henrich Kipp,
Johan Philippus Hoffman,
Johan Peter Roller,
Joh. Peter Pfankuchen,
Georg Reit,*
Henrich Scheidbach,
Nicklaus Winchel,
Martin Schmitt,
Michael Schleyer,
Michael Roth,*
Jacob Schuckman,
Johannes Becker,
Johannes Was,
Elias Schmidt,
Andreas Jäckle,
Friederich Saamm,*
Nicolas Samm,
Adam Samm,

Theobald Becker,
Peter Huth,*
Ludwig Schmidt,*
Conrad Miller,*
Peter Bär,*
Henrich Mosser,
Michael Graff, §
Jacob Klar,
Andreas Petri,
Adam Bernhart,
Dewalt Grub,
Daniel Cramer,
Michael Lauetz,
Baltzer Dickhans,*
Johannes Küstner,
Georg Seider,
Casper Lademan,
Antonius Walter,
Joh. Henrich Stanhenner,
Joh. Philip Werntz,
Joh. Benedictus Müller,
Johan Henrich Scher,
Joh. Theobald Bauer,
Philip Jacob Kehle,
Johan Jacob Siegfried,

Johan Henrich Hummel,
Johan Adam Derting,
Dewalt Dannfeltzer,
Johan Nickel Hembt,
Johan Georg Beck,
Martin Holtzhäusser,
Johan Thiel Herman,*
Henrich Müssemer,
Johannes König,
Jacob Steinbach,
Henrich Bierbauer,
Jost Schönwaldt,*
Simon Schumacher,
Johan Georg Haudt,
Johan Wilhelm Stuber,
Johan Friederich Stuber,
Johan Philip Stuber,
Hans Georg Eheller,
Johan Wilhelm Stricker,
Georg Peter Eckel,
Simon Herrmann,
Hans Jacob Gebhardt,
Peter Leonhard Henkenius,
Joh. Henrich Henkenius,
Michael Hoffman.*

---

181) Sept. 27, 1752. Ship Anderson, Hugh Campbell, Captain, from Rotterdam, last from Portsmouth.

Sept. 27, 1752. Schiff Anderson, Capitain Hugh Campbell, von Rotterdam über Portsmouth.

Leonhart Bender,
Christoph Mauerer,
Uerlich Volck,*
Georg Riegert,
Peter Willer,
Jacob Beiltel,
Johan Martin Schweitzer,
David Haussman,
Hans Georg Marquart,
Johannes Strätter,*

Johannes Weill,
Michael Heim,
Daniel Krütter,
Philip Euler,
Peter Pfeil,*
Philipp Kress,
Michael Schmidt,
Peter Dückherdt,
Friederich Steinle,
Georg Wetzel,

Christian Dürz,
Nicolaus Schunder,
David Weyfaller,
Christoph Usterle,
Michael Schelling,
Martin Betz,
Andreas Gäss,
Andreas Eppler,
Johannes Kurtz,
Pierre Lageau,
Johannes Altig,*
Adam Weisbarth,
Johannes Weber,
Andreas Weg,
Peter Ansell,*
Christoph Gisterer,
Moritz Bauer,
Thomas Knissel,
Johannes Deissher,
Wilhelm Garein,
Gottlob Herman.*
Michael Ritter,
Thomas Piel, §
Christian Peistly,*
Jacob Blessing,*
Jacob Kriser,
Jeremias Lud. Engelmann,
Johannes Schneder,
Mattheis Knügel,
Nicklaus Wenschler,

Leonhardt Gnärr,
Christian Rapman,
Johannes Waltz,
Wilhelm Fried. Schumann,
Carl Friederich Muckenfus,
Simon Zimmerman,
Jacob Friederich Fischer,
Johan Georg Breymeyer,
Wilhelm Christoph Kesebohrer,
Johan Friederich Fuchs,
Christoph Bothacker,
Andreas Scheibling,
Joh. Caspar Windesch,
Joachim Bräuchle,
Johannes Washer,
Johan David Harlacher,
Johan Georg Maul,
Johan Jacob Beltz,
Georg Michael Beltz,
Johan Jacob Fussbec,?
Hans Michael Kretel,
Georg Ernst Lindenberger,
Joh. Georg Reist,*
Joh. Georg Schilger,
Joh. Friederich König,
Matheus Kühbauch,
Joh. Friederich von Rahden,
M. Jacob Fried. Schertlein,
Balthas Triett,
Friederich Masser.

---

182) Sept. 27, 1752. Ship President, —— Dunlop, Captain, from Rotterdam, last from England.

Sept. 27, 1752. Schiff Präsident, Capitain Dunlop, von Rotterdam über England.

Johannes Enttiger,
Johannes Laufer,
Hans Bauer,
Johannes Lutz,
Johan Georg Schneider,

Joh. Martin Cranmiller,
Georg Christoph Kuss,
Johan Martin Huber,
Johannes Folmer,
Georg Albrecht,

24*

Michael Rüss,
Jacob Nast,
Gottfried Stauch,*
Michael Fischer,
Wilhelm Schneider,
Carl Killuge,
Wolfgang Hefner,
Conrad Huber,
Johan Brüning,
Michael Gantner,*
Jacob Ruppert,
Solomon Wessle,
Jacob Müller,
Christoph Strobel,
Adam Sorg,
Johann Faber,*
Peter Baltzly,*
Jacob Wildt,
George Wild,*
Andreas Weste,
Frederich Shwenk,*
Jacob Long,
Mattheis Baser,
Georg Duwerter,
Jacob Threx, §
Frantz Tulpenbaum,*
Henrich Hassler,*
Johannes Schmidt,
Bernhart Upp,
Johannes Dauchbes,?
Johan Georg Haas,

Hans Martin Shrang,
Johan Martin Pfeiffer,
Philip Jacob Nass,
Michael Pfadermiller,
Ulrich Michael Bauer,
Johan Georg Haitberger,
Ulrich Haitberger,*
Georg Friederich Scherthlen,
Johan Peter Erman,
Bernhart Höhneise,
Hans Georg Lessig,
Christoph Schmid,
Johan Georg Weidich,
Caspar Beintzighoster,
Johann Georg Wagner,
Johann Henrich Kostenbades,
Johann Christoph Peter,
Johannes Schnecke,
Melchior Beltzhuber,
Hans Georg Looser,
Johann Jacob Long,
Johannes Schwencke,
Adam Augermeyer,
Martin Schillinger,
Johan Bernhard Bauer,
Andreas Schwartz,
Hans Georg Baser,
Johannes Schärthle,
Georg Friederich Hengel,
Philip Samuel Pühl.

---

183) Sept. 27, 1752. Ship Nancy, John Ewing, Captain, from Rotterdam, last from Cowes.

Sept. 27, 1752. Schiff Nancy, Capitain John Ewing, von Rotterdam über Cowes.

Jacob Schweiler,
Jacob Schmidt,
Jonas Bastian,*
Georg Hauher,

Samuel Müsse,
Philip Mall,
Johan Friederich Danninger,
Jacob Mussgenug,

Carl Fr. Biebert,?
Philip Jacob Wunder,
David Xander,
Johann Michael Hauss,
Konradt Weiss,
Andreas Bastian,
Georg Wenig,*
Matheis Deibel,*
Friederich Baisch,
Jacob Baish,*
Christoph Breisser,
Johannes Butz,
Michael Eyroh,*
Joseph Stündel,
George Grass,*
Jacob Dietrich,
Joseph Bernhart,*
Joseph Bernhart jr.,*
Hans Kintz,*
Johannes Shwitzer,*
Jacob Zinchffer,?
Jaque Peirot,
Jaque Molan,
Michael Doser,
Balthas Baumm,
Christoph Embich,
Israel Eberlin,
Philip Fallen,
Valentin Hagner,
Ludwig Erich,
Martin Fromm,
Andreas Jäger,
Henrich Schlachter,*
Christoph Mast,§
Paul Waag,
Rudolph Klaar,*

Hans Stöts,
Jacob Kautz jr.,
Joh. Philip Bietrighoffer,
Adam Friederich Weiss,
Joh. Georg Friederich Bayer,
Jacob Bauerschmiedt,
Jacob Bauerschmied jr.,
Georg Friederich Jauss,
Christoph Rothbaust,
Johann Andreas Roth,*
Johann Friederich Uhlandt,
Jacob Armbrüster,*
Georg Michael Spatz,
Jacob Stützmann,
Johann Ludwig Seiler,
Christian Hamberg,
Johannes Herrmann,*
Hans Georg Kautz,
Hans Jacob Lersch,
Frantz Saltzman,
Peter Halteman,*
Johan Martin Doser,
Christian Mühlheim,
Jos. Jacob Ernst,
Hans Jacob Neustätt,
Hans Georg Heilikel,
Georg Balthas Ernst,
Casper Underweg,
Johann Marx Klopfer,
Joh. Martin Rüdelmayer,
Herman Matsh,*
Georg Friederich Schwartz,
Hans Georg Krebs, §
Hans Paul Henrich,
Johann Georg Braun,
Johannes Griess.

184) Oct. 4, 1752. Ship Neptune, John Mason, Captain, from Rotterdam, last from Cowes.

Oct. 4, 1752. Schiff Neptune, Capitain John Mason, von Rotterdam über Cowes.

Adam Hartman,
Valentin Letman,
Christophel Feichtner,
Nicolas Boron,*
Johann Ludwig Leib,
Hans Michel Gutknecht,
Hans Michael Dock,
Hans Georg Hartman,
Nickel Nählich,
Henry Henly,*
Georg Mewes,
Christian Schmidt,
Johannes Bernhart,
Stephan Nicklaus,*
Georg Werner,
Michael Hoak,*
Stoffel Hussung,
Daniel Stattler,*
Daniel Conrad,*
Anthony Roth,
Johannes Conrad,
Casper Fell,*
Paul Hoffmann,
Jacob Schwartz,
Adam Pence,*
Nicklaus Hoh,
Michael Busch,
Matheus Andræ,
Wendel Biesel,*
Jacob Haberstich,
Balthasar Schwartz,
Paulus Seip,
Theobald Schwartz,
Philip Seip,
George Meyer,*
Jacob Kuhn,*
Thomas Straub,
Johannes Hortig,
Johannes Kress,
Henry Kress, §
Caspar Kress,*

Carl Kress,*
Nickolas Schall,
Andreas Schall,
Conrad Rösch,
Jacob Zieget,
Simon Schmitt,*
George Unckel,
Johannes Feyly,*
Matheas Ebener,
Johann Jacob Wolff,
Hans Peter Hertzog,
Johan Valtin Walter,
Hubert Baumgärtner,
J. Christian Bohnenblust,
Hans Nicolaus Pesser,
Hans Georg Kurtz,
Joh. Jacob Becker,
Johan Henrich Nöl,
Hans Georg Kucher,
Georg Friederich König,
Philip Jacob Roth,
Christian Rohrbacher,
Christian Hoffmann,
Johann Georg Werner,
Philip Christian Weller,
Joh. Sigmund Hagelgans,
Johann Jacob Dietrich,
Johann Michel Harfer,
Johan Adam Wild,
Wilhelm Trautmann,
Christian Haberstich,
Hans Georg Schwartz,
Wilhelm Stauch,
Michael Hutzner,
Johan Adam Tietz,*
Dewalt Witterspohn,*
Johan Peter Asseim,
Nickolas Schall jr.,
Christopher Blumer,
Johan Georg Weber,
Johan Philip Griech,*

Johann Jacob Friess,
Hans Adam Weber,
Georg Lautenschläger,
Johan Michael Heinecke,
Johan Adam Heinecke,
Nicklaus Schweyer,
Johann Sebastian Gross,
Johann Andreas Gross,
Johan Henrich Niess,
Johan Wilhelm Schneider,
Joel Dormeier,
Andreas Dormyer,*
Jacob Dormyer,§
Peter Schneider,
Conrad Schneider,
Samuel Schultz,
Ludwig Küster,
Philip Wentzel,*
Johannes Geiss,*
Mattheis Haller,
Peter Molsbach,
Johannes Schäffer,
Henry Lipps,*
Johannes Nickellas,
Joseph Bernhart,
Christian Lauer,
Peter Uhrich,
Johannes Züplie,
Johannes Hirni,
Johannes Arris,
Johannes Glass,
Hans Kuntzi,
Georg Meyer,*
Ulrich Sterchi,
Christian Sterchi,
Michael Spatz,
Michael Hessler,*
Johannes Blöckinger.
Ulrich Feitz,*
Peter Shneyder,*
Peter Dunter,*

Johannes Hoffer sen.,
Johannes Hoffer jr.,
Nicolas Lotz,
Jacob Gross,
Johannes Kautz,
Johannes Conrad Streuber,
Gebhart Bertholt,
Georg Philip Küster,
Joh. Henry Lohmiller,
Johann Georg Rübsaamen,
Johann Georg Jung,
Johannes Hufnagel,
Joh. Michael Schmidt,
Johann Philip Haffner,
Christophel Keller,
Heinrich Schäffer,
Johan Philip Breuning,
Johan Adolph Gilman,
John George Nicholas,
Peter Zöngrig,*
Johann Jacob Baumann,
Johann Michael May,
Johann Casper Domm,
Johannes Schwatzer,
Johan Heinrich Heiss,
Joh. Adam Arris,
Johann Jacob Hipge,
Friederich Zurbüchen,
Johan Philip Müller,
Johann Peter Müller,
Valentin Lautenschläger,
Johan Georg Kriegenmeyer,
Johan Wilhelm Lotz,
Johannes Lohmöller,
Christoph Ensling,
Johann Peter Schmidt,
Johan Daniel Becker,
Christian Kautz,
Johannes Diehl,
Johan Caspar Kindt,
Johann Georg Nonyus.

185) Oct. 11, 1752. Ship Forest, Paterick Ouchterlony, Captain, from Rotterdam, last from Portsmouth.

Oct. 11, 1752. Schiff Forest, Capitain Paterick Ouchterlony, von Rotterdam über Portsmouth.

Michel Danner,
Johannes Schreiner,
Johann Jacob Wilbrandt,
Johan Georg Englerdt,
Jacob Reinardt,
Balthas Maute,
Peter Sauder,
Johannes Rubemiller,*
Peter Pfeill,
Jacob Heller,
Peter Girstohber,
Johannes Wolff,
I. Daniel Junger,
Conrad Feuch,
Johannes Hirschman,
Valentin Braun,
Johannes Clauss,
Johannes Schell,
Johannes Tillman,
Conrad Jung,
Christoph Gerhardt,
Jacob Notz,
Johannes Lademacher,
Johannes Helters,
Henry Kahlbach,
Johannes Amgontert,
Caspar Hubert,
Johannes Schoyrer,
Hans Erling,
Jacob Digel,
Michael Englest,
Johannes Hayner,
Mattheis Miller,
Johannes Mayer,
Johannes Huss,
Henrich Creutz,
Wilhelm Creutz,

Daniel Leicht,*
Joh. Jacob Swartz,*
Joh. Jacob Lerch,
Johann Engelschreter,
John Henry Shram,*
Jacob Tillinger,*
Emanuel Heintz,
Johan Jost Georg,
Christoph Stattel,
Hans Georg Bader,
Johan Ludwig Henner,
Johan Peter Schönfelter sen.,
Johan Peter Schönfelter jr.,
Johann Georg Hoffmann,
Johann Caspar Fitting,
Johann Adam Schissler,
Friederich Jacob Kuntz,
Johann Adam Wolff,
Johan Carl Wolff,
Johan Dietrich Schwartz,
Georg Martin Vött,
Hans Georg Suliger,
Christian Scheckenberger,
Johann Conrad Wack sen.,
Johan Conrad Wack,
J. Henry Herman,
Johan Junges Jung,
Johann Peter Clossmeyer,
Johann Conrad Hay,
Johann Henrich Wiesteir,
Johann Christ. Reis,
Johann Peter Jung,
Johann Georg Leuder,
Johann Jacob Vaymer,
Johann Simon Schreyer,
Adam Leonhart Schreyer,
Johan Peter Steinbach,

Johan Henrich Humerich,
Johann Georg Hänner,
Joh. Teis Reichel,
Johan Friederich Gass,
Johan Engel Röder,
Johann Philip Weller,
Georg Henrich Gross,
Hans Martin Wiser,
Johan Leonard Harriger,
Johann Georg Oltenwaldt,
Johan Michael Büntzel,
Johann Dietrich Riess,
Hans Adam Werner,

Johann Peter Sprecher,
Michael Bitzer,
Mattheis Bitzer,
Johannes Retter,*
Peter Grimm,
Michael Kegereiss,
Johannes Adam Adam,
Jean Christoph Marekel,
Johan Georg Benck,
Johann Peter Archbiss,
Johann Martin Walter,
Johann Henrich Beil,
Johannes Jacob Dowart.

Sick—Matheis Bader, Nicolaus Ruth, Conrad Luntz, Johannes Teis, Henrich Gross, Christian Freilich.

186) Oct. 16, 1752. Snow Ketly, Theophilus Barnes, Commander, from Rotterdam, last from Portsmouth.

Oct. 16, 1752. Seeschiff Ketly, Commandant Theophilus Barnes, von Rotterdam über Portsmouth.

Friederich Jarquart,
David Welsch,
Wilhelm Lenhardt,
Christian Closs,
Philip Bideljung,*
Daniel Klein,*
Joseph Mey,
Johannes Gachon,
Leonhart Seuffert,
Georg Schneyder,
Johannes Hen,
Andreas Heck,
Henrich Miller,
Christian Wentz,
Johan Bluth, §
Philip Scheffer,
Philip Albrecht,
Caspar Bauer,
Andreas Mack,
Christian Sand,

Georg Brauss,
Christoph Süss,
Joseph Weber,
Henrich Weidner,
Jacob Hän,*
Georg Wolff,
Jacob Welde,
Martin Grün,
Michael Baker,*
Johan Dieter Marckbach,
Johann Daniel Mütschler,
Johan Conrad Œsterich,
Johan Conrad Ruth,
Johan Christian Burg,
Johan Christophel Volck,
Johann Peter Niedenthal,
Johann Jacob Nunymeyer,
Johann Philip Schneider,
Johan Wilhelm Strempel,
Jonas Rinderdust, ?

Johan Joachim Tölcker,
Johan George Frey,
Johann Georg Hertranft,
Johan Michael Leid,
Johan Jacob Decker,
Johann Peter Höll,
Johann Jacob Müller,
Johann Henrich Heyl,
Philip Jacob Mack,
Johann Tobias Ebele,
Joh. Daniel Weisenberger,
Georg Philip Lied,
Conrath Thomas Lied,
Philip Carl Schenckel,
Georg Michael Egert,*
George Michael Hain,*
Johan Jacob Heintz,

Nickolas Salladin,*
Friederich Müller,
Henry Hess,
Georg Gass,
Jacob Heyl,
Henry Süs,
Georg Welde,
Nicklaus König,
Peter König,
Abraham Sontag,
Johannes Kallenberger,
Hans Georg Brenner,
Jacob Shuster,
Philipp Schenckel,
Heinrich Schenckel,
Balthaser König.

187) Oct. 20, 1752. Ship Duke of Wirtemberg, Daniel
Montpelier, Commander, from Rotterdam, last from Cowes.

Oct. 20, 1752. Schiff Duke of Wirtemberg, Commandant
Daniel Montpelier, von Rotterdam über Cowes.

Jacob Guth,
Michael Stöhr,
Georg Ziegler,
Jacob Bosch,
Michael Meng,
Christian Zürn,
Johannes Kleiss,
Mathäus Kibler,
Tobias Baab,
Johannes Blickly,*
Tobias Mick,*
Christian Lutz,
Mattheis Bruder,
Johannes Wehing,
Balthasar Lotz,
Jacob Schaibler,
Friederich Stöhr,
Friederich Kilgus,

Matheis Zeiger,*
Hans Hemiger,
Heinrich Schwab,
Christian Drion,
Friederich Dehm,
Matheus Stahl,
Michael Fohme,?
Johannes Lemle,
Michel Lömle,
Jacob Wessener,
Matheus Lang,
Johann Michael Guth,
Johan Georg Guth,
Samuel Banher,
Johan Martin Bat,
Conrad Feuerbohnen,
Jacob Bernhart Schwab,
Johann Friederich Gross,

Immanuel Fred. Weckerlin,
Johannes Schwartzwölder,
Anthony Katterer,*
Johannes Deschler,
Johann Ludwig Uber,
Johann Michael Fissler,
Johann Georg Fissler,
Hans Georg Kellner,
Hans Jacob Kellner,
Sebastian Wegner,
Johann Fritlauf,?
Johann Conrad Hesser,
Jacob Simon Vogler,
Johannes Schwartz,
Jacob Michel Hel,
Hans Georg Heitzman,
Johannes Seitz,
Michael Hauer,
Johannes Fachmeyer,
Michael Goodner,*
Johann Jacob Lauman,
Johann Georg Ott,
Johannes Miller,
Michael Bach,
Jacob Bauman,
Christian Braun,
Andreas Gering,
Matheis Bruchli,*
Joel Waltz,
Georg Haber,
Friederich Mag,
Michael Hart,
Peter Haller,*
Jacob Hewass,
Jacob Schuler,*
Jacob Weyn,*
Martin Haug,
Asaph Lantz,
Jacob Heitter,
Johannes Braun,
Johannes Braun jr.,

Jacob Mass,
Martin Lang,
Jacob Stehly,
Jacob Lanck,*
Jacob Morhardt,
Jacob Gündner,
Jacob Walter,
Mattheis Wessener,
Jacob Beyerly,
Jacob Braun,
Jacob Braun sen.,
Mark Mattheis,
Christian Haas,
Jacob Bub,*
Christian Stahl,
Mattheis Van,
Hans Geo. Zinkblei,
Elias Finslaimer,?
Johannes Zinsser,
Michael Leichs,*
Johannes Leichs,*
Hans Michael Schatz,
Johannes Raible,
Hans Martin Raible,
Christian Getz,
Christian Ziegler,
Johannes Kugler,
Johannes Lochmeier,
Albrecht Walter,
Johannes Shutz,
Christian Karch,
Joseph Bontaux,
Friederich Schmeltzle,
Ulrich Scheermesser,
Christian Singer,
Mattheis Kirsch,
Friederich Gasser,
Johannes Leix,
Hans Martin Lang,
Hans Georg Fritz,
Andreas Wasserman,

Friederich Schmidt,
Augustin Stahl,
Johannes Vigeld,
Christian Hebling,
Georg Haffner,*
Johannes Hetzel,

Anthoni Burell,
Johannes Fleit,*
Johann Jacob Masser,
Hans Georg Haak,
Hans Georg Göttle,
Christoph Fried. Biller.

Sick—Johan Jacob Keyser, Michael Frick, Hans Jacob Van.

188) Oct. 23, 1752. Ship Bawley, George Grove, Captain, from Rotterdam, last from Plymouth.

Oct. 23, 1752. Schiff Bawley, Capitain George Grove, von Rotterdam über Plymouth.

Adam Ship,*
Adam Tesch,*
Heinrich Klein,
Jacob Wann,
Christoph Reyter,
Christian Metzger,
Johannes Heil,
Georg Heil,
Peter Schwab,*
Johannes Bauss,*
Hans Bauss,
Johannes Koch,*
Jacob Hottenstein,
Johannes Schmit,*
Moritz Schadig,*
Jacob Frey,*
Daniel Hätzel,
Gottfried Schutz,
Andreas Haag,
Michael Rüttger,
Andreas Jauch,
Martin Jäger,*
Henry Bauth,*
Peter Simmon,
Andreas Vey,*
Michael Kitz,
Kilian Bauer,
Baltzer Simon,*

Andreas Berge,
Conrad Ahster,
Valentin Stall,
Henrich Simon,
Georg Hartman,
Andreas Höhl,
Christian Hügel,
Nicolaus Böhm,
Johannes Roth,
Justus Derbert,
Stephanus Lotz,
Johannes Lotz,
Ulrich Miller,*
Georg Braun,
John Georg Bager,?
Henrich Peter Tesch,
Philip Henrich Gross,
Joh. Friederich Gackly,
Joh. Michael Breiner,
Melchior Katteman,*
Leonhart Bauman,*
Hans Georg Schmitt,*
Georg Wilhelm Dönges,
Conradt Dönges,
Johan Friederich Wübel,
Joh. Nicklaus Graushar,
Johannes Graushar,
Bernhart Mauer,

Joh. Wilhelm Engesbach,
Johan Adam Zey,*
John George Wendel,
Johann Georg Gross,
Nicholas Miller,*
Johan Henrich Cress,
Johannes Müller,
Nickolas Gräffenstein,
Hans Peter Lein,
Johann Simmon,
Johannes Thurm,*
Daniel Machleit,
Joh. Philip Titshler,*
Johannes Glassler,*
Wilhelm Gottlieb Jaysser,
Johan Georg Strobig,*
Johannes Lincker,*
Joh. Georg Eberly,
Leonhart Spang,
F. Peter Bauer,
Johan Nicklas Ott,
Andreas Frischkorn,
Joh. Nicklas Staus,*
Jacob Gumeringer,*
Hans Georg Steedinger,
Joh. Philip Fretz,
Lorentz Haushalter,
Joseph Burgstahler,
Johannes Seitz,
Michael Lang,
Matheis Miller,*
Jacob Neiell,?
Matheis Kron,
Conradt Endres,
Friederich Kern,§
Elias Most,
Philip Fisher,*
Daniel Schmidt,
Leonard Gohl,

Elias Gohl,
Johannes Stocker,
David Jung,
Christian Kress,
Michael Wilhelm,
Andreas Brauss,
Carl Bentz,
Johannes Stehr,
Philip Caryess,*
Gottfried Weyland,
Johannes Hebeisen,
Christian Herrmann,
Johannes Möller,
Johannes Bohn,
Christoph Hancker,
Hans Georg Mock,
Hans Georg Wächter,
Johan Gottlieb Fröhlich,
Georg Henrich Bentz,
Johan Jacob Schuppert,
Johann Georg Wunderlich,
Hans Georg Gardner,*
Georg Friederich Klein,
David Hottenstein,
Georg Eberhart Döring,
Lenhard Schweitzer,
Jacob Schweitzer,
Joh. Nickolas Bender,
Johannes Ommerth,
Jacob Sultzberger,
Georg Adam Kern,
Johan Henrich Gattung,
J. Henry Staubach,*
Theobaldus Eberhardt,
Johan Tobias Kenner,
Joh. Conrad Trünckler,
Georg Christoph Steinertz,
Jost Henrich Möller.

189) Nov. 2, 1752. Ship Phœnix, John Spurrier, Commander, from Rotterdam, last from Portsmouth.

Nov. 2, 1752. Schiff Phönix, Commandant John Spurrier, von Rotterdam über Portsmouth.

Bastian Kender,*
Lorentz Michel,
Georg Hore,
Johannes Riess,
Peter Ahlemann,
Heinrich Becker,
Conrad Ross,
Joachim Ströver,
Thomas Geissler,
Philip Herdel,
J. Jacob Shellbecker,*
J. Henry Sholtes,*
Jacobus Sautranck,
Johann Henrich Schleich,
Johann Jacob Wetzel,
Joh. Baltzer Kleinschmidt,
Hans Michael Fries,
Philip Jacob Hore,
Matheis Wilhelm Heming,
Johann Michel Wissler,
Johann Wolf Wissler,
Johann Casper Wissler,
Johan Henrich Katzbach,
Joh. Philip Schelbacher,
Johan Wilhelm Bäcker,
Johan Michael Bürger,
Johannes Stehlert,
Johannes Wassum,*
Leonhart Wassum,*
Christoph Kuhn,
Frantz Ihmme,
Philip Kurtz,
Abraham Eduman,
Johannes Schmid,
Johannes Schmid,
Andreas Bauer,
Stephan Bauer,
Michel Bauer,
Hans Seubert,
Georg Hörner,
Andreas Seuberth,
Peter Dihm,
Jacob Bauer,
Andreas Drach,
Veit Garrecht,
Friederich Hirsch,
Michael Hoffman,
Johann Bausch,
Conrad Kurtz,
Adam Rochia,*
George Bier,*
Michael Leiberich,
Jeremias Œsterlein,
Jacob Gibler,
Nicklaus Strauss,
Johannes Hörner,
Ludwig Wejuatius,?
Lorentz Kuntz,
Andreas Dressler,
Peter Ross,
Andreas Hörauff,
Georg Müller,
Johannes Fintzel,
Jacob Wolff,
Andreas Eyrich,
Andreas Büttel,
Hans Fertig,
Joh. Georg Hoh,
Hans Philip Dosch,
Johan Conrad Wassum,
Joh. Georg Wassum,*
Hans Christoph Schlesman,

Johan Ludwig Feister,
Johan Christian Heydt,
Johannes Satzman,
Hans Michel Uetzel,?
J. Jacob Götzelman,
Johan Adam Einner,
Joh. Melchior Hörner,
Joh. Jacob Hörner,
Jacob Oberdorff,
Veit Fetterling,
Hans Thomas Dihm,
Hans Caspar Haag,
Ludwig Haltemeyer,*
David Haltemeyer,*
Hans Melchior Stieffel,
Hans Adam Stieffel,
Joh. Georg Sauselin,
Johan Georg Wimmer,
Johan Friederich Berger,
Joh. Phil. David Spindler,
Joh. Henrich Kinsel,
Joh. Conrad Duntz,
Hans Peter Meyer,*
Johan Caspar Wisener,
Johan Michael Schrom,
John Christoph Weydner,
George Adam Frederick,
Johan Nicklas Klein,
Johann Peter Weichell,
Johan Christoph Bütner,
Christian Tobias Hensel,
Hans Georg Egenschweller,?
Johan Friederich Volck,
Joh. Henrich Schlessman
Hans Georg Hand,
Johan Michael Lutz,
Hans Michael Beck,
Johan Nicklaus Ott,
George Hoppengartner,*
Conrad Onkel,*
Andreas Aleberger,*

Michel Schülein,
Johan Eissendal,
Christoph Schaad,
Nicolaus Weyant,
Michael Hundt,
Philip Sieur,*
Sebastian Leybolt,
Johannes Kraus,
Nicklas Ingelhoff,
Johannes Scholthes,
Johannes Weisgerber,
Johannes Endress,
Johannes Miller,*
Jacob Danner,
Christian Schäffer,
Valtin Ehrhart,
Johann Schäffer,
Christoph Waltz,
Barthel Schötzlie,
Andreas Klein,
Simon Beleni,?
Carl Schmid,
Hans Gerbrich,
Hans Georg Sell,
Andreas Sell,
Jacob Krächman,
Jacob Will,
Tobias Ketter,
Joseph Sommer,
Johannes Hotman,
Lorentz Heffner,
Johann Heffner,
Johannes Honnig,
Lorentz Rörich,
Peter Fleischer,
Peter Müller sen.,
Hans Georg Lang,
Hans Georg Fintzel,
Hans Martin Franck,
Johann Peter Reeg,
Nicklas Weitzenhöller,

25*

Carl Ludwig Mäckelburg,
Johan Melchior Stader,
Paulus Jacob Wolff,
Caspar Beuschlein,
Hans Henry Forster,*
Baltzer Lantz,
Hans Adam Schäffer,
Hans Peter Schäffer,
August Henrich Schröter,
Johan Henrich Mönch,
Hans Adam Hoh,
John Ludwig Bender,
Johan Georg Strauss,
Christoph Kuhlemann,
Joh. Conrad Bütefisch,
Johan Martin Noll,
Carl Fried. Dan. Christian,

Johan Adam Härdel,
Johan Georg Kallemeyer,
Lorentz Joseph Dennschertz,
Hans Georg Engelbert,
Joh. Christoph Schaber,
Joh. Niclaus Schlessman,
Joh. Stephanus Horn,
Johan Philip Eich,
Hans Georg Büttel,
Hans Antonius Seger,
Joh. Ferdinandus Leiss,
Johann Heinrich Muth,
Heinrich Fleischer,
Christian Denner,
Joh. Peter Müller,
Hermanus Cronenberg,
Johan Conrad Stödter.

Sick—Andreas Drach, Johan Heyser, Johann Leonhart Wieder, Johan Henrich Scholtes, Henrich Bed, Joh. Henrich Koch, Michael Kuchel, Henrich Kuhn.

---

190) Nov. 3, 1752. Ship Queen of Denmark, Georg Parish, Commander, from Hamburg, last from Cowes.

Nov. 3, 1752. Schiff Queen of Denmark, Commandant Georg Parish, von Hamburg über Cowes.

P. Wortman,
Christopher Pabst,*
Zacharias Bach,
A. Dietrich Schell,
Johan Zwiebeller,
Andreas Schott,
Jacob Schott,
P. Matheis Abel,
Lambrecht Philip,
Johan Egen,
Magnus Schröder,
Peter Bruns,*
Johann Schlüter,
Simon Marcus,*
J. Jacob Lanten,*

Andreas Ulsch,
Conrad Schäffer,
Georg Gärtner,*
Christian Nagel,*
Michael Stahl,
Hen. Van Hoven,
Johan Croyer,*
Joachim Harloff,*
Christoph Meyer,
J. Fried. Lutzer,*
Ernst Hornäffer,*
Christ. Wilgenson,*
J. Henry Shultz,*
Henrich Magnus,
Joh. Ernst Heim,

Peter Weis,
Joh. Ohnschild,*
H. Mich. Menneke,*
Joh. Adam Gartner,*
F. Christo Torson,*
H. Fred. Laub,*
Zacharias Straubel,*
Frantz Schütz,
Johan Meyer,*
Friederich Schreyer,*
Henrich Burchard Gabriel,
Georg Thomas Gimpel,*
Georg Christian Fischer,
Casper Friederich Lutz,
Hans Zacharias Longer,*
J. Christian Morgenroth,
G. Leopold Heinig,
Georg Gottlieb Fass,
Johan Casper Oberman,
G. Henrich Herold,*
Johan Adam Stoltze,
J. Nicolas Tränckner,
J. Daniel Metzler,
Joachim Henrich Detloff,
Hans Casper Batram,*
Nicholas Daniel Nas,
Johan Henrich Bauer,
Joh. Casper Fried. Grümmet,
L. Ludwig Winckler,
Christoph Ludwig Grümmet,
M. Friederich Kippenberg,*
Georg Christoph Günder,
Georg Christoph Mück,
H. Zacharias Hagelberg,
Georg Michael Hamscher,
J. Christian Nesselroth,
Georg Christian Klem,

Christian Henrich Habicht,
Henrich Andreas Nagel,
Hen. Jacob Struckmeyer,
Joh. Henrich Sackman,
Joachim Andreas Bräutigam.
Joh. Sebastian Voght,
Joh. Joachim Görtler,
Christ. Dietrich Meyer,
Johan Georg Golhell,
Henrich Caspar Putscher,
J. Martin Röttger,
Joh. Valentin Dantius,
Johan Carl Menneke,
Henrich Nothdarf,*
J. Christo Schletz,*
Casper Gab. Miller,*
Joh. Geo. Barfuss,
Christ. Ludwig Münt,
Carl Fred. Grobler,
Christian Henrich,
Fried. Solomon Weis,
Friederich Zimmer,
Dietrich Volkman,
Johannes Bibe,
Joh. Henrich Sänger,
J. Andreas Hornäffer,
Dietrich von Bieren,
Joh. Gottfried Zerhiger,
Johan Daniel Eckebert,
Hen. Rudolph Stoltze,
Joh. Friederich Grässler,
Joh. Bartho. Nühlhahn,
Casper Henrich Grimm,
Joh. Georg Reinhold,
Johan Zacharias Jahn,
Johan Christoph Winter.

Sick—Joh. Henrich Hefthar, J. Thomas Kuhn, Gottfried Wilhelm Allhelm, Johannes Minck, Johan Gustavus Kuntz, H. Christian Willfeld, Georg Christian Mayer, Johan Friederich Günter, Johan Ernst Holland, Georg Friederich Tesch, Johan

Henrich Klem, Henrich Rudolph Nagel, Christoph Mayer, David Mörson, Gottfried Reinknecht, Joh. Ernst Simon, J. Friederich Berghaus, Friederich Albrecht Scheller, Joh. Henrich Wendel, David Henrich Heyer, Nicklaus Ruel, A. Matheis Molin, Hans Georg Breihahn, Johan Ludwig Schlotterman, Johan Adolph Flock.

---

191) Nov. 8, 1752. Snow Louisa, John Pittcairne, Captain, from Rotterdam, last from Cowes.

Nov. 8, 1752. Seeschiff Louisa, Capitain John Pittcairne, von Rotterdam über Cowes.

Michael Deeg,
Matheus Kepstner,
Christoph Kuntz,
Jacob Holder,
Ulrich Meyer,
Johannes Feiler,
Johannes Meyer,
Johannes Ullman,
Casper Krieger,
Adam Pabst,*
Christian Hofman,
David Mellinger,
Jacob Hoffmann,
Frantz Carl von Campe,
Hans Georg Hausser,
Hans Georg Reisch,
Johan Herman Rosenblatt,
Johan Leonardt Kopp,
Johan Christian Friess,
Johann Martin Holder,
Johan Michael Geiger,
Hans Georg Lantzer,
Georg Michael Schmidt,
Albrecht Michael Felder,
G. Friederich Hottenbacher,
Hans Adam Statell,*
Wilhelm Fortenbacher,
Johannes Geiler,
Leonhardt Schindler,

Conrad Schindler,
Johannes Romig,*
Frantz Schmid,
Konrad Hepfoh,
Balthaser Scholl,*
Peter Diem,
Georg Gobel,
Christoph Gülberth,
Joseph Beyrer,
Tobias Stahl,*
Christian Kast,
Johannes Schneider,
Jacob Hag,
Johannes Bader,
Johannes Hoss,
Jacob Grieg,
Georg Karr,
Friederich Schrader,
Hans Michael Carl, §
Johan Georg Koch,
Johann Peter Scholl,
Johann Georg Sturm,
Georg Baltzer Schelling,
Johann Georg Gilbert,
Johann Jacob Kuckhen,
Johann Jost Bruno,
Johan Georg Laubinger,
Andreas Gilbert,
Jac. Balthasar Volcampe,*

Hans Georg Kautz,
Joh. Philip Schwartländer,
John Philip Welsh,*
Johann Georg Meyer,
Georg Philipp Bock,
Hans Michael Schmidt,

Georg Michael Müller,
Johann Michael Päth,
Johan Martin Haussleither,
Johan Jacob Stoll,
Georg Christian Nüsser,
Simon Leitel Huber.

---

192) Nov. 22, 1752. Ship Phœnix, Reuben Honor, Captain, from Rotterdam, last from Cowes.

Nov. 22, 1752. Schiff Phönix, Capitain Reuben Honor, von Rotterdam über Cowes.

Peter Antel,*
Josias Schertzer,
Johann Klass,
Jacob Hüwit,
Rudolph Hoffman,
Michael Burgin,
Ulrich Nüssly,
Friederich Weiler,
Leonhart Uller,
David Zimmermann,
Lambert Smyets,
Johannes Mohr,
Johannes Roth,
Valentin Scheurich,
Jacob Scheurich,
Christoph Dosch,
Ludwig Henrich Nussbürckel,
Johan Adam Lotz,
Johan Nicklas Allhäll,*
Johann Peter Gittin,
Georg Christoph Bauman,
Johan Adam Geiger,
Johann Henrich Breser,
Jean Jaques le Roy,
Han Georg Rohrer,
Johan Henrich Becker,
Jacob Friederich Schneider,
Johan Philip Albert,
Frantz Joseph Pfeifer,

Johan Matheis Scheurich,
Johan Martin Dostman,
Hans Michael Adelman,
Ludwig Weimer,
Johannes Frölich,
Philip Jacobi,
Hans Shneyder jr.,*
Jean Botisnion,
Christian Kuhbach,
Daniel Gingenhan,
Abraham Peter,
Michael Peter,
Paul Walleysen,*
Jacob Ogli,
Johannes Statler,*
Bartholomeus Hoffman,
Augustin Fieng,
Abraham Frioth,
Henrich Lolleninger,
Andreas Kutz,
Johannes Fischer,
Jacob Gartman,
Jacob Grauss,
Christian Roth,
Rudolph Döbely,
Johann Schaidt,
Henry Geisler,*
Joseph Imfeld,
Ulrich Ott,

Rudolph Egy,
Jacob Haller,
Johann Waltz,
David Jugnal,*
H. Weytzel,*
Peter Gilliona,*
Daniel Lawall,
Henry Straub,
Jacob Guyer,
Matheis Krauth,
Johannes Düff,
Peter Jung,
Wilhelm Albert,
Simon Schneider,
Christoph Henrich,
Jacob Lüper,
Johannes Heltenmeyer,
Burchard Zendmeyer,
Joh. Jacob Winter,
Johann Georg Suber,
Guiliam Silbirit,
Johann Adam Speck,
Johann Georg Heck,
Johann Georg Gingenhan,
Hans Georg Dosh,*
Johann Peter Lehmann,
Jean Michel Lanblene,
Johan Peter Conveer,
Hans Michael Claus,
Johann Jacob Schelling,
Johan Georg Merckling,
Hans Georg Zaimger,
Johann Michel Ihl,
Johann Henrich Schaff,
Johann Thomas Beck,

Johann Burckhard,
Hans Georg Meyly,
Mich. Friedrich Buch,
Johan Peter Pfannkuchen,
Johan Adam Klein,
Michael Ullmann,
Hans Michael Hoff,
Georg Nebeling,
Johan Ludwig Lawall,
John David Henkel,
Hans Michael Lutz,
Hans Martin Scheurich,
Adam Le Roy,
Johan Peter Frembes,
Johann Georg Roth,
Johan Rudolph Ferrer,
Georg Henrich Kop,
George Henry Koch,
Georg Bernhart Kapp,
Johan Michael Christian,
Martin Johann Bauer,
Hans Jacob Back,*
Johan Melchior Ensle,
Daniel Kuhn,
Piere Guillons,
Frantz May,
Kilian May,
Anthon Weinbrener,
George Hoffman,*
Wolfgang Winebrener,*
Johann Jacob Miller,*
Johann Philip Straub,
Michael Schäffer,
Johann Rudolph Graff,
Johan Theobald Closs.

Sick—Johannes Lenschy jr., Hans Georg Backofen, Thomas Leyerig, Johan Ludwig Mickel, Johann Dietrich Eckel, Jacob Reigert, Jacob Döbly, Hans Georg Beicht, Georg Hinleer, Abraham Freilich, Jacob Lupfer, Johan Gottfried List, Jacob Scheywisch.

193) Sept. 8, 1753. Ship St. Michael Michael, Thomas Ellis, Commander, from Hamburg, last from Cowes.

Sept. 8. 1753. Schiff St. Michael Michael, Commandant Thomas Ellis, von Hamburg über Cowes.

John Henry Deer,*
Joh. Fried. Deer,*
Henry A. Deer,*
Christian Warner,*
Peter Gunckel,*
Andreas Shweishelm,
Andreas Böger,
J. George Saxe,
Johannes Rehr,*
Friederich Rauberg,*
Wilhelm Latink,*
Christian Latink,*
Lorents Shüler,
J. Henry Krape,*
J. Peter Millberg,*
J. Christian Heyl,
Michael Kind,
Christoph Wegener,
Conrad Eichler,
Ludwig Töpper,
Christian Aterholt,*
Johannes Resch,
Ehler Herse,
Andreas Linden,
Herman Inbuss,
Henrich Meyer,
Fred. Henrich Barthals,
John Jacob Port,
Joh. Josephus Meinersen,
John Henry Keller,
John Henry Gross,

Johann Henrich Ahrens,
Joh. Henrich Billingesleben,
J. Henry Messershmit,*
J. Friederich Fischer,
Johann Christian Sachse,
Johan Nicklaus Rehcopp,
J. Caspar Latink,*
J. Henry Seydling,*
J. Friederich Allter,*
J. Andreas Vogt,
G. Christoph Warinken,*
Conrad Henry Sander,*
Clas Casten Kröger,
Johann Daniel Klemm,
Hieronimus Eichler,
H. Christoph Gall,
Joh. Hen. Eberhart Hensen,
Joh. Benedictus Breittenfeldt
Friedrich Henrich Stern,
Johann Gerhart Mayer,
Hans Henry Tete,*
Frantz Con. Rose,
J. Henry Ratiker,*
J. Henry Gutjahr,*
Johann Kirscher,
Matheis Kersher,*
Johann Erich Reuter,
Johan Friederich Sachse,
John Henry Saxe,
Christian Wilhelm Cöll,
George Wilhelm Hooker.*

194) Sept. 10, 1753. Ship Beulah, —— Richey, Captain, from Rotterdam, last from Cowes.

Sept. 10, 1753. Schiff Beulah, Capitain Richey, von Rotter= dam über Cowes.

Jac. Bishop Berger,*
Joh. Georg Rab,
Vinsintzius Beggari,
Johan Perass,?
Friederich Züron,
Christian Scheitt,
Stephan Lay,
Andreas Lay,
Moses Bauer,
Simon Walther,
Peter Uber,
Thomas Dich,
Friederich Gruber,
Jacob Michel,
Baltius Zweyk,*
Christoph Zweig,
Conrath Schief,
Ludwig Schick,
Andreas Frey,
Jacob Stein,
Friederich Cast,*
Hans Georg Wilt,
Albrecht Heckman,
Georg Arnolt,
Michel Kuhn sen.,*
Michael Kuhn,
Sebastian Hoffman,*
Johannes Hoffman,*
Valentin Korn,
Martin Bürger,
Lorentz Hössert,
Hans Waltz,
Martin Hedinger,
Johan Michael Greffenstein,
Stephan Frantz Volch,
Georg Friederich Volch,
Johan Michael Bauer,
Georg Friederich Braun,
Johann Simon Schmieg,
Johann Friederich Freund,

Johann Matheus Braun,
Johann Henrich Hoffmann,
Georg Heinrich Alter,
Johann Jacob Alter,
Johann Albrecht Fessler sen.,
Johann Albrecht Fessler,
Johann Andreas Fessler,
Georg Conrad Braun sen.,
Johan Stephan Riegler,
Georg Conrad Braun,
Johann Michael Krauss,
Johann Georg Braun,
Johann Matheus Mayer,
Henrich Martin Ebele,
Johan Philip Vohleder,
Johan Michel Ungerer,
Johan Philip Berberich,
J. Friederich Hiltzbeck,*
Georg Friederich Schweitzer,
Johann Henrich Gebert,
Johan Georg Ziegler,
Johan Michael Lang,
Johan Christoph Nitz,
Johann Peter Bauer,
Johann Friederich Bauer,
Johann Wilhelm Ruth,
Georg Scholler,
Peter Truckenmiller,*
Jacob Sammit,*
Andreas Klein,
Georg Schimmel,
Joh. Jacob Keppner,
H. Adam Brenner,
Joh. Ernst Sattelthaler,
Joh. Andreas Schmieg,
Georg Henrich Schäffer,
Georg Friederich Schall,*
Johan Michael Franck,
Joh. Ludwig Sommer,
Johan Georg Dietz,

Georg Christoph Dietz,
Hans Georg Kamm,

Georg Ludwig Rosenmüller,
Georg Michael Däueber.

---

195) Sept. 11, 1753. Ship Queen of Denmark, Geo. Parish, Captain, from Hamburg, last from Cowes.

Sept. 11, 1753. Schiff Queen of Denmark, Capitain Georg Parish, von Hamburg über Cowes.

Caspar Krönberg,
Ludwig Raffgarn,*
Henry Bergfeld,
Georg Bossman,
Thomas Fugnicht,*
Ernst Delitz,
J. Ernst Kort,*
John Ewald,*
Christian Arrent,*
P. Zangenberg,
Ludwig Brall,*
J. Henry Frey,
Lorentz Petry,*
Andreas Grotheim,*
Nicolaus Schäffer,
J. Jost Werning,*
Johannes Taubert,
David Albrecht,
J. Jacob Voigt,
J. August Freyberg,
J. Friedrich Desern,*
Christoff Endike,*
J. George Gerang,*
George Fischer,*
Christian Heippe,*
Christian Luig,*
Wilhelm Brenner,
Johann Reichman,
Christoph Gut jr.,*
Johann Valentin Elte,
Hans Georg Disseler,*
Johan Henrich Mastenberg,
H. Christopher Shadike,*

Dieterich Proptenslad,*
Jost Henrich Behe,
Joh. Friederich Ungar,*
J. Andreas Rudolph,*
J. Andreas Balthauer,*
Joh. Henry Engel,*
Hans Herman Arrent,*
Johann Christian Tenne,
Johan George Distner,*
J. Valentin Neimeyer,*
Ludwig. Wil. Bockrantz,
Anthon Barthol. von Brunck,
Joh. Carl Rauschenbach,
Joh. Wilhelm Schiele,
Johann David Fischer,
Johan Christian Bolle,
Johan Valentin Rausch,
Johan Christian Schneider,
Jost Henry Kinige,*
Joh. Christoph Gobrecht jr.,
Georg Wilhelm Reburg,*
Joh. Christian Gobrecht,
Frantz Henrich Ernst,
Johann Ernst Blanssart,
Geo. Wilhelm von Lüde,
Johann Dingler,
Christian Gollstäd,*
Wilhelm Krelss,
Peter Fred. Niemeyer,
Nicolaus Christian Otto,
Joh. Friederich Wambeck,*
Henrich Julius Boths.

26

Sick—Johan Ludwig Starck, Georg Demme jr., Friederich Jordan, J. Dietrich Welde, Hans Herman Brand, Christoph Weidener, Joh. Philip Preising, Christian Neiss, Johan Georg Müller, Erhart Reindel, Christoph Gut sen.

---

196) Sept. 14, 1753. Ship Edinburgh, James Russel, Captain, from Rotterdam, last from Portsmouth.

Sept. 14, 1753. Schiff Edinburgh, Capitain James Ruffel, von Rotterdam über Portsmouth.

Johann Achintopfs,?
Michael Halberstadt,
Julius Brecker,
Samuel Maus,
Peter Miller,*
Dewald Creutz,*
Johannes Miller,*
Abraham Miller,*
Jacob Braun,
Philip Lantz,
Philip Mülhof,
Conrath Kleim,
Jacob Dewalt,
Conrath Guth sen.,
Conrad Guth,
Andreas Hesterich,
Peter Schuh,
Heinrich Schupp,
Jacob Müller,
Bastian Mohr,
Michael Lang,
Ludwig Busch,
Adam Hamscher,
Joseph Zwieshig,
Carl Arnth,
Andreas Scher,
Georg Marthin,
Johannes Limberger,
Peter Steiner,
Philip Henry Gabel,
Johann Jacob Ham,

Johann Jacob Wissinger,
Philip Jacob Mühlhoff,
Michael Zimmerman,
Johann Georg Kuhn,
Johann Adam Kreischer,
Johann Sebastian Kreischer,
Ernst Christoph Adam,
Johann Jacob Ross,
Conrad Klenter,*
Johann Peter Bade,
Johannes Schwalb,
Balthaser Pemeller,
Johann Jacob Beck,
Johann Reinhardt Rahmer,
Johann Georg Jost,
Johann Friederich Vogeler,
Johann Christoph Mauerer,
Christoph Treydel,
Jacob Kauffmann,
Johann Nickel Michel,
Johann Georg Leonard,
Conrad Wagner,
Christian Jutzener,*
Johannes Herguth,
Johann Nickel Jacoby,
Johann Nickel Jacoby sen.,
Johann Peter Jacoby,
Wilhelm Stein,
Jacob Krier,*
Carl Bernhart,
Peter Kuntz,

Jacob Schott,
Johannes Laffer,
Peter Rödtler,
Friederich May,*
Jacob Threye,
Jacob Zombro,
Jacob Knab,*
Philip Preiss,*
Johan Rauffbem,*
Jacob Bauer,
Jacob Bachman,
Jacob Heck,
Daniel Heck,
Peter Beder,
Samuel Wertz,
David Schmitt,
Belann Lantz,
Martin Geldt,
Peter Klein,
Wilhelm Spira,
Johannes Fellentzer,
Adolph Meyer,
Daniel Hann,
Jacob Bollinger,
Johannes Stötzel,
Philip Weber,
Andreas Hamstein,
Ulrich Wäber,
Johannes Frey,
Bernhart Beck,
Matheis Ehhalt,
Martin Braun,
Conrad Foltz,
Marcus Angst,
Paulus Hartman,
Georg Göhringer,
Ludwig Folmer,*
Friederich Jäckle,
Christoffel Renner,
Valentin Hoffmann,
Jean Pierre du Corbier,

Johann Adam Böhm,
Valentin Kohlmann,
Theobald Angene,
Friederich Schwartz,
Philip Henry Lein,
Johann Jacob Bachman,
Lorentz Bachman,
Eberhart Schmitt,
Ludwig Jung,*
Johann Entzmenger,*
Johann Bientzel,
Joh. Henry Bintzel,*
Johannes Bintzel,*
Paulus Spirandin,
Jacob Bollinger,
Johann Kraffgoss,
J. Henry Shrohr,*
Peter Flickinger,
Joh. Christ. Huffnagel,
Johan Georg Weyshaar,
Johann Georg Steinbock,
John Henry Wunderling,
Justus Henrich Weber,
Conrad Mentzinger,
Johan Wilhelm Wäber,
Johannes Kornhaas,
Johannes Rechtlos,
Johannes Buchstel,
Christian Fischer,
Gregorius Büsche,
Friederich Hartman,
Wilhelm Hartman,
Friederich Weidmeyer,
Andreas Huttenbach,
Jeremias Hüsterle,
Johan Christian Dörr,
Johannes Schmidt,
Heinrich Adam Hoffman,
Georg Melchior Hiebner,
Johannes Auer,*
Jacob Knodel,

Adam Roser,
Johannes Kreiner,
Jacob Polweller,*
Henrich Strack,
Jacob Miller,*
Jacob Ott,
Philip Lehrer,
Johan Georg Märcker,

Paulus Hochstrasser,
Valentin Fleck,
Johan Michael Hauber,
Johann Conrad Metz,
Friederich Stephan,
Elias Kneller,
Solomon Gabel,
Johan Jacob Albert.*

Sick—Friederich Kramer, Michael Decker, Rudolph Welde, Henrich Rodhaf, Friederich Hartman.

---

197) Sept. 17, 1753. Ship Patience, Hugh Steel, Captain, from Rotterdam, last from Cowes.

Sept. 17, 1753. Schiff Patience, Capitain Hugh Steel, von Rotterdam über Cowes.

Gottfried Haberly,
Jaques Balme,
Paul Caffarel,
Mortier Ture,
Jaques Gouriie,
Lorie Nerien,
Jacob Gerhart,*
Adam Seihs,
Jacob Fisher,*
Jaque Berger,
Joseph Knittel,
Johannes Singer,
Jacob Borman,
Friederich Jensel,
Michael Scheible,
Charles Shommet,*
Martin Käyser,
Martin Jauss,
Pierre Gautier,
Jean Bonnet,

Elias Nastes,?
Jaque Bac,
Jacob Singquet,
Lenhart Heller,
Pierre Armin Jean,
Jean Pierre Chappelle,
Jeremie Chappelle,
Pierre Rouchon,
Henri Rouchon,
Jean Jaques Servai,
Michael Rüstler,
Joh. Georg Knidel,
Hans Georg Feller,
Jean Richardon,
Hans Georg Sholter,*
Georg Valentin Reinhardt,
Andreas Münchinger,
Fried. Haux, *a*
Johannes Würmle,
Gottlieb Heinrich Harindus,

---

a To this name is prefixed *Ehw. Dom.*, i. e. *Rev. Mr.* ; thus: *Ehw. Dom. Fried. Haux.*—(*Editor.*)

a Vor diesem Namen steht Ehw. Dom., d. h. Pastor Fried. Haux.—(Herausgeber.)

Hans Conrad Hogoodus,
Hans Georg Bross,
Ferdinand Würtz,
Friederich Reinholdt,
Christoph Hehr,
Johann Caspar Gross,
Johann Georg Strödinger,
Johannes Preyss,
Daniel Stauber,
Jacob Banchle,?
Michael Aller,
Johannes Bodner,
Hans Hentzinger,
Johannes Hiller,
Philip Weiss,
Bernhart Jung,
Henrich Kendel,
Matheas Heber,
Tobias Kurch,
Johannes Kleintopf,
Johann Jackobi,
Adam Winhart,
Johannes Breinig,
Casper Hassler,
Peter Gröbil,
Bastian Erig,*
Peter Landig,*
Leonhard Schauer,
Peter Bühler,
Michael Gerber,
Simon Gerber,
Christoph Schmit,

Etienne Breun,
Jacob Gerber,
Gabriel Lausch,
Michel Röm,
Georg Martin Kreidler,
Johannes Schweitzer,
Georg Michel Descher,
Jacob Ochsenreiter,
Johan Friederich Werner,*
Joh. Friederich Ochsenreiter,
Joh. Friederich Stähle,
Johan Caspar Sieg,
Georg Adam Wiet,
Hans Georg Roller,
G. Wilhelm Rieser,
Christoffel Kleintopf,
Hen. Christo. Bleicherodt,
Joh. Matthias Schmidt,
Hans Georg Schättinger,
Hans Georg Adtelberger,
Philip Adtelberger,
Hans Adam Schäffer,
Heinrich Hackmann,
Hans Michael Mann,
J. Dietrich Steinbrecher,
J. Lenhart Gerwig,*
Sebastian Knartsch,
Johan Daniel Rau,
Samuel Bosserman,
Friederich Osswald,
Johan Georg Federhoff.

Sick—Isaac Grad, Christoph Larg, Christian Bauer, Hans Georg Leib.

---

198) Sept. 17, 1753. Ship Richard and Mary, John Moore, Commander, from Rotterdam, last from Cowes.

Sept. 17, 1753. Schiff Richard und Mary, Commandant John Moore. von Rotterdam über Cowes.

Joseph Phillipp,
Ulrich Seuberlich,
Peter Juncker,
Joh. Martin Jacob,
F. Wilh. Zürn,
Joh. Knabschneider,
Geo. Adam Schober,
Johan Caspar Gayer,
Hans Michael Rau,
Johan Jacob Gayer,
Johan Henrich Juncker,
Johan Carl Siegle,
Johann Ernst Juncker,
Johan Christian Kniess,
Martin Sührer,
Andreas Diehm,
Johannes Siglin,
Conrad Lampater,*
Joseph Lampater,*
Johannes Lampater,*
Joseph Wild,
Casper Weschune,?
Adam Stall,
Adam Grim,
Abraham Lang,
Michael Vollmer,
Friederich Kucher,
Josephus Friederich,
Peter Janson,
Paulus Bäutigam,
Joh. Ernst Nagel,
Christoph Mahl,*
Johannes Kuchen,
Han Jacob Adam,*
J. Georg Metzger,*
Peter Rahm,*
Adam Obendorff,
Peter Hitschner,
Jacob Schlauchter,
Johannes Sack,
H. Albert Hörner,*

Johannes Schreiber,
Jacob Wittmann,*
Paulus Hopp,
Valentin Schobig,
Christoff Waltz,
Christoph Heinickel,
Peter Nass,
Christophel Gref,
Peter Seiler,
Johannes Hollscheit,
Johannes Gürtz,*
Simon Sark,*
Johannes Peroing,*
David Reiff,*
Philip Hammerschmit,*
Joh. Nicolaus Schubert,
Joh. Michael Schubert,
Joh. Casper Wurm,
Johan Georg Stump,*
Georg Friederich Pflieger,
Joh. Georg Maisch,
Joh. Georg Gelinder,
Hans Martin Gelinder,
Hans Jacob Kemmerli,
Johan Adam Körner,
Joh. Georg Gerstenmayer,
Georg Friederich Weiss,
Joh. Lenhart Zembt,?
Carl Friederich Weydo,§
Joh. Christoph Herth,
Joh. Daniel Druss
C. Friederich Hutman,*
Joh. Friederich Hess,
Joh. Friederich Satler,*
Joh. Wilhelm Engelhardt,
Georg Paul Langenbach,
Hans Ludwig Mall,
Hans Georg Kreis,
Joh. Henrich Oberlender,
Johan Adam Wolff,
George Nicklas Straus,*

Joh. Philip Stein,
Joh. Christoph Beck,
Joh. Conrad Steinmetz,
Joh. Henrich Müller,
Joh. Michael Spannagel,
Georg Adam Wittmann,
Johann Georg Klein,
Hans Barthel Heck,
Hans Geo. Schöllhammer,
Johan Caspar Auen,
Ernst Wilhelm Kageroth,
J. Gottfried Knapper,*
Georg Friederich Heininger,

Hans Adam Oswald,*
Johan Georg Bick,
Johan Peter Ruhter,
Herman Weyskirk,*
Michael Kolb,
Jacob Schenck,
Johannes Schmit,*
H. Georg Gramly,*
Hans Georg Seydelmeyer,*
Philip Grindelmeyer,*
Hans Georg Harst,
Joh. Matheus Pfanner,
Joh. Georg Braun.

199) Sept. 19, 1753. Ship Leathley, —— Lickey, Captain, from Hamburg, last from Cowes.

Sept. 19, 1753. Schiff Leathley, Capitain Lickey, von Ham= burg über Cowes.

Anercus Foll,
Christian Schlemer,*
Christoph Amelon,*
Christoffel Termel,*
J. Christoph Bömer,*
H. Henry Cöffer,*
Caspar Hillebrecht,*
C. Rudolph Rechner,
Daniel Lange,
Henry Busman,*
Henry Neymeyer,
Andreas Busman,*
J. Carsten Thorman,*
Ludwig Schmit,*
J. Henry Hinsey,
Michael Uhl,
Christian Ramberg,
Henry Shreeder,*
Hiram Alleman,
Johan Heneman,*
Henry Werner,
J. Henry Probe,*

Conradt Shmit,*
Friederich Veiher,*
Valentin Wegmeyer,
John Henry Hening,*
Johan Peter Koch,
J. Wilhelm Voss,
J. Dieterich Sehr,*
Joh. Gottfried Golde,
Christophel Schlencker,
Fried. Wilhelm Schlencker,
Frantz Hen. Schlencker,
Christ. Andreas Nichtedt,
Joh. Ludolph Wehmeyer,
Joh. Andreas Meyer,
Johan Just Müller,
Hans Henry Busman,*
Ernst Henrich Stölle,
Joh. Philip Fertinbach,
Johan Stats Koch,
Joh. Christoph Appache,
Johan Nicklaus Klein,
Casper Ludwig Siwert,

Johan Henrich Siwert,
Johan Christian Ale,
J. Cort Halster,

Georg Casper Höppener,
And. Christoff Meinsken,
Joh. Fried. Christian Alleman.

---

200) Sept. 24, 1753. Ship Neptune, John Mason, Master, from Rotterdam, last from Cowes.

Sept. 24, 1753. Schiff Neptune, Capitain John Mason, von Rotterdam über Cowes.

Friederich Melcher,
Johann Wilhelm,
Peter Dümmig,
George Keytel,*
Joh. Michael Schärphlein,
Georg Nicolas Weugäterr,
Johan Georg Wenckert,
Hans Michael Rather,
Peter Keytel,*
Sebastian Hore,
Peter Klünth,
Nicklas Hebling,
Sebastian Werlein,
Michael Kretz,
Andreas Bolch,
Philip Riesser,
Andreas Schneffer,
Jacob Oberdorff,
Joh. Peter Riess,
Georg Weiss,
Johannes Ross,
Conrad Winckler,
Michael Hollenbach,
Caspar Dollmann,
Johannes Riess,
Nicklas Hollebach,
Simon Irst,?
Georg Falock,
Georg Leming,
Melchior Eisnert,
Johannes Fleischer,
Christian Reysing,*

Michael Hollenbach,
Philip Weiss,
Adam Hauck,
Peter Lennich,
Sebastian Hämer,
Joh. Adolph Ott,
Johannes Schreiner,
Wilhelm Würtz jr.,
Wilhelm Würtz sen.,
Joh. Georg Raab,*
Bernhart Shop,*
Andreas Crieby,
Sebastian Riess,
Casper Henkel,
Johannes Hue,
Geo. Wilh. Morash,*
Andreas Hommer,*
Jacob Beyer,
Lorentz Friederich Croy,
Georg Schwenckert,
Johannes Trump,
Bartel Raunberger,
Johann Michael Werlein,
Johan Georg Schwab,
Joh. Christoph Breitenhardt,
Joh. Philip Eyrich,
Joh. Michael Erdners,
Joh. Michael Heidt,
Johan Paul Schwab,
Hans Adam Dierhein,
Johan Adam Sauer,
Johann Georg Wunder,

Johann Michael Desch,
Joh. Lenhart Wüttninger,
Joh. Sebastian Hammeter,
Joh. Christoph Feemhaber,
Joh. Philip Mewe,
Hans Jacob Winckler,
Hans Thomas Winckler,
Johan Georg Hollenbach,
Joh. Bernhardt Pahosuch,
Johan Nicklas Saul,
Johan Georg Harmoff,
Georg Peter Fuchs,
Joh. Nicklaus Heckser,
Hans And. Weickert,
Ephraim Benedict Kaubel,
Georg Henry Bauer,*
Johan Thomas Lennich,
Hans Georg Stautz,
Hans Casper Fuchs,
Hans Georg Carl Volck,
Joh. Henrich Graf,
Joh. Georg Conrad Hinck,
Johan Caspar Schnerr,
Johan Adam Saull,*
Hans Michael Hörner,
Johan Georg Oberdorff,
Johan Georg Beck,
Hans Michael Köller, §
Johan Meyer,*
Jacob Schäffer,
Andreas Sahm,
Baltzer Oberdorff,
Georg Wollf,
Adam Scheck,
Paulus Plitz,
Jacob Scholl,
Christoph Büttel,
Johannes Horn,
Balthaser Seuberth,

Hannes Schnepper,
Nicklas Reinhart,
Nicklaus Beringer,
Christoph Horn,
Martin Semmel,
Michael Seubert,
Simeon Bürger,
Jacob Willier,*
Johannes Stihling,
Peter Höbling,
Carl Mildy,*
Hans Schreck,
Andreas Seuberth,
Valentin Oberdorff,
Christian Ernst Nieman,
Johan Heinrich Ord,
Johan Christian Keyser,
Johan Michael Seelig,
Johann Adam Bolch,
Johann Adam Schatz,
Joh. Henrich Schlösser,
Georg Philip Roth,
Philipp Hoffman,
John Michael Schatz,
Johan Peter Stumpf,
Baltzer Georg Christian,
Georg Philip Bürger,
Johann Peter Flick,
Johann Paulus Platz,
Johan Philip Meyer,
Johann Bernhart Saull,
Johannes Burkhardt,
Hans Meckelein sen.,
Johan Henrich Meckelein,
Hans Meckelein,
Johann Michael Wassem,
Johan Adam Schantz,
Adam Nicolaus Platz.

201) Sept. 24, 1753. Ship Peggy, James Abercrombie, Commander, from Rotterdam, last from Plymouth.

Sept. 24, 1753. Schiff Peggy, Commandant James Abercrombie, von Rotterdam über Plymouth.

Martin Bauer,
Christian Roth,
Johannes Lutz,
Christoph Frantz,
Christoph Hast,
Michael Voltz,
Holfern Holtzman,
Jacob H. Herly,*
Johannes Hütterly,
Jacob Miller,
Casper Mäuele,
Fortunatus Geney,*
Nicklas Schreck,*
Johan Andreas Buch,
Christian Friederich Panse,
Johan Jacob Kautz,
Johann Adam Zweuer,
Johannes Eiminghoff,
Johann Carl Erhardt,
Johannes Bachman,
Johan Casper Nill,
Johan Michael Schumacher,
Philip Leonard Schwartz,
J. George Pluner,*
Johan Adam Oberweiler,
Carl Friederich Waag,
Casper Schaff,
Jacob Hohr,*
Michael Ban,?
Johann Forttmeier,
Johannes Steinman,
Ignatius Vogt,
Johannes Fihs,
George Baker,*
Jacob Eberhart,
Conrad Wiettemeyer,
Jacob Armschild,*

Wilhelm Gonder,
Peter Heiss,
Jacob Hetrich,
George Lange,
Michael Müller,
Diebolt Sorg,
Conrad Jäger,
Michael Brauer,
Martin Beck,
Jacob Schmidt,
Georg Matzon,*
Johannes Walder,
Jacob Berger,
Valentin Schäffer,
Philip Krebs,
Jacob Grininger,
Jacob Hirsch,
Carl Ebersohl,
Henry Hassler,
Abraham Correll,
G. A. Daser,
Conradt Huber,
Martin Schneider,
Philip Jacob Meyer,
Joseph Graff,
Isaac Müller,
Anton Cantzle,
Jacob Nagel,
Carl Degreiff,*
Jacob Haller,
Philip Zorge,
Hans Michel Zomel,
Carl Weinmiller,
Georg Philip Ziegler,
Jean Frans Battez,
Johan Jacob Zucker,
Georg Anton Linder,

Johan Andreas Schrödlie,
Johan William Engel,
Hans Jacob Steigelmann,
Johan Jacob Kleinbub,
Joh. Michael Hero,*
J. Dieterich Oppenheim,
G. Wilhelm Albrecht,
Henrich Philipp Brumm,
H. George Leysig,*
Friederich Dannwind,
Joh. Theobald Sternberger,
Johan Michael Sorg,
Johan Martin Bettinger,
Johan Jacob Blecker,
Georg Peter Delp,
Joh. Wilhelm Kempff,
Joh. Wolfgang Zeilen,
Johannes Francisculur,
Peter Casper Schön,

Johan Jacob Walther,
Georg Adam Geiss,
Nicklas Turmeyer,*
Georg Adam Siegrist,
Michael Feierstein,
Joh. Georg Sautter,
Jos. Conrad Haussman,
Joh. Nicolaus Bartholomæ,
Johan Casper Rumetsch,
J. Georg Schweickhart,
Georg Christ. Reinholdt,
Joh. Friederich Engelhart,
Joh. Wolfgang Leiter,
Johan Adam Schackh,
Johan Friederich Uebel,
Johan Carl Jacqueart,
Johan Conrad Kagel,
Johann Christian Krebs.

Sick—Johannes Rudel, Johan Jac. Müller, Nicklas Harter,
J. Jacob Selwinger, Paulus A. Daser, J. Casper Weitzenfelder.

---

202) Sept. 26, 1753. Ship Brothers, William Main, Commander, from Rotterdam, last from Cowes.

Sept. 26, 1753. Schiff Brothers, Commandant Wm. Main, von Rotterdam über Cowes.

Peter Eysenbreit,
Christian Diem,
Matheis Blocher,
Michael Wäsener,
Johannes Karch,
Jacob Haipser,
Ludwig Fischer,
Lorentz Kölcket,
Daniel Wunderlich,
Melchior Minalt,
Johannes Kuss,
Burckhart Bindeman,
Melchior Rieckhed,
Johannes Jödder,

Friederich Mergel,*
Philip Hoffman,
Jacob Hester,
Lenhart Diterich,
Christoph Müller,
Jacob Müller,
Friederich Müller,
Ludwig Hertz,
Johannes Strohm,
Martin Flisterer,
David Kind,?
Andreas Keyser,
Isaac Vendner,
Paulus Bohler,

Michael Setzer,
Stephan Kreidler,
Jacob Mann,
Johannes Koch,
Johannes Zaberer,
Stephan Reybolt,*
Nickolas Miller,*
Hans George Hop,*
Hans Jacob Finfleher,
Michael Schittenhelm,
Martin Shittenhelm,*
Johann Casper Koch,
Hans Georg Hay,
Johann Simon Jäger,
Hans George Baltsonderweg,*
Georg Christoph Eberle,
Johan Ludwig Weltz,
Philip Jacob Kreidler,
Johan Martin Kreidler,
Johan Philip Freher,
Christoph Jacob Käucher,
Johan Philip Kliestadt,?
Hans Wendel Huber,
Georg Friederich Reinhard,
Johan Paul Schott,
Hans Georg Marsteller,
Hans Georg Frauenfelder,
Georg Friedrich Andræ,
Georg Alberth Dill,
Melchior Fliesbach,

Eberhart Sallener,?
Georg Peter Wilhelm,
Friederich Henrich Knabe,
Lenhardt Beckermann,
Christoph Schenck,
Hans George Mann,
Bernhart Schneider,
Friederich Lay,
Johannes Weyerbacher,
Mattheis Röstlin,
J. Andreas Ehrman,
Johann Casper Marburg,
Johannes Limbach,*
Johannes Herlein,
Philip Geyer,
Jacob Mann,
Friederich Leinbach,
Friederich Künstler,
Johannes Steidle,
Johannes Mann,
Jean Hartman,
Martin Schneider,
Michael Schneider, §
Hans Georg Fischer,
Johan Jacob Müller,
Hans Georg Mann,
Hans Georg Schweitzer,
Georg Jacob Schramm,
Jacob Schweitzer,
Valentin Klein.

203) Sept. 27, 1753. Ship Windsor, James Good, Captain, from Rotterdam, last from Cowes.

Sept. 27, 1753. Schiff Windsor, Capitain James Good, von Rotterdam über Cowes.

Rudolph Banninger,
Marcus Tomer,*
Daniel Schneider,
Martin Fazler,
Christian Schober,

Sigmund Bondeli,
Henrich Pfister,
Johannes Gräber,
Henry Boner,*
Christian Deiss,

Daniel Speck,
Caspar Lütz,
Heinrich Sättel,
Samuel Sättel,
Christian Keller,
Johannes Thomas,
Georg Hoff,
Georg Mossbach,
Casper Cabbas,*
Johan Nicklin,
J. Jacob Martin,
Philip Rice,*
Simeon Reiss,
Jacob Reive,*
Henry Eschrich,*
Joh. Peter Diehm,
Jacob Shrey,*
Adam Libhart,
J. Wilhelm Tistel,*
Joh. Jacob Boshart,
Joh. Reinhart Batz,
Joh. Martin Kietzmiller,
Johan Ludwig Beck,
Georg Stephanus Wallhauer,
Johann Georg Mann,
Johann Georg Schmidt,
Johan Wilhelm Cromer,

Reinhart Dietrich Kercher,
Johan Ferdinand Lehrer,
Johann Christoph Rein,
Hans Georg Lütz,
Joh. Martin Truckenmüller,
Hans Adam Schatzman,
Henrich Gottfried Murr,
Johan Peter Hörn,
Johann Joachim Jaysor,
Johann Jacob Friess,
Johann Peter Grub,
Johan Peter Eltz,
Michael Milberger,
Johannes Baumann,
Johann Casper Diehl,
Johan Jacob Osterwald,
Wilhelm Berckhäuser,
Georg Friederich Steidgers,
Johan Jacob Striby,
Johann Philippus Pix,
Simon Peter Strauch,
Andreas Grünau,
Nicklas Mensch,
Adam Hoppacher,
Johann Georg Betz,
Johann Michael Hobbär,
J. George Sommer.

204) Sept. 28, 1753. Ship Halifax, Thomas Coatam, Cap
tain, from Rotterdam, last from Cowes.

Sept. 28, 1753. Schiff Halifax, Capitain Thomas Coatam,
von Rotterdam über Cowes.

Friederich Keener,*
Johannes Colle,*
Heinrich Thönei,
Ludwig Luther,
Adam Syroa,*
Andreas Seydlle,*
Daniel Brenner,
Henrich Merki,

Daniel Ammon,
Andreas Staub,
Felix Gerber,
Jost Conrad,
Andreas Ingan,*
Johannes Kuhn,
Conrad Bornn,
Christoph Weber,

27

Christian Banner,*
Paulus Wolffe,
Jacob Rein,
Johannes Buch,
Johannes Bassert,
Johannes Wagner,
Isaac Budeman,
Talio Repair,*
Andreas Hath,?
Christoph Schütz,
Joseph Schmitt,
Jacob Streder,
Johannes Happener,
Gottfried Streidtz,
Johannes Haass,
Henrich Kohn,
Ludwig Würtz,
Johannes Henckel,
Johannes Mayer,
C. Friederich Maag,
Christian Heillmann,
Johannes Peter Hann,
Georg Michael Vollerman,
Georg Michael Megerth,
Georg Baldas Ungerer,
Johannes Danwisch,?
Solomon Hartman,
Heister Hängärten,
Michael Grossclaus,*
Rudolph Meyer,*
Jost Fischbach,
Bernhart Schmid,
Paulus Weygant,
Daniel Zacharis,
Mattheis Zacharis,
J. Henry Stoffel,
Herman Göbel,
Johan Georg Becker,
Hans Michael Gock,
Joh. Daniel Haga,

Joh. Ludwig Hesser,
Joh. Caspar Weiss,
Ludwig Henrich Karcher,
Johan Jacob Welter,
Joh. Georg Stöcker,
Johan Conrad Hess,
Johan Georg Moritz,
Johann Georg Schräster,
Johan Conrad Betis,
Johan Georg Hinroth,
Johan Georg Prost,
Johann Georg Krauskob,
Johan Georg Fillibs,
Johan Peter Heun,
Jacob Ringwald,
Martin Mayer,
Johannes Heyr,
Nicolaus Kremer,
Georg Bishoff,*
Mattheus Gromlich,
George Führling,
Adam Fays,
Michael Laub,
Jacob Urban,
J. Georg Steyb,*
Johannes Laub,
Johannes Theis,
John Adam Bald,
Johannes Achenbach,
Johann Jost Schmidt,
Johan Georg Sanborn,
Johan David Drüber,
Christian Rohrbach,
Peter Katzenmeyer,
Hans Nicklas Börger,
Johann Casper Koch,
Johan Adam Forsch,
Gottfried Körschnöck,
Adam Milchsack,
Johannes Georg Henny.

Sick—Christopher Getzelman, Jacob Meyer, Felix Miller,

Johannes Monbauer, Jacob Kreyder, David Beistel, Jacob
Schaafbahn, Johannes Schwartz.

---

205) Sept. 28, 1753. Ship Two Brothers, Thomas Arnot,
Captain, from Rotterdam, last from Portsmouth.

Sept. 28, 1753. Schiff Two Brothers, Capitain Thomas
Arnot, von Rotterdam über Portsmouth.

Johannes Späth,
Mattheis Dischong,
Wilhelm Dischong,
Frantz Klein,
Conrad Lützing,
Leonhart Lützing,
Johannes Wagner,
Martin Jung,
Johannes Müller,
Debalt Bosseng,*
Peter Stauber,
Johannes Lein,?
Johannes Wirtz,
Joh. Philip Fus,
William Tillboner,*
Johannes Grau,
J. Georg Volck,
J. Joachim Seebert,
J. Adam Kohlman,
Hieronimus Bruner,*
Michael Hotman,
Jacob Hering,
John Friederich Schuy,
Rudolph Zimmerman,
Joh. Jacob Helpfish,*
Johan Henrich Lütsch,
Johann Theis Schütz,
Joh. Henrich Heesman,
Johan Frantz Koch,
Johan Philip Heyman,
Johan Peter Jung,
Johan Matheis Schneider,
Christian Tressenstütt,
Johan Philip Gesseler,
Johan Wilhelm Müller,
Johan Philip Dill,
Johan Adolph Gesseler,
Johann Peter Hahn,
Johan Adam Wirth,
Johann Adam Meyer,
Joh. Gerhard Müller,
Johan Jung Richler,
Johannes Elias Arnoldt,
Johan Adam Pfetzer,
Johannes Schneider,
J. George Winter,*
Johannes Neydig,*
J. Adam Lang,
Heinrich Schmaus,
Conrad Shmaus,*
Johannes Schmaus,
Matthias Nied,
J. Adam Shwartz,*
J. Wilhelm Shütz,*
Johannes Feck,
J. Henry Jäckel,
J. Georg Jäckel,
Israel Wetzfeld,
Johannes Jung,
Joseph Beck,
Conrath Pfillibs,
Johannes Schey,
Jacob Hann,
Johannes Seiser,
Johannes Pauly,
Friederich Kroh,

Joh. Valentin Wieber,
Jacob Kohl,
Johan Kohl,
Friederich Hamman,
Johan Leonhart Müller,
Johan Adam Pabst,
J. George Bechtol,
Johan Peter Koch,
Joh. Nicklaus Lehnes,
Johan Stephan Dieter,
J. Jacob Eisenhauer,
Joh. Wilhelm Hardtstang,
Johan Adam Schmit,
Johann Baltaser Götz,
Johann Adam Götz,

J. Ludwig Shook,*
Johannes Peter Halt,
Johannes Wirthsman,
Johann Philip Schneider,
Johan Georg Bechtoldt,
Johan Wilhelm Schäffer,
Joh. Paulus Shäffer,*
Franciscus Schmidt,
Johan Philip Klein,
Johan Christian Zuprian,
Joh. Henrich Heymann,
Joh. Henrich Sägnisch,
Elias Conrad Stegman,
Johan Georg Seiffert.

206) Sept. 29, 1753. Snow Rowand, Arthur Tran, Captain, from Rotterdam, last from Cowes.

Sept. 29, 1753. Seeschiff Rowand, Capitain Arthur Tran, von Rotterdam über Cowes.

Philippus Schmidt,
Daniel Flender,
Joh. Peter Weyel,*
Johannes Buchner,
Christian Mann,
Jonas Mann,
Ludwig Lupp, a
Johann Georg Starck,
Johann Christian Weinbrenner,
Johan Stephan Klöckner,
Christ. Henrich Greb,
Johan Deis Greb,

Johan Wilhelm Jung,
Johan Peter Meyer,
Joh. Z. Schruntz,
Bernhart Pfeiffer,
Martin Helfeysen,*
Joh. Phil. Siesfass,
Johannes Selbach,
Johan Engelpruck,
Joh. Jacob Hass,
Frantz Zeiller,
Conrad Becker,
Johannes Selbach,*

a Rev. *Ludwig Lupp*, a German Reformed Minister at Lebanon, Pa., from 1786 to 1798. He was born January 7, 1733, and died June 28, 1798. His remains rest in the German Reformed grave yard at Lebanon.—See H. Harbaugh's Lives of German Reformed Ministers.

a Pastor Ludwig Lupp war von 1786 bis 1798 deutsch-reformirter Geistlicher zu Lebanon, Pa. Er war am 7. Jan. 1733 geboren und starb am 28. Juni 1798. Seine Gebeine ruhen im deutsch-reformirten Kirchhofe zu Lebanon.—Siehe Harbach's Lebensbeschreibungen reform. Geistlicher.

G. Peter Bear,*
George Hoover,*
David Giessler,
Jacob Hetering,*
Peter Müller,
Johannes Miller,
Joh. Hen. Brutz,
Johan Hindert,*
Joh. Conrad Gra,
Christian Rübsamen,
Joh. Henry Held,
Johannes Thomas,
Johannes George,
Johannes Freund,
Philip Pool,*
Peter Kolb,
Philip Schuman,
Jacob Shütz,*
Sebastian Weber,
Johannes Keller,
Jacob Böller,*
Theiss Lauer,
Henrich Lauer,
Johan Frantz,
Henry Wastenhaber,*
Johannes Schäffer,
Matthias Schütz,
Martin Diel,
Henry Kämpffer,*
Johannes Kregeloch,
Christian Mann, §
Paulus Crum,
Johan Friederich Schmidt,
Johan Philip Sonner,
Johan Christian Greebel,*
Joh. Wilhelm Böhmer,
Johan Peter Köll,
Joh. Martin Buckner, §
Johan Henrich Buchner,
Johan Theis Erand,
Jost Henrich Meller,

Johan Philip Seye,?
Joh. Heinrich Böhm,
Johan Elias Steneroloh,?
Johan Peter Schlämacher,
Christian Blickensdörffer,
Jost Blickensdörffer,
Joh. Jacob Lingenfelter,
Johan Peter Rach,
Johann Theis Hissgen,
Joh. Gerhart Humbel,*
Johan Henrich Helt,
Johan Engel Thomas,
Joh. Georg Georg,
Joh. Georg Knörtzer,
Johan Christ. Bentz,
Johan Philip Späth,
Joh. Henrich Späth,
Joh. Bastian Heun,
Joh. Henrich Schäffer,
Joh. Gerlach Schäffer,
Wilhelm Becker Grün,
Joh. Henrich Kicherman,
Johan Theis Kicherman,
Joh. Wilhelm Schäffer,
Johan Theis Schmidt,
Joh. Henrich Felger,
Joh. Henrich Strunck,
Johann Peter Leiss,
Johan Theis Rübsamen,
Joh. Christ. Stahl,
Joh. Gerlach Stahl,
Bastian Shneyder,*
Matheus Zimmerman,
Johannes Crum,
Andreas Ecker,
Johannes Creutz,
Henry Panix,*
Hermanus Zimmerman,
John Peter Krammer,*
Johan Engel Braun,
Johan Peter Braun.

27*

207) Oct. 1, 1753. Snow Good Hope, John Trump, Captain, from Hamburg, last from Cowes.

Oct. 1, 1753. Seeschiff Good Hope, Capitain John Trump, von Hamburg über Cowes.

Ulrich Reling,
Peter Knobe,*
H. George Becker,
J. Henry Klapper,
J. Henry Niederhut,*
Andreas Feigner,
Christoph Michael,
Christofel Ohms,*
Christofel Ahllborn,*
J. Henry Nederman,*
Johan Kinerimen,*
Simon Shroder,*
Jeremias Pflug,*
Christopher Pok,*
Elias Au,
J. Henry Worm,
Christian König,
Conrad Hartman,
Christoph Reinman,
Christoph Kneply, §
Simon Eberle,
Jacob Riemann,
Gerdt Hurrelman,
Joh. Peter Pügner,
Carl Ahlborn,

Joh. Hen. Christo Runcker,
Hans Henry Steedeberger,*
J. Henry Selligman,*
Joach Conrad Steinwehn,
Johan Peter Dippel,
H. Andreas Wigman,
Joh. Erich Schneeberg,
Johan Georg Laumann,
Hans Christoph Engel,
Henrich Christoph Diedrich,
Johan Jacob Niecke,
Joh. Henrich Ziegeler,
Joh. Andreas Forster,
J. Christoph Leman,*
Hans Joachim Meissner,
Joh. Gottlieb Wecker,
Joh. Urban Kaulitz,
Joh. Christoph Mohmeyer,
Joh. Theodor Martini,
Justus Carl Wil Martini,
Joh. Wilhelm Röber,
Joh. Christian Bachman,
Jean Jaque Lapierre,
Joh. Andreas Friederichs,
Georg Henrich Doieges.

208) Oct. 2, 1753. Ship Edinburgh, James Lyon, Captain, from Rotterdam, last from Cowes.

Oct. 2, 1753. Schiff Edinburgh, Capitain James Lyon, von Rotterdam über Cowes.

Joh. Engel Jung,
Joh. Conrad Scherer,
Joh. Hen. Knodt,
Friederich Köhler,
Joh. Georg Christoph Hering,
Joh. Henrich Wessing,

Joh. Henrich Otto,
Joh. Philip Schneider,
Friederich Bömer,
Johannes Denig,
Johannes Rudrauf,
Wilhelm Cossler,

Philip Wagner,
Gottfried Krum,*
Andreas Gerlach,
Urban Schäddell,
Johannes Heyl,
Henry Gimper,*
Anthon Keusch,
Christian Dötter,
J. Henry Cronro, §
Anthon Gersterkorn,
Friederich Schrieg,
Christian Jauch,
Jacob Looss,
J. Peter Lehr,
J. Jacob Wiesser,
Joh. Adam Krum,
Michael Hauss,
J. George Rosdorff,
Joh. Wilhelm Buhl,
Joh. Georg Stahl,
J. Dan. Maunshagen,*
Andreas Schnyder,
Johannes Aurandt,
Joh. George Shwartz,*
Johannes Jüngst,
Adam Klöckner,
Christophel Hebener,
Johannes Renschmit,
Daniel Schlappy,
Georg Schäffer,
J. Peter Meyer,*
J. Christian Schmit,*
Michael Tasch,
Anthon Krim,
Johan Schneider,
Johannes Fregele,
J. Peter Kirchhöffer,
J. Wilhelm Wisser,
Joh. Wilhelm Höffer,
Jost Henrich Weyerhaussen,
Joh. Friederich Schall,

Joh. Gottfried Höhle,
Philip Valentin Kurseli,
Joh. Solomon Heim,
Johan Georg Müller,
Johann Peter Baldus,
J. George Friedrich Löser,
Andreas Erdman Leinan,
Johan Wilhelm Æhl,
Joh. Wilhelm Steer,
Johan Conrad Schneider,
Johann Georg Looss,
Johan Jacob Katz,
Johann Daniel Ruppert,
Johann Henrich Kuntz,
Johan Henrich Printz,
Johan Philip Göbel,
Johan Jacob Schweitzer,
Johan Jacob Hoffman,
Johann Georg Schneider,
Joh. Ludwig Schweitzer,
Joh. Baltzer Ducker,
Joh. Gerlach Born Hütter,
Johan Anthonius Hun,
Joh. Friederich Weitzell,
Philip Hen. Arndorff,
Johan Gerlach Klein,
Joh. Gerlach Muttersbach,
Joh. Wilhelm Stump,
Joh. Henrich Steinseiffer,
Joh. Georg Kinsel,
Joh. Conrad Orndorff,
Joh. Wilhelm Wullenweber,
Johan Georg Wäller,
Joh. Wilhelm Weller,
Hieronimus Schneider,
Ernst Ludwig Krauss,
Johan Henrich Stoltz,
Johan Peter Stoltz,
Johan Georg Schneider,
J. Gerlach Wisser,*
F. Conrad Schmit, §

Johannes Müller,
Johannes Gräff,
Johan Peter Orndorff,

Joh. Henrich Jung,
Joh. Jost Schlappig.

---

209) Oct. 3, 1753. Ship Louisa, John Pittcairne, Captain, from Rotterdam, last from Cowes.

Oct. 3, 1753. Schiff Louisa, Capitain John Pittcairne, von Rotterdam über Cowes.

Conrad Kühl,
Balthaser Vorbach,
Ernst Jacoby,
Mathias Becker,
Philip Klein,
Johann Dach,
Johannes Buhlman,
Phillippus Zech,
Johannes Preyss,
Christian Weber,
Andreas Kratz,
Johannes Fuss,
Hans Georg Jansy,*
Christophel Schöpf,
Friederich Heyer,
Conrad Röberling,
Johannes Wärffer,
Joh. Georg Braun,
Stephan Riel,
J. Henry Wemeyer,*
Friederich Dürck,
Johannes Müller,
Philip Lutrich,
Henrich Schmidt,
Herman Emrich,
Johannes Bauman,
Peter Tran,*
Johannes Leipp,
Peter Mauer,
Lothering Richan,
Henry Fleck,
Carl Emrich, §

Jacob Henendorff,
Philip Brendtle,
Benedictus Neidlinger,
Johan Philip Hehnel,
Johan Adam Dach,
Joh. Georg Hemmersbach,
Johan Peter Spielman,
Johan Christian Lauer,
Joh. Wilhelm Rück,
Georg Wilhelm Hard,
Johan Georg Grub,
Johan Peter Stadel,
Johann Philip Innlab,*
Johann Carl Vöttel,
Johann Albert Maurer,
Johan Conrad Strott,
Johann Henrich Schmit,
Johan Philip Hinnlaub,
Georg Adam Mandel,
Johan Christian Mandel,
Johann Jacob Neiman,
Henrich Wilhelm Becker,
Johan Christian Schweiler,
Johan Peter Grub,
Johan Philip Wachs,
Georg L. Gundrum,
Hans Michael Müller,
Hans Cansfluderman,
Joh. Georg Hasselbacher,
Johan Peter Nickel,
Johann Peter Schmick,
Philip Friedrich Warth,

Georg Friederich Hoolböck,
Johan Henrich Seeberger,
Johan Georg Zenlaub,
Johannes Blocher,*
Michael Pflocher,
Andreas Heister,

Achilles Stau,
Carl Veny,*
Joh. Wilhelm Völbel,*
Joseph Geiger,
Friederich Zillow,*
Hans George Priere.*

---

210) Oct. 3, 1753. Ship Eastern Branch, James Nevin, Captain, from Rotterdam, last from Portsmouth.

Oct. 3, 1753. Schiff Eastern Branch, Capittain James Nevin, von Rotterdam über Portsmouth.

Johannes Dutt,
Johan Brey,
J. Martin Fanau,*
Sebastian Stauzer,
Christoph Curfes,
Joh. David Fuss,
Conrad Fausser,
Christ. Mäusfall,
Henrich Leiner,
Jacob Schmidt,
Sebastian Schaber,
Johannes Hopff,
Ulrich Stierlein,
Johannes Löbss,
Jacob Anthoni,
Johannes Lieck,?
Peter Bilhinger,
Jacob Schneider,
Johannes Kirme,*
Johan Christian,
Ludwig Christian,§
Gottlieb Müschlitz,
Matheis Stoll,
Friederich Schäffer,
Peter Klees,
Tobias Wandel,
Christoph Wölffe,
Wilhelm Decker,
Daniel Parisien,

Friederich Glasser,
Johannes Glasser,
Adam Dornberger,
Jacob Weininger,
Henrich Stollzol,
Johan Michael Röller,
Johan Friederich Bleich,
Johan Martin Feyl,
Joh. Andreas Lohrman sen.,
Joh. Andreas Lohrman,
Johan Martin Kielman,
Hans Ulrich Stohonen,
Hans Michel Ketterer,
Georg Wilhelm Schlatterer,
Christoph Henrich Spiegel,
Michel Ludwig Feitter,
Georg Philip Feuerstein,
Johan Michel Schöneck,
Hans Georg Dehts,
Johann Caspar Hopff,
Joh. Henrich Krauss,
Johan Georg Förg,
Johan Jacob Reneb,
Joh. Philip Vogelgesang,
Johan Georg Beck,
Hans Philip Klein,
Johan Lorentz Siegrist,
Georg Friederich Taxis,
Michael Hörmann,

Johann Michael Brodbeck,
Georg Eysemann,
Johann Ludwig Hellers,
Johannes Dörflinger,
Johan Nicklaus Zeitz,
Hans Georg Heintzelman,
Philip Daniel Gross,
Johannes Ronner,
Hans Georg Schenck,
Joseph Haanelam,*
Casper Kreiter,*
Michael Basseler,
Conrad Hadt,

Andreas Schnabel,
Michael Vogel,*
Andreas Deg,
Joseph Crisby,*
Jost Peter,
Johan Peter Lorie,
Friederich Deeg,
Jacob Friederich Schenck,
Jacob Schmertzka,
Johan Conrad Giessler,
Hans Georg Michael,§
Johan Conrad Ludwig,
Henrich Friederich.

211) Nov. 19, 1753. Ship Friendship, James Seix, Master, from Hamburg, last from Cowes.

Nov. 19, 1753. Schiff Friendship, Capitain James Seix, von Hamburg über Cowes.

Johann Petz,
Gottfried Nebe,
Johan Tabel,*
George Kneeling,*
Christoph Wächter,
Valentin Reyling,
Johan Volks,
Christophel Auhagen,
Gottfried Förster,*
Gottfried Leman,*
Jacob Bramer,
Andreas Blötz,
Conrad Hage,
Andreas Singneitz,
H. Ulrich Rossel,
Christoph Matthesen,
Joachim Dietrich Mohl,
Adam Stein,
Andreas Gerlach,
Lorentz Rüschle,
Johan Lorentz Vogel,

Joh. Heinrich Schneider,
Joh. Fred. Franciscus Sorsini,
Christ. Henrich Lutterman,
Joh. Fried. Landgraff,
Joh. Henrich Reventlau,
F. Michel Lorentz,
Conrad Henrich Törentz,
Johan Andreas Klein,
Johan Georg Görtller,
Johann Christian Zeise,
Johan Peter Schmit,*
Henry Jacob Noll,
Joh. Henrich Comülder,
Joh. Henrich Bauermeister,
Hen. Christoph Delikamp,
Johan Friederich Pelss,
Andreas Henrich Lanneger,
Johan Hartman Emmel,
Joh. Henrich Sammann,
Joh. Henrich Paffland.

☞ Sworn sick on board whose names are not in the List.

☞ Als krank an Borb beeidigt, beren Namen aber nicht auf ber Liste sind.

---

212) Sept. 14, 1754. Ship Nancy,——Ewing, Captain, from Rotterdam, last from Cowes.—Inhabitants from Lorraine. †

Sept. 14, 1754. Schiff Nancy, Capitain Ewing, von Rotter= bam über Cowes.—Einwohner von Lothringen. †

Abram Huguelet,
Antoni Hogar,
Charles Huguelet,
Jeania Quepic,
Johannes Adolphf,
Peter Rämmy,*
Simon Keppler,
Johannes Seyser,
Friederich Kramer,
Abram Joray,
Johannes Bär,*
Abraham Gobat,
Frederick Showay,*
Peter Smith,*
Carl Steiss,*
Thomas Bauer,
Adam Maine,
Michel Haag,
Christian Cölly,
Christoffel Welss,
Jacob Müller,
Johannes Ull,
Pierre Vautie,
Franc La Mero,

Pierre Griene,
Abram Duille,
Georg Got,
Pierre Dechin,
Philip Hasslinger,
Philip Spannseiler,
Wilhelm Bahr,*
Frantz Bahr,*
Christian Böss,
Caspar Riegel,*
Jean Mathiat,
Georg Dessloch,
Alexandre Guille,
Jacob Bauer,
Jacob Brautwald,
Joh. Georg Steubesant,
Mattheus Schendt,
Nicklaus Schwartz,
Johan Jacob Völl,
Joh. Daniel Meyländer,
Adam Le Roy,
Abram Le Roy,
Ludwig Keiner,
Abram De Die,

---

† *Lorraine*, an old province in the North-East of France, and since the treaty of peace, at Frankfort, 1871, again became attached to Germany In ancient times this name was applied to the countries of Germany and the Netherlands, northward to the mouth of the Rhine.—(*Ed.*)

† Lothringen, eine alte beutsche Provinz, norböstlich von Frankreich ge= legen unb seit bem Frankfurter Frieben 1871 wieber mit Deutschland ver= bunben. In alter Zeit wurbe bieser Name ben Ländern Deutschland's unb ber Nieberlanbe beigelegt, welche nörblich von ber Münbung bes Rheins lagen.—(Herausgeber.)

Albert Otto Steg,
Johan Peter Wedel,
Johan Henrich Stentz,
Christoph Scharlle,*
Hans Michael Conradt,
Johann Adam Wagner,
Henrich Eisenhuth,
Michael Klenck,
Joh. Daniel Zimer,*
Joh. Conrad Zäumer,
Johan Jacob Kuntzmann,
Johan Dietrich Gompff,
Johan Jost Lap,
Jean Pierre Monin sen.,
Jean Pierre Monin,
Johan Jacob Willer,*
Johan Nickel Bauer,
Jaque Barberat,
David Marchand,

Jean Jaque Allemand,
Johan Henrich Häusser,
Michel Amacher,
Valentin Heidenberg,
Jean Christoph Pechin,
Joh. Gottfried Herring,*
Alphonse Louis Willemin,
Abram Rathend,
Frantz Philip Weis,
J. N. Pechin,
Daniel Fischer,
Gabriel Seger,
Jean Periter,*
Johannes Schelling,
David Putner,*
Jean Periter jr.,*
Johan Thomas Bernhard,
John Pierre Bellie,*
Johannes Shullobak.*

213) Sept. 14, 1754. Ship Barclay, John Brown, Captain, from Rotterdam, last from Cowes.—Inhabitants from Alsace and Lorraine.

Sept. 14, 1754. Schiff Barclay, Capitain John Brown, von Rotterdam über Cowes.—Einwohner von Elsaß und Lothringen.

Georg Voltz,
Abram Duton,*
Nicklaus Bauer,*
Johannes Craus,
Daniel Weiss,
Ludwig Haas,
Nicklas Ash,*
Georg Schmit,*
David Pfeller,
G. Peter Lange,*
Jacob Traub,
Michael Rüeb,
Jacob Kräber,
Friederich Schenck,
Tobias Reisener,

Joseph Miller,*
H. Peter Engels,*
Ludwig Schuster,
Johannes Karch,*
Matheus Reuchler,*
Andreas Kreissel,
Martin Hechler,*
Michel Eissge,
Bastian Rust,*
Joseph Sudtner,
Nicklaus Ehrhardt,
Johannes Köhler,
Michael Hauch,
Ludwig Stanger,
Georg Näwiss,*

Johannes Jüngst,
Jacob Geissler,
Johan Conrath Mock,
George Michael Fautzer,*
John Adam Fass,*
Michael Hostman,
Nicolus Steinman,*
Jean Pierre Rottei,
Joh. Adam Traub,*
Georg Peter Bock,
Christoph Inpierman,
Bernhard Winder,
Valentin Zaneichel,*
H. George Hechler,
Samuel Tallebach,*
H. Michael Unangst,*
Lorentz Schönman,*
Joh. Friederich Haller,*
Wilhelm Jacob Fack,*
Philipp Kattenmann,
Bernhart Mirbach,
Christian Hoffbauer,
Johan Carl Greiss,*
Frantz Ludwig Uehle,
Georg Waffunong,*
Johann Adam Dörr,
Johannes Schnarrenberger,
H. Georg Haffner,
Hans Georg Stauch,
Michael Kornwalther,
Bernhart Ochsenbacher,
Hans Michael Berr,
Johan Martin Unangst,
Johan Conrad Ber,
Johannes Bahs,
Andreas Baum,
Gottlieb Nagel,
Matheis Schreiner,
Johan Backofen,
Johan Schranck,

Caspar Ganz,
Michael Knecht,
Jacob Böckhle,
Martin Schranck,
Peter Thum,
Frantz Rotham,*
Matheas Wagner,*
Han Nickel Künel,
Otto Bürgestrass,
Michael Stauch jr.,
Jacob Eichely,
Philip Hentzer,
Wilhelm Zetzel,
Bernhart Meyer,
Christoph Gans,
Matheus Alt,
Andreas Stauch,
Bernhart Rebhuhn,
Hans Georg Feyl,
Jacob Rathacker,
Joh. Jacob Strohmenger,
Helfrich Knieriemen,
J. Michael Seiffer,
Christoph Laichinger,
Dewald Braunholtz,
Hans Georg Fuchs,
Johannes Schuman,
Ludwig Bernh. Zwissler,
Joh. Christian Jauss,
Joh. Nicklaus Martin,
Sebastian Muschler,
Johan Jacob Rauch,
Michael Stauch sen.,
Philip Jacob Griedler,
Mattheus Fautz, §
Michael Œrthler,
Hans Michael Bleich,
Johan Jacob Seitz,
Johannes Kleinfeld.

214) Sept. 25, 1754. Ship Adventure, Joseph Jackson, Captain, from Hamburg, last from Plymouth.—Inhabitants from Franconia. † — 245 passengers.

Sept. 25, 1754. Schiff Adventure, Capitain Joseph Jackson, von Hamburg über Plymouth.—Einwohner von Franken. † — 245 Reisende.

Johann Hartmann,
Christian Schäffer, §
Johan Georg Ilger,
Andreas Weiss,
Johannes Weiss,
Johannes Andriola,
Frantz Hautuss,
Christian Letzbeyer,*
Johannes Vell,
Joh. Andreas Hoffner,
Joh. Adam Kohlass,
John George Shmit,*
Hans Peter Rehvan,*
Johan Philip Wagner,
Johannes Andriola sen.,
Johan Jacob Weinman,
Johan Adam Rollbach,
Joh. Conrad Spongenberg,
Johannes Fritz,
Johannes Keim,
Balthaser Raab,
Johannes Reidiger,
Joseph Gasser,
Philip Michael,
J. Zacharias Stökel,
Herman Massemer,
Anthon Lembach,*
Christian Nehrlich,
Henrich Urich,

George Köhle,
J. Jacob Cornelius,
Johannes Liebrich,
Johannes Didrich,
Joh. Jost Will,
Joh. Nickel Bech,
Caspar Schreiber,
Johannes Ditmar,
Philip Thiringer,*
Joh. Georg Shmit,*
Johannes Mardersteck,
Christian Funck,
Johan Eberth,
Adolph Urbach,
J. Friederich Ebnie,*
Georg Steinweg,
Johannes Rütiger,
Georg Steinweg jr.,
Christian Gasser,
Johan August Straube,
Johan Georg Gütsell,
Joh. Christoph Diemer,
Joh. Dietrich Baltdauss,
Johan Christian Eser,
Joh. Henrich Neumann,
Joh. Michael Weiss,
Joh. Henrich Kohrman,
Johan Georg Jung,
Joh. Daniel Franck,

† *Franconia*, an old duchy, afterwards a circle of the Germanic Empire, between Upper Saxony and Lower Rhine, Swabia, &c.—(*Editor.*)

† Franken ist ein altes Herzogthum und war nachher ein Kreis des deutschen Reiches. Es liegt zwischen Obersachsen, dem unteren Rhein, Schwaben u. s. w.—(Herausgeber.)

J. Philip Tamhöffer,
Joh. Jacob Renneck,
Joh. Wilhelm Schaf,?
Joh. Gottfried Nagel,
    Minist. Candit. a
Johann Jost Heck,
Johan Jacob Rühlein,
Joh. Martin Gardert,
Joh. Frid. Ermetraud,
Joh. Martin Matterstek,*

Joh. Nicklaus Handt,
Joh. Georg Rausch,
Joh. Matthias Müller,
Joh. Henrich Ruppel,
Joh. Christoph Müller,
Johan Conrath Con,?
Joh. Leonard Rohrmann,
Math. Andonius Rütiger,
Nicklaus Gorshbotte.*

215) Sept. 30, 1754. Ship Richard and Mary, John Moore, Master, from Rotterdam, last from Cowes.—Inhabitants from the dukedom of Wirtemberg,—six Roman Catholics.—230 passengers.

Sept. 30, 1754. Schiff Richard und Mary, Capitain John Moore, von Rotterdam über Cowes.—Einwohner vom Herzogthum Württemberg,—sechs Römisch-Katholische.—230 Reisende.

Michael Fischer,
Conrad Fischer,
Caspar Kust,
Hans Casper Geyer,
Michael Staiger,
Johannes Schnerenberger,
Andreas Zinckh,
Jacob Zinckh,
Christoph Zinckh,
Gottlieb Tuche,?
Jacob Saltzer,
David Kohl,
Michel Wolff,
Jacob Adam,
Jacob Wolff,
Ludwig Strobel,
Johannes Bether,
Adam Knoblig,*

George Heisel,
Georg Heisel jr.,
Martin Schmidt,
Henrich Kost,
Jacob Blessing,
Friederich Deiler,
Friederich Burr,*
Jacob Marier,
Johannes Wetzel,
Casper Hincke,
Jacob Steudtle,
Jacob Busch,
Wolfgang Ulmer,
David Wolff,
Christoph Walters,
Jacob Zuch,
Jacob Ramsberger,
Christian Zinck,

a Joh. Gottfried Nagel is written in a very bold *Latin script.*—(*Ed.*)

a Joh. Gottfried Nagel ist in sehr deutlicher lateinischer Schrift geschrieben.—(Herausgeber.)

Michael Wolff,
Johannes Hohl,
Georg Hohl,
Johannes Lauer,
Georg Grau,
Daniel Stumpp,
Johannes Schlotz,
Valentin Leman,*
Herman Fonnedus,
Henrich Kägele,?
Johannes Schauer,
Christian Kramer,
Jacob Schnerenberger,
Johannes Gürthner,
Michael Libelt,
Hans Martin Müller,
Johan Michael Strobel,
Michael Welthe,
Jacob Welthe,
Ludwig Müssi,
Johannes Schiessle,
Hans Georg Bether,
Hans Georg Welte,
Hans Georg Meyer,*
Jacob Adam Wendel,
Michael Herman,
Christoph Fleisser,

Georg Fried. Dockesladel,?
Johannes Machler,
Hans Martin Schäffer,
Johan Georg Busch,
Jean Jac. Foulquier,
Joh. Michael Mössinger,
Daniel Blumenschein,
Ludwig Zimmermann,
Anthonius Schmidt,
Joseph Feinrür,
Joh. Christoph Beyrle,
Mattheis Süss,
Hans Georg Ramsberger,
Wolfgang Wolff,
Georg Friederich Dietz,
Johan Caspar Dietz,
Georg Adam Engell,
Hans Georg Meyer,*
John Martin Alisch,
Hans Georg Heidle sen.,
Hans Georg Heidle,
Hans Georg Rössel,
Hans Friedrich Klinger,
Georg Ludwig Kraft,
Ludwig Wilhelm Heller,
Friederich Reninger,
Johannes Bernhard.

216) Sept. 30, 1754. Ship Brothers, William Muir, Captain, from Rotterdam, last from Cowes.—Inhabitants from the Palatinate and Mentz,—seven Roman Catholics, twenty-seven Mennonites.—251 passengers.

Sept. 30, 1754. Schiff Brothers, Capitain William Muir, von Rotterdam über Cowes.—Einwohner der Pfalz und von Mainz,—sieben Römisch-Katholische, sieben und zwanzig Mennoniten.—251 Passagiere.

Joh. Georg Kol,
Johannes Miller,*
Joh. Peter Hahn,
Johannes Aller,

Conrad Wagner,
Daniel Sander,
Conrad Mercky,
Johannes Klein,

Henry Weidman,
Jacob Bernhard,
Wilhelm Staut,*
Joh. Ansthoch,
J. Georg Lucker,
Carl Heinrich,
Jacob Kauffman,
Johannes Schadel,
Michael Räsch,
Jacob Huber,
Henrich Graff,
Valentin Noldt,
Jacob Shable,*
Johannes Küny,
Johannes Forrer,
Jacob Brubacher,
Johannes Schöri,
Peter Weitzel,
Anthony Weitzel,
Stephan Weber,
Frantz Burghart,
Joseph Zieff,
Jacob Pfister,
Daniel Ott,
Valentin Urlettig,
Hans Georg Krauss,
Frederick Andreas,
David Hemgerberer,
Christophel Volckrath,
Johannes Bartel Misihni,
Johan Georg Humbert,
Philip Jacob Späth,
Georg Christoph Dauber,
Johan Conrad Schmidt,
Johan Diehl Kleinman,
Johan Balthas Schmidt,
Johann Tiel Werss,
Johann Peters Werss,
Hans Jacob Geist,
Johann Georg Spies,
Johan Nicolaus Stimmel,

Joh. Lud. Ernst Schiller,
Abraham Mellinger,
Johannes Herschberger,
Johannes Eicher,
Georg Michael Schultz,
Abraham Hackman,
Joh. Jacob Brubacher,
Michael Burghart,
Georg Ludwig Meittinger.
Johan Christian Trump,
Hans Georg Zieff,*
Friederich Beher,
Augustus Schaad,
Heinrich Zumbrun,
Christian Wolst,*
Johannes Ritschart,
Hans Müldaler,
Joh. Wolfgang Möhring,
Balthas Reiner,
Christian Eicher,
Abraham Bleistein,
Johann Georg Diemes,
Johan Valentin Webel,
Hans Jacob Schaffner,
Joh. Christian Wittmer,
Joseph Lemann,
Jacob Dettwiller,
Martin Herman,
Adam Kuntzel,
Philip Metzger,
Johannes Frey,
Jacob Becker,
Peter Frey,
Wendel Gilbert,
Johannes Seithss,
Philip As,
Caspar Knag,
Johan Jacob Wittmer,
Christian Huber,
Johannes Müller,
Abraham Strickler,

28*

Oswald Andreas,
Leonhart Krumbein,
Johann Georg Becker,
Hans Mich. Koppenhäffer,

Wilhelm Eschelman,
Henrich Heistandt,
Joseph Bubickofer,
Johannes Kantz.

---

217) Sept. 30, 1754. Ship Edinburgh, James Russel, Master, from Rotterdam, last from Cowes.—Inhabitants from the Palatinate and Wirtemberg,—five Roman Catholics, and one Mennonite.

Sept. 30, 1754. Schiff Edinburgh, Capitain James Ruffel, von Rotterdam über Cowes.—Einwohner der Pfalz und Württemberg's,—fünf Römisch-Katholische und ein Mennonite.

Jacob Schlotter,
Henrich Weil,
Herman Gerlach,
Georg Hilt,
Johannes Hirsch,
Philippus Spetzius,
Christophel Gühtt,
Melchior Schimpf,
Paulus Löshorn,
Herman Summer,*
George Wessig,*
Anthon Petry,
Andreas Wegel,
Ludwig Rahm,
Casper Zahn,
Andreas Dein,
Philip Besteres,
Johannes Bott,
Johannes Lincker,
Jacob Ludwig,
Andreas Hübner,
Rudolph Drack,
George Lohr,
Friederich Wilhelm Frich,
Georg Eberhart Mühl,
Johan Henrich Pfeiffer,
Johan Conrad Schäppler,
Johan Henrich Blecker,

Johan Georg Wilhelmi,
Johan Peter Walschner,
Johannes Matthäus,
Bernhard Matthäus jr.,
Bernhard Matthäus,
Georg Henry Rahm,
Conrad Wüchart,
Johannes Ludwig,
Conrad Ludwig,*
J. Jost Bingeman,
Friederich Schimpf,
Daniel Vetzberger,
Heinrich Walther,
J. Henry Langsdorff,
Engelhard Ludwig,
Ludwig Winckler,
Joh. Jacob Schmess,
Balthaser Faulstick,
Casper Erb,
Johannes Haubt,
Peter Hecht,
Conrad Lohr,
Philip Ludwig,
Johannes Huber,
Conrad Bauer,
Conrath Enders,
Johannes Weber,
Georg Kopp,

Adam Strehm,
Valtin Beltzer,
Henrich Huey,
Casper Weber,
Jacob Kern,
Matheus Kern,
Michael Wentz,
Christoph Essig,
Peter Paul,
Adam Maurer,
Johann Henle,
Michael Georg,
Conrad Grim,
Johannes Grim,
Conrad Philips,
Georg Grim,
Peter Kiel,
Conrad Mieser,
Werner Tickel,
Peter Tickel,
Hans Deme,
Jacob Giebel,
Georg Diel,
Ernst Menge,
Peter Pigger,*
Reinhart Weiss,
Conrad Geysel,*
Herman Geysel,*
George Sorge,
Jacob Hoffman,
George Börstler,
Jacob Fondenie,
Samuel Haubt,
Joh. Nickel Haubt,
Jacob Hammerstein,
Valentin Ulrich,
Eberhard Diehl,
Henrich Wenckler,
Henrich Gebhart,
Peter Weissman,
Joh. Daniel Krug,

Adam Böchteldt,
Joh. Henrich Strehm,
Heinrich Hock,
Anthoni Hecht,
Johan Georg Weitzell,
Christoph Rebele,
Georg Henrich Haas,
Anthon Merckell,
Johann Chrunz,?
Joh. Conrad Schneider,
Andreas Krauthamel,*
Joh. Sebastian Fritz,
Joh. Dan. Langsdorff,
Joh. Conrad Langsdorff,
Friederich Hildebrand,
Herman Matheus,
Johannes Bender,
Joh. Conrad Bender,
Conrad Schneider,
Johannes Rupp,
Johannes Kemmerer,?
Heinrich Lupp,
Peter Derdler,
Johannes Menge,
Lorentz Albahn,
Gerhardt Allbahn,
Jacob Hellebrich,
Christoph Hellebrich,
Johannes Geisel,
Hans Conrad Diehl,
Frank Baltzer Schalter,
Johannes Knaab,
Joseph Nadtheimer,
Michael Künstler,
Georg Renner,
Jacob Renner,
Henrich Herter,
Johannes Becker,
Casper Becker,
Henry Stecker,
Jacob Renner jr.,

Hans Michael Esper,*
Georg Gottfried Völcker,
Christian Merckell,

Johannes Schmeh,
Hans Georg Kroh.*

Sick—Philip Sommer, Philip Riess, Philip Tauberman, Georg Metzger, Jacob Rehble, Johannes Kopping, Henrich Peterson, Casper Ziegler, Georg Holl, Mathias Ludwig.

---

218) Sept. 30, 1754. Ship Neptune, —— Ware, Captain, from Rotterdam, last from Cowes.—Inhabitants from Darmstadt and Zweibrücken,—four Roman Catholics.

Sept. 30, 1754. Schiff Neptune, Capitain Ware, von Rotterdam über Cowes. —Bewohner von Darmstadt und Zweibrücken,—vier Römisch-Katholische.

George Meyer,*
Jacob Bersding,
Mathias Heiner,
Andreas Bingel,
Gottfried Gebhard,
Georg Boltz,
Johannes Rebe,
Friedrich Schneider,
Georg Hoffman,
Daniel Stegner,
Johannes Hoch,
Henry Klein,
Philip Wilt,
V. Brücker,
Jacob Weynant,
Friederich Preis,*
Jacob Weynant jr.,
Johannes Schober,
Phillippus Frey,
Christian Rietz,
Philip Wild,
Georg Hechler,
Benedictus Forster,*
Henry Schäffer,
Valentin Dalick,
Christoph Speck,
Joh. Georg Decher,

Geo. Mich. Vitzthum,
Georg Michel Löhr,
Joh. Henrich Brumbach,
Joh. Henrich Kurcht,
Joh. Adam Michael,
Johann Peter Decher,
Johannes Schuman,
Joh. Georg Traxel,
Joh. Thomas Bisshantz,
Georg Jacob Haussman,
Johann Carl Hermsdorff,
Hans Adam Beckenhaub,
Johan Bernhard Meck,
Johan Adam Edelman,
Joh. Nicklaus Hauer,
Phil. Friedrich Wünger,
Hans Adam Bleier,
Joh. Paul Gemberling,
Hans Nickel Ensminger,
Joh. Carl Gemberling,
Aug. Sigfried Eichler,
Eberhart Kriechbaum,
Philip Jacob Fösig,
Joh. Henrich Schneider,
J. Adam Angold,
Philip Dietrich,
Peter Rubel,

Conrad Wagner,
Valentin Clementz,
Christian Hoch,
Heinrich Cappis,
Johannes Böckel,
Jeremias Herbel,*
George Weyman,
Jacob Graulich,
Henry Shneyder,*
Christian Bauer,
Peter Stötzel,
Michael Miller,*
Friederich Betz,
Christian Andreas,
Henrich Holtzhausser,
Friederich Betz,
Conrath Nie,
Henrich Haun,
Johannes Schmitt,
Johannes Lentz,
Frederick Brand,
Andreas Riehl,
Jacob Becker,
Jacob Schoff,
Peter Step,*
Ludwig Herring,
Daniel Schrein,
Conradt Wirl,
Reinhart Stein,
David Miller,*
Peter Shamar,*
Johannes Keyser,
Wilhelm Grauss,
Johannes Völck,
Henry Hain,*
Burchart Shneyder,*
Philip Lang,
Peter Hilliger,
Arnold Becker,
Philip Becker,
Georg Reiger,
J. Henry Shneider,*

Joh. Christian Wissbach,
Joh. Georg Grundloch,
J. Jost Stuberling,*
Johannes Kleinbehl,
Johan Philip Nold,
Joh. Philip Kölb,
Joh. Bernhart Wolff,
Joh. Philip Bresel,
Joh. Georg Mentz,
J. Adam Thomas,
J. Peter Schrot,
Daniel Hoffman,
Johannes Bartenbach,
Balthaser Bergmann,
Joh. Michael Schrot,
J. Jacob Zimmerman,
G. Michael Andreas,
Johan Henrich Hauff,
Abraham Holtzhausser,
Adam Höllerman,
Johannes Keller,
Johan Peter Haun,
Johan Christian Haun,
Joh. Nicklaus Eitenmüller,
Johannes Herman,
Joh. Peter Scheuerman,
Reinhold Scheretz,
Joh. Conrad Meiger,
Joh. Georg Kribel,
Joh. Philip Dietz,
J. Jacob Dorsham,*
Johann Georg Gack,
Valentin Gösper,
John William Kurtz,
Johan Peter Denger,
Ludwig Gach,
Martin Neimiger,
Joh. Henrich Grantz,
Johan Michael Rapp,
Johannes Krayly,*
Johan Just Gack,
Conrad Scherrer.

219) Oct. 1, 1754. Ship Phœnix, John Spurrier, Captain, from Rotterdam, last from Cowes.—Inhabitants from Franconia, the Palatinate and Zweibrücken,—seventeen Roman Catholics, twenty-five Mennonites.—554 passengers.

Oct. 1, 1754. Schiff Phönir, Capitain John Spurrier, von Rotterdam über Cowes.—Einwohner Franken's, der Pfalz und Zweibrücken's,—siebenzehn Römisch-Katholische, fünf und zwanzig Mennoniten.—554 Passagiere.

Johannes Jung,
Jacob Schneider,
Ludwig Göttgen,
Abraham Stein,
Peter Streier,
Peter Henrichs,
Philip Wesger,
Hans Reisch,
Ulrich Fesel,
Johannes Alberth,
Johannes Gebhart,
Johannes Sauer,
Johannes Andreas,
Peter Müller,
Lorentz Alberth,
Daniel Doss,?
Hans Kisecker,
Johannes Beck,
Andreas Hath,
Andreas Fertig,
Johannes Hilbert,
Johannes Schäffer,
Lenhardt Ott,
Henrich Ott,
Adam Gieg,
Michael Bertrie,
Matheus Stumpf,
Adam Miller,*
Georg Schäffer,
Peter Schäffer,
Adam Dihm,
Peter Heiges,
Heinrich Dann,

Caspar Jost,
Andreas Schmidt,
Andreas Gerberich,
Valtin Hörner,
Carl Henrich Werckhäusser,
Johan Nickel Dibs,
Johannes Henrichs,
Jost Schönauer,
Michael Fletter,
Lorentz Mangel,
Burckhardt Küch,
Marcus Weidinger,
Frantz Weidinger,
Hieronimus Grünewald,
Hans Adam Sauer,
Hans Michael Sauer,
J. Michael Teubel,*
J. George Ruttenwalder,*
Joh. Lenhart Binzel,
Joh. Bernhard Bob,
John Georg Bob,
J. Henry Unckelbach,*
Christoffel Schum,
Andreas Schwartz,
G. Philip Epsenhaar,
Hieronimus Gieg,
Jean Jaque Aiquel,
Jean Pierre Zoisin,
Johannes Hartman,
Nicolaus Bindder,
Casper Oberdorff,
Hans Senffbeber,
Andreas Brüschlein,

Thomas Dihm,
Hans Adam Dihm,
Thomas Biemmer,
Melchior Weppert,
Johan Georg Katz,
Andreas Cunckel,
Peter Cunckel,
Joh. Heinrich Müller,
Martin Sentiner,
Johannes Gabel,
Heinrich Haag,
Michael Seitner,
Dietrich Gerhart,
Balthas Holl,
Lorentz Rütes,
Matheis Reinhart,
Conrad Kern,
Lorentz Cramer,
Johannes Hertz,
Martin Shreyer,*
Valentin Keyser,
Peter Thomass,
Ludwig Cuntz,
Caspar Haas,
Michael Krühl,
Hartman Haas,
Matheas Pop,
Andreas Ferdig,
Johannes Geyman,
Simon Bechler,*
Johannes Beyl,*
Andreas Grub,*
Philip Wagner,
Jacob Fries,
Frederick Christian,
Daniel Ditloh,
Peter Guth,
Ludwig Schott,
Peter Ney,
Georg Rau,
Dietrich Weirig,

Wilhelm Weiss,
Peter Rohrbach,
Wilhelm Alberth,
Andreas Hüter,
Wendel Kremer,
Daniel Schmidt,
Johannes Schmidt,
Nickel Neuman,
Reinhart Wolff,
Nicklaus Schindtelman,
Joh. Philip Schindtelman,
Balthaser Rabanus,
Abraham le Roy,
Baltzer Schneider,
Lorentz Sandmann,
Henrich Messerschmidt,
Joh. Nicklaus Armhiener,
Georg Philip Diehl,
Johann Helffer Cramer,
Johan Peter Fischer,
Bernhart Thomass,
Wilhelm Metzger,
Johan Jacob Helder,
J. Nicklas Gerhart,
Philip Adam Paulus,
Jacob Schneider,
Philipp Schuch,
Johannes Schneider,
Hen. August Grimler,
Joseph Reinhard,
Jacob Bernhart,
J. Wilhelm Zwib,*
Johann Jacob Angst,
Phil. Friederich Schäffer,
Bernhart Franckfürter,
Nicklas Lehmer,
Joh. Henrich Sackss,
Johann Lehmer,
Hans Peter Schott,
Johannes Kauffman jr.,
Johannes Kauffman,

Abraham Edinger,
Adam Heinbach,
Johan Georg Gerlach,
Thomas Hunsicker,
Daniel Hunsicker,
Joh. Adam Batziuss,
Joh. Daniel Pfeil,
Joh. Albrecht Stimmel,
Johan Peter Stimmel,
Michael Dietrich,
Jacob Herman,
Peter Dörrnis,*
Jacob Miller,*
Adam Schmit,*
Henry Shedle,*
Henry Hather,*
Peter Biehl,
Daniel Biehl,
Georg Friess,
Philip Hess,?
Adam Müller,
Christian Koch,
Johannes Zinn,
Ludwig Wird,*
Conrad Dewa,*
Friederich Miller,*
Johannes Veith,
Peter Dick,
Nicklas Paul,
Elias Jentes,*
Henry Gielman,*
Daniel Führer,
Peter Æshelman,*
Hans Jantz,
Joseph Wänger,
Ulrich Engel,
Frantz Zechler,
Ulrich Richty,
Hans Schwartz,
Hans Schütz,*
Christoph Pantzly,*

Peter Balzey,
Christoph Widerich,*
Peter Schwartz,
Christian Schwartz,
Nicklaus Moser,
Georg Hartwieg,
Lorentz Enders,
Christoffel Müller,
Friederich Herman,
Johan Georg Tinius,
Joh. Henrich Schmitt,
David Schröder,
Jacob Rathebach,
J. Nicklas Lorentz,
Gerhart Martins,
Johann Michael Sauer,
Georg Magnus Conrad,
Wendel Wendeling,
J. Lenhart Burchart,
Matthias Müller,
Jacob Theissinger,
Christian Brengel,
Jacob Brengel,
Jacob Hussing,*
Christian Conrad,
Wilhelm Becker,
Christian Brächtbül,
Christian Führer,
Nicklaus Schantz,
Hans Æschliman,
Jost Neuenschwander,
Hans Uelireist,
Ulrich Burckhalter,
Hans Jacob Moser,
Hans Burckhalter,
Christian Burckhalter,
Sebastian Neuenschwander,
Ulerich Newcomer,*
Christian Geimmer,
Christian Geimmer jr.,
Abraham Brechbühler,

Christian Newcomer,*
Christian Helhoff,*

Bartholomais Beringer.

---

220) Oct. 16, 1754. Ship Peggy, James Abercrombie, Captain, from Rotterdam, last from Cowes.—Inhabitants from the Palatinate and Wirtemberg,—ten Roman Catholics.

Oct. 16, 1754. Schiff Peggy, Capitain James Abercrombie, von Rotterdam über Cowes.—Einwohner der Pfalz und Würtemberg's,—zehn Römisch-Katholische.

Marcus Weckfort,
Henrich Hust,
Frantz Stichling,
Wendel Warner,
Ferdinand Frantz,
Jacob Freyberger,
Peter Gebel,
Andreas Bonjour,
Jacob Shutt,*
Georg Köhl,
Henry Rubrecht,
Bernhart Egel,
Jacob Frey,
Abraham Trestel,
Peter Wudo,
Johannes Luppoldt,
Hans Luppoldt,
Matheus Zenaldt,
Friederich Koch,
Johannes Hässer,
Matthäus Die,
Friederich Hausehl,
Andreas Heckenleib,
Michael Koster,
Johann Daniel,
Johannes Hummel,
Joseph Boger,
John Shuster,*
Stephan Kraus,
Johannes Wersum,
Martin Haas,
Johannes Cläss,
Michael Krebs,
Johannes Ricker,
Jacob Thum,
Hans Glee,?
Johannes Meyer,
Johannes Meyer,
Michael Klein,
Hans Schüle,
Michael Köller,
John Carl Krumholtz,
Antony Kettinger,
Balthasar Wisser,*
Christ. Henrich Fiedler,
Georg Adam Dürstler,
Hans Michael Shmit,*
Hans Philip Flachs,
Jacob Friederich Mayer,
Johan Valentin Meyer,*
Daniel Hingerer,
Hans Georg Kraus,
Georg Schweiger,
Michael Schenck,
H. George West,*
Hans Martin Tram,
Hans Georg Tram,
Ludw. Fried. Freisinger,
Hans Georg Armbrüster,
Joh. Adam Schnelleberger,
Jacob Hikenleibly,*
Matthias Wassermann,

29

Hans Georg Zinn,
Jacob Henrich Pluhan,
Georg Henrich Bauer,
J. Johannes Herrmann,
Johan Friederich Linck,
Hans Michael Dies,
Joh. Conrad Möschler,
H. Michael Hüpbisch,
John George Braucher,
Henrich Ludwig Wörn,
Hans Georg Rätze,
Johannes Schumacher,
Johannes Biecheler,
Michael Wuster,
Johannes Walckher,
Lorentz Martin Scherer,?
Michael Rossnagel,

Christian Reck sen.,
Georg Nickel Reck,
Christian Reck jr.,
Hans Meyer,*
Martin Marckel,*
Johannes Vaubel,*
Johannes Butz,
Wilhelm Reichly,*
Adam Grund,*
Christoph Gress,
Johan Adam Pfisterer,
Georg Adam Grombeer,
Johann Peter Schlemb,
Johann Georg Kress,
Hans Georg Schiettinger,
Georg Peter Kochendörffer,
Jacob Andreas Sprecher.

Sick—Georg Weber, Johan Friederich Hauser, Melchior Jordan, Anthon Wallbeyer, Jacob Graaf, Johan Georg Kreyer, Michael Tietz, Jacob Eberhart.

---

221) Oct. 21, 1754. Ship Friendship, Charles Ross, Captain, from Amsterdam, last from Gosport, England.—Inhabitants from Franconia and Hesse,—seven Roman Catholics.

Oct. 21, 1754. Schiff Friendship, Capitain Charles Roß, von Amsterdam über Gosport, England.—Einwohner von Franken und Hessen,—sieben Römisch-Katholische.

Gabriel Reber,
Johannes Zeller,
Joseph Weissert,
Albrecht Miller,*
Martin Shnyder,*
Jacob Feiner,*
Gregorius Grim,
Deis Dersch,
Andreas Bommer,
Johannes Manckell,
Henrich Steller,
Johannes Koch,
Johannes Schmitt,

Philip Schweiger,*
Jacob Stahl,
Conrath Spenner,
Lorentz Althart,
Johannes Immel,
Christoph Stedtler,
Moritz Göbel,
Georg Steiner,
J. Friederich Korn,
Johannes Harff,
Johannes Freyling,
Johannes Wihrrem,
Henrich Reyel,

Adam Neubeck,?
Joh. Christoph Lang,
Johannes Shellenberger,*
Joh. Philip Schöberger,
Johan Georg Weissert,
Johann Jost Berger,
J. Henry Cautz,*
Johann Wedelscheider,
Reinhard Werkheiser,
Johan Peter Hasbach,
Joh. Dietrich Kalckbrenner,
John George Shmit,*
John Michael Hoch,
Johan Georg Hen,
Johan Casper Freyberg,
Johann Georg Stahl,
Johann Michael Stahl,
Joh. Balthaser Harff,
Johan Henrich Euhricheim,
Johan Henrich Schmidt,
Johan Wilhelm Mohr,
Johan Jacob Mohr,
Henrich Wilhelm Müller,
Georg Friederich Auger,
Joh. Wilhelm Becker,
Joh. Marcus Weylthöffer,
Johannes Straull,
Johannes Reuber,
Balthaser Stittz,
Christian Diehl,
Martin Bender,
Carl Wender,
Johannes Müller,
Jacob Fries,
Philip Seybolt,
Anthon Russ,
Nicklas Rab,
Johannes Vogt,
Georg Krüg,*
Bernhart Spesser,
Reinhart Schmitt,

Johannes Ammon,
Conrad Schmitt,
Peter Klein,
Balser Saltzer,
Johannes Kick,
Peter Stein,
Peter Buss,
Johannes Buss,
Philip Luar,*
Anthon Dauber,
Johannes Nold,
Henrich Scherr,
Johannes Mebür,
Georg Pott,*
Mattheus Diehl,
Johan Philip Schreidt,
Johan Jacob Laux,
Johannes Seybolt,
Nicolaus Heister,
Joh. Wilhelm Bender sen.,
Johan Philip Bender,
Konrad Freitenberger,
Joh. Henrich Rathschlag,
Joh. Michael Reinhart,
Wil. Henrich Lautenber,
Johan Conrad Krüg,
Matheus Achenbach,
Herman Wetzler,
Reinhard Kuntz,
Johannes Riell,
Conrath Langsdorff,
Arnold Dannhöffer,
Johann Peter Bernhardt,
Heinrich Esch,
Johannes Weber,
Johannes Schaffstall,
Joh. Daniel Büshart,
Johannes Danneheim,
Johan Georg Meyreiss,
Johan Henrich Vos,
Johann Georg Vos,

Joh. Henrich Scheid,   Johan Ludwig Bernhart,
Henrich Peter Köllmer,   Johan Christian Schmidt.
Sick—Friederich Stein, Johannes Müller, Michael Dinges.

---

222) Oct. 21, 1754. Ship Bannister, John Doyle, Captain, from Rotterdam, last from Cowes.—Inhabitants from Wirtemberg, Westphalia and the Palatinate,—four Roman Catholics.

Oct. 21, 1754. Schiff Bannister, Capitain John Doyle, von Rotterdam über Cowes.—Einwohner von Württemberg, Westphalen und der Pfalz,—vier Römisch=Katholische.

Jacob Hörman,	Joh. Peter Wolff,
Bastian Wittmer,	Abraham Gehr,
George Wittmer,	Adam Mirtorum,*
Andreas Eberharth,	Conrad Kemp,*
Hans Michael Miller,*	Johannes Delp,
Johan Peter Rademacher,	Peter Meister,*
Joh. Conrad Jauch,	Ludwig Lang,
Matheis Heinlein,	Elias Hartmann,
Johannes Kintsch,	J. Peter Weber,*
Konrath Weber,	Johannes Weber,*
Johannes Geisler,	Leonhart Weber,*
Joseph Cormet,*	Conrad Gildner,*
Martin Torward,*	Jacob Ludwig Beimling,
Martin Torward jr.,*	Georg Reissdorff,
Jaques Talmon,	Joh. David Krauss,
Jaques Caral,	Christoph Scharfrichter,
Jaques Caral,	Friederich Schiebel,
Simon Ege,*	Alexander Finck,*
Adam Ege,	G. Daniel Uhll,*
Balthes Müller,	Hans Mich. Bühlheim,
Christoph Diger,*	Hans Georg Ruass,
Georg Wirst,	Hans Jacob Ruass,
Peter Butz,	Johannes Laucher,
Philip Modi,*	Joh. Michael Schickel,
Johannes Weber,	Philippe Rouchon,
Johannes Benner,	Johan Valentin Keller,
Joh. Peter Kebler,*	S. Bastian Geyer,*
Matthias Buchman,	Phylippe Sarijons,
Valentin Jäger,*	Hans Georg Dölcker,
Joh. Jacob Wolff,	Johan Jacob Weber,

Johan Georg Jäger,
Joh. Nicolaus Derscher,
Nicklaus Baserman,
William Leeb,*
J. Henry Ashman,*
Joh. Conrad Georg,
Joh. Jacob Modi,*
Joh. Georg Hofman,

Joh. Burchart Häusser,
Johan Nickel Mick,
Christoffel Müller,
Johan Henrich Müller,
Georg Wärthmann,
Wenzel Bolteschwag,
Johan Adam Gebhart,
Johan Peter Emrich.

Sick—Johan Christoph Borell, Johannes Bernhard Wench, Johannes Fiedler, Jacob Kress, Pierre Tolman.

223) Oct. 22, 1754. Ship Henrietta, John Ross, Captain, from Rotterdam, last from Cowes.—Inhabitants from Franconia, Wirtemberg and Hesse,—three Roman Catholics.

Oct. 22, 1754. Schiff Henrietta, Capitain John Roß, von Rotterdam über Cowes.—Einwohner von Franken, Württemberg und Hessen,—drei Römisch=Katholische.

Johannes Keipp,
Christian Schwartzwelder,
Jacob Seyboldt,
Peter Dietrich,
Georg Stöhr,
Jacob Knödler,
Noah Hagy,*
Simon Pier,*
P. Henry Pier,*
Philip Badert,*
Jacob Volmer,*
Hartman Rausch,*
Friederich Haysner,
Jacob Haysner,*
Peter Stroh,
Philip Gruss,
Simon Higdal,
Conrad Bohl,
David Ernstmeyer,
Simon Leible,
Johannes Karch,
Balthas Thüringer,
Christoph Sauther,

Georg Vetter,
Georg Franck,
Elias Tomm,*
Michael Tomm,*
Albertus Roosin,
Peter Franck,
Jeremias Eckert,
Ludwig Zucker,
Michael Kohr,
Joseph Schmidt,
Johannes Koch,
Jacob Œhler,
Jacob Sehner,
Johan Christoph Preiss,
Jacob Kaltmiller,*
Joh. Bernhard Ressing,
Johan Reinhard Steiner,
Johan Daniel Pier,
Johan Georg Reith,
Jacob Schiefferdecker,*
Johan Georg Herbst,
Georg Adam Klee,
Hans Mich. Scheer,

Joh. Henrich Schwalbach,
Joh. Caspar Stropp,
Johan Georg Bader,
Joh. Anthon Graff,
Joh. Georg Neuman,*
Georg Henrich Beck,
Johan Michael Peter,
Johannes Rothenbürger,
Johan Georg Schneider,
Joh. Georg Franck,
Conrad Schlemmer,
Johan Adam Rohlandt,

Albrecht Schweinfarth,*
Johannes Reinhart,
Joh. Wolrath Krüger,
Johan Georg Heiges,
Georg Friederich Stübert,
Joh. Henrich Günther,
Bernhard Speck,
Johan Philip Beuerle,
Hans Jacob Mayer,
Johan Georg Ihle,
Gottfried Ludwig.*

224) Oct. 22, 1754. Ship Halifax, Thomas Coatam, Captain, from Rotterdam, last from Cowes.—Inhabitants from Wirtemberg, Hesse, Franconia and the Palatinate,—ten Roman Catholics.

Oct. 22, 1754. Schiff Halifax, Capitain Thomas Coatam, von Rotterdam über Cowes.—Bewohner von Württemberg, Hessen, Franken und der Pfalz,—zehn Römisch-Katholische.

Johann Haas,
Johann Förch,
Hans Georg Merling,
Johan Georg Best,
Michael Schneck,
Leonhard Schmith,
Bongre Nietzel,*
Bastian Geringer,*
Henry Heinnisch,*
Albrecht Rabenstein,
Anthoni Sultzer,
Andreas Schober,
Johan Gunderbusch,*
Johann Reckert,
Conrad Büchler,
Hans Oberzeller,*
Bernhard Kreith,
Anthony Gruber,*
Lorentz Senkeler,*
Michael Klein,
Johannes Geiger,

Elias Gordan,
Jacob Darm,
Georg Richter,*
Gustavus Reeb,
Jacob Strach,
Johann Ihle,
Jacob Grassel,*
Adam Breck,
Henrich Heiss,
Nicolaus Felix,
Andreas Frantz,
Anthony Dirner,
Conrath Casper,
Peter Zegels,
Jacob Wolfinger,
Jacob Weis,
David Blanck,*
Jacob Stegman,*
Martin Rarr,*
Henrich Wereni,
Anthony Braun,

Michael Poobagh,*
Johannes Hoch,
Martin Briell,
Johannes Schwab,
Joh. Michael Kleinschrot,
Peter Matheis Ganshon,
Joh. Georg Getinbaur,?
Hans Georg Oberholtzer,
Joh. Philip Hofmann,
Joh. Wolfgang Dietrich,
Joh. Michael Tristers,
Joh. Michael Abelman,
Joh. Michael Kauffman,
Hans Adam Schmidt,
H. Friederich Schmit,*
Johan Caspar Wahl,
Johan Georg Riess,
Johan Michael von Berg,
Paulus Fussweg,
H. Thomas Schlösser,*
Hans Georg Ihle,
Johan Jacob Roth,
Johan Nickel Wetterhardt
J. Jacob Wetherholt,*
Hans Adam Haner,*
Johann Michael Koch,
Martin Dorschheimer,

Joh. Henry Amrein,*
Hans Jacob Ferre,?
Joh. Fried. Albrecht Bürckert,
Johan Simon Schelberger,
Joh. Leonhard Ilgenfritz,
Johan Adam Ewa,
Valentin Weebehandt,
Johan Daniel Heck,
Johan Christian Guth,
Johan Dietrich Brecht,
Hans Michael Swenk,*
Christophel Heil,
Johannes Bachman,
Johan Jost Koch,
Joh. Henrich Briehll,
Hans Martin Schierch,
Hans Jacob Dirner,*
Johan Georg Maull,*
Joh. Bernhart Willer,
Philip Gresel,
Jacob Lang,*
Martin Pfeiffer,
Hans Georg Schütz,*
Jacob Hanengrath,
Joh. Lenhart Kochendörffer,
Hans Michael Düssing.

Sick—Martin Volckmeyer, Johan Michael, Matheis Tar, Nicolaus Remberger, Andreas Schopp, Nicolaus Geringer, Johan Henrich Haas, Johan Albrecht Henrich.

225) Oct. 23, 1754. Snow Good Intent, John Lasly, Captain, from Amsterdam, last from Gosport.—Inhabitants from Hesse, Hanau, the Palatinate, and a few from Switzerland,—seven Roman Catholics.

Oct. 23, 1754. Seeschiff Good Intent, Capitain John Lasly, von Amsterdam über Gosport.—Bewohner von Hessen, Hanau, der Pfalz und einige aus der Schweiz,—sieben Römisch-Katholische.

Friederich Holtzappel,*
Johannes Linck,*

Conrad Heyser,*
Johannes Heyser,*

Jost Marthin,
Johannes Ortt,*
Casper Schwing,
Paulus Fabin,
Johan Fillibich,
Andreas Zwanzger,
G. Friederich Klein,
Andreas Schäffer,
Peter Staub,*
Matheas Staub,
Christian Meyer,*
Conrath Aumüller,
Johannes Aumüller,
Johannes Bock,*
Johannes Lang,*
Johannes Vogel,
Conrad Loray,*
Anthon Zollmann,
Johannes Glück,
Christoph Kopp,*
Friederich Deussinger,
Mich. Leinberger,*
Mich. Rehbock,*
Nicklas Tillman,*
Frantz Peter Schultz,
Marcus Anthon Schultz,*
Joh. Nicolaus Hoffmann,
Joh. Bernhart Heckardt,
Johannes Wohlemder,
Ludwig Hen. Krutter,
Johan Georg Göss,
Johan Christoph Lang,
Joh. Bernhart Rost,
Joh. Wilhelm Weiss,
Joh. Jacob Schäffer,
Johan Wilhelm Lieber,
John Valentin Henkel,*

John Peter Lob,*
Johan Georg Hoff,
John Jost Meyer,*
Joh. Peter Bleichenbacher,
Georg Friederich Walber,
Joh. Caspar Loray,
Georg Henrich Vogel,
Joh. Wilhelm Christian,
Joh. Wilhelm Becker,
Johan Adam Zollmann,
Joh. Henrich Schwärtzel,
Johann Teitzwortzer,
Johann Teitzwortzer jr.,
Joh. Philip Klück,
Joh. Georg Hinckel,*
Nicholas Resch,*
Jacob Köller,*
Friederich Stüntzel,
Friederich Pepler,
Lorentz Arnold,
Johannes Hauck,
Wilhelm Arnold,
J. Friederich Nebel,*
Philip Rieth,*
Balthasar Frietz,*
Peter Asper,
Johannes Abachlender,
Johan Adam Blihle,
Johan Christian Heintz,
Johannes Breidenbach,*
Joh. Philip Kleiss,
Johannes Stephanus,*
Sam. Friederich Rügerr,
Joh. Caspar Bock,
F. Reinhardt Fischer,*
Christian Scheidt.

Sick—Frantz Jacob Miller, Johan Wilhelm Niese, Michael Sommer.

226) Oct. 26, 1754. Brigantine Mary and Sarah, Thomas Brodrich, Captain, from Amsterdam, last from Portsmouth.— Inhabitants from Franconia, Wirtemberg and the Palatinate,— six Roman Catholics.

Oct. 26, 1754. Schnellsegler Mary und Sarah, Capitain Thomas Brodrich, von Amsterdam über Portsmouth.—Einwoh= ner von Franken, Württemberg und der Pfalz,—sechs Römisch= Katholische.

Jacob Visser,
Michael Lehn,*
Michael Wenhart,*
Adam Breydinger,*
Carl Menges,*
Peter Volck,*
Jacob Störner,
Jacob Shumbert,*
Adam Schäffer,
Jacob Haller,*
Joseph Dohner,
Anthony Rohr,
H. Peter Carel,*
Nicholas Seewald,*
Anthon Kling,
Nicolaus Carl,
Johannes Roll,
Peter Edelman,
Herman Neyman,*
Lorent: Mauerer,*
Peter Menges,
Jacob Carel,*
Johan Christoph Heiss,
Joh. Wilhelm Schneider,
Nicolaus Œllenschläger,
J. Adam Schwäbel,*
Joh. Bernhart Kessler,
J. Conrad Menges,*
Johan Georg Brincker,
Hans Georg Aeuchler,
Johan Nickel Lehr,
J. Michael Schlauch,*
J. Dieterich Zieller,*

Johannes Brunner,
Joh. Jacob Helm,*
H. Adam Reybolt,*
Nickolas Leberman,*
Johannes Edelmann,
Johann Bartman,
Georg Adam Käiser,
Philip Sommer,*
Hans Peter Menges,
Johann Georg Menges,
Adam Menges,
Jacob Schmit,*
Matheas Krauss,*
Michael Hubert,*
Peter Weygand,*
Michael Wirth,*
Friederich Volck,*
Conrad Geyer,*
Peter Schnurr,*
John Ihrig,*
Adam Neidig,
Jost Reichel,*
Samuel Löfe,*
David Löfe,
Philip Naab,
Hertz Kiest,*
Johannes Pfeiffer,
Martin Kistner,
Johannes Reist,*
Georg Schöff,
Peter Joh,
J. George Krauss,*
Joh. Peter Krauss,*

J. Leonhart Neidig,*
Hans Adam Meister,*
Joh. Adam Weber,*
H. Philip Hartman,*
Johan Philip Kuhl,
J. Leonhart Trumheller,*
Hans Peter Joh,*
Philip Jacob Schwenck,
J. Adam Heckman,*

Georg Lud. Nonnenmacher,
Bastian Schraader,
Daniel Neidig,
Johan Michael Schall,
Joh. Bernhart Mayer,
Joh. Leonhart Kistner,
Joh. Jost Schletz,*
Johan George Michel,
Johan Jacob Helm.

Sick—Joh. Georg Edelman, Hans Edelman, Jost Witt, Hans Schnellenberger, Georg Kauffman, Johannes Breslauer.

---

227) Nov. 7, 1754. Ship John and Elizabeth, —— Ham, Captain, from Amsterdam, last from Portsmouth.—Inhabitants from Hanau, Wirtemberg and the Palatinate,—eleven Roman Catholics, one hundred and twenty Protestants.—330 passengers.

Nov. 7, 1754. Schiff John und Elisabeth, Capitain Ham, von Amsterdam über Portsmouth. — Einwohner von Hanau, Württemberg und der Pfalz,—eilf Römisch-Katholische, hundert und zwanzig Protestanten.—330 Reisende.

Nicklaus Lang,
Conrad Herman,
Wendel Fritzius,
Georg Hochreitter,*
Henry Wölfling,*
Martin Krebs,
Henry Eyler,*
Nicolaus Desch,
Johannes Nees.
Johannes Winholt,*
Johann Schillers,
Leonhart Peteri,
Berthold Henry Pott,*
J. Georg Birckenmeyer,*
Carl Friederich Schultz,
Joh. Fried. Thebards,
Johan Henrich Schmid,
Melchior Meichler,*
Johannes Roley,?
Friederich Adam Derst,

Martin Reinharth,
Joh. Georg Gerner,*
Joh. Gebhart Leichtheisser,
Johan Georg Heck,
Jacob Ammon,*
Georg Meissner,
Johannes Klein,
Herman Henger,
Theobald Pein,
Johannes Hahn,
Christian Kramer,
Jacob Wagner,
Paul Hoffman,
Jacob Ende,
Wilhelm Shneyder,*
Johannes Roth,
Johannes Blecher,
Georg Uder,
Christoph Mengel,*
Martin Cachler,

Johannes Weygandt,
Michael Scheck,
Burchart Hentz,*
Johannes Shuster,*
Nicklaus Klein,
Friederich Margel,
Johannes Flinner,
Johannes Mäning,
Johannes Horatz,
Henry Shneyder,*
Michael Homan,
Michael Krug,
Peter Fischer,
Henry Bachy,*
Albert Schunck,
Adolph Flohri,
Christian Aldt,
Johannes Rentz,*
George Flohri,*
Michael Schmit,*
Jacob Gander,
Philip Boger,*
Andreas Schwartz,
Jacob Dogent,*
Adam Bartholomæ,*
Joseph Debeer,*
Daniel David Heiner,
Bartholomi La Gneau,
Johan Jost Süsser,
Johannes Heldmann,
Johannes Meister,
Joh. Henrich Schmidt,
Joh. Ernst Fronheuser,
Johannes Schumacher,
Daniel Leuckel,
Henrich Dresbach,
Philip Achebach,
Jean Jaque Kifie,
Joh. Henrich Franck,
Johannes Gräffenstein,*
Georg Wilhelm Schneider,
Johan Adam Männig,

Casper Darner,
Michael Staub,
Michael Neyff,*
Joh. Adam Zehnen,
Jacob Werthmüller,
Johan Martin Lösch,
Joh. Georg Küllmann,
Joh. Jacob Schlötzer jr.,
Joh. Jacob Schlötzer sen.,
Johan Wendel Lent,
Johann Georg Fey,
Johann Peter Hauss,
H. Georg Miller,*
Hans Georg Abel,
Joh. Michael Uhting,
Jacob Bernhardt,
Hans Nicolaus Dech,
Andreas Gebhart,
Hans Georg Kleinpeter,
Johannes Därendinger jr.,
Johannes Därendinger sen.,
Johan Henrich Schuster,
Henry Schwartzenbach,*
Christian Hauswirth,
Joh. Wendel Königsfeldt,
Joh. Nicklaus Seidel,
Jacob Wenigart,
Christoph Mey,*
Carl Gleim,
Christian Keller,
Daniel Pfadt,
Jacob Müller,
Joh. Conrad Geil,
Joh. Peter Bannot,
Johan Philip Klein,
P. Christian Gross,*
Joh. Jacob Gross,*
Joh. Andreas Götz,
Johann Georg Schütz,
Johann Peter Herrmann,
Joh. Valentin Brünckmann.

Sick—Caspar Fahrenstock, Johan Adam Nees, Richard Nees, Hans Minnich.

---

228) Dec. 13, 1754. Ship Neptune, William Malam, Captain, from Hamburg, last from Cowes.—Inhabitants from Hamburg, Hanover and Saxony.—149 passengers.

𝔇ec. 13, 1754. Schiff Neptune, Capitain William Malam, von Hamburg über Cowes.—Bewohner von Hamburg, Hannover und Sachsen.—149 Passagiere.

Andreas Schindler,
Gottfried Ficke,
J. Andreas Knochen,*
Nicolaus Albers,
Joh. Georg Bolich,
J. Gottlob Basler,
Anthon Günther,
Wilhelm Antheis,*
Ludwig Leib,
Adam Müller,
Conrad Zorn,*
Elias Israel,*
B. Christian Barkel,*
Joh. Ernst Ziegler,
J. Peter Usbeck,
J. Christoph Urich,*
Joh. Offenhäuser,
W. Claar,*
Johannes Lebentraut,
J. Christian Kucher,*
Walter Wittmann,
J. Caspar Œrrig,*
J. Christian Kühnman,
Christian Kalckbrenner,
Friederich Wiederhohl,
Johann Holler,*
Christopher Guitelman,
Joh. Henrich Schäffer,

Johan Simon Kähler,
Hen. Anthon Bestenbast,
Joh. Martin Martine,*
Joh. Christoph Zachriss,
Julius Casper Strebig,*
Joh. Christian Werlisch,
Andreas Jacob Emeyer,
Johan Henrich Weidner,
Jerome Diederich Solfon,
Georg Christoph Maschcat,
Joh. Christian Schrader,
Joh. Gottlob Küntzelman,
Joh. Abraham Glimpff,
Christian Gebhart Ziegler,
Johan Henrich Schlesse,
Conrad Schnogheim,
Johan August König,
Jac. Friederich Shröder,
Henrich Frid. Stammann,
Christ. Hen. Jacobi,
Georg Hen. Heller,
Joh. Philip Alberti,
Joh. Julius Sorge,
Joh. Gottfried Ritter,
Johann Arntberger,
John Kotter,*
Peter Henry Trotz,
Johan Philip Stein.*

---

229) Oct. 7, 1755. Ship Neptune, George Smith, Master, from Rotterdam, last from Gosport.—226 passengers.

Oct. 7, 1755. Schiff Neptune, Capitain George Smith, von Rotterdam über Gosport.—226 Reisende.

Reimer Landt,
Bodo Otto,
Christian Ocker,
Philip Grieg,
Israel Josep, *a*
Henrich Metz,
Joseph Steinman,
Christian Reutter,
Jacob Bertsh,
Nicklaus Rein,
Jacob Würtz,
Friederich Dietz,
Peter Finck,*
Thomas Hütz,
Albrech Shabert,*
Jacob Stierle,
Adam Wenigeck,
Hans Reinger,
Michael Blaass,
Johan Kaiser,
Wilhelm Walder,
Casper Ulerich,
Christian Stöhr,
Hans Buch,
Jacob Buch,
Michael Wer,
Michael Wörer,
Christoph Mayer,
Friederich Ege,
Johannes Schitz,*
Andreas Missner,
Mathias Preissgärtner,

Georg Peter Hässer,
Christoph Kauffman,
Joh. Ludwig Dantzebecher,
Joh. Adam Chretschenbach,
Thomas Dantzebecher,*
Joh. Casper Bittonff,
Joh. Conrad Eirheim,
Georg Friederich Dillman.
Johan Henrich Finck,
Henrich Henckell,
Gottfried Zergiebel,
Sebastian Schmidt,
Casper Hinderstieff,
Hans Michael Krauss,
Johannes Biendser,
Michael Schindel,
Joh. Jacob Schock,
Joh. Casper Zincke,
Christ. Ludwig König,
Joh. Henrich Möser,
Hans Georg Schneider,
Hans Georg Scheffer,
Christian Baumann,
Conrad Baumann,
Johannes Erbshusser,
Andreas Höfflinger,*
Mathäus Obergefäll,
Johan Nickel Gast,
Johann Christian Gast,
Philipp Jacob Bär,
Joh. Peter Hickman,
Joh. Adam Helmställer,

a This name is written in *Hebrew*. The final letter *Pe*, having a *dot inscribed*, I have written *Josep;* for reason known to those who read Hebrew.—(*Editor.*)

a Dieser Name ist in hebräischer Schrift. Da der Schlußbuchstabe *Pe* punktirt ist (Dagesch Lene), so habe ich Josep geschrieben, und zwar aus Gründen, welche Diejenigen, die in der hebräischen Sprache bewandert sind, wissen.—(Herausgeber.)

30

Johannes Steiney,*
J. Philip Fischer,*
Sebastian Senlieder,
Conrath Müller,
Johannes Walther,
Friederich Adam,
Christian Bausman,
Matheas Weis,
Henrich Emert,
Johan Petter,
Friederich Schirdt,
Georg Klinger,
Jean Frentier,

Johan Michel Körner,
Johan Melchior Hirth,
Georg Christ. Webrecht,
Johan Michael Weise,*
Adam Lorentz Dietrich,
Johannes Schneider,
Jacob Albrech Haass,
Bernhart Eilsheimer,*
G. Michael Schwab,*
Hans Georg Keller,
Johann Georg Volck,
Joh. Georg Blanckenbiller,
Samuel Fraatsrach.?

---

230) Nov. 1, 1755.† Ship Pennsylvania, Charles Lyon, Captain, from London.

Nov. 1, 1755.† Schiff Pennsylvania, Capitain Charles Lyon, von London.

Friederich Leydig,*
Lorentz Seitz,
Andreas Rietel,
Georg Friederich Weber,
Johannes Jung,
Joh. Philip Fischer,
Conrad Timpe,
Joh. Heinrich Albers,

Johan Valentin Reuter,
Georg Ludwig Hochheimer,
Johan Georg Koch,
Joh. Daniel Bräutigam,
Joh. Henrich Fischer,
Joh. Melchior Hornung,
Johan Just Hopman,
Andreas Nicolaus Salling.

---

231) Nov. 10, 1756. Snow Chance, —— Lawrence, Captain, last from London.—109 passengers.

---

† The *Rev. John Conrad Bucher*, a name associated with *Church and State* in this country, came to Pennsylvania in 1755, resided for some time at Carlisle, then a frontier settlement. He died, while pastor of the German Reformed Church of Lebanon, at Millerstown (Annville), Aug. 15, 1780.—See *Rupp's History of Lebanon*, p. 459; *Harbaugh's Lives of German Reformed Ministers.*

† Paſtor John Conrad Bucher, ein in Kirche und Staat in dieſem Lande wohlbekannter Name, kam 1755 nach Pennſylvanien und wohnte eine Zeit= lang in Carlisle, das damals noch eine Grenzanſiedlung war. Er ſtarb am 15. Auguſt 1780 als Paſtor der deutſch = reformirten Kirche zu Lebanon in Millerstown, jetzt Annville. — Siehe Rupp's Geſchichte von Lebanon, S. 459; Harbach's Lebensbeſchreibungen ref. Geiſtlicher.

Nov. 10, 1756. Seeschiff Chance, Capitain Lawrence, über London.—109 Reisende.

Bernhard Uehlein,
Paulus Kamp,*
Ehrhardt Conradt,
Georg Doll,
Leonhard Dürr,
Georg Ludwig Eberle,
Caspar Bernhart,
Johann Andreas Klünck,
Johann Peter Klünck,
Johann Michael Kuhn,
Simon Hengel,
Nicklaus Hahn,
Michael Müller,
Nicklas Pauly,
Johannes Sombero,
Baltes Schinf,?
Adam Schmidt,
Johan Sack,
Friederich Schöff,
Frantz Waner,
Casper Biener,

Johannes Weytzel,
Friederich Walther,
Christian Segnitz,
Johannes Haas,*
Valentin Dürr,
Georg Ludwig Crucius,
Hans Wolff Gundel,
Wolfgang Nicolaus Heymann,
Johann Peter Körner,
Johann Heinrich Klöpper,
Johan Valentin Panzer,
Joh. Wilhelm Stiernkorb,
Johan Georg Schmidt,
Johan Georg Weining,
Johann Peter Weber,
Johan Nickel Wagner,
Joh. Nickel Basserman,
Christian Pauli,
Hans Epplinger,
Rudolph Fulleweiler,*
Johan Michael Wagner.

232) Oct. 21, 1761.† Snow Squirrel, John Benn, Master, from Rotterdam, last from Cowes.

Oct. 21, 1761.† Seeschiff Squirrel, Capitain John Benn, von Rotterdam über Cowes.

Peter Mischler,
Eberhart Disinger,
Christophel Bamberg,
Johannes Beyerle,
Andreas Graff,
Stephan Danner,
Daniel Schaab,*

Nicolaus Schweitzer,
Georg Vogelgesang,
Wilhelm Becker,
Hans Eckardt,
Henrich Holtzapfel,
Joh. Jacob Vogelgesang,
Friederich Probst,*

† Owing to the hostilities between France and England, German immigration was completely suspended from 1756 to 1761.—(*Editor.*)

† Während der Jahre 1756 bis 1761 hörte die deutsche Einwanderung wegen der zwischen Frankreich und England bestehenden Schwierigkeiten ganz auf.—(Herausgeber.)

Friederich Lieberknecht,*
Caspar Knoblauch,
Valentin Annawaldt,
Johan Simon Mayer,
Johann Wilhelm Serger,
Johann Conrad Serger,
Joh. Nickel Hertzler,
Johan Nickel Becker,

Georg Friederich Rohrer,
John Henry Diessinger,*
Johann Jacob Hackman,
Johann Friederich Diehl,
Johann Nicolaus Diehl,
Johan Ludwig Probst,
Johan Jacob Probst,
Johann Dietrich Taub.

233) Oct. 5, 1763. Ship Richmond, Charles Young Husband, Captain, from Rotterdam, last from Portsmouth.—162 passengers.

Oct. 5, 1763. Schiff Richmond, Capitain Charles Young Husband, von Rotterdam über Portsmouth.—162 Reisende.

Joh. Jacob Peiffer,
Johannes Zimmerman,
Johannes Schütz,
Johannes Klappert,
Johannes Schütz,
Rudolph Hehr,
Peter Gatz,
Jacob Gatz,
Heinrich Daum,
Ludwig Agricola,
Johannes Schneider.
Joseph Fischer,
Frantz Mültz,
Georg Bender,
Conrad Betis,*
P. Pautz,
Joseph Bohn,*
August Hemerlein,*
Johannes Hänner,
Paul Grin,
Henrich Dietz,
Peter Götz,
Johannes Claus,
Daniel Paulus,
Peter Humberd,
Jacob Otho,
Jost Heintz,

Johannes Basel,?
Casper Müller,
Andreas Dress,
Wilhelm Eck,
Andreas Mertz,
Matthias Lockner,
Henry Wagner,*
Johann Daub,
John Sollberg,*
Martin Hasch,
Johannes Just,
John Marbes,*
Johannes Schaff,
Henry Banroth,*
Georg Bastian,*
Johan Jacob Hoffmann,
Johann Theis Cromm,
Johann Herman Klappert,
Johann Engel Becker,
Johann Michael Becker,
Johan Henrich Schneider,
D. Dieterich Burchardt,
Andreas Holtzmann,
Johan Thomas Noll,
Friederich Schönleber,
Johan Daniel Royscher,
Johann Georg Hibler,

Johann Henrich Niess,
Joh. Philip Wahrenholtz,
Johann Jost Hänner,
Johann Jost Dietz,
Johan Christian Scheidt,
J. Henrich Läck,
Johann Henrich Paulus sen.,
Johann Henrich Paulus,
Johann Friederich Stüll,
Johann Michael Matz,
Hermanus Janler,
Wilhelm Völtmer,
Johann Georg Giesberg,
Johann Peter Giesberg,
Johannes Engel Giesberg,

Hermann Donat,
Johann Engelhut,
Jacob Glässner,
Lorentz Knöri,
Heinrich Beinöller,
Martin Schaffner,*
August Eissinger,*
Dilmanus Becker,
Phillipp Warner,
Jacob Bergmann,
Friederich Bergmann,
Georg Friederich Huber,
Johan Henrich Wensell,
Conrath Wolff,
Johannes Wickel.

234) Nov. 1, 1763. Ship Chance, Charles Smith, Captain, from Rotterdam, last from Cowes.—193 passengers.

Nov. 1, 1763. Schiff Chance, Capitain Charles Smith, von Rotterdam über Cowes.—193 Reifende.

Joseph Seifferdt,
Valentin Gänssel,
Philip Casner,*
David Goltir,
Johannes Ludy,
Georg Ebert,
Philip Schappert,
Nicolaus Schappert,
Henrich Alsbach,*
Philip Schmit,
Jacob Spielman,
Casper Huber,*
Georg Günther,
Jacob Jentz,
Johannes Gern,
Andreas Feger,*
Jacob Baltzel,
Carl Baltzel,
Adam Samuel,*
Georg Jantz,

Georg Fischer,
Jacob Schädt,
Johannes Dorst,
Jacob Schlick,
Jacob Behr,
Peter Wolff,
Christian Wangolt,
Friederich Arnold,
Peter Krafft,
Adam Schmid,
Michael Schmidt,
Daniel Zütter,
Balthasar Zütter,
Henry Schwantz,*
Johannes Weller,
Johannes Engelbert,
John Henry Miller,*
Anthon Hausam,
Martin Braun,
Samuel Müller,

30*

Johannes Schellenberger,*
Henrich Deberts Häusser,
Jean Henri Gaijdon,
Johann Georg Vetter,
Joh. Jacob Schnorss,
Johannes Schnorss,*
Johan Peter Kessler,
Johan Christian Schwab,
Philip Zumstein,
Johan Georg Dornch,
Georg Ludwig Kesselrinck,
Bernhard Ranhert,
Johann Nickel Kotter,
Johann Georg Mühlheim,
Johann George Henninger,
Georg Jacob Baltzel,
Johann Peter Hauck,
Hans Peter Studi,
Michael Becker,*
Hans Georg Zeiner,*
Michael Zeiner,*
Johan Henry Shuntz,*
Johann Michael Altz,
Jacob Ebersohl,
Johann Jacob Sonntag,
Johann Jacob Hoffman,

Johan Valentin Hauck,
Georg Henrich Flanckenhardt,
Johannes Dörbaum,
Friederich Wilhelm Stahl,
Johann Benedictus Grieben,
Johann Wendel Fackler,
Johan Thomas Gil,
Johannes Jacob Hud,
Johann Peter Munner,
Johann Engel Œrter,
Johan Eckart Œrter,
Jost Henrich Schmidt,
Johann Henrich Keil,
Johannes Becker,
John Bernhart,*
Michael Stoffel,
Heinrich Menges,
Samuel Cyriaci,
Balthaser Christ,
Johannes Strätzer,
Johann Ernst Thiel,
Valentin Nicodemus,
Michael Spielman,*
Emanuel Meisterer,*
Nicolaus Wistadius,
Philip Georg Kneiht.

235) Nov. 25, 1763. Brigantine Success, William Marshall, Captain, from Rotterdam.

Nov. 25, 1763. Schnellsegler Succeß, Capitain William Marshall, von Rotterdam.

Abraham Neu,
Jacob Helm,
Leonhardt Wass,
John George Bauman,*
Anton Näryes,
Johann Kayser,

Johann Henrich Hedrich,
Johan Jacob Müller,
Charles Christman,*
Mathias Christman,*
Joh. Matheis Steffen,
Johan Henrich Fetzer.

236) Nov. 25, 1763. Ship Pallas, Richard Milner, Master, from Rotterdam, last from Cowes.—198 passengers.

Nov. 25, 1763. Schiff Pallas, Capitain Richard Milner, von Rotterdam über Cowes.—198 Reisende.

Isaac Droqunt,
George Kuhnele,
Conrad Mayer,
Georg Wagner,
Johannes Schmidt,
David Jansohn,
Jacob Weissert,
Johannes Schaaff,
Ludwig Amaus,
Gottlieb Koll,
Peter Opp,
Johann Wendel,
Martin Helder,
Jacob Hauser,
Lewis Stutz,*
Jost Vohl,
Johannes Georg,
Jacob Heintz,
Henrich Flick,
Henrich Graff,
Johannes Blum,
Henrich Just Röhrig,
Georg Friederich Hammer,
Ulrich Bürckholder,
Georg Wilhelm Janson,
Johann Henrich Strauch,
Friederich Holtzhausser,
Michael Braun,
Conrad Scherer,
Johann Georg Höchst,
Martin Schneider,
Johannes Friehruff,

Wilhelm Bleiniger,
John Henry Miller,*
Johan Martin Merck,
John Henry Freind,*
Johann Conrad Kryser,
Johann Jacob Schweitzer,
Johann Adam Hoffheintz,
Johann Daniel Hoffheintz,
Wilhelm Ritter,
Georg Thomas Gerhardt,
Peter Schütz,
Caspar Reider,
Andreas Obmann,
Lorentz Obmann,
Martin Steffen,
Henry Pfeiffer,
Baltzer Schock,
Friederich Hüttner,
Philip Faust,
Philip Miller,*
Christian Pfeiffer,
Valentin Seipel,*
Peter Wercken,*
Abraham Senner,
Jean Andrie Stockinger,
Jean Louis Seiz,
Johann Georg Prestel,
Leonhart Frischkorn,
Johann Schittenhelm,
Johann Christian Schreiber,
Gerlach Wittenstein.

237) Aug. 8, 1764. Ship Chance, Charles Smith, Captain, from Rotterdam.—208 passengers.

Aug. 8, 1764. Schiff Chance, Capitain Charles Smith, von Rotterdam.—208 Reisende.

Sebastian Bender,
Peter Neyer,*
Henry C. Shiel,*
Johannes Schneider,
Philip Shiffere,*
Balthas Kappes,
Valentin Metzger,
Bernhard Ginger,
Johannes Strenger,
Michel Bandelo,
Adam Wanner,
George Sleig,*
Matheus Roth,
Friederich Altherr,
Philip Brogli,
Johannes Tandt,?
Peter Grosh,*
George Haag,
Andreas Amon,
Ludwig Schad,
Johannes Rittesheim,
Antoni Vogt,
Andreas Scholl,
Peter Arandt,
Jacobus Arandt,
Peter Krapff,
Michael Bremich,
Joh. Ludwig Dexheimer,
Daniel Dexheimer,
Johann Peter Schmidt,
Johann Philip Thoma,
Johann Adam Schiffer,
Johann Martin Hes,
Joh. Michael Habtüzel,
Joh. Friederich Müller,
Johann Georg Haass,
Georg Peter Beck,
Johann Wilhelm Weiss,
Johann Jacob Sties,
Johann Nickel Mayer,
Johan Herman Mayer,

Johan Peter Durst,
Georg Leonhart Stutz,
Johannes Gerhard,
Stephan Freundt,
Johan Georg Gebhardt,
Johannes Wench,
Johan Jacob Grob,
Johan Jacob Schiffer,
Matheus Bremich,
Johan Stephan Saam,
Johann Adam Bremich,
Johann Georg Hundt,
Philip Abraham Hornich,
Johannes Kelter,
Jacob Eckfeldt,
Heinrich Schäffer,
Peter Zürn,
Philip Blum,
Andreas Bartel,
Johannes Wahl,
Andreas Meisch,
Ludwig Feter,
Joseph Gaser,*
Peter Rücker,
Peter Haas,
Johannes Theissen,
Philip Will,
Ludwig Huber,
Georg Gielberth,
Friederich Ringer,
Michael Wilhelm,
Johan Georg Strein,
Friederich Wahl,
Herman Zonnerer,
Simon Descher,
Johan Christian Descher,
Johannes Späth,
Johannes Rick,
Johann Georg Theiss,
Friederich Hoffman,
Daniel Weniger,

Frantz Schwartz,
Matthias Kempe,
Andreas Druckenbrodt,
Georg Scherer,

Johannes Weinberger,
Sebastian Seyberth,
Valentin Bauer,
Geo. Wendel Zimmerman.

---

238) Sept. 19, 1764. Ship Polly, Robert Porter, Captain, from Rotterdam, last from Cowes.—Six Roman Catholics.—184 passengers.

Sept. 19, 1764. Schiff Polly, Capitain Robert Porter, von Rotterdam über Cowes. — Sechs Römisch = Katholische. — 184 Reisende.

Bernhardt Beck,
Nichl Shluhtes,*
Johannes Schadt,
Friederich Galle,
Hans Grimm,
Joh. Jacob Reudt,
Jacob Berchel,
Joh. Jacob Mann,
Christian Bergman,*
Caspar Wenger,
Jacob Wenger,
Nicklaus Lugebül,
Joh. Daniel König,
Geo. Adam Graff,
John Martin Stoll,
Johannes Beiser,
Johannes Eulman,
Peter Steigelman,
Christian Lang,*
Johann Christoph Schmidt,
Joh. Jost Schreckenangst,
Johann Jacob Graff,
John Melchior Hollebach,
Johan Georg Schmidt,
Johann Peter Trein,
Johann Georg Eller,
Joh. Casper Güttenberg,
Joh. Michael Bergman,
Johan Friederich Strass,

Johan Conrad Strass,
Johann Carl Laubach,
Johan Henrich Ehls,?
Johan Georg Weyckel,
Johan Nicklas Franck,
Johan Adam Franck,
Johan Henrich Schell,
John George Schwaab,
Johan Nickel Heibst,
Peter Marks,*
Andreas Grebiel,
Peter Grebiel,
Leonhart Bauer,
Conrad Bauer,
Antoni Jutz,
Peter Dietrich,
Adam Mishell,*
Carl Schmidt,
Anthoni Welte,
Frantz Peter Hacket,
Johan Valentin Dumm,
Joh. Fried. Zimmermann,
Peter Thormeyer,
Anthon Noschang,
Johan Mathias Hoffman,
Christian Ernst Beschler,
Jacob Neblinger,
Wilhelmus Moser.

239) Sept. 20, 1764. Ship Sarah, Francis Stanfield, Captain, from Rotterdam, last from Portsmouth.—230 passengers.

Sept. 20, 1764. Schiff Sarah, Capitain Francis Stanfield, von Rotterdam über Portsmouth.—230 Reisende.

Paul Hoffman,
Godfrey Keyser,
Conrad Bischoff,
Georg Scherer,
Michael Lauth,
Adam Göttel,
Peter Göttel,
Henrich Eich,
Theobold Lehman,
Jacob Hoch,
Israel Grob,
Peter Schwaab,
Peter Hüb,
Theobold Weber,
Adam Lüdy,
Frantz Kettering,
Christian Meyer,*
Jacob Allspach,
Daniel Frick,
Conrad Frick,
Michael Hoffecker,
Jacob Kieffer,
Joh. Peter Weber,
Leonhard Lenckner,
Johann Büthenfeldt,
Andreas Vollprecht,
Johannes Welte,
Michael Funck,
Martin Hoffman,
Georg Jacob Scherer,
Johan Ludwig Betz,
Johan Urban Betz,
Johan Adam Schaff,
Friederich Conrad Scheffer,
Henrich Wettern,?
Theobold Itzberger,
J. Henry Kisauer,*

Christian Främdling,
Jacob Altvatter,*
Johann Jacob Kaufman,
Simon Friederich Schober,
Johannes Spielman,
Johan Daniel Fuhrman,
Daniel Dausman,*
Philip Hoffecker,
John George Hubacher,
Johan Michael Thran,
John George Drachsel,
Henrich Ochssenbecher,
Hans Georg Schyre,
Johann Henrich Hoff,
Hans Dietrich Hoff,
Johann Georg Grossglass,
Johann Matheis Dibel,
Johann Friederich Küchner,
Johann Philip Welde,
Jacob Schantre,
Jacob Feiock,*
John Schüster,
Michael Metzger,
Jacob Gänsel,
George Fischer,
Johannes Finniger,
Johannes Dörr,
Johan Herman,
Carl Gerhardt,
Peter Kuhn,
Arend Krissing,
Wendel Sheets,*
Christel König,
Georg Schog,
Georg Riehm,
Johannes Hitz,
Johannes Gass,

Johannes Blitz,
Oswald Rap,
Peter Göttel,
Moritz Master,
Johann Christ. Schaub,
Johannes Georg Specht,
Conrad Fischer,
Jacob Trein,
Heinrich Schreiner,
Martin Rauch,
Johan Henrich Fashaus,
Johann Wilhelm Weber,
Johann Jost Strack,

Johann Peter Ottershelt,
Johannes Hegenstill,
Frantz Thomas Hartman,
Johan Christoffel Bintz,
George Henry Hartman,
Johann Georg Wetzel,
Johann Philip Kuhn,
Henrich Nickel Raque,
Hans Christ. Raque,
Johann Daniel Löhr,
Conrad Schäffer,
Johan Peter Steiler,
Johann Michael Jung.

---

240) Sept. 26, 1764. Ship Brittania, Thomas Arnot, Captain, from Rotterdam.—260 passengers.

Sept. 26, 1764. Schiff Brittania, Capitain Thomas Arnot, von Rotterdam.—260 Reisende.

Christoph Heger,
Johannes Einzopp,
John Weber,
Augustus Weiss,
Nicholas Smith,*
Daniel Rieg,
Theobald Roth,
Martin Jetter,
Andreas Vogt,
Johannes Gitt,
Jacob Gitt,
Adam Fink,
L. Herschheimer,
Jno. Geo. Reiff,*
Johann Baum,
Casper Erhardt,
Gottfried Lampart,
Joh. Paulus Grabsteinbrenner,
Andreas Ketteman,
Georg Michael Schmitt,
Johann Henrich Wölker,
Georg Haudler,

Friederich Zäntler,
Johan Carl Schmitt,
Georg Philip Karwin,
Georg Adam Zepp,
Henrich Marschheimer,
Jacob Tieschmar,
Johan Wilhelm Werger,
Georg Michael Oeltinger,
Adolph Carl Schneider,
Philip Lautenschläger,
Thomas Wagner,
Christian Schellman,
Johannes Waibel,
Stephan Waibel,*
Adam Miller,*
Andreas Freyberger,
Justus Lechleider,
Carl Garaus,
Valentin Stettler,
Jacob Masohlder,
David Schneider,
Christian Fleckstein,*

Peter Wiser,
Johannes Wambach,
Jacob Schäfer,
Johannes Hoch,
Peter Paulus Leicht,
Joh. Andreas Velck,
Joh. Valtin Horter,
Joh. Adam Rau,
Erhard Bodenstein,
Joh. Friedrich Koch,
Phil. Henry Miller,*
Jacob Brückert,
Christoph Brückert,
Johannes Kalbfleisch,
Abraham Messer,
Fried. Jocheim,*
Christian Eberhard,*
Andreas Jäger,
Georg Lehner,
Georg Lambarth,
Georg Kuntz,
Henrich Wegner,
Jacob Bätzerlein,
Christian Rupp,
Nicklas Staller,*
Friederich Bachman,
Dietrich Gerhart,
Christoph Keller,
Johann Bernhart Oth,
Johann Andreas Schmidt,
Christian Haushalter,
Georg Heinrich Schmitt,
Johannes Georg Freyberger,
Johann Martin Ott,

Johann Friederich Vogel,
Georg Wilhelm Schmitt,
John Conrad Wambach,
Johann Philipp von Nieda,
Johan Friederich Mopps,
Gerhart Steinbreucker,
Georg Friederich Helids,
Johann Georg Graff,
Johann Adam Graff,
Johann Georg Cautz,
Georg Valentin Dengen,
Joh. Philip Seidenstricker,
Johann Jacob Schmidt,
Philip Henrich Engel,
Johan Philip Racke,
Johann Henrich Spitzer,
Johann Andreas Spitzer,
Johan Friederich Beyermeister,
Johan Dietrich Hauck,
Hans Georg Schusterdreher,
Johann Philip Schösser,
Henry Seidenstricker,*
Hans Michael Lampart,
Johann Ludwig Schäffer,
Joh. Henrich Fabricius,
John George Menges,*
Johann Michel Michel,
Christian Sachsman,*
Hans Adam Taxler,
Jacob Bartscherer,
Hans Michael Rosser,
O. P. Dieter Ticker,?
Martin Bühler.

241) Oct. 3, 1764. Ship King of Prussia, James Robinson, Captain, from London.—94 passengers.

Oct. 3, 1764. Schiff King of Prussia, Capitain James Robinson, von London.—94 Reisende.

Jacob Vadel,
Henrich Schell,
Johann Müller,
Jacob Weber,
Gerlach Gran,
Philip Rescher,*
Ludwig Schell,
Sem. Urckart,
Frantz Schweitzer,
Johan Nickel Herst,
Andreas Zinck,*
Johannes Stutz,*
Wendel Apffel,
Georg Schlemb,*
Henrich Strohm,
Georg Appel,*
Georg Ridle,
Paul Schreck,
Nicklas Scherrer,
Christian Wickert,
Albertus Häffer,
George Kenttner,*
Elias Appel,*
Jacob Specht,
Christian Appel,*
Georg Doll,*

Johann Peter Vadel,
Johann Georg Ther,
Georg Peter Deisert,
Christian Weber,
Johannes Ott,
Matthias Hendrich,*
Joh. Philip Rauschkopf,
Philip Jacob Breszler,*
Johan Nicolaus Dippel,
Johan Philip Steinmetz,
Johan Philip Matter,
Ernst Ludwig Reinbold,
Georg Schwerdt,
Thomas Salade,
Johan Georg Ernst,
Joh. Nicolaus Schwerdt,
Michael Salade,
Johan Peter Fischer,
Philip Jacob Suder,*
Johannes Delb,
Georg Michael Hart,*
Johan Martin Heidt,
Johann Georg Gantz,
Johann Nickel Wagner,
Johannes Häffer,
Joh. Philip Mühlmichel.

242) Oct. 20, 1764. Ship Richmond, Charles Young Husband, Captain, from Rotterdam.—224 passengers.

Oct. 20, 1764. Schiff Richmond, Capitain Charles Young Husband, von Rotterdam.—224 Reisende.

Jacob Nill,
Friederich Gebberdt,
Jacob Sherber,*
Christoph Weber sen.,
Christoph Weber,
Bernhart Schneider,
John Allman,
Samuel Starck,
Johannes Anpert,

Daniel Weichel,*
Johann Christian Thiel,
Johann Peter Gerhard,
Johann Georg Diebert,
Eberhard Kirsheyer,*
John George Fullman,*
Johan Conrad Kauffman,
Johann Adam Sebeinzer,*
Johann Martin Anpert,

Joh. Wendel Bartholmæ,
John Adam Heckman,
Michel Halm,
Conrad Jacoby,
Jacob Hasbirch,
Wendel Runckel,
Albert Gülcher,
Michel Keiser,
Frantz Kuhn,
Balthas Steiner,
Sebastian Stier,
Johannes Glück,
Samuel Stauffer,
Henrich Kurtz,
Georg Taub,
Michael Reiner,
Gottfried Schott,
Daniel Sätzler,
Johannes Seitz,
Michael May,
Paul Kober,
Peter Müller,
Jacob Metz,
Henrich Allman,
Abraham Jacob,
Jno. Geo. Ord,*
Jno. Geo. Haffner,
Conrad Minger,
John Erlenheiser,*
Jacob Kleh,
Jacob Schneyder,
Michel Becker,
Jacob Breisch,
Christian Jung,
Jacob Bardon,
Wilhelm Feickert,
Nickel Kämerer,
Peter Hardtman,
Peter Hanner,?
Adam Rieth,
Nickel Götz,

Michael Mayer,
Gottlieb Börckle,
Georg Stattler,
Wendel Heiss,
Johann Peter Schell,
Valentin Hackenbach,
Johann Friederich Henrich
Friederich Hirschfeldt,
Matheich Koch Weber,
Joseph Breisch,
Christoph Martin Henerdt,
Hans Georg Kurtz,
John Geo. Geiger,
Hans Georg Hagenbach,
John Martin Knobloch,
Nicklas Lächner,
Johann Andreas Kolb,
Michael Reidebach,
Johan Philip Müller,
Johann Adam Schütz,
Wendel Gutdänder,
Johannes Mensch,
Johann Michel Stoff,
Joh. Jacob Engelhardt,
Wolfarth Reinhart Edinger,
John Peter Beckel,
Johannes Jacob Quandel,
Johannes Henrich Harn,
Johannes Erlenheiser,
Frederick Kühlman,
Georg Leonhard Pfeiffer,
Hans Michael Wills,
Johan Nickel Grimm,
Peter Reidebach,
Hans Michael Henrich,
Conrad Dieffenbacher,
Johann Dietrich Heiss,
Philip Friedrich Müller,
Wilhelm Spengler,
Johan Peter Chypfeius,
Johan Adam Weber,

Johan Balthaser Häusser,   Johann Nickel Reidenbach,
Johannes Spengler,   Melchior Edinger.
Joh. Christopher Ulrich Kenser,

---

243) Oct. 27, 1764.   Ship Hero, Ralph Forster, Captain,
from Rotterdam, last from Cowes.—500 passengers.

Det. 27, 1764. Schiff Hero, Capitain Ralph Forster, von
Rotterdam über Cowes.—500 Reisende.

Johannes Hufer,*
Jacob Karch,
Johannes Weiss,
John Berg,
Andrew Wolff,
Jacob Hass,*
Peter Müller,
Georg Sicl,
Jost Meyer,
Georg Etter,
Jacob Lössle,
Matheis Petter,
Jacob Hauck,
Johannes Hauck,
Peter Schauer,
Peter Scheide,
Martin Herwald,
Gustavus Schlosser,
Peter Wedel,
Gottfried Eppling,
Friederich Eppling,
Johannes Will,
Daniel Strickler,
Michel Shub,*
Lazarus Herby
Jacob Hönich,
Johannes Ludwig,
Johannes Gress,
Jacob Schibb,
Conrath Dörr,
Johannes Dürr,
Lorentz Dürr,

Dietrich Jäger,
Philip Ecker,
Michael Philipi,
Adam Philipi,
Johannes Deehr,
Adam Fägle,
Adam Neiss,*
Ulrich Eyman,
Johann Georg Wagner,
Johannes Welsch,
Johann Andreas Schad,
Johann Christian Gernet,
Leonhard Büchler,
Wilhelm Henrich Biegel,
Johann Lorentz Beck,
Johann Adam Rudolph,
George Adam Weickel,
John Reinhard Cauffman,*
Henrich Schwerdt,
Jacob Sauerheber,
Johann Schuman,
Rudolph Schuman,
Christopher Radebach,
Johannes Fuhrmann,
Johan Ludwig Sewaldt,
Martin Heylman,
Johann Georg Wetzel,
Johann Adam Wausch,
Johannes Dage,?
Johann Ernst Daniel,
Johan Adam Seyberth,
Hans Georg Götz,

Johann Michel Walter,
Johan Philip Küntsch,
Abraham Fetter,
Jacob Düssardt,
Johann Michael Klein,
Hans Nickel Bauer,
Johannes Hoffmann,
Johannes Fellman,
Johannes Ring,
Joh. Georg Weydenmeyer,
Urban Weidenmaier,
Eberhardt Weydenmeyer,
Nicholas Anthony,
Ludwig Freibürger,
Johann Jacob Gross,
Conrad Bingman,
Peter Nickles,
Johannes Gerent,
Adam Meyer,
Paulus Pauly,
Henrich Fuchs,
Johannes Frietsch,
Michael Scheff,
Georg Wintz,
David König,
Conrad König,
Georg Wilhelm,
Egidius Jung,
Henrich Sohl,
Nicholas Ott,
Johannes Sellheim,
Joseph Hertel,
Georg Heyman,*
Martin Schupp,
Andreas Reck,
Simon Fischer,
Bernhard Steiner,
Jacob Kiportz,
Joseph Renau,
Henrich Baum,
Johannes Wittig,

Henrich Roth,
Michael Nieth,
Gottlieb Nieth,
Georg Sachs,
Georg Deg,
Michael Walter,
Samuel Schober,
Andreas Michael,
Michael Schaffer,*
Martin Heitz,
Nicolaus Breidebach,
Daniel Brennemann,
Christian Brubacher,
Jacob Seitz,
Daniel Joder,
Rudolph Kägy,
Peter Grebil,
Georg Altschuh,
Johann Georg Adam,
Johann Nickel Raab,
Johan Adam Bruchhauser,
Johann Henrich Lutz,
Friederich Haffner,
Abraham Schantz,
Conrad Haftenträger,
Jacob Kauffman,
Johann Henrich Heyl,
Johann Georg Heyl,
Johann Conrad Heyl,
Johann Jacob Heyl,
Johann Peter Hoffstadt,
Johann Jacob Leiman,
Johann Henrich Bausch,
Johann Valtin Becker,
Christian Schowalder,
Jost Dettweiler,
Johann Michael Breidebach,
Georg Philip Pettry,
Carl Ludwig Baum,
Johannes Prenser,?
Melchior Weydenmeyer,

Johann Daniel Franck,
Johann Georg Scherer,
Albrecht Schumacher,
Benedictus Gälle,
Johann Philip Gättman,
Johann Gottfried Weiss,
Johann Ludwig Weber,
Johann Michael Hirschlag,
Johannes Kugelwerth,
Johann Martin Klein,
Johannes Kiester,
Johannes Kundelmann,
Christian Stauffer,
Henrich Schneider,
Johan Henrich Lannert,*
Adam Herman,
Nicholas Ueberroth,
Johann Jacob Nagel,
Valentin Volck,
Peter Harris,*
Georg Bortz,
Nickel Herisch,
Adam Ruth,
Peter Ambrose,

Peter Ziefus,*
Peter Jung,
Christopher Hess,
Simon Klos,
Jacob Klamm,
Abraham Petter,
Johann Glasser,
Michael Büttner,
Philip Beck,
Johann Adam Büch,
Friederich Lofinck,
Hans George Baumantz,
Herman Wittscher,
Georg Peter Zenteler,
Johann Michael Nagel,
Johann Andreas Unangst,
Michael Resmeyer,
Georg Michael Klamm,
Georg Simon Rieger,
Johann David Schaadt,
Friederich Würtzbacher,
Johann Henrich Schöneberger,
Johann Martin Mäder,
Conrad Höldebrand.

---

244) Nov. 5, 1764.   Ship Jeneffer, Georg Kerr, Captain, from Rotterdam, last from Cowes.—247 passengers.

Nov. 5, 1764. Schiff Jeneffer, Capitain Georg Kerr, von Rotterdam über Cowes.—247 Reifende.

Johannes Futerman,
Hans Perger,*
Frantz Krämer,
Jost Rauter,
Frantz Krämer,
John Jäger,
Antonius Cromm,
Henrich Cromm,
Simon Georg,
Georg Schön,
Peter Hürstman,

Andreas Braum,
Johannes Ochsa,
John Cond. Steibel,
Jno. Geo. Upper,*
Jno. Diet. Fehring,
Thomas Weller,
Johannes Rübelandt,
Friederich Decker,
Jno. Charles Hetrig,
Martin Scheller,
Johann Wantzbach,

31*

Christian Roth,
Johann Ludwig Degen,
Johann Philip Endres,
Johann Gottfried Meyer,
Johan George Leininger,
Frantz Rübsamen,
Johann Martin Neb,
Johann Tönges Cromm,
Johann Christ. Lindorff,
Johann Best Weber,
Johann Gerlach Traut,
Johann Gerlach Finck,
Johann Peter Weber,
Johann Wilhelm Strunck,
Johann Henrich Au,
Johann Peter Petery,
Johann Georg Reyman,
John George Faust,
Johann Jacob Schlosser,
Joh. Dieterich Schmidt,
John Christ. Fuhrsbach,
Jost Henrich Frantz,
Johann Jacob Frantz,
Johann Wilhelm Frantz,
Johannes Volck,
Gottfried Stock,
Conrad Braun,
Christian Zimmer,
Jacob Landes,
Johannes Landes,
Ulrich Bieber,
John Miller,

Henrich Stöckel,
Nicklaus Meisset,
Jacob Meisset,*
Philip Schmidt,
Jno. Wm. Miller,
John Schwab,
Christian Hantzel,
Abraham Schapler,
Jacob Werns,*
Stephan Petri,
Peter Grebihl,
Joh. Engel Stöhr,
Johann Christ. Heusser,
Johannes Georg Reusch,
Johann Andreas Wentzell,
Johann David Mehn,
Johan Adam Steinwax,*
Johann Henrich Gihl,
Valentin Schuster,
Hans Georg Vuter,
Hans Georg Schmidt,
Johann Michael Braun,
Heinrich Wilhelm Gruck,
Johann Henrich Helensteuer,
Johann Adam Bieger,?
Johann Jacob Batz,
Balthasar Dieffenbach,
Johannes Gerhard Klein,
Johan Wilhelm Weynan,
Jacob Brennemann,
Johann Peter Hachenberg,
Johann Wilhelm Klein.

---

245) Nov. 5, 1764, Ship Prince of Wales, James Edgar, Master, from Rotterdam, last from Cowes.—131 passengers.

Nov. 5, 1764. Schiff Prince of Wales, Capitain James Edgar, von Rotterdam über Cowes.—131 Reisende.

Peter Römen,
Johannes Muth,
Philip Becher,

Casper Fries,
Ludwig Mader,
Peter Julien,

Philip Golb,*
Carl Uhl,
Nicolaus Booss,
Henrich Happel,
Jacob Dorsheimer,
Peter Dörr,
Johannes Eckel,
Peter Rorbach,
Peter Harbarger,
Paul Bichler,
Christoffel Schneit,
Johannes Schertzer,
Johannes Strack,
Adam Henneberger,
Johann Philipp Bittman,
Jacob Schenckweiler,
Conrad Korffmann,
Georg Wilhelm Resler,
Johannes Manderfelth,
Georg Peter Hessler,?
Charles Norheimer,*
Wilhelm Henrich Kuss,
Johann Nicklas Schneider,
Johann Valentin Schneider,
Philipp Mittmann,
Johannes Schnell,
Wilhelm Stuntz,
Johannes Stuntz,
Georg Jäger,
Adam Käiser,

Carl Stoltz,
Johannes Orth,
Gottlieb Becker,
Philip Barth,
Peter Wann,
Adam Gless,*
Peter Umstatt,
Jacob Petry,
Georg Schmit,
Sebastian Thiel,
Thomas Polhaus,
Peter Hesler,
George Horster,
Martin Seybert,
Johann Conrad Stoltz,
Johan Jacob Mattheis,
Johan Christoph Pruch,
Peter Laubenstein,
Johan Peter Laubenstein,
Johann Philip Schuey,
Jacob Espenschied,
Georg Schäffer,
Henrich Rihm,
Peter Cärius,
Georg Adam Dückel,
Christopher Heidrich,
Henrich Berninger,
Johannes Schneider,
Joh. Burchardt Culman,
Johannes Weisgerber.

---

246) Nov. 10, 1764. Ship Boston, Matthew Carr, Master, from Rotterdam, last from Cowes.—203 passengers.

Nov. 10, 1764. Schiff Boston, Capitain Matthew Carr, von Rotterdam über Cowes.—203 Reisende.

Henrich Spahr,
Johannes Schwerm,
Anthony Boley,
Johannes Wentz,
Johannes Walther,

Philip Glass,
Johannes Kessler,
Peter Wentz,
Peter Kendemer,?
Georg Reidenauer,

Johannes Pflaum,
Diebolt Lertz,
Andreas Köppel,
Lorentz Jung,
Ludwig Scheffer,
Michael Georg,
John Scheffling,
Diebolt Beit,
Jaque Depre,
Isaac Bertsch,
Adam Lampart,*
Johan Andreas Fuchs,
Henrich Bachmann,
Johan Casper Keipper,
Johann Peter Schahl,
Johan Georg Muth,
Johan Valentin Dickes,
Hans Georg Büttner,
Johan Carl Boley,
Georg Dannefeltzer,
Hans Adam Hartman,
Nickolaus Reidenauer,
Andreas Schneider,
Simon Peter Baidemann,
Christian Jacob Klein,
Johann Teobald,
Lewis Shimfassel,
Johan Philip Weytzel,
Henrich Herbach,

Frantz Lambert,
Christian Mühleisen,
Peter Castermann,
John Lampart,*
Jacob Buss,
Henry Bauer,*
Michael Weck,*
Peter Halm,
Justus Eckhard,
Henry Scheffer,*
Henrich Fuchs,
Peter Geiss,
Peter Fuchs,
Henrich Fuchs,*
Nicklas Hittel,
Peter Steffen,
Johan Nickel Weck,
Jacob Conrath,
Andreas Baussmann,
Rupertius Waller,
Bernhart Döss,
Philip Jacob Bausmann,
Casper Bernhardt,
Wilhelm Bernhardt,
Johann Diter Bledel,
Conrad Fried. Bientelheimer,
Johann Georg Stättler,
Johannes Sponknöbel,
Philip Gerber.*

---

247) Dec. 4, 1764. Snow Tryall, John Clapp, Master, from Rotterdam, last from Plymouth.—48 passengers.

Dec. 4, 1764. Seeschiff Tryall, Capitain John Clapp, von Rotterdam über Plymouth.—48 Reisende.

Jacob Keppel,*
Georg Bender,
Andreas Emrich,
Johannes Greast,
Johannes Bender,
Henrich Strocher,

Philippus Stein,
Johannes Jung,
Bastian Bender,
Anthony Opp,
Carl Dost,
Johan Daniel Gross,*

Heinrich Lautzenheisser,*
Peter Lautzenhäusser,
Abraham Schäffer,
Christopher Mathias,*
Johannes Roscher,

Nickolaus Aberthal,
Johann Jacob Enck,
Johannes Gaull,
Kaspar Schönbruck,
Valentin Braun.

248) Aug. 24, 1765. Ship Polly, Robert Porter, Master, from Rotterdam, last from Cowes.—211 passengers.

Aug. 24, 1765. Schiff Polly, Capitain Robert Porter, von Rotterdam über Cowes.—211 Reisende.

Jacob Huntzicker,*
Andreas Heintz,
Jacob Nägele,
Jacob Gay,
Joseph Stecher,
Jacob Gemberling,
Christian Wunder,
Conrad Hauenstein,*
Elias Werner,
Joh. Adam Friedrich Doll,
Jacob Gemberling sen.,
Georg Jacob Hauenstein,*
Christoph Spriegel,
Joh. Leonard Devil,*
Andreas Ehresmann,
Andreas Buchhecker,
Lorentz Gronninger,*
Joh. Michael Gronninger,*
Peter Sigrist,
Conrad Münch,
Jacob Mays,*
Peter Zeiler,
Jacob Wunder,
Elias Wigandt,
Jacob Faus,*
Peter Gram,
Jacob Treuttle,
Jacob Schultz,*
Jacob Behr,*
Samuel Behr,*

Jacob Thorwarth,
Jacob Hetzel,
Jacob Schneck,
George Stadtler,*
Henrich Hopff,
Friederich Hippel,
Georg Uffer,?
Christian Maurer,
Rudolph Mambeck,
Johannes Voltz,
Johannes Müller,
Johannes Schmidt,
Michael Hoff,
John Mich. Bishop,
Johannes May,
Jacob Müller,
Anthony Rhein,*
Michael Mensebach,*
Peter Gress,*
Johan Bernhart Dietrich,
Gottfried Münch,
Georg Adam Bressler,
Michael Widerick,*
Valentin Kauffmann,
Georg Simon Haushalter,
George Adam Teis,*
Christoph Dieterich,
Henrich Wilhelm Mayer,
Henrich Berthgiss,
Christian Häuffrer,

Johann Philip Harttung,
Jacob Schwenck,?
Paulus Sturm,
Johannes Rathacker,
Christoph Ginähle,
Hans Georg Schneck sen.,
Hans Georg Schneck,
Christopher Hanmüller,
Johan Jacob Hanmüller,
Johann Bardtmann,

Johann Jacob Hofelen,
Johann Georg Hoff,
Johann Jacob Schressel,
Johann Nickel Fischer,
Johann Wilhelm Bender,
Frantz Arnold Lein,
Martin Klaubach,*
Johan Jacob Mohr,
Johan George Kähler,
Peter Rudolph.*

249) Sept. 9, 1765. Ship Chance, Charles Smith, Master, from Rotterdam, last from Cowes.—216 passengers.

Sept. 9, 1765. Schiff Chance, Capitain Charles Smith, von Rotterdam über Cowes.—216 Reifende.

Peter Kebbler,*
Georg Krebs,*
Charles Grim,*
Jacob Müller,
Jacob Geiger,
Peter Schmidt,
Jacob Deinius,
Johannes Schissler,
Caspar Roth,
Henrich Lambert,
Balthas Breitenbühr,
Johann Georg Bauer,
Tobias Hafferstock,
Christopher Kessler,*
Jacob George,*
Johannes Fecher,*
Daniel Meyers,*
John Dauchawirt,
Jacob Krafft,
Henrich Kägel,
Jacob Guth,
John Klein,
Jacob Kendel,
Jacob Kehl,
Johan Erendorff,

Christian Höhl,
Eberhard Lüttig,*
Michael Heyl,
Martin Weber,
Israel Bockreider,
Friederich Keller,
Peter Beixitsch,*
Nicklaus Ludi,
John Dinius,
Jonas Dill,
Christoph Kettering,
Wendel Schanck,
Johannes Preiss,
Rudolph Brengel,
Jacob Kebbel,
John Russ,
Valentin Röbach,
Isaac Frantz,
John Geo. Firer,
Michael Hütler,
Matheis Hora,
Michael Müller,
Joh. Georg Philip Lessig,
Johann Christian Lessig,
Johan Gottlieb Gampffer,

Valentin Metzger,
Georg Christian Müller,
Johan Philip Melter,
Michael Kettenring,
Johan Jacob Kettenring,
Joh. Georg Paul Christmann,
Johann Wilhelm Nützer,
Philip Henrich Mayer,
Joh. Christophel Kurtz,
Joh. Wilhelm Schäffer,
Joh. Conrad Escher,
Joh. Wendel Gübeller,
John Henry Reichard,
Matheis Hartmeyer,

Joh. Adam Græim,
Johannes Ernst Kaps,
Apothicaire,
Johan Friederich Weyrer,
Joh. Burchard Krels,
Joh. Henrich Gernardt,
Joh. Michael Seitzer,
Abraham Breitenbüher,
Johann Philip Müller,
Johan Daniel Müller,
Johannes Giedelmann,
Johan Michael Hoyer,
Christian Brützius.

---

250) Sept. 19, 1765. Ship Betsey, John Osman, Commander, from Rotterdam, last from Cowes.

Sept. 19, 1765. Schiff Betsey, Commandant John Osman, von Rotterdam über Cowes.

Ludwig Barer,
Jacob Frietz,
Daniel Cobbit,
Henrich Pfeiffer,
Jacob Idler,
Isaac Gassman,*
Henrich Hermann,
Johan Matheus Dollmann,
Michael Löwenstein,
Hans Michael Brattler,
Johan Jacob Brattler,
Phil. Gottfried Mathias,
Abram Schming,
Martin Becker,
Jacob Zekerr,
Wilhelm Schäfer,
Joh. Georg Pletz,
Peter Schneider,
Wilhelm Freund,
Joh. Ebert Œrter,
Johann Gastlied,

Daniel Zwigart,
George Schiff,
Peter Garthner,
Michael Zehner,
John Heins,
Martin Hegner,
Jacob Hauss,
Benedict Schmit,*
Hans Merckle,
Johannes Wolff,
Jacob Blaus,
Darius Strauss,
Jacob Hiller,
Martin Ostertag,
Christian Wehr,
Andreas Heckel,
Jacob Licht,
Josua Metzger,
David Gottschall,
Conrad Schuler,
Johannes Braun,

Johann Henrich,
Benjamin Gassmann,
Gottfried Grumbach,
Joh. Carl Gabriel,
Hans Georg Ochs,
Jacob Friederich Schäffer,
Gottlob Jacob Löffler,
Johan Jacob Thiel,
Johann Georg Schneider,
Johan Henrich Ohrendorff,
Johan Adam Schneyder,
Johann Christian Betz,
Johann Adam Arnsterger,
Stephan Höpffer,
Philip Jacob Stockel,*
Lorentz Rinckle,*

Hans Georg Frietz,
Abraham Gleding,
Johan Philip Müller,
Johannes Riemer,
Georg Deschner,
Johannes Peter Zepper,
Johan Jacob Birki,
Friederich Heckel,
Johan Ruben Weller,
Johan Nickel Licht,
Johan Conrad Lang,
Johan Henrich Clement,
Johan Philip Schreder,
Philip Peter Laplace,
Johan Friederich Ernst,
Jacob Rockenbäuch.

251) Sept. 21, 1765. Ship Myrtilla, James Cayton, Captain, from London.—81 passengers.

Sept. 21, 1765. Schiff Myrtilla, Capitain James Cayton, von London.—81 Reisende.

Martin Schmidt,
Christian Hauss,
Jacob Kapp,
Martin Frey,
Martin Behr,
Philip Behr,
Jacob Dieterich,
Johannes Burgholdter,
Samuel Funck,
Christian Burgholdter,
Andreas Friederich,
Christoffel Dieterich,
Jacob Burgholdter,
Henrich Keller,
Adam Eckel,
Jacob Meyer,

Henrich Frey,
Johannes Krebüll,
Jacob Räumann,
Ulerich Wissler,
Jacob Wissler,
Henrich Küny,
Joh. Michael Meyer,
Sebastian Nill,
Ludwig Schehlman,
Johann Christian,
Josue Dedie, a
Jean Dedie, a
Abraham de Roche, a
Jean Jaque Etienne, a
Jean Richar Vierisard. a

a Swiss-French Protestants.
a Schweizerisch-französische Protestanten.

252) Oct. 7, 1765. Ship Countess of Sussex, Thomas Gray, Captain, from Rotterdam.—50 passengers.

Oct. 7, 1765. Schiff Counteß of Suffer, Capitain Thomas Gray, von Rotterdam.—50 Reifende.

William Hagher,*	Joh. Christ. Schönfelder,
David Vohl,	Frantz Carl Beaujacque,
Rudolph Käphffer,	Joh. Leonhard Hirsch,
Henry Stephan,	Johan Theodor Hofius,
Georg Michel Hertle,	Joh. Jacob Scheppach,
Joh. Thomas Metzler,	Joh. Gottlieb Ponce sen.,
Melchior Metzler,	Joh. Gottlieb Ponce jr.,
Jacob Sandemeyer,	Joh. Henrich Bender,
Christian Schneider,	Joh. Henrich Hepde,?
Conrad Brombach,	Johan Henrich Mell,
Johannes Brombach,	Joh. Christoph Schultz.
Andreas Hubert,	

253) Sept. 23, 1766. Ship Chance, Charles Smith, Master, from Rotterdam, last from Cowes.—200 passengers.

Sept. 23, 1766. Schiff Chance, Capitain Charles Smith, von Rotterdam über Cowes.—200 Reifende.

Conrad Störckell,	Johann Peter Faist,
Johannes Gröll,	Johan Franciscus Faist,
Johannes Hoch,	Johannes Meister,
Peter Blass,	Johannes Vogt,
Johannes Muller,	Philip Blitz,
Johannes Lipp,	Johannes Emrich,
Johannes Conradi,	Martin Lantz,
Conrath Eurich,	Johannes Graub,
Jacob Reitzel,	Joh. Georg May,
Henrich Gross,	Johannes Leis,
Nicholas Arnold,	Friederich Lüderitz,
Johann Georg Freytag,	Joh. Adam Flick,
Johan Friederich Altvetter,	John Haster,*
Johan Friederich Ulrich,	Johann Borthlehr,
Michael Sulheimer,	Gabriel Becker,
Johann Georg Ernold,	Henrich Frey,
Johann Georg Eurich,	Johannes Mates,
Johan Peter Mehrling,	Zacharias Endres,
Johan Henrich Kern,	Henrich Bossel,

32

Paul Conrad,
Andreas Weiss,
Friederich Locher,
Henrich Haher,
Henrich Dewalt,
Johannes Miesemer,
Sebastian Heckman,
Adam Schäffer,
Peter Burging,
Georg Tramp,
Geo. Conrad Seip,
Joh. Georg Weber,
Heinrich Ehrhart,
John Peter Tramp,
Johan Hirschbirg,
Johannes Kehl,
Peter Weber,
Simon Bichller,
Joseph Schmidt,
Johannes Reb,
Christoph Huger,
Johannes Huger,
Johannes Weber,
Anton Mundorff,?
Francis Beler,*
Joh. Christian Kunckel,
Johan Jacob Vögler,
Michael Grünewald,
Johan Peter Hör,
Johan Friederich Helm,
Johann Adam Ohl,
Johan Georg Seib,
Joh. Benedict Schneider,

Joh. Ludwig Waltmann,
Joh. Nicklaus Seitz,
Joh. Wilhelm Klöpper,
Joh. Valentin Klöpper,
Joh. Gabriel Gröber,
Joh. Michael Weingärtner,
Joh. Henrich Deetzel,
Joh. Dietrich Koster,?
Hannes Waldtmann,
Joh. Daniel Frischmuth,
Johan Nickel Martin,
Georg Gramlich,
Henrich Jüngst,
Joh. Jacob Reinhart,
Johan Peter Löw,
Joh. Friederick Müller,
Joh. Jacob Matzenbacher,
Hans Georg Schnepp,
Johan Wilhelm Seip,
John Adam Sand,
Johan Christoph Simon,
Joh. Georg Zimmermann,
Simon Peter Deubard,
Christopher Unger,
Philip Colman Rämlander,
Johan Michael Kuh,
Joh. Christoph Kämpff,
John Michael Lauer,
Johan Georg Ott,
Johan Nicolaus Wiebel,
Johan Georg Allsbach,
Joh. Henrich Leuthäusser,
Simon Gickert.

---

254) Oct. 13, 1766. Ship Betsey, John Osmond, Master, from Rotterdam, last from Cowes.—154 passengers.

Dct. 13, 1766. Schiff Betsey, Capitain John Dsmond, von Rotterdam über Cowes.—154 Reisende.

Johannes Breinckhart,
Nicolaus Böhler,

Johannes Schmid,
Jacob Henckel,

Michael Rath,
Daniel Brenner,
Joseph Stauch,
Johannes Benner,
Jacob Schäffer,
Jacob Kauffmann,
Joseph Singer,
Gottlieb Geyer,
Fred. Hoffman,
F. G. Hirschmann,
Johannes Mæyer,
Johannes Dahm,?
Jonas Barone,?
Lorentz Boris,*
Jacob Kern,
Jacob Günther,
Louis Robert,
Johannes Höckert,
Jacob Hähn,
Jacob Wagner,
Johannes Linck,
Valentin Schürling,
Peter Lütter,
Michael Weiss,
Johan Hage,
Peter Reyt,
Christoph Willemann,
Jacob Greuther,
Christian Wolff,*
Johannes Häuser,
Johannes Mosser,
Valentin Hamm,
John Keller,*
Peter Guite,
Georg Bub,
Jost Kuntz,*
Daniel Zimmermann,
Johan Helman Karle,

John Jacob Karl,
Johann Georg Becker,
Johannes Gelessener,
Jost Henry Volmer,
Georg Schiltwächter,
Johann Georg Volmer,
Johan Georg Miller,
Johann Jost Miller,
Johann Georg Fiesser,
Joh. Melchior Endlich,
Joh. Henrich Bär,
Joh. Henrich Frantz,
Joh. Philip Lambach,
Friederich Schittenhelm,
Georg Michael Schäher,
Johan Jacob Haussmann,
Johan Bernhard Borst,
Johann Henrich Fessler,
Johann Jacob Fessler,
Georg Friederich Immich,
Henrich Frantz Feck,
Johann Christoph Götz,
Johan Georg Lichtenberger,
Hans Martin Ziegler,
Johan Georg Knell,?
Johan Michael Keyser,
Johan Michael Schäffer,
Johan Filbert Gleh,
Johannes Wüst,
Lenhart Eckert,
Johan Bernhard Körtz,
Christian Frey,
Philip Buchman,
Lorentz Ladenberger,
Joseph Haller,
Christian Becker,
David Wathman,
Joh. Georg Schneyder.

255) Oct. 16, 1766. Ship Palladium, Richard Hunter, Master, from Lisbon, Portugal.

Oct. 16, 1766. Schiff Palladium, Capitain Richard Hunter, von Lissabon, Portugal.

Pedra Oberländer,
Ignacio Onder,
Francis Frey,
John Meyer,*
Francis Fisher,*
Peter Polo,*

Peter Schotter,
Paul Abzieger,
Carl Grissinger,
Erhard Schlagel,
Johannes Kreck.

256) Oct. 18, 1766. Ship Polly, Robert Porter, Master, from Amsterdam, last from Cowes.—181 passengers.

Oct. 18, 1766. Schiff Polly, Capitain Robert Porter, von Amsterdam über Cowes.—181 Reisende.

Christian Reiss,
Georg Schättel,
Nicolas Stoltzfus,
Christian Stoltzfus,
Jacob Holler,
Jacob Helfer,
John Brodnier,
Jacob Diemer,
Joh. Jacob Lentz,
Johannes Reuther,
Joh. Hen. Müller,
Ernst Wilh. Christ,
Johannes Geitling,
Johan T. Lupp,
John Edelmaan,
Johannes Schwen,
Johannes Bloch,
Philip Walter,
Peter Müller,
John W. Herman,
Hans Jacob Motz,
Andreas Stetzel,
Johannes Schrag,
Valentin Weld,
Frantz Schmidt,
Michael Friederich Gutekunst,

Michael Schättel,
Johann Nickel Werns,
Hans Georg Horn,
Frantz Herman,
John Georg Herman,
Philip Henrich Hechs,
Hans Georg Cuntz,
Johan Philip Jacob,
Hans Jacob Duchman,
Johan Jacob Schreiner,
Johannes Peter Stockmann,
Johan Adam Widerstein,
Johan Hen. Eissenberger,
Johan Philip Gielberth,
Johan Eberth Michael,
Georg Friederich Steiner,
Johan Georg Schreiber,
Joh. Philip Weltzheimer,
Hans Georg Petry,
Joh. Philip Schreiner,
Georg Valentin Steiner,
Joh. Henrich Herdel,
John Conrad Erick,*
Johann Jacob Henninger,
Johan Caspar Trump.

257) Nov. 4, 1766. Ship Sally, John Davidson, Master, from Rotterdam, last from Cowes.

Nov. 4, 1766. Schiff Sally, Capitain John Davidson, von Rotterdam über Cowes.

Paulus Amecker,	Georg Jacob Elsass,
Johannes Lemp,	Georg Friederich Göbss,
Jacob Brandenberger,	Joh. Georg Sturmfels.
Christoph Henrich Augustinus,	

---

258) Jan. 23, 1767. Ship Juno, John Robinson, Master, from Rotterdam, last from Berwick-on-Tweed, England.—36 passengers.

Jan. 23, 1767. Schiff Juno, Capitain John Robinson, von Rotterdam über Berwick-on-Tweed, England.—36 Reisende.

Johann Bekenne,	Johan Georg Seuberth,
Michael Götz,	Johan Georg Huber,
John Henry Hirsh,*	Johann Henrich Kiesy,
John Peter Böll,	Joh. Hen. Holdinghaus,
Johannes Moss,	Johan Clemens Gulich,
Joh. Hen. Lebo,	Georg Mich. Kittelmeyer.

---

259) Oct. 5, 1767. Ship Sally, John Osman, Master, from Rotterdam, last from Cowes.—116 passengers.

Oct. 5, 1767. Schiff Sally, Capitain John Osman, von Rotterdam über Cowes.—116 Reisende.

Henrich Kleiber,	Adolph Dill,
Georg Kleiber,	Theobald Fischer,
Georg Leidich,	Adam Dörr,
Jacob Durweeg,	Christian Müller,
Johannes Sommer,	Andreas Sperling,
Peter Wilrich,	Leonhart Beyer,
Stephan Tuchman,	Johannes Kemperling,
Philip Krimmel,	Gabriel Leon,
Joh. Emerich Adam,	Georg Henrich Focht,
Bernhart Eglin,	Adam Knoblauch,
Michael Gütchrel,	Friederich Gamssendahl,
Peter Auchementer,	Martin Bornträger,
Wendel Bernhardt,	Joh. Theodore Hartman,
Georg Bernhardt,	Hans Georg Mattheis,

32*

Christo. Ludwig Detweiler,
Hans Adam Bauer,
Johan Georg Würtzer,
Johan Andreas Seuling,
Georg Henrich Keitz,
Adam Philip Kietz,
Johan Philip Huff,
Wilhelm Diewalt,
Johann Petrygandt,
Joh. Conrad Bertsch,
Joh. Nicklaus Weyandt,
Georg Kilian Werth,
Joh. Henrich Krafft,
Joh. Nicolaus Ludwig,
Joh. Michael Bast,
Joh. Hieronimus Augustine,
Johannes Müller,
Joh. Jac. Heiser,
Frantz Hoch,
Jacob Eckenberger,
Jacob Berndt,*
Jacob Berndt jr.,*
Henrich Weber,
Nickel Huber,
Caspar Acker,
Adam Huber,
Michael Miller,
Adam Müller,
Valentin Hoch,
Philip Huber,
Jacob Lein,
Jacob Küffer,
Jacob Kerst,
Peter Diehl,
Kunrad Heier,
Peter Miller,*
Frantz Wilhelm,
Adam Reyter,*
Jacob Lambert,

Walter Heyl,
Jacob Zebalt,*
Frederick Kass,
Henrich Kiess,
Jacob Görtlerr,
Caspar Spies,
Jacob Reder,
Jacob Rümmel,
Hans Georg Graberth,
Johann Adam Lechler,
Johann Philip Lutz,
Johann Simon Hoch,
Joh. Bernhard Hoffmann,
Hans Schonenberger,
Philip Frölich,
Johann Georg Miller,
Daniel Lauth,
Jacob Luntz,
Johann Adam Reb,
Georg Adam Keffer,
Johan Henrich Fückes,
Hans Adam Palm,
Wilhelm Reuter,
Leonard Albrecht,
Michael Klein,
Peter Schweitzer,
Hans Georg Buchman,
Joh. Friederich Schlemb,
Adam Eckenberger,
Joh. Carl August Kiess,
Johann Jacob Appel,
Philipp Rottmann,
Joh. Wilhelm Bonyneburg,
Jacob Stellwagen,
Johan Caspar Schneider,
Phil. Leonhart Hartman,
Balthaser Heinrich,
Nickolaus Cabbett.

260) Oct. 6, 1767. Ship Hamilton, Charles Smith, Commander, from Rotterdam.—302 passengers.

Oct. 6, 1767. Schiff Hamilton, Commandant Charles Smith, von Rotterdam.—302 Reisende.

Christophel Henritzy,
Joh. Phil. Toninger,
Geo. Leon. Zeller,
Peter Rothrock,
Friederich Satler,
Nicklaus Schäffer,
Michael Wambach,
Johan Nicklaus Frick,
Joh. Henrich Baydeman,
Joh. Henrich Grosshard,
Joh. Friederich Anstbach,
Johann Peter Grumm,
Hans Michael Dreher,
Andreas Dreher,
Matheus Cuntz,
Michael Merlock,
Christ. Wineman,*
Henrich Felty,
Johannes Hoch,
Peter Krassle,
Peter Neuschwander,
Peter Neuschwander jr.,
Peter Diether,
Caspar Fitrius,?
Henrich Seyler,
Johannes Weiss,
Jacob Euher,
Jacob Nuss,
Leonhart Knor,
Wendel Heuntz,
Johannes Huber,
Conrath Rau,
Conrad Wachter,
Jacob Veiock,
Johannes Dis,?
Philip Baltzer,
Joh. Nic. Smith,*

Michael Endres,
Conrad Henrich,
P. E. Leonie,
Georg Cuntz,
Daniel Stollberger,
Caspar Walter,
Christian Steiner,
Jacob Schneider,
Johannes Hedinger,
Johannes Schneider,
Peter Seekatz,
Adam Lotz,
Henry Wagner,
George Hoock,*
Frantz Hopp,
Ludwig Horst,
Joseph Blisch,
Leonard Gramm,
John Vestermeyer,
Joseph Schleser,
Joh. Christ. Kirschenmann,
Jacob Hochstrasser,
Georg Jacob Baumann,
Henrich Nickel Heynich,
Geo. Michael Roth,
Geo. Michael Vuss,*
Joh. Nickel Stück,
Joh. Michel Kulman,
Christoph Seiler,
Conrad Böhmer,
Friederich Böhmer,
Johann Georg Butz,
Conrad Wagard,
Michael Heuntz,
Georg Jacob Süss,
Christophel Shitertz,*
Heinrich Walther,

Diebolt Kelchoffner,
Philip Christian Schrader,
Johan Conrad Schlüpp,
Johan Gottlieb Blümler,
Friederich Möllinger,
John Peter Hees,
Johan Melchior Reuschling,
Johan Friederich Heuntz,
John Bernhard Hoch,
Frid. Wilhelm Rauhman,
Peter von Hulen,
Johan Jacob Beuckler,
Christoph Hartman,
John Philip Menick,*
John Adam Peck,
Johannes Bürcket,
Johann Jacob Frick,
Christian Winseher,
Johan Georg Biss,
Hartman Schneider,
Peter Michael Klein,
Martin Kalckhaufen,
Johann Conrad Reiss,
Georg Peter Stoffel,
Johan Zacharias Donselt,
Henrich Medart,
Friederich Hert,
John Ewig,
Daniel Barch,

Adam Humbert,
Henrich Horn,
Sebastian Ettel,
Fried. Vogel,
Michael Kiesser,
Gottlieb Geiss,
Jacob Badel,*
Jacob Albrecht,
Michael Erhart,
Jacob Schell,
Peter Bollinger,
Johan Schultz,
Andreas Neuman,
Friederich Stimmel,
Phil. Jacob Cuntzmann,
Friederich Conrad Hoff,
Casimir Bernhard Alberti,
Georg Friederich Knobelloch,
Frau W. Sehwig,
Lorentz Schmidt,
Johan Gottlieb Hauck,
Johannes Fütter,
Philip Eullmann,
Hans Philip Bott,
Quirinus Michael,
Johan Peter Klatz,
Mattheis Grässel,
Joseph Dubernock.*

---

261) Oct. 26, 1767. Ship Brittania, Alexander Hardy, Master, from Rotterdam, last from Portsmouth.

Oct. 26, 1767. Schiff Brittania, Capitain Alexander Hardy, von Rotterdam über Portsmouth.

Johannes Han,
Casper Dietrich,
Henrich Gorgi,
Michael Göhler,*
Johannes Hirsch,
Henrich Hesser,

Johannes Bauer,
Johannes Staub,
Johannes Kunckel,
Henrich Kunckel,
Friederich Stegel,
Adam Dieterich,

Johannes Kister,
Johannes Keyser,
Carl Rörig,
Lorentz Schuster,
Michael Güntzler,
Jacob Plat,*
Johannes Glück,
Johannes Hem,
Johannes Kleinpeter,
Friederich Steygerwalt,
Johann Peter Hoch,
Johannes Steigerwalt,
Friederich Flehmann,
Michael Jacob Bach,

Johan Philip Falck,
Leonhart Krämer,
Johannes Kunckel,
Johan Michael Alstat,
Johannes Breitenbach,
Valentin Breitenbach,
Johan Henrich Bory,
Johannes Christian,
Johannes Kohler,
Johannes Bach,
Peter Schuster,
Johan Peter Uhl,
Matheus Köhler.

262) Oct. 29, 1767. Ship Minerva, John Spuriers, Master, from Rotterdam, last from Cowes.—194 passengers.

Oct. 29, 1767. Schiff Minerva, Capitain John Spuriers, von Rotterdam über Cowes.—194 Reisende.

Johannes Nauman,
Johannes Nauman jr.,
Jeremiah Nauman,
Nicholas Blacher,
Johann Tetwelder,?
John Miller,*
Peter Schumacher,
John Fischer,
Johannes Houer,
John Miller,*
Jacob Hellman,
Friederich Gaey,
H. Hambach,
Christian Faber,
Valentin Faber,
Jacob Faber,
Jacob Gorsch,
Peter Fuchs,
Anthony Schoch,
Joh. Mausshalder,
Jacob Weiss,

Michael Buch,
Jacob Drill,
Henrich Laux,
Jeremias Algeir,
Philip Hitzler,
Michael Seitz,
Peter Müller,
Valentin Stahl,
Johannes Schmidt,
Johannes Fusser,
Jacob Hohlwein,
Hans Georg Mayer,
Hans Bernhart Mayer,
Johan Peter Schumacher,
Johann Simon Schuey,
Joh. Dietrich Hennenberg,
Johan Wilhelm Endres,
Johannes Georg Hefer,
Johan Jacob Zechiel,
Joh. Valentin Kattinger,
Georg Adam Teutsch,

Christian Kauffman,
Joh. Matheis Schleemann,*
Valentin Faber sen.,
Georg Wilhelm Meyer,
Georg Adam Wetterbauer,
Johan Martin Motzer sen.,
Johan Martin Motzer,
Valentin Kamper,
Johan David Bordili,
Hans Georg Haaga,
Conrad Schneider,

Johann Georg Schäffer,
Nicolaus Albrecht,
Diterich Reidenmeyer,
Nicodemus Ungerer,
Johan Wolfgang Bolschner,
Johan Daniel Wilhelm,
Johann Jacob Lang,
Johann Adam Pfeiffer,
Johan Daniel Schmoltze,
Johan Ludwig Dieterich.

---

263) Nov. 4, 1767. Brigantine Grampus, Henry Robinson, Commander, from Rotterdam.

Nov. 4, 1767. Schnellsegler Grampus, Commandant Henry Robinson, von Rotterdam.

Adrian Granget,
Christian Muinber,
Peter Dertwa,*
Nicolaus Müller,

Johan Peter Gläkler,
Michael Unseld,
Johan Bernhard Welte.

---

264) Nov. 10, 1767. Ship Sally, Patrick Brown, Master, from Rotterdam, last from Cowes.—62 passengers.

Nov. 10, 1767. Schiff Sally, Capitain Patrick Brown, von Rotterdam über Cowes.—62 Reisende.

Adam Hertzerger,
Johannes Egel,
Lorentz Huber,
Hans Tschopp,
Martin Wäller,
Martin Stohler,
Simon Stein,
Friederich Bäntz,
Conrad Hering,
Johann Gänssle,
Simon Boni,
Valentin Neissel,*
Henrich Dölle,
Johannes Glotz,

Johann Tschudy,
Jacob Gobell,
Martin Tschudi,
Martin Müller,
Daniel Ernst Hirach,
Jacob Ersteberger,
Johannes Hänner,
Christian Althaus,
Hans Michael Boni,
Georg Fried. Weidmayer,
Johannes Burman,
Adrian Hablützel,
Michael Länhart,
Joh. Rudolph Bapp,

Martin Nicolaus Schudy,
Georg Wachter, *aus Memmin-*
      gen,
Georg Carl Mändel,

Christoph Lochner,
Philip Jacob Fuchs,
Johan Christian Roth,
Henrich Schaab.

---

265) Oct. 3, 1768. Ship Pennsylvania Packet, Robert Gill,
Master, from London. †

Oct. 3, 1768. Schiff Pennsylvania Packet, Capitain Robert
Gill, von London. †

Martin Pontzius,
Ludwig Brenner,
Jacob Linder,
Wilhelm Pynni,
Jacob Koch,
Jacob Kulmann,
David Pontzius,
Jonas Apfel,
Jacob Mauss,
Johan Georg Jung,

Frans Peter Brenner,
Reinhart Schell,
David Higernell,
Johannes Schumacher,
J. Frantz Helm,
Nicklas Kulmann,
Hans Jacob Hoffman,
Johan Georg Würtz,
Johan Peter Müller.

---

266) Oct. 10, 1768. Ship Minerva, Thomas Arnott, Master,
from Rotterdam, last from Portsmouth.—247 passengers.

Oct. 10, 1768. Schiff Minerva, Capitain Thomas Arnott,
von Rotterdam über Portsmouth.—247 Reisende.

Johannes Mohr,
Johannes Kunckel,
Friederich Stapf,
Rudolph Dersch,
Wendel Engel,
Philip Höhl,
Jacob Höhl,
Wendel Decker,
Johan Strohbau,

Johannes Busser,
Michael Latsch,
Ludwig Orth,
Daniel Weber,
Friederich Brand,
Conrad Braun,
Michael Wolff,
Peter Karp,*
Michael Ehrman,

---

† In List B, the only one preserved, are found the names of only
nineteen, although *twenty-eight* were to be qualified. Diligent search for
the nine missing names has been made, yet without success.—(*Editor.*)

† In Liste B, der einzig erhaltenen, finden sich die Namen von nur neunzehn, obgleich acht und zwanzig qualifizirt werden sollten. Es wurde fleißig
nach den verlorenen neun gesucht, jedoch ohne Erfolg.—(Herausgeber.)

Johannes Söstner,
Philip Gruntzge,
Christian Phül,
Henrich Müller,
Georg Mühl,
Jacob Frauenfelder,
Johann Bernhardt,
Michael Illgentz,?
Christian Koch,
Michael Schiesler,
Jacob Clautsch,
Jeremias Gleim,
Thomas Seyberth,
Jost Götz,
Maximilian Netzert,
Jacob Neu,
Christian Echternacht,
Frantz Hammet,
Michael Lang,
Erhard Giebelhauss,
Paul Büchert,
Johan Klemer,*
Joh. Peter Meier,
Philip Scheckler,
Johan Christian Helland,
Wilhelm Philip Knecht,
Johan Jacob Höhl,
Hans Jacob Rippas,
Henrich Straumay,
Johannes Schrath,
Casimer Hembd,
Conrad Lückhaub,
Valentin Sandel,
Johann Raffensburg,
Johan Wolfgang Seybots,
Johan Lenhard Wagner,
Christian Wilhelm Frütz,
Joh. Andreas Wiest,
Joh. Georg Mich. Strecker,
Johannes Stückerdts,
Joh. Georg Eisenman,

Johan Christoph Weick,
Johan Peter Graff,
Joh. Balthasar Graff,
Joh. Christian Steymenn,
Joh. Balthaser Kroh,
Johan Anthon Stephan,
Johannes Schmidt,
Joh. Conrad Rau,
Georg Adam Rau,
Paul Weitenbacher,
Jacob Zimmerman,
Johan Adam Meyer,
Georg Henry Seyberth,
Mathäus Kockenbauch,
Philip Peter Hautz,
Johannes Theis Müller,
Philip Jacob Ohler,
Johan Peter Merckel,
Johann Mathias Müller,
Johan Wilhelm Kleman,
Georg Henrich Haug,
Johan Jacob Walther,
Johan Jacob Dietrich,
Johan Jacob Härmann,
Johan Peter Sieffert,
Michael Hieber,
John Peter Meyer,*
Josephus Hybler,
Philip Sahl,
Wilhelm Frühs,
Michael Mauerer,
John Hasselberger,
Melchior Schmidt,
Peter Obersheimer,
Jacob Zoll,
Peter Feitne,
Georg Emmiger,
Johan Wilhelm Paulus,
Joh. Matheis Best,
Joh. Georg Scheuerman,
Johan Tobias Mohr,

Johan Valentin Krauss,
Joh. Peter Schmidt,
Joh. Nickel Huber,
Joh. Philip Schleicher,

Joh. Henrich Haubt,
Johan Jacob Schaffner,
Joh. Daniel Kauff,
Johannes Scheyzer.

267) Oct. 26, 1768. Ship Crawford, Charles Smith, Master, from Rotterdam, last from Cowes.—205 passengers.

Oct. 26, 1768. Schiff Crawford, Capitain Charles Smith, von Rotterdam über Cowes.—205 Reisende.

Gottfried Schlaug,
Jacob Schmidt,
Franc Gouche,*
John Gersto,*
Peter Farry,
Johannes Schäffer,
Georg Erlinger,
Andreas Ussener,
Conrad Scheffer,
Johannes Schütz,
Jacob Welcker,
Johannes Welcker,
Michael Welcker,
Johannes Kreiter,
Henrich Blum,
Abraham Saruain,
Isacque Dedie,
Samuel Saldret,
Abram Doisin,
Jacob Stehm,
Gottlob Schwartz,
Henrich Herschberger,
Philip Götz,
Hannes Weickert,
Georg Hoffmann,
Martin Schnabel,
Joh. Jacob Escher,
Johan Samuel Amweg,
Johan Georg Scher,
Christian Aescher,
Gabriel Aescher,*

Jacob Echman,
Joh. Jacob Kümmel,
Johan Valentin Friehs,
Johan Christophel Keller,
Carl Ludwig Staudehauer,
Georg Wilhelm Becker,
Johan Philip Haass,
Johan Dönius Frölig,
Friederich Hoffmann,
Fried. Samuel Heller,
Johan Georg Grün,
Jean Pierre Welle,
Martin Gerhardt Utes,
Johan Samuel Güdtner,
Jacob Ulrich Siltzel,
Johan Henrich Fohrman,
Johann Philip Michell,
Michael V. Huber,
Ignatius Zengerle,
Joh. Friederich Schnabel,
Joh. Conrad Schnabel,
Daniel Spies,
Conrad Frühs,
Martin Paff,
Joh. Philip Fries,
Caspar Lütschy,
Peter Galloe,
Joh. Jacob Dietz,
Joh. Hen. Leis,
Ludwig Kiehl,
Joh. Adam Staud,

33

Jost Hen. Müller,
Philip Hoff,
Isaac Cochet,
Joh. Wil. Hartman,
Joh. Nick. Hartman,
Sebastian Hinderle,
Joh. Matthias Hartman,
Georg Henrich Fischer,
Emanuel Waltmann,
Georg Jacob Waltmann,
Johan Isaac Cochet,

John Georg Beilstein,
Johan Wilhelm Diehl,
Joh. Nicklaus Heckmann,
Joh. Henrich Walterscher,
Joh. Herman Obermeyer,
Jost Henrich Schneider,
Joh. Erhardt Schneider,
Georg Dietrich Cochet,
Johan Henrich Strom,
Johan Wilhelm Waltman,
Andreas Gotthard Löbe.

---

268) Oct. 16, 1768. Ship Betsey, S. Hawk, Captain, from Rotterdam, last from Cowes.

Dct. 16, 1768. Schiff Betsey, Capitain S. Hawk, von Rotterdam über Cowes.

Solomon Stenger,
Peter Kämmes,
Jacob Andoni,
Joh. Philip Naahs,
Jacob Berentz,
Michael Bieber,
Jacob Stenger,
Jacob Naschi,
Johannes Niess,
Philip Münsch,
Adam Anthony,
Valentin Bieber,
Johann Gerst,
Jacob Bieber,*
Gerhard Krug,
Jacob Motz,
Adam Steger,
Andreas Hauck,
Adam Horn,
Frantz Schnell,
Joseph Emrich,
Jacob Stenger,
Johan Gerhard Thiel,
Jacob Anthony Mannwiller,

Joh. Matheis Mannwiller,
Ch. Frantz Christman,
Abraham Madsseil,
Christian Seyfert,
Johan Peter Gerhart,
Nicklaus Rauscher,
Theobald Pfaff,
Peter Reissdorff,
Jacob Schulheiss,
Johan Philip Opp,
Peter Armenbefer,
Johannes Schulheis,
Johann Friederich Leich,
Henrich Borckel,
Johann Henrich Marx,
Johann Nicklas Müller,
Johannes Schweyer,
Martin Weisshardt,
Fried. Wilh. Hoffmann,
Mathias Müller,
Daniel Stenger,
Christian Kuntze,?
Wendel Günther,
Georg Dupont,

Stephani Felix,
Martin Felix,
Michael Lang,
Georg Schütt,
Martin Bauer,
Nicolas Shirra,*
Valentin Müller,
Jacob Mayer,
Peter Sieber,
Henry Bender,
Peter Mennel,
Hannes Greissell,
Friederich Mahler,
Georg Mutz,
Peter Driebler,
Nicolas Gläzer,
John Matheis,
Jacob Scholl,
Andreas Schmidt
Johannes Gess,
George Huber,
Andreas Bach,
Nicholas Hardt,
Michael Raum,
Henrich Zibig,
Nickel Ber,
Philip Gippel,
Adam Klein,
John Cottringer, a
Johannes Felix,
Christopher Kirchsettin,

Hans Georg Honher,
Johan Jacob Lorentz,
Johan Georg Threin,
Johann Nickel Lintz,
Johann Nickel Lintz jr.,
Philip Micher,
Johann Nickel Scholl,
Philipp Schammo,
Hans Adam Müller,
Johannes Tedweiler,
Friedrich Brandtohr,
Johan Peter Frick,
Hans Ludwig Herman,
Michael Wilhelm,
Daniel Gerhard,
Hans Adam Schory,
Michael Zimes,
Johannes Pfau,
Hans Georg Bau,
Georg Wendling,
Daniel Kämmer,
Johann Peter Facquart,
Joh. Henrich Hermann,
Jacob Hausknecht,
Joh. Hen. Krächmer,
Adam Bernhart,
Johan Adam Stenger sen.,
Georg Etelwein,
Daniel Kämmer,
Christian Stenger.

---

269) Sept. 1, 1769. Ship Nancy and Sucky, William Keys, Captain, from London.

Sept. 1, 1769. Schiff Nancy und Sucky, Capitain William Keys, von London.

Friederich Roth,
Wilhelm Usener,

Jacob Grob,
Joan Guilielmus Pythan,

---

a John Cottringer was only qualified Feb. 14, 1769.—(*Editor.*)
a John Cottringer wurde erst am 14. Febr. 1769 qualifizirt.—(Herausg.)

388 NAMES OF GERMAN, SWISS

Joh. Balthaser Dernheimer,
Joh. Hen. Christoph Roth,
Uli Schrack,
Christian Roth,

Nicklaus Ernst,
Johann Georg Wunder,?
Johannes Gabriel.

---

270) Sept. 29, 1769. Ship London Pacquet, James Cook, Captain, from Lisbon, Portugal.

Sept. 29, 1769. Schiff London Pacquet, Capitain James Cook, von Lissabon, Portugal.

Wentzel Serb,
Martin Long,*
Johannes Miller,
Thomas Brüst,
Martin Gütt,
Friederich Diess,
Adrian Brüst,
Pitre Incler,

Hermanus Cazo,*
John Henry Block,
Hen. Michael Dhämer,
Joseph Schmeuell,
Frantz Gamb,
Joel Franciscus Todf,
Joh. Her. Fried. Lippenkan.

---

271) Oct. 13, 1769. Ship Minerva, Thomas Arnott, Captain, from Rotterdam, last from Portsmouth.

Oct. 13, 1769. Schiff Minerva, Capitain Thomas Arnott, von Rotterdam über Portsmouth.

Andreas Heyer,
Lorentz Heier,
Friederich Grommel,
Hans Georg Bopp,
Conrad Bock,
Joh. Jacob Lentz,
Michael Baus,
Friederich Kesseler,
Abraham Mellinger,
Peter Ulrich,
Philip Moses,
Bernhard Karg,
Philip Seyfrit,*
Joseph Farni,

Jacob Farny,
Jacob Müller,
Michael Hertz, a
Conrad Hoffman,
Michael Neff,
Michael Dosch,
Daniel Scheffer,
Jacob Berg,
Johan Philip Hecker,
Johan Georg Göltmann,
Johan Christoph Ferdig,
Philip Henrich Bohlender,
Joh. Matheis Katzenbach,
Johan Nicklas Schaffer,

a Michael Hertz, written in Hebrew, undoubtedly a *Jew.*—(*Editor.*)
a Michael Hertz ist in hebräischer Schrift geschrieben, und ist zweifelsohne der Name eines Juden.—(Herausgeber.)

Johan Theobald Emrich,
Johann Adam Klein,
Johann Adam Weller,
Johannes Theis Arnd,
Joh. Henrich Manderbach,
Joh. Henrich Manderbach jr.,
Joh. Henrich Dischardt,
Johann Wilhelm Schu,
Georg Friederich Rück,
Johan Georg Zundel,
Johann Nicklaus Döbler,
Hans Georg Jacob,
Jacob Musselmann,
Jacob Sülger,
Johan Matheus Dock,
Johann Jacob Walter,
Henrich Klein,
Nickelas Weber,
Nich. Bernet,*
Jacob Diehl,
Christoph Pasch,
Jacob Fryer,*
John Bolliek,*
Heinrich Fentz,
Johannes Herd,
Christian Jung,
Anthon Fuchs,
Andreas Heger,
Johannes Weber,
Georg Siemath,*
Joh. Jacob Fritz,

Theobald Hess,
Hans Vass.?
Peter Säwel,
Manuel Eberth,
Antoni Drexel,
Johann Hemrier,
Henrich Porster,
Georg Martin Jentz,
Theobald Schramm,
Jacob Henrich Arnold,
Philipp Conrad Häussler,
Henrich Carl Steutz,
Philip Peter Rothenheusser,
Georg Henrich Ziegler,
Johann Bernhard Frietzel,
Daniel Naumann,
Johannes Schneider,
Johann Philip Frey,
Johan Jacob Walther,
Johan Henrich Pfeffer,
Johan Casper Pauli,
Johan Ludwig Wasser,
Johan Christoph Scherrer,
Johan Adam Stock,
Joh. Andreas Strasbürger,
Johann Adam Steuer,
Johan Valentin Klein,
Johan Jacob Kiefer,
Johan Michael Rademacher,
Johan Philip Hennstz,
Stanislaus Matter.

272) Oct. 24, 1769. Ship Crawford, Charles Smith, Commander, from Rotterdam.

Oct. 24, 1769. Schiff Crawford, Commandant Charles Smith, von Rotterdam.

Georg Rüncker,
Michael Caff,
Johannes Hinckel,
Friederich Kneiss,

Dieter Beyerle,
Johannes Hoff,
Peter Thorn,
Wilhelm Nadler,

Anthon Müller,	Jost Henrich Thiel,
Johan Adam Bariedet,	Christopher Schmidt,
Johan Wilhelm Stoll,	Johann Theis Kempff,
Valentin Hoffman,	Johann Bernhart Kempff,
Johann Wilhelm Flick,	Johan Theis Miller.*

273) July 27, 1770. Snow Neptune, Thomas Edward Wallis, Commander, from Lisbon, Portugal.

Juli 27, 1770. Seeschiff Neptune, Commandant Thomas Edward Wallis, von Lissabon, Portugal.

John Nuttler,*	Georg Heinrich Cremer,
Francicio Weytzer,	Philip Jacob Michael,
Johann Paul Karz,	Johann Georg Bradtfisch.
Jean Baptiste,	

274) Aug. 29, 1770. Brig Dolphin, George Stephenson, Captain, from London.

Aug. 29, 1770. Brigg Dolphin, Capitain George Stephenson, von London.

Joseph Solomon,	Johann Jost Klein,
Peter Miller,*	Jean Siesrieux,
George Alizon,	Nicola Pavit,
Jaque Monie,	Piere Pavit.

275) Sept. 10, 1770. Snow Rose, George Ord, Master, from Lisbon, Portugal.

Sept. 10, 1770. Seeschiff Rose, Capitain George Ord, von Lissabon, Portugal.

Johannes End,	Johann Krüsser,
Peter Mohr,*	Petro Claude,
Antoine Dore,	Gille Sarier.*
Louise Patier,*	

276) Oct. 1, 1770. Ship Minerva, Thomas Arnott, Master, from Rotterdam, last from Cowes.

Oct. 1, 1770. Schiff Minerva, Capitain Thomas Arnott, von Rotterdam über Cowes.

Georg Mengs,
Michael Schmitt,
Johannes Schell,
Georg Müller,
Jacob Kuntz,
Jacob Marx,
Valentin Hess,
Philip Frantz,*
Lorents Vix,
David Ott,
Georg Gelli,*
Adam Bieber,
Adam Wolff,
Theobald Büsch,*
Jacob Greiner,
Sebastian Heiss,
Jacob Schmit,*
John Leiffer,*
Georg Lück,
Jacob Lück,*
Peter Schmit,
John Weyer,
Johannes Sprötz,
Georg Jacob Sturm,
Hans Georg Schell,
Johann Georg Hammerer,
Michael Nonnenmacher,
Johann Georg Schnepp,
Andreas Eyrich,
Caspar Pletsch,
Mathias Weber,
Johann Peter Bössinger,
Friederich Hehlhofher,
Friederich Greiner,*
Johan Georg Pfäll,
Georg Heinrich Maurer,
Johannes Scheib,
Johann Georg Müller,
Jacob Lück,
Mathias Scheuermann,
Christian Weiss,

Johannes Becker,
Martin Kerner,*
Philip Preissman,*
Johan Georg Bastian,
Joh. Henrich Bastian,
Georg Nickel,
Conrad Holstein,
Heinrich Freyer,
Jacob Paulus,
Peter Miller,
Michael Schock,*
Philip Simon,*
Jacob Heintz,
Georg Wier,*
Johan Frantz,
Christian Schultz,*
Michel Gerst,
Jacob Coblentz,
Michael Schafter,
Georg Ferber,
Henrich Gärthner,
Jacob Doll,
Jacob Stambach,
Dieterich Stambach,
Johannes Gaul,?
Andreas Kiefer,
Johannes Humbolt,
Georg Paul Freyer,
Matheis Weidner,
Philip Jacob Bessinger,*
Wilhelm Schlemilch,
Hans Georg Herrmann,
Stephan Fünfrock,
Michael Fünfrock jr.,
Hans Georg Mallo,
Joh. Henrich Hornberger,
Joh. Geo. Zimmerman,*
Hans Georg Weidman,
Michael Kammer,
Georg Henrich Braunig,
David Hirschberger,*

Conrad Sebastian Köller,
Jacob Philip Harn,
Michael Pessinger,*

Martz Olftheintz,
Johan Henrich Wäldte.

---

277) Oct. 30, 1770. Snow Brittania, Richard Eyer, Master,
from Lisbon, Portugal.

Oct. 30, 1770. Seeſchiff Brittania, Capitain Richard Eyer,
von Liſſabon, Portugal.

Z. Didiers,
De Labeaume,
Jean Hissard,

Guilliaume Mommaton,
Jean Vinettier,
Matheis Kreis.

---

278) Oct. 29, 1770. Ship Sally, John Osmond, Master, from
Rotterdam, last from Cowes.—143 passengers.

Oct. 29, 1770. Schiff Sally, Capitain John Osmond, von
Rotterdam über Cowes.—143 Reiſende.

Joh. Anton Frazer,*
Christoph Müller,
Francis Stein,*
Joh. Geo. Altefried,*
Peter Joseph,*
Paul Mingel,*
Burchart Seipp,
Daniel Solmer,*
Johannes Ditman,
Georg Christian Völcker,
Dietrich Wilh. Bücking,
Thomas Engelhardt,
Johan Friederich Hester,
Joh. Jost Sasmanshaussen,
Johan Krafft Achebach,
John Henry Denner,
Johann Henrich Eul,?
Johan Jost Birckelbach,
Andreas Lichti,
Johannes Lichti,
Johannes Criess,
Jacob Schneyder,
Jacob Schnell,

Johannes Reichel,
Henrich Weitherstein,
Martin Hebeisen,
Joh. Georg Dentzel,
Christian Furbi,
Paulus Welbemeir,
Henry Wernley,
Johannes Bibighauss,
Johannes Vollmer,
Johannes Stick,
Johannes Franck,
Johannes Weyandt,
Justus Schmidt,
C. G. Hauck,
Henricus Horn,
Jacob Bühler,
Peter Vogt,
Jacob Hubacher,
Paridon Petersen,
Friederich Borsch,
Rudolph Miller,*
Hans Christian,
Daniel Mise,

Christoph Beil,
Johannes Gaul, a
Johan Henrich Affterbach,
Johan Henrich Weyand,
Joh. Christopher Dietz,
Johan Theobald Franck,
Ludwig Daniel Stendli,
Johann Nicklaus Walter,
Johann Georg Schleicher,
Johan Balthas Klein,
Johan Henrich Klieberstein,
Johann Adam Haar,
Georg Andreas Wagner,
Johan Christian Breitner,*
Johann Nickel Haas,
Johann Nickel Bach,

Johann Jost Weyandt,
Johan Christ. vom Hoff,
Johann Peter Grüb,
Georg Ludwig Fischer,
Johannes Bachneid,
Johan Martin Gaul,
Joh. Martin Baumann,
Friederich Wilh. Baumann,
Christian Aeschlimann,
Johan Jacob Heinriegel,
Balzar Heinriegel,
Christ. Ludwig Heinriegel,
George Emmert,
Johannes Hothem,
Johan Valentin Franck.

279) Nov. 23, 1770. Ship Crawford, Charles Smith, Master, from Rotterdam, last from Cowes.—60 passengers, including *Newlanders.*†

Nov. 23, 1770. Schiff Crawford, Capitain Charles Smith, von Rotterdam über Cowes. — 60 Reisende, einschließlich der Neuländer. †

Daniel Stauffer,
Jacob Rohrer,
Wilhelm Gramm,
Johannes Hiestand,
Cornelius Gramm,
Tobias Hartmann,
Peter Müller,
Johannes Uff,

Jacob Uff,
Francis Kuhlman,
Ernst Berg,
Johannes Jauss,
Henrich Haub,
Andreas Gutting,*
P. F. Droz,
Jacob Geiger,

a A memorandum on this list states, "*nine absent of those to be qualified.*"—(*Editor.*)

a Eine Anmerkung auf dieser Liste sagt: „neun der zu Qualifizirenden abwesend.—(Herausgeber.)

† *Newlanders,* such persons as had been in Pennsylvania before.—See *Rupp's History of Germans in Penna.*, Chap. "*Neuländer.*"

† Neuländer sind solche Personen, die schon vorher in Pennsylvanien gewesen waren.—Siehe Rupp's Geschichte der Deutschen in Pennsylvanien. Kap. „Neuländer."

Carl Wilhelm Keck,
Johannes Ginther,
Johannes Diehl,
Carl Adolph Seitz,
Andreas Serenius,

Georg Kleiderlein,
Johannes Hummy,
Onesimus Schwend,
Heinrich Geiger,
Cornelius Braun.

---

280) June 17, 1771. Ship Pennsylvania Packet, Peter Osborn, Master, from London.

Juni 17, 1771. Schiff Pennsylvania Packet, Capitain Peter Osborn, von London.

Conrad Bachman,
Abraham Mayret,
Ludwig Rohrer,
Johannes Heyler,

Philip Jacob Weiss,
Joh. Georg Fried. Bechtel,
Johann Adam Bauth.

---

281) July 27, 1771. Brig America, William Copeland, Commander, from London.

Juli 27, 1771. Brigg America, Commandant William Copeland, von London.

Johannes Belmann,
Johannes Hepp,
Justus Kornschur,?
Lorentz Stahl,
Jacob Ruff,

Johann Georg Helff,
Johann Dietrich Hepp,
Joh. Georg von Nieder,
Joh. Martin von Nieder,*
John Jacob von Nieder.

---

282) Sept. 17, 1771. Ship Minerva, Thomas Arnott, Captain, from Rotterdam, last from Cowes.—204 passengers.

Sept. 17, 1771. Schiff Minerva, Capitain Thomas Arnott, von Rotterdam über Cowes.—204 Reisende.

Jacob Wentz,
Henry Spiess,
George Miller,
Gabriel Gascha,*
Philip Müller,
Christian Kneber,
Jacob Beier,
Peter Hertel,*
Henrich Schäffer,

Henry Dieterich,
Joh. Barth. Röhm,
Johan Daniel Schröder,
Wilhelm Friederich Seeger,
Carl Philip Ebert,
Johan Henrich Schmaltz,
Georg Jacob Stoltzel,
Johan Georg Jordy,
Johan Peter Lütsch,

Johann Peter Kuntz,
Johann Peter Heissler
Jacob Weiss,*
Caspar Osser,
Conrad Osser,
Jacob Jung,*
John Werge,*
Alexander Oranu,
John Geo. Noth,*
Jacob Wentz,
Adam Wagner,
Michael Waldenaus,*
Wilhelm Hirsch,
Friederich Hirsch,*
Valentin Linn,
Carl Welcker,
Jacob Welcker,
Philip Helick,
Henrich Kurtz,
Ulrich Käyser,
Mattheis Engel,
Andreas Hertziger,
Friederich Dewald,
Johannes Böst,
Jacob Reiff,*
Christian Gaul,
Michael Schmidt,
Jacob Hanhor,
Anton Glantz,
Ludwig Stegner,
Peter Kurtz,
Jacob Laux,
David Drexler,
Petrus Meyer,
Joh. Peter Lehr,
Erasmus Busch,*
Dionisius Busch,
Henrich Weidlandt,

Johann Geo.Friederich Scheller,
Henrich Matterkens,*
Johann Georg Christmann,
Johan Henrich Sche,
Johannes Güntlert,
Johannes Reinhold,
Michael Pilerge,?
Johann Michael Schmidt,
Johan Jacob Meder,
Andreas Hettmansterger,
Johann Georg Stierle,
Johann Michael Hoel,
Friederich Seigmüller,
Jacob Grünenwaldt,
Johann Adam Malle,
Johann Georg Süss,
Johann Friederich Dörsch,
Johan Conrad Roth,
Johann Conrad Schneider,
Hans Baltzer Peterman,*
John Henry Peterman,*
Johann Philip Schenckel,
Valentin Saslavo Stadecker,
Theobald Leibrock.
Philip Jacob May,
Sebastian Marcker,
Jacob Kuhlman,
Adam Molitor,
Johan Michael Straub,
Jacob Huthmacher,
Joh. Gerhard Kaltschmidt,
Joh. Stephan Guck,
Johan Jost Otterback,
Joh. Erhardt Räyer,
Philip Henrich Knapp,
Philip Conrad Christ,
Georg Christoph Hebebold.

283) Sept. 19, 1771. London Packet, —— Cook, Captain,
from Lisbon, Portugal.

Sept. 19, 1771. London Packet, Capitain Cook, von Lissabon, Portugal.

Henrich Berger,	Michael Esteuer,
Peter Schunke,*	Michelle Devignair,*
Paulus Gottlob Griell,	Etienne Teisser,
Gerardius Vestens,	Pier Gabori.*
Jean Baptiste,	

284) Oct. 31, 1771. Brigantine Recovery, —— Bull, Master, from Rotterdam, last from Cowes.

Oct. 31, 1771. Schnellsegler Recovery, Capitain Bull, von Rotterdam über Cowes.

John Havel,	Gottfried Lebrecht Schmidt,
Jacob Schupp,	Johann Georg Reiss,
Michael Gundery,	Joh. Henrich Ortmann,
Johannes Ortmann,	Gottfried Henrich Diehoff,
Christian Furman,*	Johannes Nicklaus Neu,
Johannes Herschman,	Johann Michael Lahm,
Paul Ackerman,*	Christophel Zäntyes,
Philip Burbach,	Johann Peter Schneider sen.,
Daniel Niederhauss,	Johannes Peter Schneider,
Nicholas Becker,	Johannes Christian Horster,
Peter Schneider,*	Johann Jacob Denkircher,
Albert Delir,	Jacob Henrich Wilhelm,
Christian Weber,	Ludwig Schneider,
Albertus Kratz,	Alexander Schumacher,
Johannes Benner,	Johann Nickel Welsch,
Andreas Schneider,	Johann Jost Schneider,
Philip Gräff,	Johann Adam Leonhardt,
John Martin,*	Hans Jacob Schäffer,
Jacob Welsch,	Johan Conrad Spangenberg,
Wilhelm Œrtter,	Johannes Eckstein,
Valentin Thomas,	Wilhelm Ernst Felbach,
Jacob Schäffer,	Johannes Schnell jr.,
Michael Schäffer,	Johann Martin Hisger,
Peter Becker,	Johann Henrich Filger,
Johannes Schnell,	Johann Jacob Becker.

285) Nov. 19, 1771. Ship Tyger, Georg Johnston, Master, from Rotterdam, last from Cowes.

Nov. 19, 1771. Schiff Tyger, Capitain Georg Johnston, von Rotterdam über Cowes.

John Kreble,*
Peter Wagner,*
Nicholaus Scheuerman,*
Jacob Wagner,*
Ludwig Schneider,
Johannes Müller,
Hans Georg Benner,
Johann Jacob Beyerle,
Sebastian Wille,
Dominicus Heyrom,*
Nicholas Grünenwald,
Johann Lautenschläger,
Peter Wasser,
Adam Steiner,
Henry Apple,
Henry Webber,
Anthony Klein,
Nicholas Jost,
Johannes Sigile,
Matheis Fauth,
Caspar Beyer,
Johannes Motte,
Nicklaus Köhler,
Friederich Foltz,
Jacob Burg,
Jacob Hoffman,
George Hann,*
Nicholas Hoffman,
Jonas Blesch,
Jacob Ihrig,
Gustavus Müller,
Johannes Lupp,
Peter Odern,
Christoph Störner,
Wilhelm Kumpf,
Henrich Mülberger,
Johannes Ihrig,
Martin Grahn,
Henrich Rickos,

Johannes Weller,
Johannes Nitzel,
Leonard Kessler,
Georg Volck,
Johannes Schneider,
Peter Kessler,
Carle Benner,
Johannes Benner,
Martin Benner,
Jacob Marx,
Adam Grosshart,
Peter Trexler,
Michael Trexler,
Jacob Kessler,*
Conrad Haasse,
Georg Michael Weiss,
Joh. Daniel Schwanfelder,
Jacob Samuel Golde,
Johann Nicolas Fuchs,
Johann Michael Beltz,
John Le Port,
Georg Mich. Raffenberger,
Hans Georg Ackermann,
Johann Wilhelm Fleck,
Georg Simon Grün,
Hen. Jac. Raubenheimer,
Johannes Wucherer,
Joh. Hen. Lautenschläger,
Johannes Willmann,
Georg Henrich Kindle,
Niclaus Samuel Golde,
Johannes Waltman,
Georg Friederich Küchle,
Johann Christ. Jäger,
Wilhelm Schmidt,
Johann Peter Weill,
Johan Georg Scheuermann,
Johan Daniel Cleiss,
Johann Michael Ihrig,

Johann Friederich Dörr,
Georg Eissenring,
Johann Peter Schrig,
Joh. Gottlieb Stein Becker,
Johann Georg Horn,
Johann Adam Löw,
John Bernard Leyer,
Johan Caspar Lorentz,
Hann Heinrich Zimmerman,
Johan Wilhelm Schneider,
Gottfried Kihnner,
Johann Nickel Martin,
Johannes Bernhardt Henn,
Johann Ludwig Starck,
Johann Adam Dracker,
Johan Conrad German,
Johann Bernhard Ragel,
Johannes Peter Reusch,
Conrad Meyer,*
Johannes Schott,

Lewis Ney,
John Ney,
Sebastian Dheuch,
Johannes Schletzer,
Martin Eberts,
John Jorts,*
Jacob Scheibly,
Philip Egle,
Adam Als,
Christ. Jeremias Schmidt,
Johannes Reusch,
Conrad Radman,
Johann Jacob Menges,
Jacob Sanner,
Johannes Niebel,
Johan Georg Laudenschläger,
Hans Mich. Lautenschläger,
Conrad von Halt,
Adam Eberhardt,
Andreas Ehmer.

286) Nov. 25, 1771. Ship Crawford, Charles Smith, Commander, from Rotterdam, last from Cowes.

Nov. 25, 1771. Schiff Crawford, Commandant Charles Smith, von Rotterdam über Cowes.

Michael Mohrlock,
Daniel Wolff,
Mathias Krauss,
Gottfried Stoll,

Jacob Friederich Höckhlen,
Johann Peter Kuch,
Johann Stephan Sulger,
Christoph Gottlieb Thieleman.

287) Dec. 1, 1771. Brig Betsey, Andrew Bryson, Commander, from London.

Dec. 1, 1771. Brigg Betsey, Commandant Andrew Bryson, von London.

Jacob Frey,
Jacob Schneider,
Heinrich Meier,
Friederich Bänley,
Jacob Bäy,
Jacob Stügger,

Johannes Schmidt,
Johannes Staub,
Jacob Kugler,
Heinrich Fichter,
Peter Stein,
Jacob Heer,

Henrich Dicke,
Hermanus Dicke,
Rudy Funck,
John Koch,
Wilh. Becker,
Michael Frey,
Johannes Heintz,
Johannes Flubacher,
Jacob Flubacher,
Heinrich Busser,
Martin Thomme,
Christophel Winder,
Mattheis Füsselbach,

Paulus Bauersachs,
Johan Henrich Hester,
Jacob Zimmerman,
Jean Gaspard Hathe,
Sebastian Strauman,*
Conrad Schelerünthler,
Wilhelm Schwhenneher,
Johannes Klappert,
Johann Martin Frey,
Sebastian Harth,
Daniel Volck,
Martin Funck,
Jacob Schumacher.

288) Dec. 10, 1771. Ship General Wolfe, Richard Hunter, Commander, from Lisbon, Portugal.

Dec. 10, 1771. Schiff General Wolfe, Commandant Richard Hunter, von Lissabon, Portugal.

Charles Smith,
R. Berger,
Francs Pros,
Casper Trible,*
John Carle,*

Anton Ernits,
Nich. Biso,*
Joannes Baptista,
John Fajon,*
Johannes Schmitt.

289) Feb. 24, 1772. Ship Hope, John Roberts, Captain, from London.—26 passengers.

Feb. 24, 1772. Schiff Hope, Capitain John Roberts, von London.—26 Reisende.

Henrich Meisner,
Hieronimus Henricii,
Christian Schmidt,
Christian Wohler,
Phil. Wilh. May,
Dietrich Muntzer,
Friederich Hector,
Theobald Klein,
Lemuel Lober,
Theobald Bastian,
Martin Sudtne,

Joh. Friederich Hönninger,
Johan Ernst Ziegler,
Johann Jacob Schweutzer,
Johann Henrich Steitz,
Johann Henrich Voigt,
Johann Jacob Hartmann,
Johann Andreas Fritze,
Johan Ulrich Bäyer,
Johann Georg Trühauffer,
Johann Georg Meyer,
Johan Melchior Vast.

290) Sept. 20, 1772. Ship Minerva, James Johnston, Commander, from Rotterdam, last from Cowes.—97 passengers.

Sept. 20, 1772. Schiff Minerva, Commandant James John=ston, von Rotterdam über Cowes.—97 Reisende.

Johannes Mayer,
Caspar Wintz,
Hans Plattner,
Johannes Hauck,
Hans Schuey,
Ludwig Miller,*
Gottlob Hempel,
Henri Perret,
Jacob Schaub,
Christian Apffel,
Henrich Schweitzer,
Jacob Ballmer,
Thomas Moll,
Jacob Schwele,
Frantz Beck,
Heinrich Schäublin,
Ulrich Henberger,
Jacob Hoffacker,
John Christian Fleit,*
Hans Baltzer Büsch,

Hans Peter Kämmer,
Johan Martin Zimmer,
Johan Friederich Ulmer,
Johannes Wasling,
Hans Casper Heier,
Georg Henrich Dehn,
Hans Jacob Moller,
Johann Georg Kessler,
Johann David Bennz,
Johannes Schwerdle,
John Arnoldus,
Jacob Uberer,
Martin Rudy,
Wilm. Nycius,*
Henrich Wissich,
Hans Jacob Weier,
Gottfried Zessernick,
John George Stander,*
Johann Georg Gehr.

291) Oct. 16, 1772. Ship Crawford, Charles Smith, Master, from Rotterdam, last from Cowes.

Oct. 16, 1772. Schiff Crawford, Capitain Charles Smith, von Rotterdam über Cowes.

Andreas Hoffman,
Martin Hauck,
Jacob Demmel,
Johannes Fischer,
Jacob Schwartz,
Valentin Welcker,
Gottfried Wittman,
Friederich Beyer,
Johannes Hörner,
Jacob Scherer,
Gottfried Fechty,

Christian Schlauch,
Johann Werth,
L. Smith,*
Johannes Sauter,
Jacob Abbiter,
Henrich Vogel,
Philipp Hamman,
Andreas Weissart,
Jonathan Linck,
Frederick Feitmeyer,
Christian Mohr,

Martin Wieton,
Johannes Schmidt,
Johannes Keitzi,
Marx Schneider,
Jacob Rupp,
Samuel Schoch,
Georg Franck,
Christian Rettes,
Wilhelm Baltzer,
Henrich Zercher,
Andreas Müller,
Johan Philip Fitting,
Johan Christian Nerbler,
Johan Theobald Merckel,
Henrich Franckforther,
Johann Peter Ochsner,
Hans Martin Mayer,
Johann Henrich Wagenhorst,
Johann Carl Wagenhorst,
Hans Georg Preis,
Joh. Georg Warthman,
John Henry Zimmerman,
Matheus Lindenmeyer,
Michael Warthman,
Samuel Friederich Winter,
Georg Martin Hüchtner,
Michael Stauffer,
Jonathan Treuttle,
Peter Hamman,
Friederich Linck,
Johann Georg Baum,
Bernhardt Wieland,
Andreas Holtzbarth,
Johannes Buchmüller,
Henrich Weissmüller,
Johann Christoph Scheibe,
Jacob Friederich Lauser,
Joh. David Ziegler,
Joh. Jacob Eberly,
Joh. Georg Einwächter,

Johan Conrad Discher,
Martin Möllinger,
Johan Leonhard Fichler,
Jacob Lautermilch,
Albrecht Kümmerle,
Johann Hebeisen,
Johannes Beer,
Peter Galte,
Johann Hess,
Peter Lambert,
Andreas Lambert,
Joseph Stump,
Michael Müller,
Rudolph Seltzer,
George Shuman,*
Isaac Bergthal,
John Gramer,*
Martin Hirsch,
Balthas Bertsch,
Jonas Nothstein,
Johann Gram,
Joseph Graff,
Georg Henrich Maurer,
Friederich Wilhelm Hess,
Frantz Carl Widman,
Johann Peter Harbach,
Georg Friederich Betz,
Johann Friederich Betz,
Georg David Herm,
Philip Jacob Sartorius,
Georg Michael Miller,*
Friederich Linck,
Abraham Köhler,
Peter Weymer sen.,
Christoph Saudrich,
Johann Wendel Wiegele,
Georg Adam Zacharius,
Jacob Schmidt,
Johannes Quast,
Frantz Peter Drexler.

34*

292) Oct. 19, 1772. Ship Catharine, —— Sutton, Captain, from Rotterdam, last from London.

Oct. 19, 1772. Schiff Catharine, Capitain Sutton, von Rotterdam über London.

Francis Stephany,
Leonhard Müller,
Ulrich Otho,
Georg Keller,
George Bardeck,
Martin Schude,
Francis Geisse,
Frantz Heicks,
Henrich Gerding,

Charles Friederich Knöry,*
Johan Caspar Koch,
Christian Linderman,
Gotthard David Flickwir,
Henrich Richner,
Frantz Fideli Schreckenbürger,
Joh. Christoph Lotspeich,
Peter Mohrmann.

293) Oct. 19, 1772. Ship Pheba, —— Castle, Captain, from London.

Oct. 19, 1772. Schiff Pheba, Capitain Castle, von London.

Nicholas Jacobson,
Frederick Schröder,
Georg Rehfeld,

Joh. Reinhardt Schäbelle,
Joh. Friederich Bahlsdorf,
Friederich Klette.

294) Nov. 3, 1772. Ship Sally, John Osmond, Master, from Rotterdam, last from Cowes.

Nov. 3, 1772. Schiff Sally, Capitain John Osmond, von Rotterdam über Cowes.

Gerlach Hass,
Joh. Geo. Ostertag,
Daniel Weiss,
Samuel Reiss,
Carl Neier,
Johan Freymu,
John Holtz,
Karl Geissler,
Wilhelm Lehman,
Christian Trautmann,
Weygandt Rohr,
Henrich Rolandt,
Jacob Albrecht,
Johannes Krom,

Peter Rathenbach,
Johannes Fritzinger,
Jacob Michel,
Wilhelm Reiss,
Henrich Dieterich,
Conrad Böder,
Jean Halewyn,
J. W. Lopfer,
Jacob Theis,
Christian Schmid,
Matthias Pauli,
Christian Reete,
Johannes Theis Schnell,
Nicolaus Trautwein,

Johann Jacob Eller,
Wilhelm Henrich Ritter,
Joh. Adam Matzenbacher,
Ernst Henrich Fritzinger,
Johan Matheus Böttger,
Joh. Jost Langebach,*
Johan Henrich Hartmann,
Johannes Schieberstein,
Johan Gerlach Lupffer,
Johan Daniel Koffer,
Johann Georg Rubbel,
Johannes Peter Schneider,

Johann Henrich Georg,
Johan Georg Knebelbach,
Philip Peter Schneider,*
Burchard Heyer,*
Nicklas Paulus,
Hans Georg Hiderffer,?
John Philip Bauer,
Gottlieb Schlichter,*
Johan Jost Betz,
Johann Georg Eull,
Johann Wilhelm Meyer,
Johan Nicolaus Schuhriem.

295) Dec. 3, 1772. Ship Hope, George Johnston, Master, from Rotterdam, last from Cowes.

Dec. 3, 1772. Schiff Hope, Capitain George Johnston, von Rotterdam über Cowes.

Henrich Lehr,
Jacob Finck,
Johannes Ohlwein,
Johannes Hentz,
Johannes Cösch,
Peter Keller,
Johannes Elgerth,
Wilhelm Becker,
Jacob Binckle,
John Frickheffer,*
Arnold Peters,
Jacob Cacho,
Joh. Zacharias Langbein,
Johann Georg Pflinder,
Philip Hardmann,
Johan Philip Miller,
John George Geib,*
Friederich Jacob Laux,
Wilhelm Friederich Dampff,

Georg Wilhelm Ber,
Philip Martin Keilhauer,
Georg Kirchner,
Henrich Schuler,
Johann Adam Funck,
Paulus Huwes,
Anthon Rausch,
Anthony Auer,
Jacob Masser,
Christian Stucky,
Georg Films,
Isaac Heuman, a
Friederich Steinha
Justus Bottenfeld,
Christian Sahm,
Johann Jacob Pfautz,
Johan Jost Frickheffer,
Johan Jost Dalmer,
Carl Ohlwein.

a Isaac Heuman, written in Hebrew.—(Editor.)
a Isaac Heuman ist hebräisch geschrieben.—(Herausgeber.)

296) Dec. 24, 1772. Brig Morton Star, Georg Demster, Master, from Rotterdam, last from Cowes.

Dec. 24, 1772. Brigg Morton Star, Capitain Georg Dem= ſter, von Rotterdam über Cowes.

Gottfried Fisterer,
Jacob Weltner,
John Weickel,
Jacob Kuster,
Will. Kemp,
Conrad Underseel,
Jacob Nusser,
Abraham Richards,*
John Runkel,
Jacob Hess,
Johan Feierbrand,
Friederich Hoffmann,
Anthony Schäffer,
Peter Nauätter,
Johann Lemer,
Ludwig Reinick,
Bernhard Nickel,*
Philip Suppert,*
Friederich Winder,
Christian Wenger,
Georg Schwartz,
Frantz Mentzer,

Johan Ludwig Maxeiner,
Henrich Maxeiner,
Andreas Stettling,
Johannes Hamscher,
Nicklaus Lüdermacher,?
Jno. Jacob Nanecker,*
Conrad Langebach,
Ludwig Henrich Deisman,
Johann Henrich Küntz,
John Jacob Gerem,
Wil. Ananius Turnez,
Johann Georg Kessler,
Johann Adam Esch,
Johan Heinrich Messert,
Johan Gotfried Gressmehr,
Johann Adam Stoll,
Johann Jacob Pfeiffer,
Johann Carl Miller,*
Frantz Henricus Hegert,
Johann Frantz Kelter,
Johann Peter Ulrich,
Jacob Niebergall.

☞ February 22, 1773, Francis Caspar Hassenclever, a merchant of Philadelphia, appeared before RICHARD PENN, Esq., Lieutenant Governor of Pennsylvania, and was qualified. The time of his arrival is not stated.—(*Editor.*)

☞ Am 22. Februar 1773 erſchien Francis Caſpar Haſſenclever, ein Handelsmann von Philadelphia, vor Richard Penn, Eſq., Lieutenant=Gou= verneur von Pennſylvanien, und wurde qualifizirt. Die Zeit ſeiner Ankunft wird nicht angegeben.—(Herausgeber.)

297) April 30, 1773. Ship Pennsylvania Packet, Peter Osborne, Commander, from London.

April 30, 1773. Schiff Pennſylvania Packet, Commandant Peter Osborne, von London.

Edeme Halbon,
Gerhard Meyer,
Arnold Bödescer,
Johannes Müller,
Conrad Gabel,
Charles Klükner,*
Henrich Kese,
Philip Bahn,
Adolph Strohl,
Gottfried Hebauer,
Joseph Burchhell,

Pier Carle Pouponnot,
Johan Friederich Rintelman,
Johannes Hartman,
Anton Le Roy,
Johan Christoph Hebiegt,
Andreas Kleinschmidt,
Johan Philip Rieffenach,
Christoph Reinche,
Johann Daniel Lehmann,
Sebastian Kleinschmidt,
Friederich Basermann.

298) April 30, 1773. Ship Catharine, —— Sutton, Comıander, from London.

April 30, 1773. Schiff Catharine, Commandant Sutton, von London.

Henry Mollwitz,
Etienne Shoret,
Pierre Factzedy,
Philippe Sunbert,
Ulrich Bastig,
Jean Gourdain,*
Johannes Schmitt,
Henric Savet,
Robert Hall,

Ch. Friederich Oberländer,
Johan Christoph Schweigerts,
Henrich Conrad Boger,
Joh. Bar. Dondemand,
Georg Baumann,
Jean Daniel Pouriot,
Simeon Meyland,
Etienne Morlier,
Augustin Gage Mercier.

299) May 31, 1773. Brigantine Dolphin, Arthur Hill, Commander, from London.

Mai 31, 1773. Schnellsegler Dolphin, Commandant Arthur Hill, von London.

Friederich Heyn,
Georg Pfetzer,
Henry Cautz,
Jacob Grübe,
Michael Horn,
Niehl Bardoe,
Mathäus Borelle,
Johannes Engel,
Andreas Heinlich,

Nich. Heyer,
Miehl Flyder,*
Johann Martin Weber,
Johann Georg Kuntz,
Christian Bashedich,*
Henrich Meister,
Andreas Reinhardt,
Henrich Arcularius,
Philip Jacob Arcularius,

Ludwig Reinhart,
Erhard Ahlemann,
Johann Birstödt,
Friederich Schleiff,
Andreas Franck,
Peter Kappus,
Nicholas Gottman,
Jacob Leshong,
Friederich Frey.

John Wiseman,*
Christian Pfeiffer,
Zacharias Bohret,
Christopher Keeger,*
Johann Georg Vogeley,
Christopher Biegel,*
Balthasar Paulssig,
Eberhart Vareffens.*

---

300) June 4, 1773. Ship Carolina, Benjamin Loxley, Captain, from London.

Juni 4, 1773. Schiff Carolina, Capitain Benjamin Loxley, von London.

Gab. Valin,
Louis Demarer,
Henericus Martin,
John Ellers,

Johann Georg Egert,
Johannes Andreas Schmidt,
Joachim Hartkopff,*
Gilli Dautremer.

---

301) Aug. 23, 1773. Ship Sally, John Osmond, Commander, from Rotterdam, last from Portsmouth.—193 passengers.

Aug. 23, 1773. Schiff Sally, Commandant John Osmond, von Rotterdam über Portsmouth.—193 Reisende.

Christopher Mingel,
Mathias Ham,
John W. Petri,
Daniel Mesare,
Ernst Mengeting,
Joseph Shemmler,*
Christian Leuthe,
Heinrich Brüser,
Herman Heldich,*
Friederich Brieff,
Henry Beck,
George Wolf,
Philip Keyser,
Gerhard Nobel,
Isaac Levi,
Georg Reyninger,

Bernhard Horning,
William Ubung,*
Johannes Gadecke,
Henrich Hilgert,
Johannes Brücher,
Albertus Schilack,
Jean Peietrs,
Mathias Friederich Däübler,
Christian Ludwig Bussel,
Carl Gottlob Fridler,
Johann Mathias Hinck,
Joh. Hen. Philip Ehr,
Johann Georg Vanberg,
Johan Frantz Fuchs,
Johan Gottfried Fischer,
Johann Peter Göbrich,

Johann Henrich Thielo,
John Henry Bartram,
Johann Carl Büttner,
John Lorentz Tempel,
Johann Conrad Hasemann,
Johan Henrich Dreyman,
Adolph Gottf. Carl Rose,
Johan Friederich Kukuck,
Christopher Schlachman,
Johann Jacob Engel,
Johann Jacob Müller,
Johann Jacob Bastian,
Johann Jacob Becker,
Carl van Wuwenhuys,
J. Christ. Schultz,
G. Werner Himmel,
Jno. Nich. Harm,*
Burchardt Jung,
Andreas Jung,
Peter Lösch,
J. Daniel Weismuth,
Anton Hen. Ritter,
J. Gottfried Nestler,
W. Dollendorp,
Ernst Paul Peter,
John Daman,*
Martin Hochmeyer,
Mark Wolff,
Pierre Demje,
Adolph Unfug,
Gottfried Vogel,
John Feig,
Theobald Stephan,
J. Conrad Arnd,
J. August Just,
Frantz Mutschler,
Johannes Braun,
Andreas Wagner,
Joh. Adam Schmidt
Andreas Hampe,

Casimir Leitz,
Frantz Frischtze,
Tobias Göhnet,
Ignatius Graffenberger,
Conrad Maurer,
John Kirshner,
George Schenck,
Bartel Metilmolske,
Joh. Emanuel Klos,
Friederich Marcus Montelius,
John Henry Hasper,
John Henry Schwitger,
Johan David Mandeler,
John Bernhard Habner,
H. Conrad Hieron. Schultze,
Johan Christoph Bosse,
Joh. Gottlieb Strietzel,
Joh. Carl Rosenkrantz,
John Vanderhuyst,
John Henry Zelman,*
Johan Peter Walter,
Carl Enoch Schildbach,
Joh. Tobias Hess,
Johan Friederich Beck,
Johan Gottfried Neinrich,
John Christoph Bautz,
Francis van Bauch,
Joh. Conrad Brackmann,
Valentin Christian Lehnig,
John Herman Rudolph,
Johann Andreas Merck,
Johann Christian Merck,
Johann Christoph Fasel,
Johann Joachim Welsnack,
John Valentin Kinberg,*
Henry Fred. Shuckers,*
Henrich Wilhelm Busse,
Joh. Hen. Christ. Bremmer,
George John Rauch,
Andreas Fahrenkorn.

302) Sept. 18, 1773. Ship Brittania, James Peter, Master, from Rotterdam, last from Cowes.—250 passengers.

Sept. 18, 1773. Schiff Brittania, Capitain James Peter, von Rotterdam über Cowes.—250 Reisende.

Christoph Henri,?
Daniel Genter,
Simon Schunck,
George Miller,*
Johan Grein,
Georg Adam Vogelsang,
Johann Henrich Löhr,
Johann Georg Ehrenfreid,
Johann Dieterich Bönig,
Hans Georg Klein,
Paul Matz,
Henrich Saner,
Andreas Löb,
Jacob Lück,
Peter Eckel,
Christian Becker,
Johannes Mertz,
Anthony Weber,
Philip Conrad,
Augustin Hes,
Hans Frick,
Henrich Schultz,
Ludwig Gerlinger,
Christian Leibich,
Jacob Deque,
Christian Schütz,
Adam Kämminger,
Christophel Orth,
Mich. Runckel,
Andreas Ott,
Johannes Aal,
Daniel Spiess,
Dan. Geo. Jung,
Michael Jung,
Philip Bönning,
Jacob Wenner,
Jacob Schott,

Johannes Daub,
Michael Ruff,
Christian Nell,
Martin Kramer,
Ludwig Kramer,
Joseph Schaak,
Christoph Henckel,
Thomas Baumann,
Bernhart Webert,
Philip Runckel,
Bernhard Schmitt,
Jacob Wenner,
Jacob Neu,
Stofel Neu,
William Rockenbrod,*
Hans Georg Weyl,
Johannes Reinhardt,
Johan Friederich Cammerlich,
Johan Henrich Herbst,
Johan Nicklaus Bastian,
Johann Jacob Waiblinger,
Philipp Aberthüne,
Jacob Schauffler,
Johann Peter Schott,
Traugott Leberecht Behzer,
Johann Georg Kramer,
Johan Nickel Reuthnauer
Johan Philip Pflieger,
Johan Jacob Beheling,
Johan Martin Kramer,
Johan Georg Kramer,
Johan Philip Tück,
Johan Conrad Emich,
Johann Adam Engertt,
Johann Conrad Netscher,
Carl Anton Maas,
Johann Daniel Roth,

Joh. Georg Wenner,
Joh. Jeremias Bönning,
Hermannus Schöler,
Johann Georg Gunckel,
Johann Carl Wentzel,
Johann Georg Huss,
Georg Martin Eberhardt,
Johan Balthaser Kramer,
Johann Adam Kramer,
Johann Simon Linck,
Johann Georg Linck,
Johann Nickel Staudt,
Johann Friederich Becker,
Johan Christian Fabritzius,
Johannes Welthshans,
Joh. Michael Kirschbaum,
Hans Adam Weiss,
Johan Wilhelm Franck,
Hans Geo. Slettebauer,*
Joh. Michel Ellig,
Gottlieb Mayer,
Michel Haas,

Peter Haas,
Michael Jung,
Wilhelm Voltz,
Jacob Hertz,
Jacob Degen,*
Franc Smith,*
Henry Erb,
Daniel Schütz,
Jacob Schneider,
Michael Kieffer,
Jacob Schneider,
Johann Georg Haffer,
Conrad Voltz,
Andreas Hirsch,
Georg Henrich Geck,
Adam Schmel,
Johan Michael Füscher,
Andreas Gröner,
Johann Georg Reiner,
Adam Schneider,
Johan Michael Thome,
Michael Sath.

303) Sept. 21, 1773. Ship Catharine, James Sutton, Commander, from London.

Sept. 21, 1773. Schiff Catharine, Commandant James Sutton, von London.

Georg Lufft,
Johann Schrecka,
Philipp Wild,
Johannes Sander,
Casimir Delbig,
Johannes Klein,
Georg Baucher,

Jac. Lud. Videbant,
Conrad Trippel,
Henrich Andreas Meyer,
Johan Henrich Becker,
Christian Tihn,
Michael Habach,
Martin Eberhard.

304) Sept. 27, 1773. Ship Union, —— Bryson, Master, from Rotterdam, last from Portsmouth.—247 passengers.

Sept. 27, 1773. Schiff Union, Capitain Bryson, von Rotterdam über Portsmouth.—247 Reisende.

35

Christophel Leinn,
Balthaser Hammer,
Johannes Brand,
John Gennett,*
John Peter Fuchs,
Ludwig Bachman,
Daniel Bernhard,
Valentin Götz,
Christian Götz,
George Shreier,*
Jacob Smith,*
Johannes Schütz,
Johannes Bauss,
Johannes Kiffer,
Johann Peter Schauer,
Johannes Wicke,
John Philip Diffebach,
John Henry Dambeller,
Johan Michael Lenhardt,
Georg Philip Gruber,
Johann Jacob Hörner,
Georg Adam Wendel,*
John George Störtzemeyer,
John Adam Zeitz,
John Michael Clements,
Johan Zacharias Conradt,
Johan Henrich Bauch,
Johan Lenhart Ihrig,
John Zimmerman,
Johannes Adler,
Joh. Adam Krausser,
Johan Spannman,
Jacob Arnoldt,
Rüben Stier,
Ludwig Schenckel,
Johann Kroscher,
Hannes Schmidt,
Phil. Dan. Greiss,
John George Sheffer,*
Johannes Firnhaber,
Christian Beck,

Friederich Grames,
Nicklaus Bachert,
Andreas Fischer,
Wilhelm Spies,
Johann Pfeiffer,
Herman Spies,
Wilhelm Busch,
J. Leonard Rödel,
J. George Erig,
Joh. Bourquin,
Johannes Batz,
Conrad Marsdorff,
C. Varlet,
Joh. Egel,
Joh. Geo. Egel,
John Hartman,
Johannes Herstein,
Georg Hartman,
Jacob Garste,
Wilhelm Stickel,
Johannes Schäffer,
Philip Andreas Hadt,
Johan Matheis Flach,
Johan Jacob Aurandt,
Johann Philip Donnges,
Johann Valentin Stegmüller,
Henrich Valentin Storches,
Johan Peter Schmid,
Johan Philip Hauck,
Johann Adam Reichert,
John George Holtzschuh,
Jacob Niclaus Firnhaber,
Andreas Friederich Schwentzel,
Johann Georg Leonhardt,
Johann Leonhard Göttmann,
Johann Peter Stöhr,
Jacob von Lahnen,
Johann Gottlieb Metzger,
Johann Henrich Weber,
Johann Philip Gräber,
Johann Henrich Brausser,

Philip Peter Gruber,
Johann Georg Steilhener,
Johann Joachim Gruber,
Johann Adam Hartman,
Johann Nickel Horn,
Johann Nickel Schmaus,
Adam Rosmeissel,

John Conrad Riechels,*
Johann Jacob Hoof,
Johann Jost Lenhard,
Georg Adam Bückel,
Johan Wilhelm Krüger,
Johannes Wilheiser.

---

305) Oct. 1, 1773, Ship Hope, George Johnston, Master, from Rotterdam, last from Cowes.

Oct. 1, 1773. Schiff Hope, Capitain George Johnston, von Rotterdam über Cowes.

Andreas Dengler,
Matthias Wall,
Matthias Wexler,
Jonas Dollinger,
Johann Peter Weber,
Johann Jost Busch,
Johan Henrich Busch,
John Christian Guth,
Henry Steinbring,
Michael Stumpf,
David Niess,
John Karn,*
Christian Keberling,
Michael Bauman,
Andreas Oberdorff,
Jost Althaus,
Graff Weyand,
Conrad Gerhard,
Fried. Sölchel,
Henry Meyer,*
Johannes Huss,
Georg Wunderlich,
Johannes Hesse,
Franz Schmidt,
Andreas Annletz,
Jost Welckel,
Philip Peman,
Friederich Röser,
Henry Miller,*

Johannes Strackbein,
Leonhardt Schmidt,
Jacob Schlatter,
Joh. Hen. Klein,
Niclaus Henrich Stephan,
Johannes Wilhelm Carle,
Johann Jost Bruch,
Johann Carl Mattis,
Carl Ferdinand Conrad,
Johann Michael Conrad,
Johann Bernhart Rau,
Johann Michael Oberdorff,
Joh. Fried. Sasmanhäuser,
Johann Wilhelm Seemann,
Joh. Jeremias Ballenberger,
Joh. Wilhelm Eckhardt,
Joh. Christoph Thiel,
Philip Adam Schuck,
Johan Lorentz Dihm,
Johan Michael Hirsch,
Johann Henrich Dau,
Johann Conrad Jung,
Johann Ludwig Hantz,
Johann Friederich Welckel,
Johann Michel Seydel,
Johann Georg Seidel,
Joh. Hen. Sasmanshaus,
Johan Ludwig Offleler.

306) Oct. 22, 1773. Ship Charming Molly, Robert Gill, Master, from Rotterdam, last from Plymouth.

Oct. 22, 1773. Schiff Charming Molly, Capitain Robert Gill, von Rotterdam über Plymouth.

Christian Ernst,
Nicola Chaillot,
Valentin Dietz,
Thomas Krebs,
Cassimir May,
Johannes Steckel,
Friederich Wilhelm,
Johan Lechleitner
Pierre Miloh,
Mathias Astimer,
Engelbert Classen,*
Andreas Emmrich,
Johann Patteiss,
Johann Martin Fuchs,
Johan Henrich Hensle,
Hans Adam Weitzel,
Johan Michael Fuchs,
Joh. Conrad Leonhard,
Johann Philip Berg,
Joh. Friederich Freytag,
Johan Ludwig Schwens,
Johann Christian Letten,
Johannes Eberhart Ohl,
Johan Jost Blecher,
Johann Henrich Wentzel,
Joseph Friederich Honstein,
Jacob Elgart,*
Henry Dayberer,*
Christian Schönfeld,

Daniel Weibel,
Jacque Dubret,
Caspar Geissinger,
Friederich Dietrich,
Henrich Kleyn,
Friederich Müller,
George Reinhart,
Caspar Adam,
Johannes Hartman,
Johannes Hoch,
Christian Lambert,
Jacob Graff,
Arius Schulicus,
Johann Daniel Bonn,
Friederich Baltzer Scherer,
Nicholas Zutheimer,*
Joseph Cauffman,*
Johannes Friederich Braun,
Johann Friederich Vogel,
Johann David Steinmann,
Johann Georg Vogel,
Johann Peter Geyer,
Johann Adam Lang,
John Peter Ermolt,
Carl Heinrich Hartig,
Bernhard Bauer,
Johann Georg Müller,
Johann Georg Theys.

---

307) Oct. 25, 1773. Ship Crawford, Charles Smith, Master, from Rotterdam, last from Cowes.

Oct. 25, 1773. Schiff Crawford, Capitain Charles Smith, von Rotterdam über Cowes.

Johannes Bud,
Christian Mertel,

Jacob Trewitz,
Joh. Jost Mätz,

John Schlichter,
Joh. Math. Weber,
Wilhelm Schneyder,
Joh. Bap. Nonn,
Andreas Zahele,
Joh. Geo. Steiner,
Johannes Klappert,
Henrich Ober,
Johannes Geistweit,
Joh. Nickel Thomas,
Joh. Philip Kees,
Killian Keller,
Jno. Wm. Humer,*
Johann Fürst,
David Reich,*
Daniel Meyer,
Johannes Diebler,
Christian Meyers,*
Johann Henrich Dittman,
Johann Jost Strackbein,
Johann Conrad Triewitz,
Johannes Peter Stahl,
Johannes Henrich Kiel,
Johan Friederich Manalther,
Johann Henrich Achen,
Johan Carl Gentzheimann,
Carl Christ. Fried. Cist,
Johann Henrich Graff,
Joh. Georg Birckelbach sen.
Joh. Georg Birckelbach,

Jacob Henrich Bast,
Johann Georg Reichman,
Johan Henrich Schumacher,
Joh. Siegesmund Stedtekorn,
Georg Philip Zissle,
Ludwig Güthing,
Johan Ludwig Becker,
Johann Ulrich Sieffner,
Johan Peter Rostweiler,
Michael Müller,
Adam Michael,
Matthias Höffer,
Wilhelm Schöler,
Henry Brum,*
George Lebank,*
John Fisher,*
Joh. Geo. Hartman,
Wilhelm Walther,
Adam Hamm,
Andreas Hild,
Johannes Petermann,
Johann Henrich Dörner,
Johann Georg Schneider,
Johann Henrich Loos,
Hans Henrich Schreiner,
Johan Jacob Schwissfurth,
Johan Henrich Hoffman,
ohannes Demandt,
Joh. Daniel Schweitzer,
Joachim Stremmel.

308) Nov. 23, 1773. Snow Neptune, Thomas Edward Wallace, Master, from Lisbon.

Nov. 23, 1773. Seeschiff Neptune, Capitain Thomas Edward Wallace, von Lissabon.

Joseph Lefran,
Charles Cassell,
William Blach,

Anthony Sinclair,*
Joseph Martin.

35*

309) Nov. 24, 1773. Ship Fame, James Duncan, Master, from Lisbon.

Nov. 24, 1773. Schiff Fame, Capitain James Duncan, von Lissabon.

Geo. Shavere,*
John Martine,*

Daniel Shapue.

---

310) Dec. 7, 1773. Ship Clementia, Patrick Brown, Master, from Lisbon.

Dec. 7, 1773. Schiff Clementia, Capitain Patrick Brown, von Lissabon.

John Pesser,*
Charles Zemmer,
Maro Seroni,
Joseph Louvat,

Francis Villeneaue,*
Francois Pechenet,
Francis Duchand.

---

311) Dec. 8, 1773. Ship Montague, William Pickels, Commander, from London.

Dec. 8, 1773. Schiff Montague, Commandant William Pickels, von London.

Jacob Fürst,
Friederich Waltz,
Peter Andreas,
Joh. Ludwig,
Phillippe Engroth,
Jacob Rissner,
John Henry Lau,
Johan Friederich Pieckert,
Christian Hallitschke,
Joh. Wendel Andreas,
Johan Adam Handel,
Johan Heinrich Krauel,
Mathias Conrad,

Friederich Eberle,
Joachim Neubaier,
Joseph Walcker,
Joseph Wagner,
Joh. Matthey,
Johannes Fessler,
Joh. Friederich Zinckenritz,
Traugott Gottfried Mäyer,
Georg Ludwig Kelmold,
Anthon Henrich Gnäschler,
Johann Adam Schanckweiler,
Johan Georg Speiser,
Johann Christian Duncker.

---

312) Aug. 15, 1774. Snow Sally, Stephen Jones, Captain.

Aug. 15, 1774. Seeschiff Sally, Capitain Stephen Jones.

Conrad Bernhard,*
Conrad Seifert,

John Ulrich,*
John Sauter,*

Michael Lillienthal,*
John George Gesel,*

Joh. William Sauter,*
John Diehl.

---

313) June 21, 1774. Brigantine Nancy, Thomas Armstrong, Master, from Hamburg.

Juni 21, 1774. Schnellsegler Nancy, Capitain Thomas Armstrong, von Hamburg.

Christopher Fuse,*
Herman Schuman,
Cornelius Welck,
Johan Fried. Matz,*

Joseph Lorentz Herrmann,
John Matthias Bauer,
Carl Friederich Müller.

---

314) June 21, 1774. Ship Charming Molly, Robert Gill, Master, from London.

Juni 21, 1774. Schiff Charming Molly, Capitain Robert Gill, von London.

Henrich Küntzel,
Laurens Frost,
Christian Heyll,
Peter Stephan,
Georg Fried. Frick,
Johannes Schwenck,
Joh. Henrich Moser,

Georg Jacob Weiss,
Georg Paulus Merckle,
Christian Langspech,
Carl Christoph Nicht,
Johan Georg Schneegantz,
Johan Georg Tritzlen,
Joh. Ludwig Bettmann.

---

315) Sept. 30, 1774. Ship Union, Andrew Bryson, Captain, from Rotterdam, last from Cowes.

Sept. 30, 1774. Schiff Union, Capitain Andrew Bryson, von Rotterdam über Cowes.

Caspar Nuyne,*
Georg Rummell,
Heinrich Dörr,
Andreas Schneynow,*
Johan Wilhelm Müller,
Johan Martin Schweickart,
Matthias Wild,
Carl Eurfur,
Johannes Fuchs,
Adam Seibert,

Nicklas Grauss,
Hartman Winck,
Bernhard Schwing,
Philip Jung,
Philip Klein,
Michael Klein,
Jost Leibinger,
Carl Steinmetz,
Johannes Had,
Jacob Boss,

Adam Stam,
Laux Kochges,
Philipp Müller,
Jacob Eyler,
Christian Rossin,
Jost Spengler,
Alexander Ott,
Peter Kuner,
Leonhart Opp,
Friederich Gantz,
Nicholas Bayer,
Samuel Schenck,
Fabian Kortz,
Peter Schimmel,
Johannes Schaum,
* * * Rütticher,
Jacob Voltz,
Christian Witmer,
Friederich Weyler,
Matheis Feiring,
Friederich Bayer,
Daniel Hickert,
Martin Weimer,
Nicklas Sirer,
Peter Wallman,
Peter Sietz,
Johann Walter,
Heinrich Thering,
Johann Anthon Rühl,
Johannes Heimbach,
Heinrich Heidt,
Abraham Stoffel Jacoby,
Caspar Steinmetz,
Heinrich Steinmetz,
Carl Böhringer,
Michael Müller,
Friederich Kölheffer,
Adam Koningsfeld,
Philipp Thiebautz,
Joh. Bartholomeus Ney,
Johan Georg Gottfried,

Johan Adam Pecht,
Peter Spruckmann,
Nicklas Fitincher,
Johann Zimmermann,
Nicklaus Schneppenhäusser,
Philip Jacob Wagner,
Valentin Beyer,
Henrich Adam Weltman,
Johann Detweiler,
Gotthold Fried. Enslin,
Johan Friederich Streuch,
Johan Adam Schlott,
Johannes Stoffel,
Friederich Bergman,
Johan Carl Reutzheiner,
Peter Schwabeland,
Johan Adam Friederich,
Johann Gotthelf Paul,
        Zimmermann,
Michael David Esch,
Christ. Wilh. Rathardt,
Johannes Becker,
Christoph Eufer,
Melchior Wickert,
Johann Georg Bauer,
Valentin Göttert,
Johann Nicolehrs,
Johan Adam Steinbach,
Johann Adam Miller,
Jacob Heibenzeter,
Friederich Hehl,
Nicholas Guit,*
Joseph Fütsch,
Ulrich Webber,
Jacob Leher,
Ludwig Au,
Johan Kurtz,
Daniel Wolff,
Georg Eckhart,*
Michael Schilling,
Jacob Gucker,

Christoph Herbster,
Heinrich Engelfried,
Friederich Freytag,
Martin Schwartz,
Caspar Uhl,
Friederich Beyerly,
Johannes Carolis,
Johannes Holtz,
Israel Leypold,
Michael Müller,
Johann Nicolaus Quast,
Johan Adam Leber,
Carl Christian Loris,
Ludwig Schwabeland,
Christian Schwabeland,
John Georg Baltz,

Johan Conrad Eiselen,
John George Rutter,
Johann Jacob Roth,
Johann Jacob Medert,
Friederich Schäumenkessel,
Johan Daniel Nisler,
Johann Christian Wilms,
Johann Jacob Dieterle,
Johann Adam Stock,
Georg Jacob Häussler,
Georg Adam Marggrander,
Christian Glaufliegel,
Erhardt Freytag,
Leonard Kroneman,
Johann Georg Müller.

316) Oct. 29, 1774. Snow Patty and Peggy, Robert Hardi, Master, from Lisbon.

Oct. 29, 1774. Seeſchiff Patty und Peggy, Capitain Robert Hardi, von Liſſabon.

Jono Moraublez,*
Jono Contono,*
Franco Barkeka,
Jono Cameti,*
Jiram Cloter,*
Fran. Boz,

Jabopet Hoquedas,
Manuel Rodrigue,
Francisca Rabane,
Hipolito Poncelly,*
Juan Domingo,*
Juan Hinanso.*

317) Oct. 31, 1774. Ship Sally, John Osmond, Master, from Rotterdam, last from Cowes.

Oct. 31, 1774. Schiff Sally, Capitain John Osmond, von Rotterdam über Cowes.

Christian Müller,
Christian Ehmig,
Hans Keller,
Ludwig Seltz,
Andreas Bühler,
Caspar Miller,
Joh. Maximilian Hake,

Johann Jacob Welcker sen.,
Johann Jacob Welcker,
Frederick Mayer,
Joh. Peter Cronenberger,
Balthaser Eberhardt,
Peter Köhler,
Joseph Shem,*

Jacob Stoff,
Georg Katz,
Geo. Habel,
Adam Segel,
Peter Löwenberg,
Philip Löwenberg,
Diewalt Klein,
Wilhelm Bramer,
Peter Bartheleus,
Ludwig Fihter,
Johannes Künsinger,
Johannes Schäffer,
Daniel Zittel,
Jacob Klein,
Joel Klein,
Anthony Weber,
Christian Laros,
Pierre Maison,
John Henry Klein,

Johann Philip Weber,
Johann Jacob Sunckel,
Christoph Griebela,
Christian Schudieck,
Henrich Oberkircher,
Christian Rommel,
Friederich Löwenberg,
Carl Bartholomæ,
Michael Bartholomæ,
Georg Schaltzindt,
Johann Paul Thomas,
    Teichgräber,
Johann Conrad Schmidt,
Friederich Cronberger,
Wilhelm Wenner,
Johann Georg Burckhard,
Conrad Bindenberger,
Jacob Mussgenug.

---

318) Jan. 16, 1775. Ship Catharine, John Baron, Commander, from London.

Jan. 16, 1775. Schiff Catharine, Commandant John Baron, von London.

Caspar Beaufort,
John Adam,
David Zuber,
Thomas Klenee,

Joh. Georg Fried. Wagner,
Johan Jacob Holtzer,
Joachim Jacob Brandt.

---

319) Oct. 9, 1775. Ship King of Prussia, William Potts, Master, from Rotterdam, last from Falmouth, England.

Oct. 9, 1775. Schiff King of Prussia, Capitain William Potts, von Rotterdam über Falmouth, England.

Ludwig Eller,
Georg Bernhardt,
Jacob Müller,
Nicolaus Sandmeier,
Johannes Obersheimer,
Joh. Georg Linns,

Joh. Kilian Booss,
Jacob Kohlman,
Philip Weber,
Johann Segwalt,
Johan Friederich Huey,
Georg Conrad Busch,

Conrad Tresenreuther,
Johann Georg Weyell,
Johann Wilhelm Schilack,
Johann Michael Tannezer,
Johann Philip Kohlman,
Johann David Weber,
Johann Michael Hans,
Johann Peter Heissheiner,
Joh. Paul Lein,
Thomas Rentzheimer,
Johannes Eckenberger,
Valentin Hoch,
Nicholas Rudy,
Nicolaus Grall,
Matthias Kössler,
Leonhard Götz,
Carl Ritter,
Johannes Fauth,
Michael Kramer,
Carl Eller,
John Seip,
Jost Alstatt,
Casper Nickel,
Johan Herrman,
Christian Vätter,
Jacob Vätter,
Jacob Teutzel,
Conrad Becker,

Jacob Jost,
Thiels Zerfas,
Nicol. Heustang,
Ludwig Weiss,
Johannes Rentzheimer,
Johan Nickel Wendeling,
Johann Nickel Meyer,
Johan Friederich Meyer,
Henricus Denner,
Joh. Jacob Schmidt,
Johannes Kriedelbach,
Joh. Valentin Mündel,
Stephanus Spach,
Nicklaus Zimmer,
Nicolaus Borman,
Philip Peter Müller,
Johan Ernst Kessler,
Joh. Jacob Knabenschus,
Christian Weissbach,
Friederich Schönholtz,
Georg Friederich Grawan,
Johan Jacob Grawan,
Johan Simon Schlars,
Johannes Sahler,
Peter Horbach,
Jacob Henrich Krammer,
Christian Gottfried Willert.

ADDENDA A.

————

The *Schwenckfelders* are called after Caspar Schwenckfeld von Ossing, a Silesian Knight, and counselor to the Duke of Liegnitz, Prussia. Schwenckfeld was a contemporary with Luther, Zwingli and other Reformers, and had his adherents, who were tolerated by the German Emperors, in the arch-dukedom of Silesia, especially in the principalities of Taur and Liegnitz, for nearly two hundred years. They, like many others, had to endure persecutions in 1590, 1650, 1725, when they were compelled to seek shelter in Upper Lusatia, Saxony, under the protection of the Senate of Görlitz, and also of *Nicolaus Ludwig Zinzendorf,* who had them under his protection about eight years, when they resolved to emigrate and seek a home in Georgia; but on arriving in Holland they were persuaded to go to Pennsylvania. Some came over in 1733, but the greater part in 1734.—See pp. 90, 94, 95, 96.

————

ADDENDA B.

————

For the following List, furnished by the Rev. *Levin T. Reichel,* Salem, North Carolina, I am much indebted to Prof. *John Beck,* of Litiz, Pa., (died 1872) who not only pointed to the source, whence it could be obtained, but also very kindly *engrossed* the Mss. List at the request of the Editor.

I. *Arrivals of Moravians from Georgia in Pennsylvania, from 1737 to 1747—a period of ten years.*

NOTE.—Some ministerial brethren, as Bishop Spangenberg, Bishop Nitschmann, Peter Böhler, &c., are omitted in this List, as they were no actual settlers, but returned again to Europe, or to other fields of activity of the Moravian Church. Ministers and Missionaries are in *Italics.*

A. D. 1737.—*Georg Neiser*, born in Moravia, emigrated 1737 to Georgia, thence to Pennsylvania, died 1784; Gottlieb Demuth, Gottfried Haberecht, died 1784; George Waschke, his wife and mother; Gotthart Demuth, David Jag, David Tanneberger, the celebrated organ-builder; John Tanneberger, son of David T.— descendants near Lebanon.

A. D. 1740.—*Anton Seiffert*, returned to Europe; *Martin Mack*, died 1784 at St. Croix; George Zeisberger, Rosina Zeisberger, *David Zeisberger*, an Indian Apostle, died 1808 at Goshen, Ohio; *John Bahner*, died 1785 at St. Thomas, one of the West India Islands; Hannah Hummel, afterwards Bahner's wife.

A. D. 1742.—Hagen, Büninger—his descendants in N. Y.

A. D. 1743.—James Burnside, born in Ireland, died 1755 near Bethlehem, where his remains rest. Twice Representative of Northampton County in the Assembly.

A. D. 1744.—Hussey. 1745.—Brownfield.

II. *Arrivals of Moravians from Europe in Pennsylvania, from* 1739 *to* 1749—*a period of ten years.*

A. D. 1739.—*Christian Henry Rauch*, in New York, died 1763 at Jamaica.

A. D. 1740.—Andrew Eschenbach, *David Nitschmann*, first proprietor of Bethlehem estate, died 1758 at Bethlehem; Christian Frölich, died 1776 at Bethlehem.

A. D. 1741.—*Gottlieb Büttner*, died 1745 at Checomeko, N. Y.; *John Wilhelm Zauder*, died 1782 in Holland; *John Christian Pyrlæus*, died 1785 in Germany; Count *Zinzendorf*, only on a visit; *Abraham Meinung*, died 1769 at St. Thomas; David Bruce, was from Scotland, died 1749 at Wechquatüsch.

A. D. 1742.—*Peter Böhler* and wife, returned to Europe; David Bishop, Michael Mikseh, *Joachim Senseman*, died 1772 at Jamaica—descendants in Pennsylvania; Michael Tenneberger, David Wohmit, *John Brucker*, died 1765 at St. Croix; *Paul David Beyzelius*, a Lutheran minister, died 1771; Heinrich Almerson, George Hartin, *John Brandmüller*, died 1777 at Bethlehem; John Adolph Meyer, *Owen Rice*, died 1778 in England — descendants in Bethlehem; Thos. Yarrell—descendants in Lancaster, Pa.; Robert Huss, John Turner, Samuel

36

Powell, *Joseph Powell,* died 1774 at Sichem, N. J.; *Nathaniel Seidel,* a Bishop, died single 1782 at Bethlehem; *Gottlieb Pezold,* died 1762 at Litiz; *Philip Meurer,* died 1757 at Donegal; *Leonhard Schnell, Frederick Post,* Indian Missionary, (see Collection, p. 152, Note,); George Schneider, Matthew Wittke, George Wiesner, George Kaske, George Heidecker, John Reinhard Sommers, Joseph Möller, John Huber, George Eister, *Joseph Shar, Hector Gembold,* died 1788; John Okely, William Okely, Christian Werner, *Jacob Lischy,* (see Collection, p. 152); John Christoph Heyne, Andreas, (colored).

A. D. 1742.—*Congregation at Bethlehem Organized.* David Hurbert and wife, died 1788 at Bethlehem; *A. J. Kohn, J. C. Franke,* M. Liebisch, from Moravia; Schnell.

A. D. 1743.—In December, one hundred and twenty persons arrived at New York, who moved to Bethlehem and Nazareth; among these were thirty-three young couples, who had been married, all on the same day, at Herrnhaag, May 27, 1743.

Note.—The letter N appended to a name indicates that the individual settled at Nazareth, Pa.

A. D. 1743.—Wohmit and wife, Abraham Kessler, N; H. Biefel, N; John Tobias Hirse, N; G. Kremer, *John Henry Möller,* N, died 1760 at Bethlehem; *M. Reuz,* died 1753 at Oldman's creek, on the pulpit; Christian Fritsch, N; Matheus Otto, doctor at Bethlehem; Gottfried Grabs, N; *Wolfgang Michler,* died 1785 at Hebron—descendants in Easton; Gottlieb Anders, N; —— Herser, —— Almers; John Münster, from Moravia; Geo. Christ, N; M. Hanke, —— Schaub; Geo. Zeisberger and wife, died 1780; G. Hantsch, died 1756; Christian Höpfner, died 1760; John Jorde, N; J. Christian Weinest, N; G. Hicke; Matheus Schropp, N, died 1766 at Salem, N. C.; Jonas Wilson, —— Ostian, —— Dugion, Jno. Schaub, N; John Brandmüller, returned from Europe whither he had gone 1742; J. G. Nixdorf, died 1785 at Bethlehem, Pa.; *Anton Wagner,* died 1786 near Emaus; James Greening, D. Kunkler, N; A. Demuth, from Moravia; —— Schütze, —— Brosch, —— M. Böhmer, —— Hanke, —— Opitz; *George Ohneberg,* N, Missionary in St. Croix; Matheus Weiss, N; John Mozer, N; J. M. Micke, N; G. Bertsch, N; John Michler, N; P. Göttge, N; Andrew Kremser, N; —— Schober, —— Harding, —— Oerter, —— Döhling, —— Cook, Thomas Schaaf, N; Jacob Behringer, Thomas Fisher and wife, N; —— Lighton, Jasper Paine; *Richard*

Usley, first English Missionary in Dobbs Parish; M. Krause, died 1775 at Salem, N. C.

A. D. 1744.—*Abraham Reinke*, Bishop, died 1760—his grand-son, Moravian Minister at Litiz, his grand-daughter, wife of Prof. *John Beck.*

A. D. 1746.—J. F. Cammerhof, died 1751 at Bethlehem; —— Hendrup, —— Wacke, —— Westmann, —— Gottschalk, S. Rosun.

A. D. 1747.—The members of the Moravian Church in the region of Bethlehem numbered 316, viz: at Bethlehem 163; Nazareth 42; Frederickstown 23; Gnadenhütten 11; Gnadenthal 18; scattering 59.

A. D. 1749.—Dec. 12, the following twelve married couples moved from Bethlehem to Nazareth:

Everet Emerson; Paul Fritsch, born in Moravia; Elias Teex, born in Upper Lusatia, Germany; Gottlieb Berndt, do; Jacob Hafner, Switzerland; Gottfried Schultze, Lower Silesia; Heinrich Fritsche, do; Wenzel Bernhard, Bohemia; John Schmidt, Upper Silesia; Geo. Gold, Moravia; Melchior Schmidt, Moravia.

III. *A List of unmarried men, who arrived at Bethlehem, September 14th, 1753.*

Ludolph Gottlieb Bachoff, born in Lüneburg; Christoph Heinrich Bachmeyer, Friedensburg; Frederick Beyer, Silesia; Hans Martin Calberlahn, Norway (surgeon); Ludwig Christoph Dehne, Wernigerode; Jacob Eyerle, Wirtemberg; *George Christian Fabricius*, Denmark, was murdered, Nov. 21, 1755; *Jacob Fries*, Denmark, died 1793 at Bethlehem; George Wenzel Golkowsky, Silesia (surveyor), died 1813; Joseph Haberland, Moravia; Jacob Herr, Wirtemberg; Samuel Hunt, Yorkshire, England; Jacob Jürgensen, Finland; Henry Krause, Silesia; *Otto Christian Krogstrup*, Denmark, pastor there; Joseph Lennert, Breisgau; *Albertus Rudolph Rusmeyer*, Lüneburg; *George Sölle*, Denmark, formerly a minister; *Christian Friederich Töllner*, Pomerania; Peter Worbasse, Juttland; Christian Widsted, do; Peter Weicht, Silesia; Charles Frederick Ziegler, Pomerania; Jacob Till and his wife, Moravia, died 1783 at Bethlehem; G. Stephen Wolson, Thüringen.

Zusatz A.

———

Die Schwenckfelder werden nach Caspar Schwenckfeld von Ossing, einem schlesischen Ritter und Rath des Herzogs von Liegnitz in Preußen, genannt. Schwenckfeld war ein Zeitgenosse Luther's, Zwingli's und anderer Reformatoren. Er hatte Anhänger, die von den deutschen Kaisern geduldet wurden und sich im Groß= herzogthum Schlesien, besonders in den Fürstenthümern Taur und Liegnitz, nahe an zwei hundert Jahre fortpflanzten. Wie viele Andere, so hatten auch sie in den Jahren 1590, 1650 und 1725 Verfolgungen zu erdulden und nach der Ober=Lausitz in Sachsen, unter den Schutz des Senats zu Görlitz und des Grafen Nicolaus Ludwig von Zinzendorf, zu fliehen, welcher sie acht Jahre lang beschützte. Sie entschlossen sich auszuwandern und eine Heimath in Georgia zu suchen; man belehrte sie jedoch auf ihrer Reise durch Holland, sich in Pennsylvanien anzusiedeln. Einzelne kamen 1733, jedoch die große Masse erst 1734.—Siehe S. 90, 94, 95, 96.

———

Zusatz B.

———

Die folgende Liste von Pastor Levin T. Reichel in Salem, Nord= Carolina, habe ich Prof. John Beck von Litiz, Penns. (gestorben 1872) zu verdanken, welcher nicht nur die Quelle angab, in der sie zu finden war, sondern auf die Bitte des Herausgebers die= selbe auch für dieses Werk zurecht machte.

I. Ankunft der Herrnhuter von Georgia in Penn= sylvanien in den Jahren 1737 bis 1747—ein Zeitraum von zehn Jahren.

Anmerkung. — Einige geistliche Brüder, als Bischof Spangenberg, Bischof Nitschmann, Peter Böhler u. s. w., fehlen in dieser Liste, da die= selben sich eigentlich nicht niederließen, sondern wieder nach Europa zurück= kehrten, oder ein anderes Arbeitsfeld der Herrnhuter=Kirche aufsuchten. Prediger und Missionare sind mit gesperrter Schrift gedruckt.

1737.—Georg Reiser, in Mähren geboren, wanderte 1737 nach Georgia aus und von da nach Pennsylvanien, und starb dort 1784; Gottlieb Demuth, Gottfried Haberecht, starb 1784; Georg Waschke, seine Frau und Mutter; Gotthardt Demuth, David Jag, David Tanneberger, der berühmte Orgelbauer; Johann Tanneberger, Sohn von David T.—Nachkommen nahe Lebanon.

1740.—Anton Seiffert, kehrte nach Europa zurück; Martin Mack, starb 1784 zu St. Croix; Georg Zeisberger, Rosina Zeisberger, David Zeisberger, war Indianer=Apostel, starb 1808 zu Goshen, Ohio; Johann Bahner, starb 1785 zu St. Thomas, einer der westindischen Inseln; Hannah Hummel, hernach Bahner's Frau.

1742.—Hagen, Büninger—Nachkommen in New York.

1743.—James Burnside, in Irland geboren, starb 1755 nahe Bethlehem, wo seine Gebeine ruhen. Zwei Mal Abgeordneter von Northampton County in der Assembly.

1744.—Hussey.

1745.—Brownfield.

II. Ankunft von Herrnhutern in Pennsylvanien aus Europa von 1739 bis 1749—ein Zeitraum von zehn Jahren.

1739.—Christian Heinrich Rauch, in New York, starb 1763 zu Jamaica.

1740.—Andreas Eschenbach, David Nitschmann, der erste Besitzer von Eigenthum in Bethlehem, starb 1758 zu Bethlehem; Christian Frölich, starb 1776 zu Bethlehem.

1741.—Gottlieb Büttner, starb 1745 zu Checomeko, N. Y.; Johann Wilhelm Zauder, starb 1782 in Holland; Johann Christian Pyrläus, starb 1785 in Deutschland; Graf Zinzendorf, auf einem Besuche; Abraham Meinung, starb 1769 zu St. Thomas; David Bruce von Schottland, starb 1749 zu Wechquatüsch.

1742.—Pet. Böhler und Frau, kehrten nach Europa zurück; David Bischof, Michael Mikseh, Joachim Sensemann, starb 1772 zu Jamaica—Nachkommen in Pennsylvanien; Michael Tenneberger, David Wohmit, Johann Brucker, starb 1765
36*

zu St. Croix; Paul David Beyzelius, ein lutherischer
Geistlicher, starb 1771; Heinrich Almerson, Geo. Hartin, Johann
Brandmüller, starb 1777 zu Bethlehem; Johann Adolph
Meyer, Owen Rice, starb 1778 in England—Nachkommen
in Bethlehem; Thomas Yarrell—Nachkommen in Lancaster, Pa.;
Robert Huß, Johann Turner, Sam. Powell, Joseph Powell,
starb 1774 zu Sichem, N. J.; Nathaniel Seidel, ein
Bischof, starb 1782 unverheirathet zu Bethlehem; Gottlieb
Pezold, starb 1762 zu Litiz; Philip Meurer, starb 1757
zu Donegal; Leonhard Schnell, Friederich Post, In=
dianer=Missionar, (siehe S. 152, Anmerkung); Georg Schneider,
Matthäus Wittke, Georg Wiesner, Georg Kaske, Georg Heidecker,
Johann Reinhard Sommers, Joseph Möller, Johann Huber,
Georg Eister, Joseph Schar, Hector Gembold, starb
1788; Johann Okely, Wilhelm Okely, Christian Werner, Jacob
Lischy, (siehe Seite 152), Johann Christoph Heyne, Andreas
(farbig).

1742.—Gemeinde zu Bethlehem gegründet. David
Hurbert und Frau; er starb 1788 zu Bethlehem; A. J. Kohn,
J. C. Franke, M. Liebisch, von Mähren; Schnell.

1743.—Im December kamen ein hundert und dreißig Personen
in New York an, welche nach Bethlehem und Nazareth zogen;
unter diesen befanden sich drei und dreißig junge Paare, welche
sämmtlich am 27. Mai 1743 zu Herrnhaag getraut worden waren.

Anmerkung.—Der dem Namen beigefügte Buchstabe N zeigt, daß die
betreffende Person sich in Nazareth niederließ.

1743.—Wohmit und Frau, Abraham Keßler, N; H. Biesel, N;
Johann Tobias Hirse, N; G. Kremer; Johann Heinrich
Möller, N, starb 1760 zu Bethlehem; M. Reuz, starb 1753
auf der Kanzel zu Oldman's Creek; Christian Fritsch, N; Mat=
thäus Otto, Arzt in Bethlehem; Gottfried Grabs, N; Wolf=
gang Michler, starb 1785 zu Hebron—Nachkommen in
Easton; Gottlieb Anders, N; Herser, Almers; Johann Münster,
von Mähren; Georg Christ, N; M. Hanke, Schaub; Georg
Zeisberger und Frau, er starb 1780; G. Hantsch, starb 1756;
Christian Höpfner, starb 1760; Johannes Jorde, N; J. Christ.
Weinest, N; G. Hicke; Matthäus Schropp, N, starb 1766 zu
Salem, N. C.; Jonas Wilson, Ostian, Dugion, Johann
Schaub, N; Johannes Brandmüller, kehrte von Europa, das er
1742 besucht, zurück; J. G. Nixdorf, starb 1785 zu Bethlehem;

Anton Wagner, starb 1786 nahe Emaus; Jacob Greening, D. Kunkler, N; A. Demuth, von Mähren; Schütze, Brosch, M. Böhmer, Hanke, Opitz; Georg Ohneberg, N, Missionar zu St. Croix; Matthäus Weiß, N; Johann Mozer, N; J. M. Micke, N; G. Bertsch, N; Johann Michler, N; P. Göttge, N; Andreas Kremser, N; Schober, Harding, Oerter, Döhling, Cook, Thomas Schaaf, N; Jacob Behringer, Thomas Fischer und Frau, N; Lighton, Jasper Paine; Richard Usley, erster eng= lischer Missionar in Dobbs Sprengel; M. Krause, starb 1775 zu Salem, N. C.

1744.—Abraham Reinke, Bischof, starb 1760; sein Enkel ist herrnhuter Geistlicher zu Litiz, seine Enkelin die Frau des Hrn. Prof. Johann Beck.

1746.—J. F. Cammerhof, starb 1751 zu Bethlehem; Hendrup, Wacke, Westmann, Gottschalk, S. Rosun.

1747.—Die Mitglieder der herrnhuter Gemeinde in der Nähe Bethlehem's zählten 316, nämlich: zu Bethlehem 163, Naza= reth 42, Frederickstown 23, Gnadenhütten 11, Gnadenthal 18, zerstreut 59.

1749.—Am 12. December zogen folgende zwölf verheirathete Paare von Bethlehem nach Nazareth:

Everet Emerson; Paul Fritsch, in Mähren geboren; Elias Teer, in der Ober=Lausitz geboren; Gottlieb Berndt, ebenfalls; Jacob Hafner, aus der Schweiz; Gottfried Schultze, aus Nieder= Schlesien; Heinrich Fritsche, do; Wenzel Bernhard, aus Böhmen; Johann Schmidt, aus Ober=Schlesien; Georg Gold, aus Mäh= ren; Melchior Schmidt, ebenfalls aus Mähren.

III. Liste der unverheiratheten Männer, die am 14. Sept. 1753 zu Bethlehem angekommen sind.

Ludwig Gottlieb Bachoff, geboren zu Lüneburg; Christ. Heinrich Bachmeyer, Friedensburg; Friedrich Beyer, Schlesien; Hans Martin Calberlahn, Norwegen (Wundarzt); Ludwig Christoph Dehne, Wernigerode; Jacob Eyerle, Württemberg; Geo. Christian Fabricius, Dänemark, wurde am 21. Nov. 1755 ermordet; Jacob Fries, Dänemark, starb 1793 zu Bethlehem; Georg Wenzel Golkowsky, Schlesien (Landmesser), starb 1813; Joseph Haberland, Mähren; Jacob Herr, Würt= temberg; Samuel Hunt, Yorkshire, England; Jacob Jürgensen,

Finnland; Heinrich Krause, Schlesien; Otto Christian Krog=
strup, Dänemark, dortiger Pastor; Joseph Lennert, Breisgau;
Albertus Rudolph Rusmeyer, Lüneburg; Geo. Sölle,
Dänemark, früher Geistlicher; Christian Friedrich Töll=
ner, Pommern; Peter Worbasse, Jütland; Christian Widsted,
Jütland; Peter Weicht, Schlesien; Karl Friedrich Ziegler, Pom=
mern; Jacob Till und Frau, Mähren, starb 1783 zu Bethlehem;
G. Stephen Wolson, Thüringen.

APPENDIX (Anhang).

No. I.

NAMES OF FIRST SETTLERS AT GERMANTOWN AND VICINITY, FROM 1683 to 1710.

Namen der erſten Anſiedler von Germantown und Umgegend von 1683 bis 1710.

Names having an asterisk (*) attached were naturalized by an Act of Assembly, 1708–1709.

Die mit einem Stern (*) bezeichneten Namen wurden 1708–1709 durch Aſſembly-Beſchluß naturaliſirt.

Francis Daniel Pastorius,*	Isaac Dilbeck,*
Jacob Schumacher,	Tünes Künders,* a
Georg Wertmüller,	Arents Klincken, b

---

a Denis Kundors, or Conrad.—Pastorius had an interview with Conrad at Crefelt, April 12, 1683, on his way to America. The first religious meeting by Quakers, or Friends was held at Conrad's house, Germantown, 1683.—*Proud's Penn.*, I, p. 220.

a Denis Kundors, oder Conrad.—Paſtorius hatte Conrad zu Crefelt am 12. April 1683 auf ſeinem Wege nach Amerika geſprochen. Die erſte gottesdienſtliche Zuſammenkunft der Quäker oder Freunde wurde 1683 in Conrad's Haus in Germantown gehalten.—Proub's Pennſ., I, S. 220.

b Arents Klincken came from Holland with William Penn, in his first voyage, 1682. He became acquainted with Penn in Holland. Klincken built the first two-story house in Germantown; Penn was present, and partook of the raising dinner. The same old house stood, 1855, on Justus Johnson's premises. Klincken died at the age of eighty, and left a son whose name was Anthony Klincken, "the great hunter."—*Watson's Annals*, II, p. 20.

b Arents Klincken kam mit William Penn auf beſſen erſte Reiſe 1682 von Holland, wo er mit Penn bekannt worden war. Er baute das erſte zweiſtöckige Gebäude in Germantown; Penn war zugegen und betheiligte ſich an dem bei Gelegenheit des Aufſchlagens dieſes Hauſes bereiteten Feſteſſen. 1855 ſtand noch daſſelbe alte Haus auf Juſtus Johnſon's Grundſtück. Klincken ſtarb im Alter von 80 Jahren und hinterließ einen Sohn, Anthony Klincken, „der große Waidmann."—Watſon's Annalen, II, S. 20.

Thomas Gasper,
Cunrad Bacher, *alias* Rutter,
Dirk op den Gräff,
Herman op den Gräff,
Abraham Isaac op den Gräff,
Lenert Arets,*
Reinert Tisen,*
Wilhelm Strepers,*
Jan Lensen,*
Peter Keurlis,
Jan Simens,
Johannes Bleickers,*
Abraham Tünes,*
Wigard Levering,
Gerhard Levering,
Jan Lücken,
Johannes Jawert,*
Conrad Conrads,
Johannes Kunders,
Dennis Kunders,*
Matheis Kunders,*
Johan Kunders,*
Dirk Keyser,*
Peter Keyser,*
Johannes Döden,*
Casper Hödt,*
Cornelius Werts,*
Henrich Selen,*

Walter Simens,*
Dirk Jansen jr.,*
Richard van der Werff,*
Johannes Streper sen.,*
Cornelius Siverdts jr.,*
Peter Schumacher,*
Georg Schumacher,*
Isaac Schumacher,*
Jacob Schumacher jr.,*
Mattheis van Bebber,*
Cornelius Vandergach,*
Peter Clever,*
Georg Gödschalk,*
Hannes Reinhart van der Sluys,*
    now (jeßt) Vanderslice,
Adrian van der Sluys,*
Johan van der Heggen,*
Gödschalk van der Heggen,*
Casper Kleinhoof,*
Heinrich Buchholtz,*
Herman Tuyman,*
Paul Klümges,*
Johannes Klümges,*
Johannes de Wees,
Cornelius de Wees, now Dewes,
Mattheis Neus,* now Nice,
Johannes Neus,*
Claus Rüttynghuysen,* *a*

---

a Claus or Nich. Rittenhouse settled, says Horatio Gates Jones, Esq.,
on the eastern bank of the Wissahickon, south of Germantown, where
he erected, on a small stream, which empties into the Wissahickon,
about a mile from the Schuylkill River, the first paper mill in British
America. He died about 1730, and was the grand-father of David
Rittenhouse, the Philosopher, who was born April 8, 1732 and died
June 26, 1796.

a Claus ober Nicholas Rittenhaus siebelte nach der Angabe von Horatio
Gates Jones, Esq., auf dem östlichen Ufer des Wissahickon, südlich von
Germantown, nieber, wo er an einem kleinen Flusse, welcher etwa eine
Meile oberhalb des Schuylkills sich in den Wissahickon ergießt, die erste
Papiermühle in Britisch Amerika erbaute. Um's Jahr 1730 starb er. Er
war der Großvater des Philosophen David Rittenhaus, welcher am 8. April
1732 geboren wurde und am 26. Juni 1796 gestorben ist.

Gerhart Rüttynhuysen,
Matthias Rüttynhuysen,
Henrich Rüttynhuysen,
William Rüttynhuysen,
Casper Stahls,*
Heinrich Tubben,*
Wilhelm Hendricks,
Henrich Hendricks,*
Lorentz Hendricks,*
Gerhart Hendricks,
Heinrich Kesselberg,*
    now Casselberry,
John Rebenstock,*
Peter Verbyman,*
Johan Heinrich Carstens,*
Casper Carsten,
Johannes Radwitzer,
Johannes Cönrads sen.,*
Johannes Gorgas,*
Henrie Bartels,*
Senwes Bartels,*
Johannes Krey,*
Andreas Krämer,
Thomas Böter,
Wilhelm Krey,*
Cönrad Jansen,*

Everhart in Hoffe,*
Herman in Hoffe,*
Gerhard in Hoffe,*
Peter in Hoffe,*
Peter Jansen,*
Johannes Schmidt,*
Thomas Echelwich,*
Johannes Scholl,*
Peter Scholl,*
Gabriel Sentner,*
Heywart Hapon,
Cönrad Hermann Bom,
Dirk Vankolk,
William Potts,*
Mattheis Tison,*
Jacob Kelner,
Jacob Engell,*
Paul Engell,*
Paul Wulff,
Andreas Söplis,
Jacob Isaac von Pedden,
Arnold Kassel,
Johannes Kassel,
Jacob Isaacs,
Herman Dorst, a
Heinrich Zimmermann,* b

a Herman Dorst died suddenly near Germantown, a bachelor, past 80 years of age, Oct. 14, 1739; he lived for a long time in a house by himself.—*Penn. Gazette.*

a Herman Dorſt ſtarb plöͤplich nahe Germantown als Junggeſelle von über 80 Jahren ben 14. Oct. 1739; lange Jahre lebte er abgeſchloſſen in einem Hauſe allein.—Pennſ. Gazette.

b Heinrich Zimmermann came to Pennsylvania 1698. He returned to Europe for his family, which he brought over in 1706, to Germantown. In 1717 he removed to Chester County, now Lancaster. His son Emanuel was born 1702 in Switzerland. Emanuel died in 1780.— *Rupp's History of Lancaster County, p.* 126.

b Heinrich Zimmermann kam 1698 nach Pennſylvanien und reiſte nach Europa zurück, um ſeine Familie zu holen. 1706 langten ſie in Germantown an. 1717 zog er nach Cheſter, jept Lancaſter County. Sein Sohn Emanuel wurde 1702 in der Schweiz geboren und ſtarb 1780. — Rupp's Geſchichte von Lancaſter County, S. 126.

Philip Christian Zimmermann,
David Scherges,
Hufert Papen,
Jan Silans,
Jonas Potts,
Jacobus De la Plaine,
Simon Andreas,
Thomas Potts jr.,
Cornelius Bom,
Isaac Schefer,
Enneke Klosterman,
Claus Tamson,
Johannes Küster,
Albertus Brandt,
Johannes Pettinger,
Jacob Pelnes,
Reinhart Herman,
Anthony Loof,
Martin Seelen,
Lorento Marcus,
Christian Wammer,
Hans Peter Umbstat,
Daniel Falkner,
Johan Heinrich Mehls,
Georg Müller,
Johann Cornelius Cotweis,
Conrad Cotweis,

Peter Kenlis,
Anthoni Jerghjes,
Johan Döden,
Ludowic Christian Sprogel,*
John Henry Sprogel,* a
Mattheis Frank,
Hans Heinrich Mehls,
Heinrich Kassel,
Andreas Hartzfelder,
Johan van der Wilderniss,
Johannes van Leer,
Joseph Baumstädt,
Johannes Kelpius,
Johannes Seelig,
Heinrich Bernhardt Küster, b
Daniel Lutkins,
Ludwig Aderman,
Andreas Boney,
Heinrich Frey, c
Johannes German,
Peter Scharbon,
Mattheis Nezelius,
Johannes van der Wert,
Wilhelm Baumann,
Paul Küster,
Paul Rüttynghuysen,
Arnold von Bossen,

---

a The Sprogels were naturalized by special Act of Assembly, passed 1705.—*Col. Rec.*, II, p. 184.

a Die Sprogels wurden 1705 durch einen besonderen Assembly-Beschluß naturalisirt.—Col.-Ver., II, S. 184.

b Heinrich Bernhardt Küster, a native of the town of Blomberg, in Lippe-Detmold. He came to Germantown 1689, and was the first German and English preacher there.—*Löher*, p. 39.

b Heinrich Bernhard Küster, geboren in der Stadt Blomberg, Lippe-Detmold. 1689 kam er nach Germantown, und war der erste deutsche und englische Prediger daselbst.—Löher, S. 39.

c Heinrich Frey had been in Pennsylvania before 1682. — *Hallische Nachrichten*, p. 664.

c Heinrich Frey war vor 1682 in Pennsylvanien gewesen.—Hallische Nachrichten, S. 664.

Isaac von Sintern,
Doctor Christopher Witt, *a*
Joseph Paul,
Reiner Peters,

Jürgen Jacob Jacobs,
Wilhelm Hosters,
Hans Graaf,* *b*
Philip T. Lehnemann. *c*

---

a Doctor Witt was an Englishman and came to this country 1704. He was noted as a famous conjuror, and died 1765.—*Watson's Annals*, II, p. 22.

a Doftor Witt, ein Engländer, kam 1704 in diefes Land und war ein berühmter Wahrfager. Er ftarb 1765.—Watfon's Annalen, II, S. 22.

b Hans Graaf came to Germantown 1696. He settled afterwards in Chester County, now Lancaster, took up, as by date of warrant, 1716, in Pequæ, 1000 acres of land; on a second warrant, Nov. 22, 1717, a large tract of land in Earl Township, Lancaster County. The old homestead on this tract is now owned by Levi W. Grove, a lineal descendant of Hans.—*Rupp's History of Lancaster County*, p. 133.

b Hans Graaf kam 1696 nach Germantown. Nachher ließ er fich in Chefter, jetzt Lancafter County, nieder und nahm, wie die Urkunde befagt, 1716 taufend Acker von in Pequä zu erwerbendem Lande, und erhielt am 22. Nov. 1717 durch einen zweiten Vollmachtsbrief eine große Strecke Landes in Earl Townfhip, Lancafter County. Die alte Heimftätte auf diefem Land ift jetzt im Befitz von Levi W. Grove, ein Abkömmling in gerader Linie von Hans.—Rupp's Gefch. von Lancafter County, S. 133.

c Philip T. Lehnemann was for some time private secretary to William Penn.—*Löher*, p. 39, *Proud, Watson, Deutscher Pionier, Col. Rec.* II, p. 493, *Penn. Archives*, I, p. 63.

c Philipp T. Lehnemann war eine geraume Zeit Privat-Sekretär des William Penn.—Löher, S. 39, Proud, Watfon, Deutfcher Pionier, Col.-Ber., II, S. 493, Pennf. Archive, I, S. 63.

No. II.

NAMES OF EARLY SETTLERS OF BERKS AND MONTGOMERY COUNTIES, ORIGINALLY PHILA-DELPHIA COUNTY,
who were naturalized January 9, 1729 to 1730;
SOME FROM BUCKS COUNTY, FROM CHESTER, AND FROM THE CITY OF PHILADELPHIA.
Votes of Assembly, III, p. 131.

Namen ber erſten Anſiebler von ben Counties Berfs unb Montgomery, urſprünglich Philabelphia County,
welche vom 9. Januar 1729 an biß 1730 naturaliſirt wurben; einige von Bucks County, von Cheſter unb von ber Stabt Philabelphia.
Abſtimmungen ber Aſſembly, III, S. 131.

———

Peter Wentz,	Jacob Herman,
Martin Kolb,	Gerhart Clemens,
Dielman Kolb,	Christian Zimmerman,
Jacob Kolb,	Jacob Metz,
Michael Ziegler,	Bastian Schmidt,
Paul Fried,	Martin Gmelin,
Hans Danweiler,	Ulrich Mayer,
Valentin Hunsicker,	Christian Bauman,
Jacob Schreiner,	Abraham Schwaark,
Johannes Kooken,	Hermanus Kuster.

From Berks County.

Johan Joder,	David Kauffman,
Johan Joder jr.,	Jean Bartolett,
Philip Kielwein,	Hans Martin,
Jost Joder,	Georg Martin Schenckel,
Hans Hoch,	Jonathan Herbein,
Peter Endreas,	Johan Bauman,
Johan Dietrich Kreiner,	Arnold Huffnagle,
Peter Balio,	Johannes Langenecker,
Abraham Levan,	Johannes Buchwalter,
Isaac Levan,	Johann Eckstein,
Nicholas Lescher,	Isaac Vansintern,

Johannes Dewalt End,
Johan Georg Bentzel,
Blasius Daniel Mackinet,
Mathias Adam Hogermöd,
Hans Rupp,
Lorentz Belitz,
Johan Nicholas Kressman,
Christopher Funk,
Johan Georg Reif,
Johan Isaac Klein,
Peter Reif,
Johan Jacob Scharch,
Johan Joseph Scharch,
Antonius Halman,
Gerhard Peters,
Johannes Mayer,
Johannes Schaffer,
Jacob Seltzer,
Johannes Lefeber,

Georg Raus,
Georg Jäger,
Samuel Guldin,
Christopher Guldin,
Heinrich Pannbecker,
Hans Siegfried,
Samuel Hoch,
Johann Schneider,
Georg Merkle,
Hubbert Cassell,
Peter Traler,
Heinrich Schaut,
Jacob Hottenstein,
Daniel Langenecker,
Hans Jacob Bechtel,
Melchior Hoch,
Georg Bechtel,
Jost Henrich Sassamanhaussen.

From Bucks County.

Jacob Klemmer,
Jacob Sauder,
Philip Geisinger,

Georg Bachman,
John Dreistel.

NOTE.—As early as 1709 John Bleicher was naturalized.—*Col. Rec.*, II, p. 494.

Anmerkung.—Johann Bleicher war 1709 bereits naturalisirt.—Col.= Ber., II, S. 494.

From Chester County.

Christian Mory,
Johannes Roth,

Casper Acker,
Jacob Acker.

From the City of Philadelphia.

Marcus Kuhl,
Johan Keller,
Jacob Karsdoop,

Johann Becker,
Abraham Kintzing.

From Philadelphia County. 1734 to 1735.

Anthony Benezet,
Abraham Zimmerman,
Christian Weber,
Nicholas Keyser,

Martin Bitting,
Conrad Kerr,
Conrad Kuster,
Jacob Dubre,

Anthony Zadouski,
Hans Jacob Dubre,
Hans Bingeman,

Andreas Kreber,
Ludwig Bitting.

From Chester Co. 1734 to 1735.

Gerhart Braunbeck.

From Lancaster County.

Johan Georg Bard,
Johan Casper Stöver,
Michael Weilder,

Frederick Elberstadt,
Peter Ensminger,
Jacob Herschberger.

No. III.

SWISS AND GERMAN SETTLERS IN LANCASTER COUNTY FROM 1709 to 1730.

Schweizerische und deutsche Ansiedler in Lancaster County von 1709 bis 1730.

1709:
Johann Rudolph Bundeli,
Martin Kendig,
Jacob Müller,
Hans Graff,
Hannes Herr,
Martin Oberholtz,
Hannes Funck,
Michael Oberholtz,
Wendel Bauman,
Hans Meylin sen.,
Hans Meylin jr.,
Martin Meylin,
Samuel Gulden,
Johan Rodölf van der Werff,
Daniel Herman,
Christian Brenneman,
Johan Georg Trellinger,
Hans Mayer,

Hans Haigy,
Christian Herschi,
Hans Pupather,
Heinrich Bär,
Peter Lehman,
Melchior Brenneman,
Benedictus Witmer,
Heinrich Funck,
Christopher Franciscus,
Michael Schenck,
Johannes Landes,
Ulrich Hauerich,
Emmanuel Herr,
Abraham Herr,
Hans Huber,
Isaac Kauffmann,
Melchior Erisman,
Michael Müller,
Christopher Schlegel.

1712:

Hans Georg Schutz,
Martin Reninger,
Michael Bachman,
Jacob Hochstetter,
Jacob Kreider,
Benedictus Venerich,
Jacob Kreutzer,
Jacob Böhm,
Hans Faber,
Martin Urner,
Theodorus Eby,
Johannes Lein,
Heinrich Zimmerman,
Emanuel Zimmerman,
Gabriel Zimmerman,
Johannes Schenck,
Michael Danegar,
Marcus Oberholtz,
Christian Stein,
Edward Riehm,
Joseph Steinman,
Siegesmund Landtart.

1719:

Ulrich Brechbül,
Christian Mosser,
Andreas Schultz,
Samuel Hess,
Peter Yorde,
Hans Tschantz,
Johannes Hauser,
Francis Neff sen.,
Francis Neff jr.,
Georg Kendig,
Johannes Burchhalter sen.,
Johannes Burchhalter jr.,
Abraham Burchhalter,
Michael Bauman,
Johannes Hess,

Johann Friederich,
Christopher Brenneman,
Martin Harnish,
Joseph Buchwalter,
Felix Landes,
Heinrich Neff,
Michael Meyer,
Peter Baumgärdtner,
Melchior Hoffarth,
Johannes Brubacher,
Jacob Nüssly,
Hans Schnebele,
Jacob Guth,
Johannes Wolschlegel,
Jacob Meyer,
Joseph Steinman,
Daniel Eschleman,
Christian Bülman,
Johann Henrich Neff jr.,
Abraham Herr,
Jacob Beyer,
Hans Jacob Schnebele,
Ulrich Roth,
Rudolph Meyer,
Carl Christopher,
Henrich Musselman,
Mattheis Schleiermacher,
Jacob Kurtz,
Johan Ulrich Huber,
Johannes Lichty,
Johannes Stampfer,
Peter Neucomer,
Johan Henrich Bär,
Jacob Weber,
Heinrich Weber,
Johannes Weber,
Georg Weber,
David Langenecker,
Abraham Meyer,
Ulrich Hauser,
Johannes Meyer,

Heinrich Musselman,
Michael Schenck,
Peter Eby,
Johannes Guth,
Christian Steiner,
Adam Brandt,
Johan Jacob Lichty,
Caspar Lauman,
Friederich Stein,
Johannes Schwaab,
Bastian Rayer,
Jonas La Ru,
Simeon König,
Eberhardt Riehm,
Hans Graff,
Johannes Rupp,
Philip Dock,
Johannes Weidman,
Christian Lang,
Michael Albert,
Wilhelm Albert,
Leonard Bender,
Georg Miller,
John Buschong,
Nicholas Kendel,
Johannes Hagey,
Charles Keller,
Stephen Remsberger,
Ludwig Dettenborn,
Jacob Bär jr.,
Christian Lauer,
John Leiberger,
Michael Becker,
John Peter Kucher,
John Liebach,
Bartholomew Schäfer,
Casper Stump,
Jacob Becker,
Tobias Bickel,
Peter Ruth,
George Klein,

Paul Tittenhoffer,
Matthias Teis,
Georg Ludwig Horst,
Sebastian Graff,
John Henrich Basler,
Matthias Jung,
Jacob Schlauch,
Heinrich Michael Immel,
Felix Miller,
Martin Weybrecht,
Friederich Eichelberger,
Sebastian Fink,
Hans Adam Schreiner,
Christian Lang,
Casper Filler,
Antony Bretter,
Leonhard Ellenmacher,
Andreas Bersinger,
Jacob Hartman,
Theophilus Hartman,
Benjamin Witmer,
Abraham Witmer,
Johannes Binckley,
Turst Buchwalter,
Valentin Hergelrat,
John Stettler,
Leonhard Ramler,
Leonhard Heyer,
Peter Schell,
John Nohacker,
Nicholas Miller,
Johann Hauck,
Thomas Koppenheffer,
Christian Lehman,
George Unruh,
Jacob Schäfer,
Valentine Keffer,
Casper Rieth,
Christian Mahenschmidt,
Nicholas Kutz,
George Weyrich,

Christopher Ley,   Johannes Blum,
Jacob Lauer,   Erasmus Buchenmeyer,
Hans Mohr,   George Graff.

No. IV.

NAMES, AGE AND OCCUPATION OF THOSE WHO ACCOMPANIED REV. JOSHUA KOCHERTHAL, who settled on lands on Quassick Creek, then Dutchess County, N. Y., in the Spring of 1709.*

Rev. *Joshua Kocherthal*, aged 39; Sibylla Charlotta, his wife, 39; their children, Benigna Sibylla, 10; Christ. Joshua, 7; Susanna Sibylla, 3.—Kocherthal was furnished with 1 barrel of lime, 3 gouges, 2 formers (kind of chisel), 1 grind-stone, 1 square, 1 rule, 1 compass and several pieces more.

Lorents Schwisser, aged 25, husbandman and vinedresser; Anna Catharina, his wife, 26; their daughter, Johanna, 8.—He was furnished with 1 grind-stone, 1 square, 1 little gimlet, 2 augers, 1 smoothing plane, besides several pieces more.

Henrich Rennau, aged 24, stocking weaver, husbandman and vinedresser; Johanna, his wife, 26; their children, Lorentz, 2; Heinrich, 5 months old, and two sisters of Mrs. Rennau, Susanna Liboscha, 15; Maria Johanna Liboscha, 10 years old.—He received 1 cross cut saw, 1 mitre block, 1 adze, 2 augers, 1 gimlet, besides several small pieces.

Andreas Volck, aged 30, husbandman and vinedresser; his wife, Anna Catharina, 27; their children, Maria Barbara, 5; Georg Hieronymus, 4; Anna Gertrauda, 1.—He received 1 cross cut saw, 1 smoothing plane, 1 whipping saw, a set of gouges, besides several pieces more.

Michael Weigand, aged 52, husbandman; his wife, Anna Catharina, 54; their children, Anna Maria, 13; Tobias, 7;

* In 1710, April 20, these where furnished by Queen Anne, through Melchior Guelch, a Palatine joiner, with implements, &c.—*Doc. His. N. Y.*, V, pp. 52, 53.

Georg, 5.—He received 1 large file, 1 smaller one, 1 mortising chisel, 1 auger, besides several small pieces.

Jacob Weber, aged 30, husbandman and vinedresser; his wife, Anna Elisabeth, 25; their children, Anna Maria, 5; Eva Elisabeth, 1.—He received 1 box with knife, whitelead and compass, 1 adze, 2 gouges, 1 mortising chisel, besides several pieces more.

Johan Jacob Plettel, aged 40, husbandman and vinedresser; his wife, Anna Elisabeth, 29; their children, Margaretha, 10; Anna Sara, 8; Catharina, 3.—It appears that Mr. Plettel, husband of Anna Elisabeth, had died prior to April 20, 1710, when these implements were distributed. It is recorded "to widow Plettel," 1 whipping saw, 1 great hammer, 1 gimlet, 1 tenant saw, besides several pieces more.

Johannes Fischer, aged 27, smith and husbandman; his wife, Maria Barbara, 26; one child, Andreas, 6 months old.—He received 1 tenant saw, 1 gimlet, 1 hammer, 1 small file, 1 hatchet, 1 jointer, besides several small pieces.

Melchior Guelch, aged 39, carpenter and joiner; his wife, Anna Catharina, 43; their children, Magdalena, 12; Heinrich, 10.—He received 2 full sets of carpenter's tools.

Peter Rose, aged 34, cloth weaver; his wife, Johanna, 45; no children.—He received 1 glue pot, 1 wimble, 1 hatchet, 1 little hammer, 2 augers, 1 jointer, besides several pieces more.

Maria Wemarin, widow, 37 years of age; her daughter, Catharina, 2.—She received 1 smoothing plane, 1 file, 1 hatchet, besides several small pieces more.

Isaac Feber (*Le Fever*), aged 33, husbandman; his wife, Catharina, 30; their son, Abraham, 2 years old.—He received 1 broad axe, 1 little hatchet, 1 smoothing file, 1 rule, 1 former, besides several pieces more.

Note.—Isaac Le Fever was born March 26, 1669, and died in Lancaster County, Pa., 1736. His son, Abraham, was born April 9, 1706.— *I. D. R.*

Daniel Fiero, aged 32, husbandman; his wife, Anna Maria, 30; their children, Andreas, 7; Johannes, 6.—He received 1 broad axe, 1 square, 1 mitre block, 1 tenant saw, 1 jointer, besides several small pieces more.

Herman Schüneman, aged 28, clerk, unmarried.

Isaac Türck, aged 23, husbandman, unmarried.

Note.—In 1711, Isaac Türk left New York, went to Pennsylvania and settled at Oley.—*History of Berks County*, p. 231.

Namen, Alter und Berufsarten Derer, welche Pastor Josua Kocherthal begleiteten und im Frühjahr 1709 sich am Quassick Creek, damals Ducheß County, N. Y., niederließen.*

———

Pastor Josua Kocherthal, 39 Jahre alt; seine Frau Sibylla Charlotte 39; ihre Kinder, Benigna Sibylla 10; Christian Josua 7; Susanna Sibylla 3.—Kocherthal hatte ein Faß Kalk, 3 Hohlmeißel, 2 Stemmeisen, 1 Schleifstein, 1 Winkelmaß, 1 Richtscheit, 1 Kompaß und einige weitere Stücke.

Lorenz Schwisser, 25 Jahre, Landmann und Weingärtner; seine Frau Anna Katharina 26; ihre Tochter Johanna 8.—Er war ausgestattet mit 1 Schleifstein, 1 Winkelmaß, 1 kleinen Bohrer, 2 Stangenbohrern, 1 Planirhobel, außer anderen Stücken.

Heinrich Rennau, 24 Jahre, Strumpfweber, Landmann und Weingärtner; seine Frau Johanna 26; ihre Kinder, Lorentz 2 Jahre; Heinrich 5 Monate alt, und zwei Schwestern von Frau Rennau, Susanna Liboscha 15, und Maria Johanna Liboscha 10 Jahre alt.—Er erhielt 1 Zirkelsäge, 1 Winkelblock, 1 Hohlart, 2 Stangenbohrer, 1 Nagelbohrer, außer einigen anderen kleineren Stücken.

Andreas Volck, 30 Jahre, Landmann und Weingärtner; seine Frau Anna Katharina 27; ihre Kinder, Maria Barbara 5; Georg Hieronymus 4; Anna Gertrud 1.—Er erhielt 1 Zirkelsäge, 1 Planirhobel, 1 Brettsäge, ein Paar Hohlmeißel, nebst anderen Werkzeugen.

Michael Weigand, 52 Jahre, Landmann; seine Frau Anna Katharina 54; ihre Kinder, Anna Maria 13; Tobias 7; Georg 5.—Ihm wurde zugetheilt 1 große Feile, 1 kleinere, 1 Lochbeutel, 1 Bohrer, nebst anderen Stücken.

Jakob Weber, 30 Jahre, Landmann und Weingärtner; seine Frau Anna Elisabeth 25; ihre Kinder, Anna Maria 5; Eva Elisabeth 1.—Ihm gab man 1 Kästchen mit Messern, Bleiweiß und Compaß, 1 Hohlart, 2 Hohlmeißel, 1 Lochbeutel, nebst anderen Stücken.

———

* Am 20. April 1710 wurden dieselben von der Königin Anna durch Melchior Gülch, einem Pfälzer Tischler, mit Werkzeugen u. s. w. versehen.— Dok. Gesch. N. Y., V., S. 52, 53.

Johann Jakob Plettel, 40 Jahre, Landmann und Wein=
gärtner; seine Frau Anna Elisabeth 29; ihre Kinder, Marga=
retha 10; Anna Sara 8; Katharina 3.—Es scheint daß Herr
Plettel, Gemahl der Anna Elisabeth, schon vor dem 20. April 1710
gestorben war, an welchem Tage die Werkzeuge vertheilt wurden.
Der Bericht sagt, „der Wittwe Plettel" 1 Brettsäge, 1 großer Ham=
mer, 1 Nagelbohrer, 1 Stichsäge und andere Stücke.

Johannes Fischer, 27 Jahre, Schmied und Ackermann;
seine Frau Maria Barbara 26; ein Kind, Andreas, 6 Monate
alt.—Er erhielt 1 Lochsäge, 1 Nagelbohrer, 1 Hammer, 1 kleine
Feile, 1 Beil, 1 Schlichthobel, nebst einigen anderen Stücken.

Melchior Gülch, 39 Jahre, Zimmermann und Tischler;
seine Frau Anna Katharina 43; ihre Kinder, Magdalena 12;
Heinrich 10.—Er erhielt ein vollständiges doppeltes Zimmer=
manns=Handwerkszeug.

Peter Rose, 34 Jahre, Tuchmacher; seine Frau Johanna 45;
keine Kinder.—Er erhielt 1 Leimpfanne, 1 Windelbohrer, 1 Beil,
1 kleinen Hammer, 2 Bohrer, 1 Glatthobel, nebst anderen Stücken.

Maria Wemarin, Wittwe, 37 Jahre; ihre Tochter Katha=
rina 2.—Sie erhielt 1 Glatthobel, 1 Feile, 1 Beil, nebst einigen
anderen kleinen Gegenständen.

Isaak Feber (Le Fever), 33 Jahre, Ackermann; seine Frau
Katharina 30; ihr Sohn Abraham 2.—Er erhielt 1 breite Axt,
1 kleines Beil, 1 Glattfeile, 1 Winkelmaß, 1 Stemmeisen, nebst
einigen anderen Stücken.

Anmerkung.—Isaak Le Fever wurde am 26. März 1669 geboren und
starb 1736 in Lancaster Co., Pennsylvanien. Sein Sohn Abraham wurde
am 9. April 1706 geboren.—J. D. R.

Daniel Fiero, 32 Jahre, Landmann; seine Frau Anna
Maria 30; ihre Kinder, Andreas 7; Johannes 6.—Er erhielt
1 breite Axt, 1 Winkelmaß, 1 Winkelblock, 1 Lochsäge, 1 Glatt=
hobel, nebst einigen anderen Stücken.

Hermann Schünemann, 28 Jahre, Buchhalter; unver=
heirathet.

Isaak Türck, 23 Jahre, Landmann; unverheirathet.

Anmerkung.—1711 verließ Isaak Türk New York, kam nach Penn=
sylvanien und ließ sich in Oley nieder.—Gesch. von Berks Co., S. 231.

No. V.

NAMES AND AGES OF THE HEADS OF FAMILIES REMAINING IN THE CITY OF NEW YORK, 1710.

Namen der im Jahre 1710 in New York verbleibenden Familienhäupter und deren Alter.

☞ The females, whose names appear, were widows.

☞ Die Frauen, deren Namen hier vorkommen, waren Wittwen.

Hans Wilhelm Stuckrath, 37,
Anna Wormser, 36,
Nicklaus Jung, 32,
Frantz Lucas,
Mattheis Bronck, 50,
Johannes Jung, 32,
Baltzar Wenerich, 40,
Benedictus Wenerich, 32,
Anna Apolona Siegner, 44,
Johannes Planck, 43,
Hans Adam Zollner, 52,
Andreas Richter, 47,
Anna Maria Mengel, 27,
Maria Margaretha Scher, 23,
Peter Gerlach, 37,
Hieronimus Klein, 38,
Anna Catharina Erb, 44,
Magdalina Baum, 29,
Maria Catharina Bornwasser, 26,
Maria Catharina Schütz, 40,
Anna Maria Cramer, 38,
Maria Nies, 38,
Frances Basch, 40,
Susanna Beyer, 30,
Sitonia Melch, 41,
Anna Catharina Batz, 38,
Anna Eliza Rorbaal, 34,
Anna Elizabeth Schultz, 22,
Conrad Friederich, 52,
Johan Philip Greisler, 40,
Ludwig Bürs, 32,
Georg Ludwig Leicht, 56,
Johann Henrich Neukirch, 36,
Anna Almerod, 67,
Johann Henrich Leicht, 24,
Johann Henrich Gossinger, 31,
Friederich Maul, 31,
Christopher Dannermarker, 28,
Anna Marg. Dannermarker, 58,
Andreas Elich, 37,
Johannes Engell, 31,
Michael Päffer, 32,
Michael Storr, 38,
Joh. Diet. Wannenmacher, 28,
Conrad Lein, 56,
Peter Appelman, 42,
Anna Maria Bender, 44,
Arnold Falck, 36,
Anna Kunegunde Russ, 44,
Johannes Kautz, 40,
Maria Catharine Hebmann, 40,
Anna Maria Sack, 30,
Johann Mattheus Keiser, 23,
Johannes Trillhauser, 23,
Bernhardt Sickard, 25,
Johann Wilhelm Schneider, 28,
Valentin Bressler, 41,
Andreas Weidknecht, 40,
Johannes Bär, 40,
Melchior Dausweber, 55,

Elizabeth Lampert, 47,
Maria May, 45,
Georg Römer, 30,
Ulrich Simmendinger, 38,
Christian Kasselman, 36,
Johann Dieterich Schatz, 38,
Anna Elizabeth Maul, 42,
Peter Wickhaus, 32,
Veronica Zwick, 39,
Johannes Lorentz, 43,
Caspar Hartwig, 39,
Magdalena Off, 32,
Anna Eva Morrell, 48,
Michael Henneschied, 36,
Johann Peter Fuchs, 31,
Anna Maria Heid, 50,
Dieterich Fiebersbach, 21,
Christopher Werner, 35,
Johann Paul Badner, 19,
Elizabeth Müller, 42,
Nicolaus Heisterbach, 53,
Elizabeth Noll, 66,
Appalonia Lintz, 40,

Johanna Zenger, 33, *a*
Anna Maria Gabel, 34,
Benedictus Kühner, 36,
Anna Elizabeth Lauch, 42,
Margaretta Schmidt, 27,
Daniel Teffer, 30,
Margaretta Messer, 50,
Maria Galete, 38,
Simon Vogt, 31,
Johann Wilhelm Felten, 30,
Hermanus Hoffman, 30,
Ludolph Korning, 50,
Bernhart Ekel, 53,
Johannes Täuble, 38,
Catharina Müller, 36,
Joh. Jacob Starrenberger, 45,
Johann Friederich Neff, 34,
Anna Catharina Grau, 40,
Heinrich Schmidt, 54,
Daniel Schumacher, 30,
Philip Peter Grauberger, 29,
Johannes Roschman, 33.

In all, males and females of different ages, 430 persons.

Zufammen 430 Perfonen, Männer und Frauen verfchiedenen Alters.

---

a This poor widow was the mother of three children, *John Peter*, aged 13, Anna Catharina, 10, and Johannes, 7. Her son, *Peter Zenger*, was apprenticed to *William Bradford*, printer in New York; and afterwards became owner of the *N. Y. Weekly Messenger*. He was indicted for *libel*, 1734, on which Hamilton, a lawyer from Philadelphia, pleaded his cause.—*Doc. Hist. N. Y.*, III, p. 565.

a Diefe arme Wittwe war die Mutter von drei Kindern: Johann Peter, 13 Jahre alt, Anna Catharina, 10, und Johannes, 7. Ihr Sohn, Peter Zenger, wurde zu einem Drucker in New York, Namens Wm. Bradfore, in die Lehre gethan und nachher felbst Eigenthümer des N. Y. Weekly Messenger. 1734 wurde er wegen Verläumbung angeflagt, bei welcher Gelegenheit Hamilton, ein Advofat von Philadelphia, feine Sache führte.— Dof. Gefch. N. J., III., S. 565.

No. VI.

NAMES AND AGES OF MALE CHILDREN APPRENTICED BY GOVERNOR HUNTER, 1710 to 1714.

Namen und Alter der von 1710 bis 1714 von Gouverneur Hunter in die Lehre gethanen Knaben.

Johan Philip Lepper, 12,
Georg Friederich Weiser, 13,
Daniel Artopee Weiser, 12,
Philip Daniel Weiser, 13,
Johan Paul Denbig, 7,
Hans Georg Kuhns, 8,
Hans Philip Kuhns, 15,
Adam Greiner, 13,
Hans Georg Bär,
Joh. Ludig Trorit (Trauert), 9,
Henrich Porter (Bortner), 14,
Hans Bastian Gatian, 12,
Joh. Bernhart Ruropaw
  (Rorbach), 10,
Johann Conrad Otteene,? 9,
Frederick Otteene,? 7,
Hans Georg Schweitzer, 12,
Johan Conrad Petre, 12,
Peter Pfeiffer, 6,
Georg Kastner, 13,
Gerhardt Lamberton, 12,

Hans Gerhart Löser,? 10,
John Peter Zenger, 13,
Thomas Reich, 12,
Jacob Berleman, 10,
Johann Paul Schmidt, 12,
Georg Schneider, 15,
Joh. Con. Matheis Horner, 15,
Jacob Eysterberg, 3,
Hans Henrich Schiltz, 8,
W. Webber, 8,
Jonah Schmidt, 10,
Johannes Schiltz, 10,
Christian Engel, 12,
Arnold Schweedt, 13,
Jacobus Brauer, 14,
Peter Lohn,? 9,
Nicholas Dietrich, 14,
Peter De Mott, 13,
Johann Wilhelm Schmidt, 14,
Jacob Berleman, 11
Simon Helm, 12.

The whole number apprenticed, males and females, was 75.

Die ganze Anzahl, Knaben und Mädchen, betrug 75.

No. VII.

NAMES OF MALE PALATINES, ABOVE TWENTY-ONE YEARS OLD, IN LIVINGSTON MANOR, N. Y., IN THE WINTER 1710, AND SUMMER 1711.

Namen der männlichen Pfälzer über ein und zwanzig Jahre alt, welche im Winter 1710 und Sommer 1711 in Livingston Manor, N. Y., waren.

Johann Christopher Gerlach,
Peter Maurer,
Phillip Müller,
Johann Georg Spannheimer,
Johan Friederich Casselmann,
Johann Löher,
Friederick Merkel,
Georg Schäffer,
Johann Adam Friederich,
Valentin Bender,
—— Brandau,
—— Schäffer,
—— Arnold,
—— Wilhelm,
Henrich Hoffmann,
Georg Höhlen,
Heinrich Scherman,
Valentin Wohlleber,
Philip Wohlleber,
Peter Wagner,
Johann Henrich Krantz,
Johannes Straub,
Frantz Keller,
Johannes Becker,
Joh. Friederich Gantermann,
Philip Kilmer,
Heinrich Mann,
Thomas Ehrman,
Albert Friederich Marterstock,
Augustin Voschell,
Peter Voschell,
Johannes Eberhard,
Peter Wohlleber,
Anthony Kremer,
Herman Hostman,
Stephan Fröhlich,
Johannes Franck,
Andreas Ross,
Joseph Reichart,
Melchior Tausweber,
Rev. Joshua Kocherthal,
Jacob Mond,
Matheus Schleimer,
Georg Wilhelm Kiel,
Peter Becker,
Valentin Falkenberg,
Wilhelm Müller,
Johannes Ritzbach,
Peter Keiseler,
Johann Wilhelm Kieffer,
Johan Henrich Schram,
Peter Egner,
John Michael Emrich,
Georg Henrich Stubenrauch,
Peter Diebel,
Christian Mäyer,
Peter Oberbach,
Henrich Mohr,

Conrad Martin,
Adam Hardel,
Gottfried Fidler,
Jacob Demuth,
Gottfried Riegel,
Hieronimus Scheib,
Nicolaus Kerner,
—— Dietrich,
—— Weiden,
Hieronimus Weller,
Johann Conrad Weiser,
Mattheus Reinbolt,
Johann Peter Dopff,
Johann Jacob Reisch,
Carl Nehr,
Heinrich Jung,
Werner Deichert,
Georg Müller,
Friederich Bellinger,
Heinrich Wiederwachs,
Georg Mathias,
Christopher Hagedorn,
Frantz Finck,
Andreas Schütz,
Peter Hagedorn,
Niclaus Weber,
Wilhelm Georg,
Friederich Schäffer,
Anthony Ichard,
Johann Peter Lein,
Johann Jacob Munsinger,
Johannes Leyer,
Jacob Kuhn,
Henrich Mattheis,
Nicolaus Eckert,
Martin Dillenbach,
Nicolaus Föller,
Jacob Schnell,
Jacob Webber,
Wilhelm Nelles,
Johannes Geissler,

Georg Briegel,
Johannes Schäffer,
Georg Dachstädter,
Johannes Zeissdorf,
Heinrich Mayer,
Capt. Joh. Christopher Fuchs,
Johann Wilhelm Thales,
Johan Wilhelm Scheff,
Christian Bauch,
Peter Heidt,
Henrich Hammer,
Michael Ittich,
Johann Keyser,
Jacob Kopp,
Paulus Dientzer,
Melchior Foltz,
Johannes Segendorff,
Philip Laux,
Abraham Langen,
Johan Jacob Schultz,
Johann Wilhelm Hambach,
Nicolas Laux,
Nicolaus Göttel,
Capt. Hartman Windecker,
Johann Wilhelm Dill,
Peter Spies,
Herman Bitzer,
Johannes Schuc,
Johann Wilhelm Schneider,
Jacob Bast (Borst),
Johannes Blass,
Johan Wilhelm Kammer,
Johannes Bonroth,
Johannes Bernhard,
Sebastian Fischer,
Nicolaus Heyd,
Henrich Klein,
Henrich Balthasar Stuper,
Caspar Rauch,
Hans Henrich Zeller,
Johannes Zeller,

Samuel Kuhn,
Jacob Ess,
Gerhart Schäffer,
Ulrich Bruckhart,
Conrad Kuhn,
Friederich Mentegen,
Samuel Kuhn,
Valentin Kuhn,
Heinrich Winter,
Johann Georg Reiffenberg,
Johann Wilhelm Linck,
Johan Martin Netzbach,
Johannes Weiss,
Johann Adam Walborn,
Johann Heinrich Ahrndorff,
Daniel Busch,
Johan Henrich Conradt,
Henrich Bellinger,
Johannes Schneider,
Marcus Bellinger,
Philip Schäffer,
Johann Kraut,
Christian Sittenich,
Johann Henrich Schmidt,
Johann Philip Zerbe,
Nicolaus Ruhl,
Adam Michael Schmidt,
Conrad Meissinger,
Thomas Ruffener,
Jacob Dinges,
Henrich Fehling,
Johan Jost Petry,
Johannes Lantz,
Lorentz Zerbe,
Peter Rieth,
Conrad Schütz,
Joseph Saab,
Georg Rieth,
Gottlieb Fidler (Fitler),
Johannes Rieth,
Johan Peter Pacht,

Sebastian Pisas,
Andreas Walborn,
Antonius Scharf,
Sebastian Fischer,
Christian Lauer,
Johann Adam Lesch,
Georg Anspach,
Ludwig Wilhelm Schmidt,
Paulus Reidkopff,
Rev. Joh. Friederich Häger,
Johann Peter Kneskern,
Jacob Mauck,
Philip Peter Grauberger,
David Huppert,
Conrad Schauerman,
Henrich Sechs (Sex),
Friederich Bäll,
Jacob Kobel,
Jacob Werner,
Johannes Schultheis,
Reinhart Schäffer,
Johannes Roschman,
Carl Uhl,
Baltzer Anspach,
Conrad Keller,
Johann Georg Schmidt,
Conrad Goldman,
Georg Bender,
Johann Henrich Uhl,
Thomas Schumacher,
Peter Schmidt,
Johannes Schwall,
Georg Ludwig Koch,
Veit Müsig,
Georg Kirchner,
Christian Hills,
Rudolph Stahl,
Gottfried Wolfen,
Leonhart Anspach,
Georg Zeh,
Andreas Kapp,

Jacob Löwengut,
Johannes Noäcker,
Jacob Katterman,

Johann Philip **Theis,**
Martin Zerbe.

No. VIII.

NAMES OF THE FIRST PALATINES IN NORTH CAROLINA, AS EARLY AS 1709 AND 1710.

Namen der erſten Pfälzer in Nord=Carolina in den Jahren 1709 und 1710.

Pheneyer,	Mohr,	Müller,	Granatha,
Eslar,	Ibach,	Rished,	Riesenober,
Grumm,	Moritz,	Walcker,	Hubbach,
Ender,	Riemer,	Tetsche,	Bieber,
Bucher,	Margert,	Huber,	Ament,
Schneider,	Kinsie,	Wolff,	Lutz,
Regene,	Köhler,	Bühlmann,	Simons,
Gärtner,	Wallis,	Schäffer,	Rieser,
Buset,	Genest,	Gesibel,	Reigert.

These were still living in 1714.

Dieſelben lebten noch im Jahre 1714.

No. IX

NAMES OF MALES, SALZBURGERS, SETTLED IN GEORGIA, 1734 to 1741.

(*Sources: Ulsperger Nachrichten*, Vol. I, pp. 2307–2310.)

Namen der männlichen Salzburger, die ſich von 1734 bis 1741 in Georgia niedergelaſſen haben.

(Quellen: Ulsperger Nachrichten, Bd. I, S. 2307–2310.)

First Transport. (Erſte Ueberfahrt.)

Rev. Joh. Martin Boltzius,
Samuel Leberecht Boltzius,

Rev. Israel Christian Gronau,
Peter Gruber,

38*

Thomas Gschwandel,
Leonhart Rauner,
Matthias Rauner,
Georg Schweiger,
Thomas Schweighoffer,

Martin Hertzog,
Christian Leimberger,
Simon Reiter,
Christ. Ortman, *schoolmaster*,
(Sdjulmeifter).

In this transport there were 20, including males and females.

Auf biefer Ueberfahrt waren 20, mit Einfdjluß ber männlidjen und weiblidjen Perfonen.

Second Transport. (3weite Ueberfahrt.)

Simon Steiner,
Ruprecht Kalcher,
Thomas Pichler,
Stephan Rottenberger,
Matthias Burgsteiner,
Ruprecht Burgsteiner,
Ruprecht Eischberger,
Matthias Brandner,
Veit Lemmenhofer,
Bartholomäus Rieser,
Balthasar Rieser,
Georg Rieser,
Veit Landfelder,
Hans Maurer,
Thomas Bacher,

Georg Kogler,
Ruprecht Riedelsperger,
Johannes Riedelsperger,
Christian Riedelsperger,
Georg Sanftleben,
Gabriel Bach,
Bartholomäus Zant,
Christian Hessler,
Jacob Schartner,
Georg Brückner,
Ruprecht Zimmermann.
Paul Zittrauer,
Carl Sigismund Ott,
Heinrich Bischof.

In this transport there were 59 in all.

Auf biefer Ueberfahrt waren im Ganzen 59.

Third Transport. (Dritte Ueberfahrt).

Hans Schmidt,
Hans Flörel,
Johann Spielbiegler,
Johann Cronberger,
Leonhard Crause,
Michael Rieser,
Gottlieb Rieser,
Joseph Ernst,
Johann Ludwig Ernst,
Joh. Friederich Helfenstein,
Johann Jacob Helfenstein,

Jeremias Helfenstein,
Johannes Helfenstein,
Friederich Müller,
Johann Paul Müller,
Peter Arnsdorf,
Hans Krüsy,
Friederich Nett,
Michael Schneider,
Joh. Georg Schneider,
Peter Arnsdorf,
Andreas Grimmiger,

Frantz Hernberger,
Carl Flörel,
Peter Reiter,
Martin Lackner,
Matthias Zettler,
Joseph Leitner,
There were 59 in this transport.
59 famen mit biefer Fahrt.

Gottlieb Christ,
Johann Pletter,
Ambrosius Züblin,
Jacob Züblin, *a*
C. E. Thilo, M. D.

Fourth Transport, which arrived in June, 1741.

(Bierte Ueberfahrt, bie im Juni 1741 anfam.)

Andreas Piltz,
Caspar Gramwetter,
Martin Lackner,
Georg Eigel,
Lorentz Ludwig Eigel,
Johann Lorentz Eigel,
Georg Glaner,
Johann Frantz Eigel,
Samuel Eigel,
Balthasar Bacher,
Michael Haberer,
Abraham Haberer,
Bernhard Glocker,
Ruprecht Schrempf,
Sebastian Glocker,
Paul Glocker,
Simon Riser,

Conrad Künlen,
Johannes Künlen,
J. Ludwig Mayer, *chirurgus*,
Johann Georg Mayr,
Mattheus Bacher,
Peter Kohleisen,
Georg Klammer,
Johannes Maurer,
David Eysperger,
Johannes Scheraus,
Johann Georg Kocher,
Johan Scheraus jr.,
George Kocher,
Veit Lechner,
Ruprecht Lechner,
Joh. Georg Mayre jr.,
Johann Schefler.

There were 63 persons in this transport.

Mit biefer Ueberfchiffung famen 63 Perfonen.

---

a Ambrosius and Jacob Züblin were two brothers from St. Gall, Switzerland.—*Ulsperger Nachrichten*, I, p. 2310. See also Part II, pp. 900 and 1832.

a Ambrofius und Jacob Züblin waren zwei Brüder aus St. Gallen in ber Schweiz.—Ulsperger Nachrichten, I, S. 2310. Siehe auch Theil II, S. 900 und 1832.

No. X.

"Though," says *Peter Kalm*,* "the Province of New York has been inhabited by Europeans much longer than Pennsylvania, yet it is not by far so populous as that colony. This cannot be ascribed to any particular discouragement arising from the nature of the soil, for that is pretty good; but, I am told of a very different reason, which I will mention here.

"In the reign of Queen Anne, about the year 1709, many Germans came hither, who got a tract of land from the English government, which they might settle. After they had lived there some time, and had built houses, and made corn-fields and meadows, their liberties and privileges were infringed, and, under several pretences, they were repeatedly deprived of parts of their land. This at last roused the Germans. They returned violence for violence, and beat those who thus robbed them of their possessions. But these proceedings were looked upon in a very bad light by the government. The most active people among the Germans being taken up, they were roughly treated, and punished with the utmost rigor of the law. This, however, so far exasperated the rest, that the greater part of them left their houses and fields, and went to settle in Pennsylvania. There they were exceedingly well received, got a considerable tract of land, and were indulged in great privileges, which were given them forever. The Germans, not satisfied with being themselves removed from New York, wrote to their relations and friends, and advised them, if ever they intended to come to America, not to go to New York, where the government had shown itself so unequitable. This advice had such influence that the Germans who afterwards went in great numbers to North America, constantly avoided New York and always went to Pennsylvania.

"It sometimes happened that they were forced to go on board of such ships, as were bound for New York, but they were scarce got on shore, when they hastened on to Pennsylvania, in sight of all the inhabitants of New York."—*Peter Kalm's Travels in America,* in 1747 and 1748, Vol. I, pp. 270, 271.

---

* *Peter Kalm,* a Swedish natural philosopher and traveler, was born at Ostro Bothnia in 1715, traveled from 1748 to 1751 in North America, and at a later period in Russia; he became Professor of Botany at the University of Abo, and died 1779.

„Obschon die Provinz New York," sagt Peter Kalm,* „viel länger von Europäern bewohnt ist, als Pennsylvanien, so ist sie doch noch lange nicht so bewohnt, wie jene Colonie. Dies kann keinem besonderen Hinderniß, welches in der Beschaffenheit des Bodens liegt, zugeschrieben werden, denn derselbe ist ziemlich gut; aber ein ganz anderer Grund wurde mir angegeben, den ich hier mittheilen will.

„Während der Regierung der Königin Anna, um's Jahr 1709, kamen viele Deutsche hierher, welchen die englische Krone ein Stück Land zum Anbauen zutheilte. Nachdem sie eine Zeitlang daselbst gewohnt und Häuser, Fruchtfelder und Wiesen erbaut und angelegt hatten, griff man in ihre Freiheit und Rechte ein, und nahm unter verschiedenen Vorwänden ihnen wiederholt Theile ihres Landes weg. Dies erregte die Deutschen endlich. Sie vergalten Gewalt mit Gewalt, und vergriffen sich an Denen, die ihnen ihr Besitzthum raubten. Die Regierung nahm dieses Vorgehen übel auf. Die Tüchtigsten unter den Deutschen wurden in's Gefängniß gesteckt, hart behandelt und ihnen die äußerste Strafe des Gesetzes beigemessen. Dies erbitterte die übrigen dermaßen, daß die Meisten Haus und Hof verließen und nach Pennsylvanien zogen. Hier wurden sie sehr gut aufgenommen; sie erhielten ein bedeutendes Stück Land, und erhebliche Rechte wurden ihnen für immer zugetheilt. Die Deutschen, damit nicht zufrieden, selbst New York verlassen zu haben, schrieben ihren Verwandten und Freunden, und gaben ihnen den Rath, daß, wenn sie je nach Amerika auswanderten, sie New York scheuen sollten, dessen Regierung sich so ungerecht erwiesen habe. Die Warnung war von solcher Tragweite, daß die Schaaren Deutscher, die hernach nach Nord-Amerika zogen, New York stets mieden und Pennsylvanien als Ort ihrer Niederlassung wählten.

„Zuweilen geschah es, daß sie an Bord von Schiffen kamen, welche nach New York steuerten; kaum waren sie aber angelandet, so eilten sie im Anblick aller Bewohner von New York nach Pennsylvanien."—Peter Kalm's Reisen in Amerika, in den Jahren 1747 und 1748, Bd. I, S. 270, 271.

---

* Peter Kalm, ein schwedischer Na   alist und Reisender, 1715 in Ostro Bothnien geboren, reiste von 1748 bis 1751 in Nord-Amerika und hernach in Rußland. Derselbe wurde Professor an der Universität Abo und starb im Jahre 1779.

No. XI.

GERMAN SETTLEMENT IN NORTH CAROLINA, 1709, 1710.

"The population of North Carolina was increased, near the beginning of the eighteenth century, by two small colonies of Protestants, French and Germans. A colony of French Huguenots, encouraged by King William, had come to America in the year 1690, and seated themselves at the *Manakintown*, in Virginia, above the falls of James River. Not well pleased with the lands they first occupied, and the greater part of Carolina being unappropriated, they removed to the southward and seated themselves upon Trent River, with Rybourg their pastor, 1707. They were sober, frugal, industrious planters, and in a short time became independent citizens.

The German colony was from Heidelberg and its vicinity, on the Rhine. Those unfortunate people had suffered persecution from time to time, because they could not change their religious opinions, so as to be in constant agreement with the ruling prince. The elector palatine, Frederick II., embraced the Lutheran faith. Frederick III. became a Calvinist. Lodovic V. restored the Lutheran Church; his son and successor became a Calvinist. That prince was succeeded in the government by a Catholic family, who oppressed the Protestants.

Those people had also the misfortune to live between powerful rivals, who were often at war. In the year 1622, count Tilly, the imperial general, took the city of Heidelberg and put five hundred of the inhabitants to the sword. In the year 1634, the city was taken by Louis XIV., and many of the inhabitants killed. In the year 1688, it was taken a second time by the French, who laid the inhabitants under a heavy contribution, after which, at the approach of the imperial army, they blew up the citadel and reduced the city to ashes. The city, being rebuilt, was taken again by a French army, who committed it to the flames in the year 1693. The inhabitants, men, women and children, about fifteen thousand, stripped of their property, were turned into the fields by night. Upon the retreat of the French army, the inhabitants were again prevailed upon to rebuild the city, being promised liberty of conscience and exemption from taxes for thirty years. After some time the elector, who seems to have believed that promises made to heretics should not be observed, began to persecute his Protestant subjects. The French army having again crossed the Rhine, the distressed Palatines, persecuted by their prince and plundered by a foreign enemy, fled to England, about six thousand of them, for protection, in consequence of encouragement they had received from Queen Anne, by proclamation, 1708.

Having pitched their tents at a small distance from London, they were supported at public expense, until they could be shipped off for Ireland or the colonies. *Christopher de Graffenried* and *Lewis Michell* were attempting about this time, to mend their fortunes by purchasing lands in some of the British colonies. Michell had been several years in America,* and had obtained some knowledge of the country.

NOTE.—Michell was originally employed by the Canton of Bern in Switzerland, to search for a large tract of vacant land on the frontiers of Pennsylvania, Virginia or Carolina, to which they might send a colony. He spent some years in exploring the country. There was no scarcity of mountainous land, such as those people are accustomed to; but they desisted from the project.

The lords proprietors of Carolina had agreed with those gentlemen, April, 1706, that ten thousand acres of land should be laid off for them in one body, between *Neuse* and *Cape Fear*, they paying twenty shillings for every hundred acres, and sixpence the yearly quit-rent. The Surveyor General was also instructed to lay off an additional tract of one hundred thousand acres, which was to be reserved twelve years. One of them was to be gratified by a title, when he should pay the usual price for five thousand acres of land. *De Graffenried* made the purchase and was created a baron. This company, having secured the lands, wished to make them productive by settling them with tenants; and the poor Palatines presented themselves as an object of speculation. Commissioners had been appointed by the Queen to collect and receive money for the use of the Palatines, and to provide them with settlements. *Graffenried* and *Michell* covenanted with those commissioners, that they would transport to North Carolina six hundred and fifty of the Palatines (about one hundred families); that they would lay off for

* *Rupp's History of Lancaster County*, pp. 70, 71.

each family two hundred and fifty acres of land, to be held five years without cost, and from that period at the annual rent of two-pence currency per acre. The Palatines were to be supplied twelve months with necessary provisions, to be paid for at the end of the following year; and they were to be furnished, gratis, with tools sufficient for building houses. It was also stipulated that, within four months from their arrival, they should be provided with a certain number of cows, hogs and sheep, which were to be paid for at the end of seven years; and half the remaining issue was to be returned in lieu of interest.

The commissioners allowed five pounds sterling per head, for transporting the Palatines; and those people, who had each of them, young and old, received twenty shillings of the charitable collections, made throughout the kingdom, lodged that money in the hands of *Graffenried* and *Michell*, to be returned to them in Carolina.* The Palatines arrived in December, 1709, at the confluence of the rivers *Neuse* and *Trent*, where they erected temporary shelters until they could be put in possession of their lands. The place on which they encamped was called *New Bern*, from *Bern* in Switzerland, where *Graffenried* was born. The Palatines had too much reason to complain of their trustees; for *Graffenried*, in whose name the lands were taken up, returned to Switzerland without giving them a title to their settlements. He mortgaged the lands to Thomas Pollock for eight hundred pounds sterling; and they passed to the heirs of that gentleman.

NOTE.—Pollock, by a letter to Graffenried, Feb. 16, 1716, offered to return to him the land, fifteen thousand acres, if he would re-pay the money.

The Palatines in the meantime, being industrious and living in a country where land was plenty and cheap, increased in

---

* The commissioners were John Philips, Alexander Cairnes, Theodore Janson, White Kennet, John Camberlin, Frederick Store, Micaiah Perry.

The article of agreement was dated Oct. 10, 1709, in the eighth year of Queen Anne.

There were six hundred poor Palatines;—ninety-two families.

This article was signed by the seven commissioners; Christopher De Graffenried and Lewis Michell, in the presence of William Taylor and James De Pratt, Oct. 21, 1709.

number and acquired property. After many years, upon their petition to the king, they were in some measure indemnified, by a grant of land, ten thousand acres, free from quit-rents for ten years."

Deutsche Ansiedelung in Nord=Carolina, 1709 und 1710.

"Die Bevölkerung von Nord=Carolina wurde gegen Anfang des achtzehnten Jahrhunderts durch zwei kleine Colonien fran= zöfischer und deutscher Protestanten vermehrt. Eine Colonie französischer Hugenotten war 1690 auf Zuspruch des Königs Wilhelm nach Amerika gekommen und hatte sich am Manakintown in Virginien, oberhalb der Fälle des James=Flusses, niedergelassen. Da sie mit den Ländereien, die sie anfangs besaßen, nicht zufrieden waren, und da der größere Theil Carolina's unveräußert war, brachen sie von hier auf und zogen südlich nach dem Trent=Flusse, wo sie sich 1707 mit ihrem Pastor Rybourg setzten. Sie waren nüchterne, sparsame und fleißige Pflanzer, die in kurzer Zeit unabhängige Bürger wurden.

Die deutsche Colonie war aus Heidelberg und der Umgegend am Rhein. Diese unglücklichen Leute hatten Verfolgungen zu erdulden, weil sie ihren Glauben nicht mit jedem regierenden Prinzen ändern wollten. Der Kurfürst Friedrich II. von der Pfalz war ein Lutheraner; Friedrich III. wurde ein Calvinist; Ludwig V. stellte die lutherische Kirche wieder her; sein Sohn und Nachfolger wurde ein Calvinist; diesem wieder folgte eine katholische Familie, welche die Protestanten unterdrückte.

Ebenfalls hatten sie das Unglück, zwischen zwei mächtigen Nebenbuhlern zu wohnen, die oft gegen einander zu Felde lagen. Im Jahre 1622 nahm Graf Tilly, der kaiserliche General, die Stadt Heidelberg und richtete fünfhundert der Bewohner durch's Schwerdt hin. Ludwig XIV. nahm die Stadt 1634 und ließ viele der Einwohner niederhauen. Wiederum wurde sie 1688 von den Franzosen eingenommen und hatte eine schwere Summe Geldes zu bezahlen. Als die kaiserliche Armee angekommen, sprengten sie die Festung und brannten die Stadt nieder. 1693, als die Stadt wieder aufgebaut war, eroberten die Franzosen dieselbe zum drit= ten Male und gaben sie den Flammen preis. Die Einwohner,

39

etwa fünfzehntausend, Männer, Weiber und Kinder, wurden, nachdem ihnen Alles geraubt, in der Nacht in die Felder hinaus gejagt. Nach dem Rückzug des französischen Heeres ließen sich die Einwohner, unter Versprechung von Gewissensfreiheit und Befreiung von Steuern auf dreißig Jahre, bereden, die Stadt auf's Neue aufzubauen. Einige Zeit darauf fing der Kurfürst, welcher Ketzern geleistete Versprechen für nicht bindend hielt, an, seine protestantischen Unterthanen zu verfolgen. Die französische Armee hatte den Rhein bereits wieder überschritten; da flohen die von ihrem Fürsten verfolgten und vom Feinde peplünderten Pfälzer, etwa sechstausend an der Zahl, nach England, um nach dem von der Königin Anna im Jahre 1708 ergangenen Erlaß daselbst Schutz zu finden.

Ihre Zelte hatten sie eine kleine Strecke außerhalb London auf= geschlagen, wo sie auf öffentliche Kosten erhalten wurden, bis man sie nach Irland oder den Colonien befördern konnte. Christopher de Graffenried und Louis Michell versuchten zu dieser Zeit durch Ankauf von Land in den britischen Colonien ihr Glück zu machen. Michell war mehrere Jahre in Amerika* gewesen und hatte sich einige Kenntnisse des Landes verschafft.

Anmerkung.—Michell war anfangs vom Canton Bern in der Schweiz beauftragt, eine große Strecke leeren Landes an den Grenzen von Penn= sylvanien, Virginien oder Carolina zu suchen, auf dem der Canton eine Colonie gründen könnte. Michell brachte mehrere Jahre mit Untersuchung des Landes zu. Da war kein Mangel an gebirgigen Gegenden, wie sie jene Leute gewöhnt sind; aber der Plan wurde aufgegeben.

Die Grundherren von Carolina hatten mit diesen Herren ein Uebereinkommen getroffen, daß zehntausend Acker für sie an einem Stück zwischen Neuse und Cape Fear, gegen Bezahlung von zwanzig Schilling für je hundert Acker und sechs Pence als jähr= lichen Erbzins, abgemessen werden. Der General=Inspektor wurde ebenfalls angewiesen, eine weitere Fläche Landes von hundert= tausend Acker abzulegen, welche für zwölf Jahre zurückgehalten werden sollten. Einer von ihnen sollte nach Abzahlung des ge= wöhnlichen Preises für fünftausend Acker Landes einen Ehrentitel bekommen. De Graffenried erfüllte die Bedingung und wurde zum Baron erhoben. Nachdem diese Gesellschaft die Ländereien erworben hatten, war ihr Zweck, sie durch die Bevölkerung mit Pächtern erträglich zu machen; und da boten sich die armen Pfäl= zer zum Mittel der Speculation. Die Königin hatte Bevollmächtigte

---

* Rupp's Gesch. von Lancaster Co., S. 70, 71.

angestellt, um Geld für die Pfälzer zu sammeln und ihnen zu einer Niederlassung zu verhelfen. Graffenried und Michell mach=ten es nun mit diesen Bevollmächtigten ab, daß dieselben sechs=hundert und fünfzig von den Pfälzern, etwa hundert Familien, nach Nord=Carolina schifften, welchen sie das Land, jeder Familie zweihundert und fünfzig Acker, die ersten fünf Jahre lang unent=geldlich und von der Zeit an zu zwei Pence Courant per Acker abgeben wollten. Zwölf Monate lang sollten die Pfälzer mit Lebensmitteln versehen werden, deren Bezahlung erst am Ende des darauf folgenden Jahres fällig würde; ebenfalls sollten sie unentgeldlich mit den zur Erbauung ihrer Häuser nöthigen Ge=räthen ausgerüstet werden. Es stand ebenfalls im Vertrag, daß sie innerhalb vier Monate nach ihrer Ankunft mit einer bestimm=ten Anzahl Kühe, Schweine und Schafe versehen werden sollten, die erst nach Verlauf von sieben Jahren zahlbar würden. Statt der Interessen sollten sie dann die Hälfte der Nachzucht zurück=erstatten.

Für Ueberschiffung der Pfälzer gestatteten die Bevollmächtigten fünf Pfund Sterling auf den Kopf; und solche, welche, jung oder alt, zwanzig Schilling von den im ganzen Königreich erhobenen mildthätigen Collektionen erhielten, gaben das Geld in die Hände Graffenried's und Michell's, um es ihnen in Carolina wieder zurückzuerstatten.*

Im December 1709 kamen die Pfälzer am Zusammenfluß der Flüsse Neuse und Trent an, wo sie sich Hütten aufschlugen, bis sie in den Besitz ihres Landes gelangen konnten. Den Ort, wo sie ihre Wohnungen aufschlugen, hießen sie New Bern nach Bern in der Schweiz, dem Geburtsort Graffenried's. Die Pfälzer hatten gute Ursache zu klagen, da Graffenried, auf dessen Namen das Land aufgenommen worden war, nach der Schweiz zurückkehrte, ohne ihnen ein Grundrecht zu ihren Ansiedelungen zu geben. Er verschrieb die Ländereien dem Thomas Pollock für

---

* Die Bevollmächtigten waren John Philips, Alexander Cairnes, Theo. Janson, White Kennet, John Chamberlin, Frederick Store, Micaiah Perry.

Die Vertragsurkunde war datirt: den 10. Oct. 1709, im achten Jahre der Regierung der Königin Anna.

Die Zahl der armen Pfälzer betrug sechshundert;—zwei und neunzig Familien.

Diese Urkunde war unterzeichnet von den sieben Bevollmächtigten; Christopher de Graffenried und Louis Michell, in Gegenwart von William Taylor und James de Pratt, den 21. Okt. 1709.

die Summe von achthundert Pfund Sterling, welche dann auf die Erben dieses Mannes übergingen.

Anmerkung.—In einem von Pollock an Graffenried gerichteten Schreiben vom 16. Februar 1716 trug er ihm die fünfzehntausend Acker wieder an gegen Rückzahlung des Kaufpreises.

Die Pfälzer, die indessen das ausgedehnte und billige Land fleißig bearbeiteten, nahmen an Anzahl zu und erwarben sich Besitzthum. Nach vielen Jahren wurden sie auf eine Bitte an den König durch eine Schenkung von zehntausend Acker, die auf zehn Jahre frei von Erbzinsen waren, gewissermaßen entschädigt.“

No. XII.

GERMANNA.

"Beyond Col. *Spotswood's* Furnace, above the Falls of Rappahannock River, within view of the vast mountains, *he* has founded a town, called *Germanna*, from some Germans sent over by Queen Anne, who have now removed further up the river. Beyond this is seated by Germans from the Palatinate, with allowance of rich land, who thrive very well, and live happily, and entertain generously. These are encouraged to make wines; which by the experience, particularly of the late Robert Beverly, who wrote the History of Virginia, was done easily and in large quantities in those parts; not only from the cultivation of wild grapes, which grow plentifully and naturally in all the lands thereabouts, and in the other parts of the country, but also from the Spanish, French, Italian and German vines."— *Hugh Jones' Present Condition of Virginia, published* 1724.

Col. *Byrd*, writing of *Germanna* in 1732, says: "This famous town consists of Col. Spotswood's enchanted castle on one side of the street, and a baker's dozen of ruinous tenements on the other, where so many German families had dwelt some years ago, but have now moved ten miles higher up, in the forks of Rappahannock, to land of their own."—*Howe's His. Col.*, pp. 475, 476.

Rockingham and Shenandoah Counties are inhabited by many of German origin, who still speak the language of their ancestors.

Shenandoah Valley, in the vicinity of Harrisonburg, was almost exclusively settled by Germans from Pennsylvania, prior to 1748. A traveler through this part of Virginia, during the French and Indian war, writes: "The low grounds upon the banks of the Shenandoah River are very rich and fertile. They are chiefly settled by Germans, who gain a sufficient livelihood by raising stock for the troops, and sending butter down into the lower parts of the country. I could not but reflect with pleasure on the situation of these people, and think, if there is such a thing as happiness in this life, they enjoy it. Far from the bustle of the world, they live in the most delightful climate and richest soil imaginable. They are every where surrounded with beautiful prospects and sylvan scenes;—lofty mountains, transparent streams, falls of water, rich vallies and majestic woods, the whole, interspersed with an infinite variety of flowering shrubs, constitute the landscapes surrounding them. They are subject to few deseases, are generally robust, and live in perfect liberty. They know *no* wants, and are acquainted with but few vices. Their inexperience of elegancies of life precludes any regret that they have not the means of enjoying them; but they possess what many princes would give half their dominions for—health, contentment, and tranquillity of mind."—*Howe's Coll. of Va.*, p. 468.

Germanna.

„Draußen über Oberst Spotswood's Eisenschmelze, oberhalb der Fälle des Rappahannock-Flusses, im Anblick der unabsehbaren Gebirge, hat er eine Stadt gegründet, Namens Germanna, so genannt nach einigen von der Königin Anna herübergeschickten Deutschen, die jetzt weiter den Fluß hinauf gezogen sind. Weiter draußen wohnen Deutsche aus der Pfalz auf reichem Boden, die gut fortkommen, glücklich leben und freigebig bewirthen. Diese keltern Weine, das nach Erfahrung, besonders des verstorbenen Robert Beverly, welcher die Geschichte von Virginien geschrieben, leicht von Statten geht und in jenen Theilen auch in bedeutenden Quantitäten, nicht nur aus den in jener Gegend und angrenzenden Ländern so häufig und üppig wachsenden wilden Trauben, son-
39*

dern auch von den spanischen, französischen, italienischen und deut=
schen Reben."—Hugh Jones' Jetzige Zustände in Virginien,
herausgegeben 1724.

Oberst Byrd sagt in einem Schreiben über Germanna 1732:
„Dieses merkwürdige Städtchen besteht aus Oberst Spotswood's
bezaubertem Schlosse auf der einen Seite der Straße und einem
Dutzend und etlichen alten verfallenen Hütten auf der anderen, in
denen früher eben so viele deutsche Familien gewohnt hatten,
welche aber jetzt zehn Meilen flußaufwärts in die Gabeln des
Rappahannock gezogen sind, auf ihr eigenes Land."—Howe's
Gesch. der Col., S. 475, 476.

Die Counties Rockingham und Shenandoah sind von Vielen
deutscher Abkunft bewohnt, die noch die Sprache ihrer Ahnen
reden. Das Shenandoah=Thal in der Nachbarschaft von
Harrisonburg wurde fast ausschließlich noch vor 1748 von Deut=
schen aus Pennsylvanien angesiedelt. Einer, der während des
französischen und indianischen Krieges durch diesen Theil Vir=
ginien's gereist war, schreibt: „Die an den Ufern des Shenandoah
gelegenen Niederungen sind sehr reich und fruchtbar. Dieselben
sind hauptsächlich von Deutschen angebaut, die durch Ziehen von
Vorrath für die Truppen und durch Lieferung von Butter nach
den niederen Theilen des Landes sich einen genügenden Unterhalt
erwerben. Ich konnte nur mit Vergnügen über die Lage dieser
Leute nachsinnen, und denken, daß, wenn es in diesem Leben
Glückseligkeit gibt, sie dieselbe besitzen müssen. Weit vom Getöse
der Welt entfernt, wohnen sie im prächtigsten Klima und auf
dem reichsten Boden, den man sich denken kann. Ueberall sind sie
mit den herrlichsten Aussichten und Waldgruppen umgeben—hohe
Berge, silberhelle Ströme, Wasserfälle, reiche Thäler und maje=
stätische Wälder, mit einer Zwischensaat von duftenden, blühenden
Gesträuchen aller Art, bilden die sie umgebende Landschaft. Sie
sind nur wenigen Krankheiten unterworfen, gewöhnlich von kräf=
tigem Aeußeren und leben in völliger Freiheit. Sie kennen keinen
Mangel und sind mit wenigen Lastern bekannt. Ihre Unerfahren=
heit in der Eleganz des Lebens schließt jedes Bedauern, daß sie
nicht die Mittel zum Genuß derselben haben, von selbst aus;
ihr Theil jedoch ist ein Gut, für das die Fürsten die Hälfte ihrer
Güter geben würden: Gesundheit, Zufriedenheit und Seelen=
ruhe."—Howe's Sammlungen von Va., S. 468.

No. XIII.

NAMES OF MALES AT NEW ROCHELLE IN 1710.

New Rochelle, in West Chester County, N. Y., was early settled by Huguenots from Rochelle, a seaport-town of France. The following list embraces the names of all the males, ages annexed to the names, living in New Rochelle, December 9, 1710. The *Editor* can vouch for the true spelling of names—they have all been carefully copied.

Namen der Männer zu New Rochelle, 1710.

New Rochelle in Westchester County, N. Y., wurde frühe von Hugenotten aus Rochelle, einem Seehafen Frankreich's, ange= siedelt. Die nachstehende Liste enthält die Namen aller am 9. Dec. 1710 zu New Rochelle wohnenden männlichen Personen, nebst beigefügtem Lebensalter.

William Le Conte, 52,
William Le Conte jr., 16,
Jean Le Conte, 6,
Alexander Allear, 50,
Peter Allear, 15,
Philip Allear, 8,
Jean Allear, 3,
Isaac Allear, 1,
Peter Vallow, 47,
Josiah Le Villien, 48
Peter Le Villien, 9,
John Le Villien, 4,
Peter Martine, 45,
Andreas Nodden sen., 73,
Andreas Nodden jr., 34,
John Rannoo, 46,
Stephen Rannoo, 22,
John Rannoo, 3,
Andrew Jarro, 45,
John Jarro, 13,
Andrew Jarro jr., 11
James Jarro, 3,

John Mannion, 45,
Peter Fruteer, 22,
Isaiah Vallow sen., 72,
Peter Vallow, 10,
Daniel Bondett, 58,
William Landering, 13,
Zachariah Angevine, 46,
Zachariah Angevine jr., 6,
Daniel Angevine, 2,
James Moreye, 55,
Daniel Moreye, 9,
Ffrancis Le Conte, 45,
Josiah Le Conte, 13,
John Teast, 54,
John Lambert, 52,
Isaiah Baddo, 46,
Isaiah Baddo jr., 12,
Andris Barrett, 63,
John Barrett, 25,
Barnabas Barrett, 16,
Andris Barret jr., 13,
Peter Angevine, 44,

464   APPENDIX.

Lewis Angevine, 8,
John Barrett, 50,
John Barrett jr., 7,
Gabriel Barrett, 6,
Peter Barrett, 50,
Peter Brittain, 28,
Peter Brittain jr., 3,
Anthony Leppener, 24,
John Chance, 1,
John Neffveile, 69,
Josiah Neffveile, 18,
Lewis Guion sen., 56,
Isaac Guion, 25,
John Lammon, 28,
James Fflanders, 46,
James Fflanders jr., 4,
Peter Fflanders, 1,
Paul Pillon, 40,
Paul Pillon jr., 14,
James Sycar, 34,
John Sycar, 3,
Robert Bloomer, 76,
James Mott, 15,
Thomas Mott, 9,
Fredk. Bolt, 36,
Peter La Roue, 12,
Daniel Sycar, 40,
James Sycar sen., 75,
Daniel Sycar jr., 12,
John Sycar, 11,
Peter Sycar, 9,
Andrew Sycar, 3,
Peter Parcout, 47,
John Parcout, 15,
Andrew Parcout, 9,
John Couton, 52,
John Couton jr., 15,
Peter Couton, 12,
Frederick Scurman, 80,

Jacob Scurman, 40,
Jacob Scurman jr., 11,
Miles Scurman, 6,
Peter Symon, 47,
Peter Symon jr., 12,
Charles Fruttye, 56,
Oliver Bayley, 52,
Peter Le Doof, 46,
Daniel Le Doof, 14,
Peter Le Doof jr., 8,
John Le Doof, 5,
Andrew Le Doof, 4,
Ffrancis Geenar, 45,
Frederick Scurman, 43,
Daniel Rennœ, 55,
Theophilus Ffurtye, 68,
John Sarineer,
Stephen Garrien, 46,
John Murro, 46,
Peter Murro, 9,
John Murro, 13,
John Martine, 25,
Peter Frederick, 68,
Peter Sluce, 18,
Peter Frederick jr., 26,
John Boullie, 35,
John Boullie jr., 5,
Daniel Bonnett, 45,
Daniel Bonnett jr., 17,
John Bonnett, 15,
Peter Bonnett, 5,
Josiah Hunt, 43,
Josiah Hunt jr., 15,
John Bon Repo, 47,
Blanch Bon Repo, 13,
Gregory Guyion, 44,
Gregory Guyion jr., 7,
Peter Dais, 48.

No. XIV.

NAMES OF EARLY SETTLERS IN TULPEHOCKEN, BERKS AND LEBANON COUNTIES.

As early as 1723, thirty-three families of Germans, who had come to New York 1710, settled in Schoharie 1713, left there and located on Tulpehocken Creek; among these were:

Namen der erften Anfiedler von Tulpehocken, Berks und Lebanon Counties.

Schon im Ja͟yre 1723 ließen ſich dreißig deutſche Familien, die 1710 nach New York gefommen und 1713 nach Schoharie gezogen waren, am Tulpehocken=Fluß nieder; unter dieſen waren:

Johannes Lantz,	Johan Peter Pacht,
Peter Rieth,	Sebastian Pisas,
Conrad Schütz,	Andreas Walborn,
Lorentz Zerbe,	Antonius Scharf,
Joseph Saab,	Sebastian Fischer,
George Rieth,	Christian Lauer,
Gottfried Fitler,	Johan Adam Lesch,
Johan Nicolas Schäffer,	George Anspach.
Johannes Rieth,	

In 1728, others from Schoharie settled here.

Andere von Schoharie ließen ſich 1728 hierſelbſt nieder.

Leonard Anspach,	Georg Zeh,
Johan Jacob Holsteiner,	Andreas Kapp,
Johan Philip Schneider,	Jacob Löwengut,
Philip Theis,	Georg Schmidt,
Casper Höhn,	Johannes Nöcker,
Michael Lauer,	Jacob Werner,
Jacob Katterman,	Heinrich Six.
Conrad Scharf,	

NOTE.—In 1729, Conrad Weiser left Schoharie with his wife and five children, Philip, Frederick, Anna, Madlina and Maria, and settled near the present site of Womelsdorf, one mile east of the town. He was usefully employed in various capacities by the Government of Pennsylvania, until within a few weeks of his death. He died July 13, 1760, aged 63 years, 8 months and 12 days. His earthly remains moulder in their narrow house, near Womelsdorf.—See *Rupp's History of Berks County*, pp. 195–222.

The first settlers in Tulpehocken were Lutherans and German Reformed. Rev. Tobias Wagner was the first pastor of the Lutheran Congregation. The following is a List of the members of the Tulpehocken Church, from 1743 to 1746:

Anmerkung.—1729 verließ Conrad Weiser Schoharie mit seiner Frau und fünf Kindern, Philipp, Friedrich, Anna, Magdalena und Maria, und siedelte sich in der Nähe der gegenwärtigen Lage von Womelsdorf, eine Meile östlich vom Städtchen, an. Bis kurz vor seinem Tode leistete er der Regierung von Pennsylvanien auf verschiedenerlei Weise treue Dienste. Am 13. Juli 1760 starb er im Alter von 63 Jahren, 8 Monaten und 12 Tagen. Seine Gebeine ruhen in ihrem engen Haus bei Womelsdorf.— Siehe Rupp's Gesch. von Berks County, S. 195–222.

Die ersten Ansiedler in Tulpehocken waren Lutheraner und Reformirte. Pastor Tobias Wagner war der erste Seelsorger der Lutherischen Gemeinde. Folgendes ist eine Liste der Mitglieder der Tulpehocken-Kirche von 1743 bis 1746:

Sebastian Fischer,
Michael Nef sen.,
Erasmus Dunkenmayer,
Martin Höcker,
Peter Hohnsteiner,
Valentin Urich,
Thomas Koppenhöfer,
Michael Erhardt,
Georg Graf sen.,
Friederick Kapp,
Andreas Kapp,
Reinhold Eset,
Johannes Rickmüller,
Leonard Grau,
Christoph Kaylor,
Joh. Georg Brigel,
Joh. Georg Lechner,
Andreas Graf,
Martin Stupp,
Christian Laur,
Jacob Fischer,
Georg Unruh,
Johannes Immel,
Andreas Kreutzer,
Christian Walborn,
Andreas Saltzgeber,
Martin Batorf,
Joh. Heinrich Boyer,
Georg Anspach,
Joh. Adam Lesch,
Joh. Peter Anspach,
Joh. Georg Köhl,
Nicolaus Dek,
Johan Heinrich Dek,
Johannes Anspach,
Leonard Anspach,
Joh. Phil. Schneider,
Balthas Anspach,
Joh. Leonhard Hollsteiner,
Georg Brosius,
Abraham Lauk,
Michael Müller,
Joh. Nich. Schwengel,
Andreas Wolf,
Michel Koppenhöfer,
Simon Carle,
Joh. Phil. Gebhardt,
Michel Hof jr.,

Johann Schoss,
Abraham Nef,
Andreas Wigner,
Joh. Mich. Müller,
Joseph Keller,
Peter Gebhard,
Jacob Löwengut,
Joh. Martin Kapp,
Johan Martin Cass,
Geo. Vitus Cass,
Joh. Michel Kapp,
Joh. Georg König,
Doratha Ertzbergerin,
Margretha Baslerin,
Niclaus Hafner,
Philip Moderer,
Joh. Müller,
Joh. Adam Lang,
Peter Kreutzer,
Nichlas Gaucher,
Jacob Katterman,
Peter Zerb,
Johannes Graf,
Heinrich Schupp,
Georg Graf jr.,
Joh. Adam Christ,
Philip Kunz,
Georg Pfafenberger,
Wilhelm Leitner,
Frederick Süss,
Margr. Kreutzbergerin,
Johan Kistler,
Anna Cath. Daurin,
Melchior Debler,
Marg. Cath. Christian,
Franciscus Brosmann,
Joh. Kastner,
Anna Elisabeth Lenin,
Hermanus Batorf,
Jacob Lesch,
Leonhard Feg,

Joh. Geo. Goldmann,
Joh. Gotfried Röhrer,
Joh. Jacob Köhler,
Anna Barb. Riedin,
Daniel Schneider,
Joh. Adam Müller,
Joh. Peter Müller,
Heinrich Gruber,
Jacob Muller,
Conrad Scharf,
Christian Gruber,
Johan Dieter,
Joh. Valentin Lang,
Jacob Mautz,
Christoph Besher,
Joh. Georg Lauk,
Andreas Kraft,
Stephanus Umbenhauer,
Joh. Kettner,
Joh. Casper Stöver,
Geo. Michel Kettner,
Conrad Ernst,
Adam Scharf,
Gottfried Fiteler,
Michel Schauer,
Eva Martinin,
Martin Pfateicher,
Jacob Zorn,
Philip Straus,
Adam Schauer,
Johannes Zerbe,
Jacob Zerbe,
Adam Schmidt,
Adam Ulrich,
Leonhard Müller,
Johannes Waidmann,
Balthas Süss,
Georg Albert,
Martin Waidman,
Daniel Huber,
Georg Klein,

Jacob Klein,
Jacob Heil,
Hartman Vertries,
Leonhard Hof,
Joh. Georg Heil,
Peter Raa,
Henrich Rothe,
Johannes Bauer,
Joh. Adam Oberlin,
Geo. Eichelberger,
Michel Spieger,
Mattheus Albrecht,
Joh. Peter Kucher,
Georg Steitz,
Joh. Sigmund Herle,

Georg Zeh,
Wendel Heil,
Friderich Ruth,
Georg Günter,
Valentin Herchelroth,
Adam Stump,
Henrich Majer,
Geo. Bartel Schäfer,
Franz Wenrich,
Johannes Haak,
Georg Wenrich,
Johan Henrich Basler
Joh. Holman,
Joh. Jac. Ertzberger,
Christian Anbauer.

No. XV.

LIST OF MEMBERS OF THE GERMAN REFORMED
CHURCH, BETWEEN 1735 AND 1755.

Liste der Mitglieder der deutsch-reformirten Kirche in den
Jahren 1735 bis 1755.

Johannes Bassler,
Jonas La Ru,
Johan G. Zöller,
Wilhelm Hoster,
Hartman Zöller,
Friederich Klopp,
Georg Huber,
Johan Thomas,
Michael Spengler,
Johannes Petrus,
Nicholas Gelbert,
Johannes Zollner,
Jacob Itzberger,
Nicklaus Müller,

Johannes Müller,
Peter Becker,
Peter Loch,
Jonas Fortuny,
Johannes Lein,
Johan Adam Stein,
Jacob Dinges,
Christian Orndorff,
Jacob Simon,
Michael Gunkel,
Jacob Keller,
Johan Jacob Müller,
Peter Summois,
Georg Dollinger,

Johan Wilhelm Hoster,
Abraham Lebbo,
Peter Spycker,
John Adam Forne,
Henrich Marsteller,
Jacob Rammler,
Johannes Reiff,
Wilhelm Leitner,
Johan Georg Stahlschmidt,
Nicklaus Simon,
Michael Kor,
Peter Mayer,
Jacob Rossel,
Johan Henrich Herchelroth,
Jacob Seifert,
Johan Diehm,
Henrich Koppenhöffer,
Conrad Hartman,
Henrich Ludwig,
Daniel Maurshagen,
Johan Peter Pappel,

Isaac Mayer,
Joh. Adam Dieffenbach,
Adam Forrer,
Peter Wenkelbley,
Baltzer Noll,
Jacob Gröninger,
Conrad Goldman,
Henrich Schmidt,
Philip Ziegler,
Valentin Schuler,
Casper Kor,
Johan Michael Becker,
Michael Sänger,
Jacob Walter,
Conrad Schwartz,
Georg Deys,
Johann Dätweiler,
Martin Schell,
Augustus Wilhelm,
Jacob Zufall,
Lorentz Wolff.

NOTE.—May 10, 1728, inhabitants of *Colebrook Dale* petitioned Governor Gordon, praying for relief against what they suffered, and were likely to suffer, from the Indians, who had fallen upon the back inhabitants about *Falkner's Schwamm* and *Goshenhoppen.—Pa. Arch.*, I., p. 213.

Anmerkung.—Am 10. Mai 1728 reichten die Bewohner vom Cole= brook=Thal an Gouverneur Gordon eine Bittschrift ein, in der ?: ihn ersuchten, ihnen Abhülfe zu verschaffen von den Angriffen, die sie von den Indianern zu leiden hatten, welche bereits über die hinteren Bewohner nahe Falkner's Schwamm und Goshenhoppen hergefallen waren.— Pennf. Archiv, I., S. 213.

John Roberts,
John Pawling,
Henry Pfannebäcker,
W. Lane,
John Jacobs,
D. Bais,
Israel Morris,
Benjamin Frey,

Jacob Opdegräf,
Richard Adams,
George Boger,
Adam Sollom,
Dielman Kolb,
Martin Kolb,
Gabriel Schuler,
Anthony Hollman,

40

John Isaac Klein,
Hans Detweiler,
William Bitts,
Heinrich Ruth,
Hubrecht Cassel,
Henrich Fenttinger,
Christian Weber,
Gerhart de Hesse,
Lorentz Sinsemore,
Richard Jacob,
Herman Rupert,
Betu Bohn,
Jacob Conrads,
Christian Neuschwanger,
Conrad Cresson,
Jacob Kolb,

Hans Ulrich Borge,
John Mayer,
John Frot,
Paul Frot,
Wm. Smith,
Peter Rambo,
David Yung,
Christopher Schmidt,
Gerhart Clemens,
Mathias Tyson (Deisen),
Peter Janson,
Yost Heid,
Christian Allbach,
Hans Reif,
Daniel Stauffer,

and numerous others (und viele andere).

No. XVI.

FOUR HUNDRED AND SIXTY-FIVE NAMES OF GERMAN, DUTCH AND FRENCH INHABITANTS OF PHILADELPHIA COUNTY,
who owned land, and paid quit-rents prior to 1734.

NOTE.—*Quit-rent*, a reserved rent in the grant of land, by the Proprietary, by the payment of which the landholder was to be freed from other taxes. Quit-rents were not uniform; they varied from one shilling sterling per hundred acres, to six shillings *per annum*, and in other instances more.

Vierhundert und fünfundsechszig Namen deutscher, holländischer und französischer Einwohner von
Philadelphia County,
welche Land besaßen und vor dem Jahre 1734 Erbzinsen zahlten.

Anmerkung.—Erbzins ist eine reservirte Rente bei dem Uebertragen von Land durch den Eigenthümer, durch deren Zahlung der Pächter von allen anderen Taxen befreit wurde. Erbzinsen waren nicht gleichförmig; sie variirten von einem Schilling Sterling per hundert Acker bis zu sechs Schillingen jährlich, und in anderen Fällen mehr.

Amity Township.

Johan Jacob Roth, 100 acres, Jacob Weber, 110,
Daniel Womelsdorf, 200, Georg Ander, 200,
Elias De Hart, 100, Simon De Hart, 100.

Bibury Township.

Joseph Van Pelt, 180.

Bristol Township.

Christian Peterman, 50, Abra'm Schuhmacher, 50,
Johannes Lücken, 300, Mathias Lücken, 150.

Cresheim Township, late part of Germantown.

Wilhelm De Wees, 150, Peter Zell, 60,
Johannes Conrad, 100, Dirk Rebenstock, 50,
David Müller, 100, Peter Rüttynhuysen, 100,
Heinrich Zell, 100, Jacob Zell, 90,
Cornelius Neus, 50, Hans Schelly, 25,
Michael Acker, 25, Leonard List, 20,
Anna Rupp, 100, Johan Streper, 150,
Anthony Tünis, 150, Joh. Georg Rieser, 27.

Cheltenham Township.

Georg Schuhmacher, 100, Isaac Schuhmacher, 20.
Georg Herman, 50,

Colebrook Township.
(Number of acres not given.)

Daniel Stauffer, Hans Bauer,
Jacob Buchwalter, Peter Beidler,
Michael Bauer, Jacob Herman.

Upper Dublin Township.

Dirick Tison, 100, Johannes Herman, 100,
Dennis Cunrad, 100, Wilhelm Lücken, 200.
Johannes Cönrads, 200,

Franconia Township.

Johannes Frey, 150, Johan Griesman, 40,
Jacob Oberholtzer, 150, Conrad Küster, 100,
Jost Pfannenkuch, 100 Michael Bang, 75,
Joseph Althaus, 141, Jacob Fuhrman, 140,
Uly Hunsberger, 150, Johannes Hentz, 100,
Leonard Christoleer, 200, Ludwig Zerkel, 100,

Johannes Wilhelm, 50,
Henrich Rosenberger, 100,
Jost Schindler, 140,
Christian Mayer, 150,
Abraham Reif, 200,
Jacob Hunsberger, 50,
Georg German, 100,

Frederick Gädschalk, 150,
Wilhelm Hauk, 100,
Henrich Zerkel, 50,
Michael Hentz, 100,
Georg Hertzell, 50,
Frederick Scholl, 100.

Frederick Township.

Johannes Neus, 200,
Joh. Hein. Hageman, 100,
Henrich Stover, 100,
Henrich Stettler, 140,
Adam Barsteller, 25,
Joh. Georg Sprogel, 120,
Johannes Kraus, 150,
Jacob Fauts, 100,
Joh. Geo. Schwenhart, 100,
Gotlieb Herger, 80,
Wilhelm Frey, 150,
Geo. Phil. Dotterer, 150,

Joh. Georg Kraus, 22,
Christian Stettler, 50,
Martin Funk, 160,
Ludwig Englehart, 100,
Henrich Schmidt, 80,
Michael Kraus, 150,
Baltus Fauts, 100,
Frederick Reymer, 100,
Michael Herger, 200,
Joseph Graaf, 100,
Michael Dotterer, 150.

(The number of acres are not given in the following.)

Christian Getzendonner,
Paul Hippel,
Christian Schneider,
Michael Bastian,
Daniel Frantz,
Joh. Geo. Ganser,
Martin Husacker,
Michael Hill,
Ludwig Dotterer,

Johannes Herb,
Christian Müller,
Jacob Mecklin,
Jacob Fuchs,
Georg Trumbauer,
Abraham Pfenning,
Michael Hendricks,
Adam Hill,
Johannes Dilbeck.

Germantown.

Abraham Kauffman, 50,
Georg Wammer, 10,
Gotfried Lehman, ½,
Henrich Holtzapfel, 70,
Samuel Kerschner, 50,
Andreas Keyser, 50,
Johan Georg Knorr, 50,
Christian Wammer, 75,

Paul Engle, 50,
Jacob Keyser, 4,
Dirick Keyser, 3,
Georg Hass, 20,
Johannes Mack, 2,
Henrich Friederick, 1,
Gotfried Liebgieb, 13,
Lorentz Blitz, 15,

Bernhard Rieser, 80,
Isaac Van Sentern, 18,
Joh. Theobald Ent, 5,
Jacob Bauman, 8,
Johannes Bartel, 20,
Christopher Meng, 15,
Peter Schuhmacher, 50,
Alexander Mack, ½,
Mathias Adams, 70,
Johan Lückin, 1½,
Dirick Jansen, 100,
Jacob Müller, 50,
Casper Steinbrenner, 50,
Anthony Klinken, 100,
Joh. Friederik Ochs, 25,
Georg Traut, 28,

Joh. Jac. Pallard, 31,
Joh. Peterkoffer, ½,
Johannes Gorgas, 30,
Peter Becker, 23,
Baltzer Traut, 25,
Johannes Eckstein, 25,
Joh. Adam Gruber, 14,
Johannes Bechtel, 20,
Christopher Saur, 6,
Joh. Henrich Kalckleser, 42,
Herman Theen, 50,
Christopher Funk, 50,
Nicholas De Laplaine, 7,
Benj. Schuhmacher, 20,
Henrich Pastorius, 260,
Georg Bentzel, 15.

Hanover Township.

Stoffel Witman, 100,
Johannes Benner, 50,
Benedict Mentz, 50,
Frederich Reichard, 150,
Christian Eyster, 100,
Claus Braun, 100,
Melchior Hoch, 100,
Samuel Musselman, 50,
Henrich Wenger, 50,
Johan Linderman, 100,
Cornelius De Wees, 24,
Michael Schenk, 50,
Georg Küster, 100,
Peter Lauer, 100,
Andreas Gräber, 150,
Balthaser Huth, 150,
Henrich Kollman, 150,
Jacob Weizler, 150,
Daniel Schöner, 100,
Elias Aff, 50,
Mathias Bender, 100,
Andreas Kepler, 100,
Johannes Allbach, 100,

Jacob Hoch, 100,
Jacob Arner, 100,
Jacob Bechtel, 200,
Mathias Christman, 100,
Garret De Wees, 100,
Mathias Otto, 50,
Joh. Henrich Sprogel, 556,
Johan Bingeman, 200,
Jacob Dunkel, 150,
Ludwig Bitting, 150,
Henrich Bisbing, 150,
Georg Saalicht, 150,
Henrich Rieder, 150,
Francis Stupp, 50,
Friedrich Hillegass, 150,
Daniel Lubbar, 100,
Henrich Saalicht, 150,
Michael Schell, 150,
Jacob Mayer, 100,
Jacob Hiestandt, 150,
Johannes Zell, 100,
Georg Geiger, 50,
Ludwig Bethsill, 100,

40*

Philip Knecht, 50,
Mathias Herman, 100,
Adam Spengler, 50,
Peter Rothermel, 100,
Jacob Grus, 100,
Henrich Dehring, 100,
Henrich Antes, 150,
Henrich Bitting, 100,
Hans Martinius, 50,
Simon Krebs, 100,
Jacob Müller, 100,
Barnibus Tothero, 100,
Georg Raudenbusch, 150,
Johannes Huth, 150,
Philip Lubbar, 100,
Daniel Borleman, 100,
Conrad Kolb, 150,
Stoffel Wagenseiler, 150,
Rudolph Mauerer, 150,
Nicholas Insell, 100,
Valentin Geiger, 100,
Martin Beiting, 100,
Adam Herman, 100,
Wendel Keit, 100,
Peter Conrad, 100,
Michael Schmidt, 50,
Jacob Schweitzer, 100,

Philip Brandt, 100,
Adam Ochs, 140,
Nicholas Jost, 70,
Jacob Mayer, 100,
Henrich Krebs, 100,
Jost Freyer, 100,
Paul Hill, 100,
Casper Kemp, 100,
Bastian Reifschneider, 100,
Joh. Georg Georg, 100,
Georg Noth, 100,
Henrich Acker, 50,
Wilhelm Kehle, 100,
Martin Zentler, 150,
Johannes Eyster, 60,
Jacob Schäfer, 50,
Johan Reichelsdörfer, 100,
Jacob Frey, 100,
Johannes Schneider, 150,
Anthony Hinckle, 100,
Georg Hallenbach, 150,
Georg Steiger, 100,
Mathias Ringer, 150,
Johannes Dunkell, 100,
Casper Singer, 50,
Christopher Schlegel, 50.

(The number of acres are not given in the following.)

Nicholas Hensy,
Johan Adam Plank,
Herman Fischer,
Hans Leymeyer,
Michael Krebs,
Martin Merkle,

Stephen Reymer,
Adam Müller,
Joh. Georg Welcker,
Jacob Schmidt,
Jacob Jost,
Ludwig Burghart.

Limerick Township.

Peter Umbstat, 250,
Adolph Pennybecker, 250,
Hieronimus Has, 250,
Stephan Müller, 170,

Johannes Umbstat, 250,
Henrich Reiner, 100,
Lorentz Rinker, 50,
Martin Kalb, 150.

Maxatany Township.

(Number of acres not given.)

Jacob Hottenstein,
Peter Andreas,
Jacob Levan,
Jacob Kemp,
Wilhelm Gross,
Casper Wink,
Christian Mahnenschmidt,
Jacob Hill,
Isaac Leonard,
Peter Trexler,
Hans Hage,

Johannes Siegfried,
Nicholas Kutz,
Abraham Timberman,
Jost Hen. Sasseman,
Andreas Fischer,
Henrich Hartman,
Michael Müller,
Hans Kleimer,
Henrich Schade,
Jeremiah Trexler,
Bastian Ferr.

Oley Township.

Georg Jäger, 250,
Johannes Joder jr., 300,
Sebastian Graaf, 100,
Jacob De Plank, 100,
Andreas Bally, 200,
Johannes Bertolet, 200,
Christopher Bittle, 100,
Isaac Levan, 230,
Johannes Joder, 200,
Jost Joder, 150,
Peter Schilbert, 200,
Englo Peters, 150,
Nicholas Lescher, 150,
Arnold Hufnagel, 200,
Martin Weiler, 100,
Martin Allstadt, 150,
Peter Fornwald, 100,

Adam Weidner, 100,
Johannes Hoch, 300,
Philip Kühlwein, 200,
Jonathan Herbein, 200,
Samuel Guldin, 200,
David Kauffman, 300,
Martin Schindel, 100,
Johannes Engelhardt, 150,
Peter Bingeman, 100,
Peter Bally, 100,
Abraham Levan, 150,
Samuel Hoch, 150,
Johannes Schneider, 200,
Johannes De Turk, 300,
Johannes Leinbach, 250,
Abraham Eschelman, 150,
Rudolph Hiegler, 250.

Perkiomen and Shippack Townships.

Henrich Pennybecker, 150,
Anthony Hallman, 100,
Julius Kassel, 90,
Abraham Schwartz, 100,
Jacob Scheimer, 100,
Peter Jansen, 150,
Martin Kolb, 100,

Johannes Fried, 200,
Jacob Merkle, 200,
Paul Fried jr., 100,
Valentin Hunsecker, 100,
Johan Van Hussen, 50,
Hermanus Küster, 150,
Hupert Kassel, 60,

Georg Merkle, 150,
Jacob Updegraff, 100,
Paul Fried, 100,
Michael Ziegler, 100,
Peter Kolb, 100,
Henrich Dentlinger, 100,
Benjamin Frey, 100,

Hans Detweiler, 100,
Mathias Jansen, 50,
Leonard Van Hussen, 25,
Peter Pennybecker, 100,
Hans Heiser, 100,
Arnold Van Hussen, 50.

Providence Township.

Johannes Beidler, 100,
Conrad Rubell, 150,
Conrad Knoss, 48,
Jacob Schrack,* 250,
Jacob Müller, 80,
Han Nicholas Crisman, 200,
Bastian Müller, 100,

Dirk Ramsauer, 100,
Henrich Holtzstein, 60,
Conrad Stein, 15,
Herman Indohaven, 200,
Jacob Boblitz, 80,
Anthony Vandersluice, 100,
Joh. Georg Wagemüller, 30.

Roxburro Township.

Wilhelm Levering, 150,
Jacob Seltzer, 100.
Daniel Bergenthaler, 80,
Claus Rüttynhuysen, 50,
Henrich Schaub, 100,

Jacob Levering, 50,
Arnold Bamberger, 80,
Johannes Mack, 18,
Peter Rinker, 46.

Sulford Township.

Peter Kuntz, 100,
Valentin Crates, 100,
Hans Michael Wägly, 100,
Hans Wolleberger, 100,
Ulrich Steffe, 50,
Dewalt Jung, 100,
Hans Adam Mauerer, 100,
Jacob Kehler, 100,
Andreas Haake, 120,
Hans Weyerman, 50,
Henrich Ruth, 100,

Hans Reif, 100,
Hans Klemmer, 100,
Jacob Hoffman, 100,
Hans Georg Bucher, 100,
Jacob Reif, 150,
Vincent Mayer, 100,
Johannes Jansen, 150,
Henrich Schlinglauf, 50,
Johannes Lebo, 100,
Johannes Kemper, 100,
Galy Heffelfinger, 150,

---

* Jacob Schrack arrived from Germany, 1717, and located at the place now called *The Trappe.* He died 1742, aged 63 years.—*Hallische Nachrichten.*

* Jakob Schrack langte im Jahre 1717 von Deutschland an und wohnte in dem jetzigen Trappe. Er starb 1742 im 63ſten Lebensjahre.—Halliſche Nachrichten.

Christian Kroll, 50,
Isaac Klein, 130,
Mathias Hass, 100,
Samuel Mayer, 100,
Martin Hildenbeidel, 50,
Christian Lehman, 100,
Jost Cope,* 100,
Christopher Ankibrant, 100,
Ludwig Schäfer, 100,
Christian Allebach, 150,
Gabriel Scholer, 150,
Philip Rieth, 100,
Andreas Lederach, 150,
Thielman Kolb, 150,
Nicholas Haldeman, 100,
Georg Reif, 100,

Johannes Scholl, 100,
Christian Jüngling, 20,
Hans Wendell Hoffer, 100,
Abraham Titlo, 50,
Andreas Schwartz, 150,
Michael Moll, 50,
Christian Stauffer, 120,
Hans Mayer, 150,
Christian Mayer, 100,
Samuel Mayer jr., 50,
Henrich Funk, 150,
Hans Mayer jr., 100,
Jacob Koch, 100,
Jacob Landes, 150,
Hans Fried, 100,
Joh. Henrich Schneider, 100.

Towamoncin Township.

Jacob Frill, 100,
Nicholas Lescher, 150,
Peter Weber, 150,
Christian Brenneman, 150,
Herman Gädschalk, 100,
Henrich Frey, 50,
Jellis Jellis, 22,

Christian Weber, 50,
Jacob Frey, 200,
Peter Tison, 100,
Gerhardt Schrager, 100,
Abraham Lüken, 200,
Velty Kaufenheisen, 22.

Springfield Township.

Christopher Ottinger, 85,
Henrich Schneider, 50,

Georg Gantz, 40.

Worcester Township.

(Number of acres not given.)

Lorentz Schweitzer,
Conrad Conrads,
Stoffel Timberman,
Jacob Engel,

Johannes Van der Sluys,
   (now Vanderslice),
Henrich Schweitzer,
Johannes Lefever,

---

* Jost Cope arrived at Philadelphia, Oct. 2, 1727, with the ship Adventurer, Capt. John Davies.—See pp. 53, 54.

Joſt Cope langte am 2. Oct. 1727 mit dem Schiffe Abventurer, Capt. John Davies, in Philabelphia an.—Siehe S. 53, 54.

Adam Vanfussen,   Conrad Vanfussen,
Henrich Rüttenhuysen,   Daniel Christman.
Peter Keyser,

Whitpaine Township.

Philip Böhm, 200,   Henry Levering, 100,
Henry Conrad, 201,   Peter Indehaven, 100,
Jacob Jost, 80,   John Merckle, 100.
Jacob Levering, 100,

Whitemarsh Township.

Henry Bartinstal, 170,   Nicholas Stiegletz, 150,
Adam Kettler, 170,   Ludwig Knoss, 100.

Mooreland Township.

Joh. Van Buskirk, 180,   Garret Winecoop, 200,
Joseph Van Buskirk, 150,   Herman Yerkes, 150.

Plymouth Township.

Johannes Redwetzer, 200,   Peter Kroll, 100.

Interpretation of Baptismal Names

OCCURRING IN THE

𝕮𝖔𝖑𝖑𝖊𝖈𝖙𝖎𝖔𝖓 𝖔𝖋 𝕿𝖍𝖎𝖗𝖙𝖞 𝕿𝖍𝖔𝖚𝖘𝖆𝖓𝖉 𝕹𝖆𝖒𝖊𝖘.

Erklärung von Taufnamen, welche in der Sammlung von 30,000 Namen vorkommen.

AARON, a teacher; Hebrew, literally one that is exalted above the vulgar or common people.

ABRAHAM, father of many nations; Hebrew, from *ab*, father, and *raham*, many nations, or multitudes.

ACHILLES, one that mourns or grieves—F. Pichler. It is a Greek name, by which the son of Peleus and Thetis was known, who signalized himself at the siege of Troy.

ACHOR, Achior, trouble, disturbance of mind; Hebrew, *akhor*, troubling, or *akhan*, he that troubles.

ADAM, earthy man; Hebrew. This name may be derived from *dam*, blood, *adam*, red, or to be red, in the sense of beauty, or beautiful, *i. e.* red man, beautiful man.

ADELBERTH, Ethelbert, of noble birth; Gothic, *ædel, adel*, noble, and Anglo-Saxon, *byrd, beorth, berth*, birth, the condition in which a person is born.

ADOLPH, Adolf, a noble helper; Gothic and Anglo-Saxon, *hylpan, helpan, holpen, holph*, help, hence helper.

ADRIAN, Hadrian, one from the Gulf of Venice; Greek origin.

ÆGEDIUS, Egidius, Giles, vigilant, wakeful; Greek, and may be derived from the verb *egeiro*, to stir up, animate, to waken.

ALBERTUS, Albert, Albrecht, same as Adelberth.

ALEXANDER, one who aids, or defends; Greek, from *alexo, alexeo*, to defend, and *aner, andros*, nom. pl. *andres*, a man, men; one who protects men.

ALFRED, all peace; Anglo-Saxon, *eal*, (Greek, *holos*, all, the whole) and *freoh, freod, fread, fred*, peace.

480   INTERPRETATION OF NAMES.

ALPHONS, Alphonse, Alphonso, Olphonso, blessed, happy, one that is blessed—F. Pichler. This name may be derived from the Greek *holos*, *olos*, all, and *phone*, *phones*, sound, voice—literally, "all spoken of," much renowned. If derived from the Gothic *alfanz*, *alefanz*, *alifanz*, *alafanz*, the name signifies "a jovial man."—"Jetzt merk' ich den *alefanz*."—Wackernagel.

AMBROSIUS, Ambrose, imaginary food of the gods; Germanice, *Götterspeise;* Greek, from *ambrosios*, *a*, *on*, immortal, but mostly as appertaining to the immortals, sacred to the immortals, the food of the gods.

AMOS, one who bears a burden—F. Pichler. Burdensome, burdening, with stammering tongue—Heubner; Hebrew.

ANANIAS, the cloud of the Lord, or the Lord will answer—M. T. Bernler.

ANASTASIUS, a convalescent, one rising from the dead; Greek, *anistemi,* part. *anastesas,* arouse, arise; *anastasis,* a rising up from sickness.

ANDREAS, Andries, Andrew, a courageous man, one strong and stout; Greek, *aner*, *andros*, a man, hence *andria*, as manhood, manly courage, manly feeling—it occurs Andro.

ANTON, Anthon, Anthony, not to be valued, one who is inestimable—F. Pichler. It may be derived from the Greek verb *antheo*, to attain the highest pinnacle, hence *anthos*, *eos*, *antheon*, the excellence of anything—occurs Andoni.

AREND, a tenant-farmer; Germanice, *Pächter;* Russian, *arenda*, hence the English arendator, a farmer of the farms. It might be derived from the Greek *aroo*, to plough, sow; Latin, *aro*, *aras*, *arare*, to plough, to till. Ovid says: *arati,* *agri*, farmed fields.

ARIOVIST, honorable—F. Pichler.

ARIUS, martial, valiant; Greek, from *areios*, *arieou*, excellent, strong, valiant.

ARNOLDUS, Arnold, an honorable hero—F. Pichler. From the Gothic *æren*, *æhren*, *arn*, hence *ehren*, and *old*, *æld*, *hæld*, *held*, hero.

ASAPH, one who assembles the people; Hebrew, from the verb *asaph*, to gather, to collect, to assemble.

ASEMUS, without a mark, note or stamp; Greek, from *a*, privative, without, and *sema*, *sematos*, a sign, mark, note, stamp; Germanice, *zeichenlos*, *ungewöhnlich*.

AUGUSTUS, Augustinus,* Gustav, noble, sublime, elevated, increasing; Latin, from *augeo*, to augment, increase, elevate.

AURELIUS, the golden one, one most excellent; Germanice, *goldener*—F. Pichler. Latin, derived from *aurum*, gold, hence *aureus*, golden.

BALTHASAR, Balthas, Baltzer, Baldis, counselor of war; Germanice, *Kriegsrath*—F. Pichler. It may be derived from the Gothic *baltha*, daring, bold, audacious; Anglo-Saxon, *beald*, *bald*, bold. Iornandes, in defining this word, gives its Latin synonymn thus, *baltha*, *audax*, as *audax viribus*, der auf seine Stärke pochet.

BARTHOLOMÆUS, Bartholomew, a valiant son—F. Pichler; a son who stays the water—Heubner. It may be derived from the Hebrew, Chaldaic and Syriac *bar*, son, and Greek, *tolma*, boldness, courage, from the root; or the verb *talao*, to have boldness: undertake, hazzard, dare, support, sustain; or from the Hebrew *tal*, bear, support. This name occurs abbreviated, as Bardel, Bartel, Barthe, Bard.

BENEDICTUS, Benedict, a blessed one; Latin, from *bene*, well, and *dico, dicere, dixi, dictum*, to speak, hence benedictus—occurs abbreviated Bene, Beni.

BENJAMIN, son of fortune—F. Pichler. Son of the right hand, or most beloved son—Heubner. Derived from the Hebrew *ben*, son, and *jamin*, the right side, or the right hand.

BERNHARD, Bernhardt, Bernard, a robust child, born robust; Anglo-Saxon, *byran, baern, beran, berand*, born, and *heard*, hard or robust—abbreviated Barni.

BERTHOLD, Berchtold, Berdolf, Berdolt, worthy age, one worthy by reason of his age; Gothic, *berth, verth, werth*, worth, excellence, worthy; and Saxon, *ælde, eald*, old, advanced in years—occurs Berd, Bert.

---

* This name is variously written and abbreviated; it occurs once: *Costiniös* Ortman, p. 179. This is undoubtedly intended for *Gustinus*, Augustinus, unless it be derived from a Greek word, *kostos, kostou*, an aromatic plant.—(*Editor.*)

* Dieſer Name wird verſchiedenartig geſchrieben und abgefürzt; er fommt einmal auf Seite 179 vor—Coſtiniös Ortmann. Dieſes iſt ohne Zweifel für Guſtinus, Auguſtinus, gemeint, wenn es nicht von dem griechiſchen Worte kostos, kostou, (eine wohlriechende Pflanze) abgeleitet wird.— (Herausgeber.)

BERTHRAM, Bertram, Berdram, a stately hero, a grand champion—F. Pichler.

BLASE, Blasius, a royal one, a king—F. Pichler. It may be derived from the Swedish *blasa*; Saxon, *blaze*, to make known, hence generally known as a king.

BODO, a hero, a commander—F. Pichler.

BONGRE, good will; French, *bon*, good, and *gre*, will.

BURCHARD, Burghardt, Burkhart, one that is energetic—F. Pichler.

CAROLUS, Charles, see Karl.

CARSTEN, Karsten, a small farmer; probably from the old German, *karsten*, to hoe, to till the ground. One who tills the ground is called *Haker*, in some parts of Germany, a small farmer.

CASPAR, see Kaspar.

CLAUDIUS, Claude, one that limps, or one who is lame; Latin, *claudus*, Germanice, *hinkend*. Proverb, *Fides clauda*, lame faith.

CLAUS, see Nicolaus.

CHRISTIAN, christian, a follower of Christ; Greek, from *chrito*, to anoint, *christos*, the anointed; in Hebrew, *Messiah*—it occurs Christly, Christel, Christ.

CHRISTOPHER, a bearer of Christ; Greek, *christos*, christ, and *phero*, I bear away, bear, carry, from *pherein*, to bear or carry—it occurs Christoph, Christof, Stoffel, Stoffe.

CLEMENTIUS, Clemens, Clement, one who is benign, or indulgent; Latin, *clemens*, gentle, mild, tender hearted, indulgent—written Clem, Klemm, Klemens.

CONSTANTINUS, Constantine, one who is steadfast, firm, immovable, resolute; Latin, *constans*, firm, enduring, stable—sometimes occurs Constant, Cons, Konstans.

CORNELIUS, one that is strong, horn-like; Latin, from *cornus*, a horn, hence corneus, corneolus, horn-like. The horn is often used as a symbol of power, or strength. The principal defence and strength of many animals are in their horns.

COSTINICES, see Augustus and Note there.

DAGOBERT, Degenhart, a stately, magnificent hero—Pichler.

DANIEL, judgment of God, a righteous judge: God is my judge—Heubner; Hebrew, *dan*, judge, and Chaldaic, *el*, God.

DARIUS, he that informs himself; *conqueror*, subduer—Heubner.

DAVID, well beloved, dear; commander, governor—F. Pichler; Hebrew.

DIELMAN, see Thielman.

DIETRICH, Derrick, a patriot, or friend to the people—F. Pichler. The vulgar write Dieter; sometimes Ditrich, Tietrich, Dirk.

DIONYSIUS, divinely touched; Greek, probably derived from *dios*, divine, celestial, and the verb *nusso*, to touch, prick, spur.

DOMINICUS, Dominique in French, belonging to the Lord; Latin, *Dominus*, the Lord, as *Dominicæ habitationes*, habitations belonging to the Lord.

DURST, Dorst, if derived from the German *Durst*, it is thirst.

EBERHARD, Everhard, well reported, one that is strong and energetic—F. Pichler; Anglo-Saxon, *æfre, efre, efer, eber*, ever, constant, immovable; and *heard, hard*, unyielding, never yielding, immovably; unyielding.

ECKART, Eckard, Ekard, one who is faithful, one that has been proved—F. Pichler; Anglo-Saxon, and may be derived from *eacon*, to increase, or to complete, and *heard, hard*, unyielding.

EDMUND, a generous protector, a noble defender—F. Pichler; Anglo-Saxon, *ædel*, prefixed to the old German *mund*, a compound word, like the *vor, für*, for, and *mund*, as in *Vormund*, guardian, protector.

EDUARD, Edward, a noble watchman, truth-keeper; Anglo-Saxon, *ædel*, contracted, *æd*, noble, *weardian, ward*, a guard, or watch, act of guarding.

EGBERT, faithful and kind, one that is true and friendly— F. Pichler; Anglo-Saxon.

EGIDIUS, see Aegidius.

EGINHARD, one who has proved himself faithful, or who has been tested by experience—F. Pichler; Anglo-Saxon.

ELIAH, God the Lord, the strong Lord; God my strength— Heubner; Hebrew, *eliah, eliiahu*, Jehovah is my God; *Elisua, Elishuah*, God is my salvation; Hebrew, *elishaa*, God is salvation.

EMANUEL, Immanuel, God with us; Hebrew, *im*, with, in conjunction with; *manu*, us; *el*, God—literally, God united to man.

ENGEL, a messenger, one who is sent; Greek, *angelos*, a messenger, one who announces anything directly, or indirectly. Several names occur compounded of the prefix *angel*, and the affix *berth*, bright, fair, as Angelbert, and *hart*, *hort*, shield, rock, or defence, as Engelhart.

ENOCH, one who is consecrated, dedicated, or disciplined; Hebrew, *channok*, initiated, or initiating.

EPHRAIM, fruitful, that brings, or bears much fruit; Hebrew, *efraim*.

ERASMUS, worthy of being loved; Greek, *erasmios*, amiable, lovely, from *erao*, to love tenderly.

ERDMANN, Erdman, earth-man; Anglo-Saxon, *eard*, *eorth*, *yrth*, earth, and *man*, *mann*, man.

EHRHARD, Erhart, high-minded, magnanimous; Gothic or German, *Ehre*, *Ehr*, honor, and *heard*, *eard*, *hard*, unyielding, literally, over-honorable—of various orthography, Erhat, Erart, Erert.

ERICH, Ehrenreich, highly honorable, full of honor; German, from *Ehre*, *Ehren*, honor, honors, and *reich*, rich, wealthy, opulent.

ERNESTUS, Ernest, Ernst, serious, one that is grave or stern; Anglo-Saxon, *eornest*, *geornest*, earnest; Germanice, *ernstlich*.

ETIENNE, French; Stephan, Stephanus, Stephen, a crown, one who is crowned; Greek, *stephanos*, a crown, a wreath, a garland; from *stepho*, I crown, I decorate with a crown, hence *stephanoo*, I bestow a crown, I crown.

EWALD, one who is strong, vigorous, stout, able-bodied— F. Pichler. Probably old German, *ewalt*, *e*, *ge*, and *walt*, (*potentia* in Latin) power, strength—*Gewalt*, power, force, authority. *Er ist in seiner Gewalt*, he is in his power.

FABIAN, Fabius, one who delays, one who is dilatory. Perhaps, one who imitates Q. Fabius Maximus, avoiding battle. It occurs only once or twice as a Portuguese baptismal name.

FELIX, fortunate, happy, prosperous; Latin, *felix*, *felicis*, happy. *Vir Felix*, a happy man.

FERDINANDUS, Ferdinand, meritorious, full of merit, well deserving—F. Pichler; old German, *ferdienen*, *verdienen*, to deserve, or earn merit, *verdienend*, deserving merit.

FIDELIS, faithful, true, honest, loyal, trusty; Latin, as *Fidelis in amicitiis*, true in friendship.

FILBERT, Fillibert, Wilbertus, Philibert, most renowned, most illustrious—F. Pichler.

FORTUNATUS, fortunate, prosperous, successful, propitious; Latin, *fortuna*, fortune, success, hence *fortunatus*, fortunate.

FRANÇOIS, Franco, the first is French; Franco is Italianized, and is the Frantz.

FRANTZ, Franciscus, Francis, a freed man, freeman—unconstrained, generous, ingenious; French, *franc, franche*, free, frank, candid, sincere, open, without dissimulation.

FRIEDRICH, Friederich, Frederick, peaceable, peaceful, abounding in peace; German, *Friede*, peace, *reich*, rich, abundant, or abounding in—occurs written Frieder, Fritz, Fried, Fred.

GABRIEL, man of God, God is my strength; Hebrew, from *gabar*, to be strong, and *el*, God; *gabriel*, man of God, "a strong man of God."

GAGE, testimony, pledge, pawn, token, proof; French.

GALLUS, a leader, or chieftain; Latin. This name occurs only once as a French baptismal name.

GASPER, French, see Kaspar.

GEORG, George, a farmer, one who tills the earth; Greek, *georgos, georgios*, a husbandman, an agriculturalist—occurs strangely spelled, Yerrick, Jerg, Jurg, Yerg.

GERHARD, Gehrhart, Gerhart, a man of strength, one strong and mighty—F. Pichler. Probably derived from the old German *ger*, spear, lance, javelin, and the Anglo-Saxon *heard*, hard, powerful, forceable—one who wields the spear forcibly.

GERLACH, Gerlauch, illustrious, eminent, high; old German, *gerlauch, erlauch, erlaucht*, as *Eure Erlaucht*, your highness, same as *Durchlaucht*, now in general use.

GIDEON, one that bruises or destroys, one that cuts off iniquity; Hebrew, from *gada*, to cut down, destroy, cut off, break in pieces, hence Gideon.

GILBERT, same as Filbert, which see above.

GILLES, a Portuguese name, same import as Aegedius, which see above.

GOTTFRIED, Godfrey, Geoffry, peace of God; German, *Gott*, God, and *Fried, Friede*, peace.

GOTTHART, Gotthort, Gotthirt, inheritance of God, defence of God; old German, *Gott*, God, *hart, Hort*, a rock, shield, or safe retreat. *Mein Hort*, my rock—Ps. 28, 1. *Hort* is also

41*

something precious, a treasure or inheritance, something to be carefully preserved. Den himmlischen Hort, den Gott seinen Soldenern will geben dort—Basler Chronik, A. D. 1561.

GOTTHELF, Gotthülf, God-help; German, *Gott*, God; *hilf, hülf, hülfe*, help, assistance, support.

GOTTHOLD, God-gracious, merciful, propitious; German, *Gott*, God; *hold*, gracious, affectionate, favorable.

GOTTLIEB, God-pleasing, beloved of God; German, *Gott*, God; *lieb*, dear, beloved, pleasing, agreeable—same as Theophilus.

GOTTLOB, God be praised; German, *Gott*, God; *lob*, praise, eulogy.

GRAFF, Graf, an earl, a count; German—occurs only once or twice as a baptismal name.

GREGORIUS, Gregor, Gregory, one who is lively, sprightly; one who is watchful, vigilant; Greek, from *gregoreo*, to watch, to be vigilant, to be awake; from *egeiro*, to awaken, to stir up, to animate.

GUILLIAUME, Portuguese, see Wilhelm.

GUSTAVUS, see Augustus.

GYLLYAN, see Kilian.

HECTOR, commander, lord, ruler, master, or one who arrests and holds fast—F. Pichler; Greek.

HEINRICH, Heinerich, Henrich, Henry, a courageous man, a spirited hero—F. Pichler. Probably from the Anglo-Saxon *hentan, hæn, hent*, to seize, to lay hold of, to conquer, or to overcome, as *hæn, hentan*, sich einer Sache bemächtigen, and *ricca, ric*, rich, possessing a large portion, literally, possessing a large portion of courage, to overcome. It may be derived from the Greek *enorea*, manly courage, vigor—abbreviated Hein, Heintz, Hintz.

HELFRECHT, help-right, a suitable assistant; Anglo-Saxon, *hylp, helpan*, to assist, hence help, or assistance, and *riht, reht*, German *recht*, right, fit, suitable, proper, becoming, at a convenient time. *Helfrecht*, locally used, is "the right of selling unredeemed pledges."

HENRICUS, same as Henry, which see above.

HERRMANN, Herman, Herrmanus, Arminius, a war-man, one who is valiant; lord-man, master-man, one who subdues; Gothic, *gerr, ger*, spear or lance, and *manna*; Anglo-Saxon, *man, mann,* man, the man, the lord, or chief, who wields the lance.*

HERTZOG, Herzog, a duke, a sovereign prince, a chief, a prince; German.

HIERONYMUS, Jerome, an ecclesiastic, a person in orders, consecrated to the service of the church and the ministry of religion; Greek, from *ieros,* consecrated, and *nemo,* to pasture and rule, hence *nomos,* an ordinance, divine law, custom.

HIPOLITE, Hipolito, occurs as a Portuguese baptismal name, from Hippolitus; Greek, *ippolutos,* from *ippos,* horse, and *luo, luso,* to loose, slacken, set at liberty, hence *lutos,* loosed, susceptible of being loosed.

HIRAM, exalted life, the most high liveth—Heubner; exaltation of life; Hebrew, *hiram, herem,* something devoted to Jehovah.

HUBERT, Hubrecht, one who is renowned, famous, or celebrated—F. Pichler; Anglo-Saxon, *höb, hub,* lift, lifting, raised, exalted; and *riht, rehi, recht,* right, proper, suitable, fit—suitably exalted.

IGNATIUS, Ignace, one that is ardent, fiery, one who glows with joy; Latin, *ignis,* fire, *igneus,* fiery, glowing.

ILLES, Illos, one who squints, a person affected with strabism; Greek, *illos,* the eye, *illis,* one who rolls the eyes, from *illo,* to look askance.

IRENÆUS, Irene, one who is peaceable; Greek, *eirene, es,* peace, concord, calmness, rest.

---

* The Romans called *die Deutschen* GERMANS, from their warlike and valiant mode of thinking, a name which the *Tungi,* a body of German warriors, first bore, and was subsequently applied to all their race, to express their warlike manners, and thus to impress their enemies with terror. This name was willingly adopted by the *Germans,* as a name of honor. The man, whose heart is in the proper place, is proud of the honorable title, "*A German,*" A *Herrmann.*

* Die Deutschen wurden von den Römern wegen ihrer kriegerischen und braven Denkweise Germanen genannt, ein Name, welchen die Tungi, ein deutsches Kriegervolk, zuerst führten, und welcher allen Stämmen der ganzen Race beigelegt wurde, um ihre kriegerischen Sitten darzulegen und dadurch ihren Feinden Schrecken einzuflößen. Dieser Name wurde von den Deutschen als Ehrenname gerne angenommen. Der Mann, dessen Herz am rechten Fleck sitzt, ist stolz auf den ehrenhaften Titel: Ein Deutscher, ein Herrmann.

ISAAC, Isaque, French; laughter, or the son of laughter, son of joy; Hebrew, *itsak*, he laugheth.

ISRAEL, prince of God—Heubner. One who prevails with God; Hebrew, *israel*, a wrestler with God.

JACOB, Jaque, French; a supplanter, "who, with his hand, took hold on the heel;" Hebrew, *iakobh*, a supplanter.

JEREMIAS, Jeremiah, Jeremie, French; one exalted of God, exaltation of the Lord; Hebrew, *irmia, irmiahu*, Jehovah setteth up.

JEROME, French, same as Hieronymus, which see above.

JOACHIM, Joiakim, the resurrection of the Lord—Heubner. The Lord will arise, God will help; Hebrew.

JOEL, will, purpose; a beginner—Heubner. He that wills or commands; Hebrew, *ioel*, Jehovah is God.

JOHANNES, John, Jean, French; Juan, Portuguese; the mercy of the Lord, the grace of the Lord; Hebrew—it occurs in various spellings, Johann, Johan, Han, Hans, Hannes, Jan; it seems to be a sort of *Lieblingsnamen*, occurring in this Collection, upwards of eight thousand times, alone or connected with some other baptismal name, as Han George, Johann Jacob, Han Niclaus, Hans Peter, Hannes, Johann.

JONAH, Jonas, a dove—Heubner. He that oppresses; Hebrew, *ionah*, plural *ionim*, a dove; sometimes a word of endearment.

JONATHAN, the gift of God—Heubner. Given of God, a faithful friend; Hebrew.

JOSEPHUS, Joseph, Josephe, Portuguese, addition, increasing; Hebrew, *iasap, ioseph*, to add, to increase, enlarge, to give or bestow in abundance.

JOSIA, Josias, Josiah, the Lord burns, the fire of the Lord, essential, or real Lord; Hebrew.

JOSUA, Jesua, Joshua, a saviour, a helper, the Lord the Saviour; Hebrew, *ioshiahu*, Johovah healeth.

JULIUS, Julian, a soft-haired young man, one who is pubescent; Latin, *julus*, from the Greek *ioulos*, the first down on the cheek or chin.

JUSTINUS, Justus, Just, Jocelyn, Jocelin, sometimes Yost, in German, one that is just, honest, upright; Latin, *justus*, from *jus*. *Vir justus*, ein gerechter Mann, a just man.

KARL, Carle, Charles; one who is strong, vigorous, powerful—F. Pichler. Old German or Gothic, *charl*, *vir maritus*, a married man, *harl*, *vir senex*, an old man; Anglo-Saxon, *carl*, *cœrl*, masculus, masculine, having the qualities of a man, strong, robust, bold, brave.

KASPAR, Kasper, Casper, Jasper, Gasper, French; a royal treasurer; first Lord of the treasury—F. Pichler. Probably derived from the old German *cassa*, *casse*, *kasse*, a money-box or treasury, and *per*, *peran*, *bearan*, *byren*, to bear, to possess and use as power, to exercise; to act in any character.

KILIAN, Killian,* one who quiets, soothes, assuages, pleases, captivates by words—this is its meaning, if derived from the Greek *keleo*. If Kilian is corrupted from the Hebrew *chilion*, which signifies finished, complete, perfect, it may then be derived from *khillah*, to complete, finish; or from *khalah*, to be completed or finished—it occurs Gyllyan.

KONRAD, Konrath, Conrad, a counselor, a person who gives advice, one who is consulted by a client in a law case—F. Pichler. It may be derived from the Anglo-Saxon *cene;*

---

* *Kilian*, Killian—this name occurs frequently; its meaning I do not certainly know. The introduction of it into Germany is historically known. *Kilian* was an Irish bishop, and an apostle or missionary. Accompanied by eleven others, he crossed to the continent, and by his zealous, evangelical preaching in Germany, he persuaded *Gozbert*, governor of the city of Wurtzberg, and many others to embrace Christianity. He suffered martyrdom, A. D. 689. The cathedral erected in Wurtzburg, in the eighth century, is called *St. Kilian*. He was a contemporary with *Saints* Wolfram, Willebrand, Trudo, Lambert, Kunibert, Suidbert, Wigbert, Sturmio, Magnoald, Theodor Kempten, Offo Offonzell, Landolin, Corbinian Freissing, Emmeran, &c.—*Mentzel's Gesch. d. Deutschen*, p. 160.

* Kilian, Killian—dieser Name kommt häufig vor, allein ich kann seine Bedeutung mit Gewißheit nicht angeben. Die Einführung desselben in Deutschland ist geschichtlich bekannt. Kilian war ein irländischer Bischof und ein Apostel oder Missionar. Von eilf Anderen begleitet, reiste er nach dem Festlande, und durch sein eifriges und heilbringendes Predigen brachte er Gozbert, Statthalter von Würzburg, und viele Andere dahin, dem Christenthum zu huldigen. Er starb den Märtyrertod im Jahre 689. Die Kathedrale, welche im achten Jahrhundert zu Würzburg erbaut wurde, ward St. Kilian genannt. Er war ein Zeitgenosse der Heiligen Wolfram, Willebrand, Trudo, Lambert, Kunibert, Suidbert, Wigbert, Sturmio, Magnoald, Theodor Kempten, Offo Offonzell, Landolin, Corbinian Freissing, Emmeran, ꝛc.—Mentzel's Gesch. der Deutschen, S. 160.

Hollandish, *kœn*, pronounced *koon;* German, *kühn*, bold, keen, penetrating, and *rath*, consultation, advice, counsel—it occurs Kunrad, Conrat.

LAURENTUS, Lorentz, Laurence, Lawrence, one that has been crowned, or laureated by way of eminence, or distinction; Latin, *laurus*, laurel tree; *laurea*, a laurel leaf; *laureatus*, crowned with laurel, mit Lorbeer gekrönet.

LAZARUS, assistance of God—Heubner. "The word *lazarus*," says A. Barnes, "is Hebrew, and means a man destitute of help."—*Com. in loco.*

LEBERECHT, Lebrecht, live right; German, from *lebe*, live thou, and *recht*, right.

LEMUEL, God to them; Hebrew, from *lahem*, to them, and *el*, God.

LEOPOLD, one who is courageous, daring, intrepid; one that is magnanimus; Greek, from *leon*; Latin, *leo*, lion, and probably from *polleo, es, ere, pollens*, to be mighty, powerful.

LEVI, who is held and associated; Hebrew, from *lavah*, to adhere to any one, to be joined to any one.

LORENTZ, see Laurentus above.

LUCAS, Luke, light, luminous, shining bright; Greek, *leukos*, bright, clear, conspicuous, limpid, white lucid; derived from *leusso*, to shine, cast light.

LUDOLPH, a helper, an assistant—F. Pichler.

LUDOVIC, Ludwig, Louis, Lewis, one who is renowned, celebrated or famous—F. Pichler.

LUTHER, venerable, respectable, reverend—F. Pichler.

MARCUS, Marx, Mark, a shearer or barber, a cleanser or dresser—Heubner; polite, shining; one who contends, a champion, a warrior, or a combatant—F. Pichler; a smith's hammer—Bernler; Hebrew, *marak*, to scour, polish, furbish, to cleanse, purify; *morak*, to be cleansed.

MARTINUS, Martin, a hero, a man of distinguished valor, intrepidity or enterprise in danger, a great illustrious or extraordinary person—F. Pichler. Latin, from *Mars*, in heathen mythology, the God of war.

MATTHEUS, Matthew, one that has been bestowed, one who is given; Chaldaic, *mattan*, a present; Hebrew, *mattanah*, a gift.

MATTHIAS, Mathias, the gift of the Lord—sometimes occurs Matheis, Matteis, Matis, Teys, Deys, Theis, Deis.

MAXIMILIANUS, Maximilian, the greatest; Latin, from *magnus*, great, *major*, greater, *maximus*, greatest.

MELANCHTON, black-earth; Greek, *melas*, black, dark, and *chton*, the earth. In German *Schwartzerd*, which was his first name. At the advice of *Reuchlein*,* his teacher, Schwartzerd changed his name, according to the custom of the learned at that time, into the Greek name Melanchton.

MELCHIOR, a royal person, one of royalty—F. Pichler. Probably derived from the Hebrew *malakh*, to reign, to be a king; Chaldaic, *melekh*, king, and *hor*, *or*, riches, wealth, substance, sufficient, enough—occurs Melcher, Melchor.

MICHAEL, Michel, Michal, who is like unto God?—Heubner; who is perfect; Hebrew, derived from *mi*, who? *ca*, as, like, and *el*, God; *michael*, who is as God?

MORITZ, Maurice, dark-colored, auburn, an auburn person— F. Pichler; Greek, *mauroo*, to darken; *mauros*, dark—it occurs Moret.

MOSES, one who has been taken out of the water; Hebrew, from *masha*, to seize, to draw; *moseh*, Moses, drawn out.

NICOLAUS, Nicklas, Nicholas, victory of the people; Greek, from *nikao*, to conquer, be victorious; *nike*, *nikos*, victory, and *laos*, the people, nation, crowd, multitude—occurs Nicklas, Nickel, as in Hann Nickel, also occurs Nicola.

NOAH, repose, rest, consolation; Hebrew.

ONESIMUS, profitable, useful, one that proves profitable; Greek, from *ono*, *onemi*, *oneso*, to profit, to aid, *onesimos*, profitable.

OSWALD, Oswalt, manager, administrator, steward—F. Pichler; literally a dispenser, one who administers; German, or Gothic, *os*, *aus*, out, (as in *spenden*, *ausspenden*, to distribute, administer); *walten*, to rule, to govern, to dispose of, to distribute: *walter*, ruler, manager.

---

* *John Reuchlein* was a learned German, born in 1450, and died 1552; he was the first who introduced the study of the Hebrew among modern christians.

* Johann Reuchlein war ein deutscher Gelehrter, geboren 1450, gestorben 1552. Er war der Erste, welcher die hebräische Sprache unter den damaligen Christen einführte.

492 INTERPRETATION OF NAMES.

OTTO, Otho, father of the family, economist, manager—F.
Pichler; Gothic, *otto*, *atta*, *fadar*, father.*

PAULUS, Paul, small, little, diminutive; Latin, *paulus*, small,
little, same as *parvus*, small; *vir paulus*, a small man; *puer
parvus*, a small boy.

PETRUS, Peter, Pierre, French; a rock, *ein Fels*—Heubner;
rock or stone; one that is immovable or firm; Greek, *petros*,
a stone or rock, hence the word *petra* in Greek, a stone, a
rock. The French word *pierre*, Peter, and *pierre*, rock or
stone, are spelt alike, *e. g.* su ei Petros, kai api tautei tei
petrai—es Pierre, et que sur cette pierre. Petros and Pierre
are masculine, and petra and pierre feminine.

PHILLIPPUS, Philipus, Philip, a lover of horses—Heubner;
a knight—F. Pichler; Greek, *philippos*, that delights in
horses; fond of riding; from *philos*, a lover, a friend, and
hippos, a horse.

REINHARD, same as Richard.

REMIGIUS, an oarsman, a rower, a navigator—F. Pichler;
Latin, from *remigo, are*, to row, to impel a vessel or boat on
water.

REUBEN, Ruben, who sees the son, vision of the son;
Hebrew, from *raah, rao, rau*, to see, perceive with the eye,
and *ben*, a son.

---

* *Otto, atta, fadar*, father of a family, means literally, one who be-
gets, provides and governs his children; the word *"father,"* in various
languages, conveys a similar idea—as in the Sanscrit *pitr*, Zend *pata*,
Persian *pader*, Latin *pater*, Italian *padre*, French *père*, Greek *pater*,
Ancient German *fatar*, German *Vater*, Anglo-Saxon *faeder*, Swedish
fader, Hollandish *vader*, Irish *athair*, Welsh *tad*, Russian *otetz*, Polish
ojciec, Bohemian *otec*, Finnish *isa*, Hebrew *ab*, Arabic *abon*, Malaic
bappa, Coptic *babb*, Spanish *padre*, Britannic *taad*, Icelandic *bader*,
Dalmatian *otcse*, Croatian *ozhe*, Lusatic *wosch*, Hungarian *atyanc*, &c.

* Otto, atta, fadar, Vater einer Familie, bedeutet eigentlich: Einer,
welcher seine Kinder zeugt, für sie sorgt und dieselben regiert. Das Wort
„Vater" bedeutet in vielerlei Sprachen dasselbe, z. B.: Sanscrit pitr.
zendisch pata, persisch pader, lateinisch pater, italienisch padre, französisch
père, griechisch pater, alt-deutsch fatar, deutsch Vater, anglo-sächsisch faeder,
schwedisch fader, holländisch vader, irländisch athair, welsch tad, russisch
otetz, polnisch ojciec, böhmisch otec, finnisch isa, hebräisch ab, arabisch
abon, malaisch bappa, coptisch babb, spanisch padre, brittisch taad, islän-
disch bader, dalmatisch otcse, croatisch ozhe, lausitzisch wosch, ungarisch
atyanc ıc.

RICHARD, richly honored; Saxon, from *ric, ricca,* rich, *earen, ered, eard,* honored.

ROLANDT, Roland, one who is honest, a just man—F. Pichler; probably Gothic.*

RODOLPHUS, Rudolphus, Rudolph, Ralf; in Hollandish, *Rœlf,* a counselor, adviser; any person who gives advice; but properly, one who is authorized, by birth, office, or profession, growing out of that relation, to give advice to another, in regard to his future conduct and measures—*Ein Rathgeber,* einer der Jemanden Gründe vorführt, seinen Verstand zu gewinnen, um ihn zum Nachdenken zu bringen. Probably derived from the old German *ræd, ræt, Rath,* consultation, advice, counsel, and Anglo-Saxon *helpan, hylpan, hylph, hulf;* German, *Hülf, Hülfe,* help, to help, to aid, to assist; aid, assistance.

RUPERTIUS, Rupert, Robert, red-beard; Gothic.

SALOMO, Solomon, peaceable, peaceful, peacefulness; Hebrew, *shele,* quietness, peace, prosperity; Chaldaic, *shleah,* rest, tranquility; *shlomin,* peaceable.

SAMUEL, asked of God, heard of God; Hebrew, *shmuel,* heard of God; from *shama,* to hear, and *el,* God.

SEBASTIAN, august, exalted, elevated; Greek, from *sebo, sepso,* to venerate, to stand in awe; *sebas,* veneration, *sebastos,* venerated, worshipful, venerable, august.

SEM, Sema, Shem, a name, renown; Hebrew, *shem,* a name, authority, fame, renown, a good name; a rumor, report, a monument.

SETH, a law—Heubner; put, or who puts; Hebrew.

SEVERIMUS, more earnest, one who is very austere or stern; Latin, from *severus,* stern, earnest, serious, austere, as *severus judex,* an austere judge.

SIEGFRIED, victory of peace, peace-conquest; German, *Sieg,* victory, triumph, and *fried, Friede,* peace.

SILAS, or Silvanus; the former is a contraction of the latter— one who loves the woods, or delights in the forest; Greek,

---

* A distinguished general, *Feldherr,* mentioned in German history, A. D. 778, was called *Roland,* whose fame has been spread by ancient and modern poets.

* In der deutschen Geschichte wurde Roland um's Jahr 778 als ein ausgezeichneter Feldherr bezeichnet, dessen Ruhm von den älteren und neueren Dichtern verbreitet wurde.

42

silas etiam *silovanos*, hence the Latin *sylvanus*, the god of the woods; *sylva*, woods.

SILVESTER, Silvius, one who lives in woods, or country; Latin, derived from *sylva*, woods; *Sylvestres homines*, Bauernleute, peasants; *musa sylvestres*, or *musa sylva*, a peasant's song, ein Bauernlied.

SIMEON, Simon, heard, one that is heard; Hebrew, *shamea*, to hear; *shimon*, a hearing.

STANISLAUS, praiseworthy constancy, glorius stability, laudable firmness; Greek, *stasis*, a fixed state, immovable, constant; Latin, *status*, fixed, certain, hence *stanis*, and *laus*, praise, from *laudo*, I praise.

STEPHANUS, Stephan, Stephen, a crown, crowned; Greek, from *stepho*, *stepso*, to crown, to decorate with a crown; *stephanoo*, to crown; *stephanos*, a crown, a wreath, a garland—occurs Stefan, Steffy, Steff, Steven.

TACITUS, silent, tacit; Latin, *tacitus*, a name from Cajus Cornelius Tacitus, a celebrated Roman historian, orator and statesman under Vespasian, Titus and Domitian. He was born A. D. 56.

TALIO, occurs as a Portuguese baptismal name; retribution, remuneration, recompense; may be derived from the Latin *talio*, *talionis*, retribution.

THEOBALD, Theobold, one that is valiant, bold, brave, valorous; a compound name, from the Greek *theos*, a god, a prince, a ruler, a judge, a person in station or office, and Anglo-Saxon, *beald*, *bald*, bold—occurs Debald, Dewalt, Diewald, Siebald, Siebalt, Siebold.

THEODOR, Theodore, gift of God; Greek, *theos*, God, and *doreo*, *doreso*, to bestow anything as a gift; *doron*, a gift, a present.

THEOPHILUS, see Gottlieb above.

THOMAS, twin, a twin brother; Hebrew, from *taam*, a twin, to be doubled, and *Hiphel*, to bear twins; in Greek *Didymus*, from *didumos*, double, two-fold; *dis*, twice, and from the root *doo*, *dosi;* *didomi*, *doso*, to give, to offer, to present.

TITUS, honorable, illustrious, noble; Greek, *tio*, *tiso*, to estimate, to value, to esteem, to prize, to honor; *titos*, honorable.

TOBIAS, the goodness of the Lord; God's kindness; Hebrew.

TRAUGOTT, trust God, confide in God; German, *trauen*, to trust, to rely upon, to have confidence in, and *Gott*, God.

ULRICH, Ulric, Ulrique, French; one who is richly endowed, of strong and vigorous intellect; endowed with reason—F. Pichler. May be derived from the Gothic *olos, ull;* Greek, *olos;* Latin, *ullus;* Anglo-Saxon, *æl,* all; wholly, completely, and *ricca, ric,* rich, possessing a large portion—it occurs Uldrich, Uly, Ury, Ullerich.

URBAN, polite, courteous, urbane; Latin, *urbanus, urbanitas,* urbane, urbanity, politeness.

VALENTIN, Valentine, strong, powerful, a man of valor, one of strong affections; Latin, from *valeo, valere,* to be healthy and strong; *valens homo,* a strong person—occurs Felty, Felten, Velde, Valtin.

VINCENT, one who conquers, or overcomes; (same as Victor, which occurs abbreviated Vict.); Latin, from *vinco, vincere,* to conquer.

VITE, celerity, speed, quickly, fast, nimble; French, as *parler vite,* to speak fast.

WALTHER, Walter, one who governs or rules; German, *walten,* to rule, to govern, to manage; *Walter,* a manager or ruler.

WENCESLAUS, victory of the people or subduer of the people—F. Pichler—occurs Wendel, Wentz, Wenslas, Wenzel. Perhaps derived from the Latin *vinco, vincere,* to conquer, and Greek, *laas,* the people.*

WILHELM, William, Guilliaume, Portuguese; a defender of many, a potent shield, a strong protector—F. Pichler; Anglo-Saxon, from *willa;* Gothic, *wilja,* determination, ability, power, and *helma,* helm, a defensive armor.

WOLFGANG, an assistant, a helper—F. Pichler.

ZACHARIAS, Zachariah, the memory of the Lord; Hebrew, *zakhar,* think of, remember; *zikharon,* memory, remembrance; *z'khariah,* Jehovah remembereth.

---

* Wenceslaus is a Bohemian name, written *Wenceslaw,* and is derived from *wenec,* wreath of honor, chaplet of honor; and *slawa,* praise, honor, celebrity, glory, hence one that has been crowned with glory.

* Wenzeslaus ist ein böhmischer Name und wird Wenceslaw geschrieben; es wird abgeleitet von wenec, Ehrenkranz, und slawa, Ruhm, Ehre, Berühmtheit, Glorie; also Einer, der mit Ehren gekrönt ist.

INDEX

by

Ernst Wecken

Aal 408; Aam 79; Aarond 89; Abachlender 344; Abbiter 400; Abel *80, 129, 294, 347; Abelman 343; Abendscho(e)n *222; Abercrombie *161, *195, 250, 251, *277, *310, *337; Aberly 98; Aberman 82; Abert 257; Aberthal 369; Aberthuene 408; Able 78, 80; Ablin 57; Ably 89; Abraham 18, 36; Abzieger 376; Ache *276; Achebach 347, 392; Achen 413; Achenbach 314, 339; Achintopfs 302; Achtung 185; Acker *80, 110, 225, 378, *435, 471, 474; Ackerman(n) 64, 124, 126, 186, 226, 233, *242, 396, 397; Ackert *131; Adam 201, 218, 246, 259, 277, 287, 302, 306, 327, 350, 364, 377, 412, 418; Adams 50, *189, 218, 257, 469, 473; Adelman 240, 297; Aderman 432; Adest 55; Adich 136; Adler 202, 410; Adolphf 323; Adtelberger *305; Aechstein 53; Aegender 68, *70; Aehl 319; Aengne 101; Aerig 188; Aescher *385; Aeschliman(n) (Aeshelman) *336, 393; Aeuchler 345; Aff 473; Affterbach 393; Agricola 352; Ahl 156; Ahlbach *97, *98, 272; Ahlem 257; Ahlemann 292, 406; Ahles 196; Ahl(l)born *318; Ahls 147; A(h)ner 98, 99, 269; Ahrens 299; Ahrndorff 448; Ahrnold 51; Ahster 290; Aiquel 334; Albenaecht 161; Alber 174; Albers 348, 350; Albert(h) 69, 106, 116, 131, *137, 253, *297, 298, 304, *334, 335, *438, 467; Alberti 348, 380; Albirger (s. Eulenber) 272; Albrecht 49, 72, 73, *76, 84, *85, 112, 147, 161, 173, 198, 210, 234, 242, 244, 264, 281, 287, 301, 311, 378, 380, 382, 402, 468; Albright 84; Aldorffer 73; Aldt 347; Ale 308; Aleberger 293; Aleiss 231; Alenbach 231; Algeir 381; Algeyer 222; Alisch 328; Alizon 390; Alloigre 7, 25; Allan 254; Allbach 470, 473; Al(l)bahn *331; Allbrecht 251; Alldoerffer 86; Allear *463; Allebach 477; Alleman 277, 307, 308; Allemand 324; l'Allemand (s. Lallemand); Allen 134, 138, 139, *140, *247; Aller 192, 200, 272, 277, 305, 328; Allerth 192; Alles 221; Allhaell 297; Allhelm 295; Allimang *180; Allman 361, 362; Al(l)sbach (-pach) *118, 279, 374; Allspach 358; Allstadt 475; Al(l)ter 299, 300; Alman 204; Almerod 443; Almers 152, 422, 426; Almerson 421, 426; Als 398; Alsbach 353; Alstadt 10, 29, 59; Alstat(t) 381, 419; Alt 120, 125, 264, 267, 325; Altefried 392; Altenberger 109; Altendorff 267; Alter 247; Althart 338; Althaus(s) *126, 186, *202, 222, 382, 411, 471; Altheer 276; Althen 162; Altherr 356; Alt(h)onius(s) *140;

---

* vor den Zahlen bedeutet mehrfaches Vorkommen des Namens auf dieser Seite.

497

Altig 281; Altik 198; Altlandt 103; Altman *203, *204; Altneth 222; Altoch 126; Altorffler 52; Altrich 265; Altschuh 364; Altvater 206; Altvatter 358; Altvetter 373; Altz 354; Amacher 324; Amandus 100; Amaus 355; Amborn 71; Ambrecht *126; Ambrose 365; Ambrossi 83; Ambruester 115; Amecker 377; Amelon 307; Amend(t) 74, 122, 162; Ament 162, 449; Amgontert 286; Amhyser 186; Amman 215; Amme (s. Omme) 191; Ammich 243; Ammo 199; Am(m)on 63, 98, *166, 313, 339, 346, 356; Ampel 232; Amrein 343; Amstedt 209; Amweg 61, 108, 146, 385; Anard 132; Anbauer 468; Anckenbrant 63; Ander 95, 152, 471; Anderbach 143; Anderegg 266; Anderich 94; Anders 17, 36, *96, 141, 182, 271, 422, 426; Anderson 166, 167; Andich 115; Andoni 104, 386; Andrae 238, 284, 312; Andrea 249; Andreae 170; Andreas 63, 71, 108, 216, 329, 330, *333, 334, *414, 432, 475; Andres(s) 72, 169; Andrews 63; Andriola *326; Aner 233; Angculy 278; Angel 159; Angelberger 90; Angene 303; Angevine *463, 464; Angny 175; Angold 332; Angst 131, 185, 303, 335; Angstet *92; Anhorn 260; Ankibrant 477; Annawaldt 352; Annletz 411; Anpert *361; Ansel(l) 269, 281; Anselt 87; Anspach 116, 154, *448, *465, *466; Anspacher 49; Anstbach 379; Anstein 261; Ansthoch 329; Antel 297; Anter 214; Antes 149, 182, 474; Antheis 348; Anthon 172; Anthoni 148, 203, 236, 237, 321; Anthony 364, 386; Anton 236; Apfelbaum 104; Apf(f)el (s. Appel) 85, 185, 361, 383, 400; App 268, 277; Appache 307; Appel (s. Apffel) 76 109, 209, *210, *361, 378; Appelman 443; Apple 93, 397; Arand 89; Arandt *356; Arb 231; Arbeiter 247; Arbengast 247, 255; Arcularius *405; Archbiss 287; Ardt 186; Arend 187; Arets 430; Arhndorff (s. Orendorff) 147; Armbriest 150; Armbriester 279; Armbruester 261, 283, 337; Armenbefer 386; Armgast 172, 209; Armhiener 335; Armrester 180; Armschild 310; Armstrong *415; Arnd 389, 407; Arndorff 319; Arndt 51, *67, 258; Arner 473; Arnis 7, 25; Arnold(t) *110, 129, 140, 153, *179, *218, 229, 248, 251, 271, 315, *344, 353, 373, 389, 410, 446; Arnoldus 400; Arnolt 300; Arnot(t) *179, 184, 185, *199, 270, 271, *315, *359, *383, *388, *390, *394; Arnoul 261; Arnsdorf *450; Arnsterger 372; Arnt *234; Arntberger 348; Arnth 302; Arrent *301; Arris *285; Artger 97; Arth 141; Artz(t) 78, 79, 262; As 329; Aschenbacher 209; Aschenbrenner 144; Aseby 148; Ash 324; Ashman 341; Aso 52; Aspech 110; Asper 125, 344; Asseim 284; Astimer 412; Aterholt 299; Au 318, 366, 416; Aubertien 134; Auchementer 377; Auchenbach 122; Auen 307; Auer 303, 403; Auert 146; Augenstein 258, *269; Auger 339; Augermeyer 282; August 154; Augustine 378; Augustinus 377; Auhagen 322; Auler 198; Aul(l)enbacher 90, 105; Aumueller 227, *344; Aune 168; Aurandt 319, 410; Auterbach 80; d'Avier 82; Ax 162; Axer 157, 201.

Baab 175, 288; Baal 149; Baarsteyn 79; Bab 102, 274; Babb 250; Babenmayer 66; Bac 304; Bach 115, *123, 133, 289, 294, *381, 387, 393, 450; Bacher 207, 450, *451; Bacher (alias Rutter) 430; Bachert 215, 410; Bachler 136; Bachman(n) *132, 156, 159, 198, 218, 228, 254, 266, *303, 310, 318, 343, 360, 368, 394, 410, 435, 437; Bachmeyer 423, 427; Bachneid 393; Bachoff 423, 427; Bachy 347; Back *59, 134, 184, 298; Backastos 166; Backofen 298, 325; Baddo *463; Bade 302; Badel 380; Badenheinner 200; Bader 119, 131, 224, 278, 286, 287, 296, 342; Badert 341; Badner 83, 444; Baecker (s. Baker) 112, 200, 252, 276, 292; Baeder 170; Bähr 52, 206; Baell 448; Baeninger *132; Baenly 398; Baenssle 263; Baentz 382; Baer *56, 65, *83, 134, *139, *158, *164, 176, 177, *197, 201, 224, 231, 256, 280, 323, 349, 375, 436, 437, 438, 443, 445; Baerger 157; Baetz 74; Baetzerlein 360; Baeuerle 198, 251; Baey 398; Baeyer 399; Bager 73, 120, 239, 246, 290; Bahlsdorf 402; Bahn 69, 405; Bahner 421, 425; Bahr *323; Bahret 118; Bahrt 218, 219; Bahs 325; Baidemann 368; Baire 103; Bais 469; Bais(c)h 263, *283; Baker (s. Baecker) *164, 168, 199, 200, 260, 287, 310; Balbierer 228; Bald 127, 314; Baldesberger 130; Baldus 319; Balick 218; Baliett 118; Balio 434; Ball 82, *93; Balledium *216; Ballenberger 411; Ballmer 400; Bally *475; Balmas 249; Balme 304; Balmer *73, 110, 124, 125; Balsam 231; Balsbach 72, 248; Balt 50; von de Balt 228; Baltdauss 326; Balthas 220; Balthauer 301; Baltsonderweg 312; Baltz 76, 417; Baltzel *353 354; Baltzer 124, 277, *279, 379, 401; Baltzly 282; Balzey 336; Bamberg 351; Bamberger 476; Bambergher *135; Ban 310; Banchle 305; Banckauff 71; Bandelo 356; Bang 157, 471; Bangman 278; Banher 288; Banner 314; Banninger 312; Bannot 347; Banroth 352; Bansche 96; Bantlion *268; Banton 7, 25; Bantz 130; Bapp 382; Baptista 399; Baptiste 390, 396; Barberat 324; Barch 380; Bard 228, 436; Bardeck 402; Bardoe 405; Bardon 362; Bardtmann 370; Barer 371; Barfuss 295; Barher 203; Barhitz 204; Bariedet 390; Baritschwerd 278; Barkeka 417; Barkel 348; Barle 247; Barnes *287; Barnitz 199; Barthals 299; Baron 180, *418; Barone 375; Barr 197; Barrett *463, *464; Barsch *68; Barsteller 472; Bart 89, 197; Bartel 356, 473; Barteleme 50; Bartels *431; Bartenbach 333; Barth 49, 65, 101, 114, 124, 134, 154, 207, 219, 239, 367; Barthel 143; Bartheleus 418; Barthelm 115; Bartheus 164; Barthnies 250; Barthol 181; Bartholmae 362; Bartholomae 311, 347, *418; Bartholomaeus 74, *181; Bartholome 129; Bartholomy 117; Bartholt 234; Bartinstal 478; Bartle 79; Bartman(n) 132, *133, 345; Bartoleme 146; Bartolett 434; Bartolomes 164; Bartram 407; Bartruff 277; Bartscherer 360; Barttel 234; Bartz 125; Basch 242, 443; Basel 102, 352; Baser *282; Baserer 83;

Baserman(n) 341, 405; Bashedich 405; Basler(in) 348, 467, 468; Bass 250; Bassel 155; Basseler 322; Basserman 183, 185, 351; Bassert 314; Bas(s)ler 82, 83, 223, *244, 438, 468; Bast 77, *218, 230, 378,'413; Bast (Borst) 447; v. Basten 109; Bastenmeye 230; Bastian *59, *76, 219, 263, 282, 283, 352, *391, 399, 407, 408, 472; Bastig 405; Basting 161; Bat 288; Bath 218; Batorf 466, 467; Batram 295; Battelm 116; Battenberg 206; Battenfeld *234, 235; Batter 62; Battez 310; Batur *204; Batz 174, 213, 233, 313, 366, 410, 443; Batziuss 336; Bau 81, 387; Bauch 123, 410, 447; van Bauch 407; Baucher 409; Bauchler 131; Baudemont 241; Bauer 66, *76, 90, 107, *113, 148, 151, 156, 162, 163, 164, 180, *201, *212, 213, 216, 225, 228, *229, 230, 232, 238, 239, 245, 250, 254, *263, *273, 277, 280, *281, *282, 287, 290, 291, *292, 295, 298, *300, 303, 305, 309, 310, *323, *324, 330, 333, 338, *357, 364, 368, 370, 378, 380, 387, 403, 412, 415, 416, 468, *471; Bauerdt 158; Bauerman 255; Bauermeister 322; Bauersachs 229, 399; Bauerschmied(t) *283; Baueshar 211; Bauinger 231; Baum 71, 75, *105, 165, 184, 190, 227, 239, 248, 260, 269, 325, 359, *364, 401, 443; Bauman(n) 53, 55, 71, 97, 103, 111, *112, *132, 135, 153, 171, 175, 176, 188, 195, 197, *206, *207, 216, 265, 267, 269, 273, 285, 289, 290, 297, 313, 320, *349, 354, 379, *393, 405, 408, 411, 432, *434, 436, 437, 473; Bauman(n) (s. Bowman); Baumantz 365; Baumberger 179; Baumer 131; Baumgaerd(t)ner 76, *103, 109, 437; Baumg(a)ertner 73, 113, 130, 217, 222, 225, 284; Baumgardner 158; Baumgertel 184; Baumm 283; Baumstaedt 432; Baunich 263; Baur 133; Bausch 292, 364; Bausel 49; Bausman 350; Baus(s) 203, *290, 388, 410; Baus(s)man(n) *176, 179, 186, *368; Bausser *91, 92; Bauster 215; Bausum *258; Bauth 290, 394; Bautz 407; Bawder 76; Bawer 207; Bawmann 176; Bawngwar 180; Baydeman 379; Bayer 57, 114, 164, 226, 343, 265, 283, *416; Bayley 464; Beaber (s. Beaver, Rieber) 171; Beach *124, *208; Bear *65, 143, 173, 317; Beatt 260; Beaufort 418; Beaujacque 373; Beavenaw 205; Beaver (s. Beaber) 233; van Bebber 430; Bebertz 137; Bebighausen 180; Bech 326; Becher 111, 123, 250, 366; Bechler 335; Becholdt 121; Becholt(t) 113, 216; Becht 142; Bechtel(l) (s. Begtel) 55, 165, 274, 394, *435, *473; Bechtle 83; Bechtol 316; Bechtol(d)t 115, 123, 316; Beck 91, *92, 119, *140, 142, 178, 180, 193, 211, *212, 213, 218, 223, 224, 232, 236, 244, *252, *253, 271, 272, 273, 280, 293, 302, 303, 307, 309, 310, 313, 315, 321, 334, 342, 356, 357, 363, 365, 400, 406, 407, 410, 420, 424, 423, 427; Beckel 362; Beckeles 140;' Bekke(n)bach *267; Beckenhaub 332; Becker (s. Boecker) 61, 79, 80, *89, *105, 106, 114, 130, 133, *134, 137, *142, 143, 146, *148, 150, 157, *159, *160, 186, 197, 199, *200, *201, 202, 210, *213, 215, 217, 233, 235, 240, 241, 258, 259, *277, 279, 280, 284, 285, 292, 297, 314, 316, 318, *320, 329, 330, *331,

*333, 336, 339, 344, 351, *352, 353, *354, 362, 364, 367, 371, 373, *375, 385, 391, *396, 399, 403, 407, 408, *409, 413, 416, 419, 435, *438, *446, 468, 469, 473; Beckermann 312; Beckley 246; Beclie (s. Böckle) 72; Bed 294; Beder 303; Bederie *133; Beed 194; Beege 187; Beegel 100; Beel *232; Beem 127; Beensly 229; Beer 104, 260, 401; Beetel 83; Beggari 300; Begly 151; Begtel (s. Bechtel) 165; Begtholt 228; Behe 301; Beheling 408; Beher 329; Behl 268; Behler 148, *217; Behlerdt 72; Behm 271, 279; ¡Behn 71, 75, 127; Behning 273; Behr 52, 245, 353, *369, ,*372; Behringer 126, 164, 422, 427; Behrt 246; Behzer 408; Beicht 298; Beick 147; Beickle 258; Beidelmann 63; Beidler 471, 476; Beier 67, *114, 159, 394; Beiffweg 194; Beiger 197; Beihn 135; Beil 97, 108, 287, 393; Beiler 111, 112; Beilstein 386; Beiltel 280; Beimling 340; Beinder 50; Beinoeller 353; Beintzighoster 282; Beisbeker 199; Beiser 357; Beissel 85, *86, 194, 214; Beistel 315; Beit 368; Beiterman *239; Beitert 103; Beiting 474; Beitzel 111, 186; Beixitsch 370; Bekenne 377; Bele 241; Beleni 293; Beler 191, 374; Belitz 57, 435; Bell *50, *145; Bellie 324; Bellinger 447, *448; Bel(l)man(n) 124, 195, 394; Belscher 64; Belsner 82; Beltz 190, *281, 397; Beltzer 331; Beltzhuber 282; Bem 237; Bence (Bentz) *205; Benck 287; Bencker 56; Bender 52, 66, 72, 82, *122, 136, 141, 150, 153, 161, 165, 186, *202, 204, 212, 218, 220, 225, 234, *242, *251, 252, *253, 258, 259, 280, 291, 294, *331, *339 (s. Wender), 352, 356, *368, 370, 373, 387, 438, 443, 446, 448, 473; Bendler 72; Bene 126; Benedick 157; Benedict 79, 117, 212; Bener 129, 224; Benezet 435; Bengel 57; Beni 50; Beniger 136; Benin 7, 25; Benish 273; Benn *92, 230, 233, 239, *351; Benner 161, 190, *222, 260, 340, 375, 396, *397, 473; Bennz 400; Benoedes 170; Bensch 124; Bense 54; Bensel(l) 227, 274; Bensinger 164; Benter 60; Bentheis 189; Bentli 160; Bentz 80, 82, 113, 143, 183, 259, 273, *291, 317; Bentz (s. Bence); Bentze 55; Bentzel 435, 473; Bentzinger 163, 178; Ber 83, 178, 387, 403; Berberich 300; v. Berbisdorff 57; Berch 235; Berchel 357; Bercher 230; Berckhaeuser 312; Berckhyser 140; Berdos 10, 29; Berensteher 256; Berentpeller 154; Berentz 386; Bereth (s. Berret) 73; Berg 244, 265, 363, 388, 393, 412; von Berg 343; Berge 290; Bergenstott 57; Bergenthaler 476; Berger (s. Zerger) 73, 115, 116, 126, 130, 140, 148, 150, 168, 169, 187, 218, 229, 235, 237, 293, 300, 304, 310, 339, 396, 399; Bergerhoff 153; Berges 185; Bergfeld 301; Berghaus 296; Bergh(eimer?) 73; Bergheimer 73; Bergher 225; Beringer 309; Bergman(n) 120, 124, 154, 250, 333, *353, *357, 416; Bergströsser 67; Bergthal 401; Bergtohlt 195; Bergtoll 188; Beringer 129, 337; Beriss 190; Berkel *93, 134; Berkle 93; Berleman *445; Berlett 78; Berlib 262; Berlin *129; Bermes 160; Bern 139; Bernath 247; Bernauer 234; Berndt *378, 423, 427; Berne 80; Bernet 389; Bernhard 324; Bernhardi 236, 278;

Bernhard(t) 52, 110, 116, 117, 229, 273, 328, 329, 347, *368, *377, 384, 410, 414, 418, 423, 427, 447; Bernharth 198; Bernhart(t) 111, 117, 145, *146,ı148, 171, 189, 202, 246, 266, 279, 280, *283, 284, 285, 302, ı335, 340, 351, 354, 387; Bernheisel (-heusel) *73, 190; Berninger ı240, ı367; Berntz 114; Ber(r) *195, *325; Berret (s. Bereth) 72; Berringer 251, 274; Bersch 250; Berschman 191; Bersding 332; Bersey *275; Bersinger 438; Berth 188, 208; Berthgiss 369; Bertholt 240, 285; de Bertholt 110; Bertolet 475; Bertolets 10, 29; Bertrie 334; Bertsch 220, 368, 378, 401, 422, 427; Bertsh 349; Bertz 153; Besa 128; Besch 207; Bes(c)har 98, *99; Beschler 357; Besel 190; Besenger 168; Beser 83; Beserer 143; Besher 467; Besicker 77; Besinger 89; Besmer (s. Bressmer); Bessinger (s. Pessinger) 391; Best 115, 267, 342, 384; Bestenbast 348; Besteres 330; Beswanger 63; Beter 86; Bether ı327, 328; Bethsill 473; Betis 314, 352; Betsch 263; Betschen 71; Betschler 124; Better 131; Bettinger 311; Bettmann 415; Betz 142, 174, *182, 248, 252, 281, 313, *333, *358, 372, *401, 403; Betzele 119; Betzer 141; Betzler 236; Beuckler 380; Beudler 72; Beuerle 342; Beuschlein 207, 294; Beut(h)ler 193, 275; Beverly 460/1; Bevier 6, 25; Beydeler 53; Beyer *67, *68, *69, 75, 76, 90, *101, 105, 113, *114, 115, 126, 132, 140, 145, 149, *178, 194, ı226,ı *227, 264, 272, 308, 377, 397, 400, 416, 423, 427, 437, 443; Beyerle 64, 83, 129, 351, 389, 397; Beyerly 269, 289, 417; Beyermeister 360; Beyl 49, 177, 179, 335; Beylstein 258; Beyrer 249, 296; Beyrle 328; Beysely 178; Beyzelius 421, 426; Bibe 295; Bibighaus(s) 126, 127, 392; Bichel *235; Bichler 367; Bichller 374; Bick 307; Bickel(l) 82, 105, 176, 438; Bicker 77, 265; Bickes 125; Bickler 53, *172; Bideljung 287; Biebel 245; Bieber (s. Reaber) 85, 135, *171, *201, *204, *257, 366, *386, 391, 449; Biebert 283; Biebler *251; Biecheler 338; Biedeman 201; Biedenbender 187; Biedniger 105; Biefel 422, 426; Bieg *266; Biegel 363, 406; Bieger 366; Biehel *57, 128; Bi(e)hl 188, 190, *336; Biehler 119; Biehn 223; Biemmer 335; Biendser 349; Biener 351; Bientelheimer 368; Bi(e)ntzel 303; Bier 106, *185, 292; Bierbauer 280; v. Bieren 295; Biesang 118; Biesel 284; Bietch *258; Bietrighoffer 283; Biettel 108; Biever 135; Bigler 91, 145, 221, *267; Bihlmeier 70; Bilbo 7, 25; Bildhous 171; Bildman(n) 190, 273; Bilger 262; Bilhinger 321; Biller 122, 290; Billheimer 235; Billig 92; Billiger 81; Billing 207, 275; Billinger 257; Billingesleben 299; Billlng (Billing?) 272; Bil(l)-man 103, 277; Bimmesdoerffer 231; Bin *114; Binackel 157; Binckle 403; Binckley 438; Binckly *103; Bindder 334; Bind-eissen 70; Bindeman 311; Bindenberger 418; Binder 155, *156, *172, *242; Bindschaedler 163; Biner 221; Bingel 332; Bingeman 330, 436, 473, 475; Binger 261; Bingli 7, 25; Bing-man 364; Bininger 251; Bintnagel 80; Bintz 359; Bintzel 190; Binzel 334; Birckelbach 392, *413; Birckenmeyer 346; Birckenstock

122; Bircker 220; Birger 180; Birkenbeyly 232; Birki 372;
Birkingbey 199; Birle 83; Birstler 81; Birstoedt 406; Biry
72; Bisbing 473; Bisch 110; Bis(c)hof(f) 67, 85, 105, 121, 133,
*144, 152, *179, 183, 269, 314, 358, 450; Bischon 269; Bischop
*180, 425; Bisecker 178; Bishop 369, 421; Biso 399; Bison 203;
Biss 380; Bissahr 205; Bisser 135; Bisshautz 332; Bitilion 267;
Bitinger 256; Bitsferker 231; Bittenbender 17, 36, 126, 172;
Bitter 255; Bitterwein 186; Bitting 435, 436, 473, 474; Bittle
475; Bittmann 367; Bittner 62, 145; Bittonff 349; Bitts 470;
Bitzer 241, *287, 447; Blaass 349; Blach 413; Blacher 381;
Blader 226, *277; Bladman 158; Blaeser (Blazer, Blesser)
*265; Blaesser 233; Blanck *266, 342; Blanckenbiller 350;
Blank 89; Blanssart 301; Blaser 92, *93, 134, 188, 264,
273; Blass 373, 447; Blasser 238; Blattenberger 162; Blat(t)ner
69, 70, 136; Blauch 244; Blaus 371; Blazer (s. Blaeser);
Bleakly 174; Blecher 200, 275, 346, 412; Bleck 279; Bleckens-
torfer 188; Blecker 311, 330; Bledel 368; Bleibtreu 104;
Bleich 244, 321, 325; Bleichenbacher 344; Bleicher 104,
435; Bleicherodt 305; Bleickers 430; Bleier 332; Bleininger
355; Bleistein *136, 329; Bleigestaufer 176; Blesch 397;
Bleshor 249; Blesinger 263; Blesser (s. Blaeser); Blessing
281, 327; Bley 144, 226; Bleymeyer 216; Blicher 68;
Blickensdoerffer *317; Blickest(o)erfer *196; Blickly 288;
Blihle 344; Blim(m) 59, 277; Blintzinger 249; Blisch 379;
Blisky 174; Blitz 359, 373, 472; Bloch 376; Blocher (s.
Pflocher) 311, 321; Block *250, 388; Bloeckinger 285;
Blömen 57; Bloemhauer 84; Bloetz 322; Blom *272;
Blonk 191; Bloom 77; Bloomer 464; Bloss 155, 218, 235;
Blosser 239; Bluecher 126; Bluegner 252; Bluemler 380;
Blum 64, 255, 257, 355, 356, 385, 439; Blumenschein 194,
234, 328; Blumenstein 258; Blumer 190, 284; Bluth 287;
Boach 114; Bob 151, 204, *334; Bobe 237; Bobenheiser
*117; Boblitz 476; Boce 218; Bochner 175; Bock 68, *70,
168, 218, 219, 249, 297, 325, *344, 388; Bockius 147, 202;
Bockrantz 301; Bockreider 370; Bodenheimer 259; Bodenreider 197; Bodenstein 360; Bodner 305; Bodomer 220;
Böchle (s. Boeckle) 72, 73; Boechtel 135; Boechteldt 331;
Boechtold 78; Boeckel(l) 108, 333; Boecker (s. Becker) 130;
Boeckhle 325; Boeckle (s. Beclie, Boechle) *72; Bockney
148; Boeder 402; Boedescer 405; Boeger 299; Boehler 73,
135, 374, 420, 421, 424, 425; Boehm 126, *160, 180, 218,
228, 236, 290, 303, 317, 437, 478; Boehmer 199, *235,
*260, 317, *379, 422, 427; Boehner 195; Boehringer *188,
264, 416; Boell 377; Boella 56; Boeller 317; Boem 164;
Boemer 307, 318; Boemmer 116, 117; Boemper 17, 36;
Boenig 408; Boenning 408, 409; Boerckle 362; Boerger 314;
Boerner 240; Boerns 52; Boerstler 331; Boesch 187;
Boeshar 17, 36; Boesher 69; Boesler 189; Boess 323;

Boessinger 391; B(o)es(s)mer *223; Boest 395; Boeter 431; Boettger 272, 403; Boettle 49; Boetz 223; Boetzer 111; Boger 67, 72, 73, 337, 347, 405, 469; Boger(d)t 55, 79, 171; Bogner 88; Bogus 261; Boher 100; Bohl 341; Bohlender 388; Bohler 311; Bohm 155, 271; Bohn 113, 156, *174, 291, 352, 470; Bohnenblust 284; Bohner 178, 187; Bohr 196, *197; Bohre 227; Bohrer 211; Bohret 406; Bohrman(n) 273, 278; Bohset 239; Bolander 151; Bolch 308, 309; Boley 367, 368; Bolich 348; Bolland 202; Bolle 301; Bollenbacher 142; Boller 209; Bolliek 389; Bollinger 107, 135, *245, *303, 380; Bollman 129; Bollmar *137; Bollon 75; Bolschner 382; Bolt 464; Bolteschwag 341; Boltz 113, 189, 277, 332; Boltzius 14, 32, *449; Bom 205, 431, 432; Bombach 144; Bome 157; Bommer 338; Bond *127; Bondeli 312; Bondett 463; Bondurant 7, 25; Boner 142, 312; Bonet 87, 88, 226; Boney 432; Bongart 159; Boni *382; Bonjour 337; Bon(n) *244, *272, 412; Bonner 76; Bonnet(t) 110, 304, *464; Bon Repo *464; Bonroth 447; Bontaux 289; Bontz 58; Bony 60; Bonyneburg 378; Books 103; Boor 149, 197; Boorlinger 54; Booser 191; Boos(s) 116, 118, 130, 367, 418; Boous 261; Bopenmeier 156; Bop(p) 161, 233, 388; Boracker 149; Borckel 386; Bordili 382; Borell 341; Borelle 405; Boret 123; Borge 470; Borich 146; Boris 375; Borleman 53, 474; Borman 304, 419; Born 78, 107, 125, 144, 240; Bornn 271, 313; Borntraeger 377; Bornwasser 443; Boron 284; Boronii 180; Borsch 392; Borst (s. Barst) 58, 375; Borthlehr 373; Bortner (s. Porter) *79; Bortz 52, 365; Bory 381; Bosch 124, 198, *242, 266, 288; Boschung 68, *70, 84, *85; Boserman 189; Bosfeld 126; Boshart *99, 132, 213, 231, 313; Boss 151, 415; Bossart 166; Bosse 179, 407; Bossel 373; v. Bossen 432; Bosseng 315; Bos(s)er 141, 158, 159; Bosser(d)t 60, 98, *131, 263; Bosserman 305; Bosshardt 178; Bossler 128; Bossman 301; Boswell *223; Bothacker 281; Bothner 105; Boths 301; Botisnion 297; Bott 76, 159, 160, 184, 330, 380; Bottenfeld 403; Botz 232; Bouger 137; Bough 137, 228; Boullie *464; Boumer 158; Bourquin 410; Boushy 205; Bouse *138; Bousman 232; Bouton 132; Bower *116, 246, 262; Bowman (s. Bauman(n) 50, 53, 54, 59, 112; Bown *382; Boyd 63; Boyer 466; Boz 417; Brabek (s. Browbak, Brubeck) 191; Brabnith 214; Brackmann 407; Bradford *444; Bradtfisch 390; Brady 197, 198; Braechtbuel 336; Braeitinger 268; Braetscheri *167; Braeuchle 281; Braeutigam 295, 306, 350; Brakebill 84; Brall 301; Brallion 78; Bramer 322, 418; Brammeret 230; Brand 101, 263, 278, 302, 333, 383, 410; Brandau 446; Brandenberger 377; Brandenbuerg 141; Brandenbuerger 272; Brandmüller 153, 421, 422, *426; Brandner 228, 450; Brand(t) 72, 76, 78, 120, *135, 195, *220, 251, 418, 432, 438, 474; Brandtohr 387; Brang 228; Branner 112; Braseur

78; Brattler *371; Braubeck 139; Brauch 123, 201; Braucher 338; Brauchler 150; Brauer 239, 310, 445; Braum 365; Braun 18, 37, 93, 101, 113, 116, 118, 123, 125, 128, 146, 148, 159, 170, *185, *198, *200, 214, 229, 235, 237, 248, *274, 278, *279, 283, 286, *289, 290, *300, 302, 303, 307, *317, 320, 342, 353, 355, *366, 369, 371, 383, 394, 407, 412, 473; Braunbeck 436; Braunefelder *167; Braunholtz 325; Braunig 391; Braunmiller 132; Braunsberg 240; Brauss 126, 287, 291; Brausser 410; Brautwald 323; Bray 110; Brech 159, 245; Brechbil(l) 72, *84, 85; Brechbuehler 336; Brechbuel 437; Brechbue(h)ll 73, 122; Brecht 70, 229, 343; Breck 342; Brecker 302; Breelinger 246; Bre(e)m *142; Breidebach *364; Breidenbach 190, 344; Breidengross 94; Breihahn 296; Brein 143, 151; Breinckhart 374; Breiner 290; Breinig 267, 305; Breining 219; Breininger 219; Breisah 214; Breisch *362; Breisser 283; Breitenbach 176, *381; Breitenbueh(e)r 370, 371; Breitenhardt 308; Breitner 393; Breittenfeldt 299; Breitzinger 235; Brem 255; Bremer 126, 277; Bremich *356; Bremmer 407; Brendel *118; Brendley 256; Brendlinger 268; Brend(t)le 258, 320; Breneissen *64; Brener 264; Brengel 105, *336, 370; Brenhauer 229; Brenholtz 100; Brenighoff *255; Breninger 93; Brenneman(n) 364, 366, *436, 437, 477; Brenner 86, 113, *207, 288, 300, 301, 313, 375, *383; Brent 145; Brentz 257, 276; Brentzer 141; Brentzinger 254; Bresel 333; Breser 297; Breslauer 346; Bresler *218; Bressler 369, 443; Bresthle 175; Breszler 361; Bretter 438; Bretz *161, 169, 230, *232, 233; Bretzius 185; Breun 305; Breuning 285; Breuninger 93, *118; Brey 321; Breydinger 345; Breyer 215; Breymayer (-meyer) 177, 281; Breys 245; Breyvogel 170; Brian 7, 25; Bricker 118, 119, 161, 213, 246; Brickli 243; Brickner 220; Brieff 406; Briegel 447; Briegner 139; Briehll 343; Briell 343; Brientz 124; Brigel 466; Brightbill 122; Brill 211; Brimmer 89; Brin(c)ker 17, 36, 99, 231, 345; Bring 276; Brinkman 227; Brittain *464; Brittschedt 242; Britzing 233; Brobeck 139; Brock *89, 265; Brod 198, 225; Brodbeck *218, 268, *269, 322; Brodnier 376; Brodrich 345; Broeder 142; Broening 227; Brogli 356; Brombach 275, *373; Brommer 182, 211; Bronck 443; Bronholtz 182; Bronk 241; Bronnen 182; Brosch 422, 427; Brosius 140, *157, 187, 466; Brosmann 467; Bross 225, 305; Brossman 136; Brost 189, 204; Brotsman 128; Brotzmann 128; Browbak (s. Brabek, Brubeck) *191; Brown 59, 79, 108, 119, *165, 182, *187, 193, 211, *324, *414; Brownfield 421, 425; Browning *209; Brownwart 75; Brows 127; Brua 135; Brubacher *329, 364, 437; Brubacher (s. Bruebacher); Brubeck (s. Brabek, Browbak) 192; Bruce 421, 425; Bruch 101, 107, 143, 162, 411; Bruchhart *276; Bruchhauser 364; Bruchli 289; Brucker 111, 275, 421, 425; Bruckhart 448; Bruder 173, 288; Bru(e)bacher *196, 202; Bruecher 406;

Brueckbauer 160; Bruecker 118, 152, 186, *219, 332; Brueckert 243, 360; Brueckner 450; Bruederle 104; Bruenckmann 347; Bruenckner *99; Bruening 282; Bruensholtz (s. Printzholtz) 226; Brueschlein 334; Brueser 406; Bruest 210, 388; Bruettschiett 273; Bruetzius 371; Bruker 191; Brulasher 56; Brum 413; Brumbach 239, 332; Brumm 311; v. Brunck 301; Brunder *132; Brundich 17, 36; Brundle 235; Bruner 102, 163, 192, 203, 211, 231, 233, 236, 315; Brungart 276; Bruning 227; Brunner 56, 61, *71, 83, 98, 99, 101, 163, 166, *194, 203, 345; Brunnholtz *173, 230; Brun(n)ing(h)er 69, *70; Bruno 296; Bruns 294; Brutz 317; Bryson 398, *409, *415; Bryzelius 153; Bub *125, 187, 289, 375; Buber 182; Bubickofer 330; Buch 57, 119, 179, 182, *262, 277, 298, 310, 314, *349, 381; Buchaker 180; Buchenmeyer 439; Bucher 18, 37, 54, 64, 78, 83, 99, *100, 115, 132, *137, 156, 158, 188, *231, *260, *350, 449, 476; Bucher (al. Rutter) 2, 20; Buchharner 202; Buchhecker 369; Buchholtz 430; Buchman 170, 208, *237, 340, 375, 378; Buchmueller 401; Buchner 316, 317; Bucholtz 182; Buchstel 303; Buchter 194; Buchty 103; Buchwalter 434, 437, 438, 471; Buchy 159; Buck 235, 273; Buckbeck 235; Bucke 201; Buckenmeyer 126; Bucki 165; Buckner 317; Bucks 225; Bud 412; Buda *192; Budeman 314; Buden 133, 134; Budniger 105; Buebel 228; Buebelt 187; Buebinger 122; Buech 158, 365; Buecher 99, 175; Buechert 384; Buechler 90, 91, 108, 342, 363; Bueckel(l) 143, 215, 264, 267, 411; Buecking 392; Buecksell 227; Buehler 136, 277, 305, 360, 392, 417; Buehlheim 340; Buehlmann 449; Buehlmayer 81; Buehrly 166; Bueller 52; Buelman 437; Buembel 263; Bueninger 421, 425; Buentzel 287; Buer 197; Buerckert 343; Buercket 380; Buerckholder 355; Buerge 176; Bürger 64, 94, 108, 133, 292, 300, *309; Buergestrass 325; Buergi 130; Buerkhardt 264; Buerki 88, 112; Buers 443; Buerth 244; Buesch 391, 400; Buesche 303; Bueschler 278; Bueshart 339; Buessung 276; Buetefisch 294; Buethenfeldt 358; Buetler 101; Buettel 292, 294, 309; Buet(t)ner *176, 232, 293, 365, 368, 407, 421, 425; Bufle 118; Bugner 153; Buhl 147, 319; Buhler 97; Buhlman 320; Bull 106, 107, *396; Bullher 119; Bullinger *76, 107, 115; Bumgardner 72; Bumgarner 59; Bundeli 436; Bundry 148; Burbach 396; Burchard *90; Burchardt 352; Burchart 336; Burchert 136; Burchhalter 92, *437; Burchhardt 237; Burchhart 253, 255, 256; Burchhell 405; Burckart 163; Burckhalter *336; Burckhard(t) 90, 253, 298, 418; Burckhart 213, *329; Burckner 153; Burell 290; Burg 198, 241, 287, 397; Burgener 153; Burger 94, 166, 254; Burghalter 91; Burghart 80, 81, *137, 474; Burghen 275; Burgher *135; Burgholdter *372; Burgin 297; Burging 374; Burgstahler 291; Burgsteiner *450; Burkard 224; Burkhard(t) 221, 309; Burkhalter 72; Burman 382; Burn 128; Burnside 421, 425; Burr 327; Burye 173;

Busch 103, 142, 166, *178, *189, 260, 267, 284, 302, 327, 328, *395, 410, *411, 418, 448; Buschong 438; Buset 449; Bushart 144; van Buskirk *478; Busman *307; Buss 74, *339, 368; Bussart 213; Busse 89, 407; Bussel 406; Bus(s)er *191, 383, 399; Bussy 214; Buth 190; Butterfass 115, 160; Butterweh 147; Buttman 166; Butz 129, 165, 178, 279, 283, 338, 340, 379; Buyghart 207; Byrd 460, 462; Byshall 212.

Caarel 233; Cabbas 313; Cabbett 378; Cabel 233; Cachler 346; Cacho 403; Cackey 18, 36; Caeppele 268; Caerius 367; Caff 389; Caffarel 304; Caffroth 182; Cairnes 456, 459; Calb 57; Calberlahn 423, 427; Cambeck 199; Camerer 110; Cameti 417; Cammerhof 423, 427; Cammerlich 408; Camp (s. Kamp) 207; Campbell *246, *280; v. Campe 296; Campo 278; Cansfluderman 320; Cantick 241; Cantz (s. Gans?) 239; Cantzle 310; Cap *112; Caplinger 76; Capp *74, 256; Cappis 333; Caquelin *103, 104; Caral *340; Carel *345; Carl 68, 102, 103, 128, 182, 199, 277, 296, 345; Carle 74, 107, 121, *188, 249, 260, 264, 267, 399, 411, 466; Carmane (Carmone) *266; Carn 78; Carolis 417; Carr *367; Corson *78; Carsten 431; Carstens 431; Carter *112; Carver 59; Caryess 291; Cashnetz (s. Castnitz) 105; Casman 67; Casner 353; Casper 166, 245, 342; Caspering 74; Cass *467; Cassel 470; Casselberry (s. Kesselberg); Cassell 119, 413, 435; Casselmann 446; Casser 187; Cast 300; Castermann 368; Castle *402; Castnitz (s. Cashnetz) 105; Cattler 81; Cauffman 231, 363, 412; Cautom *238; Cautz 339, 360, 405; Cayton *372; Cazo 388; Cellier 188; Cene (s. Le Cene); Cerber 155; Chaillot 412; Chamberlin 456, 459; Chambon 7, 25; Chance 464; Chap(p)elle 249, *304; Charle 115; Charmely 202; Chasrood 55; Chastain 7, 25; Chavlier 204; Cheert 169; Che(e)sler 81, *82; Cheesman *183; Cheseches 231; Chilton 140, 141; Chitzrieth 228; Chrestien 103; Chretschenbach 349; Chriesmerg 74; Chrisback 246; Christ 56, 72, *91, 106, 129, *157, 183, 228, 260, 354, 376, 395, 422, 426, 451, 467; Christein *264; Christen 77; Christi 241; Christian *74, 136, 159, 189, 238, 259, 294, 298, 309, *321, 335, 344, 372, 381, 392, 467; Christler 102; Christman(n) 64, 103, 151, 186, 188, 193, *354, 371, 386, 395, 473, 478; Christoleer 471; Christopher 437; Christy 139; Chron 53; Chrunz 331; Chypfeius 362; Cist 413; Claar 348; Claess 337; Clain 246; Claither 127; Clamdy 247; Clap(p) 51, *368; Classen 412; Clatley (s. Glattl[e]y) 132; Claude 390; Clauser *241; Claus(s) 132, 181, 182, 238, 272, 286, 298, 352; Claussenius 223; Clausser 166; Clautsch 384; Cleiss 203, 397; Cleiver 135; Clem 145, 209; Clemens 434, 470; Clement 372; Clements 410; Clem(m)entz 119, 185, 218; 333; Clemmer 64; Clever 430; Clewer 79; Click 82; Cline 77; Cloder 121; Clos(s) 116, 287, 298; Clossheim 161; Clossmeyer 286; Cloter 417; Clucksclear 55; Cludy 125; Clymer

*64, *91; Coatam *145, 192, *256, *275, *313, *342; Cobbit 371; Coblentz 391; Coblet 243; Cochenderff 81; Cochet *386; Coeffer 307; Coell 299; Coelly 323; Coelus 275; Coen 121; Coenrads 431, 471; Coesch 403; Coger 56, 127; Colle 313; Collep 228; Coller 228; Comer 103; Commens 149; Comrath 239; Comuelder 322; Con 327; Conkell 80; Conrad (s. Kuendors); Conradi 228, 373; Conrads (s. Kunders) 430, 470, 477; Conrad(t) 74, 107, *109, 111, 112, 142, 143, 179, *201, 202, 210, 224, 225, 255, 276, 278, 279, *284, 313, 324, *336, 351, 374, 408, 410, *411, 414, 448, 471, 474, 478; Conrath 147, 176, 213, *224, 279, 368; Conrieu 175; Conselman 149; Consul 175; le Conte *463; Contono 417; Gontter 189;ᵢ Conver 250, 298; Cook *388, *395, 396, 422, 427; Coon 118; Coope 54; Coos 140; Coots 172; Cope *477; Copeland *394; Copenhäer *74; Copia 186; Coppelger 155; Coppy 213; du Corbier 303; Corbo 110; Corell 116, *147, 152, 196, 217; Cormet 340; Cornelius 86, 87, 326; Corngibel 227; Corngiber 240; Cornman 151; Correl 135, 310; Corrt 129; Cosia 262; Cossler 318; Cottringer 387; Cotweis *432; Cotz 261; Coughly 158; Coultas 55, 58; Coulties 262; Courpenning 253; Courteuer 204; Couton *464; Couwald 140; Cowie 153, 154, *159; Craessmann 140; Crafft 248; Craigie 60; Cramer 71, 78, 213, 280, *335, 443; Cranch *150; Cranester 115; Cranmiller 281; Crapy 205; Crassan 219; Crates 476; Cratz 101, 217; Craus 324; Crause 450; Creat (s. Gratt?) 204; Creagh *208; Crebil 59; Crebler *230; Creesh 262; Creesle 204; Creesman 156; Creeter 59; Creim 151; Creiner 64, 203; Cremer 390; Crentz 151; Cresman 151; Cress *143, 165, 291; Cressap 12, 30; Cressel 176; Cresson 470; Creuccas 113; Creutz 129, 239, *286, 302, 317; Creyebiel (s. Crybile) 55; Creysmeyer 118; Crieby 308; Criess 392; Crietz 242; Criger 80; Criling 146; Crisby 322; Crisman 476; Crispell 6, 25; Crobf 61; Crocket *51, *57, *75; Croes(s)man 54, *59, 60, 107, *143; Croll 59; Cromberg 259; Cromer 107, 313; Cromm 352, *365, 366; Cron 109, 121, 183; Cronbach 101; Cronberger 418, 450; Cronenberg 294; Cronenberger 154, 417; Cronro 319; Croo 55; Crope 261; Crop(p) *61, 158; Croy 308; Croyer 294; Croyter 107; Crub 133; Crucius 351; Cruir 75; Crum 222, *317; Crybile (s. Creyebiel) 55; Cryle 76; Cuenrad 260; Cünter 62; Culman 367; Cumm *89; Cummer 230; Cump 212; Cunckel *335; Cunius 116; Cunkel 240; Cunner 184; Cunningham *266; Cunrad 471; Cuntz 49, 65, 74, 101, 155, 164, 186, 217, 224, *228, 232, 236, 335, 376, *379; Cuntzmann 380; Cuny 198; Curfes 321; Curr *248; Cuschuah 75; Cusick 171; Cussack *157, *164; Cyriaci 354.

Daam 203; Dach *320; Dachstaedter 447; Dadinger 117; Daegen 139; Daehn 209; Daenderich 211; Dänig 87; Daeppen 103; Daerendinger *347; Daesterr 202; Daetweiler

469; Daetwyler 192; Daeublin 244; Daeueber 301; Daeuebler 406; Dage 363; Dagon 212; Dahleth 238; Dahlheimer 117; Dahm 375; Dais 464; Dalick 332; Dalmer 403; Dalwig 134; Daman 407; Dambeller 410; Damfuchs 199; Dam(m)er (s. Thamer) *174, 274; Dampff 403; Damselt 222; Danbach 220; Dandoner 163; Danecker 249; Danegar 437; Danesus 214; Dang 187; Dangoranslo 215; Daniel 119, 150, 235, 337, 363; Danler 77; Dann 334; Dannahauer (s. Dannenhauer); Dannefelser 159; Dannefeltzer 368; Danneheim 339; Dannenhauer (Dannahauer) *112; Danner 51, 86, 153, *158, 177, 191, 198, 286, 293, 351; Dannerinborgen *247; Dannermarker *443; Dannether 225; Dannewald 156; Danney (s. Denigh?) 137; Dannfeltzer 280; Dannhoeffer 339; Danninger 250, 282; Dannwind 311; Dannwolff 264; Dantius 295; Dantzebecher *349; Danweiler 434; Danwisch 314; Danzel 220; Dapper 186; Darm 342; Darner 347; Dartwiller (Doertweiler) *205; Dascher 106; Daser 310, 311; Daterer 155; Datismann 198; Dau 411; Daub 116, 117, 352, 408; Daubenberger *251; Daubenspeck 101; Dauber 180, 185, 256, 329, 339; Daubnuestel 186; Dauchawirt 370; Dauchbes 282; Daudt 242; Dauerschauer 173; Daum 149; 352; Daumer 228; Daumiller 261; Daunneberger 227; Daur(in) 467; Dausman 358; Dausweber 443; Dautderer 161; Dautremer 406; Dauttel 174; Davahrt 146; David 7, 25; Davidson *377; Davies 53, 54; Dayberer 412; Deato 165; Debald 237; Debeer 347; Debilbissen (Debelbissen) *69, 70; Debler 467; Delong 122; Debues 166; Debuss 245; Dech 347; Decher *332; Dechin 323; De(c)k *96, 101, 114; Decker 17, 36, 131, 150, *258, 259, 275, 288, 304, 321, 365, 383; Decreiff 170; Dederer 52, 251; Dedie *372, 385; Dedigman 92; Deederich 184; De(e)g 296, *322; Deehr (s. Doerr, Duerr) 363; Deen 7, 25; Deer 249, *299; Deeter 76; Deetzel 374; Deffithal 183; Deg 364; Dege 192; Degen 190, 366, 409; Degenbeck 129; Deghe 241; Degler 205; Degreiff 310; Dehlbauer 138; Dehm 288; Dehn 400; Dehne 423, 427; Dehr 72; Dehring 474; Dehts 321; Deibel 283; Deible 192; Deichert 447; Deiler 327; Deilinger 274; Dein 330; Deinberger 245; Deinie 129; Deininger 247; D(e)inius *370; Deisen (s. Tyson); Deisert 361; Deisman 404; Deiss 145, 146, 188, 269, 312; Deissher 281; Deissinger 187; Deiswers 271; Deitschmall 250; Deitt 256; Dek *466; Delangs 10, 29; Delatter 148; Delb 102, 361; Delbig 409; Delcher (s. Telcher) 227; Delebach 244; Delikamp 322; Delir 396; Delitz 301; Dellen 212; Dellinger 87, 88, 126, 235; Delman 62; Delon 204; Delong 18, 36; Delp(p) 109, 128, 195, 311, 340; Demanche 247; Demandt 413; Demarer 406; Deme 331; Demje 407; Demme 302; Demmel 400; Demott (s. de Mott); Demster *404; Demuth 264, *421, *425, 422, 427, 447; Denbig 445; Dencey 147; Denckelberg *56; Dencker 225; Dengeiss 218; Dengen 360; Denger 333; Dengler 232, 411; Denig(h)

Den—Dim

(s. Danvey) 137, 185, 318; Denkircher 396; Denler 263, 273; Denner 109, 140, 294, 392, 419; Dennschertz 294; Dentlinger 476; Dentzel(l) 225, 392; Dentzer 242; Dentzler *99; Deobalt 217; Deobeld *172; Depre 368; Depu 17, 36; Deque 408; Derber 76; Derbert 290; Derdamer 191; Derdler 331; Deremot 224; Deretinger 205; Derffus 224; Dering 205; Derker 252; Dernheimer 154, 388; Derr 198, 232; Derrick 127; Dersch 338, 383; Derscher 341; Dersler 195; Derst 85, 165, 346; Derstenbecher 215; Derting 280; Dertwa 382; Des 108; Desch 150, 309, 346; Descher 305, *356; Deschler 89, 289; Deschner 209, 372; Desern 301; Dessler 156; Dessloch 323; Dester 111, 112; Destermueller 251; Deterich (Deterig) 218, 238; Detloff 295; Dettenborn 438; Dettmer 56; Dettweiler 364; Dettwiller 329; Detweiler 103, 378, 416, 470, 476; Deubard 374; Deull (s. Peul) 245; Deussinger 344; Deutsch 261; Devignair 396; Devil 369; Dewa 336; Dewald 395; Dewalt 166, 172, 173, 175, 251, 302, 374; Dewes (s. de Wees); Dewess 88; Dewetten 253; Dewys 166; Dexheimer *356; Dexter 169; Deyh 185; Deymen 84; Deyo (s. Dian); Deys 469; Dhaemer 388; Dheuch 398; Dian (s. Deyo) 6, 25; Dibel 358; Dibs 334; Dich 300; Dick 119, 201, 202, *230, 241, *243, 336; Dicke *399; Dickes 368; Dickhans 280; Dickhoff 109; Dickinson 10, 28; Dickleder 78; Didah 184; Didel 129; Didiers 392; Didrich 250, 326; Die 337; de Die 323; Diebel 109, 446; Diebert 361; Diebler 413; Diebolt *135, 208; Dieckert 170; Diedrich 224, 225, 318; Dieffenbach 366, 469; Dieffe(n)bacher 110, 228, 362; Diehhart 202; Diehl 67, *133, 135, *142, 148, 157, *182, 201, 221, 253, 285, 313, *331, 335, *339, *352, 378, 386, 389, 394, 415; Diehlbeck 279; Diehm 313, 306, 469; Diehoff 396; Diehrig 231; Diekenschiedt (s. Dinckenschiet) 170; Diel 49, *116, 126, 317, 331; Dielbohn 146; Dielinger *56; Diell 52; Diem 207, 267, 296; 311; Diemer 143, 237, 241, 326, 376; Diemes 329; Dieminger 87; Diemus 218; Diener 254; Dientzer 447; Dieppel 17, 36; Dierenberger (Durrenberger) 238; Dierhein 308; Dierlhoffner 170; Diersen 251; Dierstein 195; Dies 338; Diesbergen 226; Diesch 264; Diess 388; Diessinger 352; Dieter 52, 61, 75, 174, 316, 467; Dieterich 129, 142, 187, 238, 276, 369, *372, 380, 382, 394, 402; Dieterle 417; Dietewig 220; Diether 267, 379; Dietmar 242; Dietrich 172, 264, 271, 273, 274, *276, 283, 284, 332, 336, 341, 343, 350, 357, 369, 380, 384, 412, 445, 447; Dietrichs 66; Dietterich 177; Dietz 127, *128, 146, *189, 202, 251, 300, 301, *328, 333, 349, 352, 353, 385, 393, 412; Dietzel 250; Diewalt 378; Diffebach 410; Digel 286; Diger 340; Dihl(l) 61, *96, 200; Dihm 292, 293, 334, *335, 411; Dilbeck 2, 20, 429, 472; Dilier 272; Dilgard 180; Dilhart 185; Dill 93, 107, 192, 312, 315, 370, 377, 447; Dillan 171; Dillenbach 447; Dillman(n) *107, 258, 349; Dil(l)s(s) 271, *272; Dimott

141; Dinck 236; Dinckenschiet (s. Diekenschiedt) 170; Dincky 159; Dinger 217; Dinges 149, 159, 201, 242, 340, 448, 468; Dingis 257; Dingler 301; Dinius (s. Deinius); Dippberger 238; Dippel 227, 318, 361; Dirkerhoff 266; Dirner 342, 343; Dirr *82; Dirstein 72, 264; Dirwess 199; Dis 379; Dischardt 389; Discher 229, 401; Dischler 235; Dischong 272, *315; Disinger 351; Dispionit 131; Disseler 301; Distner 301; Diterich 311; Diterichs 66; Ditloh 335; Ditman 392; Ditmar 326; Ditrich 140; Dittis 123; Dittman 413; Ditz 199, 201, 227; Ditzler 17, 36; Diwall 211; Dob(b)ler 172, 241; Dobeler 224; Dochman 172; Dochterman 166; Dock *198, 284, 389, 438; Dockesladel 328; Doctor 275; Doderer 56; Doeb(e)ly 297, 298; Doebler *72, 129, 389; Doeden 430, 432; Doehling 422, 427; Doelcker 340; Doelle 382; Doenges *290; Doerbaum 354; Doerffling 218; Doerf(f)linger 93, 207, 322; Doering 291; Doerner 144, 413; Doerr (s. Deehr, Duerr) 57, 81, 82, 120, 154, 162, 186, 196, 303, 325, 358, 363, 367, 377, 398, 415; Doerrnis 336; Doersch 395; Doertweiler (s. Dartwiller); Doertzbach 129; Doess 368; Doest 181, 182; Doetter *216, 319; Doetzter 255; Doganer 87; Dogent 347; Dohl (Doll) 62, *268; Dohner 345; Dohster 174; Doieges 318; Doisin 385; Dolch 147; Doldt 97; Doll 105, 106, 132, *133, 137, 145, 156, 219, 351, 361, 369, 391; Dollendorp 407; Dollinger 115, 411, 468; Dollmann 308, 371; Domey 102; Domie 154; Domingo 417; Domm 285; Domme (s. Thome 103, 191; Dommer 119; Dommi 65, 277; Don 7, 25; Donat 353; Donbach 57; Dondemand 405; Donner 192; Donnges 410; Donselt 380; le Doof *464; Doopel 85; Dopff 447; Dore 390; Doren 254; Dorest 59; Dorff 269; Dormeyer (—meier) 203, 204, 205, *285; Dormyer (s. Dormeier); Dorn 219; Dornbach 168, *169; Dornberger 321; Dorneh 354; Dornhauer 175; Dornig 164; Dorschheimer 343; Dorsham 333; Dorsheimer 367; Dorst 353, 431; Dortst 119; Dosch 292, 297, 298, 388; Doser *283; Doss 334; Dost 368; Dostman 297; Dotterer *472; Dowart 287; Doyle *340; Drabach (s. Trarbach) 250; Drach 292, 294; Drachsel 86, *87, *105, 205, 358; Drack 330; Dracker 398; Drackes 187; Draichler 121; Drapet 236; Drasbart 103; Drass 109; Draugh 62; Drauth 114; Drear 234; Dreher 116, 148, 194, 273, *379; Dreibelbiss 82; Dreichler 109; Dreis(s)bach *162, 234; Dreistel 435; Drenth 190; Dresbach 347; Drescher *96; Dress 174, 352; Dressler 133, 292; Drexel 389; Drexler 395, 401; Dreydel 147; Dreyerling 189; Dreyman 407; Dreysbach 266; Driebler 387; Dries *92; Driesch 229; Drill 381; Drion 268, 288; Drog 125; Drollinger *123; Drom 133; Droqunt 355; Droz 393; Druck 149, 196; Druckenbrodt 357; Druebe 70; Drueber 314; Druechsel 261; Drugrare 203; Drumberg 115; Drum(m) 105, 116, 157; Druss 306; Drybler 272; Dubach 96; Dubernock 380; Dubo 84, 85; Dubois 6, 25; Duboy 57;

Dubre 435, 436; Dubret 412; Dubs 59, 101, 103; Dubydorffer 159; Duchand 414; Duchman(n) (s. Tuchmann) 220, 376; Ducker 319; Duckwell 107; Ducy 7, 25; Dübendöffer 49, *99; Duebinger 166; Dueckel 367; Dueckherdt 280; Duedi 229; Dueff 298; Duemmig 308; Duenck *132; Duenschman 141; Duentz 112; Duerck 320; Dueringer 226; Duer(r) (s. Deehr, Doerr) 118, 197, 212, 236, 262, 270, 273, 275, *351, *363; Duerstler 337; Duery 93; Duerz 281; Duessardt 364; Duessing 343; Duesto 175; Duett 268; Düttenhoeffer 63; Duey *230; Dugion 422, 426; Duille (s. Guille) 323; Dulany 12, 31; van Duliken 96; Dull 250; Dullnick 269; Dum 228; Dumbaldt *104; Dumernicht 121; Dumm 357; Dummer 215; Dummey 207; Duncan *414; Dun(c)kel 62, 132; Dunckelberg 56; Duncker 414; Dunkel(l) 473, 474; Dunkenmayer 466; Dunlap (-lop) 62, *281; Dunter 285; Duntz 293; Dupel 148; Dupont 386; Dups 103, 158, 232, 235; Dupuy 7, 25; Durabercher 119; Durell *172; Duren 191; Durie 123; Durny 149; Durrenberger (s. Dierenberger); Durschman *200; Durst 246, 356; Durweeg 377; Dust 115; Dute 268; Dutoi 7, 25; Duton 324; Dutt 321; Duval 203; Duvinger 212; Duweiler 275; Duwerter 282; Dykar 7, 25.

Eader 143; Easterly 118; Eatter 166; Ebaertz 148; Ebbly 269; Ebby 72, 73; Ebeland (s. Evelandt) *76; Ebele 288, 300; Ebeler 101; Ebener 178, 284; Ebenno 82; Ebenth 229; Eberam *55; Eberhard 236, 242, 360, 409, 446; Eberhar(d)t *54, 104, 105, *114, 126, 166, *170, *179, 182, 193, 210, 229, 259, *270, 275, 291, 310, 338, 398, 409, 417; Eberharth 216, 340; Eberhartt 178; Eberle (s. Oberle) 73, 111, 221, 234, 277, *278, 312, 318, 351, 414; Eberli 51; Eberlin 283; Eberling 188; Eberly 272, 291, 401; Eberman(n) *76, *81; Ebersohl 51, *135, 310, 354; Eberst 185; Ebert(h) *69, 80, *182, 185, 199, *255, 278, 326, 353, 389, 394; Eberts 207, 398; Ebes 259; Ebi 173; Ebirhardt (s. Eberhardt); Ebler 105; Ebly *89; Ebnie 326; Eby 437, 438; Eche 235; Echelen 67; Echelwich 431; Echman 385; Echternach 213; Echternacht 384; Eck 158, 225, 352; Eckardt 351; Eckart 162, 225; Eckebert 295; Eckel(l) 155, 210, 211, 244, 280, 367, 372, 408; Eckenberger *378, 419; Eckenroth 161; Ecker 112, 123, 220, 268, 317, 363; Eckerdt 224; Eckerlein 18, 37; Eckert 66, 83, 193, 212, *270, 274, 341, 375, 447; Ecket 156; Eckfeldt 356; Eckford 71; Eckhard(t) 190, 211, 368, 411; Eckhart 416; Ecki 198; Eckinan (s. Eckman) 50; Eckler 81; Eckman (s. Eckinan) 49, 217, 251; Eckroth 162; Ecks 277; Eckstein 396, 434, 473; Ecron 149; Edelberger 249; Edeler 274; Edelmaan 376; Edelman(n) 64, *91, 92, *194, 234, *274, 332, *345, *346; Edenborn 147; Edeborn 184; Ederle 57; Ederly 249; Edesma 56; Edgar *366; Edinger 109, 336, 362, 363; Edlinger 249; Edmond 7, 25; Eduman 292; Eerlman 206; Egart 211; Ege *123, 270, *340, 349; Egel 337, 382, *410; Egen 128, 294; Egenbrohen 174; Egener 53; Egenschweller 293; Eger 212; Egert 288, 406; Egg 98; Eggler 238; Egle 398; Eglin 377; Egnel 110; Egner 446; Egolf *174; Egy 298; Egyr 202; Ehart 249; Ehele 242; Eheller 280; Ehemann 110; Ehhalt 303; Ehley 80; Ehli 176; Ehls 357; Ehmer 398; Ehmig 417; Ehr 406; Ehrait 198; Ehrenfeichter 134; Ehrenfelter 157; Ehrenfreid 408; Ehrenhard(t) 76, 171; Ehrenstieger 191; Ehresmann 274, 369; Ehrgott 136; Ehrhard 133; Ehrhardt 324; Ehrhart 228, 293, 374; Ehrholt 124; Ehring 207; Ehrman 169, 238, *251, 265, 312, 383, 446; Eibach 278; Eich *211, 294, 358; Eichart 199; Eichede 203; Eichelberger 57, 89, 438, 468; Eichely 325; Eicher *329; Eichhart 140; Eichholtz 105, 175, *216; Eichhorn 166; Eichler *299, 332; Eickert 53; Eidenes 244; Eigel 276, *451; Eigelberger 258; Eiglebonner 121; Eiler 161; Eileshauer 118; Eilheim 242; Eill 60; Eilsheimer 350; Eilting 264; Eimann 196; Eimiger 86; Eiminghoff 310; Eindesweiler 278; Einner 293; Einsel 253; Einwaechter 401; Einzopp 359; Firheim 349; Eischberger 450; Eischby 224; Eise 50; Eiselen 417; Eiselman 74; Eisely 222; Eiseman 86; Eisenman(n) (s. Eisseman) *203, 384; Eisenbeiss 261; Eisenhardt 268; Eisenhauer (s. Isenhauer) *151, 316; Eisenhuth 324; Eisenm(a)enger 202, 252, *271; Eisnert 308; Eisseman (s. Eisenmann) *203; Eissenberger 376; Eissendal 293; Eissenhardt 264; Eissenring 398; Eissge 324; Eissinger 353; Eister 422, 426; Eiszele 241; Eitenmueller 333; Eitergall 150; Ekel 444; Elberscheidt 65; Elberstadt 436; Elch 148; Elgart 412; Elgerth 403; Elias 279; Elich 443; Elie 114; Ellenberger *135, 195; Ellenmacher 438; Eller 141, 163, 175, 178, 357, 403, 418, 419; Ellers 406; Ellig 409; Ellinger 121; Ellis *299; Elsass 377; Elser 214; Elte 301; Elter 275; Eltz 313; Ely 80; Embich 283; Embright 82; Embs *149; Emder 152; Emerson 423, 427; Emert 350; Emeyer 348; Emich 84, *85, 408; Emig *165; Emmel 322; Emmerich 279; Emmert 64, *80, 195, 279, 393; Emmiger 384; Emminger 261; Emmrich 412; Emrich 117, 195, 229, *320, 341, 368, 373, 386, 389, 446; Emy 74; Enck *161, 179, 250, 369; Enckisch 249; End 390, 435; Ende 346; Ender 449; Enderly 237; Enders 212, 330, 336; Endes 165; Endi 178; Endike 301; Endler 106; Endlich 375; Endreas 434; Endres(s) 191, 207, 291, 293, 366, 373, 379, 381; Endt *90, 174; Enes 267; Engel 10, 29, 107, 136, 142, 146, 147, 171, 172, *183, *185, *186, 210, 220, 231, 237, 275, 301, 311, 318, 336, 360, 383, 395, 405, 407, 445, 477; Engelbert(h) 263, 294, 353; Engelbret 124; Engeler 57; Engelfried 417; Engelhard(t) 134, 306, 362, 392, 475; Engelhart 238, 311; Engelhut 353; Engell 116, 328, *431, 443; Engel(l)man(n) 146, 149, 150, 267, 281; Engel-

pruck 316; Engels 324; Engelschreter 286; Engert(t) 56, 408;
Engesbach 291; Engle 472; Englehart 472; Engler 217, 218;
Englerdt 286; Englert(t) 57, 76, 235; Englest 286; Engroth
414; Enler 148; Enogel (s. Engel?) 185; Ensle 298; Enslin
416; Ensling 285; Ensminger 86, *87, 127, 128, 151, 238,
332, 436; Ent 473; Entes 187; Entiemann 257; Entzmenger
303; Enttiger 281; Entzminger 257; Epgardt 141; Eppelman
159, 196; Eppenzeller 262; Epple 110, 142; Eppler 179, 241,
281; Eppli 131; Eppling *363; Epplinger 351; Epsenhaar 334;
Epson 249; Er 56; Erand 317; Eranmach 147; Erb 100, 103,
*111, 112, 191, 198, 330, 409, 443; Erbach 169, 182; Erben
154; Erbolt 265; Erbshusser 349; Erch 215; v. Erden (siehe
v. Erdre) 147; Erdman(n) 73, *109, 249; Erdmayer 183; Erdners
308; v. Erdre (s. v. Erden) 146; Erdroth 195; Erdt 55; Erendorff 370; Erferdt 247; Erford 116; Erhar(d)t 135, *148,
*236, *261, 310, 359, 380, 466; Erich 210, 251, 283; Erick 376;
Erig (s. Ihrig) 198, 305, 410; Erisman 436; Erlegner 141;
Erlenbach 187; Erlenheiser *362; Erlewyne 66; Erling 286;
Erlinger 385; Erlwein 164; Erman 282; Ermel 151; Ermentraudt *133; Ermetraud 327; Ermich 75; Ermolt 183, 412;
Ern 173; Ernits 399; Ernold 373; Ernsperger 112; Ernst 81,
*113, *134, 145, 175, 206, 207, 249, 264, *283, 301, 361,
372, 388, 412, *450, 467; Ernstmeyer 341; Ersame 110; Ersteberger 382; Ertel 134; Erter 130; Ertinger 208; Ertz 126;
Ertzberger(in) 467, 468; Ervig 262; Esbenstein 225; Esch
164, 228, 269, 339, 404, 416; Es(c)hbach 114, 245; Eschbacher (s. Eshbagh) 111, 112, 170, 195, 196; Eschbalt 278;
E(s)chelman(n) (s. Eschleman) 56, 59, 69, *89, *196, 199,
330, 475; Eschenbach 139, 421, 425; Escher 371, 385; Eschleman (s. Eschelma[n]) 89, 437; Eschrich 313; Eser 326; Eset
466; Eshbagh (s. Eschbacher) 221; Eshwyn 267; Esich 142;
Eskusen (Escoque) *119; Eslar 449; Esler 126; Esling 143;
Eslinger 206, 225; Esman 151; Espenschied 367; Esper 332;
Espidt 218; Esping 97; Ess 448; Essig 102, *103, 151, 182,
202, 331; Essy 262; Ester 274; Esteuer 396; Estu 109; Etel-
wein 387; Etienne 372; Etimers 129; Ettel 380; Etter 100,
153, 170, 185, 233, *237, 363; Ettinger 115; Etzler 258;
Etzweiler 163; Euerling 221; Eufer (s. Eurfur) 416; Euher
379; Euhricheim 339; Eulenber (s. Albinger) 272; Euler 280;
Eulert 227; Eul(l) 392, 403; Eullmann 380; Eulman 357;
Eulon 207; Eumler 191; Eurfur (s. Eufer) 415; Eurich *373;
Eurvett 148; Eusinger 241; Evald(t) *90, 91; Evar 275; Evelandt (s. Ebeland) 76; Everhard 127; Everhart 118; Ewa 343;
Ewald 120, 194, 310; Ewers 276; Ewert 115, 155; Ewick *75;
Ewig 110, 261, 267, 380; Ewing *282, *323; Ewy 56; Exell
54; Eyb 87, 88; Eydam 179; Eyer 172, 214, *392; Eyerle
423, 427; Eyerman 232; Eygenbrod 186; Eyler 182, 346, 416;
Eyman 363; Eymeyer 266; Eyrich *229, 292, 308, 391;

Eyroh 283; Eyrt 212; Eysen 100, 102; Eysenbreit 311; Eyserloh 242; Eysperger 451; Eys(s)e(n)man 86, 177, 322; Eys(s)enmenger *252, 262; Eystelohr 215; Eyster 259, 473, 474; Eysterberg 445; Eytel 277; Ezle 81.

Faas(s) 74, *115, 241; Faber 87, 88, *113, *202, 282, *381, 382, 437; Fabin 344; Fabricius 17, 36, 360, 423, 427; Fabritzius 409; Fachler 111, 112; Fachmeyer 289; Fack 325; Fackert 168; Fa(c)kler 216, 218, 242, 354; Facquart 387; Factzedy 405; Faegelman (s. Fogelman) 249; Faegle 363; Faehr 248; Fahren *244; Fahrenkorn 407; Fahrenstock 348; Fahringer 274; Fahrion 115; Fahrismann 92; Fahrne 245; Fahss 255; Faigile 222; Faist *373; Fajon 399; Falbeystan 114; Falch 214; Falck 83, 243, 381, 443; Falckenhahn 228; Falick 210; Falkenberg 446; Falkenstein 175; Falkner 432; Fallen 283; Faller 88; Falock 308; Fanau 321; Fanner 165; Fannes 187; Fannheel 209; Fans 188; Fantler 188; Fantz 82; Fanz 193; Farckart 249; Farenthal 157; Ferne 50, 136, 205; Farni(e) (s. Farny) 97, 105, 257, 388; Farny 388; Farringer 237, 276; Farry 385; Fasel 407; Fashaus 359; Fass 186, 229, 295, 325; Fas(se)nacht *210, 227; Faulstick 330; Faure 7, 25; Faus 369; Fausser 321; Faust *87, *133, *155, 156, 170, 183, 229, 355, 366; Fauth 397, 419; Fauts *472; Fautz 239, 325; Fautzer 325; Favon (s. Favian) 84; Favian (s. Favon) 83; Fayerbach 171; Fays 314; Fazler 312; Feber (le Fever) 440, 442; Feber (s. Fuehre); La Febre 6, 25; Fecher 370; Fechty 400; Feck 315, 375; Fecks 214; Fedel 211; Feder 66; Federhoff 239, 305; Federolff 63; Feeler 192; Feelt 114; Feemhaber 309; Feerer 176; Feg 467; Fege 120; Fegely *86, *89; Feger 139, 353; Fegert 259; Feglin 101; Fehl 119; Fehler 128; Fehling 448; Fehr 131, 207; Fehring 365; Feichtner 284; Feick 252; Feickert 362; Feierbrand 404; Feierstein 311; Feig 407; Feigner 318; Feiler 296; Feillem 244; Feilter 53; Feiner 338; Feinruer 328; Feiock 358; Feiring 416; Feister 293; Feitmeyer 400; Feitne 384; Feitter 321; Feitz 285; Felbach 396; Felbaum *164; Felber 247; Felder 296; Feldmayer 178; Feler 77; Felden 137; Felger 317; Felix 342, *387; Felker 78; Fell 17, 36, 284; Felle 175; Fellenberger 202; Fellentzer 303; Feller 304; Fellman(n) 101, 364; Felsinger 120; Feltberger 159; Felte 124, 185; Felten 444; Feltman(n) 143, 247; Felty 230, 379; Feltz 275; Fendig 207; Fengel 201; Fennima 55; Fens 273; Fenstenmacher 106; Fenstermacher (s. Finstermacher) *116; Fenttinger 470; Fentz 389; Feppel 210; Fer 176; Ferber 171, 237, *255, 391; Ferdig 183, 335, 388; Ferdinandt 162; Feree (s. Führe); Fernsler 58, 110; Ferr 475; Ferre 343; Ferrer 298; Ferschbach 271; Ferster 221, 239; Fertig 292, 334; Fertinbach 307; Feruser 50; Fesbely 229; Fesel 334; Fessingen (s. Fissnand) 71; Fessler 86, *300, *375, 414; Feter 356; Fetter *59, 125, 364; Fetterley 139; Fetterling 293;

Fet—Fon

Fetzer 225, 244, 252, 253, *273, 354; Feuerbohnen 288; Feuerstein 227, 321; le Fever (s. Feber); La Fevre (s. Fuehre); Fey 80, 140, 164, 211, 259, 347; Feyl 321, 323; Feyler 207; Feyly 284; Feyzer 169; Ffister 162; Fflanders *464; Ffurtye 464; Ficcus (Fickus) *113; Fichgus 160; Fichker 159; Fichler 401; Fichter 398; Fichthelm 143; Fick 119, 232; Ficke 348; Fickel 97; Ficus 59; Fide 55; Fidler (Fitler) 179, 230, 447, 448; Fiebersbach 444; Fiedler 337, 341; Fiehl *170; Fiehlt 170; Fiehman 62, 149; Fieng 297; Fieohr 70; Fiere (s. Fuehre); Fiero 440, 442; Fiersler 61; Fiess 245; Fiesser 375; Fiett 176; Fig 109; Fihr 212; Fihs 310; Fihter 418; Filbert 105; Filger 396; Filler (s. Foeller) 54, 240, 438; Fillibich 344; Fillibs 314; Fillinger 115; Fillkeysinger 50; Films 403; Fincher 18, 36; Finck 105, *207, 237, 340, *349, 366, 403, 447; Fincky 163; Finderer 217; Finfleher 312; Finger 195; Fink 359, 438; Finniger 358; Finslaimer 289; Finstermacher (s. Fenstermacher) 116; Fintzel 292, 293; Fircus 170; Firer 370; Firnhaber *410; Fisar 248; Fischbach 97, 136, 147, 314; Fischborn *169, 170; Fis(c)hel *154; Fischer 65, 73, 79, *86, 91, 103, 107, 113, 116, 132, *141, *163, 166, 176, 194, 200, 205, *213, 217, 218, *220, 221, 223, 231, *237, 253, 256, 264, 273, 276, 277, 281, 282, 295, 297, 299, *301, 303, 311, 312, 324, *327, 335, 344, 347, *350, 352, 353, 358, 359, 361, 364, 370, 377, 381, 386, 393, 400, 406, 410, 427, 440, 442, 447, 448, 465, *466, 474, 475; Fiser 62, 74, 141; Fishahason 146; Fisher 54, 65, 70, 135, 193, *213, 220, 237, 244, 264, *266, 291, 304, 376, 413, 422; Fissel 154; Fisser 228, 269; Fissler 77, *289; Fissnand (s. Fessingen, Visanant) 71; Fisterer 404; Fiteler 467; Fitheim 113; Fitincher 416; Fitler (s. Fidler) 465; Fitrius 379; Fitterer 160; Fitting 286, 401; Fitz 224; Fixe 226; Flach 209, 247, 410; Flachs 337; Flak 177; Flamerfeld 97; Flanckenhardt 354; Fleck 125, 129, 254, 304, 320, 397; Fleckser 103; Fleckstein 275, 359; Flehmann 381; Fleischer 189, 293, 294, 308; Fleischman(n) 216, 254; Fleiser 72; Fleisher 246; Fleisser 328; Fleit 290, 400; Flender 316; Fletiger 129; Fletter 334; Fleur *247; Fleury 81; Flick *260, 309, 355, 373, 390; Flickiner 86; Flickinger 303; Flickwir 402; Fliegel 125; Fliesbach 312; Flinner 347; Flisterer 311; Flock 296; Floerel 450, 451; Flohri *347; Florans 136; Florer 136; Florig 172; Flour 227; Flournoy 7, 25; Flubacher 191, 399; Flueck 170; Flückiger 61; Flug(h) 170, 227; Flure *88; Flyder 405; Focht 377; Foehl 207; Foelix 249; Foelker 234; Foell 212; Foeller (s. Filler) 240, 447; Foerch 118, 342; Foerg 321; Foerster 171, 210, 322; Foesig 332; Foess 178; Fogelmann (s. Faegelman) 249; Fohl 155, 162; Fohme 288; Fohrman 385; Folber 146; Folberg 140; Fol(c)k (s. Volck) 194, 216, *269; Foll 307; Folmer 161, 281, 303; Folock 55; Fols 146; Foltz 183, 224, 303, 397, 447; Fondenie 331;

Fon—Fri

Fonderburgh 122; Fonn 200; Fonnedus 328; Fooks *237; Fo(o)st *168; Forbringer 236; Ford 64; Fordene (s. Fortineh) *105; Forne 469; Fornwald 475; Forqueran 7, 25: Forrer 55, 329, 469; Forsch 314; Forschberge 220; Forst 98; Forster 172, 188, 294, 318, 332, *363; Fortenbacher 296; Fortine(h) (s. Fordene) 105, 151; Fortineaux 63; Fortinnix 154; Fortney 137; Forttmeier 310; Fortuny 468; Fossbendler 161; Foth 251; Foulquier 328; Fraatsrach 350; Fraemdling 358; Fraetz 173; Francisculur 311; Franciscus 436; Franck 71, 82, 92, 101, *136, 158, 181, 196, *197, 234, 247, 248, 293, 300, 326, *341, 342, 347, *357, 365, 392, *393, 401, 406, 409, 446; Fran(c)ke(n)berger 101, 102, 269; Franckerfeld 270, 271; Franckforther 401; Franckfuerter 335; Franckfurther 182; Fran(c)khauser 56, 245; Franger 213; Frank 74, 122, 248, 432; Franke 422, 426; Frankenfelt 190; Frankfelder 132; Franklyn 67, 68; Frans 53; Frantz 18, 36, 52, *72, 73, 104, 105, 109, 110, 118, 128, *137, 141, 142, 180, *181, 185, 195, 236, 248, 258, 270, 310, 317, 337, 342, *366, 370, 375, *391, 472; Frarry 236; Frasch 241; Frauenfelder 312, 384; Frawiener 63; Frazer *104, 392; Frech 263; Fredcrick 50, 115, 293, *464; Fredrick 110; Free 139; Freeman(n) 67, 132; Fregele 319; Freher 312; Freibuerger 364; Freidel 96; Freilich (s. Froelich?) 287, 298; Freind 355; Freir 6, 25; Freisinger 337; Freitag 122, 250; Freitenberger 339; Frelich 128; Fremauer 189; Frembes 298; Freneir 131; Frentier 350; Fretter 206; Fretz 291; Freueller 121; Freund 300, 317, 371; Freundt 356; Frevel 168; Frey 49, 68, 70, 76, 77, 85, *85, *86, 90, 91, *96, 98, 99, 117, *118, 125, 139, *154, 162, 165, 180, 195, 212, 233, 234, 243, 244, 261, 262, 271, 276, 288, 290, 300, 301, 303, *329, 332, 337, *372, 373, 375, 376, 389, 398, *399, 406, 432, 469, 471, 472, 474, 476, *477; Freyberg 301, 339; Freyberger 337, 359, 360; Freydinger 112; Freyer *391, 474; Freyhofer 159; Freyling 123, 338; Freymann 175; Freymiller *208; Freymu 402; Freysh 234; Freysinger 215; Freys(s) 133, 145; Freytag 373, 412, *417; Frich 330; Frick 74, 91, *139, 246, *251, 268, 290, *358, 379, 380, 387, 408, 415; Fricker 231; Frickheffer *403; Fridler 406; Fridli 266; Fridrich 255; Fridtel 136; Friebele 233; Fried 233, 273, 277, 434, *475, 476, 477; Friedburg 156; Friederich 81, *110, *118, 119, 123, 213, 273, 278, 306, 322, 372, 416, 437, 443, 446; Friederichs 318; Friederick 107, 472; Friedland 257; Friedle 69, *70, 75, 251, 252, 267; Friedler 51; Friedly 92; Friedrich 99, 102, 251; Friedt 176; Frieh 162; Friehruff 355; Friehs (s. Fruehs) 385; Frier 54; Fries(s) 86, 108, *121, 122, 188, 213, 226, 256, *266, 285, 292, 296, 313, 335, 336, 339, 366, 385, 423, 427; Friessner 233; Frietsch 364; Frietz 344, 371, 372; Frietzel 389; Frih 56; Frill 477; Frioth 297; Frischkorn 291, 355; Frischmuth 374; Frischtze 407; Frison

517

236; Frit(h) 72, 261; Fritlauf 289; Fritley 54; Fritsch 108, 422, 426, 423, 427; Fritsche 423, 427; Fritz 49, 51, 129, *140, 182, 202, 224, 264, 265, *269, 289, 326, 331, 389; Fritze 399; Fritzinger 402, 403; Fritzius 346; Froch(e) 84; Froeli 130; Frö(h)lich 59, 106, 144, 291, 297, 378, 421, 425, 446; Froelig 385; Froely 231; From(m) 105, 139, 283; Fronheuser 347; Fronkhousen 166; Froschauer 81; Frost 415; Frot *470; Frounwalder 167; Frueh *102; Fruehs (s. Friehs) 384, 385; Fruetschie 197; Fruetz 384; Fruteer 463; Fruttye 464; Fryer 389; Fuchs 52, 57, 77, 101, 132, *140, 144, 156, 160, 163, 166, 169, 170, 178, 179, 182, 189, 193, 196, 200, 211, 217, 224, *230, 245, *252, 263, 269, 274, 281, *309, 325, 364, *368, 381, 383, 389, 397, 406, 410, *412, 415, 444, 447, 472; Fuechthorn 164; Fueckes 378; Fuehr 154, 232; Fuehre (Feree, Fiere, Feber, La Fevre) 8, 27; Fuehrer *336; Fuehrling 314; Fuenfrock 246, *391; Fuerber 263; Fuerer 131; Fuerst 413, 414; Fuerster *247; Fuerstner 215; Fuescher 409; Fuesel 126; Fuesselbach 399; Fuetsch 416; Fuetter 380; Fughs 171; Fugnicht 301; Fuhrman(n) 112, 358, 363, 471; Fuhrsbach 366; Fulker 77; Fulleweiler 351; Fullman 361; Fullmer 179; Fulmer (s. Vollmer) 123; Fultz 52; Funck 92, 93, 109, 111, 118, 146, 147, 175, 176, 178, 196, 197, 226, 231, *245, 255, 270, 326, 358, 372, *399, 403, *436; Funk 52, 150, 435, 472, 473, 477; Furbi 392; Fur(ch)tig *157; Furkill 80; Furman(n) *151, 192, 396; Furny 180; Furrer 243, 244; Furster 51; Furtuly 154; Fuse 144, 415; Fus(s) 67, 315, 320, 321; Fussbec 281; Fusser 381; Fussweg 343; Futerman 365.

Gaab 269; Gaar 79, 80; Gabel 121, *133, 274, 302, 304, 335, 405, 444; Gabele 76; Gaberd 147; Gabori 396; Gabriel 295, 372, 388; Gach (s. Gack) 333; Gachon 287; Gack (s. Gach) *333; Gackenbach 166; Gackly 290; Gadecke 406; Gaedschalk 472, 477; Gaelle 365; Gaensel 358; Gaensle 163, 164; Gaenssel 353; Gaenssle 382; Gaerdner 102; Gaerniger 117; Gaerthner 391; Gaertner 166, 180, 182, 294, 449; Gaess 281; Gaettman 365; Gaetzinger 194; Gaey 381; Gaijdon 354; Galete 444; Gall 207, 277, 299; Gallater 225; Galle 357; Galler 61, 131, 189; Gallman(n) *197, 214, 268; Galloe 385; Gally 249, 252, 253; Galte 401; Gam 79; Gamb 388; Gambach *159; Gamber 83, 230, *234; Gambert 220; Gamooroon 86; Gampffer 370; Gamssendahl 377; Gander *79, 347; Ganderman 168; Gandner 216; Ganger *103; Gangwyer 52; Gan(n)s(s) (s. Cantz) *234, *239, 267, 272, 325; Ganser 472; Ganshon 343; Ganshorn 234; Gansle 192; Gantermann 446; Ganther 230; Gantler 185; Gantner 282; Ganty 142; Gantz 132, 361, 416, 477; Ganz 325; Garaus 359; Gardert 327; Gardner 91, 291; Garein 281; Garner 68, 196; Garrecht 292; Garrien 464; Garste 410; Garster 191; Gartnner 371;

man 297; Gartner 295; Gartom 220; Gascha 198, 394; Gaser
356; Gash (s. Gass); Gasner 71; Gasper 2, 7, 20, 25, 430;
Gass (s. Gash) *51, 143, 186, 191, 192, 245, 287, 288, 358;
Gasser 81, 90, *91, 190, 289, *326; Gasserd 145; Gassinger
248; Gassler 214, 226; Gassman(n) 131, 245, 371, 372; Gassner 163; Gast 192, *349; Gastlied 371; Gastner 162; Gatian
445; Gattermyer 17, 36; Gattung 291; Gatz *352; Gaucher
467; Gauer 164; Gauff 74, 148; Gauffs 211; Gaul(l) *88,
162, 182, 369, 391, *393, 395; Gausfres 123; Gauss 241,
242; Gautier 304; Gavin 7, 25; Gay 369; Gayer *306;
Gebberdt 361; Gebel 337; Geber *68, 70; Gebert(h) 66, *67,
300; Gebhard(t) 146, 280, 332, 356, 466, 467; Gebhart 116,
180, 190, *210, 219, 272, 277, 331, 334, 341, 347; Geck 84,
409; Gedelo 219; Geeber 204; Geebs 184; Geenar 464;
Gees 236; Geesseler 266; Geest 147; Gehemann 253; Gehr
67, 221, 275, 340, 400; Gehrich 247; Gehringer 264; Geib
132, 180, 403; Geidlinger 219; Geier 104; Geigenberger 217;
Geiger 17, 36, 83, 105, 111, 112, 118, 134, 155, *164, 189,
*221, 247, 251, *253, 296, 297, 321, 342, 362, 370, 393,
394, 473, 474; Geigle 264; Geil 347; Geiler 296; Geimmer
*336; Geiner 248; Geis 202, 263, 264, 311; Geisel 331;
Geiser 156; Geisinger 194, 198, 435; Geisler 267, 297, 340;
Geiss 106, *261, 285, 368, 380; Geisse 402; Geissel 120;
Geisselmann 122; Geisser 266; Geissert 244; Geissinger 412;
Geissler 292, 325, 402, 447; Geist 140, 210, 329; Geistweit
260, 413; Geitling 376; Gelbach *198; Gelberee 229; Gelbert
468; Geldt 303; Gelehren 69; Gelessener 375; Gelinder *306;
Gelisen *219; Gell 147, 149; Geller 154; Gelli 391; Gelsendorf 115; Geltbach 109; Geltz 235; Gemberlin 135; Gemberling *332, *369; Gembler *194, 218; Gembold 422, 426;
Gemling 100; Gemmer 200; Gemser 273; Genberger 127;
Genest 449; Geney 310; Gennett 410; Gensemer 123; Gensheimer 279; Gensle 115; Gensly 270; Gensman 89; Genter
408; Genther 76; Gentzheimann 413; Georg 50, 72, 116,
180, 224, 225, 229, 286, 317, 331, 341, 355, 365, 368,
403, 447, 474; George 317, 370; Georgey 259; Georjan 265;
Geradewohl 208; Gerahn 139; Gerang 301; Gerber 89, 97,
101, *111, 129, 156, 166, 194, 211, *238, 254, *305, 313,
368; Gerberich 334; Gerbrich 252, 253, 293; Gerckenhauser
86; Gerdheir 146; Gerding 402; Gerdner 233; Gerem 404;
Gerent 364; Geres 133, 138; Gerg 194; Gergerich 274;
Gerges 148; Gerham 64; Gerhard(t) 72, *132, 147, 181, 271,
278, 286, 355, 356, 358, 361, 387, 411; Gerhart 17, 36, 101, 117,
142, 155, 229, 250, 258, 260, 278, 304, *335, 360, 386; Geri
135; Gerig 257, 274; Gering 289; Geringer 342, 343; Geris
*157; Gerizeh 242; Gerlach 72, 222, 228, 319, 322, 330, 336,
443, 446; Gerlart 236; Gerligh 180; Gerling 108, 258; Gerlinger 408; German *72, 145, 174, 177, 179, 194, 195, 229,

256, 398, 432, 472; Germerjung 154; Gern 128, 353; Gernandt 109, 172; Gernardt 371; Gernaut 221; Gerndt 196; Gerner 234, *235, 346; Gernet 363; Gerra 175; Gerret 203; Gerringer 56, 249; Gerro 175; Gerry 135; Gers 121; Gerst 150, 213, *224, 386, 391; Gerstenmayer 306; Gersterkorn 319; Gerster 103, 188; Gersto 385; Gerth 115; Gerttner 57; Gertz *227; Gertzinger 268; Gerwig 305; Gesel(l) 52, 77, 99, 113, 162, 171, 415; Geseller 110; Gesibel 449; Gesler 119; Gess 173, 387; Gessel 200; Gesseler *315; Gessner 207, 261; Gestner 186; Getinbaur 343; Gett 113; Gettling 239; Gettner 260; Getts 84; Getz 192, 194, 289; Getzelman 314; Getzendonner 472; Geused 225; Geyer 106, 169, *190, *210, 211, 246, 257, 275, 312, 327, 340, 345, 375, 412; Geyger 67; Geyler *274; Geyman 335; Geysel *331; Gibbo 176; Gibler 207, 292; Gickert 374; Giebel 331; Giebeler 239; Giebelhauss 384; Giebler 248; Giedelmann 371; Gieg *334; Gielberth 356, 376; Gielman 336; Giersbach 259; Gies 260; Giesberg *353; Giesie 191; Gi(e)s(s)e *71, 149; Giessler 144, 317, 322; Giesy 148; Gihl 366; Gil 354; Gilbert (s. Guelberth) 75, *165, 215, 216, *239, 248, *296, 329; Gild 158; Gildner 117, 340; Gill *383, *412, *415; Giller 72; Gillinger 79, 165; Gillion(a) 115, 298; Gil(l)man(n) 149, 285; Gimpel 295; Gimper 319; Ginaehle 370; Ginder 176, *203; Gingenhan 297, 298; Ginger 356; Ginter 194, 278; Ginterman 254; Ginther 394; Gintner 216; Gippel 387; Gir 161; Girstohber 286; Gisch 90; Giss 74; Gist 109; Gistelbarth 247; Gisterer 281; Gitt *359; Gittelman 159; Gittin 297; Gitting 239; Givodan 7, 25; Gladman *152; Glaeffer 245; Glaekler 382; Glaesser 199; Glaessner 353; Glaezer 387; Glaner 451; Glantz *79, 395; Glasbrenner 73, 83; Glaser 105, 122; Glass 90, 233,ı 285, 367; Glassbrenner 229; Glasser 57, 207, 239, *321, 365; Glassler 291; Glattly (s. Clatley) *131; Glaufliegel 417; Gleding 372; Glee 337; Gleh 375; Glehas 232; Gleim 66, 86, 87,ı 190, 347, 384; Gleis 85; Gleissinger 259; Gless 367; Glesser 138; Gleysler 276; Glick 186, 207; Glimpff 348; Glisser 198; Glocker *451; Gloekil 276; Glohser 241; Gloninger 154; Gloss 209; Glotz 382; Glueck 219, 344, 362, 381; Glug 146; Gmelin 434; Gnaerr 281; Gnaeschler 414; Gnaessle 248; la Gneau 347; Gniser 187; Gob 249; Gobat 323; Gobel(l) *89, 175, 239, 296, 382; Gobrecht *301; Gochnat 267; Gochnauer 72; Gock 314; Godfried 149; Godschalk 174; Goebe 120, 189; Goebel 314, 319; Goebeler 200; Göbel(l) 80, 197, 338; Goebler 259; Goebrich 406; Goebss 377; Goedeke 73; Goedschalk 430; Goedtel 211; Goehler 380; Goehnet 407; Goehr 186ı; Goehringer 303; Goelb 235; Goeltmann 388; Goenner 215; Goer 164; Goeress 276; Goerges 225; Goerich 76; Goertlerr 378; Goertl(e)er 295, 322; Goesel 267; Goesper 333; Goess 344; Goeth 261; G(o)et(h)er *187;

Goetschy *99; Goettel *93, *358, 359, 447; Goettert 416; Goettge 422, 427; Goettgen 334; Goettges 254; Goettle 290; Goettlich *143; Goettman(n) 261, 410; Goetz 91, 111, 169, 268, *316, 347, 352, 362, 363, 375, 377, 384, 385, *410, 419; Goetzelman 293; Gohl *291; Goin 7, 25; Golb 367; Gold 423, 427; Golde 307, *397; Goldenberger 125; Goldman(n) 448, 467, 469; Goldner 166; Golhell 295; Golkowsky 423, 427; Gollstaed 301; Goltir 353; Gomer *106; Gompff 324; Gonder 310; Gondermann 17, 36, 232, 260; von Gondie 17, 36; Gonger 50; Gontler 190; Good 158, 164, *312; Goodbrood 66; Goodman *118, *134, *143, 162, *202; Goodner 289; Goonner 256; Goos 201; Gordan 342; Gordner 90; Gordon *469; Gorgas 431, 473; Gorgi 380; Gorm 195; Gorsch 381; Gorshbotte 327; Gosner 192; Goss 274; Gossinger 443; Gossler 182, 190; Gossweiller 209; Got 323; Gotter 172; Gottfried 119, 416; Gottman 406; Gottschalck 142, 156, 240, 274; Gottschalk 423, 427; Gottschall 180, 371; Gottwalt 262, 270; Gottwals 121, 133; Gotz 90; Goub 176; Gouche 385; Gourdain 405; Govan *188; Gouriie 304; Gra 317; Graaf 338, 472, 475; Graaf (später Grove) 433; Grabeman 239; Graber 194, 210; Graberth 378; Grabs 422, 426; Grabsteinbrenner 359; Grack *240; Grad 305; Graeber 171, 312, 410, 473; Graeff 49, 150, 154, *255, 320, 396; op den Graeff *430; Graeffenstein 291, 347; Graeim 371; Graell 211; Graessel 380; Graessler 295; Graetsch 219; Graetz 259; Graeuttler 268; Graf *222, 245, 309, *466, *467; Graff (s. Groff) *57; 64, 74, 82, 97, 102, 103, *107, 110, 134, 172, 173, 182, 195, 210, 224, 258, 266, 280, 298, 310, 329, 342, 351, 355, *357, *360, *384, 401, 412, 413, 436, *438, 439; Graffenberger 407; de Graffenried 3, 21, 455—460; Graffhos 222; Grahn 397; Grall 419; Gram 401; Gramer 401; Grames 410; Gramlich *206, 248, 271, 274, 278, 374; Gramly 206, 307; Gram(m) 263, 369, 379, *393; Gramp 89; Gramwetter 451; Gran 249, 361; Granable 161; Granatha 449; Grandadam (Grantadam) *204; Graner 119; de Grange 205; Granget 123, 382; Graninger 260; Grantz 333; Grantzer 143; Grass 283; Grassel 342; Grassert 170; Gratt (s. Creat?) 204; Gratze 205; Grau 148, 315, 328, 444, 466; Graub 373; Grauberger 444, 448; Grauel(l) 87, 126, 142, 209, 253; Grauer 194; Graul 101; Graulich 333; Graushar *290; Grauss 266, 297, 333, 415; Grawan *419; Grawius 79; Gray *81, *373; Greast 368; Greb *213, *316; Greber 126, 177, 192, 231; Greberger 204; Grebiel *357; Grebihl 366; Grebil 364; Greebel 317; Green 143; Greenblat *192; Greenemeyer 180; Greenewald 254; Greening 422, 427; Gref 306; Greffenstein 300; Greib 91; Grei(d)er *102, 103, 130, 192; Greier (s. Grei[d]er); Greim *246; Grein 408; Greiner *83, 241, 268, *391, 445; Greiser 118; Greisler 443; Greiss 199, 200, *260, 325, 410; Greissell 387;

Greiter 224; Grell 261, 266; Grem 217; Grendel 188; Gresel 343; Gress (s. Kress) 150, 179, 180, 338, 363, 369; Gresser 170; Gressmann 260; Gressmehr 404; Gretter 249; Greulich 162; Greuther 375; Grevener 127; Gribel 161; Gribeler (s. Griebel); Grieb 209; Griebel (Gribeler) *206; Griebela 418; Grieben 354; Griech 284; Griedler 325; Grieg 296, 349; Grieger 139, 204; Griell 396; Griene 323; Griese 275; Griesemer 66; Grieser 237; Griesinger 86; Griesman 471; Griess 221, 283; Griessemann 217; Grietzinger *269; Griffe 80; Grim 306; Grimb 230; Grimler 335; Grim(m) (s. Krimm) 58, 91, 101, 102, 107, 112, 121, 143, *151, 237, 252, 287, 295, *331, 338, 357, 362, 370; Grimmiger 450; Grin 352; Grindelmeyer 307; Grindler 225; Gring 162, *259; Grininger 310; Grisemer 62; Grisse 206; Grissinger 376; Grist 121; Gro 142; Grob (s. Grop) 128, 139, 155, 158, *171, 229, 356, 358, 387; Grobler 295; Groeber 374; Groebil 305; Groell 373; Groener 409; Groeninger 146, 469; Groether 216; Groetz 122; Groff (s. Graff) 58, *191, *224; Groh 160, 179, 221, 224, 233; Grohmann 106; Groll 189; Groller 107; Grombeer 338; Gromlich 314; Grommel 388; Gronau 14, 32, 449; Grondt 91; Gronninger *369; Gronsaum 91; Grop (s. Grob) 139; Gropff 277; Grosch 160; Groscost 62; Grosh 356; Grosmuck 190; Grosnickel 176; Gross *78, *97, 101, 111, 112, *151, 156, 161, 178, 190, 193, 203, 204, 222, 237, 245, 248, 271, 272, *276, *285, *287, 288, 290, 291, 299, 305, 322, *347, 364, 368, 373, 475; Grossclaus 314; Grossert 160; Grossglass 358; Grosshard 379; Grosshart 397; Grosskopff 160, 248; Grossman 216; Groundler 245; Grotheim 301; Grove (s. Graaf) 183, *290; de Grove *215; Grow 221; Grub 116, 119, 132, 154, 280, 313, *320, 335; Grube *118; Gruber 82, 93, 94, 144, 199, *200, 261, 300, 342, 410, *411, 449, *467, 473; Gruck 366; Grueb 393; Gruebe 405; Gruebel 170; Gruell 101; Gruellmann 177; Gruemmet *295; Gruen 124, 154, 213, 287, 317, 385, 397; Gruenau 313; Gruendell 221; Gruenenwald(t) 395, 397; Gruenewald 334; Grund 338; Grundloch 333; Grundrum 320; Gruene(n)wal(d)t 175, 205, 217; Gruener 266; Gruenewald 374; Gruenwald 176; Gruenzweig 217; Grull 195; Grumbach 166, *221, 372; Grumbacher 88; Grumm 191, 379, 449; Gruntzge 384; Grusius 202; Grus(s) 341, 474; Grydelbach 206; Gryffing 208; Gschwandel 450; Guck 395; Guckel 240; Gucker 67, *157, 416; Guckert 133; Guckes 117; Guebeller 371; Guebler 193, 197; Guebrit 201; Guecker *162; Guedtner 385; Guefi 80; Guehtt 330; Guelberth (s. Gilbert) 296; Guelch 439, 440, 441, 442; Guelcher 362; Guellam 166; Guender 240, 295; Guendner 289; Guenter 185, 295, 468; Guenther *122, 342, 348, 353, 375, 386; Guentlert 395; Guentzler 381; Guerthner 328; Guertz 306; Guetchrel 377; Guething 206, 413; Guetinger 158; Guetsell 326; Guett 388; Guettenberg 357; Guetting 276; Guetzinger 197; Gugerle 119; Gugesk 181; Guille (s. Duille?)

323; Guillons 298; Guion *464; Guit 416; Guite 375; Guitelman 348; Gulde 192; Gulden 436; Guldin 17, 36, *435, 475; Gulich 377; Gullmann 103; Gum 80; v. Gumden 205; Gumeringer 291; Gumpp 76; Gun(c)kel 121, 211, 299, 409; Gundacker 147; Gunde 60; Gundel 351; Gundelfinger 244; Gunderbusch 342; Gunderman 232; Gundery 396; Gun(d)t 68, 69, 70; Gunkel 468; Gunst 75, 225; Gunstenhauser 191; Güntzerhausser 238; Gurdner 238; Gurlach 84; Gurtz 57; Gusman 251; Gustav 225; Gut *52, 72, 98; Gutbrod 66; Gutdaender 362; Gutekunst 376; Gutelius 239; Gut(h) *52, 116, 134, 155, 178, 256, 274, *288, 301, *302, 335, 343, 370, 411, 437, 438; Guthard 105; Gut(h)man(n) 130, 161, 162, 165, 226; Gutjahr 299; Gutknecht 199, 284; Gutt 63, 121; Gutting 393; Guttinger 231; Guyion *464; Gyer 50, 298; Gyser *127; Gysler 128.

Haag 134, 196, 256, 290, 293, 323, 335, 356; Haaga 382; Haak 290, 468; Haake 476; Haalling 103; Haan 112, 195, 245; Haanelam 322; Haar 193, 393; Haartz *171; Haase 247; Haas(s) 104, 114, 142, 150, 187, 190, 222, 229, 274, 282, 289, 314, 324, 331, *335, 337, 342, 343, 350, 351, *356, 385, 393, *409; Haasse 397; Ha(a)ss(e)-ler *231; Habach 409; Habacker 122; Habeger (s. Hapeger) 111; Habel 418; Haber 213, 237, 254, 289; Haberacker 49; Haberecht 421, 425; Haberer *451; Haberland 423, 427; Haberling 238; Haberly 213, 304; Haberman 237; Habermehl 210; Habersod 160; Haberstich *284; Haberstick 238; Haberstueck 151; Habgehes 246; Habicht 295; Habinger 187; Habluetzel 382; Habner 407; Habtuezel 356; Hach 219; Hachenberg 366; Hachman 68; Hack 56, 136; Hacke 178; Hackeler 256; Hackenbach 362; Hackensmitt 134; Hacker 162, 214; Hacket 357; Hackir 257; Hackman(n) 101, *196, 198, 305, 329, 352; Had 415; Hadorn 141; Hadt 322, 410; Haeberlin 216; H(a)eckman(n) 157, 186, 194, 223, *274, 300, 346, 374; Haeffer 169, *361; Haeffner 207; Haege 51; Haegele 263; Haeger 448; Haehn 375; Haelle 148; Haeltz 198; Haeman 269; Haemer 308; H(a)en *287; Haendsche 18, 36; Haengaerten 314; Haenner 287, 352, 353, 382; Haenrich 87; Haensell 133; Haeny 219; Haerdel 294; Haerfstenbach 169; Haermann 384; Haershy 162; Haerther 203; Haesser 337, 349; Haetzel 290; Haeuffrer 369; Haeuser 375; Haeusser 324, 341, 354, 363; Haeussler 222, 278, 389, 417; Haeut 172; Haeyden 71; Haeydt 273; Haeyer 253, 273; Hafer 226; Haffelee 113; Haffer 199, 218, 228, 260, 409; Hafferstock 370; Haffner 206, 213, 227, 228, 252, 285, 290, 325, 362, 364; Hafner 423, 427, 467; Haftentraeger 364; Hag *183, 262, 296; Haga 314; Hage 17, 36, 275, 322, 375, 475; Hagea *83; Hagedorn *447; Hagelberg 295; Hagelgans 284; Hageman 472; Hagen 246, 421, 425; Hagenbach 362; Hagenbuch 112, 267; Hagert 211; Hagey 438; Hagg 79; Hagher 373; Hagman 54; Hagner 187, 283; Hagy 341; Haher 374; Hahn 66, *133, 135, 170, *174, 188, 222, 243, 255, 262, 267,

268, 315, 328, 346, 351; Hahns 271; Hai 163; Haible 172; Haigy 436; Haillman 101; Haimes 124; Hain 288, 333; Hainman 182; Haipser 311; Haisch 193; Haitberger *282; Hake 417; Halber 155; Halberstadt 302; Halbon 405; Haldeman 54, 477; Halder 59; Haldriter 148, *149; Haledii 137; Halewyn 402; Halftzmer 125; Hall 65, *177, 262, 405; Hallenbach 474; Haller 86, 87, *163, 181, 187, 231, 285, 289, 298, 310, 325, 345, 375; Hallifas 226; Hallitschke 414; Hallman 475; Halm 224, 362, 368; Halman 435; Halshaus 69; Halster 308; Halt 316; v. Halt 398; Halte 195; Halteman 283; Haltemeyer *293; Halter 118; Haltsbieller 56; Ham 232, 279, 302, *346; Hambach 232, 381, 447; Hamberg 283; Hambrecht *126; Hambro 229; Hamburgeis 227; Hame 201; Hamels 216; Hamen 224; Hamer 195; Hamerich *71; Hamilton *444; Ham(m) 184, *208, 375, 406, 413; Hamma 62; Hammacher *141; Hamman 150, 198, 201, 316, 400, 401; Hammel 66, 219; Hammer 61, 93, 159, 179, *183, 210, 219, 247, 256, 275, 355, 410, 447; Hammerer 391; Hammerschmit 306; Hammerstein 331; Hammet 384; Hammeter 309; Hampe 407; Hamscher 189, 295, 302, 404; Hamstein 303; Han 189, 203, 380; Hanck 155; Hancker 291; Hanckstein 146; Hand 173, 249, 293; Handeise 149; Handel 414; Handschuh *183; Handshy 191, 230; Handt 327; Handtwerch 102; Handwerck (Hant-) *138; Handwercker 164; Hanengrath 343; Haner 200, 343; Hanet 143; Hanfwerck 218; Hang 263, 277; Hangerer 143; Hanhor 395; Hanick 276; Hanke *422, 426, 427; Hanmueller *370; Han(n) *66, 106, 112, 171, 303, 314, 315, 397; Hannar 76; Hannecker 123; Hanner 362; Hannewald (Hannewalt) 100, 122; Hannold 264; Hanroth 143; Hans 142, 419; Hansberger 55; Hanslay 131; Hanst 251; Hant 161; Hantsch 422, 426; Hantz 411; Hantzel 366; Hap 183; Hapeger (s. Habeger) 111; Hapon 431; Happel 80, 367; Happener 314; Happes 266; Harbach VI, VIII, 401; Harbarger 367; Harberger 217; Hard 320; Hardel 447; Hardi *417; Harding 422, 427; Hardmann 403; Hardt 150, *160, 165, 189, 387; Hard(t)man(n) 254, 273, 362; Hardtner 153; Hardtstang 316; Hardy *380; Harfer 284; Harff 338, 339; Harger 52; Hargesheimer 202; Hargrave *82; Harhaussen 141; Harindus 304; Harlacher 53, 92, 127, 281; Harloff 294; Harm 407; Harmoff 309; Harmonie 218; Harn 392; Harneist 231; Harner 159; Harlas 115; Harle *100; Harn 362; Harnisch 78; Harnish 437; Harriger 287; Harris 365; Harrison *131; Harsch 272; Harst 146, 307; Harstlich 78; Hart 206, 289, 361; de Hart *471; Hartenstein 140; Harter 157, 311; Harth 180, 399; Hartig 412; Hartin 421, 426; Hartkopff 406; Hartlieb 212; Hartman(n) 17, 36, 49, 63, 72, 73, 75, 117, 123, 142, 154, 165, 169, *182, 188, 202, 205, 206, *212, 215, 229, 240, 259, 266, *284, 290, *303, 304, 312, 314, 318, 326, 334, 340, 346, *359, 368, 377, 378. 380, *386, 393, 399, 403,

405, *410, 411, 412, 413, *438, 469, 475; Hartmeyer 371; Hartsoc 107; Hartt 157; Hart(t)ing 210, 240, 272; Harttoffel 174; Harttung 370; Hartung 212; Hartweg 139; Hartwich 210; Hartwieg 336; Hartwig 444; Hartzel 245; Hartzfelder 432; Harwich 75, *76; Harz 264; Hasbach 339; Hasber 225; Hasbirch 362; Hasbroucq (Hasbrouck) 6, 25; Hasch 352; Hase 114; Hasee 206; Hasele 86; Haseman 407; Hasenbuerger 233; Hasler 191; Haspelhorn 212; Hasper 407; Has(s) 62, 81, 124, 146, 205, 316, 363, 402, 472, 474 477; Hasselbach 190; Hasselbacher 255, 320; Hasselberger 137, 384; Hasseler 195; Hasselwanger 134; Hassenclever *404; Hassinger *186; Hassler 192, 282, 305, 310; Hassleton *243; Hasslinger 323; Hast 310; Haster 186, 373; Hath 314, 334; Hathe 399; Hather 336; Hattebach 202; Hattenbach *278; Hatz 129; Hatzinger 237; Haub 81, 393; Hauber (s. Hauher, Huber) 197, 264, 304; Haubersack 239; Haubt 142, 218, 330, *331, 385; Hauch 137, 193, 324; Hau(c)k 90, 91, *214, 215, 232, 234, 257, 308, 344, *354, 360, *363, 380, 386, 392, *400, 410, 438; Haudenscheidt (s. Haudesch, Heydersh) 221; Haudesch (s. Haudenscheidt, Heydersh) 221; Haudler 359; Haudt 280; Hauenstein 229, *369; Hauer *113, 147, 198, 257, *258, 264, 272, 289, 332; Hauerich 436; Hauff 56, 198, 333; Haufstein 264; Haug 186, 220, 225, 256, 289, 384; Haugendobler 242; Hauher (s. Hauber) 264, 282; Hauk 472; Haun *333; Haup 107; Haupt 116, 198, 199; Hauptman 178; Hausam 353; Hause 258; Hausecker 130; Hausehl 337; Hauselmann 193; Haushalder (Haushalter) 136, 267, 291; Haushalter 360, 369; Hausknecht 124, 151, 387; Haus(s) 62, 74, 163, 236, 283, 319, 347, 371, 372; Haussaman 276; Haus(s)er 52, 74, 118, 131, 139, 166, 197, 207, *208, 218, 222, 231, 232, 245, 253, 264, 267, 273, 277, 296, 338, 355, *437; Haus(s)er (s. Housser); Haussleither 297; Haus(s)man(n) 132, 155, 160, 176, 219, 223, 280, 311, 332, 375; Haust 106, 213; Hauswirth (Hauswird) 130, 199, 267, 347; Haut 249; Hauth 113; Hautuss 326; Hautz 62, 123, 239, 384; Hautzenbieler 241; Haux 304; Havecker 135; Havel 396; Havervass 71; Hawk *386; Hawly *191; Hay 236, 256, 257, 286, 312; Hayd 115; Hayle 82; Hayn 212; Hayner 286; Haysner *341; Hayt *119; Haytzmer 210; Hayvigh 84; Hazelwood *245; Heanz 228; Hebauer 405; Hebebold 395; Hebeisen 178, 291, 392, 401; Hebel 232; Hebener 319; Heber 305; Heberling *79; Hebiegt 405; Hebling 290, 308; Hebmann 443; Hebrecht 158; Hechelman 198; Hechler 324, 325, 332; Hechs 376; Hecht 190, 209, 330, 331; Heck (s. Hoeck) 66, 91, 92, 107, 185, 210, 227, 237, 287, 298, *303, 307, 343, 327, 346; Heckardt 344; Heckel 371, 372; Heckendorn 224, 261; Heckenleib 337; Hecker 206, 260, 388; Heckert 100, 185; Heckman (s. H[a]eckman); Heckman(n) 346, 362, 386; Heckser 309; Hector 399;

Hedinger 300, 379; Hedly 277; Hedrich 354; Hedrigh 121; Hee 114; Heegy 263; Heenig 128; Heer 398; Heerbuerger 82; Heerd 273; Heerreder *210; Hees 380; Heesman 315; Hefer 237, 381; Heff 184; Heffelfinger 476; Heffeling 139; Hef(f)ner 282, *293; Hefft *108; Hefling 170; Hefthar 295; Hegel(le) 75, 80, 146; Hegendorn *103, 107; Hegenstill 359; Heger 101, 111, 162, 172, 181, 196, 359, 389; Hegert 404; van der Heggen *430; Hegi 82, 237; Hegli 166; Hegner 371; Hegnetsweiller 159; Hehbel 162; Hehl 416; Hehlhofher 391; Hehnel 320; Hehnle 270; Hehr 305, 352; Heibenzeter 416; Heiber 224; Heibly (Heiply) *216; Heibst 357; Heichel 235; Heicks 402; Heid 109, 444, 470; Heide 239; Heidecker 422, 426; Heidenberg 324; Heides 59; Heidle *328; Heidrich 367; Heidschuh 56; Heidt 308, 361, 416, 447; Heier 107, 378, 388, 400; Heiges 334, 342; Heigis (Heygis[s]) *242, 253; Heilbrunn *228; Heileger 143; Heilikel 283; Heil(l) 83, 201, 216, *290, 343, *468; Heil(l)man(n) *80, 207, 233, 314; Heim 109, 114, 185, 269, 280, 294, 319; Heimbach 161, 211, 416; Heimer 157; Hein *51, 149, 269; Heinbach 336; Heinberger 259; Heindel 175; Heinder 115; Heindt 175; Heine 149; Heinecke *285; Heiner 332, 347; Heinetsch 165; Heiney 191; Heinickel 306; Heinig 295; Heininger 307; Heinle 228; Heinlein 340; Heinlen *207; Heinlich 405; Hein(n)inger 104, *223; Heinnisch 342; Heinnoldt 113; Heinrich 67, 112, 126, 147, 158, 197, 199, 214, 216, 242, 248, 268, 329, 378; Heinrichs 177; Heinriegel *393; Heins 264, 371; Heinsman (=Heissman?, Keinsman?) 97, 98; Heintz 65, *116, 117, 155, 255, 259, 286, 288, 344, 352, 355, 369, 391, 399; Hein(t)zelmann *270, 322; Heiply (s. Heibly); Heippe 301; Heisch 253; Heisel *327; Heiser 137, 237, 238, 258, 378, 476; Heiss *111, 121, 218, 228, 248, *261, 278, 285, 310, 342, 345, *362, 391; Heisser 124, 195; Heissheiner 419; Heissler 187, 395; Heissman (s. Heinsman?) 97; Heist *194, 262; Heistand 68; Heistandt 330; Heister 321, 339; Heisterbach 444; Heisy 261; Heit 98, 257; Heitter 289; Heitz *212, 364; Heitzman 289; Hekendorn 102; Hel 289; Helbach 271; Helburgher 135; Held 208, 209, 268, 276, 317; Heldebrand 140; Helder 335, 355; Heldich 406; Heldmann 347; Heldt 253; Helensteuer 366; Helfenstein *450; Helfer *85, 376; Helfeysen 316; Helff 394; Helffenstein 133; Helford 72; Helhoff 337; Helick 395; Helids 360; Hell 208, 226; Helland 384; Hellebrich 331; Hellebrun 84; Hellenthal 161; Heller 56, *114, 154, 205, *252, 286, 304, 328, 348, 385; Hellers 322; Helligas 64; Helling 231; Hellman(n) 17, 36, *274, 381; Helm 234, 273, 345, 346, 354, 374, 383, 445; Helmstaeller 349; Helpfish 315; Helsel (s. Hoeltzel?) 184; Helt 109, 200, 317; Heltenmeyer 298; Helters 286; Helweg 196; Helwig 149, 189, 230; Hem 169, 381; Hembd 384; Hembel 244; Hemberger 165; Hembt 280; Hemerlein 352; Hemgerberer 329; Hemiger 288; Heming 292; Hemler (s. Hengher!) 75, 208; Hemmersbach 320; Hemming 231; Hemmle *213; Hempel 400; Hempele 110; Hemrier 389; Hen 339; Henberger 400; Henche 193; Hencke 113; Henckel(l) 210, 314, 349, 374, 408; Henckels 100; Hencker 144; Hendel 185, 273; Henderich 66; Hendershit 201; Hendrich 361; Hendrick *133, 249; Hendricks *431, 472; Hendrup 423, 427; Hene 271; Heneberger 72; Heneman 307; Henendorff 320; Henerdt 362; Henerich 64; Hengel 282, 351; Henger 214, 346; Hengher (s. Hemler?) 208; Hengst 56, 214; Henhey 246; Hening 307; Henke 56; Henkel 205, 298, 308, 344; Henkenius *280; Henle 120, 331; Henlein 213; Henly 17, 36, 284; Hen(n) *169, 170, 398; Henneberger *110, 252, 367; Hennel 91; Henneman 215; Hennenberg 381; Henner 123, 286; Henneschied 444; Henning 69, 70, 163, 248; Henninger 354, 376; Hennold 231; Hennstz 389; Henny 314; Henri 408; Henrich 50, 84, 109, 151, 155, 216, *225, 251, 253, 254, 255, *259, 261, 283, 295, 298, 343, *362, 372, 379; Henrichs *334; Henricii 399; Henritzy 379; Henry 118, 196, 260; Hensel 293; Hensen 299; Hensi 139; Hensle 412; Hens(s)el 56, 136, 143, 239; Hensy 474; Hentz 219, 347, 403, 471, 472; Hentzel 232; Hentzelmann 223; Hentzer 325; Hentzinger 305; Hepde 373; Hepfoh 296; Hepp *217, 218, *394; Heppel *211; Herals 163; Heranus 153; Herb 150, 206, 472; Herbach 150, 368; Herbalt 239; Herbein 12, 29, 434, 475;ι Herbel 145, 333; Herber *157; Herbert(h) 64, 125, 169; Herbertz 68; Herbes 164; Herbig 196; Herbold *128; Herbolt 136, 239; Herbst 248, 341, 408; Herbster 192, 227, 417; Herby 363; Herchelroth 468, 469; Herd 389; Herde 134; Herdel 292, 376; Herdlein 106; Herdte *173; Herer 56; Herford 173; Herge(d)ι 182, 215, 234; Hergelrat 438; Herger *472; Hergle 120; Herguth 302; Heriger 54; Hering (s. Hoering) 249, 250, 261, 265, 268, 315, 318, 382; Herisch 365; Heritho 193; Herker 176; Herle 468; Herlein 312; Herlieman 150; Herly 310; Herm 401; Hermanes 200; Herman(n) 57, 71, 76, 91, *92, *161, 172, 178, 179, 204, 236, 237, 245, 259, *264, 269, 275, 280, 281, 286, 328, 329, 333, *336, 346, 358, 365, 371, *376, *387, 432, 434, 436, *471, *474; Hermannis 199; Hermes 123; Hermsdorff 332; Hernberger 451; Hero 311; Herold(t) 163, 194, 295; Herr 84, 104, 207, 253, 423, 427, *436, 437; Herrgeroeder 88; Herring 324, 333; Herrman(n) 180, 185, 218, 263, 274, 280, 283, 291, 338, 347, 391, 415, 419; Herry 49; Herschberger 112, 195, 196, 329, 385, 436; Herschfänger 182; Herschheimer 359; Herschi 436; Herschman 396; Herse 299; Herser 422, 426; Herst 361; Herstein 410; Herster 209; Hert 380; Hertcher 242; Hertel(l) 207, 274, 364, 394; Herter 222, 263, 331: Herth (s. Hirt?) 148, 262, 306;

Herther 242; Hertle 373; Hertlein 106; Hertranft 288; Hertsel 134; Hertt 126; Hertteranf(f)t *96, *97; Hertz 220, 222, 311, 335, 388, 409; Hertzberger 112; Hertzel(l) 77, *78, *130, 187, 472; Hertzer 49; Hertzerger 382; Hertziger 395; Hertzler *195, *244, 352; Her(t)zog 118, 146, 205, 229, 236, 240, 259, 284, 450; Herwald 363; Hes *62, 63, 356, 408; Hesler 185; Hess 53, 101, 124, 128, 145, *150, 199, 209, *210, 216, 233, 250, 261, 266, 276, 288, 306, 314, 336, 365, 389, 391, *401, 404, 407, *437; Hesse 166, 411; de Hesse 470; Hesselbeck 124; Hesser 81, 289, 314, 380; Hes(s)ler 285, *367, 450; Hester 311, 392, 399; Hesterich 302; Hesterman 124; Hetering 317; Hetle 239; Hetrich 310; Hetrig 365; Hetter 252; Het(te)rich 87, *88, 120, 174; Hetterling 100; Hettich 219; Hettinger 265; Hettler 178; Hettmansterger 395; Hettrich 210; Hetz 258; Hetzel(l) 50, *94, *226, 260, 267, 290, 369; Hetzer (s. Hitzer) 105, 223, 264; Hetzler 194; Heu (s. Hey) 263; Heucher 154; Heuer 257; Heugeld 254; Heuler 255; Heuling 239; Heuman 403; Heun 314, 317; Heunemeyer 155; Heuntz *379, 380; Heuschkell *238; Heuse 203; Heusser 366; Heussler 242; Heustang 419; Hevener 136; Hewass 289; Hey (s. Heu) 79, 137, 192, 263; Heyd 278, 447; Heydecker 153; Heydel 256; Heydelbach 173; Heydenreych 190; Heyderich *174; Heydersh (s. Haudenscheidt, Haudesch) 221; Heydrich *96, 97, 118, 119; Heydrig 156; Heydrukee 56; Heydt 157, 293; Heyel 119; Heyer 100, 133, *162, 296, 320, 388, 403, 405, 438; Heygis (s. Heigis); Heyl 72, 73, *136, 219, 240, 270, *288, 299, 319, *364, 370, 378; Heyle 227; Heyler 165, 253, 394; Heyll 415; Heylman(n) 73, 117, 274, 363; Heyly 123; Heym 259; Heyman(n) 142, 315, 316, 351, 364; Heyn 405; Heyndel 210; Heyne 153, 422, 426; Heynich 379; Heyr 314; Heyrom 397; Heys 243; Heyser *109, 218, 257, 294, *343; Heyshe 198; Hibler 352; Hibscher 273; Hicke 422, 426; Hickenauer 220; Hicker 57; Hickert 416; Hickman 274, 349; Hiderffer 403; Hidler 110; Hieber 384; Hiebner 303; Hiegler 475; Hieman 198; Hieppel 184; Hier 50; Hierlyman 159; Hieronymus *179; Hierte 168; Hiestand(t) 54, *55, 277, 393, 473; Hig 249; Higdal 341; Higernell 383; Highart 254; Hikenleibly 337; Hilbert 334; Hilbisch 199; Hild 413; Hildebrand(t) 96, 247, 253, 331; Hildenbeidel 477; Hildenbrandt 263; Hilfisch 200; Hilgert 179, 406; Hill 47, 48, 145, *405, *472, 474, 475; Hillebrandt 143; Hillebrecht 307; Hillegas(s) 73, 175, 473; Hiller 193, 305, 371; Hilligass 49; Hillinger 235, 333; Hills 448; Hilssheimer 181; Hilt 330; Hiltenbeittel 216; Hiltenbrandt 126, 237; Hiltzbeck 300; Hims *123; Himler 75; Himmel 407; Himmelberger 110, 207; Himroth 272; Hina 131; Hinanso 417; Hinck 309, 406; Hincke 327; Hinckel 203, 344, 389; Hinckle 474; Hind 236; Hinderle 386; Hinderstieff 349; Hindert 317; Hindertruther

126; Hingerer 337; Hinkel 186; Hinleer 298; Hinnlaub 320; Hinroth 314; Hinsch 177; Hinsey 307; **Hipge** 285; **Hipp** 279; Hippel 143, 369, 472; Hipscher (s. Huebscher) 263; Hirach 382; Hirdt 275; Hirni 285; Hirnneise *269; Hirnschall 103; Hironimus 101; Hirsch *70, 133, 140, 141, 264, 292, 310, 330, 373, 380, *395, 401, 409, 411; Hirschberger ᵢ391; Hirschbirg 374; Hirschfeldt 3,62; Hirschi 135; Hirschlag 365; Hirschman(n) *269, 286, 375; Hirse, 422, 426; Hirsh 222,ᵢ377; Hirt (s. Herth?) 126, 148, 155, 227; Hirter 168; Hirth 350; Hirtzel 155; His 238; Hisch 199; Hisger 396; Hisle 61; Hisly 54 Hisner 276; Hissard 392; Hissgen 317; Hissle 61; Hissong 136; Hister 204; Hite 92; Hitman 251; Hitschner 306; Hittel 368; Hitz 158, 358; Hitzer (s. Hetzer) 264; Hitzler 381; Hoak 284; Hobbach 154; Hobbaer 313; Hobbecher 111; Hobel 228; Hobert 139; Hobian 149; Hobler 196, 252; Hoch 134, 193, 215, 268, 332, 333, 339, 343, 358, 360, 373, *378, 379, 380, 381, 412, 419, 434, *435, *473, *475; Hochgenug 63; Hochheimer 350; Hochlaender 115; Hochmann 61, 62; Hochmeyer 407; Hochreitter 346; Hochreutener *181; Hochstaedt 163; Hochstaedter (s. Hochstedler) 102; Hochstaetter (Hostetter) 205, *206; Hochstetter 130, 437; Hochstrasser 304, 379; Hochzig 195; Hock 261, 331; Hodely 128; Hodg(e)son 52, *128; Hoebel 155; Hoeberling 183; Hoeblich 170; Hoebling 309; Hoechst 355; Hoeck (s. Heck) 185, 210; Hoecker 134, 148, 466; Hoeckert 375; Hoeckhlen 398; Hoedt 430; Hoeffelbauer *187; Hoeffer 160, 319, 413; Hoeffler 263; Hoeffling 172; Hoefflinger 349; Hoeffner 89; Hoeflich 170; Hoehl 290, 370, *383, 384; Hoehle 319; Hoehlen 446; Hoehn 223, 465; Hoehneise 282; Hoeldebrand 365; Höl(l) 73, 288, 395; Hoeller 143, 199; Hoellerman 262, 333; Hoelley *244; Hoelsel 227; Hoeltzel (s. Helsel?) 184; Hoeltzer 228; Hoelty 163; Hoenich 363; Hoenig 159; Hoenninger 105, 399; Hoepffer 372; Hoepfner 422, 426; Hoeppener 308; Hoeppe; 187; Hoepster 149; Hoer 374; Hoerauff 292; Hoerch 202; Hoerg 194; Hoering (s. Hering) 234, 250, *261; Hoerman(n) 321, 340; Hoern 313; Hoerner 156, *241, *292, *293, 306, 309, 334, 400, 410; Hoernlie 205; Hoersch 275; Hoertzel 211; Hoessert 300; Hoeth (Huth) 17, 36; Hoetz *185; Hoetzele 257; Hoetzer 86; Hof 466, 468; Hofelen 370; Hoff 62, 65, 86, 117, 161, 298, 313, 344, *358, 369, 370, 380, 386, 389; vom Hoff 393; Hoffacker 81, 400; Hoffart 61; Hoffarth 437; Hoffbauer 325; in Hoffe *431; Hoffecker 197, *358; Hoffener 125; Hoffer 84, 97, 118, 126, 160, 253, *285, 477; Hoffheintz 258, 259, *355; Hoffman(n) 52, *54, 65, 80, 82, 83, 84, 87, *93, *95, *97, *107, 110, 111, *112, *115, 124, *125, *126, 127, 132, 134, *135, 136, 141, 142, *147, 148, 160, 161, *162, 164, 174, *178, 182, 189, 190, 196, 197, *200, 202, 207, 212, *215, 216, *217, 220, *221, 228, 230,

Hof—Hot

234, 259, *262, *263, 266, 267, 272, 275, 276, 279, 280, *284, 286, 292, 296, *297, 298, *300, *303, 309, 311, 319, 331, 332, 333, 344, 346, 352, 354, 356, 357, *358, 364, 375, 378, 383, *385, 386, 388, 390, *397, 400, 404, 413, 444, 446, 476; Hof(f)ner 182, 187, 207, 243, 326; Hoffstadt 364; Hoffstaettle 212; Hofius 373; Hofman(n) 52, 63, 215, 265, 296, 341, 343; Hofmeister 278; Hofminich 66; Hogar 323; Hogermoed 434; Hognon 205; Hogoodus 305; Hoh 284, 292, 294; Hohenschilt 102; Hohl 174, *328; Hohlman 125; Hohlstein 74; Hohlwein 381; Hohn 210; Hohnsteiner 466; Hohr 310; Hohsteter 197; Hohwerder 149; Holbe 110; Holbein 155; Holber 110; Holder 251, *296; Holderbaum 250; Holdinghaus 377; Holdt 157; Holl *111, 112, *119, 145, 188, *233, 252, 332, 335; Holland 295; Holle(n)bach 279, *308, 309, 357; Hol(l)enberger *140; Holler 108, 348, 376; Hollich 229; Hollinger 101, 107, 112, 183, 263, 272; Hollman 469; Hollobach 261; Hollscheit 306; Hollstein 267; Hollsteiner 466; Holly 244; Holman 468; Holsbacher 49; Holschuh 143; Holsinger 68; Holstein 391; Holsteiner 58, 74, 465; Holtz 93, 130, 183, 235, 267, 402, 417; Holtzapfel *69, 351, 472; Holtzappel 343; Holtzbarth 401; Holtzeder *79; Holtzer 418; Holtzhaeusser 280; Holtzhausen 65; Holtzhausser *333, 355; Holtzhefer 118; Holtzinger *71; Holtzleeder 149; Holtzman(n) 229, 310, 352; Holtzschuh 275, 410; Holtzstein 61, 476; Holwer 163; Homan 120, 178, 347; Homberger 99; Hombert 260; Hombro 254; Hommer 271, 308; Honegger 192; Honher 387; Honi *135; Honnig 81, 293; Honor *297; Honstein 412; Hoock 59, 115, 379; Hoof 411; de Hooff 154; Hoofman 54; Hoogh 67; Hooghstadt 53; Hook 90, 246; Hooker 299; Hoolboeck 321; Hoon *226; Hoorle 74; Hoot 57; Hoover *255, 317; Hoozer 246; Hop 190, 312; Hopbach 61; Hope *121; Hopff 178, 210, 256, *321, 369; Hopman(n) 83, *132, 350; Hopp 306, 379; Hoppacher 313; Hoppe 242; Hoppengartner 293; Hoquedas 417; Hora 370; Horatz 347; Horbach 419; Horch 52; Hordt 193; Hore *292, 308; Horein 177, 221; Horlacher 67, 249; Horlogh 54; Horn 78, 106, 109, 146, 261, 273, 277, 294, *309, 376, 380, 386, 392, 398, 405, 411; Hornaeffer 294, 295; Hornberger *64, 83, 239, 391; Hornecker *176 177; Horner *130, 445; Horngacher 239; Hornich 356; Hornig 104; Horning 73, 406; Hornung 145, 350; Horny 226; Horrester 53; Horrst 249; Horsh 68; Horst 118, 159, 175, 232, 379, 438; Horster 367, 396; Horsveldt 88; Hort 204; Horter 360; Hortig 284; Hortung 132; Hoschar *205; Hoss 296; Host 249, 263; Hoste 71; Hostedler (s. Hochstaedter) 100; Hostein 151; Hosteller 73; Hostender 247; Hoster 149, 468, 469; Hosters 433; Hostetter (s. Hochstaedter, Hosteller) 72; Hostman 131, 211, 325, 446; Hothem 393; Hotman 293, 315; Hotner 110; Hottel(l) 75, 78; Hotten-

Hot—Jac

bacher 296; Hottenstein 290, 291, 435, 475; Hotz 229, 236;
Houer 381; Hough 137; Houpt 177; Houser 192; Hously
85; Housser (s. Haus(s)er *231; Houston *127; Hovell 135;
van Hoven 294; Howell *106; Hoyer 371; Hoyst 193; Hub
*251; Hubach *122; Hubacher 358, 392; Hubbach 449; Hubele
111; Hubely 166; Hubeny 150; Huber (s. Hubler?) 52, 56,
*77, *78, *82, *98, 99, 102, 112, 118, 123, 131, 153, *156,
163, 164, 170, *176, *197, 213, 215, *222, 228, *232, 235,
*250, 264, 281, 282, 297, 310, 312, *329, 330, *353, 356,
377, *378, 379, 382, *385, 387, 422, 426, 436, 437, 449,
467, 468; v. Huber 231; Hubert 68, 117, *148, 286, 345, 373;
Hubler 18, 36; Hubler (s. Huber?) 99, 107; Hublich 85;
Hubrich 123; Huby 170; Huck 227; Hud 354; Hudere 263;
Huders 271; Hue 170, 308; Hueb 358; Huebbert 267; Huebbertz
265; Hueb(e)ner *95, *96, 109, 158, 218; Hueber 59; Huebner
330; Huebscher (s. Hipscher) 264; Huebschman 108; Huebster
125; Huechtner 401; Huefrefege 139; Huegel 290; Hueller
141, 166, 234; Huenche 162; Huenckel 253; Huenler 205;
Huenner 214; Huepbisch 338; Hueppel 116, 179; Huerd 155;
Huerstman 365; Hu(e)selman *89; Huesterle 303; Hüster(r)
(Hiester) 41, 45, *109; Hueter 108, 252, 335; Huethler 273;
Huetig 184, 250; Huetler 370; Huetter 137, 319; Huetterly
310; Huettner 105, 355; Huetwohl 186; Huetz 349; Hützel
*64; Huewit 297; Huey 144, 150, 331, 418; Hufer 363;
Huff 219, 235, 378; Huffnagel 303; Huffnagle 434; Huffshmit 245; Hufnagel 285, 475; Hug 158, 213; Hugel 84;
Huger *374; Hugett 105; Hugly 221; Huguelet *323; Huhn
*202; Huisiner 77; Hukabach 127; v. Hulen 380; Hull
199; Hultzler 236; Humbel 317; Humberd 352; Humberger
195; Humbert 241, *268, 329, 380; Humbold 199; Humbolt
391; Humer 413; Humerich 287; Hummel 75, 101, *163, 175;
198, 215, 273, 280, 337, 421, 425; Hummer 262; Hummerle
*209, 246; Hummy 394; Hun 319; Hundt 293, 356; Huner
271; Hunkinger 216; Hunolt *259; Hunsberger 471, 472;
Hunsecker 67, *107, 475; Hunsicker *336, 434; Hunt 423,
427, *464; Hunter 5, 24, 375, 376, *399, *445; Huntz 175;
Huntzecker 91, 185; Huntzicker *127, 369; Huntzinger 119;
Huppert 448; Hurbert 422, 426; Hurrelman 318; Husacker
472; Husar (s. Huser) 97; Husband 352, *361; Huser (s. Husar)
97, 254; Huss 170, 273, 286, 409, 411, 421, 426; van Hussen
475, *476; Hussey 421, 425; Hussing 336; Hussung 284; Hust
115, 211, 337; Hutekunst 242; Huth 49, 160, 180, *181, 196,
240, 248, *252, 273, 280, 473, 474; Huth (s. Hoeth); Huthmacher 395; Hutman 306; Huttenbach 303; Hutter 18, 36,
276; Huttich 270; Hutzner 284; Huwes 403; Huyet 117, 217;
Hybler 384; Hyches 120, 121; Hyder 246; Hyl 157; Hyltel
115; Hyndman *221.
    Jaac 237; Jabbes 215; Jack 136; Jacke 103; Jackle (s.

531

Jaeckel, Jakele) 96; Jackobi 305; Jacks 140; Jackson *326; Jacob 102, *103, 124, 146, 159, 175, 220, 225, 237, 241, 271, 276, 306, 362, 376, 389, 470; Jacobi (Jacoby) 123, 137, 190, *224, 234, 267, 297, *302, 320, 348, 362, 416; Jacobs 116, 433, 469; Jacobson 402; Jacoby (s. Jacobi); Jacqueart 311; Jaeckel (s. Jackle, Jakele) *95, *96, 97, 192, *315; Jaeckle 279, 303; Jaeger 96, 101, 115, 154, 159, 200, 218, 240, 283, 290, 310, 311, 340, 341, 360, 363, 365, 367, 397, 435, 475; Jägi 84; Jaeky 101; Jag 421, 425; Jagel 261; Jagi 113; Jahller 213; Jahn 295; Jakele (s. Jaeckel, Jackle) 95; Jakly 166; James *190; Janckbach 189; Jani 115; Janler 353; Jans 195; Jansen 430, *431, 473, 475, *476; Janso(h)n 154, 306, *355, 456, 459, 470; Janss 114; Jansy 320; Jantz (s. Jentz) 182, 189, 336, 353; Jarquart 287; Jarro *463; Jauch 290, 319, 340; Jauss 283, 304, 325, 393; Jawert 430; Jaxthemer 194; Jaysor 313; Jays(s)er 100, 291; Jayter 166; Iba 221; Ibach 449; Ichard 447; Ichle 216; Ick 145; Ickrath 161; Idler 371; Jean 304; Jeffervs *252; Jegel 194; Jegner 75; Jeidler 278; Jeil 202; Jellis 477; Jemel 244; Jensel 304; Jentes 336; Jentz (s. Jantz) 353, 389; Jerger 64; Jerghjes 432; Jerholtz 254; Jerling 108; Jeserding (s. Iserding) 137; Jetter 175, 359; Jeune 243; le Jeunes 214; Jewdie 103; Igelsbach 90; Ihl 298; Ihle *342, 343; Ihllig 52; Ihmme 292; Ihrich 195, 251; Ihrig (s. Erig) 345, *397, 410; Ihringer 251; Jirarden 185; Ilgenfritz *112, 343; Ilger 326; Illgentz 384; Illig 83, 136; Imberman 103; Imboten 272; Imbsweiller 217; Imfeld 297; Imhoff 230, 246; Imich 218; Immel 438, 466; Immerhausser 183; Immich 375; Im(m)ler 82, *94; Immel *74, 145, 338; Imno 215; Imoberstuech 231; Imschmiedt 275; Inaebmit 278; Inbuss 299; Incler 388; Indehaven 478; Inder 255; Indohaven 476; Indorff 176; Ingan 313; Ingebrand 179; Ingelhoff 293; Ingold 91; Inhof 107; Innlab 320; Inpierman 325; Insel(l) 225, 474; Joan 171; Jocheim 360; Jochim *100; Joder 266; 364, *434, *475; Joedder 311; Joek 125; Joh 110, *194, 345, 346; Johe 118; John 96; Johnle 89; Johnloft 147; Johnston 396, 397, *400, *403, *411; Jollgo 155; Jommel 239; Jonas 154, 190; Joner *103, 104; Jones *414; Jonger 204; Jooghly 163; Joram 247; Joray 323; Jordan 263, 267, 275, 302, 338; Jorde 422, 426; Jordin 7, 25; Jordte 196; Jordy 394; Jorger 81; Jorts 398; Josep *349; Joseph 250, 392; Jost 49, 56, 86, *88; 108; *116, 123, 142, 151, 190, 203, 237, 238, 255, 302, 334, 397, 419, *474, 478; Jotter *156, *194; Joughein 114; Irrendt 217; Irst 308; Isaac *75; Isaacs 431; Isbod 178; Isch 203; Ischadt 191; Isele 249; Isenhauer (s. Eisenhauer) 151; Iserding (s. Jeserding) 137; Ish 78; Israel 348; Isseller 197; Issener 261; Ittich 447; Itzberger 55, 358, 468; Juedii 250; Juenghen 112; Juengling 269, 477; Juengst 230, 319, 325, 374; Juergensen 423,

427; Jugnal 298; Julien 366; Julius 179, 182; Juncker 173, 224, 276, *306; Jundt(t) 204, 253; Jung 18, 36, 51, 76, 80, 87, 97, 98, 111, 123, *128, 149, 150, 151, 154, 162, 169, 170, 177, 189, 196, 198, 199, *200, 201, 206, 211, *217, 218, *222, 223, 225, 229, *232, 235, 239, 240, 254, *258, 260, 274, 285, *286, 291, 298, 303, 305, *315, 316, 318, 320, 326, 334, 350, 359, 362, 364, 365, *368, 383, 389, 395, *407, *408, 409, 411, 415, 438, *443, 447, 476; Jungblud 147, 213; Jungck 172; Junge 224; Junger 185, 286; Jungmann 71, 247; Jurdan 123; Jurgeins 50; Jurian 83; Just 352, 407; Jutz 357; Jutzener 302; Jutzy 173.

Kabel *194, 195; Kachel 240; Kachelriess 106; Kaeffer 140; Kaegel 370; Kaegele 328; Kaegy 364; Kaehler 348, 370; Kaeiser 345, 367; Kaeller 98, 99; Kaellner 209; Kaelsch 108; Kaemerer 362; Kaemmer 275, *387, 400; Kaemmerer 267, *269; Kaemmerlin *86; Kaemmes 386; Kaemminger 408; Kämpff 86, 87, 374; Kaempffer 317; Känele 68; van Kännen 182; Kaephffer 373; Kaepple 193; Kaeppler 244; Kaerber 110; Kaerch (s. Kirch) 179; Kaercher 217; Kaeschstler 155; Kaeucher 312; Kaeyser 304, 395; Kagel 262, 311; Kagelberger 140; Kageroth 307; Kagie 139; Kahlbach 286; Ka(h)n 86, 87; Kaiser 349; Kalb 474; Kalbach 147; Kalbfleisch 360; Kalcher 450; Kalckbrenner 339, 348; Kalckglässer 61; Kalck(g)l(o)eser *61, *259, 473; Kalckhaufen 380; Kalladay 122; Kallemeyer 294; Kallenberger 288; Kalm 184, 185; Kalteisen 236; Kaltmiller 341; Kaltschmidt 395; Kamm 301; Kamman 278; Kammer 253, 391, 447; Kammerer 102; Kamp (s. Camp) 131, 146, 207, 351; Kamper 382; Kantz 207, *220, 330; Kantzer 276; Kapp 139, 145, 202, 237, *256, 298, 372, 448, 465, *466, *467; Kappeberger 229; Kappel 159; Kappes 258, 271, 356; Kappis 263; Kappler 83, 270; Kappus 406; Kaps 371; Karch 119, *274, 289, 311, 324, 341, 363; Karcher 92, 93, 122, 123, 279, 314; Karg *269, 388; Karger 250; Karl(e) 112, 123, *375; Karli 111; Karn 411; Karnagel 188; Karne 84; Karner 229; Karp 383; Karr 296; Karsdoop 435; Karst 90, 124; Karwin 359; Karz 390; Kascht 146; Kase 81; Kaske 422, 426; Kasper 179; Kass (s. Kiess) 378; Kassel 54, 55, *431, 432, *475; Kasselman 444; Kast 152, 207, 242, 255, 296; Kastinitz 124; Kastner 187, 445, 467; Kater 163; Katler 187; Katteman 290; Kattenmann 325; Katterer 289; Kat(t)erman(n) 126, 127, 278, 449, 465, 467; Kattinger 381; Katz 193, *209, 254, 269, 270, 319, 335, 418; Katzbach 292; Katzenbach 388; Katzenbacher 212; Katzenmeyer 314; Katzenstein 157; Kau *219; Kaubel 309; Kaucher 263; Kaufenheisen 477; Kauff 125, 142, 385; Kauffeld 116, *175, 176; Kauffer 276; Kauffman(n) 52, 86, 111, 112, 123, 125, 148, 174, 175, 177, 195, 203, *205, 207, 233, 241,

244, 256, 267, 277, 302, 329, *335, 343, 346, 349, 361, 364, 369, 375, 382, 434, 436, 472, 475; Kaufman 205, 358; Kauger 74; Kaulbach 169; Kaulitz 318; Kaupt 198; Kautz 172, *283, *285, 297, 310, 443; Kautzman(n) 216, 229, 248; Kawffman 224; Kawtzman 233; Kaylor 466; Kayser 108, 206, 354; Keanig(h) *227, 235; Keamigh 241; Kebbel 370; Kebbler 370; Kebelbe 74; Keberling 411; Keble 235; Kebler 340; Keck 150, 394; Keef(f)er 189, 205; Keeger 406; Keel 52; Keellenthal 224; Keener 313; Keeper *230; Keer 56, 103; Kees 215, 413; Keesey 71; Keffer (s. Kueffer) 137, 378, 438; Keg 104; Kegel 227; Kegereiss 287; Keher 154; Kehl 370, 374; Kehle 280, 474; Kehler 126, 128, 213, 476; Kehm 219; Keich 210; Keil 57, 354; Keiler 221; Keilhauer 403; Keilinger 222; Keilman 142; Keim 10, 29, 57, 62, 109, 205, 222, 326; Keiner 323; Keinsman (s. Heinsman?) 97; Keipp 341; Keipper 368; Keiseler 446; Keiser 59, *97, 362, 443; Keisser 254; Keit 474; Keith *9, 27, 28; Keitz (s. Kietz) 378; Keitzi 401; Kelch 151; Kelchner 67, 90; Kelchoffner 380; Kelhover 226; Kelinsteller 253; Kelker (s. Köllicker) *167; Kell 168, *169; Keller 58, 64, 83, 89, 93, *103, 104, 113, 121, 122, 141, 159, 188, 192, *196, 204, 207, 214, 219, 220, 223, *233, 243, 273, 285, 299, 313, 317, 333, 340, 347, 350, 360, 370, 372, 375, 385, 402, 403, 413, 417, 435, 438, 446, 448, 467, 468; Kelling 222; Kelter 404; Keltinger 206; Kellner *289; Kelmold 414; Kelner 431; Kelpius 432; Kelter 356; Kemmerer 331; Kemmerli 306; Kemp 340, 404, 474, 475; Kempe 357; Kemper 124, 146, 476; Kemperle 124; Kemperling 377; Kempff 311, *390; Kempt 228; Kendel 305, 370, 438; Kendemer 367; Kender 292; Kendig 8, 9, 10, *27, 28, 436, 437; Kendtel 239; Kener 121; Kenlis 432; Kennamer 82; Kennel 181, 257; Kennely 256; Kenner 291; Kennet 456, 459; Kenneway *278; Kensel 119; Kenser 363; Kensinger 59; Kent 164; Kenttner 361; Kentzel 119; Kentzler 259; Kepele 130; Kepler 473; Keppel 368; Keppert 268; Keppler 323; Kep(p)linger 63, 215; Keppner 300; Kepstner 296; Ker 204, 255; Kerber 129; Kerch 157, *201; Kerchel 264; Kercher 157, 313; Kerchner 170; Kerffer 273; Kerkes 68; Kerlin 274; Kerlinger 234; Kern 54, 68, 70, 78, 100, 105, 108, 123, 132, 137, *166, 179, 180, 189, 195, 197, 198, 223, 230, 264, 269, *291, *331, 335, 373, 375; Kerner 391, 447; Kerr 88, *365, 435; Kerschner 220, 472; Kersher (s. Kirscher) 299; Kerst 378; Kerstrich 147; Kese 103, 405; Kesebohrer 281; Kesselberg (später Casselberry) 431; Kesseler 388; Kesselrinck 354; Kessinger *113; Kessler 129, 157, 162, 188, 196, 223, 245, 262, 345, 354, 367, 370, *397, 400, 404, 419, 422, 426; Kestenholtz 130; Ketteman *224, 267, 359; Kettenring *371; Ketter 293; Ketterer 321; Kettering 358, 370;

Ketterman 163; Kettinger 337; Kettler 478; Kettner *93, *94, *467; Ketzendander 61; Keuchert 278; Keuffer 248; Keuler *256; Keurlis 430; Keusch 319; Keyger 118; Keys *387; Keyser 53, 68, 77, 78, 83, 128, *140, 144, 149, 160, 163, *209, 240, 254, 290, 309, 311, 333, 335, 358, 375, 381, 406, *430, 435, 447, *472, 478; Keytel *308; Kibler 288; Kicherman *317; Kichler 140, 142; Kick 339; Kiderer 263; Kiebel 61; Kiechner 264; Kiefer 221, 389, 391; Kieffer *72, *73, 84, *146, *185, 358, 409, 446; Kiehl 126, 385; Kiel 331, 413, 446; Kiele 193, 243; Kielman 321; Kielwein 434; Kiener *51, 134; Kienser 125; Kienstein *242; Kientz 208, 276; Kiesecker 187; Kiess (s. Kass) 273, *378; Kiesser 380; Kiest 345; Kiester 107, 153, 170, 365; Kiesy 377; Kietz (s. Keitz) 378; Kietzmiller 313; Kiffer 110, 237, 410; Kifie 347; Kihnner 398; Kilgus 288; Kilian 65, 78, 149, 206, 212; Kill 194; Kille 56; Killhaver 59; Killinger 277; Killuge 282; Kilmer 446; Kilner 59; Kimmel 233, *251, 261; Kimmerlein *256; Kinberg 407; Kind *217, 299, 311; Kinder 246; Kindigh 52; Kindle 397; Kindlishberger 204; Kind(t) 186, 188, 285; Kinerimen 318; Kinige 301; Kinsel 293, 319; Kinsie 449; Kinss 71; Kint 81; Kinter 127; Kintsch 340; Kintz 283; Kintzel 126, 129; Kintzer 106, 108, 125; Kintzing 435; Kintzinger 194; Kiportz 364; Kipp 218, 279; Kippenberg 295; Kipper 145; Kipping 60; Kirbach 97, *141; Kirch (s. Kaerch) 179, 181, 190; Kircher 151, 257; Kirchhoeffer 319; Kirchhoff 51, 140; Kirchner 115, 181, 257, 258, 403, 448; Kirchsettin 387; Kirme 321; Kirsch 289; Kirschbaum 229, 251, 409; Kirschberger 196; Kirschenmann 379; Kirscher (s. Kersher) 240, 299; Kirschman 273; Kirs(c)hner 65, 69, 87, *88, 155, 182, 227, 407; Kirsheyer 361; Kirst 159; Kisauer 358; Kisecker 334; Kiser 81; Kissel 278; Kisselberg 268; Kister 118, 381; Kistler 467; Kistner 78, 129, 345, 346; Kitsmiller 56; Kittelmeyer 377; Kittwiler 215; Kitz 290; Klaar 283; Klaeppinger 108; Klaerr 201, 202; Klages 181; Klagh 129; Klam(m) 189, *365; Klammer 451; Klan 149; Klapp 51; Klapper 318; Klappert *352, 399, 413; Klar 280; Klarwein 259; Klases 262; Klass 297; Klatz 124, 182, 380; Klaubach 370; Klauser 61; Klawer 175; Kleber 188; Klebsattel 88, *89; Klee(h) 116, 217, 248, 341; Klees 178, 321; Kleffer 84; Kleh 116, 137, 362; Klehass 221; Klehr 184; Kleiber *377; Kleidens 220; Kleiderlein 394; Kleim 68, *145, 181, 193, 208, 239, 302; Kleimer 475; Klein 17, 36, *78, *82, 98, 105, 106, 116, *128, 129, *133, 134, *135, *137, *141, 144, 148, 149, 150, 154, *155, 169, *170, 171, 172, 182, 190, 199, 201, 202, *204, 205, *217, 220, *222, 224, *227, 235, 240, 246, *253, 255, 257, 260, 275, 287, 290, 291, *293, 298, 300, 303, *307, 312, 315, 316, 319, 320, 321, 322,

328, 332, 337, 339, 342, 344, 346, *347, 364, 365, *366, 368, 370, 378, 380, 387, *389, 390, 393, 397, 399, 408, 409, 411, *415, *418, 435, 438, 443, 447, 467, 468, 470, 477; Kleinbach 261; Kleinbehl 333; Kleinbub 311; Kleine 213; Kleinfeld 325; Kleinfelter 240; Kleingenny 127; Kleinhauss 73; Kleinhoof 430; Kleinman 329; Kleinpeter 158, *253, 347, 381; Kleinschmidt 292, *405; Kleinschrot 343; Kleintopf *305; Kleiss 188, 288, 344; Kleman 384; Klemer 384; Klem(m) 83, *90, 91, 94, 95, 178, 295, 296, 299; Klemmer 64, 262, 435, 476; Klenck 324; Klenee 418; Klengler 114; Klenter 302; Kleppert 147; Kless 116; Kletle 113; Klett 256; Klette 402; Kletter 162; Kley 50, 204; Kleyn 412; Klieberstein 393; Kliestadt 312; Klincken 429; Kling 61, *81, 345; Klingel *178; Klinge-meyer 269; Klingen 74; Klingenschmidt *119; Klinger 123, *194, 261, 328, 350; Klingman(n) 72, 73, 164; Klinken 473; Klippel *213; Klobly 248; Kloeckner *97, 144, 316, 319; Kloepper 351, *374; Kloepster 245; Kloeti 238; Klonninger 179; Klopert 173; Klopfer 283; Klop(p) *51, 468; Klos 365, 407; Kloss(e) 193, 226, *227; Klossmayer 218; Klosterman 432; Klotz 129, *193; Kluck (s. Klug); Klueck 344; Kluekner 405; Kluemges *430; Kluenck *351; Kluenth 308; Klug (Kluck) 17, 36, *183; Klump 262; Klunt 119; Knaab 331; Knab 115, 253, 303; Knabe 174, 244, 312; Knabenschus 419; Knabschneider 306; Knaeg 156; Knag 329; Knapff 180; Knapp 395; Knappenberger 199; Knapper 307; Knartsch 305; Knauer 71, *252, 253; Knauss *166, 218, 226, 245; Knebel *244; Knebelbach 403; Kneber 394; Knechell 72; Knecht 61, 77, 177, 185, 325, 384, 474; Kneeling 322; Kneerster 130; Kneiht 354; Kneisel 234; Kneiss 218, 389; Kneith 188; Knell 375; Kneller 304; Kneply 318; Knepper 61, 109, 201; Knerr 243, 279; Kneskern 448; Kness 254; Kney 241; Knidel 304; Knieriemen 325; Kniesel 133; Kniess 306; Knipe 209; Knipp 209; Kniss 227; Knissel 281; Knittel 304; Knob 231; Knobe 318; Knobelloch 380; Knoblauch 352, 377; Knoblig 327; Knobloch 188, 362; Knoch 277; Knochen 348; Knockel 72; Knodel 303; Knodt 318; Knoebel(l) 86, 186; Knoedler 156, *242, 341; Knoeri 353; Knoertzer 317; Knoery 402; Knoess 216; Knoll 87, 262; Knop(p) 65, *66, 90; Knor(r) 379, 472; Knoss 476, 478; Knotz 242, 261; Knuegel 281; Kob(b)ler 87, 107; Kobel 52, 68, 88, *178, 448; Kobelentz 166; Kober 64, 156, 185, *255, 362; Koberstein 242; Koble 171; Koch 51, 61, 66, 77, 91, 108, 116, 117, *120, *131, 134, 142, *145, 149, 157, 161, 169, 180, 182, 183, 217, 218, 219, 225, 231, 233, 245, 246, *252, 253, 260, 270, 290, 294, 296, 298, *307, 312, 314, 315, 316, 336, 337, 338, 341, *343, 350, 360, 383, 384, 399, 402, 448, 477; Kochenauer 101; Kochendoerffer 251, 338, 343; Kocher 108, 128, *451; Kocherthal 4, 8, *10, 22, 27, *29, 439, 441, 446; Kochges 416; Kochlein 155; Kochler 255; Kochling 260;

Kockart 132; Kockenbauch 384; Kockert 133; Koder *256; Koehl 69, 70, 337, 466; Koehle 326; Koehler *56, *93, 109, 112, 115, *156, 163, 164, 169, 171, 185, 318, 324, 381, 397, 401, 417, 449, 467; Koelb 333; Koelcket 311;' Koelheffer 416; Koell 317; Koeller 165, 309, 337, 344, 392; Köllicker (s. Kelker) *167, 168; Koellin 76; Koellmer 340; Koemmele 253; Koenig 123, 137, *144, *172, 190, 193, 202, 258, *267, 271, 280, 281, 284, *288, 318, 348, 349, 357, 358, *364, 438, 467; Koenigsfeldt 347; v. Koennen *212, 264; K(o)eppel *203, 368; Koepplinger 63; Koerber 86; Koergert 245; Koerner 233, 246, 306, 350, 351; Koerper 72, 114; Koerschnoeck 314; Koertz 375; Koessler 419; Koettring 276; Koffel 111; Koffer 403; Koger 84; Kogh 175; Kogler 450; Kohde 137; Kohl 82, 104, 146, 162, 169, 184, *316, 327; Kohlass 326; Kohleisen 451; Kohler 89, 256; 271, 275, 381; Kohlman(n) 303, 315, 418, 419; Kohn 141, 314, 422, 426; Kohr 105, 341; Kohrman 326; Kolb 58, 61, 65, 83, 105, 109, 119, 151, 155, *169, 170, 253, 307, 317, 362, *434, 469, 470, 474, 475, 476, 477; Kol(l) 328, 355; Koller *100, 117, 185, 201, 214, 253; Kollman 473; Kollmer 235; Kolman 156; Kolmangreuer 165; Kolmer 79; Kolp *118, 180; Kolter 212; Kommell 217; Kommer 103; Konder *107; Konig(h) 74, 184, 244, 265, 267; Koningsfeld 416; Koogh 79; Koohn 156; Kooken 434; Kookes 153; Koonts 247; Koop 234; Kop 172, 236; Kopenhaver 58; Koplin 57; Kop(p) 127, *128, 296, 298, 330, 344, 447; Koppe 187; Koppelberger 171; Koppenhaeffer 330; Koppenheffer 119, 438; Koppenhoefer *466; Koppenhoeffer 469; Kopping 332; Kor *469; Korffmann 367; Korn 147, 300, 338; Korndoerfer 189; Kornhaas 303; Korning 444; Kornmann 105; Kornschur 394; Kornwalther 325; Korr 58; Korst 147; Korstmann 149; Kort 301; Kortz 416; Kost (s. Kust) 327; Kostenbades 282; Koster 207, 337, 374; Kotter 348, 354; Kouten 153; Kraeber 203, 230, 324; Kraechman 293; Kraechmer 387; Kraeffeller 141; Kraemer *67, 80, 150, 159, 161, 196, 200, 222, 234, 271, 272, *365, 381, 431; Kraess *277; Kraeuter 189; Kraffgoss 303; Kraf(f)t 68, 105, 114, 115, 153, 156, 166, 216, 248, 328, 353, 370, 378, 467; Kraffthorn 276; Krahl 171; Krahmer 216; Kram 68, 74; Kramer 78, 143, 195, 231, 251, 304, 323, 328, 346, *408, *409, 419; Krammer 150, 182, 317, 419; Kranmer 149; Krantz 116, 446; Krape 157, 299; Krapff 356; Krasch 204; Krassle 379; Krater 86; Kratringer 219; Kratz 54, *97, 320, 396; Kratzer 103, 106, 205; Krauel 414; Kraun 197; Kraus 230; Krause 109, 110, *423, 427, 428; Kraushar 17, 36; Krauskob 314; Kraus(s) 52, 66, 89, 136, 174, *212, 214, 253, 293, 300, 319, 321, 329, *337, 340, *345, 349, 385, 398, *472; Krausser 228, 410; Kraut 217, 223, 448; Krauth 111, 112, 298; Krauthamel 331; Krautter 162, 267; Krayly 333; Krebe 170; Kreber *144, 436; Krebil(l) 52, 173; Kreble 397; Krebs 123,

125, 169, 171, 182, 210, *213, 241, *253, 283, 310, 311, 337, 346, 370, 412, *474; Krebuell 372; Kreck 376; Kregeloch 317; Kreger 144, 259; Kreider(r) 73, 437; Kreidler 305, *312; Kreil 76; Kreiling 267; Kreiner 223, 304, 434; Kreis 306, 392; Kreischer (Kreuscher) 145, 189, *190, 227, *302; Kreiss 215; Kreissel 324; Kreisseman 89; Kreiter *80, 322, 385; Kreith 342; Kreitzer *129; Krels(s) 301, 371; Kremer 49, 67, *73, 132, 141, 219, 222, 265, 314, 335, 422, 426, 446; Kremmer 271; Kremser 422, 427; Kresler 83; Kress (s. Gress) 61, 280, *284, 291, 338, 341; Kressman 435; Kretel 281; Kretz 308; Kreuel 76; Kreuller 248; Kreuscher (s. Kreischer); Kreuss 244; Kreutter 89; Kreutz 242; Kreutzberger(in) 467; Kreutzer 437, 466, 467; Kreutzwisser 234; Krey *431; Kreybach 275; Kreyder 315; Kreyer 338; Kreyser 275; Kreysh 194; Kreyter 108; Kribel 333; Krichbaum *195; Kricht 277; Kri(e)bel *95, *96, 97; Kriechbaum 274, 332; Kriedelbach 419; Kriegenmeyer 285; Kri(e)ger 63, 124, 126, *152, 199, 233, 296; Krieharst 273; Krier 302; Krieve 127; Krim 319; Krimb 277; Krimm (s. Grimm) 121, *142; Krimmel 377; Kring 272; Kriser 281; Krissing 358; Kristmann 259; Kroeber 179; Kroebs 85; Kroeger 299; Kroenberg 301; Kroft 194; Krogstrup 423, 428; Kroh 147, 255, 315, 332, 384; Kroll 59, 248, 477, 478; Krom 113, 184, 402; Kron 150, 291; Kroneman 417; Kropf(f) 61, 189; Kropp 61, 66; Kroscher 410; Krueber 80; Krueck *67, 100; Krueg *339; Kruegele 263; Krueger 342, 411; Kruehl 335; Kruesser 390; Kruesy 450; Kruetter 280; Krug 139, 331, 347, 386; Krum *319; Krumbein 330; Krumholtz 337; Krumlauf 221; Krumm 260; Krumrein 74, 182; Krutter 344; Kryebiel 52; Kryser 355; Kuber 187; Kubhold 135; Kuch 398; Kuchel 294; Kucheller 183; Kuchen 306; Kucher 81, 284, 306, 348, 438, 468; Kuckhen 296; Kuebarts 221; Kuebatz 182; Kueber 273; Kuebler 112; Kueblinger *196, 244; Kuebortz 136, 148; Kuech 334; Kuechle 113, 397; Kuechler 263; Kuechli 264; Kuechner 358; Kueder 111; Kueffer (s. Keffer) 278, 378; Kuegel 265; Kuehbauch 281; Kueher 219; Kuehl 145, 320; Kuehlein 249; Kuehler 264; Kühller 80; Kuehlman 362; Kuehlmer 17, 36; Kuehlwein 239, 475; Kuehner 122, 177, 216, 444; Kuehnman 348; Kuellmann 347; Küllmer 67; Kuem 200; Kuemell 272; Kuemmel 385; Kuemmerle 401; Kuemmerley 242; Kuenbe 268; Kuendors (s. Conrad) 429; Kuenel 325; Kuener 134; Kuenerein 126; Kuenlen *451; Kuensinger 418; Kuenstler 312, 331; Kuenther 253; Kuentsch 364; Kuentz 404; Kuentzel 80, 150, 175, 415; Kuentzelman 348; Kueny 329, 372; Kueper 190; Kuepperter 144; Kuerntglein 139; Kuerr 166; Kuestener 160; Kuester (s. Kuestler) 255, *285, *432, 471, 473, 475; Kuesterman 150; Kuest(l)er *110; Kuestner 181, *197, 280; Kugel 110; Kugelwerth 365; Kugler 198, 289, 398; Kuh

Kuh—Lan

374; Kuhbach 297; Kuhl 346, 435; Kuhlemann 294; Kuhler 85; Kuhlman 393, 395; Kuhm 239; Kuhn 58, *85, 86, 118, 121, *145, 146, 158, 170, 214, 243, 248, 284, 292, 294, 295, 298, *300, 302, 313, 351, 358, 359, 362, 447, *448; Kuhnele 355; Kuhns *445; Kuhntz 151; Kuhrbocker 274; Kukuck 407; Kullem 262; Kulm 122; Kulman(n) 202, 379, *383; Kumm 181; Kumpf 397; Kun 62; Kun(c)kel 120, 121, *187, *188, 374, *380, 381, 383; Kundelmann 365; Kunders (s. Conrads) *430; Kuner 416; Kunkler 422, 427; Kunrad 213; Kunst 197; Kunstman 97, 187; Kuntz *51, 74, *76, *80, 85, *86, 105, 109, 116, *129, 131, 144, 145, *170, 176, 179, 185, *197, 203, 217, 220, 225, 226, 237, 241, 242, 275, 278, 286, 292, 295, 296, 302, 319, 339, 360, 375, 391, 395, 405, 476; Kuntze 275, 386; Kuntzel 329; Kuntzer 83; Kuntzi 285; Kuntzly 231; Kuntzman(n) 254, 273, 324; Kunz 112, 467; Kunzig 130; Kupferschmidt (-schmied) 102, 254; Kupper 278; Kurch 305; Kurcht 332; Kurseli 319; Kurtz 53, 100, 111, 143, 155, 172, *173, 179, *183, *205, 207, 213, 223, 253, 281, 284, *292, 333, *362, 371, *395, 416, 437; Kusche 199; Kusig 171; Kuss 187, 281, 311, 367; Kust (s. Kost) 327; Kuster 108, 404, 434, 435; Kutern 214; Kutz 77, 119, 297, 438, 475; Kuyl 187; Kylbach 206.

Laaber 155; Laabour 82; Labach 96; de Labeaume 392; Labengyger 50; Lach 196; Lachart 148; Lachbaum 89; Lack 67; Lackner *451; Lademacher 286; Lademan 280; Ladenberger 375; Ladsher 145; Laechner 362; Laeck 353; Laedtermann 102; Laegerhaen 56; Laegner 148; Laemmer 150; Laemmle 103; Laengle 123; Laenhart 382; Laepli 191; Laerer 159; Laffer 303; Laffersweiler (s. Lauffersweiler) 159; Lageau 281; Lahm 396; v. Lahnen 410; Laichinger 325; Laidyg 214; Lale 105; Lallemand 253; Lamb 240; Lambach 375; Lambarth (s. Lampart) 360; Lambe 201; Lambert 104, 201, 368, 370, 378, *401, 412, 463; Lamberton 445; Lamberty 245; Lambrecht 172, 262; Lamenick 132; Lamm 140; Lammon 464; Lamot 204; Lampart (s. Lambarth) 359, 360, *368; Lampater *306; Lampert *125, 444; Lanblene 298; Lanciscus *64; Lanck 289; Lanckes 53; Lanckhaer 64; Land 202; Lander 266; Landering 463; Landert 213; Landes 101, 165, 189, 213, *366, 436, 437, 477; Landfelder 450; Landgraff 115, 210, 214, 322; Landig 305; Landis 77; Landmann 210; Lands 169; Landt 349; Landtart 437; Lane 469; Lang 17, 36, 78, 79, *86, 93, 94, 100, *105, 106, 115, *130, *140, 154, 172, 190, *201, 217, 221, 255, 256, 278, 288, *289, 291, 293, 300, 302, 306, 315, 333, 339, 340, 343, *344, 346, 357, 372, 382, 384, 387, 412, *438, *467; Langbein 403; Lange 113, 125, 225, 307, 310, 324; Langebach 403, 404; Langen 447; Langenbach 306; Langenberger 176, 213; Langenecker 434, 435, 437; Langer 189;

539

Langerfeld 97; Langnecker 51; Langsdorff 330, 331, 339; Langspech 415; Lanish 227; Lann 151; Lanneger 322; Lannert 365; Lanius 66; Lans 205; Lanten 294; Lantz *127, *128, 134, *180, 189, 205, 266, 289, 294, 302, 303, 373, 448, 465; Lantzer 296; Lapierre 318; Laplace 372; de Laplaine 473; Lap(p) 93, *267, 324; Lappe 259; Larber 268; Larg (s. Long?) 305; Laros 418; Lasch 136, 252, 275; Laschett 114; van Laschet *101; Lasher 213; Lasly *343; Lassall 124; Latink *299; Latsch 383; Latshow 56; Lau 84, 85, 414; Lauall 249; Laub 136, 137, 169, 201, 262, 295, *314; Laubach *120, 185, 245, 357; Laubenhauer 238; Laubenstein *367; Laubinger 216, 296; Laubs(c)her *243; Lauch 89, 137, 225, 444; Laucher 340; Laucks 123; Laudenberger 188; Laudenschla(e)ger (s. Lautenschleger) 193, 195, 201, 234, 398; Lauderbach 110; Lauderbrunn 226; Laudermilch 81; Lau(e)r (s. Louer) 73, 76, 90, 263, 285, *317, 320, 328, 374, 438, 439, 448, *465, 466, 473; Lauerer 178; Lauetz 280; Laufaner 263; Laufer 263, 281; Lauffer *260; Lauffersweiler (s. Laffersweiler) 159; Laufflenter 154; Lauk 466, 467; Lauman 55, 87, 88, 126, *174, 289, 318, 438; Laure 204; Lausch 305; Lauser 401; Lautenbach 133, 277; Lautenber 339; Lautenschla(e)ger (s. Laudenschla[e]ger) 194, 261, 263, *285, 359, *397, 398; Lauter 273; Lauterbach 110, *210; Lautermann 124; Lautermilch 401; Lauth 358, 378; Lautzenhaeusser (-heisser) *369; Lautermilch 69, 103; Laux 187, 339, 381, 395, 403, *447; Laver 264; Law 12, 31; Lawall 202, *298; Lawer 212; Lawmeister 240; Lawrence 47, 48, 350, 351; Lawson *184; Lay 80, 100, 178, 200, *300, 312; Layar 208; Lazarus 225, 226; Leaber 144; Leaderer 268; Leap *120; Leavy 163; Leazer 124; Lebank 413; Lebbo 469; Lebegood 91; Lebemith 139; Lebenguth (s. Leibegood) 18, 36, 92, *94, 108; Lebentraut 348; Leber 211, 417; Leberger 76; Leberle 210; Leberling 272; Leberman 345; Lebing 215, 216; Leble 246; Lebo 377, 476; Lebolt 107; Leby 226; Le Cene *79; Lechleider 359; Lechleiter 149; Lechleitner 412; Lechler 378; Lechner *451, 466; Lechteni 77; Lechtenwallner 85; Lederach 477; Lederer 76, 273; Lederholt 184; Lederman(n) 69, 109, 238; Ledig 226; Lee *87; Leea 158; Leeb 341; Leeder 56, 197; Leeman 54, 76; Leemer 55; Leer 158; van Leer 432; Lees (s. Lisch) 161, 226; Leeseman 234; Leeser 207; Leesher 176; Leety (s. Luet[i]e) 192; Leey 147; Lefeber 435; Lefever 477; Lefran 413; Legire 142; Legler 163; Leh 275; Leher 85, 246, 416; Lehman(n) 53, 69, 70, *71, 111, *112, 237, 244, 262, 298, 358, 402, 405, 436, 438, 472, 477; Lehmbacher 255; Lehme 257; Lehmer *335; Lehn 154, 345; Lehnemann 433; Lehner 79, 360; Lehnert 102; Lehnes 316; Lehnig 210, 407; Lehr 140, 180, 200, 210,

321; Lied *288; Lieman 51; Lienberger 63; Lieppert *121; Lier 197; Lieser 135; Lies(s) 148, 165, 170; Liesser 137; Liettel 153; Liewel 207; Liff 241; Light 114, 126; Lighton 422, 427; Likwilder 181; Lilie 128; Lillienthal 415; Limbach 312; Limbacher 198, 199; Limbech 225; Limberger 302; Limbert 192; Limper 276; Lin 108; Linck *89, 213, 338, 343, 375, 400, *401, *409, 448; Lincker 291, 330; Lindeman *142, 237, 254; Linden 299; Lindenberger 281; Lindenmeyer 401; Lin(d)e(n)muth 206, *207, 274; Lindenschmidt *182; Linder *87, 88, 101, 310, 383; Linderman(n) 17, 36, 402, 473; Lindner 250; Lindorff 366; von der Lindt 202; Lingel *108; Lingenfel(d)ter 115, 317; Lingeveldt 143; Link 261; Linke 195; Linn 395; Linns 418; Linsenbigler 74; Linss 218; Lintell 115; Lintz 128, 237, 277, *387, 444; Lintze 120; Liphart 54; Lipking 60; Lipp *91, 373; Lippenkan 388; Lippert 214; Lippoth 260; Lip(p)s 79, 237, 271, 285; Lisa 81; Lisch (s. Lees) 161; Lischy 152, 422, 426; Liser 128; Lishire 80, 81; Liss 251; List 147, 298, 471; Litz 250; Litzler 192; Lloyd *71; Loadig 224; Loatz 87; Lob 344; Lobach 171; Lober 399; Lobstein 274; Lobwasser 178; Loch *136, 227, 468; Locher 374; Lochmann 229; Lochmeier 289; Lochner 383; Lochtner 75; Lockner 352; Loeb 408; Loebe 386; Loeble *219; Loebss 321; Loefe *345; Loeffel 86; Loeffler 106, 177, 234, 264, 372; Loeffner 189; Loehe 258; Loeher 446; Loehmer 200; Loehner 141; Loehr 199, 200, 332, 359, 408; L(o)emle *288; Loer 272; Loerch 87, *120, 161; Loere 169; Loesch 244, 347, 407; Loescher *93; Loeser *151, 319, 445; Loeshorn 330; Loessle 363; Loetterhe 193; Loew 239, 374, 398; Loewenberg *418; Loewengut 449, 465, 467; Loewenstein 103, 371; Lofinck 365; Logan 8, 26; Lohman(n) 164, 251; Lohmiller 285; Lohmoeller 285; Lohmueller 115; Lohn 445; Lohr 54, 75, 237, *330; Lohrman(n) *66, 112, *321; Lohss 140; Loie 140; Lolleninger 297; Lomger 151; Long 77, *130, *138, 229, *282, 388; Longenacre 59; Longer 295; Longhauer 204; Loninacre 89; Loof 432; Looh 173; Loomyer 247; Looser 282; Loos(s) 162, *319, 413; Lopfer 402; Loras 10, 29; Loray *344; Lorentz 84, 85, 100, 140, 154, 179, *181, 197, 209, 245, 248, 274, 322, 336, 387, 398, 444; Lorey 211; Lorie 322; Lorig 86; Loris 417; Loritz 142; Loroh 212; Loroy 120; Lostatter (Lostetter) *231; Lostetter (s. Lostatter); Lotspeich 402; Lotter 121; Lotz 80, 122, 219, 227, 240, *285, 288, *290, 297, 379; Louer (s. Lauer) 74; Loucadou 7, 25; Louvat 414; Low 84; Lower *105; Lowra 110; Lowrence 116; Loxley *406; Luar 339; Lubbar 473, 474; Lubek 214, 215; Lucas 233, 443; Lucker 329; Ludwick 238; Lucas 140; Luckenbach *141; Ludewig 248; Ludi 93, 263, 370; Ludwig *90, 198, *207, 212, 230, 242, 245, 248, 257, 276, 278, 322, *330, 332, 342, 363, 378, 414, 469; Ludy 353; Luebcken 97; Luebrick 139; Lueck 264, *391, 408; Luecken 430, *471;

Lueckhaub 384; Lueckin 473; v. Luede 301; Luedenboerg 100; Luederitz 373; Luedermacher 404; Luedy 358; Lueken 477; Lueper 298; Luesbes 225; Lueta 203; Luethy 232; Luet(i)e (s. Leety) *192; Luetsch 315, 394; Luetschy 385; Luetter 375; Luettig 370; Luetz *313; Luetzing *315; Luetzler 107; Lufft 409; Lugebuel 357; Lugenbiehl 244; Luick 194; Luig 301; Lukebill 63; Lukenbell 63; Lummel 252; Lunenmacher 264; Lung *258, 259; Luntz 287, 378; Lupfer 298; Lupffer 403; Lupp 200, *258, 274, 316, 331, 376, 397; Luppoldt *337; Luteer 204; Luteinger 117; Lutes 84; Luther 254, 313; Lutkins 432; Lutrich 320; Lutterman 322; Luttman 229, 277; Lutwig 203; Lutz 69, 88, *121, 125, 146, 178, 201, 206, *210, 219, *239, 260, 272, *277, 281, 288, 293, 295, 298, 310, 364, 378, 449; Lutzer 294; Lyme 232; Lynter 172; Lyon *318, 350.

Maag (s. Moag) 105, 159, 160, 243, 275, 314; Maas 248, 408; Machleit 291; Machler 328; Macholt (Makhold) *192; Macht 187; Mack *60, 61, 62, 86, 287, 288, 421, 425, 472, 473, 476; Mackhart 213; Mackinet 435; Mackler 164; Mackly 157; M'Nair *274; Mader 257, 366; Madery 191; Madler 98; Madlung 113; Madoeri 138; Madriger 66; Madsseil 386; Mäck 79, 278, *279; Maeckelburg 294; Maeder 365; Maegli *213; Maehlich 204; Maeintzer 258; Mäncher 71; Maendel 383; Maening (s. Maennig, Minnich) 347; Maennig (s. Maening, Minnich) 347; Maercker 304; Maertz 109, 159; Maesner 223; Maetz 412; Maeuele 310; Maeuer *217; Maeuerle (s. Maeurly) *256; Maeurly (s. Maeuerle) 256; Maeusfall 321; Maeusslin 100; Maeyer 82, 271, 375, 414, 446; Mag 258, 289; Magasch 206; Magel 143; Magnus 294; Mahenschmidt 438; Mahl 306; Mahler 123, 387; Mahnenschmidt 475; Mahr 78; Mahrsteller 110; Mahrt 185; Main 152, *311; Maine 323; Maintzger 198; Maisch 268, 306; Maisheller 261; Maison 418; Maitlin 232; Majer 468; Makhold (s. Macholt); Malfier 197; Mall 282, 306; Malle 238, 395; Mallert 200; Mallet 7, 25; Mallo 204, 391; Mallycoat 262; Maltzberger 259; Mambeck 369; Manalther 413; Manckell 338; Mandel *320; Mandeler 407; Manderbach 260, *389; Manderfelth 367; Maneubach 160; Mang 137; Mangel 334; Manich 221; Mann 78, 116, 139, 147, 182, 206, 229, 305, *312, 313, *316, 317, 357, 446; Mannion 463; Mannwiller *386; Mans 137; Mansinger (s. Mantzinge) *130; Mansperger 122; Mante 278; Mantz 124, 149, 245; Mantzinge (s. Mansinger) 130; Marbes 352; Marburg 312; Marburger 222, 276; Marchand 324; Marckbach 287; Marckel 338; Marcker 96, 395; Marckert 190; Marcus 228, 294, 432; Mardersteck (s. Matterstek) 326; Mardtin 52; Marekel 287; Margel 188, 347; Margert 449; Marggrander 417; Marheffen 255; Marich 235; Marier 327; Markly (s. Merckly) *191; Marks 357; Markwart 163; Maron 134; Marot 90, *91; Marquard(t) (-quart) 232, 275, 280; Marret 105; de Mars 153; Marschall 103; Marschheimer 359; Marsdorff

410; Marsh 59, 202; Marshall *99, *117, 205, *354; Marsteller 59, 102, 312, 469; Martain 7, 25; Marte 64, 78; Marteler 54; Marterstock 446; Martger 137; Marthin 187, 302, 344; Marti (Marty) 100, *191, 242; Martin 18, 36, 70, 77, 84, 85, 101, 119, 134, 145, 165, 201, 207, *235, 245, 248, *250, *265, 268, 313, 325, 374, 396, 398, 406, 413, 434, 447; Martine 348, 414, 463, 464; Martini *318; Martin(in) 467; Martinius 474; Martins 336; Martloff 18, 36; Marttin 52; Martz 246; Martzloff 135; Marx 144, 151, *239, 386, 391, 397; Maschcat 348; Mashberger 196; Masohlder 359; Mason *153, *161, *171, 202, 203, 236, *261, *283, *308; Maspeck 127; Mass 289; Massemer 326; Massener (s. Mesemer, Messner) 191; Masser 281, 290, 403; Masserly 164; Massiman 156; Mast 50, 111, 244, 283; Mastenberg 301; Master 359; Matern 75, 82; Mates 373; Math 249; Matheas 259; Matheis 217, 235, 387; Matheus 331; Mathias *255, 369, 371, 447; Mathiat 323; Mathis 86; Maties 255; Matinger 228; Matler 61, 237; Matsh 283; Matter 223, 250, *254, 268, 361, 389; Matterkens 395; Matterstek (s. Mardersteck) 327; Mattes 84, 115; Matthaeus *330; Matt(h)eis 146, 149, 189, 268, 289, 367, 377, 447; Matthesen 322; Matthey 184, 414; Mattinger 170; Mattis 411; Mattler 278; Matz 84, 98, *99, 123, 353, 408, 415; Matzenbacher 374, 403; Matzon 310; Mauch 250; Mauck 169, 178, 448; Maud 246; Mauden 232; Mauer 201, 202, 250, 290, 320; Mauerbach 259; Mauerer 101, 129, 136, 147, 153, 178, 201, 217, 231, 251, 273, 277, 280, 302, 345, 384, 474, 476; Maul(l) 84, 183, 184, 257, 281, 343, 443, 444; Maunshagen 319; Mauntz 111; Maurer 17, 36, 98, 99, 103, 113, 117, 130, 142, 144, 161, 166, 173, *192, 211, 213, 225, 254, 263, 320, 331, 369, 391, 401, 407, 446, 450, 451; Maurshagen 469; Mausch 218; Mauser 84, *256, *276; Maus(s) 90, 144, 157, 164, 189, 240, 274, 302, 383; Mausshalder 381; Maute 286; Mautz 69, 467; Mawer *197; Maxeiner *404; May (s. Mays) 144, 160, 165, 180, *181, 246, 285, *298, 303, 362, 369, 373, 395, 399, 412, 444; Mayer 52, 54, 55, *65, 67, 72, *73, *75, 76, *77, 78, 102, *114, 122, 126, 131, *136, 166, 172, 173, 179, 182, *183, 186, *193, 199, *206, 214, 223, 240, 246, *256, 264, *268, *269, 273, 278, 286, 295, 296, 299, 300, 313, *314, 337, 342, 346, 349, 352, 355, *356, 362, 369, 371, *381, 387, 400, 401, 409, 417, 434, 435, 436, 447, 451, *469, 470, 472, 473, 474, 476, *477; Mayr *451; Mayret 394; Mays 369; Mebel 195; Mebuer 339; Mechel 213; Mechling 58; Meck (s. Maeck) 198, 243, 332; Meckel 105; Meckelein *309; Meckes 172; Meckle 268; Mecklin 472; Meckling 58; Medart 380; Meder 86, 87, 268, 395; Medert 417; Medh 120; Medtler 58; Meeder 206; Meeke 172; Meerbagh 227; Mees 146; Meesmer 124; Meetzler 182; Meffet 257; Megerth 314; Mehl *255; Mehls *432; Mehn 366; Mehriam 127; Mehrling 373; Meichler

346; Meidelman *63; Meidinger 166; Meier 98, 106, 108, 128, 131, 142, *158, 162, 165, *196, 204, 221, 247, 384, 398; Meierhofer 191; Meiger 268, 333; Mein 101; Meinersen 299; Meingaestner 176; Meininger 189; Meinsken 308; Meinterfeer 61; Meintz 106; Meintzer 257; Meinung 421, 425; Meisch 356; Meisenheim 170; Meishter 96, 177; Meisner 187, 399; Meiss 129; Meisset 366; Meissinger 448; Meissner 318, 346; Meister 97, 113, 172, 248, 340, 346, 347, 373, 405; Meisterer 354; Meisters 128; Meisteuch 179; Meisther 95; Meittinger 329; Melber 225; Melch 443; Melcher 101, 233, 308; Melchert 217; Melchior 149; Melchner 85; Mell 235, 373; Meller *75, 317; Mellinger 195, 196, 296, 329, 388; Melter 371; Meltzer 147; Memart 100; Memminger 124; Menchen 74; Mendinger 135; Mendung 122; Menein 84; Mener 224: Meng 56, 231, 288, 473; Menge *331; Mengel(l) 266, 346, 443; Mengen 254; Menges *194, 220, *345, 354, 360, 398; Mengeting 406; Mengs 391; Menick 380; Menigh 62; Menneke *295; Mennel 387; Menner 84; Mensch 146, 233, 313, 362; Mensebach 369; Menser 258; Mentegen 448; Mentz 82, 245, 330, 473; Mentzer 110, 266, 404; Mentzel *96; Mentzinger 261, 303; Merchand *71; Merchant 99, 100, *102; Mercher 126; Mercier 405; Merck 355, *407; Merckel(l) 118, 182, 183, 225, 257, 275, 331, 332, 384, 401; Mercker 254, 257; Merckhaeusser 230; Mercki 257; Mer(c)kle *227, *269, 371, 415, 435, 478; Mercklin 226; Merckling 298; Merckly (s. Markly) 199; Mercky 328; Mergel 166, 311; Merk 98; Merkel 446; Merki 313; Merkle 474, 475, 476; Merky *103, 197; Merling 342; Merlock 379; la Mero 323; Merschrath 102; Mertel 412; Mertens 154; Mertz 74, 88, *91, 92, 99, 158, 161, 187, 190, 201, 214, 218, 223, 266, 352, 408; Mesare 406; Meschler 96; Mesling 103; Mess 83; Mes(s)emer (s. Massener, Messner) 191, 217; Messer 126, *219, 360, 444; Mes(s)erly 191, 203; Messerschmi(d)t 64, 76, 170, 185, *256, 299, 335; Messert (s. Moesser) 185, 186, *210, 404; Messner (s. Massener, Mesemer) *123, 192; Mestenbach 203; Meth *132; Metilmolske 407; Metz 57, 87, 88, 146, 147, 150, 208, *217, 232, *247, 252, 256, 272, 304, 349, 362, 434; Metzem 271; Metzger 66, 99, *154, 155, 157, 193, 201, 234, 236, 272, 290, 306, 329, 332, 335, 356, 358, *371, 410; Metziger 221, 228; Metzler 150, 169, 295, *373; Meundel 201; Meurer 422, 426; Mevius 108; Mewe 309; Mewes 284; Mey 50, 63, 217, 287, 347; Meyer *49, 54, *64, *68, 69, 74, *79, 85, *98, *99, *101, *102, 105, 107, *108, 114, 118, 119, 121, 122, 123, *124, *126, 129, *131, *132, 134, 141, *145, *148, *150, 151, 153, *155, 157, 158, 159, 161, 163, *168, 169, 173, 177, 178, 180, 186, 192, 193, *195, *197, *208, 214, *218, 222, 223, *231, 233, 235, *237, 241, 242, 244, 253, 255, 260, 261, 263, *265, *266, *269, *272,

*275, 276, 277, 284, 285, 293, 294, *295, *296, 297, 299, 303, 307, *309, 310, *314, 315, 316, 319, 325, *328, 332, *337, 338, *344, 358, 363, 364, 366, *372, 376, 382, *384, 395, 398, 399, 403, 405, 409, 411, 413, *419, 421, 426, *437; de Meyerer 85; Meyerhoffen 130; Meyers 370, 413; Meylaender 323; Meyland 405; Meylander 150; Meylin *436; Meyly 298; Meyreiss 339; Meys 59; Meysel 273; Michael *71, *117, 133, 148, 168, 170, 228, 242, 276, 318, 322, 326, 332, 343, 364, 376, 380, 390, 413; Michaels 64; Michele 198; Michel(l) 3, 21, 71, 147, 182, 292, 300, 302, 346, 360, 385, 402, 455—460; Micher 387; Michler 211, *422, 426, 427; Mick 288, 341; Micke 422, 427; Mickel 298; Micklein 104; Middeldorff 61; Middle 59; Miech 248; Miedel 201; Mier(e) 68, 81; Miesch 152, *230; Miesemer 374; Mieser 331; Mieß 18, 36; Mihller 244; Mihm 90; Mikseh 421, 425; Milberger 313; Milchsack 247, 314; Mildeberger 248; Milder *50, *51; Milderd 50; Mildy 309; Milhaus 139; Mill 116, 175; Millberg 299; Millburger 66; Millefelt *257; Millend 243; Miller 47, 48, 51, 52, 53, *55, *56, 57, 64, 65, *69, 72, 75, 76, *80, *81, 82, 83, 86, 89, 111, *113, *114, 116, 117, 118, 120, 128, *129, *133, 134, 135, 136, 144, 149, *156, *157, 159, 160, *161, *164, 165, 169, 172, 175, 177, 183, 186, 187, 188, 190, 197, *200, 202, *204, *205, 208, *211, 213, 215, *218, 219, 224, *226, 232, *233, 234, 237, 241, 242, 243, *247, *250, 251, 253, 254, 261, 272, 274, 279, 280, 286, 287, 289, 290, *291, 293, 295, 298, *302, 304, 310, 312, 314, 317, 324, 328, *333, 334, *336, 338, 340, 344, 347, 353, *355, 359, 360, *366, *375, *378, *381, 388, *390, 391, 392, 394, 400, 401, 403, 404, 408, 411, 416, 417, *438; Millerschurl 230; Millhouse 86; Milling 207; Milner 354, 355; Miloh 412; Mils 263; Minalt 311; Minch 243; Minck 295; Mindisch 252; Mineehr 105; Mingale 54; Mingel 392, 406; Minger 362; Minhard 74; Minjan 247; Minich 105, 133; Minier *82; Minler 211; Minnich (s. Maening, Maennig) 348; Mintz 220; Mirbach 325; Mire 91; Mirtorum 340; Mischat 171; Mischeb 198; Mischler (Misseler) 100, 128, *205, 206, 351; Mise 222, 392; Mishell 357; Misihni 329; Misseler (s. Mischler); Misser 178; Missner 349; Mitchell *212; Mi(t)shit *203; Mittelberger 242, 265; Mittelburger 249; Mittelkauff 56; Mittmann 367; Mitzler 116; Moag (s. Moog) 159; Moak 83, 165; Moan (s. Mohn) 180; Moch 114; Mochel 237; Mock 116, 214, 291, 325; Moclotz 219; Moderer 467; Modi 340, 341; Modus 146; Moebs 250; Moecklei 93; Moeggy 245; Moehner 160; Moehring 329; Moeler 227; Moelich 56, 98, *99; Moelig 204; Moeller 66, 70, 152, *228, 240, *291, *422, *426; Moellinger 380, 401; Moench 294; Mörson 296; Moeschler 338; Moeser 120, 349; Moesser (s.

Messert) 210; Moessinger 75, *76, 244, 328; Moestmer 192;
Moeths 194; Mofhel *242; Mohl 227, 322; Mohler 63, 217;
Mohmeyer 318; Mohn (s. Moan) 87, *88, 180; Mohr 104,
142, 159, 170, 184, 202, 220, 256, *257, 297, 302, *339,
370, 383, 384, 390, 400, 439, 446, 449; Mohrlock 398;
Mohrmann 402; Molam *348; Molan 283; Molin 296; Molitor 395; Moll 59, *67, 70, 106, 171, 178, 245, *277, 400,
477; Moller 400; Mollwitz 405; Molsbach 285; Molssberger
259; Moltz 149, 274; Mombau(e)r 116, *133; Momma 179;
Mommaton 392; Monbauer 315; Mond 446; Mondshauer 160;
Monford 7, 25; Monie 390; Monin *324; Monitzer 258;
Montandon 59; Montelius 407; Montpelier *268, *288; Moog
131, 236; Mook 147, 182, 248; Moor 58, 132, 211; Moore
147, 257, *279, *305, *327; Mopps 360; Morash 308; Moraublez 417; More 171; Moret 249, 264; Moretz 93; Moreye
*463; Morgedaller 209; Morgen 169; Morgenroth 295; Mor-
genstern 56, 196; Morhardt 289; Morian 170; Morietz 121;
Moris 192; Morith 246; Moritz 241, 242, 314, 449; Morlier
405; Morrell 444; Morris 469; Morriset 7, 25; Morth 76;
Morty (s. Marti); Mory 435; Mosemann *90; Moser 57, *79,
81, 209, 269, *336, 357, 415; Moses 159, 388; Mosieman
173; Mosock 98; Moss 377; Mossbach 313; Mosselman 173;
Mosser 18, 36, 52, 58, 78, *79, 119, 173, *178, 198, 231,
280, 375, 437; Most 291; Motheri 215; Mothes 68; Mott
*464; de Mott 445; Motte 397; Motz 18, 36, 186, 376, 386;
Motzer *382; Mozer 422, 427; Much 74; Muckenberger 178;
Muckenfus 281; Mueck 295; Mueckli 89; Muedtschi 188;
Mueh 273; Muehl 147, 330, 384; Muehleisen 368; Muehl-
eissen (Muehleysen) 178, 179, *224; Mühlenberg *158; Muehl-
heim 283, 354; Mue(h)lhof(f) *197, *302; Muehlmichel 361;
Muehlschlaegel 225; Muehr 128; Muelberger 66, 397; Muel-
daler 329; Mueller 17, 36, *51, 53, 55, *59, 63, *64, 66,
72, *74, *75, 76, *77, *78, *80, 81, *8,_ *85, *87, 88, *97,
98, 99, 102, *105, 111, 112, 114, 115, 117, 119, *122,
123, 127, 128, 129, *130, *131, 133, 134, *135, 136, *141,
142, 143, *146, *148, 149, *156, 157, 158, *163, 164, *165,
166, 168, 170, 171, *173, 174, 179, 180, 181, 182, 184, 185,
186, *188, 193, 194, 197, *204, *206, 207, 208, *209, 211,
*212, *217, *220, 222, *224, 225, 226, 227, 229, 230, *234,
*235, 237, 239, 242, 250, 252, 253, 258, *260, 262, *264,
265, 269, *271, *274, 275, *276, 277, *279, 280, 282, *285,
*288, 291, 292, 293, 294, 297, *302, *307, *310, *311, 312,
*315, 316, 317, 319, *320, 323, *327, 328, 329, 334, 335,
*336, *339, *340, *341, 347, 348, 350, 351, 352, 353, 354,
356, 361, *362, 363, *369, *370, *371, 372, 374, *376, 377,
*378, 381, *382, 383, *384, *386, *387, 388, 390, *391, 392,
393, 394, *397, *401, 402, 405, 407, *412, 413, *415, *416,
*417, 418, 419, 432, *436, *444, *446, 447, 449, *450,

466, *467, *468, 471, 472, 473, *474, 475, *476; Mueltz 352; Muench 272, *369; Muenchinger 304; v. Muenchler 254; Muenckel 198; Muencker 146; Muendel 419; Muender 252; Muenig 216; Muensch 386; Muenster 422, 426; Muent 295; Muentz 102; Mueri 52; Muerlich 229; Mueschlitz 321; Muesig 448; Muesse 282; Muessemer 280; Muessi 328; Muetschler 232, 287; Mufli 113; Mug 228; Mugler 248; Muinber 382; Muir *233, *257, *328; Mulchslager 73; Muller 255, 373, 467; Mumau 179; Mumma *67, 76, 77, 187; Mumrich 161; Mundorff 374; Muni *236, *237; Munner 354; Munsinger 447; Munster 236, 258; Muntzer 399; Muor 278; Murr 242, 313; Murro *464; Muschler 325; Muselman 72; Musgnug 258; Musloch 83; Musse 239; Musselbach 59; Musselman(n) 389, 437, 438, 473; Mussgenug 282, 418; Must 262; Muth 240, 278, 294, 366, 368; Muthhardt 113; Mutschler *253, 407; Muttersbach 319; Mutz 387; Myrteties 202.

Naab 345; Naahs 386; Naas 90; Naath 100; Nabinger 154; Nabniger 131; Nachbar 119; Nachtgall 180; Nadderman 81; Nadem 269; Nadler 389; Nadtheimer 331; Naecht 238; Naeff 98, 132, *158, *197; Naegele 369; Naegli 153; Naehlich 284; Naeryes B54; Naetter 188; Naewiss 324; Naff *158; Naffe *98; Naffzer 277; Naffzir 145; Nafzger (Nofsker) *205; Naftziger 244; Nagel 62, 84, 120, 126, 142, *194, 225, 233, 238, 255, 256, *257, *258, 262, *269, 294, 295, 296, 306, 310, 325, 327, *365; Nagle 118, 119; Nair 152; Nanecker 404; Nargang (s. Nargary, Nargarg) 101, 132; Nargarg (s. Nargang, Nargary) 100; Nargary (s. Nargang, Nargarg) 101; Naschi 386; Nas(s) (s. Nast) 267, 282, 295, 306; Nast (s. Nass) 282; Nastes 304; Nauaetter 404; Nauman(n) *233, *381, 389; Nay 189; Naycommet 56; Nazurus 246; Neas 123; Neb 366; Nebe 322; Nebel 344; Nebeling 298; Neblinger 357; Necum (Nickum, Nuekom) *190; Nederman 318; Nees 113, 164, 185, 214, 215, 227, 346, *348; Neezer 148; Nef(f) 57, 98, 99, 162, 165, 388, *437, 444, 466, 467; Neffveile *464; Negele 123, 179; Neher 241; Nehr 447; Nehrlich 326; Nehs *69, 70, 114; Neidig(h) 72, 73, 128, 187, 345, *346; Neidlinger 320; Neidung 17, 36; Neiell 291; Neier 215, 402; Neigh 144; Neihaeltzer 76; Neihart *108, 109; Neiman 217, 267, 320; Neimeyer (s. Niemeyer) 301; Neimiger 333; Neinrich 407; Neirn 7, 25; Neiser 421, 425; Neiss 302, 363; Neissel 382; Neiswanger 108; Neitlinger 202; Nell 408; Nelles 447; Neracker 231; Nerbler 401; Nerien 304; Nerlinger 273; Ness 70, 212; Nesselroth 295; Nestler 407; Netischeh 241; Nett 450; Netscher 408; Netzbach 448; Netzert 384; Netzli 98; Neu 101, *197, 354, 384, 396, *408; Neubaier 414; Neubeck 339; Neubecker 202; Neucomer 437; Neuenschwander *336; Neuer 110, 234; Neuffes 264; Neuhauser 175; Neuhauss 186; Neuhoff 196; Neukirch

443; Neuman(n) *96, 116, 117, 121, 143, *226, 245, 326, 335, 342, 380; Neumeister 98; Neumer 146; Neus (auch Nice) *430, 471, 472; Neuschwander 191, *379; Neuschwanger 155, 470; Neustaett 283; Neveling 127; Nevin *321; Newbert 71; Newcomer *155, 336, 337; Newman 240; Newmeyer 261; Newswanger 56; Ney 53, 92, 93, *248, 335, *398, 416; Neycomer 244; Neydig 315; Neyer 356; Neyff 347; Neyman 345; Neymeyer 307; Neytzert 169; Neyzart 169; Nezelius 432; Nibling 194; Nice (s. Neus); Nic(h)olas 145, *220, 285; Nicholson *228; Nicht 415; Nichtedt 307; Nichter 121; Nick 182; Nickel 133, 320, 391, 404, 419; Nickellas 285; Nicklaus 125, 284; Nickles 364; Nicklin 313; Nickom *133; Nickum (s. Necum); Nicodemus 259, 354; Nicol 136; Nicola 128; Nicolaus 146; Nicolehrs 416; Nie 333; Niebel 398; Niebergall 404; Niecke 318; Nied 315; v. Nieda 360; Niedenthal 287; Nieder *394; Niederhauss 396; Niederhut 318; Nieman 309; Niemand 161; Niemeyer (s. Neimeyer) 301; Nies 443; Niese 344; Niess 185, 285, 353, 386, 411; Nieth 189, *364; Nietzel 342; Nieve 204; Nike *204; Nill 310, 361, 372; Ninies 217; Nisch 260; Nisler 417; Niss 108; Nitschmann 14, 17, 32, 36, 420, 421, 424, 425; Nitz 300; Nitzel 397; Nitzen 65; Nixdorf 422, 426; Noaecker 449; Noah 18, 36; Nobel *97, 406; Noch 97, 98; Nodden *463; Nodhardt 130; Noecker 17, 36, 465; Noegelle 49; Noegle 247; Noel *103, 284; Noelen 169; Noell 259; Noess 69, 70; Nofsker (s. Nafzger); Nohacker 438; Nold 333, 339; Noldt 55, 329; Nolff 112; Noll 80, 85, 92, 101, 116, *169, *184, 233, 254, 255, 294, 322, 352, 444, 469; Nonn 413; Nonnemacker 203; Nonne(n)macher 235, 256, 279, 346, 391; Nonyus 285; Nordt *88; Norffkoh 223; Norheimer 367; North 143, *155, *158; Noschang 357; Noss 171; Noth 395, 474; Nothdarf 295, Nothstein 237, 401; Notoing 203; Notz 83, 118, 172, 268, 286; Nudell 177; Nudhart 121; Nuehlhahn 295; Nuekom (s. Necum); Nuesser 297; Nues(s)li 131, 132; Nuessly 297, 437; Nuetzer 371; Null 54; Nungesser 72, 73; Nunnenmacher 194; Nunymeyer 287; Nusbaum 164; Nushagen 251; Nuss 102, 105, 239, 379; Nussbaum 164; Nussbuerckel 297; Nusser 404; Nuttler 390; Nutts 194; Nutz 187; Nuyne 415; Nycius 400; Nydy 79.

Obelhart 110; Obendorff 306; Obenheyser 165; Ober 278, 413; Oberbach 466; Oberbäck 65; Oberbeck (s. Overback) *76; Oberdorff *240, 241, 293, 308, *309, 334, *411; Obere 59; Oberfeld 218; Obergefaell 349; Oberhaeussle 266; Oberheuser 211; Oberholtz 52, 64, *436, 437; Oberholtzer 72, 73, 343, 471; Oberkagler 76; Oberkehr 117; Oberkirch 250; Oberkircher 418; Oberkirsch 224; Oberländer 376, 405; Oberle (s. Eberle) *219, 234; Oberlender 306; Oberlin 468; Oberly 257; Oberman 295; Obermeyer 257, 386; Obermüller 80; Obersheimer 384, 418; Obersteg 205, 206; Oberweiler 310; Oberzeller 342;

Obmann *355; Obolt 135; Obrist 278; Ochs 372, 473, 474; Ochsa 365; Ochsenbacher 325; Ochsenreiter *305; Ochsner 401; Ochssenbecher 358; Ocker 349; Odern 397; Odewalt 267; Odewelder 159; Odt *155, *156, 166, 170; Oehl 146; Oehler 146, 166, 181, 212, 341; Oehlweiler 219; Oehrle 233; Oelgarden 272; Oellen 61; Oellenschlaeger 345; Oellinger 207; Oeltinger 359; Oerdter 254; Oerrig 348; Oerter *354, 371, 422, 427; Oerthler 325; Oertter 396; Oess 246; Oesterich 287; Oesterlein 292; Oesterle(n) (s. Oesterlin) 134, *165, 229; Oesterlin (s. Oesterle[n]) 124, 165; Oether 143; Oetzel 240; Oexle 260; Off 264, 444; Offenbacher 105; Offenhaeuser 348; Offleler 411; Offner 222; Ogli 297; Ohber (s. Weber?!) 211; Ohl 142, 374, 412; Ohle 247; Ohler 108, 384; Ohliger 74; Ohlinger 218; Ohller 62; Ohlwein 90, *403; Ohms 318; Ohneberg 422, 427; Ohnschild 295; Ohr *87; Ohrendorff 372; Ohrig 184; Okely *422, 426; Okser 207; Olenthin 275; Olftheintz 392; Oliger 149; Oliver *149; Oltenwaldt 287; Omme (s. Amme) 191; Ommell 121; Ommerth 240, 291; Onangst (s. Unangst) 272; Onas 124; Onder 376; Onkel 293; Onzemiller 276; Onzinger 209; Oordt 56; Opdegraef 469; Opitz 422, 427; Opp 179, 181, 230, 355, 368, 386, 416; Oppenheim 311; Oranu 395; Orbig 148; Ord 309, 362, *390; Orde 59; Orendorff (s. Arhndorff) 111, 147; Orich (s. Oriths) 103; Oriths (s. Orich) 103; Orndorff 319, 320, 468; Orpertag 224; Ort 254; 'Orth 59, 240, 244, 259, 277, 367, 383, 408; Ortley 130; Ortman(n) 14, 32, 179, *396, 450; Ortt 344; Osborn *394; Osborne *404; Osmon *371, *377; Osmond *374, *392, *402, *406, *417; Osseler 199; Osser 53, *395; Osswald 305; Ost 225; Oster 142; Osterman 144, 184; Osterrath 91; Ostertag *198, 371, 402; Osterwald 313; Ostian 422, 426; Oswald 76, 98, 307; Oth 360; Otho 352, 402; Otmansdorff 238; Ott 77, *90, 98, 150, *155, 165, 174, 181, *203, *226, 249, 274, 289, /291, 293, 297, 304, 308, 329, *334, 360, 361, 364, 374, 391, 408, 416, 450; Otteene *445; Otter 97; Otterback 395; Otterbein 270, 271; Otterpach 97; Ottershelt 359; Ottiner 126; Ottinger 272, 273, 477; Otto 131, 301, 318, 349, 422, 426, 473; Otz 176, 241; Ouchterlony *286; Overback (s. Oberbeck) 75; Overholser 55; Overholtz 132; Overkirs(c)h *189; Ox(e)man(n) *57, 265.

Pabst 294, 296, 316; Pacht 448, 465; Pad 170; Paeffer 443; Paeth 297; Paff 230, 385; Paffler 230; Pagman 50; Padum 83; Paffland 322; Pahosuch 309; Pahr 191; Paine 422, 427; Painter (s. Paynter) 136, 137; Palin (Palm?) 115; Pallard 473; Palm 224, 378; Palsgraff 74; Pampus 266; Pander 258; Pangert 207; Panheimer 189; Panix 317; Pannbecker 435; Panse 310; Pantzly 336; Panzer 351; Papen 432; Pappel 469; Papst 79; Par(a)et *77, 97; Parcout *464; Pargel 226; Paris *243, 248; Parish *265, *294, *301; Parisien 321; Partemer 170; Partts 212; Pasch 389; Paschon

84; Passage 69, 84; Past 258; Pastorius 2, 20, 429, 473; Path 269; Patier 390; Patt 276; Patteiss 412; Pattheuer 173; Patton *125; Patz 236; Paul 157, 331, 336, 416, 433; Paule 237; Pauli 351, 389, 402; Paulis 154; Paulssig 406; Paulus 190, 275, 335, 352, *353, 384, 391, 403; Pauly 315, 351, 364; Pausch 176; Pauser 250; Pauss 96; Paust *87, *88; Pauth 125; Pautz 352; Pavelieats 124; Pavit *390; Pavon 168; Pawling 469; Paynter (s. Painter) *114, *141; Pean 7, 25; Pechenet 414; Pechin *324; Pecht 416; Pechtluf 77; Peck 86, 117, 380; Ped 83; v. Pedden 431; Peepell 50; Peetsh 195; Peffel 59; Peffer 75, 185; Pefferle 222; Pegy 275; Peier 187; Peietrs 406; Peif(f)er 63, 177, 260, 267, 352; Pein 346; Pe(i)rcy *65, *85, *104, *132, *144, 456, 459; Peirot 283; Peisser 190; Peistly 281; Pell 6; Pelman 80; Pelnes 432; Pelss 322; van Pelt 471; Peltz 162; Peman 411; Pemeller 302; Pence *123, 284; Pendtner 278; Pengler 212; Peni 77; Penn *404; Pennybecker 474, 475, 476; Penss 201; Pentz 80; Pepler 344; Perass 300; Perdschinger 98; Perger 61, 87, 365; Periter *324; Perlet 259; Pero 7, 25; Peroing 306; Perquy 204; Perret 400; Personz 146; Perster 229; Pesser 284, 414; Pessinger (s. Bessinger) 392; Peten-koffer 61; Peteo 169; Peter 18, 36, 87, 148, 155, 157, 210, *226, 234, *236, 245, 246, 258, 282, *297, 322, 342, 407, *408; Peterey 179; Peteri 346; Peterkoffer 473; Peterly 118; Peterman(n) 187, 211, *241, 262, *395, 413, 471; Peters 83, 226, 403, 433, 435, 475; Petersen 392; Petersheim 247; Petersheimer 217; Petersohn 180; Peterson 332; Peter-welles 272; Petery 129, 366; Petre 445; Petri 280, 366, 406; Petrus 468; Petry 87, 140, 160, 201, 217, 301, 330, 367, 376, 448; Petrygandt 378; Petter 49, 350, 363, 365; Pettinger 432; Pettry 364; Petz 322; Petzold 152; Peuckert 238; Pezold 422, 426; Pfadermiller 282; Pfadt 347; Pfaeher 231; Pfaell 391; Pfafenberger 467; Pfaff 386; Pfaffenberger *93; Pfankuchen 279; Pfannebaecker 469; Pfannenbecker 202; Pfannenkuch 471; Pfanner 307; Pfannkuchen 202, 298; Pfantzler 129; Pfarr 122; Pfateicher 467; Pfatteicher 110; Pfau 387; Pfautz 49, 198, 403; Pfauty 208; Pfeffer 254, 389; Pfeifer 297; Pfeiffer 148, 175, 181, 199, 260, 261, *263, *267, 282, 316, 330, 343, 345, *355, 362, 371, 382, 404, 406, 410, 445; Pfeil 110, 148, 150, 154, 202, 217, 222, 225, 280, 336; Pfeill 286; Pfeind 187; Pfeller 111, 324; Pfenning 472; Pfester 197, 256; Pfesterer (s. Pfisterer); Pfetzer 315, 405; Pfiengstag 177; Pfiester *131; Pfiffer 191; Pfillibs 315; Pfingstag 105, 223; Pfister 159, 231, 312, 329; Pfisterer (Pfesterer) *235, 338; Pflaugner 163; Pflaum 368; Pflieger 177, 306, 408; Pfliester *254; Pflinder 403; Pflocher (s. Blocher) 321; Pflueckinger 78; Pflueger 188; Pflug 318; Pfoersching 216; Pfudere 65; Pfuester 273;

Pfü—Rab

Pfüller 238; Pfuender 123; Pheneyer 449; Phiel 119; Philip 56, 148, 294; Philipi *363; Philipin 136; Philippi 203; Philips *113, 227, 331, 456, 459; Phil(l)ipi (Philipy) *238; Phillipot 64; Phillipp 306; Phillips 236; Phillipus 199; Phuel 384; Phul 189; Pichler 450; Pichnoester 169; Pickel 82; Pickels *414; Pickeman *168; Pieckert 414; Piel 281; Pieler 130; Pier *341; Piercy 71, 72; Pier(e) 54, 82, 246; Piesch 278; Pieters 261; Piger 54; Pigger 331; Pigonie 278; Pilanus 181; Pilerge 395; Pilgram 227; Pillab 268; Piller 184; Pillon *464; Piltz 451; Piner 107; Pingley 100; Pinnet 7, 25; Pipon *130; Pisas 448, 465; Pisell 84; Pisher 54; Pisserth 252; Pitcha 54; Pittcairne *296, *320; Pix 313; Pixseler 54; Place 154; Plach *209; de la Plaine 432; de la Plaines 10, 29; Planck 277, 443; Plank 474; de Plank 475; Plantz 154, 156, *222; Plat(t) 170, 381; Plattner 400; Platz *309; Plauler 98, *99; Plause 50; Plehman 213; Plenninger 223; Plesher 233; Pletsch 391; Plettel 440, 442; Pletter 451; Pletz 371; Plitz 309; Plocher(r) 223, 264; Ploehger 140; Plott 240; Plotz 184; Plueger 66; Pluhan 338; Pluner 310; Poensy 115; Pohl 130; du Poisson 13, 32; Pok 318; Poland *224; Polch 189; Poldesberger 158; Pole 254; Polhaus 367; Poll 24; Pollock 456, 459; Polo 376; Polweller 304; Ponce *373; Poncelly 417; Pons 261; Pontius 116; Pontzius *383; Poobagh 343; Pooff 157; Pool (Puhl) 260, 271, 317; Pop 233, 335; Poriger 128; Porrath 194; Porster 389; Port 299; Porter *357, *369, *376; Porter (Bortner) 445; Possert 266; Post 101, *152, 153, 226, 422, 426; Pott *96, 339, 346; Potts *79, 129, *418, 431, *432; Potz 125; Pouponnot 405; Pouriot 405; Poutmant 264; Powell *422, 426; Prach 189; Pracht 140, 248; Prack 115; Praeuner 78; Prall 231; de Pratt 456, 459; Pregly 173; Preire 190; Preising 302; Preis(s) 110, *115, 303, 332, 341, 370, 401; Preissgaertner 349; Preissman 391; Prela 163; Prenger 148; Prenser 364; Prentz 200; Presen 140; Presler 237; Pressel 90; Presser 17, 18, *36; Prestel 355; Pretz 80; Pretzman 227; Preyss 305, 320; Prickes 147; Priem 133; Priere 321; Priest 222; Prike *229; Prill 50; Prim 254; Printly 269; Printschler 59; Printz 210, 235, 319; Printzholtz (s. Bruensholtz) 226; Pritz 104; Probe 307; Probst *85, *86, 351, *352; Prophet 234; Proptenslad 301; Pros 399; Prost 314; Protzmann 164, 236; Pruch 367; Puegner 318; Puehl 282; Puehrer 274; Puhl (s. Pool); Punch 111; Pupather 436; Purman 220; Pury 14, 15, *33; Putner 324; Putscher 295; Putterbach 272; Pynni 383; Pyrlaeus 152, 153, 421, 425; Pythan 387.

Quandel 362; Quast 401, 417; Queichel 73; Quepic 323; Quickel *104; Quinrin 276.

Raa 468; Raab 272, 308, 326, 364; Raan 56; Rab 154, 300, 339; Rabane 417; Rabanus 335; Rabe 97, 109, 227; Rabenstein 342; Rabenwalt 106; Raber 209; Rabi 228; Rach 317; Racke 196, 360; Radebach 363; Radebaugh 116; Radebusch 171; Rademacher 340, 389; Radge 143; Radman 398; Radtgaeb 98; Radwitzer 431; Raeber 174; Raedel 182; Raemer 81; Raemlander 374; Raemmy 323; Raerich 194; Raesch (s. Rish) 68, 70, 189, 240, 329; Raetze 338; Raeumann 372; Raeumer 185; Raeyer 395; Rafer 61; Raffenberger 397; Raffensburg 384; Raffgarn 301; Ragel 398; Rahausser 275; v. Rahden 281; Rahm 151, 306, *330; Rahmer 302; Rahn *108, 219, 258; Rahnfelder 239; Raible *289; Raisch 111, 239; Ralsure *84; Ram 222, 268; Rambach *93, 233; Ramberg 307; Rambo 470; Ramler 438; Rammler 469; Ramsauer *73, 476; Ramsberger 327, 328; Ramseyer 137; Ranck 56, 59, 60; Ranger 78; Ranhert 354; Rannoo *463; Rapman 281; Rap(p) 108, 219, 333, 359; Rappoldt 224; Raque *359; Rarr 342; Rat 88; Ratenbuerger 244; Ratgen 108; Rath 154, 233, 375; Rathacker 325, 370; Rathardt 416; Rathebach 336; Rathenbach 402; Rathend 324; Rathert 308; Rathgeb 264; Rathgeber 113; Rathmacher 186; Rathschlag 339; Ratiker 299; Ratsmith 146; Rattenauer 178; Rattge 109; Rau 169, 278, 305, 306, 335, 360, 379, *384, 411; Raub 80, 239, 256, 258; Raubenheimer 397; Rauberg 299; Rauch 80, 103, 116, 143, 175, 181, 184, 185, 201, 325, 359, 407, 421, 425, 447; Rauck 240; Raudenbusch 82, 83, 129, 474; Rauf(f) 89, 139; Rauffbem 303; Rauhman 380; Rauhzahn 234; Rauland 149; Raum 387; Raunberger 308; Rauner *450; Raup 80; Raus 128, 435; Rausch 104, 107, 110, 116, 125, 194, 195, 301, 327, 341, 403; Rauschenbach 301; Rauschenberger 82; Rauscher 386; Rauschkopf 361; Rausenberger 123; Rausher 85; Rauter 365; Rawher 261; Rayer 438; Rayster 242; Readwile 241; Reason *162; Reb 236, 374, 378; Rebe 332; Rebele 331; Rebell 100; Rebenstock 431, 471; Reber 118, 185, 205, 226, 338; Rebhuhn 325; Reblet 89; Rebman(n) 81, 116; Rebschleger 245; Reburg 301; Rechner 307; Rechtlos 303; Reck *338, 364; Reckert 342; Reckman 205; Reder 378; Redig 261; Redlinger 231; Redman 194; Redwetzer 478; Reeb 275, 342; Reed 207; Reedelmos 213; Reeder 153; Reeg 293; Reel 245; Reely 250; Reem *182; Reemer 54, *137; Reep 79, 80; Reese 124, 180, 204, 215; Reesher 163; Reet 91; Reete 402; Refi (Refy) 199, 200; Refschneider 142; Regel 228; Regelman 150; Regene 449; Regennas 265; Reger 204; Rehbach 239; Rehbock 344; Rehble 332; Rehcopp (-kopp) 172, 299; Rehfeld 402; Rehr 299; Rehrer 265; Rehsauer 128; Rehvan 326; Rehwalt 147; Reiber 223; Reich 92, 93, 108, 234, 236, 252, 268, 413, 445; Reichard 371, 473; Reichart (s. Reichert) 78, 120, 125, 226, 466; Reichel 287, 345, 392, 420, 424; Reichelsdoerfer 17, 36, 474; Reichenaecher 257; Reichenbach 93; Reichenerder 279; Reichert (s. Rei-

Rei—Rey

chart) 77, 224, 410; Reichhelt 238; Reichle 224, 268; Reichly 338; Reichman 232, 301, 413; Reichwein 247; Reid *88, 97; Reidenauer 179, 367, 368; Reide(n)bach *362, 363; Reidenmeyer 382; Reider 355; Reidiger 326; Reidkopff 448; Reier 80; Reif(f) 59, 60, 89, 135, 243, 244, 306, 359, 395, *435, 469, 470, 472, *476, 477; Reiffenberg 448; Reiffener (Reyffener) *199; Reiffschneider (-snyder) 120, 121, 164, 171, 185, 211; Reifschneider 474; Reiger 333; Reigert 298, 449; Reigh 121; Reilenbach 220; Reimer 63; Reimmel 107; Rein 74, 124, 125, 129, 313, 314, 349; Reinaldt 216; Reinardt 178, 286; Reinbold 361; Reinbolt 447; Reinbracht 143; Reinche 405; Reindel 302; Reiner 182, *221, 222, 223, 329, 362, 409, 474; Reinetz 123; Reinfeld 232; Reinger 349; Reinhard(t) 84, *88, 134, 139, 224, 232, 251, 253, 304, 312, 335, 405, 408; Reinhart(h) 110, 136, *176, 188, 189, 206, 219, 225, 238, 260, 276, 309, 335, 339, 342, 346, 374, 406, 412; Reinheimer 255; Reinhold(t) 97, 277, 295, 305, 311, 395; Reinholtz 223; Reinick 404; Reiniger 192; Reinke 423, 427; Reinknecht 296; Reinman 318; Reinoehl 223; Reinthaler (Reynthaler) 193, *256; Reintzel 123; Reinwald *95; Reis 59, 286; Reisch 97, 98, 296, 334, 447; Reisener 324; Reish 234; Reisinger *111, *212; Reisner 83; Reiss (Reys) (s. Rice) 118, 133, *226, 313, 376, 380, 396, *402; Reissdorff 340, 386; Reisser 129, 222; Reist 241, 281, 345; Reistebacher 238; Reistel 89; Reit 279; Reiter 277, 450, 451; Reith 341; Reithnauer (s. Reudenauer) 164; Reit(t)enau(e)r *119, 135, *139; Reitlershan 81; Reitzel *106, 373; Reitzmann 106; Reive 313; Reizer 266; Reling 318; Remberger 343; Remel 107; Remer 62; Reminger 127; Remly 219; Remmler 163; Remsberger 438; Renau *272, 364; Reneb 321; Renecker 229; Rener 147; Rengel 156; Reninger 328, 437; Renn 63; Rennau 439, 441; Renneck 327; Rennenger 71; Renner 75, 128, 201, 303, *331; Renninger 214, *227; Rennoe 464; Reno 7, 25, 249; Renschmit 319; Rentsch 101; Rentz 347; Rentzel *222; Rentzheimer *419; Repair 314; Repo (s. Bon R'); Reppert 52, 143; Resch 91, 299, 344; Rescher 361; Resh 253; Reshe 174; Resler 367; Resmeyer 365; Resseler 240; Ressener 198; Resser 77; Ressing 341; Retelsberger 93; Rett 205; Retter 287; Rettes 401; Rettig 195; Reuber 339; Reuchler 324; Reudenauer (s. Reithnauer) 164; Reudt 357; Reuel 171; Reul 164; Reusch 125, 366, *398; Reuschling 380; Reusel 260; Reushaw 243; Reussen 140; Reusswig 155; Reuter *75, 91, *113, 198, 299, 350, 378; Reuther 157, 376; Reuthnauer 408; Reutter 235, 349; Reutzel (s. Ritzel) *240; Reutzheiner 416; Reuz 422, 426; Reventlau 322; Rewold 253; Rey 80, 273; Reybold (-bolt) 261, 312; Reybolt 234, 260, 345; Reyd 160; Reydenauer 119; Reyder 181; Reydmeyer 164; Reyel 84, 85, 338; Reyer 59, 80, *192; Reyffener (s. Reiffener); Reylandt 224; Reyling 322; Reyman *119, 169, 366; Reymer 472, 474; Reynhart 175; Reyninger 406; Reynold 96; Reynthaller (s. Reinthaler); Reys (s. Reiss) 249, *255; Reysal 249; Reyser 247; Reysing 308; Reyt 375; Reyter 290, 378; Rhein 186, *255, 369; Rheiner 232; Rheinlender 49; Ribelet 198, 199; Rice (s. Reiss) 313, 421, 426; Richan 320; Richardon 304; Richards 404; Richart (Righart) *206; de Richebourg 7, 25; Richer 97; Richey *299; Richler 315; Richman 164; Richner 402; Richter 89, 97, 130, 211, 242, 258, 342, 443; Richty 336; Rick 232, 356; Rickart 201; Ricker 153, 337; Rickmueller 466; Rickos 397; Ricks *176; Ricksaker 203; Ridelsberg 205; Rider 57; Ridle 361; Ridlein 201; Riebel(l) 92, 247; Riechart 111; Riechels 411; Rieckhed 311; Riede 239; Riedel 210, 278; Riedelsperger *450; Rieder 239, 473; Ried(in) 55, 120, 467; Riedt 53, 57; Riedy *133; Rieffenach 405; Rieg 359; Riegel *79, *90, 91, 149, 323, 447; Riegeler 276; Riegelman *150; Rieger 68, 69, 96, 112, 131, 155, 166, 365; Riegert 280; Riegler 184, 300; Ri(e)hl 84, 85, 225, 333; Riehm 183, 205, 358, 437, 438; Riel(l) 320, 339; Riemann 318; Riemenschneider 122; Riemer 59, 372, 449; Riesenober 449; Rieser 305, 449, *450, 471, 473; Ries(s) 54, 105, *109, 146, *157, 177, 193, 207, 287, 292, *308, 332, 343; Riesser 53, 135, 308; Riesset 161; Rietel 350; Rieth 173, 344, 362, 438, *448, *465, 477; Rietweill 242; Rietz 332; Riffel 236; Riga 131; Riger 57, 248, 263; Rigerd 92; Righart (s. Richart); Righter 178; Rigler 251; Rihl 116; Rihm 278, 367; Rimli 149; Rimmel 249; Rimy 107; Rincker 230, 273; Rinckle 372; Rinderdust 287; Rinehart 246; Rinehold 223; Ring 52, 364; Ringer 166, 356, 474; Ringwald 314; Rinker 474, 476; Rintelman 405; Rippas 384; Rippel 266; Rippert 110; Risch 175, 235; Rished 449; Rischerd 273; Rischstein 162; Riser 54, *80, 451; Rish (s Raesh) 240; Risling 53; Riss *75, 76, 137; Rissel 277; Risser 126, 201; Rissmann 102; Rissner 414; Rister 121; Risternholtz 199; Ristnach 245; Rit 213; Ritcher 217; Riter 246; Rithmueller 238; Ritner 224; Ritschart 329; Ritt 85, *86, 87, 91; Rittelbach 206; Rittenhaus (s. Ruettyn[g]huysen); Ritter *66, 81, 103, 123, 205, 215, 258, 281, 348, 355, 403, 407, 419; Rittesheim 356; Ritz 184, 190, 247; Ritzbach 446; Ritzel (s. Reutzel) 240; Road 82; Roadebas 50; Roath 203; Roberd 7, 25; Robert 375; Roberts *399, 469; Robertus 124; Robetes 82; Robinson *360, *377, *382; de Roche 372; Rochia 292; Rockenbaeuch 372; Rockenbrod 408; Rockenstihl 239; Rod 74; Rode *113; Rodebagh 272; Rodenbach 134; Rodenburger 138; Rodennill 54; Rodhaf 304; Rodrigue 417; Roebach 370; Roeber 318; Roeberling 320; Roeckhele 253; Roedel 410; Roeder 177, 259, 287; Roedesell 50; Roedtler 303; Roeger 206, 207; Roegler 219; Roehm 248, 394; Roehn 237; Roehrer 118,

119, 467; Roehrig 155, 355; Roeller 321; Roem 305; Roemen 366; Roemer 114, 147, 444; Roer 56, 59; Roerich (s. Roerig) *141, 168, 293; Roerig (s. Roerich) 168, 381; Roesch 71, 175, *178, 251, 256, 284; Roeser 101, 126, 411; Roesli 131; Roessel 328; Roesser 203; Roessler 235, *240, 241, 249; Roestlin 312; Roeth 229; Roetter 227; Roettger 295; Rohbach 85; Rohl 59; Rohlandt 342; Rohleber 106; Rohm 215, 216; Rohr 69, *195, 230, 258, 345, 402; v. Rohr *237; Rohrbach *137, 211, 314, 335; Rohrbacher 284; Rohrer *178, 191, 244, 297, 352, 393, 394; Rohrmann 327; Rokoop 131; Rolandt 402; Roley 346; Roll 148, 345; Rollbach 326; Rollen 124; Roller 224, 235, 279, 305; Rollman 89; Roman 8, 27; Rome 233; Romel 187, 258; Romich *82, 198; Romig 296; Rommel 418; Rommigh *234; Romstein 192; Rona 153; Ronister 226; Ronner 322; Roobe 171; Roodlys 59; Roodsman 163; Roodt 67; Rooghel 176; Roorig *204; Roosin 341; Rooss 256; Root 58; Rootelee 74; Rorbaal 443; Rorbach (s. Ruropaw) 367; Rorbagh 164; Rorrer 230; Rosch 235, *269; Roscher 369; Roschman 444, 448; Rosdorff 319; Rose 299 407, 440, 442; Rosenberger 210, 472; Rosenblatt 296; Rosenkrantz 407; Rosenmann 109; Rosenmueller 301; Rosenstiel 92; Roser 304; Rosli *263; Rosmeissel 411; Ross 211, 267, *292, 302, 308, *338, *341, 446; Rossburger 267; Rossel 87, 322, 469; Rosser 178, 221, 360; Rossin 416; Rossinger 101; Rosslein *273; Rossnagel 338; Rost 122, 224, 229, 246, 344; Rostweiler 413; Rosun 423, 427; Rotenbuerger 275; Roth 17, 36, *56, 69, 70, 83, 86, 89, 105, 114, 119, 120, 124, 134, 160, *162, 170, 179, 184, 212, 215, 216, 220, 226, *240, 245, 248, 258, 263, 266, *269, *273, 274, *275, 276, 279, 283, *284, 290, *297, 298, 309, 310, 343, 346, 356, 359, 364, 366, 370, 379, 383, 387, *388, 395, 408, 417, 435, 437, 471; Rotham 325; Rothbaus 235; Rothbaust 283; Rothe 468; Rothenbuerger 342; Rothe(n)heffer 129, 156; Rothenheusser 389; Rothermel 187, 474; Rothgerber 217; Rothrock *93, 101, 379; Rothweiler 130; Rottei 325; Rottenberger 450; Rottmann 378; Rouchon *304, 340; la Roue 464; Rouller 186; Rouse 75; Rower 76; Rowp 83; Rowshower 54; le Roy 297, 298, *323, 335, 405; Royer 80; Royscher 352; la Ru 438, 468; Ruass *340; Rub 157, *244; Rubbel 403; Rubbert 230; Rubel(l) 155, 270, 271, 332, 476; Rubemiller 286; Ruber 191; Rubert 151, 215, 216; Rubi 183; Rubichon *85; Rubly 163; Rubman 89; Rubrecht 337; Ruby 119; Ruch *85, 118; Ruddiss 150; Rudel 235, 311; Rudisielie 274; Rudi (Rudy) *49, 77, 78, 253, 400; Rudolff 187; Rudolpf 101; Rudolph 122, 158, 162, 239, 275, 301, 363, 370, 407; Rudrauf 318; Rudsh 158; Rudy 419; Rueb 150, *200; Ruebelandt 365; Rübel(l) 115, 214, *276; Ruebman 206; Ruebsa(a)men 285, *317, 366; Rueck 80, 320, 389; Ruecker 356; Rueckstu(h)l

*99; Ruedelbach 228; Ruedelmayer 283; Ruedinger 201; Rueeb
324; Rueger *107, 156, *236; Ruegerr 344; Ruegner 155;
Ruehl 150, *154, 162, 183, 256, 416; Ruehlein 327; Ruehm
146; Ruehmle 121; Ruel 296; Ruemmel 378; Ruemmen 276;
Ruencker 389; Rueschle 322; Ruess 282; Ruest 242; Ruestler
304; Rueter 232; Ruetes 335; Ruetiger 326, 327; Ruetschi
98, *99, 197; Ruetsieler 204; Ruettenhuysen 478; Ruettger
290; Ruettichell 259; Rütticher 416; Ruettlinger 159; Ruettyn(g)-
huysen (Rittenhaus) *430, 431, 432, 471, 476; Ruff 105, 155,
233, 394, 408; Ruffener 448; Rughty 226; Ruhl 448; Ruhter
307; Ruibec 175; Rule 53, 132; Rulley 241; Rumel 198, *245;
Rumetsch 311; Rumffel 220; Rummel(l) 187, 198, 415;
Rump 136; Rumpfeld (-ellt) *96; Runck 115; Run(c)kel *159,
183, 185, *186, 195, 362, 404, *408; Runcker 318; Ruoff 250;
Rupert 470; Rupp 2, 20, 101, 178, 198, *205, 215, *265,
331, 360, 401, 435, 438, 471; Ruppel 327; Ruppele 100;
Ruppert 70, 282, 319; Rup(p)erter 137, 144, 245; Rurckons
159; Ruropaw (Rorbach) 445; Rush 276; Rusler 115; Rusmeyer 423, 428; Ruspag 57; Russ 76, 240, 339, 370, 443;
Russel *181, *200, 226, 227, *254, *272, *302, *330; Rust
230, 250, 324; Ruth 87, 88, 90, *91, 96, 106, 130, 133,
145, 166, 174, *287, 300, 365, 438, 468, 470, 476; Ruthlinger
266; Ruthy 156, 266; Rutisieli 105; Ruts 277; Rutschly 49;
Rutschmann 148; Ruttenwalder 334; Rutter (s. Bacher) 417;
Rutz 96; Rydenstock 118; Rymert 67; Rymisus 190; Rynert
67; Rynolle 205; Ryter *74.

Saab 448, 465; Saal 235; Saale 102; Saalicht *473;
Saam 356; Sa(a)mm *279; Saber 236; Sabererick 268; Sachs
202, 364; Sachse (s. Saxe) *299; Sachsman 360; Sack 306,
351, 443; Sackman 295; Sackreider 70; Sackss 335; Sad(d)ler
115, 208; Saebert 155; Saeger 200; Saegnisch 316; Saenger
162, 295, 469; Saettel *313; Saetzler 362; Saeusert 163; Saewel
389; Sage 169; Sahl 187, 384; Sahler *67, 419; Sahm 309,
403; Sahn 234; Sailor 205; Saipell 56; Salade *361; Salathe
214; Saldret 385; Saling 90, 236; Sallade 265; Salladin 288;
Sallam 162; Sallatin 245; Salle 7, 25; Sallener 312; Salling
350; Sally (s. Seile) 191; Saltzberger 148; Saltzer 327, 339;
Saltzgeber 466; Saltzgerber 50; Saltzman 254, 283; Samber
232; Sammann 322; Sammil 300; Sampel 248; Samsel 133;
Samuel 353; Sanborn 314; Sand 287, 374; Sandel 384;
Sandemeyer 373; Sander 226, 299, 328, 409; Sandmann 335;
Sandmeier 418; Saner 87, 150, 408; Sanftleben 450; Sanger
230, 232; Sanner 398; Sans 211; Santer 90; Sarbach 156,
165; Sarier 390; Sarijons 340; Sarineer 464; Sark 306;
Sartorius 115, 401; Saruain 385; Sasain 7, 25; Sasman-
haeuser (Sasmanshaus) *411; Sasmanhaussen 275; Sasmanshaussen
392; Sassamanhaussen 435; Sasseman 475; Sas(se)man(s)haus(e)
126, 180, 222; Sath 409; Satler 163, 306, 379; Satson 225;

Sattelthaler 300; Sattler *76, 262; Satzman 293; Sauder 75, 127, 173, 193, 286, 435; Saudrich 401; Saudter 80; Sauer 67, 92, 93, 110, 126, 149, 162, 170, 187, 200, 209, 252, 308, *334, 336; Sauerbier 105; Sauerbreu 235; Sauerheber 363; Sauerman(n) *186; Sauermilch 66; Sauerwalt 179; Sauerzapff 207; Saufert *195; Saul(l) *309; Saum 261; Saur 141, 473; Sauselin 293; Sauter 17, 36, 80, 220, 400, 414, 415; Sauther 341; Sautranck 292; Sautter 131, 181, 242, 311; Sauvage 114; Savelkorl 220; Savet 405; Saxe (s. Sachse) *299; Saxer 130; Sayler 89; Schaab 383; Schaad 74, 266, 293, 329; Schaadt 365; Schaaf 422, 427; Schaafbahn 315; Schaaff *106, 172, 200, 260, 275, 276, 355; Schaak 408; Schaal 279; Schaber 294, 321; Schackh 311; Schackie 100; Schad 2, 20, 110, 189, 356, 363; Schade 475; Schadel 329; Schadig 290; Schadt 357; Schaebelle 402; Schaeck 149; Schaecke 106; Schaeddell 319; Schaedel 171; Schaedt 353; Schaefer 80, 155, 183, 188, 227, 261, 360, 371, *438, 468, 474, 477; Schaeffer 17, 36, 65, 80, *90, *91, 113, 115, *119, 120, 122, 135, 154, 164, 168, 170, 182, 185, 186, 193, *194, *195, 198, 199, 201, 202, 213, 219, 226, 227, 228, 234, *235, 240, *243, 251, 252, 253, *262, *268, 274, 276, 277, *285, *293, *294, 298, 300, 301, 305, 309, 310, 316, *317, 319, 321, 326, 328, 331, *334, 335, *344, 345, 348, 356, 359, 360, 367, 369, 371, 372, 374, *375, 379, 382, 385, 394, *396, 404, 410, 418, *446, *447, *448, 449, 465; Schaeher 375; Schaell 154; Schaemker 96; Schaener 156; Schaeppler 330; Schaerer 78; Schaerphlein 308; Schaerschler 243; Sch(a)erthle(n) *282; Schaettel *376; Schaettinger 305; Schaeublin 400; Schaeueffele 162; Schaeumenkessel 417; Schaf 327; Schaff 231, 298, 310, 352, 358; Schaffer 134, 364, 388, 435; Schaffner 82, 86, 137, *215, 228, 329, 353, ,385; Schaffstall 339; Schafter 391; Schahl 368; Schaibler 288; Schaickel 262; Schaidt 297; Schaihing 175; Schait 90; Schalck 113; Schall 134, 183, 186, 278, *284, 300, 319, 346; Schalle (s. Shall[e]y) 165; Schallenberg 266; Schaller *106, *123, 209; Schallin 135; Schallus (Shalles) *219; Schalter 331; Schaltzindt 418; Schambach 59; Schamma 182, 387; Schanck 370; Schanckweiler 414; Schande 246; Schang 267; Schanss 264; Schantze 358; Schants 135; Schan(t)z 110, *111, 112, 113, 135, 177, 179, *219, 220, 309, 336, 364; Schapler 366; Schappert *353; Schar 177, 426; Scharbon 432; Scharch 56, *435; Scharer 214; Scharf(f) 77, 180, 228, 448, *465, *467; Scharfrichter 340; Scharlle 324; Scharmann 210, 262; Scharp *120; Schartner 450; Schatteau 137; Schatterly (s. Schnatterly) 83; Schattler 171; Schatz 163, 289, *309, 444; Schatzman 313; Schaub 10, 29, 50, 56, 107, 109, 132, 139, *167, 278, 359, 400, *422, *426, 476; Schauckert 248; Schauer 247, 259, 277, 278, 305, 328, 363, 410, *467; Schauerer 232; Schauerman

448; Schauff 204; Schauffler 408; Schaufler 243; Schaulling 214; Schaum 147, *173, *183, 416; Schaup 79, 139; Schauss 102, 133; Schaut 435; Schauwecker 192, 193; Sche 395; Schebble 273; Scheck 118, 148, 309, 347; Scheckenberger 286; Scheckler 384; Schedel 113; Schedle 117; Scheer 341; Scheermesser 289; Schefer 432; Scheff 364, 447; Scheffeler 243; Scheffer 108, 118, 120, 171, 179, 202, 229, 246, 274, 287, 349, 358, *368, 385, 388; Scheffling 368; Scheffnit 261; Schefler 451; Schehlman 372; Scheib 79, *86, 149, 187, 254, 391, 447; Scheibe 66, 401; Scheiberle 269; Scheible 256, 304; Scheibley 131; Scheibling 281; Scheibly 132, 398; Scheid 340; Scheidbach 279; Scheide 363; Scheider 147; Scheidler 102; Scheidt 344, 353; Scheier 142; Scheiffeler 193; S(c)heimer 76, *201, 475; Scheissle 126; Scheistlen 217; Scheitt 300; Schelbacher (Shellbecker) *292; Schelberger 343; Scheleren 54; Scheleruenthler 399; Schell 133, 157, 255, 286, 294, 357, *361, 362, 380, 383, *391, 438, 469, 473; Schella 213; Schellberg 144; Schellenberg 52, 132; Schellenberger 52, *73, 354; Scheller 296, 365, 395; Schelling 281, 296, 298, 324; Schellman 359; Schello 206; Schelly 471; Schemmlein 178; Schenblein *103; Schenck (s. Shank) 52, 118, 130, 155, 239, 277, 279, 307, 312, *322, 324, 337, 407, 416, 436, 437, 438; Schenckel 98, 226, 246, *288, 395, 410, 434; Schenckweiler 367; Schendt 323; Schenk 80, 473; Schenkel 67, 127; Scheppach 373; Scher 302, 385, 443; Scheraus *451; Scherban 209; Scherbeann 250; Scherch 177, 277; Scherdrong 204; Schere 77; Scheren 55; Scherer 52, *62, 72, 102, 108, *125, 134, *182, 185, 197, *201, 255, 318, 338, 355, 357, *358, 365, 400, 412; Scheretz 333; Scherffig 252; Scherges 432; Scherich 178; Scherick 256; Scherle 222; Scherman(n) 87, *88, 210, 446; Schermerhorn 9, 28; Scher(r) 85, 194, 277, 280, 339; Scherrer 63, 146, 219, 269, 279, 333, 361, 389; Schers 259; Scherstenberger 159; Scherster 252; Schertel 142; Schertlein 281; Schertz 156; Schertzer 173, 248, 297, 367; Schetterly 17, 36; Scheu 251; Scheuchzer 98; Scheu(e)rer (s. Sheyer) *158, 160; Scheuerman(n) 333, 384, 391, *397; Scheufflen *242; Scheunberger 234; Scheurer 231; Scheurich *297, 298; Schew 75; Schey 262, 315; Scheyer 108, 169; Scheywisch 298; Scheyzer 385; Schibb (s. Shub) 363; Schick 253, 300; Schickel 340; Schiebel 340; Schieberstein 403; Schiedenhelm 137; Schiedt 209; Schief 300; Schiefferdecker 341; Schieffler 109; Schiele 301; Schielie 253; Schierch 343; Schierher 241; Schierwager 97; Schiesler 384; Schiess 199; Schiessle 328; Schiettinger 338; Schiff 371; Schiffarth 253; Schiffer (s. Shiffere) 161, *356; Schilack 406, 419; Schilbert 475; Schild 137, 273; Schildbach 407; Schildemrad 159; Schilger 281; Schill 178, 262; Schiller 329; Schillers 346; Schilling 75, *83, 222, 242, 416; Schillinger 282; Schiltknecht

129; Schiltwaechter 375; Schiltz *445; Schimmel 120, 300, 416; Schimpf(f) 264, *330; Schinck 270; Schindel 261, 349, 475; Schindeldecker 108; Schindler *296, 348, 472; Schindtelman *335; Schinf 194, 351; Schipp 111, 149; Schirch 71; Schirdt 350; Schiri 112; Schirmer 237; Schissler *108, 157, 286, 370; Schirm 249; Schirmer 267; S(c)hittenhelm *312, 355, 375; Schitz 349; Schlabach 93; Schlachenhauff 198; Schlachman 407; Schlachter 283; Schladter 276; Schlaecher *120; Schlaechten 103; Schlaemacher 317; Schlagel 376; Schlappig 320; Schlappy 319; Schlarbst 212; Schlars 419; Schlater 255; Schlatter 3, 21, 173, 174, 270, 271, 411; Schlatterer (s. Schlotterer) *193, 321; Schlauch 58, 82, 83, 178, 345, 400, 438; Schlauchter 306; Schlaug 385; Schleber 236; Schleemann 382; Schleer 166; Schlegel 110, 121, *185, *268, 436, 474; Schleich 17, 36, 256, 292; Schleicher 385, 393; Schleider *229; Schleiermacher 437; Schleiff 149, 406; Schleiffer 139; Schleimer 446; Schlemb 338, 361, 378; Schlemer 169, 307; Schlemilch 391; Schlemmer 342; Schlencker 278, *307; Schlenckfer 268; Schlengeluff 59, 60; Schleppi 237; Schleppy 262; Schler 104, 114; Schleser 379; Schlesse 348; Schlesser 170; Schles(s)mann 292, 293, 294; Schletz 295, 346; Schletzer 263, 398; Schleucher 121; Schley 279; Schleyer 279; Schleyfard 119; Schleypfer 159; Schlichter 173, 264, 403, 413; Schlick 353; Schlieger 110; Schligter 122; Schlincker 258; Schlinglauf 476; Schloegel 171; Schloer 206; Schloesser 309, 343; Schloetzer *347; Schlosser 82, 182, 213, 254, 363, 366; Schlott 416; Schlotter 109, 330; Schlotterer (s. Schlatterer) 192, *193; Schlotterman 296; Schlotz 328; Schluepp 380; Schlueter 294; S(c)hma(ah)l (s. Small) 147, *160; Schmaeck 189; Schmaltz 147, 210, 394; Schmaltzhaff 156; S(c)hmaus(s) 122, *315, 411; Schmeh 332; Schmeher 251; Schmel 409; Schmeltz 274; Schmeltzer 81, 122, *230, 249; Schmeltzle 289; Schmelzer 263; Schmerber 199; Schmertzen 217; Schmertzka 322; Schmess 330; Schmeuell 388; Schmick 320; Schmid 71, 85, 86, 99, 150, 183, 186, 189, 191, 255, 282, *292, 293, 296, 314, 346, 353, 374, 402, 410; Schmidt 52, *56, 62, 63, *67, 70, 76, 79, 80, 81, 85, *88, *89, 90, 91, 97, 99, 103, *104, 108, 113, 115, *120, 123, 125, 131, 138, *141, *142, 144, 145, 153, 155, 157, 161, 162, 164, 165, *171, *179, 183, 188, 193, 198, *200, *201, 204, 207, *210, 211, 212, 218, 219, 220, 221, 222, 228, 229, 233, 245, 253, 255, 256, *257, 259, *260, *261, *264, 267, 272, 273, 278, 279, *280, *282, 284, *285, 290, 291, 296, 297, 303, 305, 310, 313, 314, *316, *317, 320, 321, 327, 328, *329, 334, *335, 339, 340, 341, 343, 347, 349, *351, 353, 354, 355, 356, *357, *360, *366, 369, 370, 372, 374, 376, 380, 381, *384, *385, 387, 390, 392, *395, 396, 397, *398, 399, *401, 406, 407, 410, *411, 418, 419, *423, *427,

431, 434, *444, *445, *448, 450, 465, 467, 469, 470,
472, *474; v. der Schmidt 229; Schmidte 203; Schmied(t)
159, 264; Schmieg 200, *300; Schming 371; Schmitgen *200;
Schmith 233, 342; Schmit(t) 76, 98, 143, *150, 157, 162,
176, 180, 181, 200, 212, 217, 226, 229, *236, 259, 279,
284, *290, *303, 305, *307, 314, 316, *319, 320, 322, 324,
333, *336, 338, *339, 343, 345, 347, 353, *359, *360, 367,
371, *391, 399, 405, 408; Schmitzer 277; Schmoehl 132;
Schmoller 241; Schmoltze 382; Schmuck 125, 253; Schmucker
146, 190, *270; Schmuckheyde 149; Schmück 89; Schmuecker
277; Schmunck 234; Schmyer 90, 91; Schnabel 213, 322,
*385; Schnaebele 275; Schnager 74; Schnarrenberger 325;
Schnatterly (s. Schatterly) 83; Schnauber 108; Schnauster
256; Schnawffer 242; Schnebele 18, 36, *89, *437; Schneb(e)li
(s. Snabily) 55, 159, 176, 195, 230; Schnebler 59; Schneck
198, 257, 259, 263, 342, 369, *370; Schnecke 282; Schneder
281; Schnedh 224; Schnee 163; Schneeberg 318; Schneeberger
266; Schne(e)bly (s. Shnabely) 197, 214; Schneeder 184;
Schneegantz 415; Schneffer 308; Schneider 10, 29, *61, 67,
73, 76, 101, 105, 108, 114, *116, 117, 120, 121, *122, 133,
135, 137, 139, *140, *141, *142, 144, 146, 147, 149, 152,
166, 169, *170, 173, 175, *179, 186, 189, 191, 192, *199,
201, *203, 204, 206, *212, 215, 218, *221, *222, 227, 230,
231, *232, 233, 235, 239, 242, 244, 247, 248, 255, 262,
264, *266, 270, 272, 275, 276, *279, 281, 282, *285, 287,
296, 297, 298, 301, 310, *312, *315, 316, 318, *319, 321,
322, *331, *332, 334, *335, 342, 345, 347, 349, 350, *352,
855, 356, *359, 361, 365, *367, 368, 371, 372, 373, 374,
378, *379, 380, 382, *386, 389, 395, *396, *397, *398,
401, *403, *409, 413, 422, 426, 435, 443, 445, 447, 448,
449, *450, 465, 466, 467, 472, 474, 475, *477; Schneiss 144;
Schneit 367; Schnelie 154; Schnell 17, 36, 119, 153, *161,
214, 242, 254, 255, *256, 257, 367, 386, 392, *396, 402,
*422, *426, 447; Schnelleberger 337; Schnellenberger 346;
Schnepf 273; Schnep(p) *86, *87, 180, 241, 374, 391; Schnep-
penhaeusser 416; Schnepper 309; Schnerenberger 327, 328;
Schnerr 309; Schney 142; Schneyder *119, 132, 149, 151,
180, 200, 216, 287, 362, 372, 375, 392, 413; Schneynow
415; Schniding 66; Schnieder 161; Schniringer *262; Schnitt
257; Schnitzer 229; Schnog 141; Schnogheim 348; Schnorss
*354; Schnuelbein *215; Schnurr 345; Schnutz 156; Schnyder
319; Schober 105, 267, 306, 312, 332, 342, 358, 364, 422,
427; Schobig 306; Schoch (s. Stotz?) 163, 237, 241, 248,
381, 401; Schock (s. Shaak) 219, 243, 271, 272, 349, 355,
391; Schoeberger 339; Schoeff 345, 351; Schoeffer 85, 133;
Schoeffler 105; Schoeler 409, 413; Schoelhorn 263; Schoel-
kopf 171; Schoellhammer 307; Schoellhorn 253; Schoeltz 71;
Schoen 169, 311, 365; Schoenauer 334; Schoenbach 204;

Schoenberger 77; Schoenbruck 369; Schoendeman 206; Schoeneberger 365; Schoeneck 321; Schoener 473; Schoenfeld 412; Schoenfelder 109, 373; Schoenfeldt 90; Schoenfelter *286; Schoenholtz 419; Schoenholtzer 54; Schoenig 74, 148; Schoenle 79; Schoenleber 352; Schoenman 325; Schoenmansgruber 92; Schoenperlen 214; Schoenwaldt 280; Schoepf 320; Schoepffer *133; Schoeppi 251; Schoeps 96; Schoerck 82; Schoeri 329; Schoerth 248; Schoesser 360; Schoester 216; Schoette 87; Schoetts 88; Schoetzlie 293; Schoeuk (s. Schuck) 194; Schof(f) 179, 279, 333; Schog 358; Scholer 477; Scholl 57, *124, 133, 137, 194, 214, *296, 309, 356, *387, *431, 472, 477; Schollenberger 154; Scholler 57, 300; Scholtes 191, 294; Scholthes 293; Scholtz *90, 94, 95; Scholtze *96, 99; Schonenberger 378; Schook 84; Schooler 192; Schopff 112; Schopp 343; Schoppenmeyer 260; Schoppert 254; Schor (s. Yor) *246; Schorb (s. Shurp) 197; Schory 387; Schoss 467; Schotebecker 263; Schott 17, 36, 79, 87, 154, 216, 226, 268, *294, 303, 311, *335, 362, 398, *408; Schotter 376; Schowalder 205, 364; S(c)howalter *244; Schoyrer 286; Schraader 346; Schrack 121, 388, *476; Schrader 296, 348, 380; Schraester 314; Schrag 376; Schrager 477; Schraidt *66; Schram(m) *125, 252, 312, 389, 446; Schranck *325; Schrantz 206; Schrath 384; S(c)hrauck *248; Schreck 309, 310, 361; Schrecka 409; Schreckenangst 357; Schreckenbuerger 402; Schreder 372; Schreiber 89, 98, 105, 111, *112, 121, 123, 144, 147, 152, 165, 213, 219, 276, 306, 326, 355, 376; Schreidt 339; Schreier 126; Schrein 333; Schreiner *114, 115, 133, 141, 183, 202, 213, 214, 228, 286, 308, 325, 359, 374, 376, 413, 434, 438; Schrempf 451; Schrenck 229; Schressel 370; Schret 278; Schreth 148; Schreyer 160, *286, 295; Schrey(i)ack(h) 83, *89, 125; Schrieg 319; Schrieger *160; Schriffele 219; Schrig 398; Schroeder 294, 336, 394, 402; Schroedlie 311; Schroegen 85; Schroeter *70, 175, 294; Schroff 97; Schrom 293; Schropp 262, 422, 426; Schrot *333; Schrotner 70; Schruntz 316; Schryack 101; Schu 389; Schubert 95, *96, *306; Schuc 447; Schuch 335; Schuck (s. Schoeuk) *194, 411; Schuckman 279; Schude 402; Schudieck 418; Schudy 383; Schueberli 274; Schuehlein 172; Schuehler 154; Schuel 229; Schuele 337; Schuelein 293; Schuenemann 10, 29, 440, 442; Schuerch *56; Schueredt 231; Schuerer 91; Schuerling 375; Schuessler 81, 156; Schuester 358; Schuett 387; Schuetterlin 209; Schuettler 248; S(c)huetz 73, 83, 105, 134, 159, 162, 165, 212, 225, *260, 276, 295, 314, *315, *317, 336, 343, 347, *352, 355, 362, 385, 408, 409, 410, 443, 447, 448, 465; Schuetze 422, 427; Schuey 76, 186, 367, 381, 400; Schuffart 92; Schug 133; Schuh *87, 254, 302; Schuhen 184; Schuhler 242; Schuhmacher 2, 20, 58, 259, *471, *473; Schuhmann 122, 207; Schuhriem 403; Schuler 64, 289, 371, 403, *469; Schulheis(s) *386; Schulicus 412;

Schuller 91; Schullmeyer 76; Schultes 81; Schultheis(s)
269, 448; Schults 67; Schultz 52, 67, 80, 91, 97, 119, 154,
*156, 200, 210, 234, 236, *238, 253, *270, 285, 329, *344,
346, 369, 373, 380, 391, 407, 408, 437, 443, 447; Schultze
65, 407, 423, 427; Schum 334; Schumacher 49, 70, 92, 106,
111, *112, *119, 141, 154, 169, 181, 199, 248, 263, *272,
280, 310, 338, 347, 365, *381, 383, 396, 399, 413, 429,
*430, 444, 448; Schumacher (s. Shoomaker); Schuman(n) *140,
200, 201, 240, 281, 317, 325, 332, *363, 415; Schunck 107,
347, 408; Schunder 281; Schunke 396; Schup(p) 118, 123,
235, 302, 364, 396, 467; Schuppert 291; Schurgh 51; Schurtz
215; Schust 102, 129, 209; Schuster 91, 144, 149, 163, 169,
180, 181, 215, 232, 234, 240, 324, 347, 366, *381; Schusterdreher 360; Schutt 18, 36; Schutten 104; Schutz 110, *131,
290, 437; Schuy 315; Schwaab 99, 351, 357, 358, 438;
Schwaark 434; Schwab 49, 186, 187, 189, 215, 241, *288,
290, *308, 343, 350, 354, 366; Schwabeland 416, *417;
Schwaebel 345; Schwaerber 131; Schwaertzel 344; Schwager
161; Schwalb 302; Schwalbach 342; Schwall 448; Schwamm
229; Schwanfelder 397; Schwanger 180; Schwanner 123;
Schwantz 353; Schwar 279; Schwarbach 250; Schwarm 149;
Schwarth 189; Schwartlaender 297; Schwartz 18, 36, 54, 55,
65, *70, *107, 118, 126, *136, 150, *162, 164, *165, 229,
244, *246, 269, *273, 274, 279, 282, 283, *284, 286, 289,
303, 310, 315, 323, 334, *336, 347, 357, 385, 400, 404, 417,
469, 475, 477; Schwartzbach 214; Schwartzenbach 347; Schwartzhaud 233; Schwartzw(a)elder *123, 247, 341; Schwartzwoelder
289; Schwatzer 285; Schwedener 121; Schweedt 445; Schweickart 415; Schweickhar(d)t 49, 212, 311; Schweigarth 242;
Schweiger 337, 338, 450; Schweigers 215; Schweigert 17,
36; Schweigerts 405; Schweighart (s. Schweinhart) 75, 199,
248; Schweighauser 143; Schweighoffer 450; Schweikharth
161; Schweiler 282, 320; Schwein 190; Schweinfarth 342;
Schweinfurth 219; Schweinhart (s. Schweighart) 74, 75;
Schweissguth 254; Schweitzer 55, 86, 98, 191, 192, 202,
220, 223, 241, 248, 280, *291, 300, 305, *312, *319, 351,
355, 361, 378, 400, 413, 445, 474, *477; Schwele 400;
Schweller 273; Schwen 376; Schwen(c)k 109, 133, 148, 217,
226, 346, 370, 415; Schwencke (s. Shwenk) 282; Schwenckel
262; Schwenckert 308; Schwenckfeld 420, 424; Schwend 394;
Schwengel 466; Schwenhart 472; Schwens 412; Schwentzel
410; Schwerber 201; Schwerdle 400; Schwerdt 107, 165,
201, *361, 363; Schwerm 367; Schweutzer 399; Schweyer 285,
386; Schweyler 266; Schwhenneher 399; Schwinck *131;
Schwindt 160; Schwinederer 279; Schwing 113, 344, 415;
Schwingel *144; Schwinkes 265; Schwisser 439, 441; Schwissfurth 413; Schwitger 407; Schwob 201, 202, 224; Schydecker
84; Schyre 358; Schyver 126; Sculpes 128; Scurman *464:

Seacoist 235; Sebaldt 178; Sebastian 52, 151; Sebeinzer 361; Sebelie 137; Sebolt 114, 143; Sechler 17, 36; Sechs (Sex) 448; Seckel 260; See 142; Seeberger 321; Seebert 315; Seeger *92, 394; Seehl 272; Seekatz 379; Seel 114; Seelen 432; Seelig 309, 432; Seeman(n) 188, 189, 411; Seemisch 259; Sees 90, 148; Seetz *139; Seewald 345; Sefues 128; Segel 418; Segen 122; Segendorff 447; Seger 109, 110, 233, 294, 324; Segman 255; Segnitz 351; Segwalt 418; Sehm 76; Sehner 341; Sehr 307; Sehwig 380; Seib(b) (s. Seip u. Sype) *82, *96, 104, 251, 374; Seibel 123; Seibert(h) 115, 116, 125, 415; Seidel 152, 279, 347, 411, 422, 426; Seidenbach 162; Seidenspinner 188; Seidensticker 240; Seidenstricker *360; Seider 100, 280; Seifert 209, 221, 414, 469; Seiffer 325; Seifferdt 353; Seiffert 316, 421, 425; Seifus(s) *128; Seig 274; Seigendaller (Siegenthahller) *236; Seigmueller 395; Seihs 304; Seile (s. Sally) 191; Seiler *114, 139, *191, 192, 205, 283, 306, 379; Seim 115; Seindel 242; Seip(p) (s. Seib) *284, *374, 392, 419; Seipel 120, 355; Seipert 145; Seiser 315; Seistel 257; Seithss 329; Seitle 177; Seitner 335; Seitz 120, 134, 156, 159, 193, 219, 244, 266, 289, 291, 325, 350, 362, 364, 374, 381, 394; Seitzer 371; Seitzius 180; Seivert 153; Seix *322; Seiz 355; Sekel *175; Selbach *316; Seleberger 74; Selen 430; Selhoff 262; Selig 251; Sell 142, 143, *293; Seller 59, 60, 264; Sellheim 364; Selligman 318; Sellser 59; Selman 198; Seltenr(e)ich 51, 170; Seltz 417; Seltzer 64, 202, 204, 236, 249, 273, 274, 401, 435, 476; Selwinger 311; Semier 151; Semmel 309; Senck 83; Sendel 269; Sender 125; Senderling 213; Senffbeber 334; Senffelder 201; Seng 180; Senger 96; Senghaass 207; Senkeler 342; Senlieder 350; Senner 355; Senseman(n) 17, 36, 152, *153, 421, 425; van Sentern 473; Sentiner 335; Sentner 431; Serb 388; Serber *87; Serenius 394; Serfass 133; Serfriedt 186; Serger *352; Seroni 414; Servai 304; Serveas 50; Sesberger 260; Setzer 312; Setzler 102; Seuberlich 150, 306; Seubert(h) 118, *292, *309, 377; Seuffert 287; Seufried *235; Seuling 378; Seusterditz 237; Seuter 237; Sevenkoel 69; Sewaldt 363; Sex (s. Sechs); Seybell 196; Seybert 367; Seyberth 357, 363, *384; Seyboldt 341; Seybolt *339; Seyboot 86, 87; Seybots 384; Seydel 109, 143, 411; Seydelman 274; Seydelmeyer 307; Seydenbender 90, 251; Seyder 219, 223; Seydler 164, 232; Seydling 299; Seydlle 313; Seyds 215; Seye 317; Seyfarth 257; Seyfeird 248; Seyfert 132, 227, 386; Seyffarth 247; Seyfriedt 207; Seyfrit 388; Seygor 206; Seyham 53; Seyl 72, 241; Seyler 58, 67, 76, 77, 146, *191, 216, 272, 379; Seyn 200, 260; Seypell 121; Seyser 323; Seysser 228; Seyter 143; Seytter 193; Seytz 50, 211; Seyvert 186; Shaad 233; Shaak (s. Schock) 67, *219; Shabert 349; Shable 329; Shack 248; Shade 117; Shadike 301; Shaeffer

122, 200, 316; Shaetz 222; Shaffer 154, 171, 204, *212, 252, 253, 268; Shaffner 192; Shak 208; Shalleberger 238; Shaller 186; Shalles (s. Schallus); Shall(e)y (s. Schalle) *165; Shamar 333; Shambach 196; Shamberger 107; Shamele 143; Shan 231; Shan(c)k (s. Schenck) 130, 151; Shanker 242; Shappy *176; Shapue 414; Shar 422; Sharff 172; Shaub 74; Shauman 249; Shaver 246; Shavere 414; Sheaneman 165; Sheck 174, 175; Shedle 336; Sheef 168; Sheel 236; Sheer 154; Sheesler 257; Sheets 358; Sheetz 142; Sheffer 127, 165, 228, 410; Shellbecker (s. Schellbacher); Shellberg 98; Shellenberg 98; Shellenberger 339; Shem 417; Shemmler 406; Shend 268; Shengle 119; Shenk 156; Shennal 273; Shep 238; Sherber 361; Sherer 181; Sherly 253; Shermillin 202; Sherr 183; Sherrer 230; Shertel 210; Shertle 79; Shertzer 126; Shetler 72; Shetz 248; Shever 65, 135; Shewerman 265; Shey 137; Sheyb 143; Sheybethal 214; Sheyco 261; Sheydecker 124; Sheyder 176, 239, 249; Sheyed 271; Sheyer (s. Scheu[e]rer) 160, 180; Shiel 356; Shiffere (s. Schiffer) 356; Shiffer *121; Shild 137; Shilling 53; Shirra 387; Shisler 120; Shimfassel 368; Shiney 247; Ship 290; Shlaybouer 226; Shlighter *238; Shloder 252; Shider 147; Shierman 219; Shitertz 379; Shitzer 191; Shleyhouff 155; Shluhtes 357; Shmaal (s. Schmaahl); Shmeyer 217; Shmit(h) 97, 114, 159, 169, 180, 199, 201, 202, 218, 227, 228, 229, 230, *232, 235, 238, 240, *241, 245, 246, 253, 307, *326, 337, 339; Shmitly 246; Shmitt 200, 224; Shmitzer 178; Shnabely (s. Schneebly) 197; Shnaudy 255; Shneering 175; Shneider 333; Shneyder 76, 119, *151, 176, 199, 203, 231, 257, 266, 273, 285, 297, 317, *333, 346, 347; Shnyder 175, 209, 211, 216, 233, 240, 241, 338; Shneid 273; Shob 266; Shock 164, 316; Shoemaker 141, 161, 198; Shoeman 204, 228; Shoenfeldt 57; Shog 168; Sholl 248; Sholter 304; Sholtes 192, 292; Sholty 248; Sholtz 260; Shoman 57; Shommet 304; Shomony 231; Shook 140; Shoomaker (s. Schumacher) 50; Shootin 191; Shop 308; Shopffer 237; Shoret 405; Shott 214, 215, 233; Shoub *229; Showalter 173; Showay β323; Shraetter 220; Shram 63, 286; Shrang 283; Shrantz 226; Shreeder 307; Shreffer 210; Shreiber 213, 260; Shreier 410; Shrey 313; Shreyer 335; Shroder 318; Shroeder 126, 262, 348; Shrohr 303; Shrout 259; Shub (s. Schibb) 363; Shuckers 407; Shueler 299; Shuenal 273; Shuetzlin 226; Shullmeyer 76; Shullobak 324; Shulty 266; Shultz 80, 294; Shumacher 53, 126; Shumaker 119; Shuman 80, 401; Shumber 251; Shumbert 345; Shuntz 354; Shup(p) 137, 214; Shurp (s. Schorb) *197; Shuster 169, 288, 337, 347; Shutt 337; Shutter *166; Shutty 214; Shutz 132, 213, 250, 289; Shwab 251; Shwaigermeyer 140; Shwalb 244; Shwartz 194, 249, 315, 319; Shweiger 267; Shweishelm 299; Shwenk (s.

Schwenke) 172, 282; Shweyart 248; Shweyzey 150; Shwitzer 158, 283; Shwob 251; Shyd *221; Sibel 121; Siber 103, 150; Sicher *243; Sickard 443; Sickenberger 227; Sieber 76, 77, 387; Sieere 50; Sieffert 384; Sieffner 413; Sieg 305; Siegel 51, 104; Sieger 239; Siegenthahller (s. Seigendaller); Siegfried 280, 435, 475; Siegle 306; Siegman *129, *130; Siegmund 62, 70, 71, 83; Siegner 443; Siegrist (s. Syegrist) 51, 244, 311, 321; Siel 363; Siemath 389; Si(e)n 75, 81; Sier 211; Siesfass 316; Siesler *150; Siesrieux 390; Sies(s) 110, 171, 212; Sietz 416; Sieur 293; Sifry 231; Sigile 397; Sigle (s. Ziegly) 174; Siglin 306; Sigrist 369; Siherrer 163; Silander 226; Silans 432; Silber 209; Silberberg 178; Silbirit 298; Sillmann 188; Siltzel 385; Silvius 120; Sim 199, 205; Simens *430; Simmendinger 444; Simmon 290, 291; Simmons 240; Simon *102, 118, 133, 145, *149, 150, 190, 219, 267, *290, 296, 374, 391, 468, 469; Simonet 53; Simons 449; Simpson 2, 20; Simre 245; Sin 126; Sinclair 413; Sinder 215; Sing 225; Singel 239; Singer 231, 233, 289, 304, 375, 474; Singneitz 322; Singquet 304; Singrove 144; Sinn *215; Sinsemore 470; v. Sintern 433; Sirer 202, 416; Sittenich 448; Siverdts 430; Siwert 307, 308; Six 122, 465; Skulpius 128; Slabach *93; Slantzeberger 73; Slaughters 61; Slawffer 196; Slebacher 139; Sleig 356; Slener 210; Slentz 87, 88; Slettebauer 409; Sligh 121; Slonacker 89; Slosser 82; Slottenbecker *101; Sluce 464; van der Sluys (Vanderslice) 477; van der Sluys (später Vanderslyce) *430; Sly 88; Small *137, *160; Smeisser *69, 70; Smidt 84; Smith (s. Schmidt) 50, *54, 82, *108, *121, 127, 135, 146, 207, 224, 254, 323, 348, 349, 353, 355, 359, 370, *373, *379, *385, *389, *393, *398, 399, *400, 409, 410, *412, 470; Smit(t) 67, 74, 76, 107, 118, 143; Smyets 297; Smyser 41, 46; Snabily (s. Schnebeli) 159; Snabley 88; Sneevele 59; Sneider 86; Sneppley 55; Snevely 71; Sneyder 132, 153; Snider 60; Snyder 50, 55; Soal 204; Sobieski, Graf (s. Zabriskie) 3, 21; Soblet 7, 25; Sochus 154; Soder 92; Sodt 271; Soeffrens 75; Soehn 161; Soehner 221; Soelchel 411; Soelle 423, 428; Soeller 58; Soelli 204; Soeplis 431; Soerger 170; Soestner 384; Soesttel 227; Sohl 364; Sohn 17, 36; Solaigre 7, 25; Solder 118; Solderman 53; Soldnier 83; Solfon 348; Solinus 259; Sollberg 352; Sollberger (s. Zolenberger) 109; Sollom 469; Solmer 392; Solomo 171; Solomon 133, 237, 390; Sombero 351; Somer 111; Somey *92; Sommer 57, 131, 166, 199, 206, 234, 247, 249, 267, 274, 275, 293, 300, 313, 332, 344, 345, 377; Som(m)erlad *184, 185; Sommers 422, 426; Sonner 317; Sonntag 354; Sontag 100, *111, 112, 150, 288; Sooper (s. Supper) 256; Sooter 93; Sorg 282, 310, 311; Sorge 331, 348; Sorsini 322; Sotz (s. Stotz); Souchonet 91; Sowber 123; Sower 54; Spaar 158; Spach

419; Spaengler 215; Spaeth 315, *317, 329, 356; Spag 93, 94; Spahr 191, 227, 367; Spang 247, 291; Spangenberg *117, 396, 420, 424; Spangler 49; Spanler 205; Spann 261; Spannagel 228, *277, 307; Spannheimer 446; Spannman 410; Spannseiler 323; Spansailer 79, 80; Spats 165; Spatz 235, 283, 285; Specht 120, 232, 359, 361; Speck *101, 123, 298, 313, 332, 342; Specker 186; Spees 186; Spegel 163; Spegt 147; Speicher 188; Speidel(l) *193, 228; Speiser 414; Spencer *211; Spengel 110; Spengler 66, *83, 92, 93, 106, 144, 228, *251, 278, 279, 362, 363, 416, 468, 474; Spenhover 192; Spenner 338; Sperger 62; Sperk 171; Sperling 377; Spery 158, 250; Spesser 339; Speth 104, 273; Spetzfendem 279; Spetzius 330; Spicker *201; Spiegel 113, 150, 253, 321; Spieger 468; Spielbiegler 450; Spieller 188; Spielman 227, 320, 353, 354, 358; Spies(s) *96, 126, 222, 272, 276, 329, 378, 385, 394, 408, *410, 447; Spiettler 229; Spiger 204; Spiker 111; Spindel 149; Spindler 293; Spira 303; Spirandin 303; Spiri 228; Spiteler *103; Spitelmayer (s. Spittlemire) 89; Spitler 17, 36, *192, 214, 246; Spittlemire (s. Spitelmayer) 89; Spitzer *360; Spitznagel 182; Spohn 91, 92, 207, 261, 278, 279; Spohnhauer 139; Spongenberg 326; Sponknoebel 368; Spotiwood 460/2; Spowner 52; Sprecher *84, 267, 268, 287, 338; Spreng 196; Sprengel 221; Spriegel 369; Spring 162, 180, 227, 248; Springel 204; Springenklee 124; Springer 107, 205, 275, 279; Sproetz 391; Sprogel *432, 472, 473; Spruckmann 416; Sprutt 208; Spurier *214; Spuriers *381; Spurrier 262, 263, *292, *334; Spycker *108, 469; Stadecker 395; Stadel 320; Stadellmaner 143; Stadelmayer 225; Stader 294; Stadtler 64, 219, 369; Staebler 277; Staedel 77; Staegenmueller 71; Staehle 239, 305; Staehlein 258; Staehler 126; Staelly 156, 191; Staerner 163; Staettel 78; Staettler 368; Staffel 175; Staffon 50; Stahl 72, 73, 114, 147, 251, 288, 289, 290, 294, 296, *317, 319, 338, *339, 354, 381, 394, 413, 448; Stahler 196; Stahlman 146, 269; Stahls 431; Stahlschmidt 469; Staiger 327; Stall 114, 163, 290, 306; Staller 81, 360; Stalley 77, 78; Stally 131; Stambach 81, 135, 136, 148, 220, 263, *391; Stamler 123; Stam(m) 64, 97, 155, 156, 161, 164, 416; Stammann 348; Stampfer 437; Stander 400; Stanfield *358; Stanford 7, 25; Stang 228, 240; Stanger 324; Stanhenner 280; Stapf 383; Starck 302, 316, 361, 398; Starffinger 147; Stark 243; Starr 120; Starrenberger 444; Startzman 119, 176; v. Starweg 219; Statell 296; Stath 200; Statily *230; Statler 297; Statt 271; Stattel 286; Stattler 225, 284, 362; Stau 321; Staub 229, 313, *344, 347, 380, 398; Staubach 291; Staube 172; Stauber 305, 315; Stauch *205, 234, 274, 282, 284, *325, 375; Staud 385; Staudehauer 385; Staudt 90, *106, *116, 137, 138, 145, 170, 409; Staudter 190, 258; Stauf 174; Stauf(f)er 51, 72,

*77, *107, 172, 195, 196, 205, 258, 278, 362, 365, 393, 401, 470, 471, 477; Staus 291; Staut 105, 107, 181, 329; Stautz 309; Stauzer 321; Stave 157; Staver 196; Stecher 79, 193, 369; Steckbek 164; Steckel 206, 238, 412; Stecker 203, 331; Stedler 74; Stedman *66, *73, 89, 90, *94, 95, *108, 110, 111, 125, 126, *129, *147; Stedt 227; Stedtekorn 413; Stedtler 338; Steeb *193; Steebly 229; Steedeberger 318; Steedinger 291; Steeg *146; Steel *206, 223, 224, *249, *304; Steer 319; Steffan 185, 225; Steffe 476; Steffen 109, 354, 355, 368; Steffer (s. Stoever); Steg 324; Stegel 128, 380; Steger 73. *79, 386; Stegman 316, 342; Stegmueller 410; Stegner 332, 395; Steheli 159; Stehle 262; Stehlert 292; Stehli 197, *266; Stehlin *91; Stehly 289; Stehm 385; Stehr (s. Stoehr) 186, 229, 291; Stehrn (s. Stirn) 263; Steibel 365; Steidgers 313; Steidle 312; Steigelman(n) 311, 357; Steiger 256, 257, 474; Steigerwalt (Steyger-) *381; Steigleder 215; Steiler 359; Steilhener 411; Stein 89, 102, 120, 125, 140, 157, 166, 172, *182, *185, 201, *208, 216, 217, 221, 227, 234, 242, 254, 257, 300, 302, 307, 322, 333, 334, 339, 340, 348, 368, 382, 392, 398, 437, 438, 468, 476; Steinbach 74, 96, 280, 286, 416; Steinbecker 398; Steinberger 240; Steinbock 303; Steinborn 218; Steinbrachel 177; Steinbrecher 305; Steinbren 89; Steinbrenner *278, 473; Steinbreucker 360; Steinbring 176, 213, 411; Steiner 67, *96, *135, 139, 143, 173, 175, *176, 201, 225, 233, 266, 268, 278, 302, 338, 341, 362, 364, *376, 379, 397, 413, 438, 450; Steinerger 51; Steinert 147; Steinertz 291; Steiney 350; Steinha 403; Steinhauer *139; Steininger 70; Steinle 280; Steinlein 64; Steinman(n) *75, *88, 132, 148, 231, 310, 325, 349, 412, 437; Steinmetz 67, 83, 105, 108, 172, 179, 202, *258, 307, 361, 415, *416; Steinroth 205; Steinseiffer 206, 276, 319; Steinuth 180; Steinwax 366; Steinweg *326; Steinwehn 318; Steirschildt 252; Steiss 323; Steitz 399, 468; Steli 79; Steller 338; Stellfeldt 57; Stelling 101; Stellwagen 378; Stellweg 146; Stelly 100; Steltz 199; Stelwag 170; Stembel(l) 105, 125; Stemler 255; Stempel 81; Stemple 81; Stendli 393; Steneroloh 317; Steng 205; Stenger 222, *386, *387; Stentz 324; Step 333; Stephan 304, 373, 384, 407, 411, 415; Stephanus 102, 344; Stephany 402; Stephen 170; Stephenson *390; Sterchi 238, *285; Sterling *116; Stern 126, 299; Sternberger 311; Sternbirger 164; Sterneman 196; Sterner 123; Sterrles 150; Sterrnn 154; Stertzenacker 165; Stes 155; Stet(t)ler 119, 121, 122, 359, 438, *472; Stettling 404; Stettz 97; Stetzel 376; Stetzler 207; Steubesant 323; Steudtle 327; Steuer 119, 389; Steutz 389; Stevenson *172; Stey 72; Steyb 314; Steyer 52; Steyerwald 183; Steyerwaldt 255; Steyger 260; Steygerwaldt 240; Steyger 79; Steygerwaldt 210, 211; Steymenn 384; Steyn 117, 267; Steyner 62, 260; v. Steysplatz (s. Steinpleis?) 57;

Stheryders 209; Stichel 121; Stichler 196; Stichling 337; Stichter 195; Stick 392; Stickel 410; Stickler *92, *93; Stiebler *221; Stieffel *293; Stieg 223; Stiegel 239; Stiegeler *169; Stieger 124; Stiegletz 478; Stiehl 225; Stier 221, 222, 362, 410; Stierle 349, 395; Stierlein 321; Stierlo 193; Stiernkorb 351; Sties(s) 269, 356; Stiffel 62; Stiganer 128; Stigel 244; Stihling 309; Still 87; Stilling 153, 255; Stimbi 150; Stimmel 183, 217, 329, *336, 380; Stindtler 253; Stinglie 123; Stirn (s. Stehrn) 263; Stis 85; Stittz 339; Stober *106, 243; Stock 56, 76, 178, 238, 254, 273, 366, 389, 417; Stockee *107; Stockel 240, 372; Stocker 70, 93, 115, 291; Stocki 264; Stockie 103; Stockhalter *128; Stockinger 355; Stockmann 222, 376; Stockschleder 150; Stockschleger 149; Stoeber 125, 276; Stoeckel 366; Stoecker 314; Stoeckly 102; Stoedter 294; Stoeffel 175; Stoegli 188; Stoehr (s. Stehr, Stroeh[e]r) *108, 186, 244, 249, 250, 269, *288, 341, 349, 366, 410; Stoekel 326; Stoelle 307; Stoemply 77; Stoer 248; Stoerckell 373; Stoerller 96; Stoerner 216, 345, 397; Stoertzemeyer 410; Stoery 160; Stoess *209; Stoets 283; Stoetzel 303, 333; Stoever *58, 467; Stoever (Steffer) 40, 44, 436; Stoey 189; Stoff 362, 418; Stoffel 241, 314, 354, 380, 416; Stoffelbein 147; Stohl 243; Stohler *117, 191, 265, 382; Stohonen 321; Stokman 222; Stoler 102; Stoll 50, 155, 165, *235, 297, 321, 357, 390, 398, 404; Stollberger 379; Stoller 203; Stollzol 321; Stoltz 125, 171, 206, 259, 264, *319, *367; Stoltze *295; Stoltzel 394; Stoltzfus *376; Stool 144; Stoop 114; Stop 104; Storch 247, 267; Storches 410; Storck 229; Storm 56, 213, 215, 220; Stormer 209; Storr 443; Stotz (s. Schoch?) 198, *241, 242, 253; Stoubig 91; Stouder 88; Stoufer 56; Stouver 156; Stove 456, 459; Stover 123, 472; Stoy 270, 271; Strach 342; Strack 74, 304, 359, 367; Strackbein 411, 413; Straeitz 180; Straetter 280; Straetzer 354; Straeueker 178; Strahling 209; Stram *174; Strasbuerger 389; Strass 73, *357; Strassbuerger 154; Straub 71, *78, 90, *91, 153, 237, 247, 259, 284, *298, 395, 446; Straube 134, 326; Straubel 295; Strauch 109, 313, 355; Straudman 214; Straull 339; Strauman 399; Straumay 384; Straus 306, 467; Straushaar 240; Strauss 81, 123, 203, 207, 217, 292, 294, 371; Streader (s. Stroeder) 209, 210; Strebig 348; Strecker 200, 384; Streder 168, 314; Strehm *331; Streicker 177; Streidtz 314; Streier 334; Streihl 175; Streilhoff 195; Strein 194, 251, 356; Streiter 109; Strele 163; Stremmel 413; Strempel 287; Strenger 356; Streper 430, 471; Strepers 430; Streter 120; Streuber 285; Streuch 416; Striby 313; Strich 202; Strickeller 55; Stricker 87, 280; Strickert 134; Strickler *112, 329, 363; Strickli 58; Striebig 91; Strietzel 407; Striey 165, 166; Strobel 129, 282, 327, 328; Strobig 291; Strocher 368; Stroebel 122, 163; Stroeder (s. Streader) *210; Stroedinger

305; Stroeh(e)r (s. Stoehr) *186, 197, 250; Stroever 292; Stroh 197, 207, 246, 341; Strohauer 85, 86; Strohbau 383; Strohl 120, 227, 405; Strohm 311, 361; Strohman 180; Strohmenger 325; Strohschneider 190, *250; Stroll 234; Strom 77, 165, 386; Strome *50; Stropp 342; Strosle 246; Strott 320; Strowman 191; Strub 105, 266; Strubel 67, 181; Strubhar 205; Struckmeyer 295; Strueckel 268; Strunck 169, 170, 317, 366; Struwel 104; Stubenrauch 446; Stuber 52, 187, *243, *280; Stuberling 333; Stucki 165, 213; Stuckrath 443; Stuckroth 86; Stucky 269, 403; Studi 354; Stueber 78, 133; Stuebert 342; Stuebigh 157; Stueck 379; Stueckerdts 384; Stueckle 128, *252; Stuegger 398; Stuell 353; Stuempel 230; Stuendel 283; Stuendter 247; Stuentzel 344; Stuer 264; Stuette 266; Stuetzmann 283; Stuhl 137; Stuky *244; Stumb 146, 223; Stumbff 235; Stumm 267; Stump 144, 306, 318, 401, 438, 468; Stumpf(f) 164, 180, 213, 216, 245, 254, 309, 334, 411; Stumpp 253, 328; Stuntz 66, *367; Stuper 447; Stupp 52, 115, 466, 473; Sturf 115; Sturm *232, 296, 370, 391; Sturmfels 377; Sturtzebach 85; Stutz 355, 356, 361; Stutzman 53; Stutzenberger 251; Suber 298; Sucher 214; Sud(d)er 101, 184, 231, 361; Sudtne 399; Sudtner 324; Sueber 229; Suefer 195; Suehn 211; Suehrer 306; Suelger 389; Suendel 268; Suerber 113, 275, 276; Suerfes 234; Suermer 177; Suesholtz 64; Sues(s) 139, 145, 150, 226, 266, 287, 288, 328, 379, 395, *467; Suesser 347; Suesz 110; Sulger 398; Sulheimer 373; Suliger 286; Sullenger 56; Suller 193; Sullinger 262; Sulsbach 121; Sultzbach 210; Sultzberger 291; Sultzer 342; Sum(m)er 171, *205, 248, 262, 330; Summerauer *188; Summois 468; Sumter 7, 25; Sunbert 405; Sunckel 418; Sunwald 107; Supper (s. Sooper) 217, 218, 256; Suppert 404; Surber 98, 148, 197; Suter 158, 265; Sutter 175; Sutton *402, *405, *409; Sutz 214; Swartz 50, 286; Swartzenberg 132; Swenk 343; Swerer 257; Swicker (s. Swyger) 50; Swiger 146; Swindel 256; Swing 243; Swisser 77; Switzer *113, 214; de Switzerdediefryer 180; Switzig 150; Swoap 50; Swonder 191; Swoob 214; Swort *65; Swyger (s. Swicker) 50; Swyng 145; Syber 67; Sycar *464; Syder 126; Syegrist (s. Siegrist) 51; Symon *464; Sype (s. Seib) 82; Sysloop (s. Zeisloff, Zeisloop) 101; Syroa 313.

Tabel 322; Tace 89; Taentzler 98; Taeuble 444; Taffelmeyer 83; Tait *186; Tallebach 173, 325; Talmon 340; Tamas 178; Tamerus 201; Tamet 202; Tamhoeffer 327; Tamson 432; Tandt 356; Taner 144; Tanneberger (s. Tenneberger) *421, 425; Tannenberger 153; Tannezer 419; Tanny *137; Tar 343; Tasch 319; Tasker 107; Tathouer 204; Tatweiler 115; Taub 352, 362; Taubenheim 247; Tauberman 332; Taubert 301; Taubetishel 154; Taules 279; Tauschhaeus 170; Tausweber 446; Taxis 321; Taxler 360; Taylor 456, 459;

Teast 463; Tecker 180; Tedweiler 387; Teele 81; Teetze 137; Teex 423, 427; Teffer 444; Teibz 248; Teich 114; Teis 140, 287, 369, 438; Teisser 396; Teitz 190; Teitzwortzer *344; Telcher (s. Delcher) 227; Tempel 407; Tenant 63; Tendelspach 78; Tenne 103, 301; Tenneberger (s. Tanneberger) 421, 425; Teny 82; Teobald 368; Termel 307; Ternantz 228; Tesch *290, 295; Test 109; Tete 299; Tetsche 449; Tetwelder 381; Teubel 334; Teuffell 264; Teul (s. Deull) 245; Teussel 263; Teutsch 251, 381; Teutscher 92, *93; Teutzel 419; Tevental 203; Textur 254; Thaeler *86; Thales 447; Thamer (s. Dammer) 174; Thar 45; Thebards 346; Thebelt 115; Theen 473; Theil 157, 236; Theiler 85; Theis(s) (s. Theissen) 64, 125, 150, 182, 221, 314, 356, 402, 449, 465; Theissen (s. Theis[s]) 356; Theissinger 336; Theobalth 142; Ther 361; Thering 416; Thesser 155; Theusler 92; Theyl 229; Theys 412; Thiebautz 416; Thieffelbach 168; Thiel 121, 354, 361, 367, 372, 386, 390, 411; Thielbon 141; Thiele 237; Thieleman 398; Thielo 407; Thilo 451; Thinges 184; Thiringer 326; Thoenei 313; Tholhaver 129; Tholl 219; Thom 202; Thoma 356; Thomas 11, 30, *64, 120, *131, *148, 173, 179, 235, 249, 250, 259, *260, 313, *317, 333, 396, 413, 418, 468; Thomass *335; Thome (s. Domme) *191, 409; Thomme *102, 119, 399; Thompson *109; Thomson *243; Thor 161; Thorman 307; Thormeyer 357; Thorn 389; Thorwarte 132; Thorwarth 369; Thoulouzan 214; Thran 358; Threer 137, 251; Threhr 59; Threin 387; Threx 282; Thron 109; Thuerig 252; Thueringer 341; Thuerwaechter 267; Thum 325, 337; Thumy 231; Thur 138; Thurm 237, 291; Tickel *331; Ticker 360; Tiebindorf 50; Tieffelmeyer 219; Tiegarden 100; Tiel 116; Tien 249, 250; Tieschmar 359; Tietz 222, 284, 338; Tiewes 140; Tieze 171; Tiffin *177; Tihn 409; Till 423, 428; Tillboner 315; Tillinger 286; Tillman 260, 286, 344; Tillshoeffer 125; Tilly 198; Timanus 83; Timberman *88, 475, 477; Timmer 125; Timothee 68, *70; Timpe 350; Tinius 336; Tisen 66, 430; Tison 431, 471, 477; Tistel 313; Titlo 477; Titshler 291; Tittenhoffer 438; Tizler 170; Toblar 4, 22; Todf 388; Toehms 209; Toelcker 288; Toellner 423, 428; Toelly 177; Toepper 299; Toerentz 322; Toerr 178; Toessler 145; Tofort *119; Toll 107, 165, 241; Tolman 341; Tomas 105; Tomer 312; Tomm 279, *341; Tomppraet 193; Toninger 379; Tonner 219; Torenberger 119, 140; Torson 295; Torward *340; Tost 105; Toster 190; Tothero 474; Tow 127; Traber 239; Trabu 7, 25; Trachsell 153; Traenckner 295; Tragher 179; Trahman 173; Traler 435; Tram *337; Tramp *374; Tran 81, *316, 320; Tranberg 115; Transu 63; Trap 124; Trarbach (s. Drabach) *250; Trasher 175; Traub 214, 245, 324, 325; Traudt *88, 215; Trauenstack 250; Trauert (s. Trorit); Traut 366, *473; Trautman(n)

*261, 262, 402; Traut(t)man(n) 103, 119, 166, 284; Trautwein 273, 402; Trawinger 192; Trawn 199; Traxel *203, 332; Tray *76; Treber 101; Treger 224; Treibel 215; Treidel 96; Treiler 78; Trein 357, 359; Treit *135; Treitter 89; Trellinger 436; Trenkel *129; Trenner 131; Trent 7, 25; Tresenreuther 419; Tressenstuett 315; Tressler 190; Trestel 337; Treuckel 163; Treuttle 369, 401; Trewer 100; Trewett 127; Trewitz (s. Triewitz) 412; Trexler *397, *475; Treydel 302; Treye 303; Triber 221; Trible 399; Triell 50; Triess 116; Triett 281; Triewitz (s. Trewitz) 413; Trillhauser 443; Trinckhauss 261; Trippel 409; Trippner 210; Trissler 130; Tristers 343; Tritzlen 415; Troelich 115; Troelly 230; Trolers 136; Trorit (Trauert) 445; Trostell 86; Trotz 348; Truckenmiller 300; Truck(en)mueller 85, 156, 165, 313; Truehauffer 399; Truemper 229; Truen 244; Truenckler 291; Truke 194; Trumbauer 472; Trumheller 346; Trummaner 262; Trump 17, 36, 79, 92, 308, *318, 329, 376; Trycler 55; Tryster 89, 96; Tschantz 437; Tschieringer 247; Tschop(p) 139, *192, 382; Tschucki 266; Tschudi (Tschudy, Tschuti) 130, *191, 214, *382; Tshakky 231; Tsober 83; Tubben 431; Tuche 327; Tuchembel 201; Tuchman (s. Duchmann) 220, 377; Tuckermann 209; Tueck 408; Tuelman 140; Tuenes 430; Tuenis 471; Tuerck 440, 442; Tuesch 190; Tulpenbaum 282; Ture 304; Turinger 154; de Turk 475; (de) Turks *10, *29; Turmeyer 311; Turner 421, 426; Turnez 404; Turny 231; Turpin *79; Tuxly 246; Tuyman 430; Tybly 235; Tymperton 84; Tyson (Deisen) 470.

Uber 199, 289, 300; Uberer 400; Ubung 406; Uder 346; Udner 179; Udry 151; Uebel 311; Ueberroth 365; Uehle 325; Uehlein 351; Uehrbass 159; Uelireist 336; Uetzel 293; Uff *393; Uffer 369; Uffner 183; Uhl 367, 381, 417, *448; Uhlandt 283; Uhle *113; Uhler 73, *112; Uhl(l) 197, 307, 340; Uhl(l)erich 148, 215, 219, 242, 258; Uhlmann 83; Uhrer 248; Uhrich 73, 251, 285; Uhrig 207; Uhting 347; Ulerich 71, 166, 349; Ull 323; Ulland 61; Uller 297; Ullerich 53, 71, 136; Ullman(n) 296, 298; Ul(l)rich 124, 157, 183, 265; Ulmer 125, 148, 219, 234, 267, 327, 400; Ulmstadt 161; Ulrich 241, 331, 373, 388, 404, 414, 467; Ulrick *53, *74, *107, 115; Ulsch 294; Umbenhauer 467; Umberger *89; Umbstat 432, *474; Umensetter *268; Umstadt *76; Umstatt 367; Unangst (s. Ungast, Urangst) 206, 271, *325, 365; Unbehand *134; Unberhent 134; Unckel 284; Unckelbach 334; Underkoffer 112, 122; Underseel 404; Underweg 283; Undetenard 64; Unfug 407; Ungar 186, 301; Ungast (s. Unangst, Urangst) 199; Ungear 163; Unger 91, 118, 150, 374; Ungerer 300, 314, 382; Unkenbacher 139; Unrath 239; Unruh 79, 274, 438, 466; Unseld 382; Unverzagt 189; Updegraff 476; Upp 182, 282; Upper 365; Urangst (s. Unangst, Ungast)

207; Urbach 326; Urban 276, 314; Urckart 361; Urering
230, 232; Urich 326, 348, 466; Urickhaus 96; Urlettig 329;
Urmi 55; Urner 437; Usbeck 348; Usener 387; Usley 423,
427; Ussener 385; Usser 158; Usterle 281; Utes 385; Utz
*92, 129, *229, 274; Utzman 126.
Vadel *361; Vaetter 171, *419; Vaintvas 175; Valck 57;
Valentin 272, 278; Valentine 216, 225; Valin 406; Valk 58;
Vallendin *196; Vallow *463; Vallstapp 147; Van 289, 290;
Vanaken 17, 36; Vanberg 406; Vandeburg 226; Vandelop 17,
36; Vandergach 430; Vanderhuyst 407; Vanderslice (s. van der
Sluys); Vandersluice (s. van der Sluys); Vandersluice 476;
Vanfloer 17, 36; Vanfussen *478; Vankolk 431; Vansant 127;
Vansintern 434; Vanterberg 262; Vareffens 406; Varlet 410;
Varninger 275; Vaser 253; Vass 389; Vast 399; Vaubel
338; Vaudalin 247; Vautie 323; Vaymer 286; d'Veau 104;
Vechtel 113; Veibert 84; Veigenbaser 263; Veiher 307; Veiock
379; Veirling 181; Veit 104; Veith 336; Velck 360; Vell
326; Velte 52; Velten 224; Velter 225; Vemisbaker 199;
Vendner 311; Venerich 437; Venig 115; Veny 321; Verbyman 431; Verley 82; Verner *177; Vertries 468; Veruch
96; Vervalson 18, 36; Vesseler 213; Vestens 396; Vestermeyer 379; Vetler 68; Vetter 61, 154, 164, 173, 209, *260,
262, 341, 354; Vetterman 224; Vetzberger 330; Vey 144,
290; Vial 115; Viantt 142; Videbant 409; Viegle 50; Viehman 185; Vielgar 84; Vieman 221; Vierisard 372; Viet 238;
Vigeld 290; Vilain 7, 25; Villeneaue 414; Villib 216; le
Villien *463; Vinettier 392; Vink 50; Vinterhelver 85;
Visanant (s. Fissnand) 71; Visser 345; Vitel 143; Vittery
*136, *139; Vitzthum 332; Viunt 214; Vivel 144; Vix 391;
Voegelin 88; Voegle 84; Voegler 374; Voelbel 321; Voelck
333; Voelcker 96, 332, 392; Voelckner *254; Voell 323;
Voeltmer 353; Voesener (s. Wessener) 217; Voett 286; Voet-
tel 320; Vogeler 302; Vogeley 406; Vogelgesang 145; 236,
321, *351; Vogelhuetter 56; Vogel(l) *66, 76, 80, 120, 143,
177, 198, 210, *322, *344, 360, 380, 400, 407, *412; Vogel-
man(n) 129, 216; Vogelsang 408; Voght 295; Vogler 70,
219, 289; Vogt *94, 207, *214, 215, 219, 229, 299, 310,
339, 356, 359, 373, 392, 444; Vohl 355, 373; Vohleder
300; Voigt *101, 147, 301, 399; Volandt 236; Volcampe
296; Volch *300; Volck (s. Folck) *105, 135, *194, 216,
251, 280, 287, 293, 309, 315, *345, 350, 365, 366, 397,
399, 439, 441; Volckmann 64; Volckmeyer 343; Volchrath
329; Volden 198; Volkman 295; Volks 322; Vollandt 226;
Vollerman 314; Vollert 262; Vollmer (s. Fulmer) 90, 123,
239, 306, 392; Vollprecht 358; Vollsteller 104; Volltzer 235;
Vollunte 225; Volmer 341, *375; Volpel 51; Volpp 263;
Volprecht 143; Voltz 111, 187, 220, 237, 246, 310, 324, 369,
*409, 416; Vonderlind 135; Vonreth 89; Vonruff 231; Vor-

bach 189, 190, 320; Voschell *446; Vos(s) 196, 307, *339; Vosselmann 84; Votrin 135; Voyt 171; Voyzin 126; Vrevel 168; Vreytach 251; Vry 59; Vundi 191; Vuss 379; Vuter 366. Waag 283, 310; Waagenaer 180; Waall 221; Waas 273; Waasser 231; Wachs 320; Wachter 201, 265, 379, 383; Wack 187, *286; Wacke 423, 427; Wacker 126, 211; Wadham *225; Waebeber 183; Waeber (s. Weber) *303; Waechter 208, 291, 322; Waegly 476; Waehrlich 267; Waelckly 198; Wäldte 392; Waeller (s. Weller) 319, 382; Waenger 336; Waerffer 320; Waerner 93; Waerthmann 341; Waesener 311; Wa(e)spy *231; Waeydemann 245; Waffunong 325; Wagard 379; Wagemueller 476; Wagenhorst *401; Wagenmann 232; Wagenseiler 474; Wag(h)eman 101, 176; Waghmer 171; Waghter 192; Wagner 74, *77, 78, 79, 80, *86, 109, 110, 112, *114, 115, 117, 123, *127, *142, 145, *152, 154, 157, 159, 164, *166, 168, *170, 175, *178, 182, 184, 189, 194, 195, 199, 200, 206, 207, 210, *211, *218, 219, *221, *228, 231, *234, 238, *245, *248, *254, 255, 257, 261, *263, 265, 267, 270, 271, 282, 302, 314, 315, 319, 324, 325, 326, 328, 333, 335, 346, *351, 352, 355, 359, 361, 363, 375, 379, 384, 393, 395, *397, 407, 414, 416, 418, 422, 427, 446, *466; Wahl 216, 222, 279, 343, *356; Wahnsidel 85; Wahnsiller 170; Warenholtz 353; Waibel *359; Waiblinger 408; Waidele 155; Waidman(n) *467; Waihdel 240; Walber 344; Walborn *448, 465, 466; Walck 82; Walcker 248, 255, 414, 449; Walckher 338; Wald 70, 126; Waldenaus 395; Walder *51, 59, 78, 81, 155, 158, 176, *177, 196, 233, 264, 310, 349; Waldman 125; Waldmer 231; Waldo *16, 34, 35; Waldschmidt 270, 271; Wal(d)tmann *374; Waldy 231; Waletein 238; Wall 108, 115, 117, 209, 411; Wallace *122, *413; Wallbeyer 338; Waller 64, 155, 211, 267, 368; Walles 215; Walleset 191; Walleysen 297; Wallhauer 313; Wallhuter 268; Wallis *390, 449; Wallman 416; Wallmiller 178; Wallrecht 123; Wallsener 191; Walmer 151; Walschner 330; Walser 194; Waltaich 155; Walters 327; Walterscher 386; Walt(h)er 49, 50, *80, 81, 90, 98, 99, 115, 116, *127, 143, 144, 148, 156, 159, 162, 165, *195, 197, 203, *204, 206, 214, 217, 228, 254, 257, 260, 264, 273, 280, 284, 287, *289, 300, 311, 330, 350, 351, *364, 367, 376, *379, 384, *389, 393, 407, 413, 416, 469; Waltman(n) *386, 397; Waltschmidt 264; Waltz 126, 130, 160, 170, 185, 235, 236, 242, 264, 269, 270, 279, 281, 289, 293, 298, 300, 306, 414; Waltzer 18, 37, 224; Wambach *360, 379; Wambold(t) 102, *108, 301; Wambolt 101, 102; Wamkessel 187; Wammer 432, *472; Wampfler 176, *177; Wandel 321; Wandlin 276; Wanenmacher *203; Waner 351; Wangolt 353; Wann 225, 290, 367; Wann(e)macher 70, *129; Wannenmacher 443; Wanner 86, 87, 193, 356; Wantlin 226; Wanton *138; Wantzbach 365; Ware *124, 332; Warembier

War—Wei

(Warenbuer) (s. Wemar); Warinken 299; Warner 96, 235, 299, 337, 353; Warth 137, 147, 320; Wart(h)man *66, 73, *401; Was 279; Waschke 421, 425; Wasey 2, 20; Washer 281; Wasling 400; Wass 354; Wassem 309; Wasser 389, 397; Wasserman(n) 289, 337; Wassum *292; Wastenhaber 317; Wathman 375; Wausch 363; Wayemer 170; Weaber 191, 233, 234; Weaver 131; Webber 127, 397, 416, 445, 447; Webel 329; Weber 51, 59, 64, *71, 74, 75, 76, 84, 91, *100, *109, 112, 114, 117, 120, 126, 130, 137, *139, 140, 149, *151, 155, 157, 162, *171, 172, 175, *182, *184, 188, *191, 196, 210, *211, *212, 213, *214, 217, *222, 232, 237, 246, 247, *252, *254, *255, *257, 260, 263, 267, 276, 281, 284, 285, 287, *303, 313, 317, 320, 329, 330, 331, 338, 339, *340, 346, 350, 351, *358, *359, *361, *362, 365, *366, 370 (s. Waeber), *374, 378, 383, *389, 391, 396, 405, 408, 410, 411, 413, *418, 419, 435, *437, 440, 441, 447, 470, 471, *477; Weber (s. Ohber); Weberd 97; Webert 408; Webrecht 277, 350; Wecher 59; Wechlid 165; Weck *368; Weckeffer (wohl Weckesser?) 198; Wecker 253, 318; Weckerlin 289; Weckerling 238; Weckerly 98; Weckesser (s. Weckeffer) 178; Weckfort 337; Wedartz 197; Wedel 237, 324, 363; Wedelscheider 339; Weder 52; Weebehandt 343; Weeber 252; Weeger 59; Weems *151; Weertz 229; de Wees (auch Dewes) *430, 471, *473; Weeser 214; Weeslin 192; Weg 255, 281; Wegel 169, 330; Wegener 299; Wegerlein 75, 76; Wegmann 158; Wegmeyer (s. Wehmeyer) 307; Wegner 289, 360; Wehing 288; Wehler 147, 206, 239; Wehmeyer (s. Wegmeyer) 307; Wehner 175; Wehr 142, 269, 371; Wehrner 177, 246; Weibel(l) (Weybel) 134, *191, 412; Weichel 361; Weick 384; Weickel 363; Weickert 309, 385; Weichel(l) 65, 293; Weichert 214; Weichstnir 253; Weicht 423, 428; Weick 162; Weickel 252, 404; Weicker 102, 115, 150, 188; Weid 247; Weidel 59, 192; Weiden 447; Weidener 302; Weidenmaier (s. Weydenmeyer) 364; Weider 50; Weidhorn 270; Weidich 282; Weidinger *334; Weidknecht 82, 443; Weidlandt 395; Weidler 212; Weidman 87, *88, *98, 99, 132, 158, 231, 276, 329, 391, 438; Weidmayer 382; Weidmer (s. Wiedmer) 99; Weidmeyer 303; Weidner 10, 29, 176, 287, 348, 391, 475; Weidt 247; Weidtmann *113; Weidy 162; Weier 258, 400; Weig 263; Weigand(t) 186, 244, 276, 439, 441; Weigell 72; Weigerich 254; Weighel 137; Weiland 109; Weilder 436; Weiler 202, 297, 475; Weil(l) 157, 280, 330, 397; Weimann 264; Weimer 297, 416; Weimmer 267; Weinandt 259; Weinberger 196, 357; Weinbren(n)er (s. Winebrener) 298, 316; Weinest 422, 426; Weingaertner 374; Weingerer 169; Weinheimer 74, 76; Weining 351; Weininger 240, 321; Weinman 326; Weinmer 253; Weinmiller 310; Weinmueller 122; Weinnert (s. Wennert) 260; Weirich 225; Weirig 335; Weis 40, 44, *49,

57, 70, 107, 146, *235, 256, *295, 324, 342, 350; Weisbarth
281; Weise 196, 350; Weisenberger 288; Weiser *58, 67,
*117, 260, *445, 447, 465, 466; Weisgerber 119, 293, 367;
Weishart 114; Weisiger 71; Weisman(n) 18, 36, *244; Weismuth 407; Weiß 67, 86, 87, 96, 98, *107, 112, 115, 119,
121, 123, 157, 159, 169, 173, *176, 184, 187, 193, 196,
197, 198, 204, 208, 210, 213, *233, 234, 235, 236, 237,
*239, 245, 248, 251, *252, *266, 276, *283, 305, 306,
*308, 314, 324, *326, 331, 335, 344, 356, 357, 363, 365,
374, 375, 379, 381, 391, 394, 395, 397, 402, 409, 415, 419,
422, 427, 448; Weissart 400; Weissbach 419; Weissel 84;
Weissenberger 276; Weisser 18, 36, 137, 268; Weissert 338,
339, 355; Weissgerber 239; Weisshardt 386; Weissig 149;
Weisskob 186; Weisskopff 160; Weissman(n) 179, 256, 331;
Weißmueller 148, 401; Weissner 53; Weitenbacher 384;
Weiter 176; Weith 155; Weitherstein 392; Weittman 184;
Weittner 89; Weitzel(l) 120, 121, *209, 210, 250, 319, *329,
331, 412; Weitzen 250; Weitzenfelder 311; Weitzenhoeller
293; Weizler 473; Wejuatius 292; Welbemeir 392; Welch
153; Welchel 134; Welck 415; Welckel *411; Welcker 49,
186, *385, 395, 400, *417, 474; Weld 376; Welde 54, 70,
230, 287, 288, 302, 304, 358; Welder 272; Weldgrau 56;
Weldi 134; Weldtli 80; Welker 194; Welle 385; Wellecker
49; Weller (s. Waeller) 109, 122, 162, 199, 204, 272, 274,
284, 287, 319, 353, 365, 372, 389, 397, 447; Wellmer 49;
Welmslehr 190; Welper 216; Wels(c)h *106, 127, 145, 146,
287, 297, 363, *396; Welsch(h)ans 132, *135; Welsnack 407;
Welss 323; Welt 262; Welte 328, 357, 358, 382; Welter
267, 314; Welterich 119; Welthe *328; Welthshans 409;
Weltman 416; Weltner 404; Weltnes 258; Weltz 86, 267,
312; Weltzheimer 376; Wemar (Warembier, Warenbuer) 8,
27; Wemar(in) 440, 442; Wemeyer 320; Wenbacher 255;
Wench 341, 356; Wenckert 308; Wenckler 331; Wendel 291,
296, 410; Wendeling 336, 419; Wendel(l) 72, 73, *110, 123,
178, 179, 328, 355; Wender (s. Bender) 339; Wendling 180,
212, 276, 387; Wendnagel 156; Wenerich *443; Wenger 53,
86, 100, 111, 112, *180, 181, *188, *196, 273, *357, 404,
473; Wengert 252; Wenhart 345; Wenig 196, 202, 283;
Wenigard 249; Wenigart 347; Wenigeck 349; Weniger 236,
356; Weninger 154; Wenkelbley 469; Wenner *408, 409, 418;
Wennert (s. Weinnert) 260; Wennertblecher 276; Wenrich
*468; Wenschler 281; Wensell 353; Wenssel 103; Wenst 66;
Wenterott 83; Wentz 66, 159, 160, 189, 208, 212, 235, 276,
287, 331, *367, 394, 395, 434; Wentzel(l) 118, 183, 285, 366,
409, 412; Weppert 335; Wer (s. Woerer) 349; Werbel 142;
Werbung 259; Wercken 355; Werckhaeusser 334; Werenfels
191; Wereni 342; Werentz 223; van der Werff 430, 436;
Werf(f)el 78, 86; Werge 395; Werger 359; Wergraf 141;

Werkheiser 339; Werlein *308; Werlie 103; Werlisch 348;
Werlle 105; Werly 236; Werner 76, 102, *136, 144, 153,
157, 166, 171, 224, 235, 237, 244, 246, 269, 270, *284,
287, 305, 307, 369, 422, 426, 444, 448, 465; Werning 301;
Wernley 392; Werns 366, 376; Werntz *173, 175, 227, 280;
Werry 108; Werss *329; Wersum 337; Wert 132; van der
Wert 432; Werth 81, 155, 161, 378, 400; Werthes 181;
Werthmueller 347; Werthon 57; Wertingisch 230; Wertmüller
2, 20, 429; Werts 430; Wertz 303; Wervel 86; Weschenbach
97, 111; Weschune 306; Wesger 334; Wessel 149; Wessener
(s. Voesener) 217, 269, 288, 289; Wessig 330; Wessing 318;
Wessinger 139; Wessle 282; West 166, 237, 337; Westberger
170; Weste 282; Westenberger 154; Wester 50; Westerberger
169; Westheber 71; Westmann 423, 427; Wetherholt 343;
Wethwein 222; Wetterbauer 382; Wetterhardt 343; Wettern
358; Wetzel(l) *70, 112, 121, 174, 280, 292, 327, 359, 363;
Wetzel 226, 239; Wetzfeld 315; Wetzler 178, 339; Weugaeterr
(Weingärtner?) 308; Wexler 411; Wey 211; Weyand(t) 211,
222, 378, 392, *393, 411; Weyant 279, 293; Weybel (s. Weibel);
Weybrecht 80, 81, 438; Weybrich 160; Weyckel 357; Weydebach 102; Weyden 219; Weydenhauer 182; Weydenmeyer (s.
Weidenmaier) *364; Weydigh 236; Weydman 231; Weydner
149, 150, 209, 293; Weydo 306; Weyel(l) 316, 419; Weyer
76, 103, 169, 391; Weyerbacher *255, 312; Weyerhaussen 319;
Weyerman(n) 213, 476; Weyes 72; Weyfaller 281; Wey-
gand(t) 56, 101, *183, 186, 345, 347; Weygant 314; Wey-
gel(l) 102, *245; Weygerdt *51; Weyhenger *268; Weyl 101,
408; Weyland 291; Weyler 264, 416; Weyll 250; Weylthoeffer
339; Weyman 151, 259, 333; Weymer 84, 85, 141, 232, 401;
Weymiller 122; Weyn 289; Weynan 366; Weynandt 70, 90;
Weynant *332; Weyre 169; Weyrer 371; Weyrich 106, 169,
438; Weys *262; Weysbach 267; Weyse 196; Weyshaar 303;
Weyskirk 307; Weys(s) 230, 231; Weyt 130; Weytzel 154,
298, 351, 368; Weytzer 390; White 256; Whitmer *88;
Wibel 269; Wichel 65, 105; Wick 101; Wicke 410; Wickel
353; Wickert 125, *217, 361, 416; Wickhaus 444; Widdenmann 270; Wideabach 107; Widemann 132; Wid(en)meyer
*263; Wiederhohl 348; Widerich 336; Widerick 369; Wider-
stein 376; Widerwenig 188; Widman(n) (s. Wittman) 166,
183, 212, 232, 401; Widmer (s. Witmer) 204, 230, 231;
Widner 64; Widsted 423, 428; Widter 130; Widtmann 228;
Wiebel 374; Wieber 316; Wieder 146, 249, 250, 294; Wiederholt 247; Wiederwachs 447; Wiedes 64; Wi(e)dmer (s. Weidmer) 99; Wieg 259; Wiegele 401; Wiegner *95, *96, 97;
Wieil 184; Wieland(t) 224, 249, 401; Wield *75; Wien 189,
227; Wier 254, *259, 391; Wiern 168; Wiesener 191; Wiesner
422, 426; Wiessener 152; Wiesser 319; Wiest 98, 122, 266,
384; Wiesteir 286; Wiet 305; Wietdemann 273; Wieton 401;

Wiettemeyer 310; Wigandt 369; Wightman 61; Wigler 50; Wigman 318; Wigner 86, 467; Wihrrem 338; Wilbrandt 286; Wild(t) 249, *282, 284, 306, 332, 409, 415; Wildanger 109; Wildenmuth 276; Wilder 49; Wildermuth 117; van der Wilderniss 432; Wildfang 96; Wildt 121, 171; Wilfanger (s. Willdanger) 245; Wilgenson 294; Wilghart 251; Wilheiser 411; Wilhelm 50, 69, 110, 120, 135, 141, 160, 183, 195, 257, 274, 291, 308, 312, 356, 364, 378, 382, 387, 396, 412, 446, 469, 472; Wilhelmi *96, 330; Wilhelmus 53, 271; Wilhertzbach 230; Wilkie *241; Wilkinson *175; Will 49, 113, 148, 163, 171, 237, 259, 293, 326, 356, 363; Willar 230; Willauer 84; Willdanger (s. Wilfanger) 245; Wille 397; Willem 175; Willemann 375; Willemin 324; Willems 101; Willer 222, 280, 324, 343; Willerich 184; Willert 419; Willet 222; Willfeld 295; Willhan 180; Willia(h)r 171, *243; Willier 309; Willing 47, 48; Willmann 397; Wills 362; Wilms 113, 417; Wilrich 377; Wilson *98, *121, *146, *163, *169, 173, 174, *240, 422, 426; Wilt 84, 110, 300, 332; Wimer 222; Wimmer 293; Winchel 279; **Winck** 415; Winckelbleck (s. Wingleplech) 79; Wincker 275; Winckler 194, 295, 308, *309, 330; Windecker 447; Windemuth 72, *102; Windenauer 203; Winder 96, 325, 399, 404; Winderbauer 113; Windermeyer *190; Windesch 281; Windlinger 129; Windmeyer 216; Windst *175; Winebrener (s. Weinbrener) 298; Winecoop 478; Winegarden 271; Wineman 379; **Winesheim** 170; **Wingert** 181, 272; Wingertmann 92, 93; , Wingleplech (s. Winckelbleck) 79; Winhart 305; Winholdt 120; Winholt 346; Wink 475; Winkelblech 18, 36; Winkelman 231; Winkler 243; Winkotz 188; Winseher 380; Winsh 243; Winter 90, *91, 106, *269, 274, 295, 298, 315, 401, 448; Winterberger 92; Winterehle 154; Wintergress 163; Winterstein 151; **Winther** 238; Wintz 364, 400; Wintzberger 279; Wirbel (s. Wervel) 86, 151; Wird 336; Wirdeberger 261; Wird(t) 162, 200, 216; Wirheiner 236; Wirl 333; Wirst 340; Wirth 140, 163, 164, 168, 181, *185, 201, 221, 272, 276, 315, 345; Wirthsman 316; Wirtz 70, 148, 177, 315; Wischhan 154; Wise 79, 89, 91; Wiseman 406; Wisener 293; Wiser 287, 360; Wisham 244; Wishong *142; Wis(h)t (s. Wuest) *241; **Wisler** 108, 126; Wiss 60; Wissbach 333; Wissel 56; Wisser 254, *319, 337; Wissich 400; Wissinger 302; Wissler 88, 270, 271, 277, *292, *372; Wis(s)man 108, 213; Wissner 176, *240, 268; Wistadius 354; Wistholtz 67; Withman 155; **Witman** 82, 473; Witmer (s. Widmer) 204, 275, 416, 436, *438; Witt 346, 433; Wittemer 247; Wittenmeyer *238; Wittenstein 355; Wittersinn 131; Witterspohn 284; **Wittgie** 152; Wittig 364; Wittke 422, 426; Wittman(n) (s. Widman) 166, 212, 242, 306, 307, 348, 400; Wit(t)mer 50, 74, 173, 176, 178, *329, *340; Wittscher 365; Wittser 50; Witz 139; **Wize** 107;

3, 21; Zach(a)rias 102. 109, 112, 222; Zacharis *314; Zacharius 401; Zachary *127; Zachriss 348; Zadouski 436;
Zaemer 129; Zaener 164; Zaentler 359; Zaentyes 396; Zaeumer
(s. Zimer?) 324; Zahele 413; Zahn 330; Zaimger 298;
Zaller 192; Zanck 254; Zaneichel 325; Zangenberg 301;
Zangmeister 206, 207; Zant 450; Zantsinger 78; Zarburger
151; Zarthmann 57; Zauder 421, 425; Zebalt 378; Zebolt
233; Zech 320; Zechiel 381; Zechler 336; Zegels 342;
Zegler 255; Zeh 448, 465, 468; Zeherman 196; Zehman
130; Zehmer 161; Zehnen 347; Zehner 371; Zehntbauer
269; Zeiger 288; Zeigner 109; Zeilen 311; Zeiler 250, 369;
Zeiller 316; Zeiner 208, 278, *354; Zeisberger *421, 422,
425, 426; Zeise 322; Zeisinger 166; Zeisloff (s. Zeislopp,
Sysloop) 17, 36, 100; Zeisloop (s. Zeisloff, Sysloop) 101;
Zeissdorf 447; Zeister 153; Zeitz 322, 410; Zekerr 371; Zell
*471, 473; Zeller 120, *222, *277, 338, 379, *447; Zellman
149; Zellner 236; Zelman 407; Zembt 306; Zemmer 414; Zenaldt
337; Zendmeyer 298; Zenger 164, 444, 445; Zengerle 385;
Zenlaub 321; Zenteler 365; Zentler 474; Zepp 359; Zepper
372; Zepter 162; Zerb 467; Zerbe *448, 449, 465, *467;
Zerch 269; Zercher 277, 401; Zerchert 135; Zerel 202;
Zerfas(s) 116, 144, 202, 419; Zerger (s. Berger?) 73; Zergiebel 349; Zerhiger 295; Zericher 178; Zerkel 471, 472;
Zerman 273; Zerr 234; Zervin 157; Zesseler 222; Zessernick 400; Zettelmeyer *261; Zettle 87; Zettlemeier 114;
Zettler 451; Zety 277; Zetzel 325; Zeuchmacher 18, 36;
Zeug 51, 52; Zey 291; Zeyler 74, 118; Zibig 387; Zichelhart 238; Ziebly 164; Zieff *329; Ziefus 365; Ziegeler 318;
Zieger 253; Zieget 284; Zi(e)gler *49, 73, 83, 105, 111,
118, 121, 122, *157, 166, 167, 168, *174, 177, 192, *198,
241, 251, 253, 263, 264, 265, 276, 288, 289, 300, 310,
332, *348, 375, 389, 399, 401, 423, 428, 434, 469, 476;
Ziegly (s. Sigle) 174; Zieller 345; Ziesser 244; Ziffe 209;
Ziffel 237; Zigel 166; Zigenfuss 257; Ziger 72; Zilchart
255; Zilling 248; Zillow 321; Zimer (s. Zaeumer) 324;
Zimerly 125; Zimes 387; Zimmer 85, 149, 188, 247, 295,
366, 400, 419; Zim(m)erle *221; Zimmerman(n) 49, 76,
77, *78, 112, 115, 133, 136, 143, *144, 166, 175, 176, 193,
205, 206, *207, *214, 216, *238, 242, 259, *260, 261, *275,
281, 297, 302, 315, *317, 328, 333, 352, *357, 374, 375,
384, 391, 398, 399, 401, 410, 431, 432, 434, 435, *437,
450; Zinchffer 283; Zinck 150, 253, 275, 327, 361; Zincke
349; Zinckenritz 414; Zinckh *327; Zinkblei 289; Zinn 62,
116, 202, 248, 336, 338; Zinsser 289; (v.) Zinzendorf *152,
420, 421, 424, 425; Zirn 211; Zissle 413; Zittel 418; Zittrauer
450; Zoblei 158; Zoebeli *188; Zoeble 231; Zoell 142;
Zoeller 121, 144, 159, *468; Zöllner 145; Zoengrig 285;
Zoepner 231; Zoerlin 172; Zoessler 257; Zohnleyter 143;

Zoi—Zyn

Zoisin 334; Zolenberger (s. Sollberger) 109; Zolinger 131; Zoll 202, 384; Zoller 86, 258, 268; Zolli 275; Zollicker 204; Zollicoffer 74; Zollinger 165; Zollmann *344; Zollner 443, 468; Zombro 303; Zomel 310; Zonnerer 356; Zook (s. Zug) *156; Zopff 109; Zorge 310; Zorn 123, 277, 348, 467; Zorr 244; Zowck 83; Zuber 418; Zuberbuehler 4, 15, 22, 34; Zubler 197; Zuch 114, 327; Zucker 310, 341; Zueblin *451; Zuegel 166; Zuehl 204; Zuend 230; Zueplie 285; Zuerch 221; Zuern 273, 288, 306, 356; Zueron 300; Zuesser 81; Zuetter *353; Zufall 469; Zug (s. Zook) *51, 114, *156, 230; Zugmayer 262; Zumbrun 329; Zumstein 354; Zundel 389; Zunfft 113; Zup(p)inger *99; Zuprian 316; Zurber 99; Zurbrueck 237; Zurbuechen 285; Zurger 112; Zurtere 59; Zutheimer 412; Zutter 159; Zwalle 103, 211; Zwaller 100; Zwanzger 344; Zwecker 110; Zweig (Zweyk) *300; Zweigle 239; Zweuer 310; Zweyer *267; Zweyk (s. Zweig); Zwib 335; Zwick 165, 444; Zwiebeller 294; Zwier 174; Zwieshig 302; Zwigart 371; Zwinger 62; Zwirner 79; Zwissler 325; Zyderman 101; Zyndelbach 212.

INDEX TO SHIPS

582